SLAVERY IN ZION

SLAVERY IN ZION

A Documentary and
Genealogical History of Black Lives and Black
Servitude in Utah Territory, 1847–1862

By Amy Tanner Thiriot

The University of Utah Press
Salt Lake City

Publication of this book is made possible in part by the John Alley Fund for Publications in the American West.

Copyright © 2022 by The University of Utah Press. All rights reserved.

 The Defiance House Man colophon is a registered trademark of The University of Utah Press. It is based on a four-foot-tall Ancient Puebloan pictograph (late PIII) near Glen Canyon, Utah.

Library of Congress Cataloging-in-Publication Data

Names: Thiriot, Amy Tanner, author.
Title: Slavery in Zion : a documentary and genealogical history of black lives and black servitude in Utah Territory, 1847-1862 / by Amy Tanner Thiriot.
Description: Salt Lake City, Utah : University of Utah Press, [2022] | Includes bibliographical references and index.
Identifiers: LCCN 2022012712 | ISBN 9781647690847 (cloth) | ISBN 9781647690854 (paperback) | ISBN 9781647690861 (ebk)
Subjects: LCSH: Slaves—Utah Territory—Genealogy. | Indentured servants—Utah Territory—Genealogy. | African Americans—Utah Territory—Genealogy. | Slaveholders—Utah Territory—Genealogy. | Slavery—Utah Territory—History—19th century. | Utah Territory—History—19th century—Genealogy.
Classification: LCC E185.93.U8 T55 2022 | DDC 323.1196/073079209034—dc23/eng/20220315
LC record available at https://lccn.loc.gov/2022012712

Errata and further information on this and other titles available online at UofUpress.com
Printed and bound in the United States of America.

Any person or persons coming to this Territory and bringing with them servants justly bound to them . . . shall be entitled to such service or labor by the laws of this Territory.

—An Act in Relation to Service,
Utah Territorial Legislature (1852)

CONTENTS

Sankofa: Remembrance   ix
Acknowledgments   xiii
List of Abbreviations   xvii

Introduction: Bound for the Promised Land   1

Part I: The Story of African American Slavery in Utah Territory   51

1. Southern Origins: Mississippi and Alabama   53
2. Southern Origins: Tennessee, Missouri, and Kentucky   62
3. Exodus and Escape   71
4. The Settlement of Utah   81
5. Going to California   98
6. Green Flake and the Tithing Myth   108
7. The Texans   115
8. Merchants, Army Officers, and Government Appointees   123
9. Free at Last   134

Part II: Biographical Encyclopedia of the Enslaved   157

10. The Enslaved   159
11. Associated Enslaved Individuals   297
12. Black Residents of Utah Territory   303
13. Former or Unproven Enslavers   313
14. Related Topics   331

Afterword   337

Appendix 1: *An Act in Relation to Service, Utah Territorial Legislature (1852)*   341
Appendix 2: *Slave Registrations and Bill of Sale*   343
Appendix 3: *Deeds of Consecration*   352
Appendix 4: *Brigham Young Correspondence*   355
Appendix 5: *Miscellaneous Documents*   359
Appendix 6: *Selected Newspaper Articles*   369

Notes   373
Bibliography   413
Index   439

SANKOFA

Remembrance

Over the past century, a Western African funerary art form called *Adinkra* has come to symbolize the African experience in America. The *Adinkra* symbol *Sankofa* is associated with a proverb, *Se wo were fi na wosankofa a yenkyi*, or "It is not wrong to go back for that which you have forgotten."[1]

An Africanist recorded three *Sankofa* in 1927, all stylized hearts, all with a meaning of "turn back and fetch it."[2] The African Burial Ground National Monument in Manhattan uses a *Sankofa* heart with the text, "For all those who were lost/For all those who were stolen/For all those who were left behind/For all those who were not forgotten."[3]

Another version of the *Sankofa* shows a bird moving forward but simultaneously turning backward to fetch an egg from its back, the egg symbolizing the burden of memory. The *Sankofa* bird appears throughout this book to symbolize the remembrance of the enslaved Black pioneers who lived in Utah Territory between 1847 and 1862.

The experience of the Redd household serves as a metaphor. In 1850, John Hardison Redd took Venus, Chaney, Amy, Luke, and Marinda Redd as chattel slaves and Sam Franklin as an indentured servant to Utah Territory. Redd kept a family record with the names and birth dates of the enslaved members of his household. Sometime in the late nineteenth or early twentieth century, a member of his family inked out the names and birth dates of the enslaved. Over time, the ink used by the unknown descendant has faded, leaving the original record just barely decipherable. The reemergence of the names together with extensive work by historians and family members has allowed a greater understanding of the identities and experiences of the enslaved members of the household.[4]

For many years, the number of enslaved, indentured, and free African Americans in Utah Territory has been an open question. While writing this book, I have found documentation for around one hundred

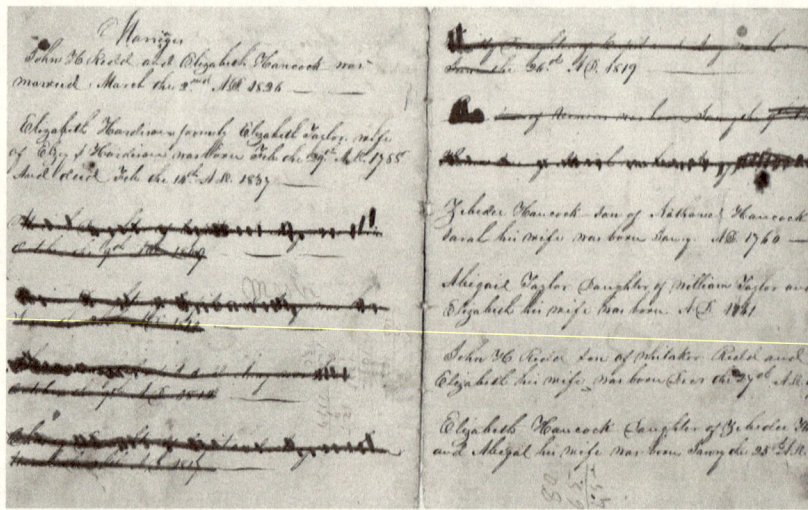

Figure 0.1 A family record by John Hardison Redd. A later family member struck out the names of the enslaved, probably in the late nineteenth or early twentieth century. Used by permission, private collection.

enslaved or indentured African American men, women, and children. Due to the nature of nineteenth-century records and particularly records about enslaved peoples, an exact number will never be known.

Little remains of the lives of the enslaved. To reconstruct their experiences, a historian must weave together wispy threads of evidence from the historical record. The autobiographical material is scarce: Green Flake wrote some memories in *The Book of the Pioneers*, Alexander and Marinda Redd Bankhead gave an interview to a reporter, Biddy Mason's daughter Ellen Huddleston described her family experiences to a journalist, and a graduate student interviewed Charles Embers near the end of his life. Despite the lack of firsthand accounts, a picture is starting to emerge of the experience of African American enslavement in Utah Territory due to the work of descendants of the enslaved, professional historians, community historians, descendants of enslavers, and archivists, plus my own work with genealogical and historical sources.

This book attempts to answer several questions. How did these enslaved men, women, and children come to live in Utah Territory? What were their experiences in the territory? What happened to them after they were freed?

Due to the long suppression and whitewashing of this history, the sheer amount of detailed work it has taken to recover these names and experiences has led to a subsequent question: How can we best honor the memory of the men, women, and children who struggled under the heavy burdens of enslavement?

The answer has become increasingly self-evident: the best way to honor their memory is to tell their stories as completely and honestly as possible.

Sankofa.

It is not wrong to go back for that which you have forgotten.

ACKNOWLEDGMENTS

Many individuals and institutions supported the work that went into this book, and there were also those who asked questions and helped me decipher the stories of hardship, loss, oppression, and grief.

Of those to whom we owe a debt of gratitude, first and foremost are those who were taken in bondage to the American West and who helped build communities there. Their descendants can be proud of their legacy of bravery, hard work, and resilience.

Many historians and authors provided research assistance and direction for this project, including W. Paul Reeve, Christopher B. Rich Jr., Thomas G. Alexander, Jeffery O. Johnson, William P. MacKinnon, William Gorenfeld, Quincy D. Newell, Kristine Shorey Forbes, Jonathan A. Stapley, Barbara Jones Brown, Sarah Barringer Gordon, Kevin Waite, Bruce Crow, Suzanne Midori Hanna, Edward Leo Lyman, DeEtta Dematarus, and Tonya Reiter, a descendant of Venus Redd and Luke Redd. Tonya's contributions to this book are extensive and immeasurable. I would particularly like to note the mentorship and assistance of historian Ardis E. Parshall, especially pertaining to all things Brigham Young and early Utah history.

Many thanks to the Fretwell family who answered a phone call from a stranger and kindly gave access to the collections lovingly created by their father, John D. Fretwell.

Among the other descendants of the enslaved pioneers, Judee Williams contributed passion for the project and practical genealogical assistance. Loretta Crump provided valuable information and collaboration on the Duncan-White family. Betty Juanita Jackson-Spillman and Juanita Ronée Reynolds consulted on naming, and Louis M. Duffy's words and encouragement heartened my research. I have often returned to his reply when he learned of a distressing story: "We're astonished, but not overwhelmed."

Many community and family historians and interested individuals contributed to this project. Among them are Eugene H. Perkins of the Perkins family; Amasa Mason Redd, Tonya and Scott Reiter, Jan Garbett, Kathryn Redd Larsen, and Rolaine Grant King of the Redd family; Ron Freeman of the Flake and Smoot families; Mindy Smoot Robbins and her father, the late L. Douglas Smoot, who donated the Smoot collection to BYU Special Collections; Devin Lewis McFarlane of the Lewis family; Carl Carter and Dennis Jones of the Dennis family; the late Ron Peterson, who helped with mining records; Pat Sagers of Spanish Fork Daughters of Utah Pioneers; the Wellsville City Historical Committee; Donald E. Burton of the Burton family; Debra Holm of the Harper family; VaLene Ewell Collings and the Ewell Family Historical & Genealogical Society; Stanley M. Jex of the Jex family; and untold others who supplied information, answered queries, or gave the valuable feedback that there were no further records preserved within a family.

Many thanks for the devoted assistance from librarians and archivists and others at many institutions: the Church History Library of the Church of Jesus Christ of Latter-day Saints, including Emily Marie Crumpton-Deason , Brian Passantino, Alex D. Smith, Jeffrey Mahas, and others; L. Tom Perry Special Collections, Harold B. Lee Library, Brigham Young University, including BYU Library Digital Collections; University of Utah Marriott Library; Utah State Archives; Utah State Historical Society; Daughters of Utah Pioneers; Logan (UT) Library; the online digital libraries of Signature Books and USU Press; California State Archives; the Schomburg Center and the Milstein Division at the New York Public Library; Genevieve Preston, San Bernardino County Historical Archives; John Cahoon, Seaver Center for Western History Research, Natural History Museum of Los Angeles County; Huntington Library, San Marino, California; Paul R. Spitzzeri of the Workman and Temple Family Homestead Museum in City of Industry, California; Charles W. Mood, Camp Floyd State Park; the National Archives; the National Archives at Denver; Susan Southwick and Peter J. Smith from the Nevada Judicial Historical Society; Kerry Petersen; and Susan Ward Payne, California Room, Feldheym Central Library, San Bernardino. I appreciate the permission for citation from Samuel H. Williamson of the *MeasuringWorth* website; the kind support of Dr. Evelyn A. McDowell, Ph.D., President of Sons and Daughters of the United States Middle Passage, *sdusmp.org*; and the friendship and support from members of the New York, New Jersey, and Utah chapters of the Afro-American Historical and Genealogical Society (AAHGS). Many cemeteries provided assistance, including Salt Lake City Cemetery, Mount Olivet Cemetery (Salt Lake City), Ogden City Cemetery, and Evergreen Cemetery (Los Angeles). Valuable large-scale digital projects included Utah Digital Newspapers; Pioneer Database, 1847–1868, including David and Judy Wood; Saints by Sea: Latter-day Saint Immigration to America; Chronicling America from the Library of Congress; California Digital Newspaper Collection; FamilySearch; and Ancestry.com.

John Alley and Thomas Krause of the University of Utah Press provided guidance as the project wore on over the years. Manuscript readers provided valuable guidance as well.

Melinda Bowers of SouthwestUS Design used a woodcarving as the model for the *Sankofa* graphic.

Finally, there are other supportive friends and family too numerous to mention, but in particular, those at the Doylestown Family History Center who listened to my stories; Mark and Deanna Butler and members of the community at *Keepapitchinin: The Mormon History Blog*; Emily Wessman and Jake Smith; Cris and Janae Baird; Eliza and Jeremy Magland; my in-laws, Steven and Merlene Thiriot; my parents, James and Ann Tanner; and, finally and most importantly, my husband David and children Clarissa, Alden, William (who helped solve the mystery of Lambson), Carina, and Daniel.

ABBREVIATIONS

CHL: Church History Library, The Church of Jesus Christ of Latter-day Saints, Salt Lake City, Utah.
FHL: Family History Library, The Church of Jesus Christ of Latter-day Saints, Salt Lake City, Utah.
FSFT: Family Tree is an online genealogical database on familysearch.org, a service of FamilySearch, The Church of Jesus Christ of Latter-day Saints, Salt Lake City, Utah.
Marriott Library: J. Willard Marriott Library, University of Utah, Salt Lake City, Utah.
Office Files: Brigham Young Office Files, 1832–1878, CR 1234 1, Church History Library, The Church of Jesus Christ of Latter-day Saints, Salt Lake City, Utah.
Pioneer Database: Pioneer Database, 1847–1868, Church History Department, The Church of Jesus Christ of Latter-day Saints, Salt Lake City, Utah.
Saints by Sea: Saints by Sea: Latter-day Saint Immigration to America (database), Church History and Family History Department, Brigham Young University, Provo, Utah.
SBCHA: San Bernardino County Historical Archives, County of San Bernardino, San Bernardino, California.
Special Collections, HBLL: L. Tom Perry Special Collections, Harold B. Lee Library, Brigham Young University, Provo, Utah.
US Census: The United States takes a census every ten years. Official copies are held in the National Archives in Washington, DC, under the category "Records of the Bureau of the Census, Record Group 29." Most census records are available, although much of the 1890 census was burned or destroyed. This book will not include the publication and roll numbers for each citation since much of the census is widely available and text searchable. Some census documents or schedules are available only from a single repository; for

example, the draft copy of the 1850 census for Utah Territory is in the Church History Library in Salt Lake City, and the nineteenth-century California mortality schedules are at the Bancroft Library at the University of California, Berkeley.

USHS: The Utah Division of Archives and Records Service (Utah State Archives) and Utah State Historical Society in Salt Lake City, Utah, are two separate organizations, but their collections appear together under this abbreviation.

Introduction

"BOUND FOR THE PROMISED LAND"

Not many contemporaneous records remain of the words of the enslaved African American population of Utah Territory, but the few words that survived their oppression and bondage almost always were of freedom. In 1850, William Crosby wrote to Brigham Young that Green Flake "supposes that if he wos free that he would never hav to do any thing on earth a gain."[1] In 1855, Theophilus (Allston) found someone to forge freedom papers for him while he was in the territory with an army officer. In 1860, Jerry (Lewis) claimed that he was a free man and told Brigham Young that Duritha Trail Lewis had no papers to prove her ownership of him.[2] Marinda Redd Bankhead told a journalist about William Taylor Dennis's enslaved workers who fled to Canada, and the journalist wrote that Marinda and her husband Alexander clearly recalled the joy "upon the faces of all the slaves, when they ascertained that they had acquired their freedom through the fortunes of war."[3] Tampian Hoye Campbell and her husband named their sons after abolitionists and emancipators, including Abraham Lincoln and Ulysses S. Grant.

The descendants of their enslavers told a sharply different story when they eventually began to tell the stories of slavery. The stories they created reshaped the yearning for freedom and self-determination into a loyalty and love that drove the enslaved to leave the South of their own free will and accompany their enslavers to the West. Flake descendants told of Green and Elizabeth who were offered their freedom in the South, but "insisted on being taken along."[4] The family said Elizabeth was later offered her freedom again and once again she refused. The story did not happen as told: the first offer of freedom would have taken place in Mississippi, a state that only allowed manumission, the emancipation or freeing of a slave, through an act of the state legislature, and the second offer of freedom would have occurred after the court action *In re Hannah* (1856) when Elizabeth already knew she was free and had arranged to lead her own life.

Manumission was rare and legally difficult by the mid-nineteenth century. Slave codes severely restricted manumission of all enslaved persons, and, in specific cases, manumission was limited due to encumbrances such as mortgages or other liens, or due to the terms, such as in a gift by will, by which an enslaver obtained ownership. Thus, despite the unsettled nature of slave law in the West, enslaved persons taken into Utah Territory continued to be held in bondage, as did most of those taken to California until they discovered they were free by early 1856. Except for the enslaved people being taken to Utah Territory by Dr. William Taylor Dennis, who liberated themselves with the help of the townspeople of Tabor, Iowa, this project includes only three instances of those in bondage leaving chattel slavery before the US Congress ended slavery in the American territories in 1862 and elsewhere in the county in 1865. US Brigadier General Albert Sidney Johnston converted Randolph Hughes from a chattel slave to a paid indentured servant while temporarily in Kentucky after being stationed in Utah Territory. The legitimate Redd heirs informally freed three of their deceased parents' enslaved workers in 1858 and granted them an inheritance. In 1856, a small group of illegally enslaved people in California sought and gained their freedom at the hands of Judge Benjamin Hayes.

Scope of the Project

This book identifies and tells the stories of the enslaved and indentured African American pioneers of Utah Territory. Despite the historical connection between Indigenous and African American slavery in Utah Territory, the book mentions Indigenous slavery only in passing. Although this book contains material applicable to a legal history or a history of race and Mormonism, its most important goal is to be a treasury of the experiences of Utah's enslaved Black residents, so the introductory history moves quickly and does not delve into topics adequately covered in other published or forthcoming works. It also serves as a demonstration of the differences between legal history and lived experience, showing what happened when Southerners transported a small number of enslaved people into the largely White settlements of the American West.

The first important writings about the experience of African American slavery in Utah Territory were from Black journalists Julius F. Taylor and Delilah L. Beasley. Taylor interviewed Alexander and Marinda Redd Bankhead and created one of the few personal narratives of slavery in Utah Territory. Beasley interviewed Ellen Mason Huddleston and wrote extensively about California's early Black history, including its connections to Utah. For decades, however, much of the telling of these stories happened within heavily fictionalized White family narratives. Jack Beller gave the topic its first academic treatment in 1929 in *Utah Historical Quarterly*. Although he collected important information, the errors he made passed largely unchallenged into later literature. In the mid-twentieth century, Kate B. Carter of Daughters of Utah Pioneers prepared a booklet called *The Negro Pioneer*. It is a mixture of important documents, accurate and inaccurate memories, and historical fiction.

Scholarly treatments of slavery and race resumed in the 1950s and 1960s with the work of James B. Christensen, Roldo V. Dutson, Dennis Lythgoe, and later Ronald G. Coleman, Helen Z. Papanikolas, Nathaniel R. Ricks, and Heather Hardy. Works related to this book include Rev. France Davis on the Black churches of Utah; Patrick Q. Mason on interracial marriage; Darren Parry on Shoshone memories; Connell O'Donovan on biography and scandal; Margaret Blair Young and Darius A. Gray's historical fiction; Larry Gerlach on the Ku Klux Klan; Leslie G. Kelen, Eileen Hallet Stone, Deidre Ann Tyler, and Jessica Nelson on twentieth-century experiences; Chester Lee Hawkins on sources; Charles L. Keller on mining; and William G. Hartley's historical biographies.

A closely related field is that of race and Mormonism, with the writings of Lester E. Bush, Armand L. Mauss, Newell G. Bringhurst, Darron T. Smith, Russell W. Stevenson, Henry J. Wolfinger, Joanna Brooks, Max Perry Mueller, Matthew L. Harris, Quincy D. Newell, Tonya Reiter, W. Paul Reeve, and others.

Historians of Utah and Mormonism are plentiful, but the work most closely related to this project is from William P. MacKinnon on the Utah War; Ardis E. Parshall on nineteenth-century Utah and Brigham Young;

Davis Bitton on Latter-day Saint diaries and autobiographies; LaJean Purcell Carruth's Pitman shorthand transcriptions; Brent M. Rogers on conflicts with the federal government; Kenneth L. Cannon about Mountain Common Law; Ronald W. Walker and Thomas G. Alexander on military, political, and environmental history; John G. Turner and Leonard J. Arrington about Brigham Young; Arrington, Feramorz Y. Fox, and Dean L. May on early Latter-day Saint economic systems; Roger B. Nielson on Camp Floyd; LaMar C. Berrett on the Southern States Mission; Juanita Brooks on Jewish communities and the Stout diaries; John W. Van Cott on place names; Polly Aird, Jeff Nichols, and Will Bagley on religious dissent; Jeffrey D. Nichols on the Black press and prostitution; and Christopher B. Rich Jr., on the legal aspects of An Act in Relation to Service. The forthcoming work of Christopher Rich and W. Paul Reeve will further illuminate the legal history of slavery in Utah Territory.

Historians of the Black experience in the American West include Stacey L. Smith on unfree labor in California; Kevin Waite on slavery and politics; George H. Junne Jr., Shirley Ann Wilson Moore, Quintard Taylor, Lawrence B. de Graaf, Monroe Lee Billington, Roger D. Hardaway, Kevin Mulroy, and others on the Western experience; John Mack Faragher about crime in Los Angeles; Paul R. Spitzzeri, Kendra Field, Daniel Lynch, and Marne L. Campbell about the Black history of Los Angeles; Dolores Hayden and DeEtta Demaratus on Biddy Mason and Hannah Smiley; Juan Caballeria, Byron R. Skinner, Edward Leo Lyman, Susan Ward Payne, S. George Ellsworth, and Kristine Shorey Forbes about San Bernardino and the Inland Empire; Mark J. Stegmaier on slavery in New Mexico Territory; Michael K. Bennion and Andrés Reséndez on Indigenous slavery; and James W. Yancy on the Black history of Tucson. Kevin Waite, Sarah Barringer Gordon, the Biddy Mason Charitable Foundation, and others are working on the history of Biddy Mason and Black Los Angeles.

Historians of slavery and race are too numerous to mention here except for a few whose writings were especially helpful for this project. They include John C. Hurd and Thomas D. Morris on legal history; Junius P. Rodriguez on resistance, rebellion, emancipation, and abolitionism; Daina Ramey Berry on the commodification of the enslaved; Jim Downs on the suffering that accompanied emancipation; Thomas A. Foster on sexual exploitation; Tera W. Hunter on marriage; Jennifer L. Hochschild and Brenna M. Powell on census racial categories; Robyn N. Smith on surnames; Stephanie E. Jones-Rogers on women enslavers; and Kimberly Wallace-Sanders on the Mammy myth.

Where original records exist, I made my best attempt to find and use them. Utah Territory and the West are the central focus of this work, although the research stretched at times back into Colonial America, through the Midwest and Eastern United States and even to Africa. I compiled a database with more than 6,000 individuals and read and reread tens of thousands of pages of censuses, church records, diaries, letter collections, court records, tax records, account books, newspapers, histories, and other records that might yield clues to piece together an extended family or discover someone's fate. Confirming a single relationship could take days or weeks, and some identities and relationships only became clear after several years of research. The search resulted in far more information than could fit into this volume, so narrative and thematic treatments are brief by necessity. If information available in prior histories is not included in this book, the likely cause is that it did not meet standards of historical accuracy. I handled every question of identity and narrative with great seriousness, especially when my conclusions contradicted popular community or family accounts. Despite my effort to find every person, there were undoubtedly additional enslaved Black settlers in the territory, especially if they lived in the territory between censuses.

Regardless of the total amount of information, there is regrettably little known of any of the lives documented in this work. Although I made every attempt to center the experiences of the enslaved, the records about them were almost always created by or about their enslavers, so this work leaves many Black experiences uncentered and unknown. However, when combined with the information here, additional research about community life and the judicious use of slave narratives and other important historical and legal material may help give a better sense of their stories, including the horrific separations, physical and sexual violence, and coercion experienced by those documented in this book.

Newly available primary source materials may further illuminate or correct this narrative and add names of additional Black pioneers. It is my hope that this book will motivate more research as families and organizations locate and digitize additional primary sources. Most to be desired are plantation or family records like the one preserved for many generations in the Redd family. It is also my hope that the enslaved children, women, and men in this book will continue to inspire art, film, literature, and public memorials, but with a word of caution. It has been all too common for descendants of enslavers to feel that they own the memory or heritage of those their ancestors oppressed. This is an offense to the memory of the enslaved. If any readers, communities, or descendants of those who enslaved household and agricultural workers in Utah Territory desire to mark a grave or create a memorial, it would be improper to begin without seeking the advice and participation of historians, African American genealogical and historical organizations, and any descendants of the enslaved.

Latter-Day Saints and Slavery

The settlement of Utah Territory is inseparably connected to the history of the Church of Jesus Christ of Latter-day Saints, historically called Mormons, LDS, Latter-day Saints, or sometimes "Saints." It was a new religion in the nineteenth century, believed by its converts to be a restoration of the original Christian church. Political, social, and religious disagreements forced early members of the church out of successive settlements in New York, Ohio, Missouri, and Illinois. The interactions of the new religion with theories of race and slavery helped form the early history of the American West and influenced long-standing racial practices and beliefs within the church. The forces that shaped the experiences of the enslaved in Utah Territory were formed on the national stage with the movement of the church to the West, the Compromise of 1850, and the ongoing tensions that led to the Civil War. Although two of the most prominent factors in the formation of the law of bondage in Utah Territory were the economic importance of the first wave of Southern immigrants in 1847 and 1848 and the decisions made by Latter-day Saint leaders about racial practices, the most important factor in the lived experiences of the enslaved was their isolation among a mostly White and Latter-day Saint population.

Joseph Smith founded the Church of Jesus Christ of Latter-day Saints in New York in 1830. In 1844, during the continued persecution of his people, he began a campaign for president of the United States.

He chose the abolition of slavery as one of the elements of his platform.[5] Smith supported the early ordination of free Black men to the church's lay priesthood, but told missionaries not to baptize the enslaved without the permission of their enslavers, and not to ordain enslaved men to the lay priesthood.[6]

After Smith's death at the hands of a mob later that year, residents of Illinois drove members of the church across the Mississippi River onto Native American lands. The church subsequently moved to temporary settlements along the Missouri River, including Winter Quarters near today's Omaha, Nebraska, and then, starting in 1847, to a valley between the Great Salt Lake and the Wasatch Mountains on the western edge of the Rocky Mountains. They compared themselves to the children of Israel fleeing Egypt and called their new home "Zion." The refugees also called their new home "Deseret," a term from the Book of Mormon used to invoke community and industry. Members of the church streamed to the Great Salt Lake Valley from Winter Quarters, and eventually tens of thousands moved to the valley from across the United States and around the world. From a central location in Great Salt Lake City, settlements spread as far as California, Colorado, Canada, and Mexico.

The church's most pressing concerns were migration, the establishment of communities with sustainable and self-reliant economies, the creation and maintenance of religious culture, care for the poor and widowed, navigation of the difficult practice of plural marriage, and interactions with the US government. However, during those early years, slavery became an issue for the church as its members encountered Indigenous slavery, and Southern enslavers eventually took around one hundred Black enslaved and indentured servants into the territory.

Brigham Young became president of the church after the death of Joseph Smith. The documentary evidence is fragmentary, but after telling three enslaved men that their entry into the Great Salt Lake Valley in 1847 meant that they were free, he learned to respect Southerners' claims to slave property. That did not mean that he cared for Southern slavery. Despite his strong racial views, he disliked both African American and Indigenous slavery, and he tried to find practical and humane solutions when presented with specific problems regarding the enslaved. When a colonizing mission left for San Bernardino in 1851, Brigham Young wrote to William Crosby, "we do not wish to encourage the sale of Blacks in these vallies."[7] Latter-day Saint apostle Wilford Woodruff wrote to Thomas L. Kane two years before, "We are a peaceful and industrious people . . . we do not wish to have any thing to do with the 'vexed question' of slavery." He explained, "[W]e deemed it expedient not to introduce a clause into our constitution prohibiting the introduction of slaves into the State of Deseret, but slavery can *never* be tolerated there."[8]

The first two presidents of the church, Joseph Smith and Brigham Young, were born in Vermont, a free state from its founding, but spent many of their early years in New York State, which ended slavery in 1827 through gradual emancipation. The first documented enslaved Africans had arrived in New York in 1626, and the enslaved population of the state was as high as one out of six residents before the state passed its first gradual emancipation law in 1799.[9] Gradual emancipation was a compromise: it gave property owners time to recoup whatever investment they had made in their enslaved workers, but it also honored the human rights of the enslaved. Brigham Young explained gradual emancipation to a congregation in Utah Territory: "After that law was passed the people began to dispose of their blacks, and to let them buy themselves off." He further explained, "They then passed a law that black children should be free, the same as white children, and so it remains to this day."[10]

Despite gradual emancipation, the White population was rarely sympathetic to abolitionism or a free Black population. Frederick Douglass wrote after visiting Vermont that it was "surprisingly under the influence of the slave power. Her proud boast that no slave had ever been delivered up to his master within her borders, did not hinder her hatred of *anti-slavery*." He explained that was also true of New York. "All along the Erie canal, from Albany to Buffalo, there was apathy, indifference, aversion, and sometimes mob-ocratic spirit evinced."[11]

The Book of Mormon, one of the sacred records of the church, provided a framework for relations with Native Americans, but not for other non-White ethnicities, except a single verse: "[God] denieth none that come unto him, black and white, bond and free, male and female . . . and all are alike unto God."[12] Despite that framework of equality, Brigham Young moved away from Joseph Smith's more expansive views on race and the lay priesthood. He believed that God appointed those of African descent to live and work as servants or slaves. He abhorred interracial marriage. His views may have been influenced by Southern enslavers in

Utah Territory, including William Crosby and John H. Bankhead, but also by earlier experiences in New York. African American activist and author Austin Steward lived near Joseph Smith and Brigham Young in New York and later wrote about the murder of a Black neighbor for marrying a White woman, an incident that may have helped form Brigham Young's well-known dislike of interracial marriage.[13]

Each of the approximately one hundred enslaved people in Utah Territory came from a system of great oppression. They could not enter contracts of marriage and had no legal rights to their families. Enslavers could separate families on a whim. Enslaved women, men, and children were subject to sexual exploitation, so family life tended to be complicated. Children sometimes did not know the identities of their parents or grandparents. An enslaved woman's children became the property of her enslaver, whether the father was White or Black, free or enslaved. When an enslaver died, his or her executors sold the enslaved or divided them among heirs. Although some enslavers may have desired to keep families together, the practicalities of estate settlements and the prices of enslaved workers meant that courts and executors often separated families.

The enslaved had little ability to direct their own work. On large plantations, enslavers may have assigned household or field work or trained a worker in a vocation, but on smaller farms, like those owned by the Latter-day Saint converts who moved to Utah Territory, there would have been limited specialization.

Disobedience was punished, often severely. Many years after she was freed, Martha Flake's family remembered that her "back was marked with whelps [welts] from beating she received from the white master." Her granddaughter Bertha Stevens Udell recalled that Martha's hand was badly burned by Elizabeth Coleman Crosby in an act of retribution. The family also remembered that Oscar (Crosby) Smith fled from his enslavers and became wedged in a rail fence. "His head was through the rails and he could not get his body through as he was a large man. He was caught & beat. He went through life with his head twisted to one side."[14]

Brigham Young and Wilford Woodruff crossed the plains in the first 1847 Latter-day Saint wagon company with three enslaved African American men sent ahead to the valley by their enslavers, and by the time Woodruff wrote to Thomas L. Kane about the local dislike of slavery, Southern converts to the Church of Jesus Christ of Latter-day Saints had already taken more than fifty enslaved people into the Great Salt Lake Valley. Over the next decade, other converts, merchants not associated with the church, officers in the US Army, and appointed federal officials would take additional enslaved people into the territory. By early 1851, the number of the enslaved in the territory was around sixty, but with the departure of Southern families for California, the number was around thirty by the end of the year and stayed between thirty and forty for the next decade, except for an additional uncounted number of enslaved servants of army officers in the territory during the Utah War or other military expeditions.

The three enslaved African American men in the first Latter-day Saint wagon company were Green Flake, Hark (Lay) Wales, and Oscar (Crosby) Smith. Nineteenth-century diarists rarely mentioned enslaved people, but when members of the first wagon company did mention the three men, it was in reference to their labor and obedience.

Two years into the settlement, an enslaved woman took refuge in Brigham Young's home. Francis McKown wrote Young and blamed her escape on an unnamed person and promised not to beat her. "She was Borne mine and I raised hur till and it seems as though there was one out of the family ever since she has bin away."[15] The same day, Benjamin Mathews wrote to Young about a man who was attempting to liberate himself, probably Rande, enslaved by Robert M. Smith. Mathews also mentioned a "Negro Boy called Jim that came through in A[masa] Lymans Company."[16] Back in Iowa, Latter-day Saint apostle Orson Hyde wrote in the *Frontier Guardian*, probably about Jim: "The counterfeiters in Pottawatamie are . . . charging us with being accessory to the running away of a negro slave to the Salt Lake."[17] Little more is known about these three attempts at self-liberation, but McKown seems to have taken the young woman back to Mississippi.

A Mississippi newspaper reported in 1850 that Utah might choose to become a slave state, since, "If the accounts of travellers are to be relied on, slavery already exists among the Mormons. . . . Quite a large number have been introduced at the Salt Lake by the southern disciples of Joe Smith."[18] A New York newspaper reported the presence of about one hundred Black residents of the Great Salt Lake Valley living with their "former masters," and editorialized that the residents of the valley believe "that 'all men are created free and equal,' and they very sensibly conclude that Slavery can have no legal existence where it has never been legalized."[19] As the national debate over slavery raged on, Georgia promised it would leave the Union if Congress banned slavery in Utah and New Mexico territories, or otherwise narrowed the reach of slavery.[20] Latter-day Saint leaders desired statehood, so they attempted to walk a delicate balance between slave and free interests. Connecticut native and Latter-day Saint apostle Orson Hyde wrote from Iowa that there "is no law in Utah to authorize Slavery, neither any to prohibit it." He claimed that any of the enslaved could "choose to remain with his master; none are allowed to interfere between the master and the slave," and that all the enslaved in the valley "appear to be perfectly contented and satisfied." Hyde either did not know or was misrepresenting the situation in Utah Territory. The history of resistance among the enslaved in Utah showed they were not "perfectly content." He also claimed that Southern converts were told, "if your slaves wish to remain with you, and to go with you, put them not away; but it they choose to leave you, or are not satisfied to remain with you, it is for you to sell them, or to let them go free." By 1850, most slave states prohibited exactly this: enslavers could not legally speak of freedom to the enslaved or let them "go free." Hyde mentioned a policy of neutrality by the church: "The laws of the land recognize slavery—we do not wish to oppose the laws of the country." He suggested that if any sin was involved in human trafficking, "let the individual who sells him, bear that sin, and not the church."[21]

No court ever considered the legal status of the enslaved in Utah Territory between the initial Latter-day Saint settlement in 1847 during its last days as part of Mexico and five years later when the territorial legislature enacted a statute codifying African American servitude. John C. Hurd published a comprehensive two-volume work in the early 1860s, *The Law of Freedom and Bondage in the United States*. Considering both national and international law, Hurd concluded that each enslaved or indentured servant taken into Utah Territory had remained "bond or free in such Territory, according to their status under the law of the place of their former domicil."[22] A *domicil* or *domicile* is the place where a person has established a permanent and principal home to which he intends to return. Most of the Utah enslavers went straight from the South to the Great Salt Lake Valley, and only a few established a domicile in Illinois, which may have freed the enslaved technically if not practically.[23]

Explorer John W. Gunnison described the situation in Utah Territory: "Involuntary labor by negroes is recognised by custom; those holding slaves, keep them as part of their family, as they would wives, without any law on the subject."[24] Hurd's opinion contradicted the common legal ideas about slavery in the territories, but he described what happened in Utah Territory: those in servitude in Utah Territory appear in almost every case to have retained their status as in the South, whether slaves for life or indentured servants.

As the United States expanded to the west, existing states fought over the slave status of new territories and states. In the contentious run-up to the Civil War, the Compromise of 1850 admitted California as a free state, with Utah and New Mexico territories given self-determination. New Mexico eventually instituted a draconian slave code that, according to an Ohio congressman, would bring "blushes to the cheek of Caligula."[25] Utah Territory, on the other hand, instituted a curious legal hodgepodge called An Act in Relation to Service (1852), identified by legal scholar Christopher B. Rich Jr. as patterned on the gradual emancipation laws of the Northeast or Midwest, rather than the slave codes of the South.[26] The Act attempted to treat slavery as contracted labor and provided unusual legal protections, including a requirement that labor could only be sold with the consent of the "servant."

The Compromise of 1850 replaced the nation's Fugitive Slave Act of 1793 with the stricter Fugitive Slave Act of 1850. In 1852, Latter-day Saint Daniel H. Wells forwarded a fugitive slave notice to the territorial marshal and encouraged him to follow the law.[27] The 1857 Supreme Court case *Dred Scott* allowed enslavers to preserve their slave property in free states, but there is no documentation that the case changed the situation of anyone held in bondage in Utah Territory.

The 1850 Federal Census

After the Compromise of 1850, Utah territorial officials desired statehood. They could not have imagined that statehood would not come until 1896. As part of their effort to gain statehood, they attempted to keep slavery in the territory from public attention. Historian Ronald G. Coleman explained that the effort extended to the 1850 federal census.[28] The territorial representative to Congress, Dr. John M. Bernhisel, advised

Brigham Young not to classify any person of African descent in the territory as a slave. He wrote that most members of Congress and most "jurists in the United States, entertain the conviction that slavery does not, and cannot exist in the Territory of Deseret, without the sanction of positive law, yet to be enacted."[29]

Since printed forms for the 1850 federal census had not arrived by 1851, territorial officials finally used forms they created themselves. The census included several "schedules." Schedule 1 showed the population of each state or territory with each free inhabitant listed by name, age, sex, color, value of real estate, and place of birth; Schedule 2 listed African American slave inhabitants by owner; Schedule 3 showed agricultural production; Schedule 4 showed manufacturing; Schedule 5 showed social statistics; and Schedule 6 listed those who died in the year preceding the census. In Schedule 2, the enslaved were to be listed only as numbers, but in what has become a historical treasure, Utah Territory's census takers, Reuben McBride and Thomas Bullock, wrote the names of most of the forty-six people they enumerated.[30] Although territorial officials initially created multiple slave schedules, they eventually sent a single schedule to Washington, DC, showing twenty-six enslaved people "Going to California."[31]

The Church of Jesus Christ of Latter-day Saints kept the draft copies of the census, and their existence was forgotten by the time anyone began to look at the practice of slavery in Utah Territory. In 2013, historian Ardis E. Parshall shared the existence of the draft census, which showed not only the twenty-six enslaved people going to California but also an indentured servant and nineteen additional enslaved people.[32]

The different drafts of the slave schedules show the confusion about what should be done. Four of the enslaved African American residents of the territory were listed only on slave schedules that did not go to Washington, DC; five were listed only in the population schedule; about eighteen were listed in both population and slave schedules; and at least nine were not listed at all.

Although Utah underreported the numbers on both 1850 and 1860 censuses, the number of enslaved and indentured servants in the territory was a tiny fraction of those held in the Southern slave states. The Southern families who used enslaved workers in the Salt Lake Valley were able to establish successful farms quickly and efficiently in the first years

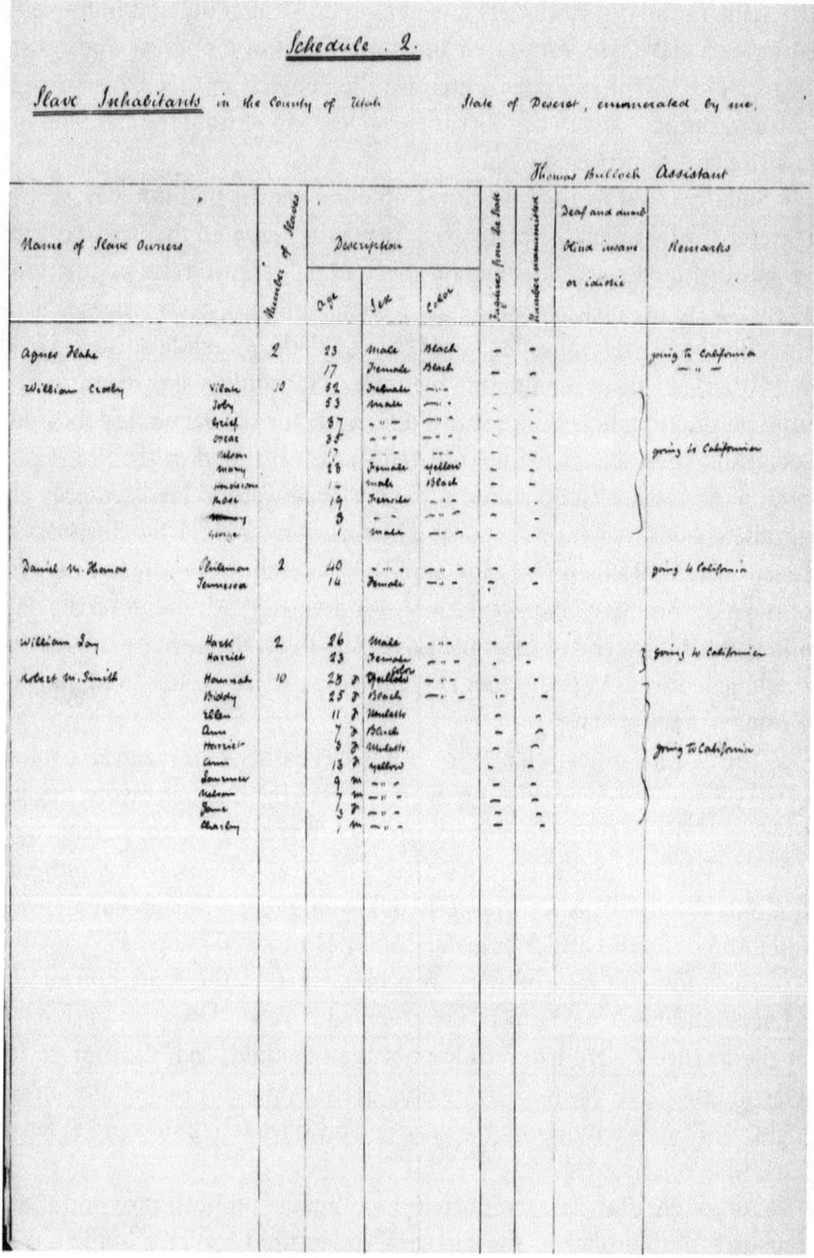

Schedule 2.

Slave Inhabitants in the County of Utah State of Deseret, enumerated by me,

Thomas Bullock Assistant

Name of Slave Owners		Number of Slaves	Description: Age	Sex	Color	Fugitives from the State	Number manumitted	Deaf and dumb blind insane or idiotic	Remarks
Agnes Flake		2	23	Male	Black	–	–		going to California
			17	Female	Black	–	–		″
William Crosby	Vilate	10	62	Female	″	–	–		
	Toby		53	Male	″	–	–		
	Grief		37	″	″	–	–		
	Oscar		35	″	″	–	–		
	Nelson		17	″	″	–	–		going to California
	Mary		28	Female	yellow	–	–		
	Henderson		14	male	Black	–	–		
	Rose		19	Female	″	–	–		
	[struck out]		3	″	″	–	–		
	George		1	male	″	–	–		
Daniel M. Thomas	Philemon	2	40	″	″	–	–		going to California
	Tennessee		14	Female	″	–	–		
William Lay	Hark	2	26	Male	″	–	–		going to California
	Harriet		23	Female	″	–	–		
Robert M. Smith	Hannah	10	28 F	yellow color	″	–	–		going to California
	Biddy		25 F	Black	″	–	–		
	Ellen		11 F	Mulatto		–	–		
	Ann		7 F	Black		–	–		
	Harriet		5 F	Mulatto		–	–		
	Ann		13 F	yellow		–	–		
	Lawrence		9 M	″		–	–		
	Nelson		7 M	″		–	–		
	Jane		3 F	″		–	–		
	Charley		1 M	″		–	–		

Figure I.1. The draft copy of the 1850 federal census slave schedule for Utah County. The census was taken in early 1851. It shows the enslaved members of Southern households leaving Utah Territory for California. Church History Library, Salt Lake City.

Schedule 2 Colored Inhabitants Utah Co Territory of Utah Enumerated by me R. McBride Assistant		Description			Fugitives from the State	No. Manumitted	Deaf or Dumb Blind Insane or Idiotic	Remarks
Name of Slave Owners	Number of Slaves	Age	Sex	Colour				
1 John H. Redd	5							
	Linus	40	m	Black				
	Chaney	38	"	"				
	Luke	19	Male	Yellow				
	Marinda	18	F	"				
	Ama	14	F	"				
	Sam Franklin	17	m	"				Free when Twenty One
2 John H. Bankhead	9	Salt Lake County						
	Sam	50	m	Black				
	Nancy	27	F	Yellow				
	Alexander	23	m	Black				
	Thomas	18	m	"				
	Nathan	22	m	"				
	Miram	17	F	Yellow				
	Sam	7	m	"				
	Ranley	4	m	"				
	Howard	1	m	Black				
3 Brigham Young	1							
	Greene	23	m	Yellow				
4 Abraham Smoot	1							
	Lucy	12	F	Black				
5 John Brown	1							
	Betsy	14	F	Black				
	Davis County							
Williams Camp								
	Charlotte	20	F	Black				
	Daniel	17	"	"	—	—	—	—
							Reuben McBride	

Figure I.2. The draft copy of the 1850 federal census slave schedule for Great Salt Lake, Utah, and Davis Counties, taken in early 1851. Church History Library, Salt Lake City.

of Latter-day Saint settlement, but arid irrigated lands and small farms did not lend themselves to the type of commercial agriculture that made slavery profitable in the American South. The 1850 census showed more than three million people enslaved in the United States, and the 1860 census showed close to four million.[33] The number of enslaved in the official 1850 census returns for Utah Territory was twenty-six, but the actual number was around fifty-four to fifty-eight. The number shown in the official census in 1860 was twenty-nine, with the actual number around thirty-three to thirty-six. The official numbers showed a slight increase, but the real numbers showed a significant decrease. If comparable to any other place in the country, the numbers in Utah Territory were most like New Jersey's change from more than two hundred "apprentices for life" in 1850 to eighteen in 1860, due to the state's gradual emancipation law.[34] Although the numbers are small compared to national totals, taking a sample of Southern slavery out of its place and setting it down again in Utah Territory revealed things about lived experience, the types of control enslavers could exercise outside the South, how the institution was handled by mostly Northerners and Europeans, the relative abundance of records about some of the enslaved in Utah compared to records for farming households in the South, and the stories people told afterward to explain the institution.

The 1851 Negotiations over Enslaved Families

Green Flake appeared three times in the 1850 census: in the official slave schedule showing Agnes Love Flake taking him to California, in the draft slave schedule showing him remaining in the Great Salt Lake Valley in the possession of Brigham Young, and in the population schedule with Rose and Violet Crosby.[35] For years, authors and journalists have repeated the myth that Green Flake was donated to the Church of Jesus Christ of Latter-day Saints as tithing. The account is based on one late and unreliable memory. The event only begins to make sense when understood as part of a series of transactions involving five or more enslavers and Brigham Young, who seems to have stepped in and hired Flake when the situation reached an impasse. Involved were enslaved Green Flake, Rose and Violet (Crosby) Litchford, Martha (Crosby) Flake, Hark (Lay) Wales, Nancy (Bankhead) Wales Valentine, Howard Egan Wales, Henry

(Bankhead) Wales Valentine, an unnamed man enslaved by one of the Bankhead brothers, Mary (Crosby) Bankhead Sampson Chism, Nancy Bankhead Jefferson, George Bankhead Chism, and possibly others, including Lucy (Lay). The enslavers involved in the negotiations were John H. Bankhead, George W. Bankhead, William Crosby, Agnes Love Flake, William and Sytha Crosby Lay, and possibly Abraham O. Smoot or Margaret McMeans Smoot.

When the Southerners took their enslaved people to the Great Salt Lake Valley in 1847 and 1848, they separated them from their families in the South. Some of the enslaved formed new families in Utah. When the Crosby, Flake, and Lay families decided to leave for California in 1851, and the Bankhead brothers decided to remain in Utah Territory, the move would separate new families. Green Flake and Hark Wales went to Brigham Young for help. When William Crosby learned about their appeal to Young, he wrote Young in a fury. Besides a vituperative personal attack on Green, he claimed that Agnes Flake found it difficult to discipline Green. If so, perhaps her new neighbors had hampered her ability to control Green's labor, since they would have had little sympathy for the physical and psychological violence required to keep Southern slavery operational. As subsequent events showed, Brigham Young disagreed with Crosby's assessment. He suggested the exchange of several of the enslaved people and wrote that it might be best to leave all of them in Utah Territory, since he erroneously concluded that "they will all go free as soon as they shall arrive in California."[36]

The negotiations kept two families together but split Hark Wales and his wife Nancy. Green Flake remained in Utah Territory with his possible wife at the time, Rose. Rose and her mother Violet left service in the Crosby household for the Bankhead household, and, in exchange, Crosby may have taken an unnamed man enslaved by John H. Bankhead so the man could accompany his wife Mary (Crosby) Bankhead. Lucy (Lay) may have been Violet's daughter, and William and Sytha Crosby Lay may have sold her to Abraham O. and Margaret McMeans Smoot so she could remain with her mother in the Great Salt Lake Valley.

Although California was a free state, the enslavers kept their workers in servitude there until a small community of free Blacks in Los Angeles helped liberate the enslaved through the *habeas corpus* action *In re Hannah* (1856), best known as the court case that freed Biddy Mason and

Hannah Smiley and their families. Their story was not unusual: many legally and illegally enslaved African Americans in California remained in bondage or had to earn money to buy their own freedom.[37] Those legally enslaved in California included eight people who lived in the Great Salt Lake Valley briefly before their owner, Latter-day Saint convert Bird B. Barnett, took them to Northern California in 1850.

Brigham Young had told Green Flake he was free when he arrived in the Great Salt Lake Valley in 1847, but around 1853, he secured Green's freedom and granted him land for a farm. When Agnes Flake tried to sell Green in 1854, Brigham Young sidestepped her request, and Green Flake remained a free man.

An Act in Relation to Service

In 1852, in the wake of unrest involving the Indigenous and Mexican slave trade, the territorial legislature crafted legislation and held a debate over African American slavery. Despite impassioned opposition from Latter-day Saint apostle Orson Pratt, Brigham Young supported legislation allowing Black servitude.[38] In a speech to the legislature, he identified the origins of slavery and race in the Bible. He said that those of African descent were created for service, but if slavery was practiced, it should be practiced humanely, since Southern slavery abused principles set forth in scripture.[39] With Young's support, the territorial legislature codified and regulated African American sales and servitude. Young's explanations to the legislature and in other settings not only ensured the passage of the Act but also began a practice that prevented most Black members of the Church of Jesus Christ of Latter-day Saints from holding the lay priesthood or participating in temple rites for more than a century.

An Act in Relation to Service attempted to shift chattel slavery into a system of contracted labor. It decreed that those who took "servants justly bound to them, arising from special contract or otherwise," into the territory "shall be entitled to such service or labor by the laws of this Territory." Those taking "servants" into the territory must register "written and satisfactory evidence [in the probate court] that such service or labor is due." The Act limited the term of service for "servants" and their children to the time required to fulfill "the debt due his, her, or their master or masters." It forbade sexual intercourse between the enslaver and enslaved or indentured of African descent, or any "white person" and "any of the African race." Although An Act in Relation to Service prohibited sexual relations between Black and White and enslavers and enslaved, it did not specifically prohibit interracial marriage. Those with "servants" must "correct and punish . . . when it may be necessary" and must provide for those in their service, including food, clothing, recreation, and at least eighteen months of education between the ages of six and twenty years.

The Act did not create an explicit mechanism for manumission. If a "master or mistress" mistreated a servant or slave, or the enslaved did not agree to a sale of his labor or removal from the territory, a probate judge would oversee the forfeiture of the enslaved or indentured servant to the territory. The Act did not specify whether forfeiture provided freedom, or whether the court would then hire out the servant or slave, as was done in the South. There are no forfeitures in the records of the probate court, although Latter-day Saint bishop Edwin D. Woolley appears to have attempted to provoke one in *Territory of Utah v. Williams Camp* (1856).

More would be known about the legal ramifications of An Act in Relation to Service if there had been more than two court cases involving the Act in the territory, but in *Utah v. Camp* (1856), the court excused the defendants for insufficient evidence, and in *A. B. Miller v. Thomas S. Williams* (1859), the federal judge set aside the jury verdict, and a court never reheard the case before Williams was murdered in California. The California Supreme Court ruled on provisions of the Act in an 1875 case about Missouri merchant Richard Pearson who married formerly enslaved Laura in Utah Territory in 1854. The court declared that the marriage secured Laura's freedom, and she was eligible to inherit Richard's estate, but the case took place a decade after the Civil War ended and did not have any bearing on the lives of those in the territory.[40]

Perhaps by design, An Act in Relation to Service gave Brigham Young the ability to emancipate Green Flake and others left in the valley when their enslavers went to California in 1851. One of those freed, Rose, gave birth to a son in 1854 and named him Daniel Freeman, his surname a celebration of their liberation from slavery. However, just weeks after the law passed, Margaret McMeans Smoot sold Lucy to Thomas S. Williams in the first African American slave sale in the Territory with existing documentation. Neither Smoot nor Williams sought approval in the probate court, but Williams recorded the sale in probate court four years later.

The Utah State Archives holds slave registrations for Shepherd, Daniel, Jerry, Caroline, Tampian, and Lucy. (See Appendix 2.) The registrations refer to a book called *Probate Register of Servants*, but it does not appear to exist anymore. None of the registrations indicate that Judge Elias Smith questioned any of the six about their desire to remain in servitude.[41]

Due to its attempt to treat slavery as contracted labor, the Act accounted for few of the situations normally encountered in Southern slavery. It was not a cohesive slave code with principles familiar to Southern enslavers, and they and the probate court mostly ignored the Act and its provisions. Although John Brown was a member of the first territorial legislature, there is no record that he or Elizabeth Crosby

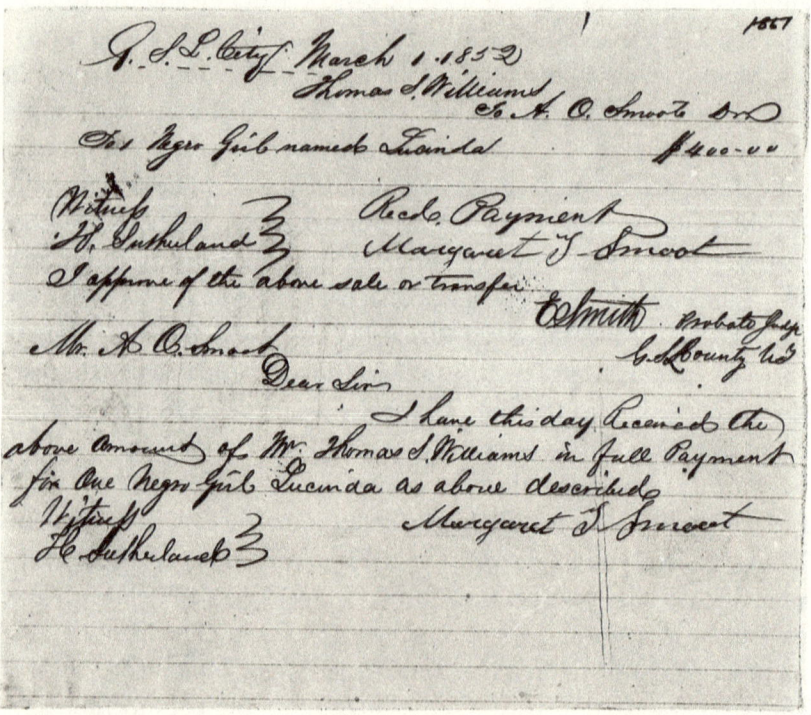

Figure I.3. In 1852, Margaret T. Smoot sold Lucy or Lucinda to Thomas S. Williams. Williams recorded the sale in probate court in 1856. Utah State Archives.

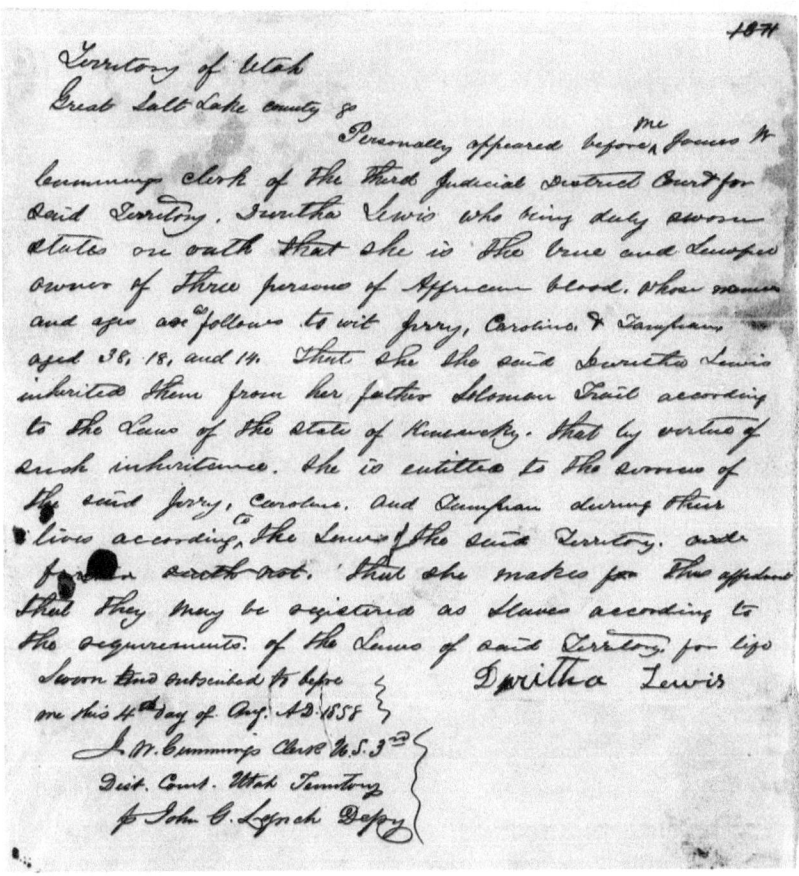

Figure I.4. In 1858, Duritha Trail Lewis registered Jerry, Caroline, and Tampian in the probate court before selling Caroline and Tampian to Thomas S. Williams. Utah State Archives.

Brown registered Betsy in the probate court, and the price he listed for Betsy in 1857 of $1,000 was a high price for a chattel slave of her age and sex and did not take into consideration any limitations on his ownership of her and her future children.[42] All known valuations or sales documents—including an 1857 price for Nancy Lines Smith of $500; the prices for Jerry, Caroline, and Tampian in the David Lewis estate; and the 1859 sale of Daniel Camp for $800—echo prices seen in chattel slavery elsewhere and do not indicate that enslavers valued their slave property any lower due to the provisions of the Act. Children born to enslaved parents in the households of Reuben Perkins and George W. Bankhead appeared in 1860 federal census slave schedules. If slavery had not ended a decade later in the territory, or if there had been more than about three dozen enslaved Black men, women, and children in the territory at any time after 1852, there likely would have been additional litigation over its provisions.

Tithing and Consecration Deeds

Before the Latter-day Saints moved to the Great Salt Lake Valley, they built a temple in Nauvoo, Illinois, which they had to abandon when they moved west. Some Southern enslavers, most still living in the South, donated cash, labor for the temple, or agricultural products, such as the tobacco donated by Seth Utley and Bird B. Barnett. Most donations from Southerners directly or indirectly involved enslaved labor. The economic contributions of the enslaved to the Nauvoo Temple ranged from any work done on the Jolley farm by six-year-old Lambson, the only person enslaved in the Henry Jolley household, to the cash donations made by the extended Crosby family from the sale of land and enslaved workers recently inherited from their father.

Tithing donations for the temple and other church uses were voluntary but strongly encouraged, and the poor were not expected to pay.[43] Tithing records show that enslavers usually donated cash or produce rather than labor. The major labor donation by enslavers was in the spring of 1845 when William Crosby, John H. Bankhead, John Brown, William Matthews, William McKown, and Samuel Heath traveled to Nauvoo to work on the temple for about a month. Tithing records and Brown's account of the trip suggest that they left any enslaved people working on their Mississippi farms.[44] Nauvoo and Utah records suggest that enslavers preserved the labor of their workers for agricultural production rather than donating their labor to the church or community.

Enslaved Venus Redd and John Burton each donated one dollar for the temple. Nothing is known about the source of their donations. Benjamin Holladay, a Black man living in Mississippi, legal status unknown, donated $1.50. Later in Utah Territory, Nancy Lines Smith and Luke Redd donated produce to the church as tithing.[45]

Known enslavers in the 1844 to 1846 Nauvoo tithing records include Henry Jolley, $124.86; the extended Crosby family, $1093.83; brothers John H., James B., and George W. Bankhead, $89.00; brothers William, James, and George W. Stewart, $195.70; brothers Bryan W. and Jabus Nowlin and their father Peyton Nowlin, $445.00; Robert D. Covington, $25.00; James M. Morehead, $10.00; Washington N. Cook, $38.50; James M. Flake, $350.00; the Redd family, $23.24; Susan Burton, $9.10; Isham and Caroline Gilliam, $25.45; Seth Utley, $83.50; Bird B. Barnett, $39.00; James Poe, $5.00; Samuel Rooker, $2.00; John M. Thompson, $16.00; George W. Brame, $2.00; Francis McKown and his son William, $33.50; and the McCorkle-Scott family, $65.98.[46] Contemporary accounts estimated the cost of the temple at between $800,000 and $1 million.[47] Donations from the Southern enslavers were occasionally much larger than the average tithing donation but total contributions were around three-tenths of 1 percent of the estimated cost of the temple.

After the Latter-day Saints began settling the Great Salt Lake Valley, a handful of Southern families used their enslaved workers to quickly create productive farms. Although church tithing books from early Utah show occasional donations from enslavers, the books do not document the direct use of donated enslaved labor.[48] Tithing donations from enslavers in the early Great Salt Lake Valley include Daniel and Ann Crosby Thomas, $210.39, the value of which would have involved the labor of Philemon and Tennessee; James M. and Agnes Flake, $128.75, labor of Green Flake and Elizabeth Flake; George W. Bankhead, $147.21, labor of Nancy Bankhead Valentine, Alexander Bankhead, and Nancy's sons; Reuben Perkins, $351.04, labor of Frank and Esther Perkins, their children, and Benjamin Perkins; and Williams Camp, $347.07, labor of Charlotte and Daniel.[49] Tithing receipts from enslavers in California beginning in 1851 include Agnes Flake, $29.50, labor of Green (hired out) and Elizabeth; the extended Crosby family, $1641.66, including the donation of an IOU for $250.00 from Thomas S. Williams to Sytha Crosby Lay, labor of Toby Embers, Grief Embers, Oscar Smith, Nelson, Henderson, Mary Crosby Bankhead and children, Philemon, Tennessee, Hark Wales, and Harriet Embers; and Robert M. Smith, $91.82, labor of Biddy Mason and Hannah Smiley and their children.[50]

In the mid-1850s, Brigham Young encouraged church members to consecrate (dedicate) their property to the work of the church. About half of Latter-day Saint households created deeds of transfer. The movement was both an effort to create a unified front as a people and an attempt to create a system by which, as Apostle Orson Pratt explained, "the Saints must eventually become perfect enough to consent to the great principles of equality in regard to property."[51] Most of the deeds still in existence show between $100 and $1,000 of property per household, but a handful show property in the tens or hundreds of thousands of dollars. An index book shows the total amount of consecrated property at close to $2 million, with $1500 of that in slave property. The deeds were symbolic; the church did not take possession of any property.[52]

Two men in Utah County, south of Great Salt Lake County, listed enslaved women in their valuations. William Taylor Dennis listed "1 African Servant Girl 500.00 [dollars]," meaning Nancy Lines Smith, then

Figure I.5. Betsy Brown Flewellen and her daughter Kate Flewellen Oglesby. From John Brown and John Z. Brown, *Autobiography of Pioneer John Brown* (1941). Used by permission.

in her forties, and John Brown listed "1 African Servant Girl 1000.00 [dollars]," meaning twenty-year-old Betsy Brown. No other enslavers listed the enslaved on their deeds although they continued to hold people in bondage.[53]

The tithing contributions made possible by their labor made the enslaved part of the Nauvoo experience, and then made them an important part of the settlement of Utah and San Bernardino. However, the Southerners' tithing and the symbolic consecration deeds were never as important to their communities as the knowledge of how to quickly begin operational communities, with contributions made through the strength and experience of Samuel Smith, Toby and Grief Embers, Philemon, John Burton, Green Flake, Violet Litchford, Hannah Smiley, and other enslaved pioneers.

The 1856 Census

The territorial government took a census in 1856 to support an attempt to gain statehood. The census is fraudulent. When recorders copied over the census, they filled blank lines with extra names. Families are full to the last line of each page without children spilling over onto the next page, many people are listed who are unidentifiable from any other record, and the census included multiple deceased people.[54] The census claims eighty-three women or girls named Rose in the territory in 1856, but most are unidentifiable, including Rose Green, Rose Flowers, and Rose Farmer. Only ten women named Rose appeared in the 1860 federal census in Utah Territory. Similarly, fifty-five men or boys named Sylvester appeared in 1856 but only twenty in 1860.

The Perkins families, both Black and White, illustrate the problem with the census. Forty-eight family members appear in Davis County, with the names of the enslaved Black family intertwined with the names of their enslavers. Although the census does not list ages, all except four of the large extended family are identifiable, and these four may either be fraudulent entries or children who died and are not remembered in family records. Five of the identifiable family members listed in the census had been dead for five or more years: Diana Anderson Perkins, Andrew Huston Perkins, Wilson Gardner Perkins, William Anderson Perkins, and James Monroe Perkins. In Great Salt Lake County, the census showed

George Bankhead in the same household as Philomela, Andrew, Allen T., Heber G., Jonathan, and James. Perhaps George W. Bankhead provided the census taker with a tally of the enslaved in his household and census clerks filled in names, so the six may be Nancy Bankhead Valentine, Alexander Bankhead, and Nancy's sons. The census could have been a valuable record of the enslaved population but must be used with a careful recognition of the patterns used in padding the census.

The Last Years before Freedom

The importation of enslaved people into the territory mostly ended by 1851, but in the mid-1850s, converts from Texas began arriving in the territory with thousands of cattle and a few enslaved people. Texan Thomas Lacy Greer married a daughter of Utah enslavers Williams and Diannah Camp. After many of their cattle froze during a disastrous winter, the extended Greer family decided to cut their losses and return to Texas. They planned to take the four enslaved members of the Camp household with them, but one of them, Daniel, did not want to return to slavery in the South. He ran away, and an ad hoc slave patrol hunted him down. Among those who were shocked at this evidence of Southern slavery was Bishop Edwin D. Woolley, a former Quaker from Pennsylvania. He had the four Southerners arrested and charged with kidnapping. The judge eventually threw out the case for lack of evidence, but Daniel remained in Utah.

In 1859, *New York Daily Tribune* editor Horace Greeley visited Utah Territory and interviewed Brigham Young. Young answered his inquiry about slavery: "We consider it of Divine institution, and not to be abolished until the curse pronounced on Ham shall have been removed from his descendants." He told Greeley that territorial laws allowed slavery. "If slaves are brought here by those who owned them in the States, we do not favor their escape from the service of those owners." Greeley asked whether Utah planned to be a slave state. "No," Young replied, "she will be a Free State." He explained, "Slavery here would prove useless and unprofitable. I regard it generally as a curse to the masters. . . . Utah is not adapted to Slave Labor."[55]

That same year, courts heard two cases involving the enslaved, both cases connected to disaffected Latter-day Saint and human trafficker

Thomas S. Williams. In 1855, shortly before David Lewis's death, Williams and Lewis entered a partnership to trade in Indigenous children.[56] In 1858, Williams purchased Daniel Camp from Williams Camp and purchased sisters Caroline and Tampian Hoye from David Lewis's widow Duritha Trail Lewis.[57] During an argument over Caroline and Tampian the next year, Thomas Bankhead Coleman shot Shepherd Camp, then enslaved by William H. Hooper. Shepherd died, and the judge sent Coleman to prison. That same year, Williams decided to invest most of his resources into a merchanting trip to California, so he dissolved his partnership with Hooper and sold him Daniel Camp.[58] As he prepared for the trip, "Charles M. Smith, Esq., filed a petition asking for a writ of replevin to recover two negro women from Mr. T. S. Williams, which he claimed was the property of A. B. Miller."[59] During *A. B. Miller v. Thomas S. Williams* (1859), Williams filed bonds with the court to keep Caroline and Tampian Hoye in his possession. The case questioned only the chain of ownership, and the jury found that Williams owned the sisters, but the judge set aside the verdict, and the case was never reheard.[60] Half a year later, Williams and his brother-in-law Parmenio Jackman were killed by Indigenous raiders on a freighting trip to California. During the long settlement of the Williams estate, attorney Seth Blair wrote an irate letter to the probate court about the ownership of Caroline and Tampian and a mortgage on one of them. The Williams estate documents show one of the women working in the home of New York native and Latter-day Saint leader Horace S. Eldredge. The murder had left the Williams and Jackman families indigent, so hiring out Caroline or Tampian may have provided the Williams widows with income. The court records do not show the resolution of the incident.

The 1860 census slave schedules showed nineteen enslaved people in Great Salt Lake County and ten in Davis County. Census takers missed several enslaved people in Iron, Utah, and Cache counties. Unlike the 1850 census, the census takers did not list names, so the identities of some of the enslaved will never be known, including at least one who would have been hired, rather than enslaved by the person listed on the schedule. Hiring out the enslaved was an important feature of Southern slavery. Those who controlled the labor of enslaved people did not always need that labor or may have needed money more than labor. During the nineteenth century, enslavers hired out between 5 and 15 percent of the

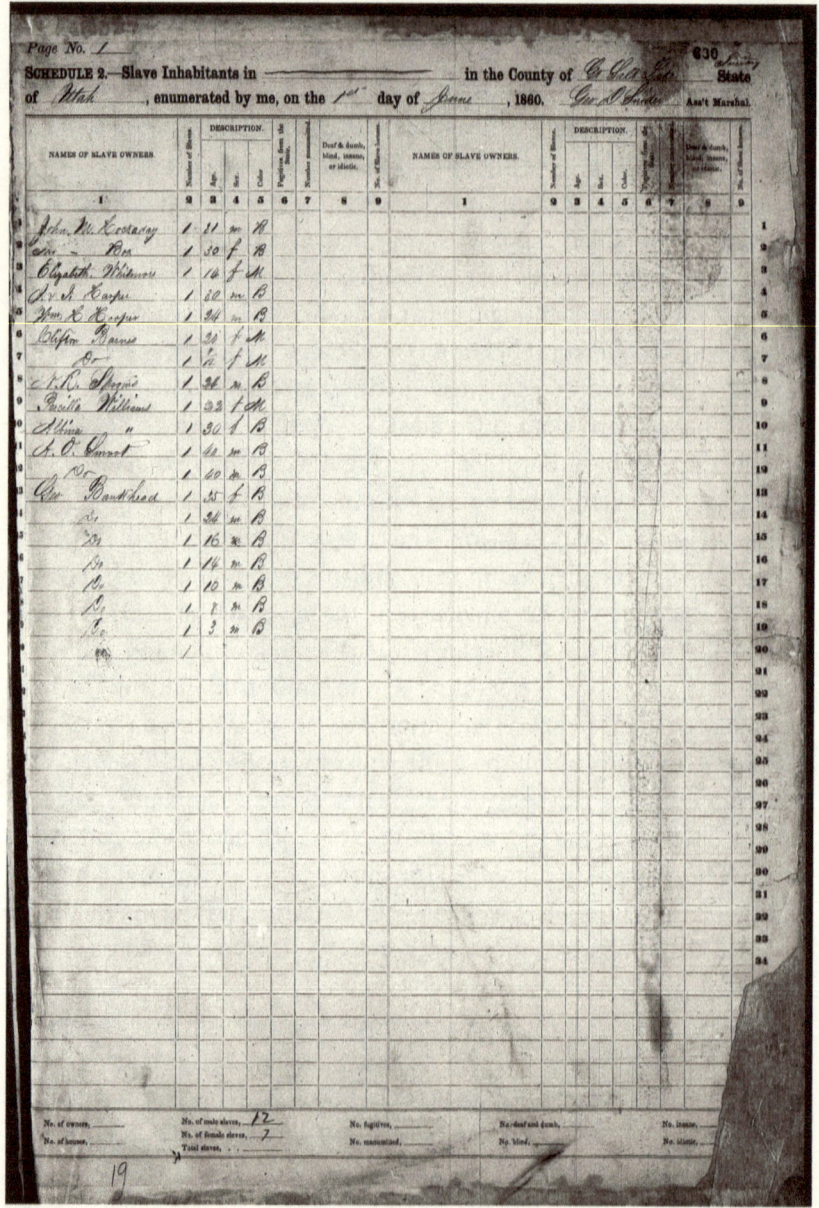

Figure I.6. The 1860 federal census slave schedule for Great Salt Lake County. National Archives and Records Administration and FamilySearch.

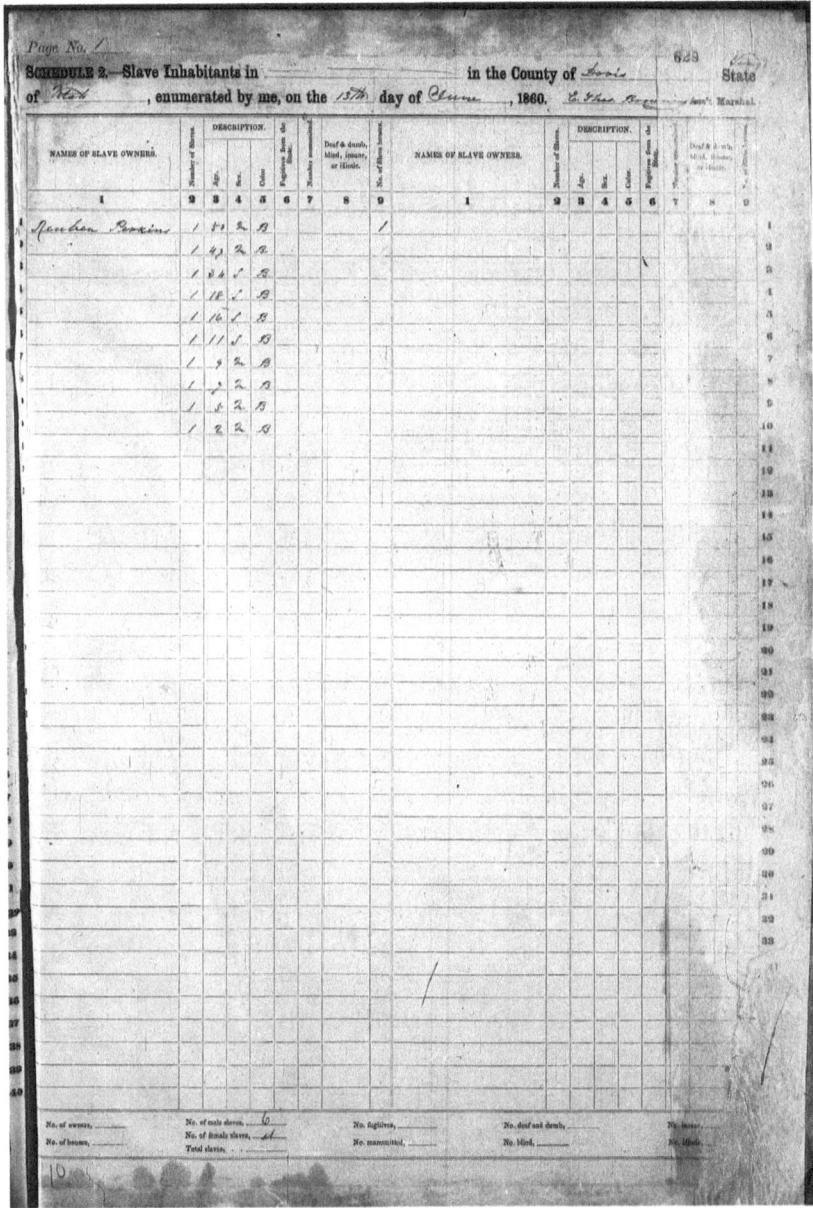

Figure I.7. The 1860 federal census slave schedule for Davis County showing the Perkins family. National Archives and Records Administration and FamilySearch.

enslaved population of the South.⁶¹ A renter assumed the cost of feeding and clothing the hired worker and returning him or her in good health. Although little documentation exists, several transactions in Utah Territory were likely to have been slave hires rather than sales, including the 1851 transaction between Agnes Love Flake and Brigham Young involving the labor of Green Flake.

In 1860, English adventurer Richard Burton recorded the presence of "an exceedingly plain middle-aged and full-blooded negro woman" in a Latter-day Saint wagon train.⁶² Burton's acerbic comments are the only known personal description of fifty-year-old Phoebe, enslaved by Emanuel M. and Nancy Easters Murphy. Phoebe was the last known enslaved African American to arrive in Utah Territory. A year later, the Talbot family smuggled a South African boy named Gobo Fango into the country and then to Utah Territory. Although the records are not conclusive, the Talbot family may have illegally hired out or sold Fango in the territory.

In 1862, half a year before the Emancipation Proclamation, Congress ended slavery in the US territories.

> CHAP. CXI.—*An Act to secure Freedom to all Persons within the Territories of the United States.*
>
> *Be it enacted by the Senate and House of Representatives of the United States of America in Congress assembled,* That from and after the passage of this act there shall be neither slavery nor involuntary servitude in any of the Territories of the United States now existing, or which may at any time hereafter be formed or acquired by the United States, otherwise than in punishment of crimes whereof the party shall have been duly convicted.
>
> APPROVED, June 19, 1862.⁶³

The Great Salt Lake City newspaper, *Deseret News*, noticed the event with a single line buried in an article about politics: "On June 20th, the President approved the bill prohibiting slavery in the Territories."⁶⁴ Dr. John M. Bernhisel sent the news to Brigham Young in a letter: "Congress has passed a bill abolishing slavery in all the Territories of the United States, and only requires the sanction of the Executive to become a law." The *Brigham Young Office Journal* skips from May 1862 to June 1863, and there is no record of reaction to the legislation in the territory.⁶⁵

The territorial government was in transition and does not appear to have taken any action: territorial secretary Frank Fuller had just become acting governor when Governor John W. Dawson fled the territory after word spread about his unwelcome advances toward widowed enslaver Albina Merrill Williams.

No family or community history reliably specifies when those enslaved in Utah Territory knew they were free, whether in 1862, or after the Civil War ended.

The Myths of Freedom and the Errors of Memory

As the years passed, the descendants of those who enslaved people in Utah Territory faced the dilemma of how to explain their existence. Multiple families independently invented the same explanation: their ancestors freed the enslaved in the South or offered them their freedom, and the enslaved accompanied their enslavers to Utah Territory out of love, respect, or gratitude at being freed. A variation of this claim first appeared in print in the 1915 obituary of Nancy Crosby Bankhead. "Mrs. Bankhead and husband were among a few of the saints to own slaves. Owing to their belief in Mormonism these slaves were liberated but came to Utah, remaining in the home of the Bankheads until . . . 1884."[66] However, many decades earlier, the family told the Utah census taker that they owned nine slaves, none of them manumitted, or freed.[67] John H. Redd descendants later claimed that while he was still in Tennessee, their ancestor "legally freed each of his slaves by an act of court and made financial provision for each."[68] However, the manumission records for his Tennessee county do not support the claim, and all appeared in the draft copy of the 1850 census slave schedule for Utah Territory.[69]

The error of claiming manumission came, partly, from not understanding what enslavers themselves understood: enslaved workers were a marker of wealth and economic status. Enslaved people were often an inheritance that enslavers received from their parents and could then provide to their children. Claims that ancestors freed the enslaved do not account for financial encumbrances that would make it difficult or impossible to free the enslaved, or for the loss of wealth, economic status, and labor that accompanied manumission. In contrast to explanations by their descendants, enslavers who left records did not make excuses for forced labor or human trafficking, with the notable exception of Lewis Ricks. Lewis and his brother, Joel Ricks, the founder of a large Latter-day Saint family, were executors of their father's estate. Lewis wrote: "We let the blacks select homes [i.e., new enslavers] and sold them as the best we could do, as the laws of Kentucky were very strict on freeing slaves." He added, "I felt very bad to be obliged to do this, but it was the best I could do under the then existing circumstances."[70]

The laws throughout other Southern states were likewise "very strict on freeing slaves." In previous generations, enslaved people could be freed in a will or by other means, but the fear of slave uprisings and a free Black population led Southern states to increasingly limit manumission. By the time Southern converts to the Church of Jesus Christ of Latter-day Saints prepared to move west, manumission required either an act of the state legislature or a visit to a county court while it was in session. Enslavers who desired to manumit the enslaved must, in most cases, provide a large bond to ensure their legal behavior, immediately remove them from the state, or send them to Africa. Anyone freed illegally, or even legally, was in danger of kidnapping and sale or arrest by the county court. It was a crime in some jurisdictions to speak of freedom to the enslaved: Tennessee made it a felony, Alabama declared a penalty of ten years' imprisonment for enticing the enslaved out of state with an offer of freedom, and Arkansas stipulated that anyone who spoke of freedom to the enslaved was subject to one to five years in the penitentiary.[71]

Some Latter-day Saints sold people on the way to Utah Territory. Widowed Ruthinda Baker Stewart sold Annaca in Missouri for two yoke of oxen, two cows, and $50.[72] Jacob and Sebrina Croft sold Patricia (age thirty-seven), Andrew (four), and Landy (two) to Cherokee leader Stand Watie as they crossed the Cherokee Nation in 1856, just before they entered Kansas Territory, then gripped with the violent conflicts over slavery that gave it the name "Bleeding Kansas."[73] Most of those enslaved by William Taylor Dennis and Talitha Bankhead Dennis freed themselves while crossing the country. Some died: Jacob (Crosby) (Bankhead) at Winter Quarters, Henry (Crosby) (Brown) in Missouri, possibly an unnamed woman enslaved by Harriet Heath Marler, and perhaps a woman named Sue enslaved by Elizabeth Thomas Morehead.

Around twenty of the enslaved or indentured men, women, and children in Utah Territory were part of the estate of John Crosby of Monroe

County, Mississippi. He died in 1840, and during the settlement of his estate, his executors valued the estate at almost $17,000, in today's currency around half a million to $12 million.[74]

Chattel slavery was lifelong, involuntary, and hereditary. In England, a child's legal status followed that of his father, but the American colonies adopted a Roman practice called *partus sequitur ventrem*, or *partus* for short, which meant that a child's status followed that of its mother.[75] This practice combined with the international and interstate slave trade meant that the American colonies brought millions of people into bondage, and thus created a large and politically powerless workforce. An alternative system of labor, indentured servitude, had a voluntary component and was limited to a certain term. The voluntary component was not always entirely voluntary, and the term was sometimes longer than the expected life of the servant, but during gradual emancipation in states such as New York or New Jersey, indentures were limited to specific terms. Although indentured servitude was the labor system under which many early White settlers came to America, even cases with an involuntary component should not be confused with hereditary chattel slavery. In one case of Black indenture, the 1850 slave schedule for Utah Territory recorded that Sam Franklin was "Free When Twenty One," which means that for a reason lost to time, he provided labor to the Redd family under indenture, not enslavement.[76]

Most converts from the American South enslaved no one in Utah Territory. A small group enslaved between one to four people.[77] Just seven households enslaved five or more African American men, women, or children in Utah Territory: John H. and Nancy Crosby Bankhead, George W. Bankhead, William and Sarah Harmon Crosby, Reuben and Elizabeth Petillo Perkins, John H. and Elizabeth Hancock Redd, Bird B. and Martha Walker Barnett, and Robert M. and Rebecca Dorn Smith. This was similar to the demographics of slavery in the South: in 1860, 20 percent of free householders in the South owned the entire enslaved population. Half of the enslavers, or 10 percent of free adults, enslaved between one and four people.[78]

Descendants of enslavers tended to inflate their ancestors' economic or social status when they retold their family stories in subsequent generations, but most of the enslavers named in this book were yeoman farmers, the large landowning Southern middle class. "All my life I have heard about how the people of that time lived in luxury, with slaves to wait on them," wrote one family historian about an ancestor's estate, including seven enslaved workers. "As poor as I think I am, I have more luxuries than Zebedee [Hancock] ever dreamed of. He apparently didn't even have a stove."[79]

Although the term "plantation" was not standardized in the nineteenth century as it is now to mean an agricultural economic unit with twenty or more enslaved workers, it is unlikely that nineteenth-century writers would describe the following small farmers as plantation owners, as was done by their descendants. "John H. [Bankhead] was the owner of a number of slaves on his large plantation."[80] Bankhead owned farms, but never a plantation. "Thomas Bedford Graham . . . owned cotton plantations in the states of Alabama and Mississippi."[81] Graham owned at most eighty acres most of the years he paid taxes in Mississippi. He may have briefly enslaved or hired one young girl. William Taylor Dennis and Talitha Cumi Bankhead "set up their own household on a beautiful plantation with *many slaves*."[82] Dennis enslaved two men and two women in 1850. Americus Greer moved to Utah Territory in 1855, and then back to Texas in 1856. Years later, his daughter Malvina Greer Skousen remembered, "My father, Americus Vespuccius Greer, was a wealthy plantation owner in Bosque County, Texas. . . . We had 25 negro servants. We were all very fond of them and treated them as part of the family."[83] However, years earlier, her father had left his own record about their "hard times in Texas" when even "corn bread was scarce." He wrote, "Our family consisted besides father and mother and eight children, [and other relatives]. . . . Also five colored viz; Ned, Jim, Judah, Lucy and Louisa—20 in all."[84]

The consistent errors in family narratives suggest common origins for the myths. Few families with enslaved workers preserved any written records, and later family histories show that children and grandchildren quickly forgot the legal and social aspects of Southern slavery. In addition, memories may have been muted or altered by efforts to explain the system to non-Southern neighbors and relatives. Finally, when descendants began to tell their family stories in the mid-twentieth century, they did not have access to reliable histories of slavery, and most had been exposed to post–Civil War Southern propaganda. After the Civil War ended, Confederate president Jefferson Davis and others reframed the war into a story of states' rights rather than an attempt to preserve an economic system based on human trafficking and enslavement, and taught slavery as a system that benefitted enslaved people. The Lost Cause mythology of Southern slavery justified the system with religious and racial theories of Black inferiority and fictionalized the system into a story of the supposedly affectionate relationships between enslaver and enslaved. Many Utah family histories that address slavery echo Lost Cause fiction. In heavily fictionalized works such as the biography of Mary Blann Ewell Jones or Charmaine Lay Kohler's *Southern Grace: A Story of the Mississippi Saints*, ancestors lived on plantations, women were refined belles, every slave was a beloved family retainer, and every "master" or "mistress" was kindhearted. Dennis family memories of their "Black Mammy," Nancy Lines Smith, include all the stereotypes: a comforting surrogate mother in voluntary servitude, cook and housekeeper, beloved and loyal, yet nameless.[85] These works of fiction consequently function mainly as an illustration of how families have adapted the experiences of their ancestors to serve the needs of subsequent generations.

In 1965, Kate B. Carter, president of Daughters of Utah Pioneers, published a booklet called *The Negro Pioneer*. She did not mention in her introduction whether she remembered her childhood neighbors, formerly enslaved African American Latter-day Saint pioneers Alexander and Marinda Redd Bankhead, but their presence must have influenced her work. *Negro Pioneer* is, at times, an infuriating collection, its information compromised by fiction presented as fact and memories confused by time, as well as only sporadic attribution or citations, but Carter did preserve names, memories, and a handful of documents that otherwise would have been lost.

The historical errors in sources like *Negro Pioneer* can be as simple as mistaking household movements, or as complex as misrepresenting economic or religious history, as in the mutilation stories of Venus Redd and "Mammy Chloe." *Negro Pioneer* claimed that Venus "had a great desire to go to the temple, and when she found that the temple was closed to Negroes, she scratched her arm until it bled and said: 'See, my blood is as white as anyone's.'"[86] "Mammy Chloe" supposedly said, "I'd be willen, honey, to be skinned alive if I could jus' go in dat Temple."[87] As much as these stories would add to the historical record, it is not possible to confirm them, and there are many reasons to disbelieve them, including the possibility that one of the women may be entirely fictional. Venus died before the Latter-day Saints built a temple in Utah Territory, and "Chloe" probably did not exist, or if she did exist, did not travel to Utah with her enslaver and live there until after the Civil War as family histories claimed, since she does not appear in multiple records that would mention her. The similarities between the two stories suggest that these supposed objections to racialized worship may have been late memories of early African American Latter-day Saint convert Jane Elizabeth Manning James and her efforts to participate in segregated temple rites, although this assumes that either family knew Manning's story. The two stories plus a supposed family memory of Gobo Fango being willing to "give his hands if he could hold the [lay Latter-day Saint] priesthood" came from an era of mythologizing and reinventing the history of slavery in Utah Territory and first appeared in the mid-twentieth century when pressure on the Church of Jesus Christ of Latter-day Saints to end racially based priesthood and temple restrictions forced many Latter-day Saints to consider questions of racial justice.[88] The creation of these mutilation stories would have been a natural result. No other sources confirm the anecdotes, there is no contemporaneous documentation given for any of the stories, and they only appear in sources filled with unreliable and incorrect information, so as much as the stories of protests against racialized Latter-day Saint worship would add to this book, none of them meet basic standards of historical reliability.

Two other myths are those of Green Flake entering the Great Salt Lake Valley and the identity of the first Black child born there, supposed to have been Daniel Freeman Bankhead. The story that Green Flake drove Brigham Young into the Great Salt Lake Valley on July 24, 1847, would provide an ironic twist to the stories of Brigham Young's strong segregationist views, but Flake had been in the valley for two or three days when Brigham Young arrived, driven by Wilford Woodruff.[89] Rather than being the first Black child born in Utah, Daniel Freeman Bankhead would have been the twelfth or fourteenth. If there were no children of African descent born to mountain men, Spanish traders, or Native Americans, the first Black children born in the area were Mary Ann James Robinson, Nancy Bankhead Jefferson, Howard Egan Wales, and Charles Embers.[90]

Although family and community histories can be valuable resources, they are unreliable due to the reinvention of narratives about slavery, the dynamic nature of memory, the scarcity of written records, and the

Figure I.8. Daniel Freeman Bankhead. His name "Freeman" celebrated the liberation of a small group of enslaved people living in the Great Salt Lake Valley. Used by permission, Utah State Historical Society.

lapse of time between the events and the retelling. When families tried to reconstruct their stories generations later, they got many details wrong. A four-sentence biography of Downey Perkins Woolridge in *Negro Pioneer* contains nine distinct errors.[91] Any family or community history must be assessed for reliability by checking every detail that can be checked against historical records and dependable histories of slavery. An "autobiography" of Henry Jolley in *Negro Pioneer* did not hold up to fact-checking. Instead, clues within the document suggest that a descendant wrote it as historical fiction about a century after Jolley's death. The history of enslavement in the family confirms that the autobiography's sentiments about slavery and race belong to the unnamed author rather than Jolley. Eighteenth- and nineteenth-century newspapers show Jolley's relatives placing numerous fugitive slave notices in attempts to preserve the labor of the enslaved who, in case after case, reportedly fled bondage to find their families.[92]

Family and community histories also tend to ignore the ethics of slavery. When a historian removes the veneer of gentility used to describe the system, what remains is unfree labor, human trafficking, sex trafficking, forced prostitution, forced or coerced reproduction, sexual assault, and rape. The 1850 federal census slave schedules for Utah Territory divided the enslaved into three categories: Black, "mulatto," and "yellow."[93] Census takers categorized eighteen of those in the census as "yellow" or "mulatto," which suggested mixed African and European descent. Although the sexual abuse and exploitation of enslaved people is a sensitive topic, it is fundamentally dishonest to pretend it did not happen and reprehensible to glorify it.

Historian Thomas L. Foster documented the various forms of sexual exploitation of enslaved men, including the hiring out of the enslaved for forced or coerced reproduction. This practice appears in an unverifiable account in the historical fiction of Charmaine Lay Kohler.

> [John Crosby] produced seed for a human crop—he ran a stud service. John was especially proud of his four "bucks." Valued well above the nine-hundred dollars a "regular" slave would bring on the market, the four were of great worth. He was able to charge high stud fees for their use and with the money continually add to his acreage. They were of top quality—tall, well-muscled and intelligent. Granted, they were almost too intelligent, for they sometimes forgot their place, but he kept them under control. He was also proud of the status this gave him in the community, for he was greatly admired by his peers. Other planters were quick to notice the prosperity of John's plantation and the quality of his "niggers."[94]

In addition to largely ignoring any sexual abuse and exploitation, family histories almost uniformly ignore the forced separation of enslaved families due to sales, deaths, or moves of the enslavers. When

Latter-day Saints took Nancy Bankhead Valentine across the plains, the father of her two young sons was not by her side. Descendants of her enslavers never include in family histories the separation of Nancy and her first husband Woodford, and then the separation of her new family with Hark (Lay) Wales when his enslavers took him to California. In the stories written by descendants of the Utah enslavers, these heartbreaking losses disappeared and instead became the fictional love and loyalty that caused the enslaved to refuse manumission and accompany their enslavers to the American West.

Those who enslaved people tended to understand the relationship to be more affectionate on the side of the enslaved than it was. In early 1856, when the enslaved men and women in San Bernardino learned they were free, they immediately planned to leave their enslavers. A granddaughter of Green and Martha Flake recalled that several of those enslaved in the Crosby household had suffered disfiguring abuses, but still members of the Crosby family were shocked to learn that the people they had enslaved valued liberty above obedience to their former enslavers.[95]

Despite the claims in later fictionalized accounts, a slave society could only perpetuate slavery in a large population by the ongoing threat of violence. The events in this book happened during the long shadow of slave rebellions, including Nat Turner's Rebellion of 1831, when a small group of enslaved Virginians took up arms and killed around sixty people. These rebellions led to panic and rumors of uprisings, including in the North Carolina county then home to the Redd family.[96] The fear of uprisings meant that the enslaved lived their lives under surveillance by their community and enslavers and under the threat or reality of violence. The amount of violence in the system led Brigham Young to wonder during a private discussion if the beginning of the Civil War would lead the enslaved population of the South to kill their enslavers and, in turn, "be slaughtered by thousands." His words echo those of Joseph Smith canonized in Latter-day Saint scripture: "slaves shall rise up against their masters, who shall be marshaled and disciplined for war."[97]

Some community and family histories incorporate the pervasive theories developed in the United States to rationalize hereditary enslavement based on skin color and African ancestry. These theories were often based in appeals to science or scripture. The family and community histories may portray enslaved people as subhuman, childlike, white in spirit, or cursed. When Brigham Young spoke to the territorial legislature in 1852 in support of An Act in Relation to Service, historian W. Paul Reeve wrote that he "laid out his views regarding slavery while articulating a firm and forceful position . . . grounded in biblical curses."[98]

Although both law and society treated the enslaved as personal possessions or chattel and allowed a wide range of abuse, the enslaved developed methods to protect themselves and their communities from violence, including the formation of family and kinship networks. The enslaved acted in the role of affectionate family servants, negotiated work conditions, created systems of play and leisure, and developed religious and cultural practices, some of which may have traced back to their ancestral homelands. Alternately, they may have controlled their labor by work slowdowns and attempted to gain some autonomy by liberating themselves temporarily or permanently, and even occasional infanticide, death by suicide, or armed rebellion.[99] The information available about the enslaved in Utah includes just a hint of some of these practices, including attempts at self-liberation and the formation of kinship networks. After their displacement from their original communities and extended families, many White Latter-day Saint converts used the practice of plural marriage to create replacement family networks.[100] This religious practice was not available to the enslaved or free Black population of Utah Territory, and the shaping and reshaping of their families due to the abuses of slavery could have created what looked like nuclear families, hence some of the later confusion.

Formerly enslaved Alexander Bankhead told a reporter late in his life that many of the enslaved in Utah were "far from being happy" and "were subjected to the same treatment that was accorded the plantation negroes of the South."[101] Their new home in the West tended to reduce the total amount of violence in their lives, but it also created loneliness as many were separated from families and friends and lived isolated among a White population. Alexander Bankhead remembered the feeling of stark isolation. He mentioned gathering "in a large room or hall on State street . . . [to] discuss their condition, and gaze in wonderment at the lofty mountains" that separated him and the other enslaved people in the valley from their former homes or any hope of liberating themselves.[102] Due to their isolation, little record remains of cultural practices or innovations. One rare exception is when a neighbor remembered that John Burton spoke of freedom in a Latter-day Saint testimony meeting in the language of the slave spiritual: "Brudders and Sisters, wen the good Lawd calls old Black John, I'se a gwine, I'se a gwine over Jordan to meet my Lawd."[103]

About the Language and Terminology
Servant or Slave

In the eighteenth century, *servant* meant an indentured servant, often European, and *slave* meant a slave for life, either a kidnapped or imprisoned African transported to North America or an African American in hereditary enslavement.[104] By the nineteenth century, the terms rarely indicated legal status. Instead "servant" normally indicated an enslaver's preferred social or economic status rather than the legal status of an individual who was in most cases a chattel slave. In the slave narrative, *Fifty Years in Chains*, Charles Ball told of an innkeeper who surprised him by using the term "servants" for those being transported in chains. "It is the custom throughout all the slave-holding States, amongst people of fashion, never to speak of their negroes as slaves, but always as servants," he wrote, "but I had never before met with the keeper of a public house, in the country, who had arrived at this degree of refinement."[105] So, on the Brigham Young Monument by Temple Square in Salt Lake City commemorating the arrival of the first wagon company in the Great Salt Lake Valley, the three men listed as "colored servants" were chattel slaves.

The Household

The migration of Southerners mentioned in this book often involved an extended family group, but the most basic migrating group consisted of a White male, his White wife and children, and their enslaved Black servants, some possibly related to the White family. When John H. Redd left for Utah Territory, he took his wife, their children, five enslaved Black women and teenagers, and an indentured Black servant. Sam Franklin was indentured, two of the enslaved belonged by life interest to Redd with ownership reverting to his wife or her heirs upon his death, and three belonged outright to him.

Elizabeth Fox-Genovese's social history of slavery, *Within the Plantation Household: Black and White Women of the Old South*, calls this group a *household*, "a basic social unit in which people, whether voluntarily or under compulsion, pool their income and resources." She explained, "As such, it has no necessary relation to family, although members of households may be related and many households may be coterminous with family membership."[106] The Southern household was both patriarchal and paternalistic, and occasionally writers would refer to "my family, white and black."[107] In an 1848 letter, John H. Redd closed with "the love of myself and family both white and black."[108] In Redd's case, at least one of the enslaved was his biological child, but the term *household* simplifies the narrative in this book.

Insulting or Dated Language

Writers used a wide variety of terms to describe members of the enslaved or free African American population, including servant, slave, colored man, colored woman, wench, Dinah, Sambo, your man, my man, mulatto, and others. *Valley Tan*, a territorial newspaper run by non-Latter-day Saint Southerners, reported in 1858 that a "darkey became obstreperous, on Main street . . . and knocked down a white man, no color was assigned for the act, except the fact that the white man called him a 'nigger.' The dusky shoulder-hitter was taken in charge by the Police."[109] Latter-day Saint apostle George Q. Cannon wrote of enslaved Nancy (Bankhead) Wales Valentine, a woman separated from her first husband Woodford in the South and her second husband Hark Wales when his enslavers took him to California: "Bro. Geo. Bankhead's . . . wench cooked a lot of biscuits for us to take along."[110] Many of the terms and sentiments in the historical record are deeply disturbing. Despite their crude nature, terms and concepts appear as is in historical documents in this book since removing them would compromise historical accuracy, and their removal would mute the evidence of the mistreatment of the enslaved and free Black members of the community.

This work also involves the changing usage of acceptable terms. During the nineteenth century and the first half of the twentieth century, "colored" was the primary acceptable descriptor for those of African descent living in the United States. In the mid-twentieth century the acceptable terms began to change. As of this writing, the generally used terms are "Black," "African American," or "people of color." Since "people of color" can encompass a variety of ethnicities, this work alternates between "Black" and the unhyphenated "African American."[111] "Colored" and "Negro" are no longer appropriate except when used in historical context. "Master" and "mistress" have modern alternatives, including "enslaver," that do not indicate approval of human trafficking, and academic standards now suggest the use of "enslaved" rather than "slave" to distinguish between legal status and identity.

Use of Dialect

Few reliable examples remain of the speech of the enslaved African American pioneers. Authors frequently render the speech of the enslaved in *eye dialect* to indicate social class and education. This practice is problematic when the language of the enslaved is reported in dialect, but White conversation is reported in pristine modern English.

The curious document "Slavery in Draper" includes the following improbable story that supposedly reproduces the speech of Samuel and Alexander Bankhead and Howard and Henry Wales, all enslaved by George W. Bankhead. Although Alexander and Samuel were too old to be involved in the story without creating an impossible dynamic, they reportedly joined the fray. "'Wha ah yo' goin' wid dat wagon, boy?' shouted Sambo [sic] as he saw Joseph [M. Smith] coming down the road." The story continued, "'Dat haint yo' wagon, chile!' chirped Howard. 'Dat am my wagon,' said Alex. 'Dat am my wagon,' said Hen and the tug of war was on." The author gave George W. Bankhead a few lines in Standard English and had him address young Walter "Rolly." "Upon one of these trips they were cutting a big tree when Roll exclaimed, 'Which way shall I run, Massa George?' 'Run the way the tree falls, you fool!' replied Mr. Bankhead." Part of the tree hit Walter, "whereupon Mr. Bankhead remarked, 'Did you get hurt, Roll?' 'No,' said the boy, 'not much.' 'Wish the hell it had killed you,' thundered Mr. Bankhead."[112]

The historical fiction about Utah slavery employs a mixture of language. In *Southern Grace*, Charmaine Lay Kohler used Standard English and light dialect for her White characters but did not give the enslaved any dialogue. In *Five Branches of Love*, Mary West Riggs had the White characters speak impeccable English, while enslaved John Burton spoke lines like, "The las time he sez dat ah say, Massa, you all knows ah won' neva leave Missa Susan—neva!" The fictionalized series *Standing on the Promises* by Margaret Blair Young and Darius A. Gray uses extensive eye dialect.[113]

Documentary Editing Standards

Historical documents are shown as written, with light editing for readability: punctuation where the lack would confuse the reader, or a correction or clarification in square brackets. Assume that any deviation from standard modern English in a quotation is from the original document, since [sic] is reserved for errors that may not be obvious. Underlining and strikeouts are left as is, and additions above the line are notated with angled brackets as follows: "*Schedule 2, ~~Slave~~ <Colored> Inhabitants Utah Co Territory of Utah.*" Missing or unreadable words are shown as [indecipherable], unless they can be assumed from the text, in which case they are shown within brackets. The second in a set of inadvertently repeated words is deleted. Periods used to mark a space are not included. Superscripts are reproduced as is; words emphasized by multiple underlines or otherwise decorated are represented by a single underline.

About the Research and Names

Traditional genealogical research cannot always trace African American family lines past the late nineteenth century. Normally, records about the enslaved were created by or for an enslaver, so a researcher tracing an enslaved individual or family before the Civil War must discover the identity of the enslaver. Recent advances can help break through this barrier, including the ongoing digitization and indexing of historical and genealogical records and DNA technology that can help tie families together and sometimes even locate relatives in Africa.

This project was unusual since it began with the identity of many of those who took the enslaved into Utah Territory. However, even this knowledge does not substitute for an overall lack of records about the enslaved. When tax records, probates, censuses, and documentation of sales exist, they rarely include more than a few identifying factors. A North Carolina official recorded an 1806 sale as follows: "Isaac R. Evera sold to William Redd for 350 dollars a negro girl named Amy."[114] In genealogy, same name does not mean same person, so this may document the mother of enslaved pioneers Chaney and Venus Redd, but without additional identifying factors, the connection is speculative.

Identifications for this project considered first and last names, approximate age, origin, location, possible movements, occupation, community members, any family members, and any possible alternate identities for similarly named persons. The data was sufficient to conclude that Oscar Smith was Oscar (Crosby) and Tampa Ann Campbell was Tampian (Lewis).

Although the historical record shows that the enslaved used both given and family names, few records during slavery included surnames. Most appeared in records with a surname only after they were freed, but when separated families sought each other after emancipation, their newspaper ads gave their surnames.[115] Toby and Grief spent over four decades laboring for the Crosby family, but after they learned they were free, they used the surname Embers, which led to the discovery of their likely original enslavers, the Embers or Embré family of Indiana.

The choice of what to call an enslaved or formerly enslaved individual is complicated by questions of personhood and agency, and further complicated when the enslaved used multiple surnames or had more than one enslaver. Where known, names in historical documents or names that men, women, and children used for themselves always take precedence. The two contemporaneous records of his life named an enslaved boy as "Lamb" or "Lambson." His enslaver's descendants later remembered him as "Sammy," but the first recorded use of that name came at about the time they were trying to exhume his body forty miles south of where he was actually buried, so he should be remembered as Lamb or Lambson, not "Sammy."

The Biographical Encyclopedia in Part 2 shows every known associated surname. Although unwieldy, it summarizes identity at a glance. Thus, Nancy Lines (Bankhead) (Dennis) Smith is distinguishable from Nancy (Bankhead) (Wales) Valentine and Nancy Bankhead Jefferson. The subjects of this book may never have used the surnames in parentheses, but the information shows a history of enslavement and indicates where to find legal or census records. Surnames listed without parentheses are names the enslaved or freed used themselves, or names their families used for them, so these names indicate personal choice and agency.

Surnames listed with a question mark indicate some uncertainty associated with the identification. Here are three examples.

Nathan Bankhead (1828-1901)

Nathan is not known to have been enslaved by anyone but the Bankhead family or to have used any other surname, so he is listed simply as "Nathan Bankhead."

Martha Morris (Crosby) (Bankhead) Flake (1828-1885)

When Martha Flake's son Abraham died in the 1930s, her granddaughter Blanche Flake Leggroan provided the information for her father's death certificate. Leggroan listed her grandmother's name as Martha Morris. Based on name usage seen elsewhere in this project, Morris may have been the given name of Martha's father, but it appears as her surname since her son's family used it as her family name. The Crosby and Bankhead families enslaved Martha, so both names appear in parentheses. Martha only appears in any known record with a surname after she married Green Flake and was freed, so Flake is her last name shown, and without parentheses.

Hark (Crosby) (Lay) Wales (1825-1887)

The man whose name is incorrectly listed as Hark Lay on monuments celebrating the first wagon company to arrive in the Salt Lake Valley was enslaved by the Crosby and Lay families, but he went by the name Hark Wales for decades after he gained his freedom, and he gave the name to his son, Howard Egan Wales, so he appears in this book with his chosen name.

Conclusion

As mentioned at the beginning of this book, many years after John Hardison Redd died, someone in his family attempted to remove the enslaved members of the household from a family record. Over time, the names reappeared: Cupit and Amy; their children Moriah, Venus, Abram, Chaney, and Fenitty; and their grandchildren Luke and Thomas.

In other cases, the community actively sought to erase or segregate memories. A picture of the first Relief Society Hall in Salt Lake City originally showed five Black members of the community, probably formerly enslaved members of the Perkins household, but the editors of a community history used primitive photo editing to replace each Black face with a White one.[116]

Not only does the plaque on the Brigham Young Monument in downtown Salt Lake City obscure the enslavement of the three Black members of the first Latter-day Saint wagon company by using the term "colored servants," it also lists two of them with their enslaved rather than free names and segregates them by an actual color line.

Figure I.9. The Fifteenth Ward Relief Society Building in Salt Lake City, n.d., probably showing several members of the Perkins or James families. Emmeline B. Wells, ed., *Charities and Philanthropies: Woman's Work in Utah* (Salt Lake City, UT: George Q. Cannon & Sons Co., 1893), 10.

Figure I.10. The picture of the Fifteenth Ward Relief Society Building from *Charities and Philanthropies*, with the faces of the Black adults and children edited to appear White for a Relief Society commemorative publication. Used by permission, Utah State Historical Society.

Figure I.11. A plaque showing the names of the three enslaved members of the first Latter-day Saint wagon company to reach the Great Salt Lake Valley in 1847. Hark Wales and Oscar Smith are shown with the names that appeared on wagon company records although those were not their own family names. Brigham Young Monument, Salt Lake City. By the author.

This book began with the introduction of the *Sankofa*, a symbol representing remembrance and the work of retrieving memory and heritage. This book provides the names and stories of those who were enslaved so they can become an integral part of the history of Utah and the American West, no longer forgotten, erased, or segregated by a color line.

Sankofa.

It is not wrong to go back for that which you have forgotten.

Part I
The Story of African American Slavery in Utah Territory

One

SOUTHERN ORIGINS

MISSISSIPPI AND ALABAMA

Perhaps the sick and desperate young Black woman found a ride on a wagon to take her the dozen miles from downtown Salt Lake City to the farming community of Union, but perhaps she walked. Cordelia Litchford went to home after home that had once housed her family and friends, but only strangers opened the doors on that cold Sunday evening in February 1891.

Finally, she arrived at the home of Rufus Forbush, an elderly family friend. He could tell Cordelia was in no condition to travel any farther and offered her a place to stay, as he had previously done for her half-brother John Priesly. Forbush's housekeeper, Lucy Ellis Wheeler, had died not long before, so perhaps he put Cordelia into Lucy's old room. Perhaps he shared memories of Cordelia's family and news of those she expected to find in Union as he settled her into her room. An hour and a half later, he found her dead.

Forbush notified the justice of the peace, and the next day, town officials convened an inquest at his home. Three jurors and the justice of the peace concluded that Cordelia Litchford died "from hemorrhage of the lungs brought on by natural causes and lack of care."[1]

Cordelia's relatives were some of the earliest Mormon pioneers. Her uncles arrived in the Great Salt Lake Valley several days ahead of Brigham Young, and her mother Rose and grandmother Violet arrived the next year with their enslaver, William Crosby. Over the years, Cordelia's extended family melted away. Some went to California in 1851. Others moved to Idaho to find a better life. Her mother and grandmother died, and her father, Miles Litchford, went to visit his childhood home in Ohio and never returned.

Cordelia, listed in the census as Martha when she lived with Green and Martha Flake as a child, may have been living in desperate poverty in downtown Salt Lake City. Due to their race, she and her sisters had few chances for marriage and families. The majority White Latter-day Saint society pushed them to its outskirts, where they may have tried to make a living as household servants but could have been exposed to traffic in prostitution and liquor and opium and become prey to unscrupulous men and women. The crowded conditions in the downtown neighborhoods of Commercial and Franklin Streets probably exposed Cordelia to her fatal illness, possibly tuberculosis.

With all her relatives gone from Union, Cordelia was fortunate to find a welcoming place to spend her final hours. Many years before her death, Rufus Forbush's father had set apart land for the Union Cemetery, and there the people of Union laid Cordelia Litchford to rest among the graves of her friends and family.

* * *

Fifty years earlier in Mississippi, the Crosby family went to heroic efforts to save the life of their husband and father, John Crosby Jr. Family members and enslaved servants waited on him day and night. Although estate documents show bills for expensive doctor visits and primitive medicines, their efforts failed.[2] When Crosby died, he left a grieving widow and six children to divide an estate valued at just under $17,000, with a modern value between half a million and more than $12 million.[3] The estate was no polished Southern plantation; it was wealth created on the far edges of the American settlements, the value of the estate mostly in land, enslaved people, and tools. The amount of inherited wealth and labor and the knowledge of agricultural production suggests that the extended Crosby family and the related Bankhead and Dennis families would have been a formidable economic force when they left Mississippi and Alabama for the new Latter-day Saint settlements in the West.

More than half of all the enslaved African American laborers and servants taken into Utah Territory or born there were connected to the Crosby or Bankhead families. The extended Crosby family took fifteen enslaved people to the Territory and had two born there, the Bankhead brothers who lived across the state line from them in Alabama took eleven and had four born there, and William and Talitha Bankhead Dennis took one. Three other families from Mississippi also took enslaved people to the Great Salt Lake Valley: Robert and Rebecca Dorn Smith took ten enslaved people and had one born there, James and Agnes Love Flake took two enslaved people, and Frances and Margaret Lockhart McKown took an enslaved brother and sister.

Many of these families and the enslaved laborers they inherited from parents or grandparents had spent much of their lives participating in the great westward migration across the American South as the US government drove Indigenous people off their lands in favor of White settlers. John Crosby Jr. married Elizabeth Coleman in Knox County, the Southern center of slavery in Indiana, then part of the Northwest Territory. French settlers had taken enslaved people into the area as early as the 1740s, and while the Northwest Ordinance of 1787 banned slavery and servitude in the territory, the practice continued for decades since enslaved people could be held in bondage indefinitely. About the time the Crosby family moved from South Carolina to Knox County, an 1805 Indiana law allowed enslavers entering the territory to hold the enslaved in a contract of service similar to Utah Territory's An Act in Relation to Service (1852).[4]

White settlers clashed with Indigenous peoples, and John and his brother Leonard Crosby left their wives and children at home to fight with territorial governor William Henry Harrison at the Battle of Tippecanoe. The historical record does not indicate whether the brothers took enslaved or indentured men with them when they fought or left them on their farms.[5]

When Indiana became a state in 1816, its first constitution banned slavery, and not long afterward, John, Leonard, and their widowed mother Sarah Jeter Crosby took their families and enslaved or indentured workers south over primitive roads to a new home in Monroe County, Mississippi. Mississippi tax records show that by 1839, John Crosby enslaved nine taxable people and owned thirteen hundred acres of land.[6] When he died in 1840, his wife Elizabeth and son William Crosby administered his estate. Crosby owned land, tools of production, enslaved people, livestock that included many goats, and a few modest luxuries. The estate documents detail the production of his cotton plantation and the selling or hiring out of enslaved workers. The probate shows a small wage paid by Crosby's son-in-law Kemp Watts to enslaved or indentured men Philemon and Toby, both later residents of Utah Territory and California. Perhaps the two negotiated the right to work for pay during a time when their labor was not needed.⁷

John Crosby Jr. died not long before his mother Sarah Jeter Crosby also died. Sarah had been a widow for more than forty years, enslaved a woman from her father's estate, and held a life interest in the estate of her husband, John Crosby Sr. When Sarah died, Leonard Crosby filed a copy of his father's four-decades-old will in the Monroe County courthouse and proceeded to finish the court-overseen distribution of his father's estate.

While Leonard served as executor for the estate of John Crosby Sr., his sister-in-law Elizabeth and her son William served as executors for the estate of John Crosby Jr. In the final distribution, they listed land and cash and twenty-four enslaved men, women, and children. Among them were Rose and Violet, mother and grandmother of Cordelia Litchford; Martha, wife of Green Flake; and Oscar and Hark, members of the first Latter-day Saint wagon company.

Owner	Enslaved Person		Value
E[lizabeth] Crosby ——	Toby —	at ——	$450
	Hardy "		700
	Edy —		450 . . .
W[illiam] Crosby ——	Oscar —	at—	$550
	Vilet —— "		325
	Rose — "		150 . . .
Ann Crosby [Thomas] ——	Phil ——	at—	$600-
	Mariah—		375-
	Tennessee—		150
	Thomas —		237 . . .
Susan A. Watts —	Ebby —	at —	$400
	Caroline — " —		100 . . .
Sytha Lay —	Hark —	at—	$550
	Milly — "		400
	Lucy — "		150 . . .
Elizabeth Crosby [Brown] —	Lewis —	at—	$400
	Sarah — " —		200
	David — "		425
	Henry — "		375
	Obadiah — "		300 . . .

Nancy Crosby [Bankhead]—	Malinda—	at—	$425
	Martha — "		275
	Benjamin — "		275
	Jacob — "		400[8]

Descendants of the enslaved did not preserve memories of how any of the twenty-four reacted to the separation of their families and division into new households although they did preserve a few anecdotes about life in slavery. Martha's granddaughter Bertha Stevens Udell recalled that her grandmother's hand was badly burned, probably by Elizabeth Coleman Crosby in an act of retribution. Udell told interviewer John D. Fretwell:

> Martha Ann Morris Flake hand was burned, withered and scarred. After Martha married Green Flake she wanted to be known as Martha Ann Morris rather than having the name of Crosby.... When Martha Ann was a young slave in the [John] Crosby's home one of her main duties was to care for the Crosby's children. One day her mistresses young girl was playing in the kitchen and during the children's play the Crosby child put her hand on a very hot kettle. The child received a large burn on her hand. The girls cries brought Mrs. Crosby who came to comfort and care for her daughters burns. Mrs Crosby was very upset with her slave girl Martha who was [tending] the children and said she was to be punished. Mrs. Crosby shouted out. "Do you know how it feels to be burned, you wicked girl?" The angry Mistress then took Martha's hand and held it on the hot iron kettle until the hand sizzled and fried. Because the girl was shouting and crying out in pain the woman forced her hand again to the hot kettle[.] She fainted and lay very still. Another slave picked up the girl and took her to the slaves quarters and tended her burns. Some of the tendons in the girls arm were damaged and after that she wasn't a good worker in the fields. The slave[s] on the Crosby plantation remembered the incident and avoided Mrs Crosby whenever possible. She was known for punishing her slaves in a cruel way.[9]

Not long after the settlement of the Crosby estates, Latter-day Saint missionary John Brown arrived in Mississippi, baptized many members of the Crosby family, and married Crosby daughter Elizabeth.[10] Brown and most of the Crosby family went to the Great Salt Lake Valley in 1847 and 1848, taking with them twelve to fourteen of the twenty-four enslaved people named in the estate documents.

While the Crosby family settled the two estates in Monroe County, Mississippi, the Bankhead family was settling the estate of their father across the state line in Marion County, Alabama. Unfortunately, the Marion County courthouse burned in 1887 and destroyed all the early county records, including probate and tax records for John Bankhead, the father of Latter-day Saint converts and enslavers, John H. Bankhead and George W. Bankhead.[11] Irish immigrant John Bankhead and his wife Jane had married in South Carolina and begun a series of moves west onto Indigenous lands, ending in 1830 in Marion (now Lamar) County.[12] Bankhead's probate would have listed the enslaved members of his household, but the 1887 fire consumed their names. Based on a reconstruction of census and Latter-day Saint records, John H. and George could have inherited two or three enslaved people each, probably including Samuel, Nancy, Alexander, Thomas, Nathan, and Miram.

In 1842, John H. Bankhead married Nancy Crosby, who inherited Malinda, Benjamin, Jacob, and Martha from her father. Malinda and Benjamin did not go west. Bankhead probably sold them to help finance the trip. Jacob went west with the family and died at Winter Quarters near today's Omaha, Nebraska. Martha went west and married Latter-day Saint pioneer Green Flake. Some of the enslaved members of the households joined the Church of Jesus Christ of Latter-day Saints, although only Thomas Bankhead Coleman was specifically identified as a Latter-day Saint.[13]

When the Bankhead brothers crossed the plains to the Great Salt Lake Valley in 1848, the wagon company roster included a tally of their eleven enslaved people but did not list names.[14] The census taker listed only nine enslaved people in the 1850 federal census, so subsequent generations have been left to puzzle over their relationships and experiences.

Nancy Crosby Bankhead died in Wellsville, Utah, in 1915. By the time she died, she and her family had begun to alter the story of slavery in her household. Her funeral notice reported that the family slaves were freed in the South.[15] Family claims of manumission can be disregarded since documents created in the 1850s and 1860s show that Bankhead and his brother eventually enslaved as many as sixteen people in Utah Territory. When Utah territorial officials began the 1850 federal census, they were still debating slavery in the territory and had been advised not to enumerate slaves. In the resulting confusion, the enslaved in the Bankhead household ended up in both the regular population schedule and in a copy of the slave schedule that was not sent to Washington, DC. The draft copy of the census showed forty-six African American slaves or indentured servants in the territory, with no indication that any of them had been manumitted, or freed.[16] The 1860 census slave schedule showed that George W. Bankhead enslaved seven people in Great Salt Lake County, probably Nancy Bankhead Valentine, Alexander Bankhead, and Nancy's five sons.[17] None of the enslaved members of the John H. Bankhead household appeared in the census in Cache Valley, but Charles W. Nibley later wrote, "negro slavery was . . . practiced to a small extent in 1860 and 1861 and 1862 in Cache Valley," so the absence of Samuel and Nathan and perhaps others from the census appears to be a mistake.[18]

Other Mississippi households included Dr. William Taylor Dennis and his wife Talitha Bankhead Dennis, who took only Nancy Lines (Bankhead) (Dennis) Smith into the territory in 1855, since the other people they enslaved freed themselves in Iowa. (See Chapter 3, "Exodus and Escape.") Frances and Margaret Lockhart McKown left for Utah Territory with two enslaved people, but Margaret died on the way, and after Francis discovered the extent of antislavery sentiment in the territory, he returned to Mississippi. Records list a few with no documented enslavers: a mother and daughter named Betty and Harriet, likely Biddy Mason and her daughter; a woman named Esther Harmon, who lived with Jane Manning James in Great Salt Lake City in 1851; and an unnamed man mentioned in a letter to Brigham Young who attempted to free himself, probably Rande (Smith).

The largest Mississippi enslaver in Utah Territory was there for three years before he left for California. Robert Mays Smith probably purchased Biddy Mason and her children, and Rande in Mississippi. His wife, Rebecca Dorn Smith, inherited Hannah Smiley and her children. They set out from their farm near Bogue Chitto, Mississippi, probably never intending to spend any time in Utah Territory.[19] When they finally left for California in 1851, Rande had disappeared, and Hannah had a son, Charles, with Toby Embers. (See Chapter 5, "Going to California.")

The final documented Mississippi enslavers were James and Agnes Love Flake, who sent Green Flake ahead in 1847 to make them a home and followed the next year with Elizabeth. (See Chapter 5, "Going to California," and Chapter 6, "Green Flake and the Tithing Myth.") An enslaved person usually entered a household by gift, probate, purchase, or birth. Family stories sometimes reported a gift of slaves upon a marriage, but few enslavers had enough excess wealth and slavery to be able to give enslaved servants to their children. Littleton Petillo did give his son-in-law Reuben Perkins an enslaved girl or woman, Rondowney, probably the mother of Black Latter-day Saint pioneer Frank Perkins. Flake descendants recalled that Elizabeth came into the Flake household as a gift from Agnes's family, but based on the physical resemblance between her and Green Flake, she is likely his sister and "Lyse," named in a Flake family will.[20] Although most enslaved people probably entered the Flake household through inheritance, if Flake needed additional labor when he moved to Mississippi, he could have purchased people from slave traders or through a private sale, auction, or estate sale. Additionally, in Southern slavery, the child of an enslaved woman became the property of her enslaver. A North Carolina census showed that Agnes Flake's grandfather, William Love, enslaved seven people. If any of them were women, their children would belong to him, and, indeed, a few years later, Love enslaved fourteen people, some of them probably the children of his enslaved women.[21]

Several generations of Flake wills still exist. In 1802, Samuel Flake left Jo, Tom, and Abraham to his wife during her lifetime and, after she died, to his children.[22] Four decades later, Samuel's son Jurden named twenty-nine enslaved people in his will: Red, Daniel, Isom, Lucy, Ruben, Cudgo, Abram and his wife, Arter, Jude, Green, Lyse (possibly Liz or Elizabeth), Allonzo, Siller and her child Claborn, Lyda, King, George, Rosan and her children Aron and Arter, Sary and her children Thaner and Tom, Aron, Jack, Cindy, Mary, and Ephram. He left them to his children, including to "my son James M Flake Two Negroes Green and Lyse and three hundred Dollars."[23] The family is not known to have kept a record of the identities and relationships of the enslaved. In contrast to recent genealogical claims about Green being the son of his enslaver, at the 1946 Arizona funeral of a grandson of James and Agnes Flake, a relative told attendees in the language of eugenics that the family had traced its genealogy back "many generations, and their blood tree has remained pure. They had guarded jealously their blood stream."[24] It was an unreliable claim given the limitations of genealogical research at the time and raises questions about how the family and their neighbors viewed the Flake heritage of slavery.

When Agnes Flake's grandfather William Love died in 1791, he left most of his enslaved people to his wife Mary during her lifetime or widowhood, but when she died or remarried, the enslaved people and their children would go to his heirs.[25] Mary Love remained a widow for almost half a century. About twenty years after her husband's death, she distributed several enslaved people to her children. When she died around 1839, their ownership was entangled, and William's heirs began a battle that went to the North Carolina Supreme Court.

Around 1842, James and Agnes Love Flake moved to join Agnes's brother Richmond Love and other relatives in former Choctaw lands in Kemper County, Mississippi. They took fourteen-year-old Green, nine-year-old Elizabeth, and probably some enslaved people from the Love estate. Mississippi tax records show that the couple enslaved eight people in 1843, nine in 1844, and eleven in 1845.[26] Flake descendants had a faint memory of a woman Edie and her children who had to be returned to Mississippi when the Flakes headed west.[27] Heirs were still negotiating the property named in *Erasmus Love v. Richmond Love* (1843) when James and Agnes moved to Mississippi. The case may explain why they left most of their enslaved people and may account for a later family memory that Agnes's brother offered her a fortune to return to Mississippi: he probably offered her the means to reclaim her own property from the Love estate.[28]

Did James M. Flake offer to free his enslaved people in Mississippi, as family legends suggest? Freeing the enslaved would have taken an act of the state legislature, and there is no record of such an act. Could he have freed them informally? It is not only legally and economically unlikely, but he would have acted in violation of law, and anyone illegally freed would have been subject to arrest and sale by the courts.[29]

The enslaved workers taken to Utah Territory and their owners provided labor to help create farms and settlements in early Utah Territory. However, within a few years, most Mississippi enslavers left for California or returned to the South. A small group of the enslaved remained in Utah Territory. Some of their descendants still live in the Salt Lake Valley.

Two

SOUTHERN ORIGINS

TENNESSEE, MISSOURI, AND KENTUCKY

In the midst of deciding whether to move west with the Church of Jesus Christ of Latter-day Saints, Tennessee farmer John Hardison Redd wrote a letter to a relative and closed by sending "the love of myself and family both white and black."[1] Although the phrase "my family both white and black" was used metaphorically among Southern enslavers, Redd was not speaking metaphorically. The ancestor of many prominent Utahns and Latter-day Saints left Tennessee shortly thereafter with his children, both White and Black, and their mothers.[2]

The enslaved from Mississippi initially outnumbered those from Tennessee, Missouri, and Kentucky, but most of the enslaved from Mississippi went to California in 1851. Those from Tennessee, Missouri, and Kentucky remained in Utah Territory, except for Camplin, Amy, John, Sandy, James, Jane, Lucinda, and Jordan, who lived briefly in the Great Salt Lake Valley before Bird and Martha Barnett took them to Northern California in 1850. Those who remained in Utah Territory included, first, John Burton of Parowan, Utah. He was born in Virginia and helped his widowed enslaver settle in Missouri and helped build Winter Quarters and Parowan. Charlotte, Daniel, Shepherd, Isaac, and Carolina (Camp) went to Utah from Tennessee and Arkansas. Three of them remained in Utah, but Isaac and Carolina's enslavers sent them back to slavery in Texas. Tom grew up in the Abraham Church household in Tennessee and helped build the settlements in Utah Territory but died months before he would have been freed by Congress. Lambson first saw the light of day as the property of War of 1812 veteran Henry Jolley and drowned not long after he reached the Salt Lake Valley. His mother died young, but during the time he and his mother were enslaved by Jolley, Tennessee neighbors, including David "Davy" Crockett, built roads and farms and hunted wolves in the lands recently occupied by Indigenous peoples.[3] Jerry and Caroline and Tampian Hoye went west from Kentucky with David and Duritha Lewis. Jerry drowned not long before he would have been freed, but sisters Caroline and Tampian each married and raised families in the Salt Lake Valley. Frank and Esther Perkins and their children lived in Missouri when their enslavers decided to take them to Utah. Venus, Chaney, Luke, Marinda, Amy, and Sam Franklin went to Utah Territory from Tennessee with John and Elizabeth Hancock Redd.

Redd

The Redd family was originally from Onslow County, North Carolina. They appeared first in county slave transaction records in 1794 when John H. Redd's father Whitaker Redd witnessed the sale of an unnamed person between Hatcher Fonville and William Redd.[4] A few years later, William Redd purchased another unnamed person for "260 Spanish milled dollars."[5] In 1832, John H. Redd sold a man named Elias on behalf of his brother-in-law Anson Hancock.[6]

Venus and Chaney and their mother Amy were originally enslaved by Redd's father-in-law Zebedee Hancock. Since Venus's grandchildren later passed as White, Venus and Chaney would have been of mixed African and European descent. Their father, Cupit or Cupid, was probably sold in 1796 between two members of the Williams family of Onslow County.[7] Southern law decreed that Cupit's children with Amy belonged to her enslaver, Zebedee Hancock, rather than Cupid's enslaver. When Hancock died in 1824, his will divided Cupit and Amy's family between his second wife and the children of his first marriage:

> In the Name of God amen. I Zebedee Hancock of the County of Onslow in the State of North Carolina, being in perfect health of body, and of sound & disposing mind, memory and understanding . . . do therefore make and publish this my last will and Testament . . .

Item. I Lend unto my wife, Nancy [Rial] Hancock four negroes by the name of Tom, Amy, Chany & Finnety, during her life and then to be Equaly divided between my three Children William, Elizabeth and Anson to them their heirs & assigns

Item. I give and bequeath unto my son William one Negro Girl by the name of Moriah to him his heirs and Assigns.

Item. I give and bequeath unto my Daughter Elizabeth one Negro Girl by the name of Venus and to her[,] her heirs and Assigns

Item. I give and bequeath unto my son Anson one Negro Boy by the Name of Abram to him his heirs and Assigns . . .

In testimony whereof I have hereunto set my hand & affixed my seal this day of May in the year of our Lord one thousand Eight hundred & twenty[8]

The Redd family did not preserve memories of what happened to Amy and Cupit, but after Nancy Rial Hancock died, Chaney went to Elizabeth and John Redd, Finnety (or Fenitty) went to Anson Hancock, and Tom went to William Hancock. Redd took Chaney and Venus and their children to Utah Territory; Anson Hancock took Abram and Finnety and her daughter to Florida Territory; and William Hancock kept Mariah and Tom in Onslow County.[9]

From the earliest days of the European settlement of North America, colonial and state legislatures and courts deliberated over details of slave law, including how to handle a woman's property and whether enslaved people should be *realty* (land and anything attached to the land) or *personalty* (movable possessions or chattel). A few years before Cupit's sale, the Virginia legislature decreed slaves to be personal estate.[10] When Elizabeth Hancock married John Redd, she entered a state of legal dependency called *coverture*. English jurist William Blackstone defined coverture as follows: "By marriage, the husband and wife are one person in law . . . that is, the very being or legal existence of the woman is suspended during the marriage, or at least is incorporated and consolidated into that of the husband."[11] The couple could have altered coverture by a prenuptial agreement, marital settlement, or trust, but there is no record of one, so a court would have handled Elizabeth's land and enslaved woman Venus using the legal practices of the time. A judge explained in 1853, "The future right of the husband to the property is a right incident to the contract of marriage, as regulated by law; the husband does not succeed to the slaves of the wife, held by her under the statute, as an inheritor or distribute of her separate estate, but they vest in him under the law, and by virtue of the contract of marriage."[12] In other words, Venus and later Chaney, since they were left to Elizabeth and her "heirs and Assigns," belonged to John by *estate of marital right*, and as with other Southern women, her property could have helped her secure a marriage.[13] Although Elizabeth was the enslaver of record of the land and people she inherited from her father, her husband controlled the use of the property. He owned outright any children of Venus or Chaney and any income generated by any of the enslaved during his lifetime, but he could not sell or hire out Venus or Chaney or leave them as an inheritance without Elizabeth's consent.[14] When Redd sold land Elizabeth inherited from her father, the court took a deposition to prove that Elizabeth agreed with the transaction, and a slave sale should have been handled similarly.[15]

Unless Elizabeth left a will making other arrangements, if there had been a court-administered probate when she died in 1853, there would have been no obvious change in their condition for Venus and Chaney and their children: they would remain enslaved by John until his death, at which point, they would become the property of Elizabeth's heirs. If both Elizabeth and John had died intestate (without wills) in the South, at John's death, Venus and Chaney would have been sold and the proceeds divided between Elizabeth's heirs. Unless John made other provisions in a will, the surviving enslaved children, Luke and Marinda, would have been sold and the money divided between his heirs, with one-third of the proceeds, the *dower interest*, going to his subsequent wife Mary Lewis Redd, and the remaining two-thirds divided between his surviving legitimate children.

The only existing probate for a Utah enslaver is from Kentucky native David Lewis, and a Utah court probably would have settled the Redd estate in a similar manner, but when Redd died in 1857, the territorial courts were in disarray, and the family divided the property among themselves. Those named in the family division of property are as follows: Redd's widow, Mary Lewis Redd, and her infant daughter; John's oldest surviving legitimate son, Lemuel Redd; legitimate Redd daughters Maria Pace and Elizabeth Pace; and enslaved or formerly enslaved Venus, Luke, and Marinda. The language and incorrect amounts shown in the document suggest that the family created it without benefit of a lawyer, and if any heir had cared to contest it, the document may not have held up in court.

Division of John H. Redd's Property
The Following is the division as made by the heirs of John H Redd Deceased.
To Mary Redd his Widow and child   1 Yoke of Cattle
"   "   "   "   "   "   2 Cows
"   "   "   "   "   "   1 Ox

One House 2 Beds & Bedding and 1 Bedstead 1 Stove and one half of the cooking utensils & one third of the grain and one third of the Hogs. ___ in money. Two ninths of the Land.
To Lemuel and Benjamin J Redd 2 Horses, 1 Wagon 1 Plough 1 Yearling Steer, 1 Gun 1 Sett of Harness 1 Bed & Beding & Bedstead 1 Pig, 20 Acres to Benjamin and 2/9 of the Land, in money.
To Maria and Elizabeth Pace 1 Yoke of Cattle 2 Cows & Calves 2 Yearlings Eighty Eight Dollars outstanding Debts, 2/9 of the Land, Cash
To Luke Redd Venus and Marinda 1 Yoke of Cattle 2 Cows 1 Plough 1 Gun, 1 Wagon 1 House 1/2 of the grain 1/2 Cooking utensils 1/2 of Hogs Cash 3/9 of the Land, 5 Acres of Land to Luke.
Mary Redd
Lemuel H. Redd[16]

Descendants later claimed that Redd "legally freed each of his slaves by an act of court and made financial provision for each" and placed the claimed manumission in time by noting that Venus and Chaney and the younger slaves "pled to remain with the family when they moved to Nauvoo."[17] Not only did the household never move to Nauvoo, the Tennessee legislature had assigned manumission to county courts and legislated that after manumission, an enslaver either needed to send a freed person to

Africa, remove him from the state, or pay a bond and petition the court for permission to leave him in Tennessee. A county court could arrest and hire out anyone illegally freed.[18] Even legally freed people lived in danger of kidnapping and sale. Redd thus had four options: sell Luke, Marinda, and Amy, and sell Venus and Chaney with Elizabeth's approval; free them legally and remove them from the state; petition the court, post a bond for good behavior, and have them remain in Tennessee at their peril; or take them to Utah Territory, where the law was unsettled, and they may or may not have become free. Not only does the 1850 census slave schedule show that they were still in bondage in Utah Territory, but they do not appear in Tennessee manumission records, so Redd chose the fourth option.[19] Despite any uncertainty, the act of taking enslaved and indentured servants into Utah Territory did not free them; as legal scholar John C. Hurd concluded, they retained the same status as in their previous domicile.[20]

Perkins

A generation after his grandfather's enslaved people were freed, Jasper Perkins remembered with puzzlement or ire that his grandfather made sure they had food, even when times got bad. "When the famine came on 'Willow Creek,' we had only four bushels of barley. Grandfather, Reuben Perkins, insisted that the Negro family was entitled to one biscuit of this a day, the same as we; with cottage cheese and milk, this was our diet until the barley ran out."[21]

After slavery ended, the children and grandchildren of enslavers quickly forgot the legal and social expectations of slavery. After purchase, inheritance, or birth, an enslaver controlled and profited from an enslaved person's labor for life. Enslaved people were not legal persons and could not enter into contracts, so they could not expect payment for their labor, but their enslavers had both legal responsibility and economic motivation to provide food, clothing, shelter, and medical care, since an enslaved person's greatest value normally consisted of the ability to work. If an enslaver failed to provide for their most basic needs, and the matter came to the attention of a court, a judge could fine an enslaver or order enslaved people sold, although courts were reluctant to involve themselves. Hurd explained the reluctance: "Every recognition of rights in the slave, independent of the will of the owner or master . . . diminishes in some degree the essence of that slavery by changing it into a relation between legal persons."[22]

Illness and death beset the Black and White Perkins families. When twice-widowed former enslaver Reuben Perkins died in 1871, only one of his seven children was still alive. When formerly enslaved, widowed, and divorced Frank Perkins died in 1888, only four of his eleven or twelve children were still alive. The time following emancipation was difficult for many newly freed people as they suffered from disease and starvation: shortly after Frank's family began life on their own, his wife and four of his children died.[23]

The first known record of Frank's family is an 1808 deed from Littleton Petillo of North Carolina: "to my beloved son-in-law [Reuben Perkins] & his wife Elizabeth . . . a Negro girl named Rondowney."[24] Rondowney or Dawney was probably Frank's mother since Frank named one of his daughters Downey, and another daughter, Mary Ann Perkins James, did a Latter-day Saint proxy baptism in 1875 for her "G[ran]dmother Dawney."[25]

Reuben Perkins was not wealthy by national standards, but by the mid-1830s, he headed one of the wealthier households in a rural district in Jackson County, Tennessee, about eighty miles east of Nashville. He owned $5,000 of taxable property, including $3,800 in slaves, or six of the nineteen taxable enslaved people in the district.[26] Perkins left Tennessee not long afterward to join some of his family in Livingston (later Grundy) County, Missouri. The 1840 census suggests he took one adult and six enslaved children with him, confirming a memory that Frank Perkins had a first wife in Tennessee and a second wife in Missouri, probably Esther, later remembered by great-granddaughter Henrietta Bankhead as a "full blooded Cherokee Indian."[27] Formerly enslaved families rarely had written records, and descendants tended to forget names and events within several generations. Henrietta Bankhead described the cost that years of heavy labor exacted: "I tell you the parents just didn't have the time to sit down and tell the generations of their generations and that."[28] However, one family memory appeared in an 1898 Montana newspaper. A reporter thought it was rare sport when Benjamin Perkins claimed he was descended from the "kings of San Domingo," but the memory may mean that the family descended from the Indigenous, African, or White populations of Hispaniola.[29]

Lewis

The scene of families being torn apart by slavery is seared into the American consciousness, but the individual and collective tragedies are largely ignored in family histories written by descendants of enslavers, perhaps from ignorance of the details or from a sense of delicacy or shame. When David and Duritha Lewis bundled Caroline and Tampian into their wagon and took them and Jerry from Kentucky to Utah Territory, the sisters must have left family or loved ones behind in the South. When Caroline died in 1904, a friend gave the names of her parents as Hagar and Nathan Hoye.[30] Were Hagar and Nathan present when Caroline, nine, and Tampian, six, started for the West? Was thirty-year-old Jerry related to Caroline and Tampian? Did he also leave family behind?

The inheritance solved a pressing problem for David and Duritha Trail Lewis. After they converted to the Church of Jesus Christ of Latter-day Saints, they moved with David's brothers to Haun's Mill in Caldwell County, Missouri. On October 30, 1838, the Livingston County militia stormed the Latter-day Saints community and killed seventeen men and children and wounded thirteen men, women, and children. The militia shot David's brother Tarlton through the shoulder and killed his brother Benjamin. David Lewis wrote, "five holes was shot threw my clot[hes] three in my pantaloons and two in my coat." After the shooting stopped, the gravely ill Lewis headed slowly home. "A little ways from my house I met my wife who had bin in prare for my deliv[rance] for she had bin in hearing of the hole seen, for she had heard the first guns that had fyered."[31] They hid until dark and then helped nurse the injured and bury the dead. They then returned to Kentucky to stay with Duritha's parents. While they stayed at the Trail home, Jerry and others would have heard about the massacre, including the death of their former neighbor, Benjamin Lewis. Perhaps Jerry saw the bullet holes in David's clothing.

When David and Duritha finished recuperating, they left Kentucky to join with the Church of Jesus Christ of Latter-day Saints in Illinois. They took no enslaved people with them. After neighbors drove many of the Latter-day Saints from Illinois in 1846, David and Duritha did not have means to travel further. Means finally came when Duritha's father died. The Simpson County Courthouse burned in the 1880s and destroyed her father's estate file, but a Utah slave registration confirms

Figure 2.1. David and Duritha Trail Lewis. Huntington Library, San Marino, California.

that Duritha inherited Jerry, Caroline, and Tampian. She must have also inherited other property since her husband's 1855 obituary reported: "In 1846 he left Nauvoo for Winter Quarters . . . but being short of means went to Missouri with some others, and in 1851 was enabled to cross the plains and join the saints again in Great Salt Lake City."[32] They had been away from Kentucky long enough that when they took possession of Duritha's inheritance, it would have been the first time they met Caroline and Tampian. Perhaps Duritha and David knew the girls' parents, Hagar and Nathan Hoye, but the Lewis family did not preserve any details.[33]

Except for the Barnett household, most enslavers from Tennessee, Missouri, and Kentucky, including the Burton-Robinson, Camp, Church, Jolley, Lewis, and Perkins households, remained in the territory, as did many of their enslaved people after their liberation from bondage. Some of the freed individuals and their families helped form Black society in Utah into the twentieth-first century.

Three

EXODUS AND ESCAPE

On July 4, 1854, six enslaved men, women, and children camped in Tabor, Iowa, while traveling from Mississippi to Utah Territory with Latter-day Saint converts Dr. William Taylor Dennis and Talitha Bankhead Dennis. Dennis had meant to cross the Missouri River farther south, but the ferries were backed up, so he continued north along the east side of the river.

Dennis probably would not have stayed in Tabor if he had known that it was a stronghold of anti-slavery sentiment and would shortly thereafter become a place of resort for famous abolitionist John Brown, but Dennis and his family and the enslaved workers camped on the west side of Main Street about halfway between Elm and Orange Streets.

It was Independence Day, and thoughts of liberty may have been in many minds. Residents approached the two enslaved men when they went to fetch water. They discovered that they and a woman and her two children wished to be free.[1] Word spread among the townspeople, and during the night, they concealed the five and arranged to send them to Canada.

Dennis woke in the morning and discovered the chores undone and only one woman remaining, Nancy Lines Smith, remembered subsequently by the family only as their "Black Mammy." Nancy had entered the household with Talitha Bankhead upon her marriage to William Taylor Dennis, a doctor whose medical qualifications are long since forgotten.[2] Talitha came from a wealthy and influential family: after she departed for the West, Talitha's mother and brothers enslaved many people at the outbreak of the Civil War, and her nephew John Hollis Bankhead served as a US senator from Alabama.[3]

When he found the five gone, Dennis located slavery sympathizers in a nearby town and organized a manhunt, but the people of Tabor hid the five too well for him to find them. Townsmen conducted the five to a Quaker settlement near Des Moines, and, from there, they reportedly made their way to Canada.[4]

The lack of wagon drivers made further travel difficult, so Nancy and the Dennis family remained in the area over the winter. The next year, Dennis joined a merchant wagon train. He drove one wagon, his daughter Dorothy drove another, and young Frank McGee, who had followed them from Mississippi, loathe to part from Dorothy, drove the third. The travelers arrived in Utah Territory in 1855.

For generations, Dennis descendants remembered the escape only as an inconvenience to the family and did not preserve the names of the fugitives from slavery.[5] Nancy Smith left no record of whether she remained with the family by chance or choice. Forty-five years later, journalist Julius Taylor preserved the story of the escape, although he incorrectly thought the story included Marinda Redd Bankhead, who with other enslaved people, "during the dark hours of the night ... made good their escape, which was a great loss to their owner."[6]

Nancy Smith was one of the last enslaved African Americans to arrive in Utah Territory. The first three, Green Flake, Hark Wales, and Oscar Smith, arrived in July 1847 several days ahead of Brigham Young. In the twenty years before the railroad crossed the continent, around sixty thousand Latter-day Saint converts made their way to Utah Territory from the United States, Europe, and as far away as India, South Africa, and Australia. It was a well-organized effort. Church leaders divided each wagon company into groups of hundreds, fifties, and tens with a captain for each group. Each wagon company was to stay together with scouting expeditions riding ahead and guards set on the camps at night. Documentation for the migration is sometimes extensive but often lacking, especially regarding the experiences of the enslaved.

During the initial cross-country movement, leadership of the Church of Jesus Christ of Latter-day Saints suggested that most of the Mississippi converts wait until 1848 to travel to the Great Salt Lake Valley, but since they had recently created new settlements in Mississippi, they knew the importance of advance parties. Most waited to go until 1848, but Daniel M. and Ann Crosby Thomas and John Brown and his small advance company went west in 1847. Brown took his wife's enslaved man Henry, his brother-in-law William Crosby sent Oscar, John H. Bankhead sent Jacob, William Lay sent Hark, and their neighbor John Powell planned to send an enslaved man but may have sold him and sent his brother David Powell instead. John Brown reported the movements of the advance company in his diary. "[I]t finally turned cold," he wrote, "& we had the severest kind of a time it was too severe for the negrows my boy whose name was Henry took cold & finally the winter feaver which caused his death on the road." Henry's companions buried him in Andrew County, Missouri.[7] Three months later, Jacob died at Winter Quarters near today's Omaha, Nebraska, and was buried in the Mormon Pioneer Cemetery. The Crosby family is not known to have preserved plantation records and since only two or three of the people enslaved by the Crosby family have living descendants who could take DNA tests to confirm relationships, when Henry and Jacob died, Hark and Oscar could have been mourning the deaths of brothers, cousins, or friends they had known since birth.[8]

The small advance group of John Brown, David Powell, Oscar Smith, and Hark Wales increased when James M. Flake decided to send his nineteen-year-old enslaved man Green Flake with them. Many years later, Flake told of traveling along the Platte River, meeting Pawnee, and seeing buffalo.[9] Thomas Bullock wrote in his diary that Brigham Young directed the men of the company not to kill game unless they needed food. Later that day, "Green Flake walked up to within two rods of a fine Buck Antelope, before the Buck got up. I wondered why he did not kill it. but the meeting held this morning was a sufficient reason."[10]

In July 1847, Brigham Young became ill with mountain fever so he sent ahead an advance party of forty men, including legendary lawman Porter Rockwell, and the three enslaved men Green Flake, Oscar Smith, and Hark Wales.[11] As they began their final approach into the Great Salt Lake Valley, Flake hitched the mules to the Flake carriage and became the first to drive into Emigration Canyon.[12] Thus, three men in bondage, either two or three of them baptized Latter-day Saints themselves, were among the first members of a Latter-day Saint wagon company to set foot in the Great Salt Lake Valley.

Green, Hark, and Oscar were joined about two months later by Tennessee "Harriet" (later Jackson) and Philemon, both enslaved by Daniel and Ann Crosby Thomas, and John Burton, enslaved by Susan McCord Burton Robinson. None of the six are in the lists of those who returned that fall to the Latter-day Saint settlements in the Midwest, so they remained in the valley over the winter and helped prepare homes and crops for the companies coming the next year.[13]

Besides the six in 1847, the total number of enslaved African American workers taken to Utah Territory by Latter-day Saint converts remains an open question but is around seventy-three to eighty-three, with most in the territory by 1851.[14] (See Table 1.) Those taken into the territory by merchants, army officers, or government appointees appear in a separate chapter.

Toby and Grief Embers, enslaved or indentured by William Crosby, crossed the plains in 1848. Homer Duncan recalled encountering a bear in the woods, running into a tree in his panic, and knocking himself out. Sidney Tanner's "little white cur dog" distracted the bear, and when Duncan regained consciousness, he "came across t[w]o negroes who belonged to the Company and they had their guns well loaded." He borrowed a firearm from one of the men and killed the bear.[15] Although Duncan did not name the men in his story, his description was of Toby and Grief. Rebellion by the enslaved was a constant fear in slave states, so even if arming the enslaved was not expressly forbidden by a state, enslavers would have taken a dim view of their neighbors providing any but the most trusted with firearms. As simple as the story of Duncan and the bear may be, it suggested that the Crosby family trusted Toby and Grief.

The buffalo were thick on the Great Plains and spooked the travelers' cattle. Margaret Gay Judd Clawson recalled an overnight stampede: "The ground shook, our wagon trembled and rocked. It flashed through my mind in a moment that a herd of buffalo was stampeding . . . so I covered up my head and prepared to die."[16] The stampede injured three men, including Frank Perkins, and it took days to gather the surviving cattle. Another stampede began when Frank's wife Esther waved a dishtowel out the end of a wagon and startled the cattle.[17] After the company split the cattle into smaller groups, the journey progressed without serious incident.

* * *

Table 1. Documented Enslaved and Indentured African Americans Taken by Latter-Day Saints to the Great Salt Lake Valley, 1847–1861

Year	Number	Names
1847	6	Green Flake, Hark (Lay) Wales, Oscar (Crosby) Smith, John Burton, Philemon (Thomas), Tennessee or Harriet (Thomas) Jackson
1848	36	Samuel (Bankhead) Smith, Martha Morris (Bankhead) Flake, Nathan Bankhead, Thomas Bankhead Coleman, Miram (Bankhead), Male (Lewis?) (Bankhead), Female (Bankhead), Nancy (Bankhead) Wales Valentine, Alexander Bankhead, Samuel Bankhead, Walter "Rolly" Bankhead, Betsy Brown Flewellen, Toby (Crosby) Embers, Grief (Crosby) Embers, Edy (Crosby), Mary (Crosby) Bankhead Sampson Chism, Violet (Crosby) Litchford, Rose Harmon (Crosby) Litchford, Nelson or Knelt (Crosby) Price, Henderson (Crosby) Houstin, Elizabeth Flake Rowan, Lambson (Jolley), Harriet (Lay) Embers, Lucy (Lay), Female (McKown), Male (McKown), Rande (Smith), Biddy (Smith) Mason, Ellen (Smith) Mason Huddleston, Ann (Smith) Mason, Harriet (Smith) Mason Washington, Hannah (Smith) Smiley Embers, Ann (Smith) Peppers, Lawrence (Smith) Smiley, Nelson "Nathaniel" (Smith) Smiley, Jane (Smith) Smiley Goins
1849	12–15	Frank Perkins, Esther Perkins, Benjamin Perkins, Mary Ann Perkins James, Sarah Perkins, Downey Perkins Woolridge, Ephraim Perkins?, Camplin Barnett?, Amy or Emily (Barnett) Rogers, John (Barnett), Sandy Barnett, James (Barnett), Jane (Barnett), Lucinda or Loucina (Barnett) Duncan, Jourdan (Barnett) Duncan
1850	8	Charlotte (Camp), Daniel (Camp), Venus Redd, Chaney (Redd) (Cunningham), Luke Ward Redd, Marinda Redd Bankhead, Amy Redd, Sam (Redd) Franklin
1851	3	Jerry (Lewis), Caroline Hoye (Lewis) Bankhead Jackson, Tampian Simpson Hoye (Lewis) Campbell
1852	1	Tom (Church) (Smoot)
1853	1	Louisa (Moody)
1854	3	Shepherd (Greer), Isaac (Greer), Carolina (Greer)
1855	1	Nancy Lines (Bankhead) (Dennis) Smith

(continued)

Table 1. Documented Enslaved and Indentured African Americans Taken by Latter-Day Saints to the Great Salt Lake Valley, 1847–1861 (continued)

Year	Number	Names
1856	0	
1857	0–2	Unnamed (Box)?, Unnamed (Whitmore)?
1858	0	
1859	0	
1860	1	Phoebe (Murphy)
1861	0–1	Gobo Fango
Unknown	1–5	Silas (Sprouse) Woolridge, possibly Thompson, possibly Esther Harmon, possibly Betty and Harriet (probably Biddy and Harriet Mason)
Total	73–83	

It was an immense effort to gather travelers and wagons to cross the plains. Haden W. Church, a former member of the Mormon Battalion, traveled in 1852 to Hickman County, Tennessee, to help settle the estate of his father, Abraham Church, who died while Haden was in England as a missionary for the Church of Jesus Christ of Latter-day Saints. No estate documents remain, but a Latter-day Saint convert named James T. Wilson who traveled with Church from England remembered that Haden inherited an enslaved man named Tom. Wilson headed for Great Salt Lake City in 1852 in a wagon company led by A. O. Smoot, but the company needed to wait in Kansas City to have wagons made. Wilson had no cash, so he walked into Jackson County, Missouri, and found work with Thomas A. Smart.[18]

In the South, if the enslaved traveled separately from an enslaver, he or she had to carry a slave or travel pass, a document stating that he had his enslaver's permission to travel. Wilson later recalled that Church sent Tom ahead with the other travelers. "When we arrived at Kansas, Tom lived among the Saints and he behaved himself first rate. Sometime after I was working for Mr. Smart, Tom was arrested as a runaway

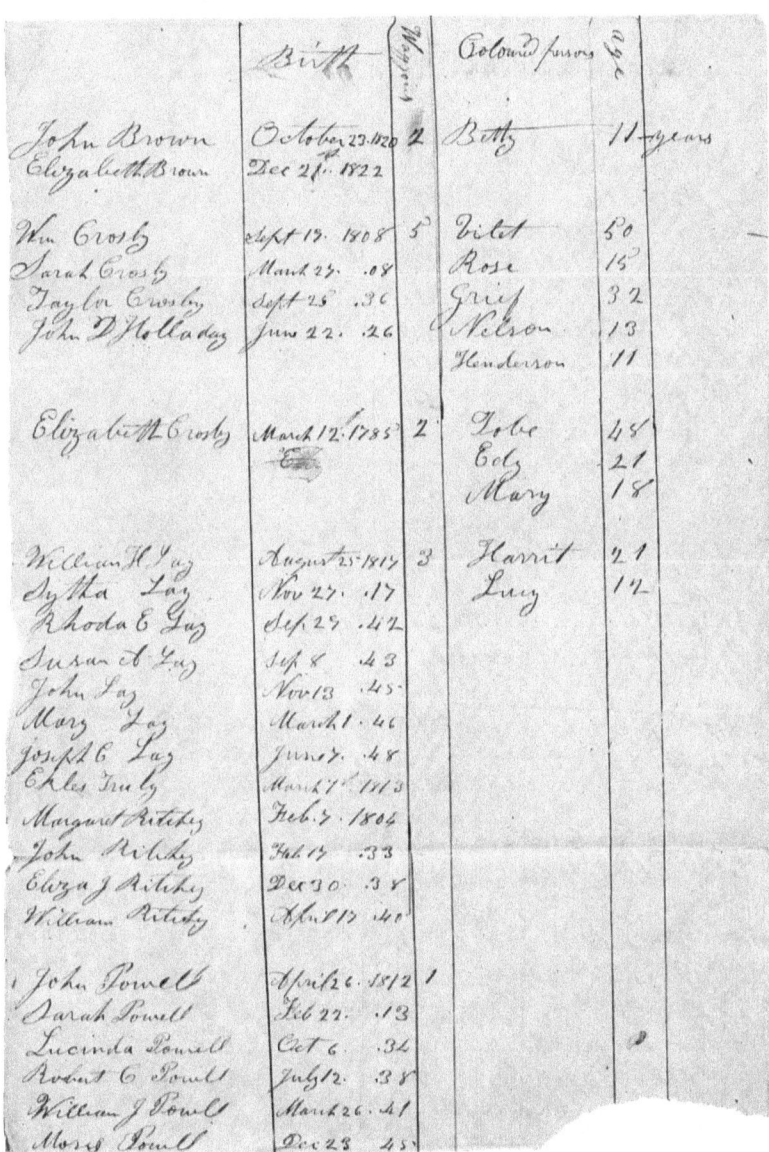

Figure 3.1. A wagon roster showing Latter-day Saint converts and their enslaved workers traveling to the Great Salt Lake Valley in 1848. All the enslaved were traveling with the extended Crosby families: Betsy, Violet, Rose, Grief, Nelson, Henderson, Toby, Edy, Mary, Harriet, and Lucy. Church History Library, Salt Lake City.

Name	Birth	Colored persons	Age
Robert M Smith	Dec 25 1814	Rande	26 years
Rebecca Smith	April 7. 10	Biddy	28
John D Smith	Oct 4. 34	Ellen	10
Elizah B Smith	Dec 15. 38	Hannah	26
William D Smith	Oct 24. 36	Harriet	3/4
James D Smith	Nov 7. 41	Ann	11
Sarah F Smith	Ap. 13. 45	Lawrence	5
Joseph L Smith	Jun 15. 47	Nat	3
Willis Boss	Jun 15. 27	Jane	1/2
Daniel Tyler	Nov 23. 1816		
Ruth Tyler	Feb 25. 20		
Perintha O Tyler	June 4. 33		
Emily Tyler	Jan 28. 47		
George Wardle	Feb 2. 1820		
Fanny Wardle	Nov 24. 21		

John Brown Captain of 1st Ten

Andrew Lytle	Dec 25 1812		
Hannah Lytle	June 4 1816		
Olive Lytle	July 17 37		
Lucina M Lytle	Sep 6 39		
Heber J Lytle	April 16 46		

Figure 3.2. A wagon roster showing Latter-day Saint converts traveling with their enslaved people to the Great Salt Lake Valley in 1848. This list shows the Robert and Rebecca Dorn Smith household with enslaved Rande, Biddy Mason, Hannah Smiley, and their children. Both Hannah and Biddy had daughters named Ann with them, but the roster is missing one of them. Church History Library, Salt Lake City.

nigger." Church had left Tom without a travel pass, and Wilson recounted the ensuing difficulties, although he was confused about the difference between a travel pass and freedom papers. (Tom would not have had freedom papers since he was still enslaved in 1860.) Tom was "asked to show his papers if he was free, but he could not as he did not have any." Wilson remembered that Church held the papers, thinking Tom would be safe with the members of the wagon company, "for if Tom had held the papers he could run away and been quite safe." He continued, "Tom refused to be taken, declaring he was Mr. Church's nigger."[19] Missouri law allowed local officials to arrest and whip a Black person without travel papers, so the Missourians beat and imprisoned Tom.[20] Smart told Wilson about the excitement, explaining that Tom "was a runaway nigger and the Mormon's were hiding him, and that it was no new thing for the Mormon's to do." He explained that the Saints had been driven from the county during the 1838 Mormon War for encouraging the enslaved to free themselves. Wilson told his employer that Tom belonged to Haden W. Church, and Smart believed him, but warned that if the situation was not as Wilson claimed, residents might raise a mob. Only then did Wilson understand he was living among participants in the 1838 Mormon War and that he and Tom were in real danger.[21] The next day, Smart secured Tom's release. The Latter-day Saint travelers took better precautions for Tom's safety and left for the Great Salt Lake Valley soon afterward.

* * *

An incident in the short life of an enslaved boy named Lamb or Lambson appears in a history of Iowa. Lambson was born in Tennessee, spent a few years in the Midwest, and then went to the Great Salt Lake Valley where he drowned at the age of eleven. An Iowa county history mentioned that his enslaver Henry Jolley's daughter Lina "attracted the attention of one John Paris . . . But the aged parents could not, for a moment, think of leaving their only child behind among the 'Gentiles,' while they themselves would join the 'saints' in the great valley." So, "the family (consisting of the old folks, the girl and a negro boy,) made a start for the west." Paris gathered a justice of the peace and townsmen "armed with old rusty muskets without locks, brass pistols out of repair, and other weapons of offense and defense" and convinced Jolley to allow the marriage. The justice of the peace wrote out a marriage license and married the couple on the road. Henry Jolley served the crowd bourbon and then "we parted—the Jolley family going toward Salt Lake, the *jolly crowd* toward Bloomfield."[22]

Although most of the enslaved went silently and uneventfully to Utah Territory, or so the records might suggest, the few records that do exist give a sense of adventure and show the role of the enslaved in providing labor for families and communities during the westward migration.

Four

THE SETTLEMENT OF UTAH

When the first wagon companies reached the Great Salt Lake Valley in 1847, the settlers discovered similarities to the lands of the Bible. They compared the Great Salt Lake to the Dead Sea and Utah Lake to the Sea of Galilee and named the river between the two the Western Jordan, later shortened to the Jordan.[1] The Holy Land's Jordan River is a powerful symbol of freedom. Enslaved Africans in America adapted and subverted themes and stories from the Bible, including Moses and the escape of the enslaved Israelites from Egypt. Songs like "Roll, Jordan, Roll" symbolized freedom, with the Jordan River marking the final passage of the Israelites into the Promised Land. The Jordan River has extra layers of meaning in the story of slavery in Utah Territory, especially in the Smoot household. While living in the Great Salt Lake Valley, Lucy (Crosby) (Lay), Jerry (Lewis), Tom (Church), and perhaps Alexander Bankhead became enslaved or hired members of the Abraham Owen (A. O.) and Margaret McMeans Smoot household. Lucy's sale is one of the few documented in Utah Territory, but she disappeared from the historical record before 1860. Both Jerry and Tom died shortly before Congress ended slavery in the territories in 1862. Jerry ironically drowned in a slough by the Jordan River.

The story of African American slavery in Utah Territory is one of bondage and deliverance, with the symbol of the Jordan River running throughout, but history seldom lends itself to uncomplicated symbolism, and the circumstances and relationships of those involved in slavery were more complex than later stereotypes would suggest. A. O. Smoot's son Reed Smoot became a Latter-day Saint apostle and US senator. In 1903, he invited Black Republicans to a political dinner, including William Wesley and Elizabeth Austin Taylor, the owners of the newspaper *Utah Plain Dealer*. The national press was aghast. "Considerable comment has been aroused in Utah over the action of Senator elect Reed Smoot in seating some negroes at a banquet with white people and having white girls serve them," wrote a journalist. "The Southerners now living in the state express themselves on the subject with especial vigor. 'And to think,' said one of them to-day, 'that Smoot's father was a Kentuckian and slaveholder. It must have made the old man turn over in his grave.'" Reed Smoot explained to the press: "If President Roosevelt is not too good to entertain a colored man [Booker T. Washington] at the White House, I don't see why I shouldn't have colored people as my guests."[2] Although the unnamed Southerner assumed that A. O. Smoot would not be seen in the same social space as Black people, a few years earlier at a celebration of the territory's settlement, Smoot and his adopted son, William C. A. Smoot, sat on the platform with Black pioneer Green Flake between them.[3] Despite any veneer of friendship, however, relationships like these were not equal. Flake's son and daughter and foster daughters did not have the same access to social, religious, and economic opportunities as the Smoot children and grandchildren. In 1897, Alexander Bankhead approached Smoot's son A. O. Smoot II for a letter supporting Bankhead's attendance at a pioneer celebration. Smoot was happy to write one. He called Bankhead "one of the 'whitest Negroes' living," both confirming the color line but also providing a reason why he thought Bankhead could cross it for the event.[4]

The story of slavery in Utah Territory played out over many decades and revealed the cost of enslavement to the enslaved. Utah Territory was a harsh environment for Black settlers, and many died early from disease, malnutrition, or violence, but others survived and helped shape the history and culture of the territory. The story of the murder of Thomas Coleman begins this chapter, which will then return to the first days of settlement in 1847.

* * *

The newspaper does not mention who found the body of Thomas Coleman on the hill behind the arsenal, now the site of the Daughters of Utah Pioneers Museum and grounds of the Utah State Capitol.[5] Reporters initially confused his identity since most knew him only as "Nigger Tom," an employee at a local hotel. People called him alternately Tom Colburn, Thomas Coleman, and Tom Coulson or Cohuson, but in his first years in Utah Territory he was known as Thomas Bankhead.[6] Coleman was probably born the property of John Crosby and his wife, Elizabeth Coleman Crosby, who may have inherited Thomas's mother from the estate of Joseph Coleman, hence Thomas Coleman's surname.

Thomas appeared on an unsigned, undated list now found in Brigham Young's "Files Relating to Marriage and Other Ordinances." Although the list appears without a word of explanation, it may document the unmarried enslaved people in the valley and suggests that their status was of concern to Brigham Young. Thomas was first, followed by Nathan Bankhead, "Harks wife" (Nancy Bankhead Wales, the Crosby-Lay family having just taken her second husband to California), "Hammon" (probably Esther Harmon), and Alexander Bankhead.[7]

Eight years after Thomas arrived in Utah Territory with John and Nancy Crosby Bankhead, he lived in Sugar House by free Blacks Isaac James and Sylvester James, enslaved Shepherd Camp, and Brigham Young's son-in-law, freighter Charles Decker. Memories of Sylvester James by his granddaughters suggest that the men were involved in freighting.[8]

Late in the summer of 1856, two handcart companies and two wagon companies of Latter-day Saint immigrants started across the plains too late in the year and became stranded by unseasonably cold weather.[9] As a General Conference of the Church of Jesus Christ of Latter-day Saints began in early October, Brigham Young learned that more than a thousand immigrants were dying of exposure and starvation in central Wyoming. It was a catastrophic emergency, getting worse by the moment, and in the rush to assemble companies of men with teams and relief supplies, no one stopped to take the names of those headed to the rescue. When Daniel W. Jones wrote his memoirs many years later, he recorded the names of everyone he could recall in his rescue company: George D. Grant, captain, Robert Burton and William Kimball, assistants, Cyrus Wheelock, chaplain, Charles Decker, guide, Daniel W. Jones, chief cook, and twenty-one others including, lastly, "Tom Bankhead, a colored man."[10] The rescuers headed up into the canyons and over the mountains into Wyoming to rescue the immigrants and suffered greatly themselves.

No documentation shows whether John H. Bankhead hired Coleman out, or whether he sold him, but three years after the rescue, Coleman was enslaved by "Col. J. H. Johnson," probably Latter-day Saint hymnwriter and colonizer Joel Hills Johnson. Coleman may have cared for Johnson's business interests in Utah Territory while Johnson headed an immigrant station in Nebraska Territory.[11]

Coleman and Shepherd or "Shep," taken by Williams Camp to Utah Territory, then sold to William H. Hooper, worked alongside each other for years, but, in 1859, they found themselves vying for the affections of Caroline and Tampian Hoye, sisters who entered the Salt Lake Valley with David and Duritha Trail Lewis, but were then enslaved by Thomas S. Williams. After Coleman and Shepherd came to blows, Coleman pulled out a firearm and shot Shepherd three times. News coverage and editorials followed in the *Valley Tan*, a local newspaper owned by Kirk Anderson and John Hartnett, non-Mormon Southern sympathizers from Missouri. *Valley Tan* wrote of the shooting in the comic manner newspapers often used for Black crime and called for the disarmament of the Black population.[12] The Latter-day Saint newspaper, *Deseret News*, kept its coverage to two short paragraphs and attributed the violence to the military presence in the city.[13] Lawmen arrested Coleman as he fled toward Wyoming. After Shepherd died from his wounds, the court indicted Coleman for murder, using the name "Colburn" or "Colebourn," perhaps a mishearing of the name "Coleman" as later found engraved on his knife. A jury found Coleman guilty of manslaughter and sentenced him to a year of hard labor and a $100 fine. Coleman went to the penitentiary with three men convicted for stealing mules.[14]

Not quite a year later, the census showed that Coleman was out of the penitentiary. At sentencing, the judge had suggested that prisoners earn their own living rather than remain at the expense of the government, so Coleman is probably the unnamed man in the 1860 slave schedule working downtown for stonecutter John Harper. When Harper moved to Southern Utah the next year, Coleman would have moved next door to work at the Salt Lake House, a hotel owned and run by relatives of Charles Decker, who guided the 1856 handcart rescue company.[15]

Five years later Coleman was dead, hit over the head, then stabbed, and his throat cut with his own knife, and a penciled note left on his chest reading, "NOTICE TO ALL NIGGERS! TAKE WARNING!! LEAVE WHITE

WOMEN ALONE!!!"[16] The *Daily Union Vedette*, the literary successor of *Valley Tan*, wrote, "The well-known colored attendant Tom Colburn, of the Salt Lake House for several years, was found with his throat cut in the rear of the arsenal last evening."[17] The next day the *Vedette* called him Thomas Coleman and said that he had lived in the community "for many years" and was a Latter-day Saint.[18]

A coroner's jury concluded that the note meant Coleman had been killed by an unknown relative of an unknown White woman. The jury described the crime, including a knife on the body engraved with Coleman's name which appeared to have been used by the murderer. The jury concluded, "The person or persons committing said murder to the jury are unknown."[19]

The *Vedette* suggested that the jury was negligent and should have located the supposed relative or friend of the suggested woman. In recent years, a suggestion arose that this was a ritualized killing, a late example of Mountain Common Law, extralegal vigilante justice used to protect Latter-day Saint women from victimization by outsiders. However, the language on the note resembled language regularly found in the *Vedette* or *Valley Tan*, and without any additional information, the murderer was as likely to have been a soldier at Camp Douglas, a non-Mormon resident, or a traveler at the Salt Lake House, as a Mormon vigilante. Law enforcement never made an arrest, so any discussion of motives and identities is speculation.[20]

Thomas Bankhead Coleman is buried in a pauper's grave in the Salt Lake City Cemetery.[21]

* * *

When the first Latter-day Saints arrived in the Salt Lake Valley, they found a wide valley watered by creeks running down from the Wasatch Mountains. Those who remained in the valley over the winter of 1847 to 1848 prepared makeshift dwellings, broke ground and planted crops, hunted, and interacted with Indigenous people. Five known enslaved men, Green Flake, Hark Wales, Oscar Smith, Philemon, and John Burton, and one girl, Tennessee, remained in the valley to prepare homes and fields for those who followed the next year. Since his enslaved man Henry had died in Missouri, John Brown hired a neighbor to prepare his land and headed back across the plains to fetch his family. His wife was expecting her first child, and she would have been without household help, so he purchased young Betsy Brown (later Flewellen) in St. Louis. Betsy was one of three dozen enslaved workers in the 1848 migration.[22]

Rather than each family living on a rural farm, settlers built their houses in town and grouped farms together in areas they often called "the Field" or "the Big Field." James M. Flake wrote to Latter-day Saint apostle Amasa Lyman in 1849, mentioning the "boys," a reference to Green and other enslaved men. Flake wrote, "I think I shall have to buy quite a quantity of provisions for the family. the boys calculate to seed all the land inside of the field." He continued, "means are rolling into our hands from the emmigration continually . . . almost evry thing is as cheap here as in the states . . . I heard from Mississippi my land is sold for one thousand dollars." He wrote that they had grown a good crop of wheat, corn, buckwheat, produce, "and almost anything you can call for."[23]

In late 1849, George W. Bankhead and James M. Flake went to California to seek gold to help fund the new settlements. The accounts of the Gold Mission do not mention enslaved people, but perhaps this trip to California, which earned Bankhead a share of a $200 gold nugget, may have been the source for a later legend that two enslaved men in the Bankhead household went to California to earn $2,000 in gold to buy their freedom. Flake died in an accident while in California, and his widow received his modest share of gold.[24]

The amount of production shown in the 1850 census agricultural schedule means that the enslaved were skilled and industrious farm workers and that much of the enslaved African American labor in the territory went into agricultural production. Nancy Crosby Bankhead later said, "We were experienced pioneers and knew how to manage and so didn't suffer so much as the other settlers."[25] The households specialized in the production of butter and cheese. The agricultural schedule shows that the ten households using enslaved Black labor by 1850 had improved almost three hundred acres, grown more than two thousand bushels of grain and corn, owned livestock worth more than $12,000, and produced more than four thousand pounds of butter and cheese. Each of the Bankhead, Crosby, and Flake households produced more butter and cheese than dozens of their neighbors combined.[26] However, by 1850, the Southerners had come to understand the costs of the climate. The weather and growing conditions were inhospitable for many of the early years of settlement, and starvation was a serious concern.[27] William Crosby wrote to Amasa Lyman, "the winter has been Long and Cold but the Spring is now here grass green and fine many cattle perished Last winter in the snow some of mine I think yours is all alive." He added, "I Bought 4 Cows and . . . it makes plenty of milk for the folks."[28]

In the spring of 1851, many Southerners gathered in Utah County on their way to resettle in California. The census takers captured their movement, noting on the slave schedule that the enslaved were "Going to California." Table 2 reconstructs known enslaved residents in 1851 since the census missed some of the enslaved, including the Perkins family.[29]

* * *

By 1850, the Barnett household with eight enslaved people had left for Northern California and the McKown household with two enslaved people had left for Mississippi, and both were not in the census in Utah Territory.[30] The presence of the enslaved in the Latter-day Saint settlements had caused discussion and dissent, but only fragments of the settlers' reactions remain in the historical record. In March 1849, the unnamed enslaved woman in the McKown household took refuge in Brigham Young's home. The same day that McKown wrote to Young about taking her back into bondage, another Southerner, Benjamin Mathews, wrote to Young about Robert M. Smith's enslaved man Rande who, at the instigation of Jim (Valentine/Banks?), took refuge with Jeremiah and Emeline Davis Root and Samuel and Julia Morris McMurtrey.[31] McKown wrote that he had received Young's letter letting him know that "my Negro Girl is at your house and is desirous to not leave the Valley" and claimed that a neighbor had encouraged her to run away. He said that he knew she expected him to "Correct hur if I get hur but this is the first offence She Ever was guilty of and I am persuaded to think my self that She is not to Blame." McKown asked Young to send her back with William Hopper and promised that he would not whip her. "She was Borne mine and I raised hur ~~till~~ and it Seems as though there was One out of the family ever since She has bin away."[32] McKown's paternalistic claim would have resonated among the Latter-day Saint leaders, so the enslaved woman McKown claimed felt like "one . . . of the family" probably returned to his household and went back with him to Mississippi. She matches the description of a woman in his household in 1860.[33] Wilford Woodruff

Table 2. Location of the Enslaved in Utah Territory, Early 1851

County	Number	Names
Davis County (Perkins, Camp)	8–10	Frank Perkins, Esther Perkins, Benjamin Perkins, Mary Ann Perkins James, Sarah Perkins, Downey Perkins Woolridge, Ephraim Perkins?, Manissa Perkins?, Charlotte Camp, Daniel Camp
Iron County (Burton-Robinson)	1	John Burton
Great Salt Lake County (Flake, Bankhead, Brown, Smoot)	15–16	Green Flake, Violet (Crosby) (Bankhead), Rose (Crosby) (Bankhead), Samuel Smith, Nancy Bankhead Valentine, Alexander Bankhead, Thomas Bankhead Coleman, Nathan Bankhead, Miram (Bankhead), Samuel Bankhead, Walter "Rolly" Bankhead, Howard Egan Wales, Lucy (Lay) (Smoot/Williams), Betsy Brown Flewellen, Martha Morris Flake, Esther Harmon?
Utah County, "Going to California" (Flake, Smith, Crosby, Thomas, Lay)	24	Elizabeth Flake Rowan, Toby Embers, Grief Embers, Oscar Smith, Nelson Price, Mary Bankhead Sampson Chism, Henderson Houstin, Nancy Bankhead Jefferson, George Bankhead Chism, Philemon (Thomas), Tennessee or Harriet (Thomas) Jackson, Hannah Smiley Embers, Biddy Mason, Ellen Mason Huddleston, Ann Mason, Harriet Mason Washington, Ann Smiley Peppers Daniels, Lawrence Smiley Embers, Nelson "Nathaniel" Smiley, Jane Smiley Goins, Charles Embers, Hark Wales, Harriet Embers, Unnamed (Lewis?) (Bankhead)
Utah County, Remaining (Redd)	6	Venus Redd, Chaney Redd, Luke Redd, Marinda Redd Bankhead, Amy Redd, Sam Franklin
Total	54–57	

Note: The Black population in 1851 also included free residents James and Iddy (unknown) and Isaac and Jane Manning James and their children.

may have had these stories in mind when he wrote to Thomas L. Kane shortly afterward, "the inhabitants of the State of Deseret will never sustain in any wise the institution of slavery in their midsts."[34]

When most of the Mississippi enslavers went to California in 1851, the Bankhead and Brown households remained in Utah Territory. John Brown served in the territorial legislature in 1852 when it created An Act in Relation to Service and should have understood its provisions. However, in 1857, he listed Betsy in a deed of consecration, a symbolic representation that he would be willing to transfer all his property to the Church of Jesus Christ of Latter-day Saints. Brown valued Betsy at $1,000. It was a high price, even for a healthy and hardworking woman entering her childbearing years, but it was an especially high valuation since she and her future children might be subject to restrictions of ownership under the vague provisions of An Act in Relation to Service. Dr. William Taylor Dennis listed Nancy Lines Smith at $500. No other enslaved people appeared on deeds.[35] (See Appendix 3.)

Before the Mississippi Saints left for California, William and Sytha Lay appear to have sold Lucy to Margaret and A. O. Smoot. Neither Margaret nor A. O. enslaved people in the South, but a few weeks after the territorial legislature enacted An Act in Relation to Service, Margaret sold fourteen-year-old Lucy to merchant Thomas S. Williams for $400.[36] Williams should have known that he needed the approval of the probate court since his father was a member of the legislature, but he ignored the requirement. He registered the sale four years later, and although the document indicates that Probate Judge Elias Smith approved the sale, it does not indicate whether Lucy approved. As such, the documentation of Lucy's sale is one of a handful of documents that showed that Utah residents rarely followed all the provisions of the Act, even if an attempt was made to adhere to any provision.[37]

During the five years that Lucy was in the Williams household, she saw her enslavers change from devout Latter-day Saints to outspoken opponents of Brigham Young's control over the economics and politics of Utah Territory.[38] Thomas S. Williams left for California shortly after Lucy entered the household, and Lucy was left with New York native Albina Merrill Williams and her four living children. Family life became more complicated when Williams returned from California with a bigamous wife, Lucy Ann Thomas, then had a failed plural marriage to Lydia

Phelps, then another plural marriage to Priscilla Mogridge, a divorced plural wife of William Smith, brother of Joseph Smith, the founder of the Church of Jesus Christ of Latter-day Saints.[39]

Their failure to abide by certain provisions of the Act did not relieve Thomas and Albina Williams from legal obligations toward Lucy. The law forbade her enslavers from sexual abuse or rape. Her enslavers had to provide her with "comfortable habitations, clothing, bedding, sufficient food, and recreation" and refrain from cruelty or physical abuse. In addition, Thomas and Albina had to send Lucy to school for at least eighteen months before she turned twenty. In return, Lucy must "labor faithfully all reasonable hours, and do such service with fidelity as may be required by his, or her master or mistress." If she violated her duty, her enslavers must "correct and punish [her] in a reasonable manner when it may be necessary, being guided by prudence and humanity." If she was not treated correctly, the probate judge could remove her from the household.[40] Fourteen-year-old Lucy was, for all practical purposes, an orphan living among strangers although Jane Manning James, Esther Harmon, and Violet and Rose (Crosby) (Bankhead) lived nearby. Violet may have been Lucy's mother, but the knowledge of any relationship is lost to time, and the only relationship a court would recognize was the one with Lucy's enslavers.

Lucy's work would have included all the duties shared by all house servants. She would have been expected to rise early in the morning to remove ashes and start a fire, perhaps from kindling and wood she had chopped. She may have cared for household animals, prepared and served food, helped with childcare, changed bed linens and diapers, emptied chamber pots, and assisted with laundry.

The unreliable 1856 Utah territorial census shows "Lucinda Williams" in the household, but then she disappeared from the public record. Thomas and Albina Williams left Utah Territory not long after their oldest daughter, Caroline, eloped with David Patten Kimball, one of the best-known rescuers of the stranded handcart companies and son of Latter-day Saint leader Heber C. Kimball. Perhaps Williams took Lucy to Missouri and sold her to finance the purchase of a hotel. After a short stay in Missouri, the family returned to Utah Territory, where Williams worked as a lawyer and merchant.

Another slave household in Great Salt Lake City was that of Duritha Trail Lewis, who remained there with Jerry, Caroline, and Tampian while her husband David Lewis worked as a Native American missionary and slave trader and lived with his plural wives in Parowan, Iron County. Duritha probably did not get word until after he was buried that David died in 1855.[41] Duritha administered David's estate, which is notable in Utah history for its valuation of both Native American and African American slaves. The probate showed "Indian boys $95.00," "1 coloured man (35 yrs old) $700," "1 [coloured] woman (16) 500," and 1 [coloured] girl (11) 300."[42]

Besides Jerry, Caroline, Tampian, the unnamed Native American boys, and some land, there was little in the estate to provide for David's

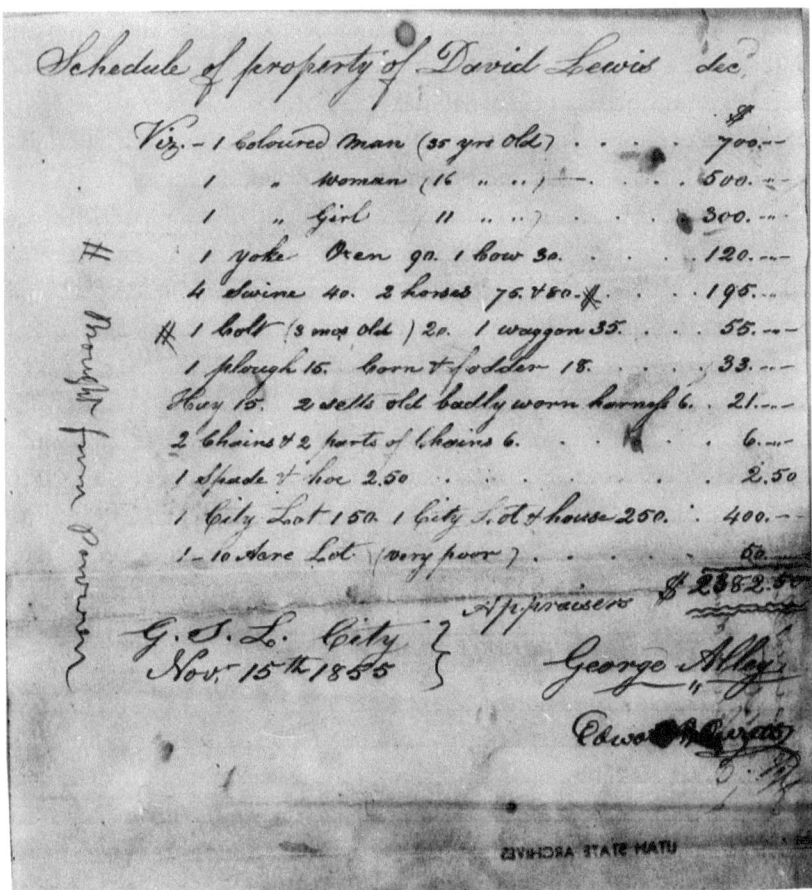

Figure 4.1. The estate of David Lewis, showing valuations for enslaved Jerry, Caroline Hoye, and Tampian Hoye. Utah State Archives.

three widows. His two widows in Parowan remarried one of his brothers as plural wives, and Duritha remarried James Hendricks, former bishop of the Nineteenth Ward. The marriage did not last, and during her ensuing poverty, she registered her three enslaved people in the probate court. She claimed to be "the true and Lawful owner of three persons of African blood, whose names and ages are <as> follows, to wit Jerry, Caroline, & Tampian, aged 38, 18, and 14 . . . inherited . . . from her father Solomon Trail."[43] (See Appendix 2.) After registering them, Lewis sold Caroline and Tampian to merchant Thomas S. Williams, just returned from Missouri. Williams also purchased Daniel from Williams Camp.[44]

As described earlier in this chapter, in 1859, Thomas Bankhead Coleman and Shepherd Camp came to blows over Caroline and Tampian, described by *Valley Tan* as "the slaves of Thos. S. Williams Esq.[,] the reigning ebony belles of Great Salt Lake City." The newspaper wrote, "[A]t their shrine the cringing knees of all cuffeedom bow down."[45] In the fight, Coleman shot Shepherd, and he died from his wounds.

Williams sold Daniel (Camp) to William H. Hooper while he was dissolving a partnership with Hooper. He also sold or mortgaged most of his property to fund a merchanting trip to California.[46] As he prepared for the trip, "Charles M. Smith, Esq., filed a petition asking for a writ of replevin to recover two negro women from Mr. T. S. Williams, which he claimed was the property of A. B. Miller."[47] Williams filed bonds with the court to keep Caroline and Tampian. The jury, including four former or current enslavers, concluded that Caroline and Tampian belonged to Williams, but the judge "set aside that verdict as against all law and the evidence adduced in the case." He refused to release the jury from service or set a new date to rehear the case.[48] Perhaps the trip to California would have made Williams's fortune and the court would have decided the case, but Indigenous raiders killed Williams and his brother-in-law Parmenio Jackman as they crossed the Mojave Desert.[49]

During the settlement of the Williams estate, lawyer Seth M. Blair wrote to probate judge Elias Smith about the ownership of Caroline and Tampian, including an unpaid mortgage on one of the girls. He asked that the administrator of the Williams estate "take possession of two Negresses belonging to the Estate of Said T. S. Williams One in the hands of Horace S. Eldridge the other in the possession of the Widow of Said Williams."[50] (See Appendix 5.) The estate file contains no reply from Judge

Smith. The letter does not specify which of the five wives of Latter-day Saint leader Horace S. Eldredge used the labor of Caroline or Tampian, or if other households also hired the girls, but their labor must have helped provide for the two Williams widows.

Either Caroline or Tampian may have been present when newly appointed territorial governor John W. Dawson propositioned widowed Albina Williams. Williams drove Dawson off, and when word spread about his conduct, he fled the territory.[51]

After they were freed, sisters Caroline and Tampian each married and raised families in Utah. Daniel (Camp) disappeared from the public record but may be remembered in the names of "Negro Dan Hollow" and "Negro Dan Spring" in rural Rich County, Utah.[52]

Table 3. Location of the Enslaved in Utah Territory, 1860

County	Number	Names
Cache	2–4	Nathan Bankhead, Samuel Smith, George A. Bankhead?, Miram Bankhead?
Davis	10	Frank Perkins, Esther Perkins, Benjamin Perkins, Mary Ann Perkins James, Sarah Perkins, Downey Perkins Woolridge, Ephraim Perkins, Wesley Perkins, Albert/Alma Perkins, Sylvester Perkins
Great Salt Lake	19	George (Hockaday), Female (Box), Female (Whitmore), Thomas Bankhead Coleman, Daniel Camp, Female (Barnes), Female Infant (Barnes), Silas Woolridge, Caroline Hoye Bankhead Jackson, Tampian Hoye Campbell, Tom (Church) (Smoot), Jerry (Lewis) (Smoot), Nancy Bankhead Valentine, Alexander Bankhead, Samuel Bankhead, Walter "Rolly" Bankhead, Howard Egan Wales, Henry Valentine, Frank Valentine
Iron	1	John Burton
Utah	1–2	Betsy Brown (Flewellen)?, Nancy Lines (Bankhead) (Dennis) Smith
Total	33–36	

Note: The Black population of Utah Territory in 1860 included twenty-nine known free residents: the Flake, Vallantyne, James, Able, and Redd families, and Francis Pope. In addition, Carson Valley, then in Utah Territory, enumerated forty-eight Black residents.

* * *

Many of the enslaved remained in Great Salt Lake, Utah, Davis, and Iron counties while Samuel Smith and Nathan Bankhead moved north with John H. Bankhead to Box Elder County.[53] As the US Army approached the territory during the Utah War, the Bankhead household fled one hundred miles south to Utah County to stay with John's cousin Talitha Bankhead Dennis. John L. Edwards told of returning to Box Elder County with enslaved Nathan Bankhead to irrigate crops. As he and Bankhead began the irrigation, a storm did all their work for them, so they returned to Utah County. The settlers found a large and successful crop when they returned home after Thomas L. Kane brokered peace between the Latter-day Saints and the federal government.[54]

John H. Bankhead then moved his household to Cache Valley. Darren Parry of the Northwestern Band of the Shoshone Nation shared oral history from his grandmother, historian Mae Timbimboo Parry. The Shoshone would go "as close as they could get without being seen and they would watch these Black people. They were so fascinated." He said, "[The Shoshone] didn't have much contact with the pioneers, so they couldn't ask who these people were [but remembered that they] were hard workers, always industrious, always doing something." The Shoshone would take members of visiting tribes to see the Black settlers.[55]

Scottish immigrant and later Presiding Bishop of the Church of Jesus Christ of Latter-day Saints Charles W. Nibley worked for Bankhead after he arrived in America. He recalled that his employers were the wealthiest in the area. "Among other property, they owned two men negroes, Nate and Sam." He explained, "It seems like harking a long way back to the days of slavery, but negro slavery was actually the law of the land and practiced to a small extent in 1860 and 1861 and 1862 in Cache Valley." Nibley continued, "I felt quite elated when I could sleep with big Nate, the big black negro that Bankhead owned. Old Sam used to ask me if I had read any news of 'de wah,' and I can remember very well him saying at one time, 'My God, I hope de Souf get licked.'" He concluded, "Only once did I see the old man Bankhead get angry at his slaves, and at that time he tore around pretty lively and threatened to horsewhip them to death if they didn't mend their ways."[56] A violent threat almost too ordinary to be mentioned in Southern memoirs was still memorable to Nibley seventy years later.

Table 4. Children Born to Enslaved Parents in Utah Territory

Names	Enslavers
Wesley Perkins (1852), Sylvester Perkins (c. 1856), Alma/Albert Perkins (1858), Ephraim Perkins (dates unknown), Manissa Perkins (dates unknown), Thomas Perkins (dates unknown), Charlotte Perkins Campbell (c. 1862)	Reuben Perkins (Davis County)
Howard Egan Wales (1849), Henry Valentine (c. 1851), Frank Valentine (c. 1857), Nancy Valentine (c. 1860)	George W. Bankhead (Great Salt Lake County)
George A. Bankhead (c. 1850/1853)	John H. Bankhead (Great Salt Lake County)
Nancy Bankhead Jefferson (c. 1848), George Bankhead Chism (c. 1849)	William Crosby (Great Salt Lake County)
Charles Embers (c. 1850)	Robert M. Smith (Great Salt Lake County)

The exact number of children born is unknowable due to infant mortality and the lack of early burial records for the town of Bountiful in Davis County, and for the towns of Union and Draper in Great Salt Lake County.

∗ ∗ ∗

Although no documentation remains of the legal details, A. O. Smoot hired or purchased Jerry (Lewis) and Tom (Church) in Utah Territory. Jerry appears to have been enslaved from birth by the Trail family and then inherited by Duritha Trail Lewis. Duritha and her husband David took Jerry, Caroline, and Tampian to Utah Territory. After David Lewis died, Jerry (Lewis) probably was the primary means of support for widowed and then divorced Duritha Lewis and her family in the Great Salt Lake Valley. In early 1860, Brigham Young wrote to Lewis since he had heard she was frequently asked to sell Jerry. He advised her that if she must sell him, "ordinary kindness would require that you should sell him to some kind, faithful member of the Church, that he may have a fair opportunity for doing all the good he desires to do or is capable of doing." He suggested that since Jerry was forty years old, he was not worth as much as a younger man, but if "the price is sufficiently made, I may conclude to purchase him and set him at liberty."[57]

Twelve weeks later, Young wrote Lewis a second letter. Someone had told him that Jerry claimed to be free and that Lewis had "no papers or <other> evidence to prove that he is [her] slave." Young met with Jerry who evidently repeated the claim but said that he would rather remain with Lewis than be sold. Young concluded that Jerry's claims to be free would imperil a sale. "For these reasons," Young wrote, "I think it much the best for you to retain him in your service."[58] (See Appendix 4.) Nine weeks later, the 1860 census showed Jerry in the service of Mayor A. O. Smoot.[59] In June 1861, after a day of work in the grain fields near the Jordan River, Jerry drowned "while bathing in one of the sloughs between the city and the Jordan, which are now filled with water, as the river is at full banks."[60]

Tom (Church) was enslaved by Haden W. Church when he started across the plains but was in the Smoot household by the mid-1850s. Margaret McMeans Smoot kept a diary between 1855 and 1859. On one occasion, she went into Big Cottonwood Canyon to cook for a crew building a road. It was laborious and dangerous work. Smoot's son Albert almost drowned, foreshadowing his drowning eight years later in the Jordan River. Margaret wrote in her diary, "the men have to work in the water and Mr Smoot too. A Bro. Hunt is sick and <Tom> to day from being in the water it is hard work."[61] Based on diary entries, Tom provided labor for both the Smoot household and Brigham Young's effort to create a sugar industry. Margaret named Tom as one of just three community members not at an 1856 Independence Day celebration. When Margaret mentioned Tom in 1859, he was usually driving a wagon for the Smoot family between Sugar House and downtown Salt Lake City. Someone later penciled "good old Tom" above a diary entry.[62] Tom died in April 1862 of "Inflam of Chest," perhaps pneumonia or tuberculosis.[63] If he had lived another seven weeks, he would have become free when the US Congress outlawed slavery in the territories. After the two men died, Smoot may have hired or purchased Alexander Bankhead. Unfortunately, no known source dates the hire or purchase, so it is not possible to conclude whether Bankhead was enslaved or free when he worked for Smoot.[64]

The labor of enslaved workers in a small number of households helped ensure the agricultural success of the earliest Latter-day Saint settlements in the Great Salt Lake Valley, but when many of the enslavers went to California in 1851, the economic impact of slavery dropped dramatically.

Around two dozen enslaved people of working age remained in the territory, many in remote settlements. Before slavery ended in 1862, Latter-day Saints took about ten more enslaved people into the territory, and merchants, army officers, and government appointees took about the same documentable number, so those in slavery experienced not only the oppression of enslavement but also the isolation of being part of a small population of enslaved people in a territory that then covered much of today's Utah, Colorado, and Nevada, plus parts of Wyoming.

Five

GOING TO CALIFORNIA

In 1867, eleven years after he was freed, Grief Embers traveled from California to Mississippi. In Mississippi, he met Latter-day Saint missionary John Brown, the son-in-law of his former enslavers. Brown wrote, "Here I met a colored man named Grief. He once belonged to Mother Crosby." Brown continued, "He was glad to see me. He is the only colored man I met in this vicinity. When the slaves were emancipated, they left the plantations and went to the cities and towns and along the railroads."[1] Embers left no record of his trip, so Brown's account leaves the reader with the wistful image of Grief looking for his loved ones in the South, and perhaps never finding them before he had to return to California.

Embers first arrived in the Great Salt Lake Valley in 1848. Three years later, Southern converts led by Latter-day Saint apostles Amasa M. Lyman and Charles C. Rich took about two dozen enslaved workers, including Embers, and headed across the Mojave Desert to California. They planned to establish a travel and mail route to the coast and grow olives, grapes, tea, sugar cane, and cotton.[2] When census takers traveled through Utah Territory in the spring of 1851, their forms showed the Southerners gathering in Utah County. The census showed five slave households: widowed Agnes Flake with Green and Elizabeth; William and Sarah Harmon Crosby with Violet, Toby, Grief, Oscar, Nelson, Mary, Henderson, Rose, Nancy, and George; Daniel M. and Ann Crosby Thomas with Philemon and Tennessee; Robert and Rebecca Dorn Smith with Hannah, Biddy, Ellen, Ann, Harriet, Ann, Lawrence, Nelson, Jane, and Charley (note: there were two girls named Ann in the same household); and William and Sytha Crosby Lay with Hark and Harriet.[3]

The Bankhead brothers decided to remain in Utah Territory so Hark had to leave behind his pregnant wife Nancy (Bankhead) and their young son Howard Egan Wales. The move would also separate Mary (Crosby) from her husband, an unnamed man in the Bankhead household. Green Flake and Hark Wales approached Young for help about the pending separations. When William Crosby found out, he wrote Young an infuriated letter. He told Brigham Young that William Lay did not have the cash to purchase Nancy from George Bankhead and that Hark wanted to go to California. "Hark is a good boy and will do right I Believe." On the other hand, he said that Green was "a mean dirty I sarvace [savage] Lying disafected Saucy to Brother Flakes wife Disobediant" and claimed that Green talked of freedom and marrying a White woman. He told Young that Green needed discipline, but that he would defer to Young's judgment.[4] (See Appendix 4.)

Despite Crosby's fury over Flake's desire for freedom, Young's reply suggests that he disagreed with Crosby's assessment, regardless of Crosby's stature in the community as a well-to-do property owner and Great Salt Lake County judge.[5] Young quickly wrote back to Crosby that it was important to keep families together, and perhaps William Lay could take Green, leave Hark in the Bankhead household, and somehow recompense Agnes Flake for Green. He wrote, "altho we do not wish to encourage the Sale of Blacks in these vallies yet it seems as tho Sister fleak might need some assistance perhaps that an Exchange might be made Either for the woman or man," especially since all the enslaved would probably "go free as soon as they shall arrive in California."[6] (See Appendix 4.)

The subsequent events only become clear through tracing the movements of all the enslaved. The slave schedule showed Green, Violet, and Rose among those "Going to California." None of them went. In its first draft, the regular population schedule showed Violet and Rose living in Great Salt Lake County and Green on the slave schedule in the household of Brigham Young. In its second draft, the population schedule showed Violet, Rose, and Green living together in a household.[7] Based on later memories from Green's family, Brigham Young hired Green Flake for a year in what must have been an important part of the negotiations. (See "Green Flake and the Tithing Myth.") Despite having to separate a family, William Lay took Hark Wales to California. An unnamed man in the Bankhead household married to Mary (Crosby) went to California, probably in place of Rose and Violet. John Bankhead was not satisfied with the reassignment of enslaved labor. Thomas Bullock wrote while traveling with Brigham Young and Heber C. Kimball, "John Bankhead came down about his 'nigger fixens [arrangements]' he feels bad about his nigger not coming back. he will not take Green."[8]

In San Bernardino, the settlers purchased a large ranch and built a fort just east of the modern San Bernardino court building. The Crosby family and their enslaved people lived in the southernmost rooms of the fort.[9] Charles C. Rich named Oscar, Grief, Toby, Hark, and Phil in a list of those loyal to the Latter-day Saint leaders of the settlement.[10] Although the enslavers were a small percentage of the community, they provided highly visible leadership. William Crosby served as Latter-day Saint bishop, and Daniel M. Thomas was probate judge. Tithing records from 1852 showed that Crosby donated eggs, butter, and $410.00 cash; Robert M. Smith donated butter, cheese, and $22.82; Agnes Flake donated cheese, a rooster, and $20.00; and Daniel M. Thomas donated produce, meat, eggs, and $30.00. Another tithing book shows that the four slave households donated $80 out of almost $6,000 of tithing paid by Latter-day Saints in Southern California. Later records show that William Lay, Daniel M. Thomas, and Robert Smith withdrew flour from tithing accounts, and William Crosby donated tithing in 1854.[11]

Besides relying on the enslaved peoples' ignorance of the law, the enslavers appear to have actively tried to create a fear of freedom. Many years later, Toby Ember's daughter, Martha Embers Beal, said she remembered her "people laugh in later years over the terror they felt on reaching California and learning they were no longer slaves." She said, "They did not know how they could live, and begged their former owners to take them back to a slave state." These words echo what Harriet Jacobs wrote after escaping from slavery in North Carolina. She told of efforts by enslavers to mislead the enslaved about freedom: "if you were to hear the enormous lies [enslavers] tell their slaves, you would have small respect for their veracity."[12]

By 1852, a man named Dick took refuge in San Bernardino. He had traveled to California during the gold rush with his enslaver, John S. Minter.[13] Minter tracked him to San Bernardino, and rancher J. D. Barker took him into custody. David Seely wrote to Amasa Lyman and Charles C. Rich: "Negro Dick was arrested and about to be taken unless we would

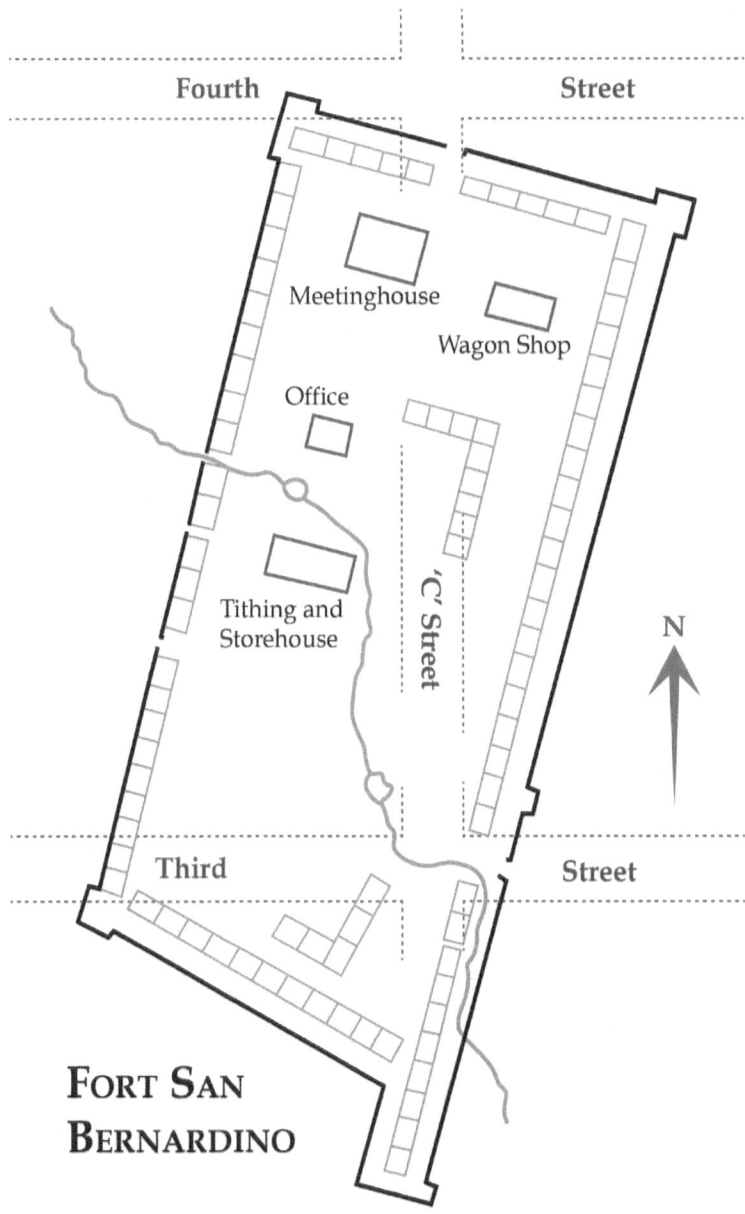

Figure 5.1. The Latter-day Saint settlers to San Bernardino built Fort San Bernardino for protection. Based on a list of residences compiled by L. A. Ingersoll, the extension on the southeast corner housed the enslaved. By the author, after L. A. Ingersoll, *Ingersoll's Century Annals of San Bernardino County, 1769 to 1904* (Los Angeles: L. A. Ingersoll, 1904), 132, 640.

pay 750 Dollars for him poor fellow it seemed as though his heart would brake the Girls thought that they could not get along with out him." San Bernardino historians later identified Dick as Richard Jackson, which meant he already had a son with Tennessee "Harriet" (Thomas) when Minter found him.[14] Seely wrote that he and Hyrum H. Blackwell arranged to either pay $500 over six months, or one hundred bushels of wheat, delivered to Minter's home. "[H]is Master came up and excepted our proposition and we let him have one hundred Bushel of your Wheat . . . [Dick] says he will stay with you as long as he lives." The bond that secured Jackson's freedom showed a payment of $750 to J. D. Barker and John S. Minter.[15] None of the documents confirm Jackson's subsequent legal status or document how long he remained in Rich's service. Jackson went with Rich between California and Utah Territory at least twice. In 1855, Rich wrote, "I in company with B^{ro} Geo. Cannon . . . [and nine others] and my negro Dick started for San Bernardino."[16] Jackson went to Utah Territory in 1857 but appears in no additional Utah records. By 1860, he and his family lived in Los Angeles. Members of his family later returned to San Bernardino.

Questions over property and autonomy within the Latter-day Saint settlement led Robert M. Smith to decide to leave for Texas in 1856. His enslaved women, Biddy Mason and Hannah Smiley, did not understand that they and their families had the legal right to remain in California. Fellow enslaved woman Elizabeth Flake (later Rowan) sent a plea for help to the small Black community in Los Angeles. Black Angeleno Charles Owens rode out to assess the situation. He notified law enforcement, and Judge Benjamin Hayes of the First District Court of California directed the sheriffs of Los Angeles and San Bernardino counties to take Mason and Smiley and their families into custody.[17]

Life in remote San Bernardino insulated the Southerners from challenges to their ability to enslave people. This also happened elsewhere in California. Hannah Cantwell lived outside Sacramento. She had her enslaved girl Mary stripped, bound, and whipped by a hired man. When word reached law enforcement that Mary had died from the beating, the coroner ruled her death accidental. The case caused little further comment, and there is no record of public inquiry into the legality of Cantwell's enslavement of Mary or her right to have her beaten to death.[18]

Figure 5.2. Ellen Mason Owens Huddleston. Miriam Matthews Photograph Collection, Library Special Collections, Charles E. Young Research Library, UCLA.

One of the enslavers in San Bernardino, probate judge Daniel M. Thomas, wrote about the battle over Mason and Smiley and their families in a letter to Amasa Lyman. He wrote in a Biblical style, highlighting the patriarchal nature of the claims to the labor of the enslaved people.

And there was one of our Brethren even Robert Smith who did abide in San Bernardino under the reign of Lym [Amasa M.] Lyman at Said city many years, and the Lord did prosper Robert in the Land untill he did possess much flocks & herds, and came to pass that there was not enough Substance in the land of San Bernardino for his flocks and herds and he Said I will depart to the land of the Gentiles where I will not have to pay tithing neither pay pieces of gold & Silver for an inheritance and after he did dwell there a few days he Said I will arise and Sell my flocks & and herd that the Lord gave me in San Bernardino and I will go and Sojourn in the land of Texas and he did according to his Saying. but It came to pass that when he was about to arise and depart those Sons of Belial the Abolishest [abolitionists] was Stired up against him because he was going to take his men and maid Se<r>vants and behold they went unto the chief men of the city and consulted togather what they Should do, and they Said we will Send the chief officer even the Sheriff and take those Servants from him which they did accordingly and Charles the Son of Toby [Embers] was at San Bernardino and the chief Judge Hays Sent up a writing to our chief officer to take charly in his care that Robert might not carry him to the Land of bondage.[19]

The case brought before Judge Hays, later incorrectly called *Mason v. Smith*, was a writ of *habeas corpus* and a curious blend of family and slave law. The case was not named *Mason v. Smith* since it was a writ of *habeas corpus* and Biddy Mason was neither the lead actor nor a plaintiff bringing the action. Its title is *In re Hannah* (1856), or in its entirety, *In the matter of Hannah and her children, Ann (and Mary, child of Ann), Lawrence, Nathaniel, Jane, Charles, Marion, Martha and an infant boy two weeks old, and of Biddy and her children Ellen, Ann and Harriet, on petition for Habeas Corpus* (1856).

Stacey L. Smith explained in *Freedom's Frontier: California and the Struggle over Unfree Labor, Emancipation, and Reconstruction* that some California enslavers tried to exploit the labor of their former slaves by gaining guardianship of minors, thereby controlling the mothers. The same year as *In re Hannah*, John and Charlotte Rowland gained guardianship of the child Rose and tried but failed to gain guardianship over Rose's mother since she was an adult.[20] Robert Smith probably assumed he would be appointed guardian of the twelve children, and thus ensure the compliance of their mothers, and once he had them back in Texas, he could sell them or continue to profit from their labor.

Judge Hayes ruled, "that all the said persons of color are entitled to their freedom and are free and cannot be held in slavery or involuntary servitude, [and] it is therefore adjudged that they are entitled to their freedom and are free forever." Hayes declared that since Smith planned to take the families to Texas "there is good reason to . . . believe that they may be sold into slavery or involuntary servitude." He also concluded that Smith exercised undue influence to convince them to go to Texas, so he denied Smith's petition to serve as guardian of the children.[21]

After the case, former enslaver Judge Hayes, stung by accusations that he was an abolitionist, detailed his legal reasoning for the newspapers and told of attempts by the Smith household to subvert the judicial process. Under state law, non-White residents of California could not testify in court, so Judge Hayes described how he held conferences with members of the two families in his chambers, with witnesses to their comments.[22]

The legal proceedings took place before the Supreme Court case *Dred Scott* could have altered its outcome, so when Judge Hayes ruled against them, Robert and Rebecca Smith gave up and left for Texas. Judge Hayes later wrote to a friend:

> In the year 1854 [*sic*], at Los Angeles, with "public opinion" against me, I tried the case of fourteen negroes, claiming the protection of the writ of Habeas Corpus. I discharged them, as entitled to freedom. I was denounced as—an abolitionist! For declaring a simple proposition of law—for granting a clear constitutional right! Even at Sacramento, I was 'damned' (so Gov. [John G.] Downey informed me.) A month passed: one day my little boy [fell] from a buggy, under the heels of the horse; one of these same poor negro women, whom Providence placed near by, rushed under the very wheels, and snatched him from death! If a Judge could be repaid, for any duty performed by him—what do you think can be the measure of my reward, in such circumstances? . . . This incident has always seemed to me one of the most singular in my "brief career."[23]

Upon the resolution of the case, about a dozen adults still in bondage in San Bernardino made plans to leave their former enslavers. Judge Thomas told Amasa Lyman about the resulting shock and confusion among the enslavers, noting that Philemon went to work for a merchant, and "Grief [Embers] and Oscar [Smith], they went and behold

Figure 5.3. Biddy Mason with friends and family. Mason is sitting just left of center facing the camera and wearing a dark dress and white collar. Miriam Matthews Photograph Collection, Library Special Collections, Charles E. Young Research Library, UCLA.

they pitched their tents in the city of the angels likewise together with that beautifull piece of Ebony called Harriet [Grief's] wife."²⁴

British traveler William Chandless visited the Latter-day Saint settlement before *In re Hannah*. He wrote, "The good bishop [William Crosby] was the husband of one, and but one wife [Sarah Harmon]; a stout old lady, who could, I fancy, in case of need have proved a thorough termagant." He continued, "Household work she did none; there were negroes to do that: niggers of all ages; half a dozen of them." Chandless reported, "The Bishop had originally owned them when slavery existed in California, and afterwards they continued with him in a voluntary servitude: now he was rather anxious to get rid of them, as they had little to do, and ate a good deal more than they worked."²⁵ If Chandless reported Crosby's words accurately, Crosby had adjusted his tale for the audience. He did not enslave anyone in California before it became a state, thus allowing him to continue to keep them in bondage; he arrived after California was a free state. Although he complained to Chandless about the cost of enslaving people, they helped build and run his hotel, the San Bernardino House.²⁶ When they left, Crosby became ill in the effort to do the work they would have done. A neighbor wrote to Amasa Lyman, "Bishop

[Crosby] has been quite sick, from over exertion and exposure while at work on the Mill."[27] Besides relying on their labor, if his illegally enslaved people had indeed been the burden he suggested, he could have hired them out, since California had a great demand for labor, as Judge Hayes told the newspapers after *In re Hannah*.[28] Diaries do note the occasional hiring out, including Amasa Lyman's record: "Went to *br* Robert Smiths to hire his colored woman to work for us."[29]

About two years later, Brigham Young called the San Bernardino settlers back to Utah Territory during the Utah War. The Crosby families left California, and those liberated from bondage may never have seen any of them again, except for Grief Embers meeting John Brown in Mississippi.

Some of the freed people became San Bernardino property owners, including Grief and Harriet (Lay) Embers, Elizabeth Flake Rowan, and Toby Embers and Hannah Smiley and their children. Others owned land in Los Angeles and Santa Monica, including Biddy Mason and her daughters and Mary Crosby Bankhead Sampson Chism. Oscar Smith, Henderson Houstin, and Nelson Price remained in the area as laborers. Hark Wales lived near San Bernardino until he returned to live in Utah Territory in the 1870s. The longest-lived of all those held in bondage in Utah Territory and California was Charles Embers, the son of Toby Embers and Hannah Smiley. He was one of the earliest Black residents of Tucson, Arizona, and died there in 1935.

Six

GREEN FLAKE AND THE TITHING MYTH

Three years after Green Flake entered the Salt Lake Valley and two years after the Flake family arrived, Green's enslaver James M. Flake went to California to search for gold to help finance the new Latter-day Saint settlements. His mule threw him outside the San Joaquin Valley, and he died of a broken neck.[1] His widow Agnes, their surviving children, and enslaved Elizabeth moved to California the next year and left Green in Utah.

When Agnes Flake died in San Bernardino in 1855, Maria Tanner Lyman, the first wife of apostle Amasa M. Lyman, took the three Flake orphans and Elizabeth into her home. When children lose their parents at a young age, are raised by acquaintances of short duration, and then go their separate ways and rarely or never see each other again, there is no one to reinforce and correct early memories. Such was the experience of Mario R. Capecchi. When he won the 2007 Nobel Prize in Medicine, he told reporters about his childhood in war-torn Europe. The Associated Press researched his story and discovered that although his childhood was traumatic, the details he had shared were largely incorrect, including a memory of his mother being taken to Dachau concentration camp. "Some of the contradictions that have since emerged might be attributed to tricks played on a child's memory or to secondhand information that eventually gelled in the mind as fact," wrote the reporters. "Capecchi might never have been given the full story, as it was quite common for those traumatized in the war to avoid talking about their experiences."[2]

Only two of seven or more Flake children lived to adulthood, married, and had children, and only one, William Jordan Flake, is known to have left written memories. Since William and his sister Sarah Flake Levie Oakden lived through numerous traumas and never lived near each other after childhood, their memories should be expected to include large gaps and inaccurate details. That the few memories Flake left are largely accurate regarding the movement of the Mormon pioneers is a testimonial to the strength of the Latter-day Saint historical narrative, but his account missed many important details of his early life.

Among the details he did not mention was the existence of at least two of his siblings. It was not until 1946 that descendants knew about a son who died as the Flake family moved across the country.[3] In recent years, Flake descendants wondered why enslaved Elizabeth was called "Carlotty" and given an incorrect age when she crossed the plains with the Latter-day Saints.[4] The original record answered that question: the wagon roster listed Elizabeth as "Elizabeth Colord," meaning "colored," and Carlotty L. Flake was not only in the roster but also in the 1840 census and records of Winter Quarters and was probably a daughter in the family. Perhaps she died during the earliest years of the Utah settlement of the same tuberculosis that later killed her mother.[5]

One of the few anecdotes Flake left of his childhood has been told and retold many times, including in the two largest Utah newspapers, the *Salt Lake Tribune* and *Deseret News*.[6] The anecdote dates to the 1890s, when Andrew Jenson, Assistant Church Historian for the Church of Jesus Christ of Latter-day Saints, began to compile a biographical encyclopedia. Flake filled out a printed form with his memories and recollections. He recalled:

> In 1851, <his> mother and family went with C. C. Rich and A. M. Lyman to settle San Bernardino. Previous to going she gave her negro slave Green Flake (one of the Pioneers of 1847) to the Church as tithing. He then worked two years for Pres Young <with his wife worked for> and Heber C. Kimball, and then got his liberty and settled near Union.[7]

The claim would have been an honest attempt to explain why Agnes Flake left Green in Utah Territory when she went to California. There would have been no one to correct William's memory or educate him in the details of early Latter-day Saint tithing or the defunct legal system surrounding Southern slavery, including the practice of hiring out enslaved people. No historical documents support the story and William's mother and Green Flake's family both contradicted his account. Negotiations between multiple enslavers as some left for California and some remained in Utah Territory in 1851 explain the story in a way that William Flake could not have remembered. Regardless of the legal situation, Agnes discovered the difficulty of managing an enslaved man who had believed briefly that he was free. Green's granddaughter later remembered, "When they reached the Salt Lake Valley B. Young said, 'Brothers [Green, Hark, and Oscar] you are now free as I am.'"[8] Despite Young's conclusion, Southern enslavers initially prevailed on questions of ownership.

If James M. Flake had lived in Mississippi at his death and died intestate, meaning without a will, the probate court may have directed that his wife would inherit a life interest of one-third of her husband's estate and given her the guardianship of her minor children with a court-overseen responsibility to preserve the remaining two-thirds of the estate for her husband's heirs, in this case, his surviving children. Agnes Flake would have had to account to the court for her handling of the estate and the sale of any property, including enslaved people. Utah Territory was in its infancy, and there is no record of a probate for Flake's estate, but as the California Supreme Court later said in *Pearson v. Pearson* (1875), the territorial courts would have been expected to act regarding slavery in Utah as they did in other parts of the country.[9]

When many Southern Saints left for California in 1851, Agnes Flake left Green in Utah Territory, probably the event her son later explained as a tithing donation to the church. Since William Crosby and John H. Bankhead were involved in the negotiations and would have checked Agnes Flake's actions, it would have been highly unusual for her to donate much of her net worth and most of the labor capacity of her household in tithing, as her son later suggested. In the previous decades, Crosby, Bankhead, and Flake had participated in complex family estate settlements and would have been familiar with slave law and custom. They would have known that Flake could not legally sell or donate an enslaved man belonging to her husband's estate. However, she could hire him out, as other widows did when they needed cash more than labor.[10] Green's granddaughter, Bertha Stevens Udell, later told an interviewer, "Brigham

Young gave a yoke of oxen for Green Flake." Based on valuations in Utah consecration deeds, the yoke of oxen Udell mentioned was worth about $100.[11] Although this fragmentary account is the only known documentation of the price of hiring an enslaved worker in Utah Territory, $100 was the price merchant Clifton Barnes paid most years to hire an enslaved man to oversee his children's property in Missouri. The price for hiring an enslaved man in Missouri ranged from 8 to 15 percent of his value, and prices in Utah Territory may have been similar.[12]

Was this a tithing donation? Bertha Udell's memory suggested that Agnes Flake received market value for the hire, which indicates there was no donation involved, but as with all late family memories, William Flake's claim should not be discarded without considering all possible meanings. One of the first questions is whether James and Agnes Flake paid tithing. Nauvoo, Great Salt Lake City, and San Bernardino tithing records confirm occasional tithing and charitable donations. James Flake donated cash or goods rather than labor to pay labor tithing assessments.[13] With James Flake's death, expectations for donations changed for the family. During the years before the move to the Great Salt Lake Valley, a few widowed or otherwise impoverished women paid tithing, but the church immediately returned their donations so they could make the gesture of paying tithing without losing any means of support.[14] Once the Saints arrived in the valley, the general labor tithing books show four women who paid labor tithing, all with older teenage or adult sons, and do not include the frail and widowed Agnes Flake, mother of three young children.[15] Flake received about $100 from her husband's gold mission, and she may have sold excess crops, household goods, and farming implements before she left for California.[16] Although the poor and widowed were not expected to pay tithing, the records show she disregarded church practices and paid modest amounts.[17]

Did Brigham Young use tithing resources to hire Green Flake? During the effort to organize and build settlements throughout the western United States, Brigham Young's finances became so intertwined with church finances that the complicated court-overseen distribution of his estate finally involved litigation between his heirs and the church.[18] Historian Leonard J. Arrington explained, "It was sometimes difficult to determine whether he had drawn on funds as trustee-in-trust or whether entries represented church expenditures in his own private capacity."[19]

However, Green Flake does not appear in the general labor tithing accounts, and Young indicated two or three times that Flake worked for him rather than the church. The first instance was in the draft copy of the 1850 federal census slave schedule, created in early 1851 as Agnes Flake started for California. It listed, "Brigham Young 1 [slave] Greene 23 [years old]."[20] The slave schedule is not a legal claim that Young enslaved rather than hired Flake since the schedule occasionally showed hired workers.

In an ambiguous statement, shortly after Flake began to work for him, Brigham Young said in a sermon, "the Abolitionest are vary fearful that we shall have the Negro or Indian as Slaves Here . . . The Master of Slaves will be damned if they Abuse their slaves." He said, "Yet the Seed of Ham will be servants untill God takes the Curse off . . . I Have two Blacks. They are as free as I am. Shall we lay a foundation for Negro Slavery[?] No God forbid And I forbid."[21] Brigham Young preached his sermon during the discussion about census slave schedules and right after he hired Flake, an event that may have occasioned comment in the community, so he may have been speaking about Flake and his coachman, New Jersey native Isaac James, or he may have been speaking about Isaac James and his wife Jane Manning James. Finally, Young wrote in an 1854 letter, "Green worked for me for about a year."[22] Flake's employment ended by 1853, since he was not on the lists of the Young household made between 1853 and 1855.[23]

During the year of the hire, the territorial legislature created An Act in Relation to Service. The law did not allow the transfer of labor without the consent of an enslaved or indentured individual, and since Flake was unlikely to provide consent, when Young hired him and kept him in the Great Salt Lake Valley, he effectively provided Flake with a gradual transition to freedom.

In 1854, Agnes Flake and her children lived in the struggling San Bernardino settlement. Flake was on her deathbed and requested help writing a will from Richard R. Hopkins and Amasa M. Lyman.[24] Lyman had sent a message to Brigham Young on her behalf almost half a year earlier:

> Sister Agnes Flake wishes me to enquire of you if there is any chance for her to receive any help by way of the negro man she left when she came here. She has a famaly on her hands for which to provide. Her health is also very delicate health and if she could

realize something from him this quarter it would be a benefit to her Thomas S. Williams told me if he could he would purchase the negro and pay for him. A word from you on this subject would be received a favor"[25]

Brigham Young wrote back: "Green Flake worked for me about a year, sometime ago & when he went into Cottonwood his health was quite feeble, & from all I learn he <is> still unable even to support himself & family entirely." He added, "[S]hould he regain his health, so as to <be> able to be of any benefit to sister Flake, I will inform you."[26] There is no way to confirm or disprove Young's claim about Flake's health. Whether or not Flake was ailing, Young sidestepped the issue of legal ownership and ensured Flake's freedom. Not long after Brigham Young refused to sell Flake to Williams, Agnes Flake died in San Bernardino. Maria Tanner Lyman took the orphaned children and Elizabeth into her home, and Elizabeth soon discovered she was free and began her own life.

In summary, Agnes Flake seems to have hired out Green Flake to Brigham Young for a year to help solve a problem involving the separation of enslaved families and the control of Flake's labor. Brigham Young then

Figure 6.1. Green Flake. *Salt Lake Tribune*, May 31, 1897.

freed Green Flake. William J. Flake reported more than forty years later that his mother donated Flake as tithing, but no known record confirms that Agnes understood tithing to be involved in the transaction, and the laws and customs of Southern slavery, the provisions of An Act in Relation to Service, the memories shared by Green Flake's family, and Amasa Lyman's letter contradict William Flake's childhood memory. Although Green Flake left no record of his understanding of the entire incident, his relationship with Brigham Young continued to be an important part of his family's heritage. Many years after both men died, a granddaughter recalled, "Green shed tears at the death of Brigham Young and helped dig his grave and was at the funeral of the beloved President."[27]

Seven

THE TEXANS

The enslaved and free population of Texas grew rapidly after it became a state. Latter-day Saint leaders sent missionaries to the state in the 1850s and created several congregations. Like other Latter-day Saint converts from the South, some from Texas were enslavers, and others were not. The known Texas Latter-day Saint enslavers were the Greer family, Nancy Reddick Greer Johnson Sprouse, Thomas and Clarkey Carpenter Box, the Moody family, and Elizabeth Carter Flaherty Whitmore.

Most of their stories exist only in fragments, but the best documented is the Greer family. After the family moved from Texas to Utah Territory, then back to Texas and later to Arizona Territory, Ellen Camp Greer preserved the memory of a beloved family song, "My Pretty Quadroon." Her family recalled the words: "I scarce knew that I was a slave / So kind was young Massa to me, / So gentle, so manly, so brave, / That I had not a wish to be free."[1] It is bitter irony that the woman who perpetuated this romantic memory of a kind "young Massa," was a daughter of enslaver Williams Camp, remembered in the diary of Hosea Stout. "To day witnessed the humiliating spectacle of seeing W. Camp thrash his wife," wrote Stout. "This is the first time in my life I ever beheld such a sight After dragging her three times by the hair of the head through the porch and finally on the ground down a flight of stone steps he struck and stamped her in the breast." Stout continued, "[He] gave her another hair pulling and chocking & knocked down & chocked another one of his wives & raised the surrounding neighborhood by the screams and cries of the family & two *thrashed* women." The city marshal arrested Camp and an alderman fined him $50 and court costs.[2]

In a second layer of complication, the historical record suggests that Williams Camp's wife and Ellen's mother, Diannah Greer Camp, sent two enslaved people she inherited from her father to Texas with Ellen in one of the few documented attempts by women in the territory to preserve slave property.³ Despite the shared name, Diannah Greer Camp was not related to Thomas Lacy Greer, the Texan her daughter Ellen married after his family arrived in Utah Territory in the mid-1850s. Most of the Greer family remained in Utah Territory for less than a year, but in that short time, they provoked one of the few court cases about African American slavery in the territory. The case led to almost all the slave registrations under the provisions of Utah Territory's An Act in Relation to Service.

Thomas Greer's father Nathaniel Hunt Greer was a larger-than-life character. He fought in the Creek Wars, served as a legislator in the Republic of Texas, and was indicted for murder in a local feud.⁴ He and his family were representative of the movement of Southerners and slavery into Texas in the 1830s, including their participation in the war with Mexico. Many members of the family joined the Church of Jesus Christ of Latter-day Saints and started for Utah Territory in 1855. Greer enslaved five or more people in Texas. The family remembered Ned, Jim, Judah, Lucy, and Louisa, but no historical record suggests that they went to Utah Territory, so the family may have sold them while in St. Louis to provision their wagon company.⁵

Nathaniel Hunt Greer and other family members died of cholera on the trail. The grieving family continued to Utah Territory. During a harsh winter, many of the cattle they drove to Utah perished in the cold. Their losses combined with the family's introduction to Latter-day Saint practices, including plural marriage and local economic controls, led most of the family to the hard decision to return to Texas. Notices in the *Deseret News* outline the story of the hasty end and messy aftermath of their businesses in Utah.⁶

Williams and Diannah Camp decided to take their enslaved people and go to Texas with their daughter who had just married into the Greer family, but after a sensational court battle, their enslaved men Daniel and Shepherd remained in Utah Territory with the Camps, and Ellen Camp Greer took enslaved Isaac and Carolina to Texas. In order to tell the story of the people enslaved by the Camp and Greer families, it is necessary to turn the calendar back many years and trace the family back across the country to the American South.

* * *

Georgia native Williams Camp moved west to Alabama as a young man. In the early 1830s, he took his family and enslaved workers north to Dresden, Tennessee, where he worked as a blacksmith. There his family joined the Church of Jesus Christ of Latter-day Saints and headed west to Utah Territory, taking an enslaved brother and sister, Daniel and Charlotte.

Ellen Camp Greer later recalled the despair teenaged Charlotte felt when she thought two Camp children in her care had drowned. Charlotte had reason to fear since her enslaver was a violent man. Williams Camp eventually had seven or eight wives, and six or seven of them left or divorced him. When Ellen's mother Diannah filed for divorce in 1861, she detailed Camp's violent abuse and said that she feared for her life.[7] In divorce proceedings the next year, another wife, Amelia Evans, told the court that Camp had "often struck, beat, choked and bruised her, with his hands and kicked her with his feet; that he at one time, whipped her severely with a horsewhip and at another stuck her with an axe."[8] The couple reconciled, but in 1863, Camp accused Amelia of killing their infant child. The jury found her not guilty, and the judge ordered Camp to pay the court costs. After the case ended, two of Amelia's relatives accosted and beat Camp, but the judge dropped charges against one and assessed the other a fine of $1 and court costs, a slap on the wrist compared to Camp's $50 fine for beating his wives. In an earlier case, another wife, Elizabeth Brooks, alleged severe abuse by both Williams and Diannah Camp.[9] The court records contain no information about how Williams and Diannah Camp treated their enslaved people, so the reader can only imagine what their lives were like, and why Charlotte preferred death by suicide to the alternative.

In 1853, Diannah Greer Camp learned that a court was settling her father's estate. She and her husband hired Daniel out to William H. Hooper and left their children with the enslaved woman Charlotte and Louisa Taylor Stout, the wife of Hosea Stout, who was a missionary in China. While the children were in their care, Louisa died, and then Charlotte died of tuberculosis at age twenty-three, leaving the children to the mercy of their neighbors.[10] Eventually the Camps returned to the territory with wagons full of trade goods and enslaved Isaac, Carolina, and Shepherd.[11]

None of the participants told the subsequent story in its entirety, but a series of seemingly unconnected documents show what happened. First, Camp wrote to Brigham Young, signing himself, "Yours etc in the Bonds of the Gospel," and asking for a plural wife: "Can I have the Privelidge to get me a young woman."[12] Several days later, Camp signed a consecration deed showing more than $10,000 of property, including an expensive piano, $500 of "merchandize," $500 of "Mrs Camp's Merchandize," and promissory notes. Like the other enslavers in Great Salt Lake and Davis counties, he did not list the enslaved on his consecration deed.[13] Just days after he signed the deed, the church excommunicated him for "nonconformity to its decisions."[14] The newspaper does not give any further explanation, but John Allen simultaneously advertised in the *Deseret News* that Williams Camp had committed fraud, and recommended that no one accept Camp's promissory notes.[15] Plural wife Elizabeth Brooks Camp then filed for divorce, alleging abuse and neglect, including a charge that Camp "has permitted [her] to be beaten like a dog by his other wife and has allowed her to be abused in a most shamefull manner until her life has become almost intolerable." Camp denied all charges, and his attorney, Thomas S. Williams, claimed that the court had no jurisdiction over a plural marriage. Probate Judge Elias Smith ignored the challenge and granted Elizabeth a divorce.[16]

During all these personal and business difficulties, Williams and Diannah Camp decided to leave for Texas with their daughter. Williams Camp met with Brigham Young, who talked him out of leaving. The next day, Diannah Camp went to the President's office "for the privilege of taking her negroes away."[17] No one left a report of the result of the consultation, but, at that point, Williams and Diannah Camp made plans to either go to Texas or to send their enslaved people with their daughter.

Daniel did not want to go back into slavery in Texas, so he ran away. An ad hoc slave patrol of Williams Camp, Stephan Decatur Greer, Americus Vespucius Greer, and Madison Foster hunted and captured him.[18]

On June 16, 1856, former Quaker, now Latter-day Saint bishop Edwin Woolley went before Judge Elias Smith to request that the court charge Williams Camp and his associates with kidnapping.[19] Brigham Young, Jesse Little, and Sheriff Robert T. Burton met to discuss the case.[20] Hosea

Stout wrote, "There was a great excitement on the occasion The question naturally involving more or Less the Slavery question and I was surprised to see those latent feeling aroused in our midst which are making so much disturbance in the states."[21]

Sheriff Burton arrested Camp and Stephan Greer. Thomas S. Williams and Hosea Stout served as their counsel and paid $1,000 bail while Daniel remained in the sheriff's custody. On June 17, Burton also arrested Americus Greer and Madison Foster. The court sent out subpoenas for Bishop Woolley, Brigham Young's son-in-law Charles F. Decker, William Crawford, who had traveled from Texas with the Greer family, and "one Dan <Camp>, a negro, to give testimony in a case."[22] Other areas of the country, including nearby California, prohibited Black and enslaved people from testifying in court, but not Utah Territory, so when the attorneys for the defense requested that Daniel be barred from testifying in court, the court ruled against them.

The case ended quickly. Judge Smith wrote in his diary, "[B]elieving that there was not sufficient proof against the accused to convict them I discharged them tho I believed truly, that they were guilty of what was alledged against them."[23] Although Smith could not find enough evidence to hold the four men, Daniel and Shepherd remained in the territory with Williams and Diannah Camp while Thomas and Ellen Camp Greer took Isaac and Carolina to Texas. The case must have caused those involved to examine the laws of the Territory because a few days later, Williams and Diannah Camp went to the probate court to register Shepherd. They documented that Shepherd was born the property of James Greer in Henry County, Tennessee, in 1837, and that when James Greer died, his property was divided between his fourteen children. Williams and Diannah Camp "did receive the said Negro boy named Shepard as aforesaid, in the month of January 1853 in the State of Mississippi, County of Marshal, of the administrator of the estate." Camp swore that, "the aforesaid Negro boy was brought by him to the Territory aforesaid a slave for life in the year 1854 . . . as is made and provided for by the statute of the Territory aforesaid."[24] (See Appendix 2.) Camp brought William Taylor Dennis with him to court, and Dennis swore that he spent two or three weeks with Williams Camp in St. Louis and crossed the plains with him, and that no one ever challenged Camp's ownership of Shepherd.[25] A week later, Camp returned to court to register Daniel.[26] Camp's lawyer, Thomas

S. Williams, also went to court to record his 1852 purchase of Lucy from Margaret McMeans Smoot. The only other known registrations were two years later when Duritha Lewis registered Jerry, Caroline, and Tampian, and then sold Caroline and Tampian to Thomas S. Williams, who then also purchased Daniel from Williams Camp. When Thomas S. Williams sold Daniel to William H. Hooper in 1859, the County Recorder's Office recorded the sale, rather than the probate court.

Besides the Greer-Camp family, other Texan Latter-day Saints also had ties to slavery, including Thomas Greer's aunt, Nancy Reddick Greer Johnson Sprouse. Before she married John Sprouse, her husband probably took an enslaved man named Silas to Utah Territory. After Sprouse died, Silas appeared in Nancy's household on the 1860 census slave schedule.[27] Silas used the name Woolridge after he was freed, which combined with his reported birthplace of Alabama suggests a series of enslavers tracing back from Nancy Greer Sprouse to his likely first enslavers, Thomas and Keziah Wooldridge.[28] After he was freed, Silas Woolridge married Downey Perkins. She and their newborn son died, and Silas left Salt Lake City for the Pioche mining area, where he lived and worked with brothers Lorenzo Dow Barton and Isaac Barton. Decades later, the three men moved to California, where Woolridge died in 1917.[29]

The Box family were also enslavers from Texas. The adventures of the extended Box family would fill a book, including the 1866 Box Family Massacre, memorialized in the writings of General George Armstrong Custer, but most of their adventures are only tangentially related to the story of slavery in Utah Territory.[30] The family's brush with slavery in Utah Territory began with Thomas and Clarkey Carpenter Box, barely literate Southerners who moved from Alabama to carve out a homestead in the Chickasaw Cession in Mississippi. Within a few years, they took one of their five enslaved people and moved to Texas where they began to build a fortune in cattle.[31] In the early 1850s, they met missionary Morris J. Snedaker and joined the Church of Jesus Christ of Latter-day Saints. Snedaker wrote in his diary one day that he "returned to Bro Thomas Box's[.] it rained and the heavens Seemed all blackined in the West from a tornado that dashed all before it . . . and Cild [killed] 9 Persons," including an unnamed enslaved girl.[32]

Box hired John Aiken to drive his cattle to Utah Territory and they started west while the US Army also headed toward the Territory to put down a supposed rebellion. Aiken told a newspaperman that in Wyoming they encountered "one hundred and fifty armed men (all Mormons); they had established an observatory to watch the approach and movements of [the] army."³³ When the men in the camp discovered that the cattle belonged to a Latter-day Saint convert, they allowed them to pass. What no one reported is whether Box took any enslaved people with him. When he arrived, he was one of the wealthier men in the territory, and within a year, he married a plural wife, Belinda Marden Hilton Pratt, a widow of murdered Latter-day Saint apostle Parley P. Pratt. The only record of the difficulties involved in the short-lived marriage was a note in a family history that Belinda's daughter "passed through many trying scenes through childhood and youth."³⁴ The 1860 census showed an enslaved thirty-year-old woman living in the household.³⁵ She is not the same woman in the household ten years earlier in Texas, and since she is unnamed, her identity is unknown.

Several days' travel south of the Box family in Grimes County, Texas, Preston Thomas baptized Alabama native Louisa into the Church of Jesus Christ of Latter-day Saints in 1853 along with members of the William C. and Harriet Henson Moody family who enslaved her. The household left almost immediately for Utah Territory where Louisa appeared in a list of rebaptisms, but by the 1856 territorial census, she was no longer in the household, and the Moody family did not preserve any independent memory of her.³⁶

Besides the Box family, another Texan shown in the 1860 census slave schedule for Great Salt Lake City was Elizabeth Carter Flaherty Whitmore, who eventually turned a Texas estate she inherited from her first husband, Irish immigrant Michael T. Flaherty, into a fortune in territorial Utah. Flaherty died around 1852 of cholera, leaving Elizabeth large holdings of land and cattle, but no enslaved people. It was not long before Elizabeth married semiliterate schoolteacher James M. Whitmore.³⁷ Although Elizabeth was raised in a slave household, she did not enslave any people until around 1856, the year that Latter-day Saint missionaries came through town and baptized the Whitmore family and the woman they enslaved. Morris J. Snedaker wrote, "11 [May 1856] Sunday We held Meeting at Brother Whitmore preaching by Eld[er] H Duncin and Eld Ostler Baptized Mr. Cunningham and Wife and a niger."³⁸ Snedaker's list of the membership in the area showed "Whitmore s Black women 1 [person]."³⁹

Within a year, Whitmore sold many cattle and two of her four enslaved people.⁴⁰ It is unlikely that she freed anyone: Texas was hostile toward a free Black population.⁴¹ The records of the Whitmore's 1857 wagon company do not show any enslaved people in the company, and the enslaved girl living in the Whitmore household in 1860 is not the enslaved woman baptized in Texas. There is no record that the unnamed enslaved girl went with Whitmore to a new home in southern Utah the next year.

Most of the documented connections between slavery in Utah Territory and Texas are concentrated in the story of the unsuccessful attempt by the Camp-Greer family to take Daniel to Texas. Other documents badly garbled the story of Silas Woolridge and forgot Louisa (Moody) and the unnamed enslaved women and teenagers in the Box and Whitmore households. All that is left are fleeting impressions of a few experiences during the western spread of African American slavery before the Civil War.

Eight

MERCHANTS, ARMY OFFICERS, AND GOVERNMENT APPOINTEES

Some enslaved people would have escaped documentation of their experiences in Utah Territory, especially those in the territory with merchants, federal government appointees, army officers, or any who spent the winter in the territory while traveling elsewhere, but several appear in records related to their time in the territory.

With Merchants

Enslaved people known to have been with merchants in the territory included an unnamed woman and infant with Missouri merchant and slave trader Clifton R. Barnes, George Hockaday with Kentucky native John M. Hockaday, and Laura Pearson and Susan Price with Missouri merchant Richard Pearson. Merchant and former Latter-day Saint Thomas S. Williams did business with a network of enslavers, including Williams Camp, William H. Hooper, David and Duritha Lewis, A. O. and Margaret Smoot, Peter K. Dotson, and John M. Hockaday, but all the enslaved in his household are mentioned elsewhere in the book and not covered separately here. They include Lucy (Lay), Caroline Hoye (Lewis) Bankhead Jackson, Tampian Hoye (Lewis) Campbell, Daniel (Camp), and perhaps a man named Bill. In addition, a community source mentioned the purchase or hiring of Benjamin Perkins of Davis County by Livingston & Kinkead, a trading firm run by New York and Pennsylvania natives James Monroe Livingston, his brother Howard Livingston, and John H. Kinkead, future governor of Alaska and Nevada.[1]

Table 5. Known Enslaved African Americans with Merchants, Army Officers, or Government Appointees

Names	Enslavers
Cato	James A. Harkreader; William W. Drummond
Woman and Infant	Clifton Barnes
Frank	Peter K. Dotson
George Hockaday	John M. Hockaday
Laura Pearson, Susan Price Halley	Richard Pearson
Randolph Hughes	Gen. Albert Sidney Johnston
Theophilus	Lt. Benjamin Allston

Unnamed Woman and Infant (Barnes)

An unnamed woman and her infant daughter appeared in the census slave schedule in Utah Territory in 1860 in the household of Missouri merchant Clifton R. Barnes. Her identity is unknown, but enough records exist about the Barnes family and slavery in Missouri to suggest some of her possible experiences, including the buying, selling, hiring, and interstate transportation of the enslaved without concern for their family relationships.

Kentucky native Clifton R. Barnes moved with his parents to Jackson County, Missouri, just after the 1838 Mormon War ended. Territorial court records show that the speculator, freighter, and small-time slave trader was in Utah by 1854 when he and his brother Sidney sued two merchants and were sued in return.[2]

When Barnes's first wife died, she left a large estate to her two children. Most years, her estate paid $100 "To Hire of Negro man [John]."[3] John may have been enslaved by a neighbor who needed cash more than labor or a widow who held a life interest in her deceased husband's property and could not sell him. The price to hire an enslaved person depended on the local market, the type of labor, and the person's sex, age, strength, and reputation.[4]

John C. Caldwell v. Richard H. Porter (1855) captured Barnes's work as a Missouri slave trader. The original bill of sale for an enslaved woman named Eliza, not the same woman later in Utah, warranted her "to be Sound in body and mind and a Slave for life."[5] Isaac Hockaday provided financing for the sale, and after the sale, Barnes sold the promissory note to John C. Caldwell, which meant that the lawsuit named Caldwell instead of Barnes after Porter found he did not have a clear title and Eliza's fitness for service was not as warranted. Porter planned to sell Eliza for a profit in Louisiana, but upon going there, found that she was well known, "and no one would buy her at any price."[6] The court reviewed her history, and a previous enslaver stated at deposition, "The Slave Eliza was a small negro woman, black <or dark color> about 20 years of age. She was brought from Independence Missouri about in March 1853 to Vicksburg by me." He reported that she would barely eat and concluded with an impersonal insight into her tragic loss: "I considered her Sound & thought her bad health was . . . brought on by being separated from her husband & child."[7]

Missouri was on several trade routes, so life for the enslaved in Missouri could be even less stable than for many of those remembered in this book. Formerly enslaved William Brown described accompanying slave trader "Mr. Walker" between Missouri and New Orleans. He recalled, "Before the slaves were exhibited for sale, they were dressed and driven out into the yard. Some were set to dancing, some to jumping, some to singing, and some to playing cards." He continued, "This was done to make them appear cheerful and happy . . . I have often set them to dancing when their cheeks were wet with tears."[8]

As Brown and Walker headed north into Missouri, they passed farms and villages where Walker purchased people. One was a new mother with a one-month-old infant who would not stop crying. Walker "took the child by one arm, as you would a cat by the leg," and went to a nearby house and offered the infant to the woman of the house, who thanked him and took it. The mother ran to Mr. Walker, begged him to let her have her child. She clung to his legs and cried, "Oh, my child! my child! master, do let me have my child! oh do, do, do. I will stop its crying, if you will only let me have it again." Mr. Walker ignored her pleas and chained her with the childless women in the slave coffle.[9]

Around 1859, Clifton R. Barnes took his second wife, Martha Dawson Barnes, their children, some employees, and an enslaved young woman, either pregnant or with a newborn daughter, and moved to Utah Territory. The enslaved woman could have been driven in chains down the dirt roads of Missouri by a slave trader like Mr. Walker, or she could have been the property of Martha Dawson when she married Barnes. The father of the enslaved infant could have been one of the White members of the Barnes household, or he could have been someone the woman had to leave in Missouri, perhaps John, whose hire was listed in the Barnes guardianship papers.

Not long after the census slave schedule showed the woman and infant in Great Salt Lake City, Barnes returned to Missouri. He then took his family to Fort Leavenworth, but Kansas had abolished slavery in 1860, and the family did not have a Black woman living with them there, so the fate of the woman and infant is unknown.[10]

George Hockaday

George Hockaday's enslaver, John M. Hockaday, was a man of adventure, passion, and learning, and a violent alcoholic.[11] George may have cared for John's business interests in Great Salt Lake City while John ran mail and trade routes between Utah Territory and Missouri.

In 1843, John Hockaday left his home in Kentucky for West Point Military Academy in New York. He was near the bottom of his class and left West Point with his coursework unfinished when his father died.[12] Hockaday probably inherited five enslaved men from his father, including two who match George's description. When John left his Kentucky farm for adventures in the American West, George probably went with him.[13]

George would have helped transport trade goods to the new settlements in the West. John ran a stagecoach line and mail route, owned part interest in a store in downtown Great Salt Lake City, and served as US Attorney for Utah Territory under presidents Franklin Pierce and James Buchanan.[14]

George may have traveled back and forth to Missouri with John, but he was alone in Great Salt Lake City in 1860. He died two months after the census and was buried in a pauper's grave in the Salt Lake City Cemetery.[15] Although his personality and experiences can only be assumed from the few existing records, his passing would have left a gap in the small Black community.

Laura Pearson and Susan Price

In 1875, the California Supreme Court decreed that an 1854 marriage in Utah Territory between a man and his enslaved woman was legal under the laws of Utah Territory and that the marriage emancipated her, "there being no local law in Utah prohibiting such marriage."[16] It was a novel reading of An Act in Relation to Service (1852), but since the court declared the standard practices of Southern slavery to have been in force in Utah Territory, the parties to the case are part of the story of slavery in the territory.

In 1847, farmer and freighter Richard Pearson purchased Laura in South Carolina and took her to Missouri. A year later, he married young Martha Powers. They lived in St. Joseph, the westernmost point on the railroad and the starting point of the Pony Express, and Pearson took advantage of the location to trade with the western settlements. In 1852, a California newspaper reported, "Money has almost ceased to be a circulating medium in Utah, and cattle are traded in exchange for merchandize ... Mr. Richard Pearson, of Mo., has also a train of stock nearly through."[17]

In 1854, Martha and Richard Pearson divorced and set in motion events that led to court battles two decades later. Martha and her young daughter, Adelaide, remained in Missouri, where her new husband raised Adelaide as his own child. Richard took his enslaved woman Laura and her two-year-old daughter Susan Price and left for California. Richard and Laura married in Utah Territory under unclear circumstances, but the California Supreme Court later found sufficient evidence of the marriage.

Twenty-one years after he divorced Martha, Richard wrote a deathbed will that gave Laura and their six children each an equal share of their productive nine-hundred-acre ranch in California's Central Valley.[18] He also left property to Laura's daughter, Susan Price, but he made a costly mistake when he did not mention his daughter from his first marriage.[19]

After word reached Missouri about his death, his daughter Adelaide contested his will. She hoped to be the sole heir of the estate since an enslaver could not marry the enslaved. She won the first case in a California district court, and a Missouri newspaper reported, "Miss Adelaide has been successful in the suit, and has gained by it 1,080 acres of land in Colusa County, worth $30 per acre." The newspaper editorialized, "This is quite a little estate for the young lady, and we congratulate her upon her deserved good fortune."[20]

Laura Pearson appealed the case to the California Supreme Court. The court overturned the district court ruling on a question of the legality of Laura and Richard's marriage and sent the case back to the lower court.²¹ Laura won the second case, and, this time, Adelaide appealed to the California Supreme Court. During the second appeal, the Supreme Court found that Laura and Richard had married legally in Utah Territory. Laura claimed to have been freed in St. Louis, but the Supreme Court said this was irrelevant since the marriage freed Laura, "there being no local law in Utah prohibiting such marriage."²² The Supreme Court denied Adelaide a new trial.²³ Much of the Pearson estate went to legal fees. After Laura's death three years later, the large and successful ranch was sold piece by piece to satisfy debts.²⁴

With Army Officers

At least two government expeditions into Utah included enslaved men. Theophilus accompanied Lt. Benjamin Allston on the Steptoe Expedition (1854–1855), and Randolph "Ran" Hughes accompanied Gen. Albert Sidney Johnston during the Utah War (1857–1858). In this book, Randolph Hughes and Theophilus represent all the unknown enslaved men and women who served military officers in Utah Territory. Of related interest, although they were not in Utah Territory, at least two enslaved men served army officers leading the Mormon Battalion on its march to California (1846–1847).

Theophilus

The further Theophilus got from the great coastal South Carolina rice plantations, the more agitated he became. Theophilus may have been born on one of the plantations of Robert F. W. Allston, later governor of South Carolina. In 1854, Theophilus accompanied Allston's son, Lt. Benjamin Allston, on the Steptoe Expedition, which surveyed military roads and investigated the massacre of the 1853 Gunnison Expedition by native raiders.

Allston wrote in a series of letters home: "Theophilus is well and so am I." Later, "Theophilus is well and is my cook." Two months after that: "Theophilus is well and sends love to all, wishes to know something about his things, wife &c." After they arrived in Great Salt Lake City, Allston was concerned that Theophilus was "not as dutiful as one might desire."²⁵

The details are scarce, but Theophilus came to believe that living in Utah Territory made him free. Allston wrote that Theophilus "took it into his head to run away after I left the City went to the Gov [Brigham Young] and showed as the Gov says free papers, and asked for employment. But thanks to Capt. [Rufus] Ingalls he was recovered and is now at Camp." Allston continued, "I feel no inclination to have him any where near me again. I am disgusted with him." He considered selling Theophilus to a Mr. Perry "without further thought were it not that the whole family belong to me and I do not like to hurt their feelings."[26]

And with that, Theophilus disappeared from further records. Perhaps Allston sold him. Perhaps he remained in the West and changed his name. Perhaps he returned with Allston to South Carolina and was among the seven hundred and fifty enslaved men, women, and children in bondage on the Allston plantations in 1860.[27]

Randolph Hughes

During the Utah War, the US Army settled at Camp Floyd about forty-five miles from Great Salt Lake City. Capt. John W. Phelps wrote, "The object in choosing this place as a military site must have been to accustom us to all kinds of unseasonableness in order to reconcile us to the greatest of all possible unseasonablenesses, viz. [namely], that of slavery."[28] Eight hundred civilians accompanied the expedition, including an unknown number of enslaved men and women.[29] Randolph "Ran" Hughes was enslaved by the leader of the expedition, Albert Sidney Johnston.

Johnston and his wealthy bride, Henrietta Preston, began their married life with an enslaved couple as servants. The enslaved couple had two sons, Randolph and John.[30] In 1855, Johnston's son claimed that John had stolen army funds to support his wife. Johnston took John to Galveston and sold him for $1,000.[31] A biographer wrote that Johnston's second wife, Eliza Griffin Johnston, would whip the enslaved, but Johnston would not. He believed that the enslaved must be trained to be subservient, and he had no sympathy for abolitionism: "If our northern brethren will give up their fanatical, idolatrous negro worshiping we can go on harmoniously, happily & prosperously and also gloriously as a nation."[32]

Johnston returned to Kentucky as he prepared to move to California. He emancipated Randolph but bound him by contract to five years of service at wages of $12 a month, plus room and board.[33] When the Civil War began, Johnston fled California under threat of arrest for treason and took Hughes with him on an arduous journey to the South. He wrote to his wife in California, "I rode on my horse from Chino to this place, except a few miles which I got Ran to *do* for me. . . . He is as good a hand with mules as need be; with my backing, Ran is *sans peur* [undaunted]."[34] The small company often traveled at night to escape the desert heat. "Though Ran is very trustworthy, I found he would go to sleep. He kept wide awake and bright, whistling at times, till about 3 A. M., when nature, not faithful Ran, gave way. Falling fast asleep, he drove square off into the desert."[35] After Johnston died at the Battle of Shiloh in 1862, Hughes is said to have continued in service to other officers, but he disappeared from the public record.

With Government Appointees

After the earliest years of settlement, the federal government appointed officials and judges for the territory. At least two officials acquired enslaved men while in the territory: Peter K. Dotson purchased or hired an unnamed man, probably Frank, and William W. Drummond purchased Cato. A newspaper claimed that Supreme Court justice John F. Kinney was involved in the slave trade, but the reporter also erroneously claimed that both Drummond and Kinney were Latter-day Saints, and Kinney does not appear in known documents about the slave trade.[36]

Frank

The Thomas S. Williams estate documents show a $10 charge for the "Use of Carriage to Grave Y[ar]d to Convey P. K. Dodson's Negro."[37] Peter Kessler Dotson was US Marshal for Utah Territory, and he left unpaid bills including the charge for the funeral when he and his family left the territory after he falsely accused Brigham Young of counterfeiting.[38] The only clue to the identity of "P. K. Dodson's Negro" is a Utah burial record documenting that Robert Taylor shot and killed "Frank Black man" in 1858.[39] A newspaper reported: "A short time past two colored gentlemen quarreled in the streets; one was stabbed and the other shot dead by his antagonist."[40] Who was Frank? How did he find himself in a fatal fight in Great Salt Lake City? Only the Williams probate offers any clue to his identity, and it is regrettably little information.

Cato

After William Wormer Drummond declared bankruptcy in Illinois, his friends arranged an appointment for him as a federal judge in Utah

Territory.[41] When he went to Utah Territory, he deserted his wife, Jemima McClenahan Drummond, and children, America Virginia, Austria Vienna, Alwilda Veria, Americus Vespucia, Angelica Vandalia, Artemica Viola (deceased), and Arabella Victoria.

Before Drummond went west, he acquired a companion in Washington, DC, identified in various sources as Ada Carroll, Ella, or Pleasant Ridgeway or Edgerton. Drummond scandalized the people of Utah Territory when she sat with him on the judicial bench, especially after friends or members of the McClenahan family living in Utah Territory learned that the woman with him was not his wife Jemima.[42] When news of Drummond's indiscretions spread after the Utah War, an Albany newspaper wrote that he was a "disreputable character, unfit to associate with decent people, and his word is as worthless as the poorest shin plaster on a Western wild cat bank. The woman he is travelling with is not his wife."[43] His morals and attempts to gain control of the executive and legislative functions of the territorial government compromised his efforts to gain control of the courts, and his subsequent claims of conditions in the territory helped begin the Utah War. After he left the territory, he failed to gain political power and died a destitute alcoholic.[44] Although this is not a biography of Drummond, his enslaved servant Cato appeared in the public record due to these scandals.

Neither Drummond's Virginia family nor Jemima Drummond's Kentucky family enslaved people, so when Drummond purchased Cato, it was probably the first time he enslaved anyone.[45] "Big Cato," as French traveler Jules Remy called him, arrived in Utah Territory with James A. Harkreader of Wilson County, Tennessee, and Sacramento, California.[46] The transaction was captured in notices in Eastern newspapers, which erroneously identified Drummond and Judge Kinney as Latter-day Saints.

WASHINGTON, Monday, April 21, 1856.

The workings of popular sovereignty in Utah are recently shown by the introduction of slavery and the slave trade. The Mormons of that Territory, not content with polygamy, desire to extend [slavery] . . . as may be seen by the following extract of a letter addressed to a Congressman in this city:

"⸺, UTAH TERRITORY, Jan. 30, 1856.

DEAR SIR: Knowing you to be 'sound' on the Negro Question, as well as on Polygamy, and as our brethren here are soon to apply for admission as a State, we just send you a note to let you see we are all right on the main question. Judge Drummond has gone a little into the negro slave trade, as the inclosed handbill will show. Judge [John F.] Kinney is also in the slave trade, as well as the principal men of the Territory. . . .

Judges Drummond and Kinney, who are file leaders of the Mormons, as well as federal officers, have thus exhibited their orthodoxy upon the Slavery question . . ."

The handbill referred to in the above letter commences in staring type as follows. The slave Cato appears to have been "sold running:"

"TAKE NOTICE.—As I have sold my Negro Man Cato to the Hon. W. W. Drummond, of this city, and for whom I recently offered $100 reward for his delivery to me: I now take this method of informing the public that as I am now about to leave this Territory, I will no longer be held liable for the said reward, the man Cato being the property of the said Judge Drummond. J. A. HARKREADER."[47]

Drummond took possession of Cato before the national press picked up the story, since he requested funds from Brigham Young "by my servant Cato."[48] Harkreader and Drummond violated the provisions of An Act in Relation to Service when they did not register the sale in probate court, but when Kentucky native and Utah lawyer Hosea Stout wrote out a list of Drummond's offenses against law and community, he did not mention the sale, so even an officer of the court was not familiar with, or interested in, the provisions of the Act.[49]

During the battles over the territorial courts, a grand jury indicted "William W. Drummond and a certain woman whose name is unknown to the Grand Jurors" for lewdness, meaning adultery or cohabitation. The grand jury called Cato to testify at a time when enslaved people could not testify in court in most jurisdictions. The grand jury indicted Drummond, but the case went no further.[50]

After the federal government moved the territorial capital from Great Salt Lake City to Fillmore, Drummond sent Cato to whip Levi

Abrams over an ongoing argument. Abrams swore out a criminal complaint for assault. Lawyer Hosea Stout represented Drummond and Cato and began the proceedings with a writ of *habeas corpus* to challenge the jurisdiction of the probate court. Utah Supreme Court Chief Justice Kinney finally decided questions of jurisdiction, and all parties withdrew from the proceedings.[51]

Not long after this episode, and with Ada agitating against remaining in the territory, Drummond took Ada and Cato and commandeered a posse to accompany him to distant Carson Valley. He held court there before he headed to California and then by way of Panama to New Orleans, and finally to Chicago. No record specifies whether Cato accompanied Drummond to Chicago; a New Orleans newspaper reported the arrival of "Judge Drummond, lady and servant," but no other records confirm the servant's identity.[52] Cato may have remained in the West: in 1860, thirty-year-old African American Cato Smith lived with John Coagner in Jacks Valley, Carson County, Utah Territory (now Nevada), close to the barn where Drummond held court. Cato Smith then disappeared from the public record.[53]

Nine

FREE AT LAST

On Old Folks' Day in 1894, four thousand people streamed into Saltair, a resort on the shore of the Great Salt Lake. The gathering was an annual event for elderly residents of Utah Territory, and that year honored the surviving members of the first Latter-day Saint wagon company to enter the Great Salt Lake Valley. Members of the organizing committee pinned badges reading "Pioneer—July 24, 1847" on the chests of each of twenty surviving members of the first wagon company and sat the men in comfortable chairs on the podium. Green Flake, who was enslaved when he entered the valley, sat in a place of honor between former enslaver A. O. Smoot and Smoot's adopted son, William C. A. Smoot.

Energetic speeches, musical numbers, laughter, cheers, and applause filled the day. Speakers included Green Flake and Wilford Woodruff, by then the president of the Church of Jesus Christ of Latter-day Saints. Flake said, "[T]hat he was proud to be of that honorable and honored body." President Woodruff told the crowd, "You see today a remnant of that band and we are now aged men.... The pioneers had a work to perform and they did and are doing it well, but labor yet remains to be done." He said, "A few days after arrival the pioneers went bathing in Great Salt Lake. Green Flake, the colored brother, had taken a swim with them and when he came out he was white." He continued, "It was the first miracle wrought in the valley. When he bathed in fresh water his original color was restored."[1]

With a single comic anecdote, Woodruff pinpointed the tension that ran through the life of Green Flake. Flake was Black in mostly White communities in Utah and Idaho, but he found meaning and camaraderie in his place in history. When Flake carved his own gravestone from limestone from the mountains above the Salt Lake Valley, he chose as the inscription the scripture, "In my Father's house are many mansions," leaving as his final words a reminder of the inclusivity and universality he found in the doctrines of the new religion, but which he and his fellow Black pioneers rarely experienced as residents of a largely White Latter-day Saint community.[2]

Flake was already free when Congress ended slavery in the US territories, but others had remained in bondage, so the 1862 legislation freed around thirty Black men, women, and children still enslaved in Utah Territory. Family accounts are unfortunately vague about when the enslaved knew they were free. Some suggest the enslaved remained in bondage until the end of the Civil War.[3]

Utah businessman and congressional delegate William H. Hooper did not take any enslaved people to Utah Territory, but he purchased Daniel and Shepherd Camp there. After he made a fortune, Hooper located his father's former enslaved man Richard Camper in Maryland and paid Camper and his wife a pension of $60 a year.[4] After Hooper and his wife died, their children discontinued the payments. The amount that the family described to a journalist as a "liberal stipend" and Daughters of Utah Pioneers later called a "generous allowance" raises questions about the ethical responsibilities of an enslaver toward the people he or she formerly enslaved and the amount and type of compensation that might be given. After John H. Redd died, his legal heirs deeded a house and other means to Marinda, Venus, and Luke, who was Venus's son with Redd. When the enslaved Perkins family was freed, however, they lived in desperate poverty in Salt Lake City, and family historian Eugene H. Perkins did not find any indication that their former enslavers provided assistance during the transition to freedom.[5] In the early 1850s, Brigham Young hired Green Flake, ensured his freedom under the terms of An Act in Relation to Service, and provided him with a transition to freedom that included a grant of land in the Salt Lake Valley and ongoing guidance and protection.

Since there was no legal requirement for enslavers to provide for the formerly enslaved, where any compensation, reparation, or settlement was given, it would have contained the meaning invested by the participants. The $5 a month paid by Hooper to Richard and Harriet Camper, when converted to 2019 dollars, was around $130 a month.[6] Rather than a liberal pension, it was a token amount given without legal obligation by Hooper and later his widow and may be viewed as a gesture of remembrance for Richard Camper's role as a substitute father figure to a young William Hooper.

Those who had help in the transition from enslavement to freedom tended to do better overall. Venus, Luke, and Marinda Redd began their lives in freedom with a home, land, and tools and were able to support themselves. The families of Nancy Bankhead Valentine and Frank and Esther Perkins, however, suffered from malnutrition and disease, lack of adequate housing, and the deaths of many family members. The 1870 census showed the value of household real and personal estate. Of the ten households with freed enslaved people in Utah Territory, most had no reportable real or personal estate. Four owned homes: Alexander and Marinda Bankhead; Miles, Rose, and Violet Litchford; Green and Martha Flake; and Sylvester and Mary Ann Perkins James. Two households owned property of more than $100: Alexander and Marinda Bankhead, and Miles Litchford. Those with no reportable net worth were Samuel and Caroline Bankhead, Nancy and James Valentine, Betsy Brown (later Flewellen), Benjamin Perkins, Chaney Redd Cunningham, and Luke Redd.[7]

One of the challenges the Black families faced was the lack of opportunity for their children to marry due to social pressures against interracial marriage.[8] Marinda and Luke Redd had no potential Black marriage partners in their county, and both had illegitimate children with White neighbors. Mary Ann Perkins raised a family after she married Sylvester James, but her sister Charlotte and sister-in-law Ellen Madora James entered the sex trade.

Due to their place in society and the nature of nineteenth-century records, there are currently no known death records for about a third of the approximately one hundred enslaved Black people of Utah Territory. Of those with death records, seventeen died before 1865, nine more by 1870, an additional twenty-two by 1900, and the final nineteen after 1900. Silas Woolridge, Charles Embers, and Benjamin Perkins each lived around ninety years. The average age at death was slightly over fifty for the two-thirds with enough information to know or estimate an age at death, but the number is barely useful due to the lack of records and insufficient knowledge of the extent of infant and childhood mortality.

The causes of death are varied. Nancy Bankhead Jefferson and Nelson Smiley died by suicide in California. Shepherd Camp, Gobo Fango, and Thomas Bankhead Coleman were murdered. Lambson Jolley and Jerry Lewis Smoot died by drowning. Sarah Perkins and Downey Perkins Woolridge died after childbirth. A significant number died from tuberculosis, including Charlotte Camp and many of the Perkins family. Tuberculosis was endemic in both White and Black Perkins families and may suggest a shared genetic susceptibility to the disease.[9]

The approximately one hundred enslaved people documented in this book are roughly divisible into four groups. First are those whose fate is unknown, such as the unnamed woman enslaved by Clifton Barnes in 1860; second are those who were taken to California in 1850 or 1851 and mostly remained there, including Toby and Grief Embers, Oscar Smith, Elizabeth Flake Rowan, and Biddy Mason and her daughters; third are those who left Utah Territory after they were freed, including Howard Egan Wales and Benjamin Perkins; and fourth are those who remained in Utah Territory, including Green and Martha Flake, Marinda Redd Bankhead, Mary Ann Perkins James, Charlotte Perkins Campbell, Rose Crosby Litchford and her daughters, and Caroline and Tampian Hoye. This chapter will tell some stories from their lives after they were freed.

Toby and Grief Embers

The departure of most of the Latter-day Saints from San Bernardino during the Utah War created instability in the town, and new settlers directed racial violence toward brothers Toby and Grief Embers. In November 1858, Toby and his family invited their neighbors to a dance in their new home. Joseph McFeely and his friends demanded to be allowed into the party. Embers objected, and McFeely beat him and drove everyone out of the home.[10] After Embers swore out a complaint with the justice of the peace, McFeely found Embers at James W. Wilson's office and drew a pistol. He threatened "a certain couloured <man> by the name of Toby Ember that he would shoot him the said Toby Ember if he did not eat a certain a paper charging him the said McFeely with doing a certain unlawful act." Wilson swore in a subsequent complaint that he believed McFeely would have shot Embers if he did not eat the paper. A jury found McFeely not guilty.[11]

The people of San Bernardino remembered Toby's brother Grief as the community musician. Not long before he died, an inebriated man named Michael Murphy "brutally accosted" Grief on the street. "Apparently Murphy was churlish to him about his ancestry, and a fight ensued." Embers broke Murphy's leg in the fight but "walked away from the fray unmolested and was not arrested."[12]

Toby and Grief Embers died within a few years of each other. Toby's children with Hannah Smiley, Charles Embers and Martha Embers Beal, inherited his property in San Bernardino after their mother died. Within a few years, Charles Embers left California for Arizona. Graduate student James Yancey interviewed him near the end of his life and took a photograph of a spare, weather-beaten man. Although he was married twice, he does not have any known living descendants, but his second wife does, as does his sister Martha. Two of Martha's grandsons, Charlie and Eddie Beal, became professional musicians and worked internationally after their military service in the Second World War.

Oscar Smith

About fifty members of the small Black community in Los Angeles gathered in 1870 to celebrate the new Fifteenth Amendment to the United States Constitution: "The right of citizens of the United States to vote shall not be denied or abridged by the United States or by any State on account of race, color, or previous condition of servitude."[13] They fired artillery and lowered the flag in respect to Abraham Lincoln and the Union Army and its Black soldiers.[14] One of those present that day was a historic figure himself. Oscar Smith, formerly known as Oscar Crosby, was one of three enslaved men in the first wagon company to enter the Salt Lake Valley in July 1847. Smith's health declined rapidly after the celebration, and he never had a chance to vote before his heart gave out.

Smith was buried in the original Los Angeles City Cemetery. The city did not take care of the cemetery, and developers paved over bones, scattered them, or moved them to other cemeteries. Unmarked graves or the cadaver trade were an all-too-common end for the enslaved, but although his final burial place is unknown, Oscar is remembered as a man of adventure who celebrated freedom and his civil liberties.[15]

Elizabeth Flake Rowan

When Elizabeth Flake helped provide freedom to the enslaved Black residents of San Bernardino, she and the orphaned children of her enslavers lived with Maria Tanner Lyman. Judge Daniel M. Thomas wrote to Amasa Lyman, "Mariah [Lyman] had also a ~~handmaid~~ <maid Servant> from the land of ham and at the end of the year when the people all were giving feasts behold the ~~handmaid~~ <maid Servant> of Mariah went down among the gentiles and behold one of the Sons of Ham Saw her even Elizabeth and promised to marry her." Thomas told Lyman, "She has made the wedding garments ~~are made~~ and all things are ready but the Son of ham has not come up yet."[16] When the census taker came around four years later, Flake was a single mother, taking in laundry to support herself and her son.

Figure 9.1. Elizabeth Flake Rowan. Courtesy of Alice Johnson Black. Used by permission, San Bernardino Historical Society.

Elizabeth Flake married Charles Rowan. He was from Maryland and had served in the Potomac Flotilla on the USS *Jacob Bell*.[17] A reporter later told about a letter of recommendation for Rowan from Abraham Lincoln in the family's possession, but the son who owned the letter died without any surviving children, and the whereabouts of the letter is unknown.[18] The Rowan family helped found the First African Methodist Episcopal (AME) Church in Los Angeles, and daughter Alice Rowan Johnson was said to be the first African American teacher in an integrated California school.[19] Elizabeth kept in touch with the White Flake family and also that of Green Flake, who may have been her brother. When Elizabeth and her daughter visited Salt Lake City in 1887, they stayed with Susan Steele Blanchard, a sister of Green Flake's daughter-in-law, Mary Ann Steele Flake.[20] Most of the other early Black San Bernardino pioneers died or moved away by the turn of the century, but in early 1901, Elizabeth became ill. She received several visitors, including Biddy Mason's daughter, Ellen Huddleston.[21]

The newspaper reported at Elizabeth's death that her funeral was at the Reorganized Church of Jesus Christ of Latter Day Saints (RLDS; now Community of Christ). "She was equally as highly esteemed as her husband, and had a host of friends who are grieved to learn of her death."[22]

Biddy Mason

Those who moved to Los Angeles when they were freed in 1856 found it a small, isolated town, divided by violence and vigilantism. "Los Angeles had its slave mart, as well as New Orleans and Constantinople," wrote Horace Bell.[23] Residents sold Native Americans at a weekly auction, paid for their work with alcohol, arrested them when they got drunk, then resold them for another week of work. The downtown area known for prostitution and saloons was *Calle de los Negros*, or in English, Negro or Nigger Alley.[24] Living in the area exposed the recently freed families to crime and addiction, but Los Angeles also provided the abundant opportunities of a frontier town, with fewer racial divides than more established communities.

Black Los Angeles couple Robert Owens (1806–1865) and Winnie Owens (1813–1883) had been enslaved themselves. Their son Charles helped free the enslaved people in San Bernardino, and Robert and

Winnie Owens provided housing to Biddy and Hannah and their families during the court proceedings until Judge Hayes put the families in protective custody in the local jail to protect them from the Smith family. Robert and Winnie helped the newly freed with their transition to freedom, and their son Charles married Biddy Mason's daughter Ellen. The Owens family were community builders. They held dinners, invited members of the press and government officials, and built bridges between Black and White communities. Together, Robert and Winnie Owens, Charles Owens, Biddy Mason, Oscar Smith, some of Hannah Smiley's family, Elizabeth Flake Rowan's husband and sons, and others built the first Los Angeles congregation of the African Methodist Episcopal (AME) Church, which still exists today.[25]

AME Bishop T. M. D. Ward visited Los Angeles in 1869. He called the community a small but "noble-hearted, public-spirited band." He said they worked hard and were respected by the entire community. "Many of them have worn the iron-yoke of oppression, still they appreciate the goodness of that Power who has broken their bonds." He wrote, "In point of liberality they excel any people I ever sojourned among. Every dwelling opened its doors; every house spread its sumptuous board. Nearly all of them own real estate, which signifies power everywhere."[26]

Biddy Mason worked as a licensed nurse and midwife.[27] She lived frugally and invested her savings in real estate. Although she helped found the First AME, she was a member of the Fort Street Methodist Episcopal Church, thus cementing her ties to both Black and White communities.

Biddy's daughter Harriet became part of the history of Los Angeles in her own right in May 1863. One morning she set off with her wealthy employers, Phineas and Rebecca Banning, and their two little boys. The five drove to the docks at San Pedro and boarded the steamer, *Ada Hancock*.

Just minutes after the steamer got underway, the boiler exploded and killed many passengers, including two Latter-day Saint missionaries and a son of General Albert Sidney Johnston. The explosion blew the rest of the passengers into deep water and spread debris up to a mile away. Harriet, called by the nickname "Darkness" in national media coverage, saved the Banning children from drowning and, as the *New York Times* wrote, "displayed undaunted courage and rendered great assistance to numbers of others. During the whole excitement she remained perfectly calm, and was the means of keeping several of the ladies' heads above water for some time after the vessel had gone down."[28]

As Biddy Mason aged, she filled her final years with philanthropy. Some years, she paid the taxes and other expenses of the First AME Church. She visited prisoners to provide comfort and aid, and she paid for the groceries of flood victims.[29] She lived to see her grandson Henry Owens become active in local politics and her other grandson Robert Owens take over the family property. However, as she aged, her family began a battle over her fortune that lasted for years after her death.[30]

Mason has become an archetype of the strong Black woman. People from around the world leave messages on her online grave memorial. "Free at last, free at last, Thank God Almighty, I'm free at last. Rest in the arms of Jesus." "In honor of a heroic woman." "Rest in peace. I'm so glad we didn't lose you to Texas."[31] Although Mason's use as an archetype has long since outstripped her actual experience, most notably her role in *In re Hannah (1856)*, Mason helped settle the West, gained her freedom, overcame adversity, helped found a church, created a large fortune, and was remembered as a philanthropist. In 1989, the City of Los Angeles dedicated a downtown public memorial to her memory. Mason is appropriately remembered in company with Hannah Smiley Embers, Judge Benjamin Hayes, Robert and Winnie Owens, Charles Owens, Elizabeth Flake Rowan, and many others. As AME Bishop T. M. D. Ward said about Mason and her associates in 1869: "Let these names through the oncoming swift-footed ages fill the speaking trump of fame."[32]

Howard Egan Wales

When William Lay took Hark Wales to California in 1851, Hark left behind his pregnant wife Nancy and their young son Howard Egan Wales. Perhaps Howard heard stories of his father's departure to California and decided to go there himself. No one kept a record of whether he ever met his father in his home in San Timoteo Canyon above San Bernardino. By 1869, Howard Wales worked in the San Joaquin Valley.[33] He was usually the only Black man in the area. In 1886, some young men plied him with whiskey and had him make political speeches until he collapsed. They dragged the unconscious Wales into a wagon box and painted his face red. Wales "was found suffering intensely, and is now in a critical condition, having taken poison into his lungs, eyes, nostrils and mouth. No arrests have been made."[34] Wales survived the poisoning, and, a year later, a newspaper reported that he shot a remarkable seven hundred and fifty ducks in one day to ship to the San Francisco market. Wales registered to vote in 1888, but then disappeared from the public record.[35]

Green and Martha Flake

Back in Utah Territory, Green Flake probably learned to read and write after 1864, because that year, he went to court to recover a bay mare and colt, and he signed a court document with a mark instead of his name. James Maxfield served as Flake's surety. Probate Judge Elias Smith found in favor of Flake and ordered him to split the costs of the suit with the defendant, Nils Mason.[36] The details of Flake's education are unknown, but he could write by 1897 when he filled out an entry for *The Book of the Pioneers*. Perhaps a neighbor, his children, or his grandchildren taught him to read and write.

Flake lived near Big Cottonwood Canyon when a mining boom began around 1870.[37] He began mining with Miles Litchford, the father of some of Rose Crosby's children. They were soon joined by more Black miners, some of them funded by African American civil rights fighter Philip A. Bell. One of their partners, Francis H. Grice, the Haitian-born son of a Maryland abolitionist, wrote about their work for Bell's San Francisco newspaper. Their mines had names like "Decomposed," "Evergreen," "Abraham Lincoln," "and "Union Blue." The shareholders in the Evergreen mine included Flake, Grice, Flake's son-in-law George Stevens, Hark Wales, Miles Litchford, and other Black neighbors and White neighbors, including Lucy Wheeler, whose room Cordelia Litchford probably occupied the day she died in 1891.[38]

Mining operations continued through the winter months. In 1882, an avalanche in Big Cottonwood Canyon swept down over the cabin of a young family. The neighbors were afraid to approach the cabin for fear of triggering a second avalanche, but Lucinda Stevens, the daughter of Green and Martha Flake, and her husband George disregarded their own safety and dug through tons of snow. Although the couple found that Charles and Eliza Hale Tackett and their four young children had perished in the avalanche, Lucinda and George retrieved their bodies. Subsequent generations of Eliza Hale Tackett's family remembered the heroic part Lucinda and George Stevens took in that bitterly cold tragedy.[39]

The miners came into conflict with Latter-day Saint economic and social policies. Since the Flakes left little record of their experiences and none about their politics, it is not known whether they agreed with those who created a petition to the US Congress, "Against the Admission of Utah as a State," or whether they were among those who, as George A. Smith alleged, "thought they were simply signing a petition against the admission of Utah as a State, without bringing personal charges against a people among whom they have lived in perfect safety."[40] However, the signers of the petition included Green Flake, Martha Flake (called Martha Green), Lucinda Flake, Miles Litchford, Violet Litchford, Rose Catlin (Litchford), Daniel Freeman Bankhead, Andrew Campbell, Frank Grice, and members of the Sion family in Cache Valley, suggesting that the politics and economy of the territory were not serving their community well.[41]

Violet's death before 1880 and Martha's death in 1885 signaled the beginning of the end of the Black community in Union. Toward the end of his life, Green Flake began to sell his land to prepare to move to Idaho to be with his children. While he was still in Utah, he spoke at Pioneer Day celebrations, held every year on July 24th to commemorate the entry of the first wagon company into the Salt Lake Valley. In 1894, he participated in the celebration held at Saltair. By 1896, he lived with his son in the Black settlement of Grays Lake, Idaho.[42]

Flake returned to Utah in 1897 for the fiftieth anniversary of the arrival of the Latter-day Saints in the Great Salt Lake Valley. Flake would have seen the new Brigham Young Monument listing the members of the first wagon company with his name as one of three "Colored Servants." The *Deseret News* reported, "This afternoon two Pioneers called at the News in the persons of Green Flake, a colored man who was one of the original Pioneers and who lived in Salt Lake for forty-nine years."[43]

Flake wrote an entry in the official record of the celebration, *The Book of the Pioneers*. He said that he "resided on Coton wood Utah for 40 years" and that he had been born in "wads burr [Wadesboro], Anson Co., North Carolina." He gave the date of his entry into the valley as July 21, 1847, and recalled meeting the Pawnee, "all in war like and demaned Pay for [our] Crossing the Country. after Presedent Young Councld with them then by

Paying them something they give us Permisson to Cross there Count[ry]." In a space where the writer could note relics for donation he wrote, "Then we cross<ed> the luck [Loup] fork of the Plat[te] then we traveled up the P[l]at[te] and I was in my wagon." In the remaining space, he told about the first time he saw a buffalo. "I haulted my team and Spoke to Ira [perhaps John Eldredge] an told him there was a Calf." The other man shot at it and "grazsed his wethers the Calf It raise to his feet," and with that, the page ended, and the binder trimmed off Flake's last words.[44]

After the celebration, Flake returned to Idaho. His death in 1903 was news throughout Utah and Idaho. His family took his body to Union and buried him alongside his family and friends. The *Deseret News* wrote, "Bro. Flake had reached the honorable age of 76, which means, to all who knew him, 76 years of honest, hard work for the betterment of humanity, and for an exaltation in his Father's kingdom."[45]

Luke Redd and Marinda Redd Bankhead

After Luke Redd and Marinda Redd accompanied their enslavers across the plains, they helped settle Utah County. For the first few years, the settlers lived in a small fort, and one can only wonder how the proximity to the Redd family and the knowledge of Luke and Marinda Redd's later illegitimate children affected the racial views of their neighbor Zebedee Coltrin, and possibly also A. O. Smoot, employer of Marinda's later husband Alexander Bankhead. The views and experiences of the two men influenced the development of Latter-day Saint racial theories.[46]

The just-freed young people were placed in an impossible situation. Interracial marriage was rare in the United States and its territories, and Marinda and Luke Redd, possibly cousins or half-siblings, were left in Spanish Fork without eligible partners. In 1862, with most of the Redd family deceased or living in different parts of the territory, Marinda gave birth to an illegitimate son, David William Pace. His father was Tennessee native John Alma Lawrence Pace, the son of the bishop of Spanish Fork.[47]

The next birth was Luke Redd's illegitimate daughter Flady Ainge. No official record remains of the court appearance of Redd and English immigrant Emma Ainge after Flady was born. Albert K. Thurber wrote to George Albert Smith in 1864 that he was at court "as a witness against Luke Redd and Emma Ainge of Spanish Fork for <u>Lewdness</u> resulting in her having a child which today she declared in open court to belong to Redd." Thurber wrote, "I trust this arest and trial will put a stop to such conduct in Spanish Fork."[48] Luke and Emma had a second child. Emma's parents raised the two children, and both eventually passed as White. When Emma married another man, Luke went to live in Southern Utah. There he fathered a son with a married neighbor. Luke's son, like his half-siblings, also passed as White.[49]

Many years later, Marinda told reporter Julius Taylor that she was "transferred" to Dr. Pinney of Salem. "Pinney" could have been the reporter's misunderstanding of "Dennis."[50] William Taylor Dennis was a hot-tempered doctor from Tennessee with one legal wife, Talitha Cumi Bankhead, two plural wives, Sarah Zabriskie and Ann Fullmer, and one formerly enslaved servant, Nancy Lines Smith. Marinda's language does not indicate that she felt she had choice in her "transfer." Perhaps the Dennis family volunteered to take Marinda and her infant son into the household to provide the guidance and stability she lacked with the Redd family gone. If so, the effort backfired. In the long tradition of the oppression and abuse of women in Southern slavery, Marinda gave birth to a second son. When baby Edward died a few months later, she named his father as Dr. William T. Dennis.[51]

Church leaders did not know the father's identity during Marinda's pregnancy. Shortly before Edward's death, Spanish Fork Bishop A. K. Thurber "denounced whoredom and said if Marinda Redd was found pregnant again death should be her portion and the same with all who whore with her." He said, "Whoredom among the young folks was also denounced and the teachers were to use their influence to stop it." The next week he "referred to whoredoms—said if there was any more whoring with black folks both black and white shall be killed."[52]

Church and civic leaders may have taken action against Dennis, but excommunication records for the Church of Jesus Christ of Latter-day Saints are inaccessible to researchers, and court records are missing. However, about this time, Talitha Bankhead Dennis left her husband, and he moved with one of his plural wives to remote Piute County. In the case of another unwed pregnancy, Spanish Fork religious leaders arranged for the young woman to marry a friend of her parents as a plural wife.[53] This option was not available to Marinda; she was of partial African descent, so the community would not allow her to marry the father of her child or another man as a plural wife. When her son David William Pace was born, the only single Black man in the county was her half-brother or cousin Luke, so she remained a single mother. However, by the time Marinda gave birth to Edward, Alexander Bankhead had moved to nearby Provo with A. O. Smoot, and Alexander and Marinda married and lived in Spanish Fork. They became respected and beloved in their community.[54]

Frank Perkins and His Daughters

After the death of his wife Esther in Great Salt Lake City, Frank Perkins married divorced Connecticut native Jane Elizabeth Manning James. Their marriage did not last long.

Figure 9.2. The man standing third from the left in the Jex Broom Factory is occasionally said to be Alexander Bankhead, who worked in the factory, but the Jex family identified the man in the picture as English immigrant George Ellis. George Edward Anderson, Jex & Sons Broom Factory, L. Tom Perry Special Collections, Harold B. Lee Library, Brigham Young University, Provo, Utah.

Jane and her first husband Isaac James had lived in Brigham Young's household, and perhaps it was due to Jane's relationship with the Young family that a small group of Black Latter-day Saints managed to negotiate the increasingly segregated Latter-day Saint worship and visited the Endowment House, a building that served as a temporary temple. The church did not allow them to participate in other sacred temple rituals, but they could do proxy baptisms for their deceased loved ones. Those in the endowment house on Friday, September 3, 1875, were Frank and Jane Manning James Perkins, Frank's daughter Mary Ann Perkins James, married to Jane's son Sylvester, and their friends who arrived in Utah after the Civil War: Samuel and Amanda Leggroan Chambers, Annis Bell Lucas Evans, and Edward and Susan Gray Read Leggroan. A list called "Record of Baptisms for the Dead for the Seed of Cain" records the names of their deceased friends and loved ones. Frank did proxy baptisms for Morris Brown; Jack Lynn Vose; a nephew, George Green; and a cousin, Jack Vose. Mary did baptisms for "G[ran]dmother Dawney" and aunts Darkous (probably Dorcas), Lousindy, Maria, and Seely.[55]

Perkins remained in Salt Lake City after his divorce. The census recorded his employment with Mary Ann Gurnsey Young and Ann Oliver Young, sisters-in-law of Brigham Young, and Washington F. Anderson, a prominent medical doctor and friend of Brigham Young.

Frank had lost most of his family to death, except Benjamin and his children: Mary, Sylvester, and Charlotte. Benjamin eventually made his way to the mining town of Butte, Montana. He was an active member of the AME Church and its debate society. As he aged, he worked as a courier for the doctors in town, but his behavior became erratic. He began to get into accidents, and after he threatened one of his employers, the town purchased him a train ticket to Salt Lake City. There the "diminutive" Perkins found work as a bootblack in a barbershop.[56] He died in the home of his brother Sylvester Perkins in Millcreek, Utah.

Sylvester and Mary Ann Perkins James also moved to Millcreek, south of Salt Lake City. They had eight children, but only William Henry James and Esther Jane James Leggroan lived longer than their parents.

Charlotte or "Lottie" Perkins was the youngest in the Perkins family. Her life is a window into the devastating situation of minority women when more respectable choices were closed to them. After her mother's death, Perkins lived with her sister Mary in downtown Salt Lake City until

Figure 9.3. Mary Ann Perkins James. Used by permission, Utah State Historical Society.

she entered domestic service. By the late 1880s, Charlotte was a chambermaid in the Salt Lake City brothel of notorious madam Kate Flint.

Salt Lake City officials decided that attempts to close brothels would drive business into other neighborhoods, and they preferred that prostitution remain under the watchful eye of the city government in the downtown minority neighborhoods of Commercial Street, now Regent Street, and Franklin Street, now Edison Street.[57] The officials developed an arrest-fine-release method to regulate and tax prostitution. The police would raid a brothel, arrest as many of the "inmates" as possible, make them post bonds, and then expect them to forfeit the bonds. Despite efforts to contain the sex trade, the establishments spilled into nearby neighborhoods, including Black Jule's on 200 East between 500 and 600 South. Larger brothels were stand-alone buildings, but smaller establishments like Black Jule's, where Charlotte worked, tended to be pioneer-era homes or outbuildings in the interior of city blocks. In Salt Lake City, each block was originally made up of eight lots, each one-and-a-quarter acres, which left a large space in the interior where business could be transacted with little public oversight. Black Jule's operated in an old home rented from Latter-day Saint George Stringfellow.

In 1886, the police arrested Perkins for vagrancy and prostitution. Rather than forfeit her $40 bond, her attorney requested a jury trial. Housekeeper Mrs. M. M. Morton, prostitute Lily Reed, and Chinese immigrant cook Jimmy Lin testified that Perkins worked as a chambermaid for Kate Flint. Charlotte's former step-uncle Isaac Manning and another witness told the court that Perkins was one of three Black women at Black Jule's and that they entertained hundreds of customers a year. Manning said, "the place was bad beyond all description; that the nightly orgies were something fearful to see and hear, that the establishment was a living disgrace in the neighborhood."[58]

Journalists tried to outdo each other in innuendo and humor in their coverage of the trial. The *Salt Lake Herald* wrote that "Lottie took the stand and denied *in toto* all the charges brought against her; she was not on the streets; had never been drunk on the streets." The reported continued, "She wept copiously before the jury; she . . . knew nothing at all—had never done anything wrong for the past four years."[59] The jury of twelve White men found her guilty but recommended mercy. She did not appear for her sentencing and forfeited her bond.[60]

The trade also reached into the James family. Jane Manning James's daughter Ellen Madora James (Robinson Kidd Early McLean) left her illegitimate daughter with her mother and went to work as a courtesan in Eureka, Nevada.[61] Although little biographical information exists on Charlotte and Ellen, their reasons for entering the sex trade may have been due largely to its proximity, since the city consciously drove the trade into minority neighborhoods. The two women had limited opportunities for legitimate relationships, education, and employment due to segregation, discrimination, and the small Black population of the territory. Ellen could read and write, but the 1880 census showed that Charlotte could not, and the money involved in prostitution would have been better than what they could earn in domestic service.[62] Finally, women or girls may have entered the trade after a rape, out-of-wedlock birth, or the end of an abusive marriage.[63]

Journalists eventually stopped using pathos in their coverage of Perkins. One journalist reported, "Hattie Clark and Lottie Perkins, two of the ebony-hued damsels who are in the habit of conducting themselves in a very loose and unlady-like manner, were arraigned on the charge of keeping a house of ill-fame."[64] Her arrests were routine, simply the way the city regulated and taxed prostitution, but things took a turn for the worse in 1894 when police arrested her for procuring, which, the newspaper wrote, "reduced to plainer terms means enticing a young girl into a house of fame for immoral purposes." Ben Naisbett swore out a complaint that Charlotte enticed his seventeen-year-old daughter into prostitution.[65] Charlotte denied the allegations. The newspaper did not mention her verdict or sentence, but she was arrested again not long afterward. The *Salt Lake Tribune* wrote about one arrest, "The sleuths penetrated the densest jungles of Coontown last night and rounded up ten of its inmates, each of whom were booked on charges of prostitution." The arrests came after an Italian immigrant "wandered into the jungles, where he was mulcted of his life savings, amounting, by his own calculations, to about $2.50." Perkins was among those arrested and assessed a fine of $8.50.[66] Prostitution is a hazardous profession, and that same year, the police court charged Idaho miner G. W. Bell with assault and battery upon Perkins.[67]

Several years later, Charlotte married prizefight organizer Charles Campbell. Not long afterward, she died of tuberculosis in her apartment above Hop Sing's laundry, so hers was a story about racial marginalization from birth, since it is likely she was born to an enslaved mother, until her early death across from the crowded, opium-scented haunts of the Commercial and Franklin Street neighborhoods.[68]

Rose and Violet Litchford

In 1860, Rose and Violet (Crosby) (Bankhead) lived with Rose's two young sons and James Vollantyne or Valentine in Union. This was not James Valentine, the husband of Nancy Bankhead; this was a younger man who later went by the surname Banks and who sometimes directed his excess energy into pranks and petty crime. In 1862, he led a group of about twenty-five youth in a rowdy celebration of a marriage called a "charivari" and was arrested along with two other ringleaders, Nephi

Figure 9.4. Charlotte Perkins Campbell. Used by permission, Utah State Historical Society.

Owen and William Woolsey.[69] James may have been Jim, who arrived in the valley with Amasa Lyman's 1848 wagon company.

Rose had five children with miner Miles Litchford, the son of Pleasant Litchford, a well-to-do Black property owner in Ohio.[70] Violet died in Union, and Rose may have died in Millcreek. James Valentine/Banks moved to Nevada. Miles Litchford went to visit his family in Ohio and never returned. Two of Rose's daughters lived for a while with Green and Martha Flake, but then Martha died, and the girls went into domestic service. Rose's daughter Catherine Litchford lived in poverty on Franklin (now Edison) Avenue in Salt Lake City when she learned in 1899 that as the only surviving daughter of Miles Litchford, she had inherited her father's estate.[71] A reporter wrote, "In a little old weather beaten shack, supported on its foundation, only because it is wedged solid between better buildings, its walls dirty and bare, its floor uncarpeted and its furnishings consisting of a table, a wood box, a stove and two chairs, there was happiness last night." The article continued, "A middle-aged, poverty-stricken colored woman lives there . . . from hand to mouth, doing all that she can to earn bread and butter, but so poor in knowledge is she that she cannot spell her maiden name." The reporter wrote that she heard that she was being sought by an Ohio lawyer and went to the police station. The police could not figure out what she wanted, since the lawyer seeking her had not mentioned that she was Black. "'My father dead? . . . and his estate being settled?' . . . It was too unnatural for the poor woman to comprehend. She simply could not believe she was an heiress to anything."[72]

Figure 9.5. Kate Litchford and an unidentified husband. Used by permission, Utah State Historical Society.

Catherine's neighbor Ella Phelps was an early community organizer. She took Catherine to Ohio to settle the estate. Catherine's sudden inheritance of $12,000 resulted in a successful marriage proposal from John Patterson, but the estate quickly disappeared, and Catherine died in the county hospital in 1917.[73] Neither Catherine nor any of her sisters have any known descendants, but her half-brothers Daniel Freeman Bankhead and Isaac Fred Valentine Banks have descendants throughout the American West who can trace their heritage back to the first pioneers to enter the Salt Lake Valley in 1847.

Caroline and Tampian Hoye

A newspaper called sisters Caroline and Tampian Hoye the "reigning ebony belles of Great Salt Lake City" when Thomas Bankhead Coleman and Shepherd Camp fought over them in 1859. The two disappeared from public records, as did many others, between the 1860 and 1870 censuses. No record tells when they knew they were free from enslavement by the two widows of Thomas S. Williams, or what they did when they learned of their liberation, but they were trained in domestic service and probably continued as household servants.

Around the end of the Civil War, Caroline married Samuel Bankhead, who had crossed the plains in 1848 and grown up enslaved in Draper, Utah. Although Samuel and their daughter Luella died several years later, Caroline continued to be close to Samuel's family, later holding the funeral for Samuel's mother in her home. Caroline remarried Civil War veteran Andrew Jackson about the same time her younger sister Tampian married Andrew Campbell, who had arrived in Utah Territory with the army.

Andrew Campbell worked to mobilize the battle for civil rights among the small Black population of the territory. Campbell, Francis Grice, and Nelson Ockry wrote to the newspapers in 1873 to support the national Civil Rights Act "in the name of those brave Colored patriots who have fought, bled and died for the independence and the preservation of our common country." They demanded "full and complete rights as citizens of the great Republic."[74] Campbell believed the Black population should affiliate with the Republican Party, as it existed at the time, and found himself on the opposite side of the question from Julius Taylor, the fiery editor of the Salt Lake City African American Democratic newspaper *Broad Ax*. Julius Taylor found Campbell a worthy foe and, in one editorial, called him the "sainted and sanctimonious Andrew Campbell, Esq., who hates the editor of the BROAD AX, with all the intensity of his being."[75] Only fragments remain of the local African American Republican newspaper, *Plain Dealer*, edited by William Wesley and Elizabeth Taylor, so little remains of Campbell's own words. Tampian did not appear in many records, but she raised children who were successful in the integrated Salt Lake City public schools.[76]

Due to the lack of records, the connection was originally unclear between Caroline Bankhead Jackson and Tampian Campbell, but when Caroline's son William Jackson registered for the draft during World War I, he listed his nearest relative not as his wife Ada, but as Tampian's son Ulysses Campbell. Although there was no field to record relationship, registrar Annie Thompson wrote "cousin" in small letters.[77] Neither Thompson nor William Jackson, a forty-five-year-old cook for the Southern Pacific Railroad, could have imagined that the one extra word would confirm the relationship between his mother and Tampian, and therefore confirm their identity as the two girls enslaved first in Utah Territory by David and Duritha Trail Lewis and then by Thomas S. Williams and his widows Albina and Priscilla.

The few seconds it took Jackson to state his relationship to Ulysses Campbell and Thompson to record it allowed the story to be told of two enslaved sisters who were taken from Kentucky to Utah Territory in 1851 and eventually made a life for themselves. The enslaved man in the Lewis household, Jerry, drowned a decade after they arrived in the Great Salt Lake Valley, but Caroline and Tampian and other freed enslaved people saw the territory progress from the earliest pioneer days past the turn of the twentieth century. The sisters' experiences were forgotten, but notable: valued in a probate, registered as indentured servants in the court, sold as chattel, used as collateral for a mortgage, fought over in court, and fought over in the streets of Great Salt Lake City. They suffered the separations and abuses of slavery and lost many loved ones to death, but along with the other Black pioneers of Utah, theirs became a story of survival, resilience, and the ties of family and friendship.

Part II
Biographical Encyclopedia of the Enslaved

Ten
THE ENSLAVED

There were undoubtedly other enslaved Black people in Utah Territory, but those shown here had at least one reliable source. The entries appear by household, which avoids repetition of sources by providing all the general sources for each household under the first person, or in the case of a discrete family within a household, in the entry for a parent. The listed sources pertain to the enslaved. Many more sources exist about communities and enslavers.

All surnames appear, including those of enslavers, as explained in the introduction. Names in parentheses are not known to have been used by the enslaved but indicate where to look for sources. For example, when Lawrence Smiley killed a man in Los Angeles, newspapers alternately gave his surname as Smith, his former enslaver's name; Smiley, his own family name; or Embers, his stepfather's name.

The category "Enslaver" lists only enslavers in Utah Territory. Historical documents often show estimated ages, so the birth dates shown are often an estimate or range based on the first known records of age. Death dates, where known, come from vital records or newspapers.

Allston

Theophilus (Allston)

Theophilus traveled west in 1854. He was the enslaved servant of Lt. Benjamin Allston, a member of the Steptoe Expedition (1854–1855), which was heading to Utah Territory to survey military roads and investigate the Gunnison Massacre. Allston was the son of rice grower Robert F. W. Allston, later governor of South Carolina.

Allston wrote home: "Theophilus is well and sends love to all, wishes to know something about his things, wife &c." The Steptoe Expedition overwintered in Utah, and while Allston was absent from the area, Theophilus presented forged freedom papers to Brigham Young. Army Capt. Rufus Ingalls took Theophilus back into captivity. Allston, angered about the attempted self-liberation, wrote home that he would sell Theophilus to a Mr. Perry without a second thought "were it not that the whole family belong to me and I do not like to hurt their feelings." Theophilus then disappeared from the public record. By 1860, Lt. Allston was back in South Carolina and enslaved more than one hundred people, while his father enslaved more than six hundred.

Enslaver: Benjamin Allston (1833–1900)

Military Expedition: Steptoe (1854–1855)

Sources: Benjamin Allston to Adele Allston, Letters, 1854–1857, Military and Personal Correspondence (1848–1960) 12/17, Allston Family Papers, 1830–1901, South Carolina Historical Society, Charleston, SC, typescript courtesy of William Gorenfeld. R. F. W. Allston, Georgetown, South Carolina Slave Schedule, *1850 Census*. Benjamin Allston, Prince George Parish, South Carolina Slave Schedule, *1860 Census*. William P. MacKinnon, "Sex, Subalterns, and Steptoe: Army Behavior, Mormon Rage, and Utah War Anxieties," *Utah Historical Quarterly* 76, no. 3 (Summer 2008): 227–46. https://www.jstor.org/stable/45063621.

Bankhead

Samuel (Bankhead) Smith (1799–1868)

Samuel Smith went west with John H. Bankhead from Marion County, Alabama. Although he was said to be Alexander Bankhead's father and Nancy Lines (Dennis) Smith's husband, he has no documented relationships except with his father, Samuel Smith, as shown in his burial record. Smith helped build the settlements of South Cottonwood, Willard, and Wellsville, Utah. Charles W. Nibley recalled, "Old Sam used to ask me if I had read any news of 'de wah,' and I can remember very well him saying at one time, 'My God, I hope de Souf get licked.'" Nibley continued, "Only once did I see the old man Bankhead get angry at his slaves, and at that time he tore around pretty lively and threatened to horsewhip them to death if they didn't mend their ways." After he was freed, Smith moved to Spanish Fork and lived with Nancy Lines Smith. He died of typhoid fever.

Documented Family: Father Samuel Smith; possibly Nancy Lines Smith

Enslavers: John Henderson Bankhead (1814–1884) and Nancy Crosby Bankhead (1825–1915)

Wagon Company: Heber C. Kimball (1848)

Burial: Spanish Fork City Cemetery, Spanish Fork, Utah

Notes: The Marion (now Lamar) County, Alabama, courthouse burned, so few records survive. ("A Big Fire," *Marion County Herald* [Hamilton, AL], April 5, 1887.) The 1840 and 1860 censuses show no Bankhead slaves, but other records confirm their presence, including the amount of production shown in the 1860 census agricultural schedule. Later sources claim that there were two men named Dan: Dan the Blacksmith and the younger Daniel Freeman Bankhead. However, the first appears to be a late memory of Smith: "He was a good blacksmith and helped the pioneers a great deal when they were crossing the plains." (Wellsville History Committee, *Windows of Wellsville, 1856–1984* [Providence, UT: Wellsville History Committee, 1985], 59.)

Sources: Thomas Bullock, 1847–1848 Emigration List, Nauvoo City Court Docket Book, February 1844–May 1845, MS 3441, 33, CHL. Sam Bankhead, Great Salt Lake County, Utah Territory, *1850 Census.* John H. Bankhead, Great Salt Lake County, Utah Territory Slave Schedule [draft], 1850 [1851] Utah Territorial Census, MS 2672, box 1, folder 6, CHL. John H. Bankhead, Great Salt Lake County, MS 2672, Utah Territory Productions of Agriculture, 1850 [1851], CHL. Jno H. Bankhead, Cache County, MS 9234, Utah Territory Productions of Agriculture, *1860 Census*, CHL. Wellsville, *Windows of Wellsville.* Samuel Bankhead, 1868, Spanish Fork (UT) Cemetery Records and Spanish Fork Cemetery Deeds (1886–1924), microfilm 1654570, FHL. Charles W. Nibley and Preston Nibley, "Reminiscences of Charles W. Nibley," *Improvement Era* 37, no. 10

(October 1934): 598. Anonymous, "1. In 1856 [excerpt from Anonymous, 'Salem Pioneers,']" Jones442 [pseud.], Family Search Family Tree (hereafter FSFT). August 26, 2013, https://www.familysearch.org/tree/person/collaborate/KWNJ-L71.

Martha Morris (Crosby) (Bankhead) Flake (1828–1885)

Nancy Crosby Bankhead inherited Martha when John Crosby died. Martha's parents may have been Violet (Crosby) and Morris. The Crosby probate set Martha's value at $275. Her granddaughters later recalled that she had scars on her back and a deformed hand from violent treatment by her enslavers.

The Bankhead family took Martha to Utah Territory. Friends later told historian Jack Beller that she went to Utah with Heber C. Kimball, and Beller understood that she was enslaved by Kimball, but the report may be a late memory that she was in Kimball's wagon train. Based on a memory from William J. Flake, it is possible that Kimball hired Martha from her enslaver, but no reliable documentation remains from the Bankhead, Kimball, or Flake families.

Martha married Green Flake, probably around 1853. Their descendants remembered that the couple paid Martha's former enslavers with produce until Brigham Young told them to stop since they owed the Bankheads nothing. The Flakes lived in Union and raised their children Abraham and Lucinda and at least two of Rose Litchford's daughters.

Documented Family: Husband Green Flake (1828–1903) and children Lucinda Flake (1854–1937, married George Stevens) and Abraham Flake (1857–1936, married Mary Ann Steele and Levora Litcherl)

Enslavers: John H. and Nancy Crosby Bankhead

Wagon Company: Heber C. Kimball (1848)

Burial: I-8, Union Fort Pioneer Cemetery, Cottonwood Heights, Utah

Notes: Martha is in the wagon roster by number, not name. Like several others, she is missing from the 1850 census although she was probably in the territory.

Sources: See Bankhead sources under Samuel Smith, Crosby sources under Toby Embers, and Flake sources under Green Flake. Martha Flake,

Salt Lake County, Utah Territory, *1860 Census*. Martha Flake, Salt Lake County, Utah Territory, *1870 Census*. Martha Flack, Salt Lake County, Utah Territory, *1880 Census*. Daughters of Utah Pioneers, Far South East, Salt Lake County, "A Bicentennial Salute & Dedication, Fort Union Pioneer Cemetery Memorial," 1976, John D. Fretwell Collection, private collection. Bertha Stevens Udell, Interview with John D. Fretwell, 1990, Fresno, CA, in John D. Fretwell, "Green Flake," 1999, typescript, 3, John D. Fretwell Collection. Notes from Bertha Stevens Udell Home, n.d., p. 2, John D. Fretwell Collection. Jack Beller, "Negro Slaves in Utah," *Utah Historical Quarterly* 2, no. 4 (October 1929): 124–25. https://www.jstor.org/stable/45057482. William Jordan Flake, box 37, folder 13, CR 100 18, Biographical Sketches, 1891–2013, CHL. Stanley B. Kimball, *Heber C. Kimball: Mormon Patriarch and Pioneer* (Urbana, Chicago, London: University of Illinois Press, 1981), 149.

Nathan Bankhead (1828–1901)

Nathan Bankhead went with John H. Bankhead to the Great Salt Lake Valley and helped settle South Cottonwood, Willard, and Wellsville. His daughter-in-law Sina Bankhead said his first wife was Mary (Miram). He was the father of George A. Bankhead and may be the father of Daniel Freeman Bankhead, son of Rose Crosby.

Charles W. Nibley remembered Nathan as "the big black negro that [John] Bankhead owned." When the settlers evacuated to Utah County during the Utah War, Nathan returned to Box Elder County to care for crops.

Around 1870, he settled on his own land in Wellsville and married Susan Jane Powell. The family was subject to social marginalization and harassment due to their race, and their children could not court or marry within the community. The family grave markers in Wellsville were destroyed repeatedly. "These blacks had been a free people for twenty years and deserved the dignity of unmolested graves, but the city fathers decided it would be best for the cemetery if the graves were left unmarked." (In 2017, the Wellsville City Historical Committee placed a marker to commemorate the family. Subsequently, Nathan's descendants used ground-penetrating radar to locate the family graves and placed another monument.) In the 1890s, Nathan and Susan Jane sold their land in Wellsville and moved to Los Angeles. Nathan died in 1901, and Susan died in 1931.

Documented Family: Wife Miram or Mary (Bankhead); son George A. Bankhead (1852–1923); possible son Daniel Freeman Bankhead (1854–) with Rose Crosby (1835–); wife Susan Jane Powell Bankhead Walton (1850–1931) and children Hyrum William Bankhead (1870–), C. Hannah Bankhead (1872–1935, married Dock Franklin Blakney and Rufus Alfred), Nathan Bankhead (1875–1885), Alexander Bankhead (1878–1916, married Olivia), Margaret Bankhead (1883–1886), William Louis Bankhead (1886–1915, married Marcella Williams), and probable other children

Enslavers: John H. and Nancy Crosby Bankhead

Wagon Company: Heber C. Kimball (1848)

Burial: Lot 7446, Evergreen Memorial Cemetery, Los Angeles, California

Notes: White Bankhead reminiscences tend to confuse Nathan and Samuel, and an occasional source confuses Nathan with Thomas Bankhead Coleman.

Sources: Nathan Bankhead, Box Elder County, *1856 Utah Territorial Census*, MS 2929, box 1, folder 2, 1, CHL. Nathan Bankhead, Land Title, January 14, 1873, Cache County, Utah, Deed Records, Vol. B, 1869–1872, Logan, UT: Cache County Courthouse. Nathan and Susan Bankhead, Cache County, Utah Territory, *1880 Census*. Nathan and Susan J. Bankhead, Los Angeles County, CA, *1900 Census*. "Items from Logan," *Ogden Standard* (Ogden, UT), October 7, 1890. "May 24, at County Hospital, Nathan Bankhead, 65 years; Gangrene." "Deaths," *Los Angeles Herald* (Los Angeles, CA), May 26, 1901. Nathan Bankland [*sic*], Evergreen Memorial Park Cemetery, Los Angeles, Records, 1877–1988 and Indexes 1877–1989, FSFT. https://www.familysearch.org/search/catalog/1143073. John L. Edwards, "The Move South Related by John L. Edwards," *Box Elder News* (Brigham City, UT), May 25, 1917. Nibley, "Reminiscences," 598. Sina Bankhead, interview by Jack Beller, in "Negro Slaves in Utah," 124. Celia Bankhead Leggroan and Carrie Bankhead Leggroan, interview, December 3, 1977, Helen Z. Papanikolas Papers, 1954–2001, MS 471, Marriott Library Special Collections, University of Utah; see also, Henrietta Bankhead, interview by Florence Lawrence, November 22, 1977, 24,

Helen Z. Papanikolas Papers. Anonymous, "History of John Henderson Bankhead, 1814–1884, and Nancy Coleman Crosby, 1825–1915" (unpublished manuscript), 79, TN-2155810, FHL. Judee Williams, "Descendants of Nathan Bankhead" August, 2015 (digital file of unpublished manuscript in possession of the author). Kate B. Carter, *The Negro Pioneer* (Salt Lake City, UT: Daughters of Utah Pioneers, 1965). Wellsville, *Windows of Wellsville*, 53–54. Warranty Deed of Nathan Bankhead, January 31, 1892, and Abstract of Title to Block 4, Plat B, Wellsville City Survey, 228, reproduced in Wellsville, *Windows of Wellsville*, 55. John Zsiray, "Wellsville Memorializes African American Settlers," May 29, 2017, *Herald Journal* (Logan, UT). https://news.hjnews.com/allaccess/wellsville-memorializes-african-american-settlers/article_3a8c57a4-5854-5232-98d9-1bd5f753c025.html. Peggy Fletcher Stack, "39 Years Later, Priesthood Ban is History, but Racism within Mormon Ranks Isn't, Black Members Say," *Salt Lake Tribune* (Salt Lake City, UT), June 7, 2017. https://www.sltrib.com/home/5371962-155/39-years-later-priesthood-ban-is. Mike Anderson, "Family Searches for Graves of Slave Ancestors in Northern Utah," KSL-TV (Salt Lake City, UT), October 11, 2018. https://ksltv.com/401856/family-searches-graves-slave-ancestors-northern-utah.

Thomas (Crosby) Bankhead Colburn/Coleman? (1833–1866?)

Thomas was probably enslaved by the John Crosby family and taken as a child into the John H. Bankhead household upon Bankhead's marriage to Nancy Crosby. Bankhead took Thomas to the Great Salt Lake Valley in 1848. Thomas was in the 1850 census twice: once in the population schedule and once in a draft copy of the slave schedule, shown as eighteen years old, Black, and neither fugitive nor manumitted. When the Bankhead family moved to Box Elder and Cache counties, Thomas stayed in Great Salt Lake County and worked as a laborer and freighter. His name was on an undated list of unmarried enslaved residents of the valley and in an 1855 newspaper list of letters at the post office. In 1856, Thomas Coleman, most likely Thomas Bankhead, lived in Sugar House Ward by Shepherd Camp, free Blacks Isaac and Sylvester James, and Brigham Young's son-in-law Charles Decker, who later that year guided a company that included Thomas to help rescue stranded handcart companies. Thomas is the only known enslaved man among approximately four hundred known rescuers. Thomas's use of the name Coleman by 1856 may connect his family back to the household of Nancy Crosby Bankhead's grandfather Joseph Coleman of Union County, South Carolina.

No documentation shows whether John Bankhead hired out or sold Thomas, but in 1859, he was enslaved by "Col. J. H. Johnson," possibly hymn-writer Joel Hills Johnson. Thomas may have taken care of Johnson's business while Johnson headed an immigrant station in Nebraska Territory.

Not long afterward, Thomas and Shepherd (Camp) (Hooper) came to blows, reportedly over Caroline and Tampian Hoye. Thomas shot Shepherd. Shepherd died from his wounds, and the court indicted Thomas for murder. *United States v. Colburn* (1859) used the surname "Colburn," but a newspaper later used the surnames Colburn and Coleman interchangeably. The court proceedings called Thomas a "negro slave" and—notably for the 1850s—called for testimony from free Black Frank Pope and enslaved Benjamin Perkins. The jury found Thomas guilty of manslaughter and sentenced him to a year of hard labor and a $100 fine.

The 1860 census showed one inmate in the county jail and eight in the state penitentiary, none of them Thomas or the two men also sentenced to a year of hard labor. At the sentencing, the judge had suggested, "In speaking of the sentence to 'hard labor,' . . . I think if your legislators would . . . set these prisoners to earn their own living, in place of letting them stay there at the expense of the Territory, it would be a very good thing." Thomas may have been on an early work release in the employ of stonecutter John Harper. Thomas then worked for several years in the Salt Lake House hotel, owned by relatives of Charles Decker.

In 1866, his body was found on the hill behind the arsenal, now the site of the Daughters of Utah Pioneers Museum and grounds of the Utah State Capitol. He had been hit over the head, stabbed, had his throat cut with his own knife, and a penciled note left on his chest reading, "NOTICE TO ALL NIGGERS! TAKE WARNING!! LEAVE WHITE WOMEN ALONE!!!" The coroner's jury did not name any suspects, and no arrests were made. Due to the lack of documentary evidence, discussion of motives or the identity of the murderer or murderers is speculation. Thomas Bankhead Coleman is buried in a pauper's grave in the Salt Lake City Cemetery.

Enslavers: John H. and Nancy Crosby Bankhead; possibly John and Isabella Mitchell Harper

Wagon Company: Heber C. Kimball (1848)

Burial: B_4_Pauper_216, Salt Lake City Cemetery, Salt Lake City, Utah

Notes: Later authors occasionally confuse Thomas and Nathan Bankhead. The newspapers called Thomas alternately Tom Colburn, Thomas Coleman, and Tom Coulson or Cohuson, but the details in the coverage suggest he was Thomas Bankhead, since he was said to have lived in the valley for many years and was a Latter-day Saint. No other known resident named Coleman or Colburn took an enslaved person to Utah Territory. Merchants or army officers were unlikely to have allowed the enslaved to become Latter-day Saints due to antipathy between the communities, and Thomas may have been one of members of the Bankhead household baptized in the South. About the identity of J. H. Johnson, the *New York Herald* reported, "Some time in August, 1858, Tom, alias Thomas Colborn, a nigger, belonging to a gambler named J. H. Johnson, shot another nigger named Shep, the property of Captain W. H. Hooper." Except for the identification as a gambler, all other clues point toward Joel Hills Johnson. ("The Utah Murders," *New York Herald* [New York, NY], January 14, 1860. Joel H. Johnson to Brigham Young, October 1, 1858, box 26, folder 11, CR 1234 1, Brigham Young Office Files, CHL [hereafter Office Files]. Joel Hills Johnson, "A Journal or Sketch of the Life of Joel Hills Johnson," 65, typescript, TN-518553, FHL.) Joel Hills Johnson was involved in the use of unpaid Indigenous labor. ("Iron County," *Deseret News*, March 5, 1853; Thomas D. Brown, *Journal of the Southern Indian Mission: Diary of Thomas D. Brown*, ed. Juanita Brooks [Logan: Utah State University Press, 1972], 111.) He was named as J. H. Johnson in an 1859 district court case, at which time, he was making his way from Nebraska to Great Salt Lake City. (*J. H. Johnson v. Elijah P. Thomas* [1859]. "Third Judicial District Court," *Deseret News* [Salt Lake City, UT], August 10, 1859. Johnson, "Journal or Sketch," 100.) In an alternate possibility for the identity of Joel H. Johnson, Hosea Stout called Albert Sidney Johnston "Col. Johnson," leaving the "t" out of his name, but based on the extensive documentation of his life, Albert Sidney Johnston only enslaved Randolph Hughes in Utah Territory. There was no known J. H.

Johnson with the army in Utah. (Roger B. Nielson, *Roll Call at Old Camp Floyd, Utah Territory* [R. B. Nielson, Fort Crittenden, UT, 2006].) Either the "gambler" operated under a pseudonym, or he did not exist, and the newspaper and Stout meant Joel Hills Johnson, the only man in the United States named J. H. Johnson traceable to the American West. The scenario of an unknown man taking another Tom into the territory is unlikely in any case, since the coverage reported that Tom had lived in the area for many years and was Mormon. One remaining complication would be if the newspaper confused Thomas for Tom (Church) (Smoot), but he died several years before Coleman was murdered.

Sources: Joseph Coleman, Union District, South Carolina *1800 Census*. Thomas Bankhead, Great Salt Lake County, Utah Territory, *1850 Census*. John H. Bankhead, Great Salt Lake County, Utah Territory Slave Schedule [draft], 1850 [1851]. Unknown to Brigham Young, c. 1851–1854, Ecclesiastical Files, 1841–1877, Files Relating to Marriage and Other Ordinances, Letters, 1845–1854, box 64, folder 1, Office Files. "List of Letters," *Deseret News*, April 4, 1855. Thomas Coleman, Sugar House Ward, Great Salt Lake County, *1856 Utah Territorial Census*. "'Uncle Charlie' Decker is Dead," *Deseret Evening News* (Salt Lake City, UT), March 23, 1901. Bankhead, interview by Lawrence. Daniel W. Jones, *Forty Years among the Indians* (Salt Lake City, UT: Juvenile Instructor Office, 1890), 63. Chad M. Orton, "The Martin Handcart Company at the Sweetwater: Another Look," *BYU Studies* 45, no. 3 (2006): 4–37, https://scholarsarchive.byu.edu/byusq/vol45/iss3/1. LeRoy R. Hafen and Ann W. Hafen, *Handcarts to Zion: The Story of a Unique Western Migration, 1856–1860* (Glendale, CA: A. H. Clark Co, 1960). David Roberts, *Devil's Gate: Brigham Young and the Great Mormon Handcart Tragedy* (New York, NY: Simon & Schuster, 2008). "Rescue Companies (1856)," *Pioneer Database*. Accessed March 31, 2017. https://history.churchofjesuschrist.org/overlandtravel/companies/11764159443600412460/rescue-companies. United States v. Colburn (1859), Salt Lake County (UT) Probate Court, Civil and Criminal Case Files, 1852–1887, Series 373, box 6, folder 12, USHS. "Shooting Affair," *Valley Tan* (Salt Lake City, UT), April 19, 1859. "Interesting from Utah," *New York Times* (New York, NY), June 17, 1859. Robert E. Fleming, "The Real Utah War: The *Mountaineer's* Efforts to Combat the *Valley Tan*" (master's thesis, Brigham Young University, 1996). "Later from Salt Lake," *Sacramento Daily Union* (Sacramento, CA), May 6, 1859. Hosea Stout,

On the Mormon Frontier: The Diary of Hosea Stout, 1844–1861, ed. Juanita Brooks (Salt Lake City, UT: University of Utah Press and Utah State Historical Society 1964), 2, 695, 699, 701. Hosea Stout, Journal, vols. 5, 7, 8, Hosea Stout Papers, Mss B 53, USHS. Editorial, *Valley Tan*, August 31, 1859. "Court Proceedings," *Valley Tan*, September 21, 1859. "Third Judicial District Court," *Deseret News*, September 21, 1859. County Jail, Great Salt Lake County, Utah Territory, *1860 Census*. Penitentiary, Warden Alexander McRae, Great Salt Lake County, Utah Territory, *1860 Census*. J. & I. Harper, Great Salt Lake County, Utah Territory Slave Schedule, *1860 Census*. "Murder," *Daily Union Vedette*, December 12, 1866. "The Recent Murder," *Daily Union Vedette*, December 13, 1866. "The Killing of Thos. Coleman Monday Night," *Daily Union Vedette*, December 15, 1866. "Coleman Thos, Known as Nigger Tom, Supposed to <be 35 years old>, [Dec] 11 [1866], found murdered Near the <Arsenal> [buried in the] Potters field." Utah Archives and Records Service, *Utah Death Registers, 1847–1966*, Series 21866. Ancestry.com. https://www.ancestry.com/search/collections/6967. Thomas Coleman, December 11, 1866, Salt Lake City Cemetery, Salt Lake City, Utah Division of State History, *Cemeteries and Burials* (Salt Lake City, UT: Utah Department of Heritage & Arts, 2014). https://utahdcc.secure.force.com/burials. Kenneth L. Cannon II, "'Mountain Common Law': The Extralegal Punishment of Seducers in Early Utah," *Utah Historical Quarterly* 51, no. 4 (Fall 1983): 308–27. https://www.jstor.org/stable/45061124. Connell O'Donovan, "'Let This Be a Warning to All Niggers': The Life and Murder of Thomas Coleman in Theocratic Utah," *Website of Connell O'Donovan*, June 2008. www.connellodonovan.com/coleman_bio.pdf. Wellsville, *Windows of Wellsville*, 51.

Miram or Mary (Bankhead) (1834–)

John H. Bankhead took Miram to Utah. She may be a woman baptized by Elder John Brown in Mississippi: "On the 18th of April I baptized Sytha [Crosby] Lay ... on the 21 of April Nancy [Crosby] Bankhed, Sarah Smithson, Margaret Mckown and a black woman by the name of Maron." The 1856 territorial census shows a woman named Maria in the Bankhead household. The government did not create an 1860 slave schedule for Cache Valley, so she may have lived there without documentation. Sina Bankhead reported that Mary was Nathan Bankhead's first wife.

Documented Family: Probably husband Nathan Bankhead and son George A. Bankhead

Enslavers: John H. and Nancy Crosby Bankhead

Wagon Company: Heber C. Kimball (1848)

Burial: Probably Utah

Sources: Miram, Great Salt Lake County, Utah Territorial Census Slave Schedule [draft copy], 1850 Census. Maria, Box Elder County, *1856 Utah Territorial Census*. Sina Bankhead, interview by Jack Beller, in "Negro Slaves in Utah," 124.

George A. Bankhead (1851/1860–1923)

George A. Bankhead was the son of Nathan Bankhead. He appears to be the son of Miram or Mary, so he could have remained in bondage until at least 1862. Bankhead, known locally as "Cooky," lived in Wellsville and homesteaded off Old Sardine Canyon Road, an area still called Cooky's Hollow. Bankhead married Sina Green Moseby of Missouri. They had nine children and moved to the Salt Lake Valley. His family is responsible for many of the existing genealogies and oral histories about slavery in Utah. Near the end of their lives, George and Sina lived with their son Nathan and daughter-in-law Henrietta Leggroan Bankhead, who remembered, "They really loved me they really did . . . And I really loved them two people." She recalled, "[George] was a wonderful person but I don't know much about his origin . . . Grandma use tell me how she use to hate to leave her farm up there and come down here. Oh I just loved that Grandma." George died in 1923, and Sina died in 1942.

Documented Family: Father Nathan Bankhead, probable mother Miram (Bankhead); wife Sina Moseby (1857–1943) and children Sina Belle Bankhead (1878–1950, married Isaac Fredric Banks/Valentine), George Bankhead (c. 1880–1881), Nathan Bankhead (1885–1944, married Henrietta Leggroan), Mary Ann Bankhead (1886–1943, married George G. Gray), Susan Bankhead (1888–1968, married Dan Gray and Daniel George Foster), Nancy Caroline Bankhead (1890–1990, married Hyrum Leggroan), Celia Bankhead (1892–1981, married Benjamin Franklin Leggroan),

Daniel Bankhead (1895–1900), and Thomas Leroy Bankhead (1897–1968, married Mary Lucile Perkins)

Enslavers: Possibly John H. and Nancy Crosby Bankhead

Burial: A_122_2, Elysian Burial Gardens, Millcreek, Utah

Notes: Do not confuse George A. Bankhead with George Bankhead Chism, the son of Mary (Crosby) Bankhead Sampson Chism. Sources suggest birth dates as early as 1849 and as late as 1860. Bankhead was not in the 1850 census, so his birth date is no earlier than 1851. He first appears in a government record in the 1880 census with a suggested birth year of 1853.

Sources: George Bankhead, Cache County, Utah Territory, *1880 Census*. George A. Bankhead, Homestead Entry, November 16, 1898, Certificate 6057, Application 10304, Cache County, Utah Territory, Bureau of Land Management and US Department of the Interior, *General Land Office Records*. https://glorecords.blm.gov. Wellsville, *Windows of Wellsville*, 54. Rose Mary Pedersen, "Her Life Story [Celia Bankhead Leggroan]—It's Based on Church, Family, Serving Others," *Deseret News*, January 20, 1977. Bankhead, interview by Lawrence. George A. Bankhead, July 11, 1923, Millcreek, death certificate 2301873, Utah Department of Health, USHS. George A. Bankhead, July 11, 1923, grave A-122-2; Sina Moseby Bankhead, August 20, 1943, grave A-122-3, Elysian Burial Gardens, Salt Lake City, Utah Division of State History, Cemeteries and Burials.

Male (Louis or Thompson?) (Bankhead)

Listed by number as a member of an 1848 Latter-day Saint wagon company, this may be an adult or child and may be Lewis or Louis, who was said by the Bankhead family much later to have gone to California to earn money to buy his freedom and died there. This unnamed man could have accompanied Mary (Crosby) to San Bernardino and been the father of Nancy Bankhead Jefferson, George Bankhead Chism, and John C. Bankhead Chism. Most likely, he is an otherwise unknown man named Thompson, shown next to Hark (Lay) Wales in the 1850 census as they traveled to California. A community memory about John H. Bankhead transporting Lewis's body from California to Utah Territory is implausible and is probably a late memory of some other connection between Bankhead and the people he and his brother enslaved.

Enslavers: John H. and Nancy Crosby Bankhead
Wagon Company: Heber C. Kimball (1848)
Burial: Possibly California; possibly Wellsville Cemetery, Wellsville, Utah
Sources: Bullock, 1847–1848 Emigration List. Carter, *Negro Pioneer*, 21. Tonya Reiter, email message to author, August 21, 2018. Thompson, Utah County, Utah Territory, *1850 Census*.

Nancy (Bankhead) Wales Valentine (1823–1894)

Nancy left no record of her origins except to tell the 1880 census taker that her parents were born in Florida. She probably had two sons with Woodford in Alabama before George W. Bankhead took her and her two boys, Samuel and Walter "Rolly," to the Salt Lake Valley in 1848. In Utah Territory, Nancy had one or two sons with Hark Wales before William Lay took Wales to California. She was mentioned, although not by name, in 1851 correspondence between William Crosby and Brigham Young, and she later appeared as "Harks wife" in a list in the Brigham Young papers.

George Q. Cannon and his entourage stayed at George Bankhead's home in 1855, and Cannon mentioned that Nancy, whom he named only as a "wench," cooked biscuits for their journey to California. A Daughters of Utah Pioneers (DUP) biography can be read as an insinuation that Nancy was sexually exploited by her enslaver. It may have been the case, but despite any possible meanings in the Cannon or DUP accounts, most of Nancy's children had known Black fathers, and she suffered as so many did after enslavers repeatedly made her a single mother.

Community members later remembered Nancy and her family in a curious but inaccurate document called "Slavery in Draper." (See Appendix 5.) It tells many stories, including the attempted lynching of one of her sons, but raises more questions than it answers, including when she knew she was free.

Nancy had another family with Canadian native James Valentine. They lived in Salt Lake City and Ogden where her husband died in 1893 and she died in 1894. Her funeral was held in the home of Caroline Jackson, her son Samuel's widow.

Documented Family: Husband Woodford and sons Samuel (1844–1871, married Caroline Hoye) and Walter "Rolly" (1845–1866); husband Hark (Lay) Wales (1825–1881/1887) and son Howard Egan Wales (1849–) and possibly Henry (Bankhead) (Wales) Valentine (1852–1888); unknown partner and children Frank (1857–) and Nancy (1860–); husband James Valentine (1809–1893) and children Mary (1864–1884) and Catherine (1865–1866); stepson Morena Valentine (1861–1883)

Enslaver: George W. Bankhead (1819–1898)

Wagon Company: Heber C. Kimball (1848)

Burial: Ogden City Cemetery, Ogden, Utah (with husband James Valentine, daughter Mary, and son Henry "John")

Notes: Do not confuse Nancy's husband James with James Valentine/Banks (1830–). Online family trees sometimes confuse Nancy's children with the otherwise unknown children of George W. Bankhead as listed in the 1850 census. *Negro Pioneer* mentioned a Jim Valentine in the William T. Dennis household, and he may have employed either James Valentine but would not have enslaved either of the men. (Carter, *Negro Pioneer*, 23, 48.)

Sources: William Crosby to Brigham Young, c. March 12, 1851, box 22, folder 6, Office Files. Brigham Young to William Crosby, March 12, 1851, box 22, folder 6, Office Files. Unknown to Brigham Young, c. 1851–1854, Ecclesiastical Files, 1841–1877, Files Relating to Marriage and Other Ordinances. George Q. Cannon, May 5, 1855, *Journal of George Q. Cannon*. Geo Bankhead, Great Salt Lake County, Utah Territory Slave Schedule, *1860 Census*. Edward L. Sloan, *The Salt Lake City Directory and Business Guide, for 1869* (Salt Lake City, UT: E. L. Sloan, 1869), 145. Nancy Valentine, Ward 9, Ward 13, Salt Lake County, Utah Territory, *1870 Census*. Nancy Valentine, Salt Lake County, Utah Territory, *1880 Census*. "Died," *Ogden Standard*, April 24, 1894. James Black, Parley Jacobsen, and Ellen Taggart, *Ogden, Weber County, Utah, City Cemetery Records* (Salt Lake City, UT, 1940–1942), 4, 995–96. Ogden City Cemetery, telephone conversation with the author, August 12, 2016. "An Aged Warrior Gone," *Ogden Standard*, July 4, 1893. Anonymous, "Slavery in Draper," 2–8, CHL.

Alexander Bankhead (1827/1836–1902)

Alexander Bankhead went to the Great Salt Lake Valley in 1848 with George W. Bankhead. His parents are unknown. He lived with Nancy and her sons in the Bankhead household in Draper, Salt Lake County. Bankhead was on a short list of unmarried enslaved African American residents of Utah Territory considered old enough to marry in the early 1850s, suggesting an earlier birth date than any age later claimed for him.

No contemporaneous documentation remains about his move from Draper to Utah County, but he and his wife Marinda later told journalist Julius F. Taylor that he "became the property of Bishop Smoot," which probably dates his move to 1868. Did Smoot enslave Alexander? Possibly, but Taylor also reported a similar claim about Marinda being "transferred" to William Taylor Dennis, which happened years after she was freed, so Smoot could have purchased or hired Alexander from George W. Bankhead, or perhaps Alexander worked for Smoot after he was freed. Bankhead subsequently worked in the Humble blacksmith shop and in Jex & Sons Broom Factory. He and Marinda Redd had no children, but he helped raise her son, David William Pace.

Many decades after his death, some Spanish Fork women remembered that Bankhead had been "casterized [castrated]," but without any more details. In a story in *Negro Pioneer*, one year at Halloween some boys "acquired" some bluing from Zebedee Coltrin and painted Bankhead's horse blue. "Alex was a kindly man and could not understand why the boys had chosen to play a joke on him." In 1897, A. O. Smoot II wrote to Spencer Clawson, "There is an old colored man, Alexander Bankhead, living in this City, who came to Utah in September 1848." He continued, "The old man called upon me this morning and stated he was very anxious to visit the Jubilee as a pioneer, and I assure you I would be glad to have him do so, as he is one of the 'whitest Negroes' living." Based on the 1899 *Broad Ax* interview, Bankhead did not attend the commemoration.

Bankhead died of a stroke in 1902. Latter-day Saint bishop Marinus Larsen served as executor of his estate, which included a town lot and home, farmland, pastureland, and $200 of stock in the local irrigation company. When Marinda died before his estate was settled, the property went to Marinda's son.

Documented Family: Wife Marinda Caroline Redd (1831–1907); stepson David William Pace (1862–1951)

Enslaver: George W. Bankhead; possibly Abraham O. Smoot (1815–1895)

Wagon Company: Heber C. Kimball (1848)

Burial: 09.09.24, Spanish Fork City Cemetery, Spanish Fork, Utah

Notes: Although *Negro Pioneer* reported that the 1897 Smoot letter was on file at the Pioneer Memorial Museum of Daughters of Utah Pioneers in Salt Lake City, Utah, the museum could not locate it. (Carter, *Negro Pioneer*, 25.) Alexander may appear in a picture of Jex & Sons Broom Factory, but the Jex family identified the man suggested as Bankhead as English immigrant George Ellis (1867–1917). Ray H. Banks and Patricia Banks, *Jex Family History* (Provo, UT: BYU Press, 2004), 44–45.

Sources: Bullock, 1847–1848 Emigration List, 33. Unknown to Brigham Young, c. 1851–1854, Ecclesiastical Files, Office Files. John H. Bankhead, Great Salt Lake County, Utah Territory Slave Schedule [draft], 1850 [1851]. Alexander Bankhead, Great Salt Lake County, Utah Territory, *1850 Census*. Geo Bankhead, Great Salt Lake County, Utah Territory Slave Schedule, *1860 Census*. Alexander Bankhead, Utah County, Utah Territory, *1870 Census*. Alex Bankhead, Utah County, Utah Territory, *1880 Census*. Alex Bankhead, Utah County, Utah, *1900 Census*. Alex Bankhead, January 10, 1902, Utah Archives and Records Service, *Utah Death Registers*. Tonya Reiter, "Redd Slave Histories: Family, Race, and Sex in Pioneer Utah," *Utah Historical Quarterly* 85, no. 2 (Spring 2017): 117, 126n66–67. https://www.jstor.org/stable/10.5406/utahhistquar.85.2.0108. "Slavery in Utah," *Broad Ax* (Salt Lake City, UT), March 25, 1899. Carter, *Negro Pioneer*, 23–24. Alexander Bankhead Probate, 1905, 1912, Marinda Bankhead Probate, 1912, Fourth District Court, Utah County, District, and Probate Courts, *Utah, Wills and Probate Records, 1800–1985*. Ancestry.com. https://www.ancestry.com/search/collections/9082.

Samuel Bankhead (1844–1871)

Samuel's parents were probably Nancy (Bankhead) Valentine and Woodford. He spent much of his childhood in Draper and moved to Salt Lake City after he was freed. He married Caroline Hoye (Lewis). Bankhead died of tuberculosis in 1871, and his daughter Luela died of the same disease the next year. The two are buried in pauper's graves in the Salt Lake City Cemetery. Bankhead is buried in William S. Godbe's lot, so perhaps he had been working for the founder of the Church of Zion (Godbeite).

Documented Family: Probably mother Nancy Bankhead Valentine and father Woodford; wife Caroline Hoye (Lewis Williams) Bankhead Jackson (1841–1904) and daughter Luela Bankhead (1866–1872)

Enslaver: George W. Bankhead

Wagon Company: Heber C. Kimball (1848)

Burial: B_4_Pauper_151, Salt Lake City Cemetery, Salt Lake City, Utah

Sources: Samuel Bankhead, Salt Lake County, Utah Territory, *1870 Census*. Samuel Bankhead, November 19, 1871, Luella Bankhead, October 29, 1872, Salt Lake City Cemetery, Salt Lake City, Utah Division of State History, Cemeteries and Burials.

Walter "Rolly" Bankhead (1846–1866)

Walter was the son of Nancy (Bankhead) Valentine and Woodford. The 1850 census listed him as "Rolly" and "Rauley." Perhaps his name was Walter Raleigh after the English explorer, or perhaps people called him "Raleigh" as a joke on the name Walter. Shortly after he was liberated, and three days after the death of his infant half-sister Catherine Valentine, he died on the Fourth of July of a pulmonary illness. The two were buried in pauper's graves in the Salt Lake City Cemetery.

Documented Family: Mother Nancy Bankhead Valentine and father Woodford; possible brother Samuel Bankhead and half-siblings

Enslaver: George W. Bankhead

Wagon Company: Heber C. Kimball (1848)

Burial: B-4-152, Salt Lake City Cemetery, Salt Lake City, Utah

Sources: Walter Bankhead <colored>, Son Woodford & Nancy, July 4, 1866, Utah Archives and Records Service, *Utah Death Registers*. Catherine Valentine, July 1, 1866, Walter Bankhead, July 4, 1866, Salt Lake City Cemetery, Salt Lake City, Utah Division of State History, Cemeteries and Burials.

Howard Egan Wales (1850–)

Howard was the son of Hark (Lay) Wales and Nancy Bankhead. His parents named him after Major Howard Egan (1815–1878), a frontiersman in the 1847 wagon company with Hark and the 1848 company with Nancy. William Lay took Howard's father to California in 1851, and Howard was raised by his mother in the George Bankhead household in Draper.

After he was freed Wales worked on farms and ranches in California's San Joaquin Valley. He was a noted marksman. The *Fresno Republican Weekly* wrote in 1887, "W. J. Browning, of Merced, killed and shipped to San Francisco this season 38,000 ducks and geese. In one day Howard Wales killed 750 ducks." He had occasional run-ins with the law and, in 1886, was poisoned in a cruel prank. The last time he appeared in a public record was when he registered to vote in 1888. He is not in Merced County death records.

Documented Family: Mother Nancy Bankhead Valentine and father Hark (Lay) Wales

Enslaver: George W. Bankhead

Burial: Unknown, probably California

Sources: "List of Letters Remaining," *Sacramento Daily Union*, June 25, 1869. Howard Woles [sic], Merced County, CA, *1870 Census*. Howard E. Wales, Merced County, California, *1880 Census*. "Verdict of Acquittal— The Indicted Ex-Officials," *Sacramento Daily Record* (Sacramento, CA), October 6, 1880. "An Earthquake Scare," *Stockton Daily Evening Mail* (Stockton, CA), March 7, 1882. "A Cruel Practical Joke," *Sacramento Daily Union*, March 20, 1886. "Just Outside," *Fresno Republican Weekly* (Fresno, CA), February 18, 1887. Merced District Cemeteries, telephone conversation, April 21, 2016. Howard Wales, 1888, Merced, California State Library, *California Voter Registers, 1866–1898*. Ancestry.com. https://www.ancestry.com/search/collections/2221.

Henry (Bankhead) (Wales?) Valentine (1851–1888)

Henry Valentine was enslaved from birth, the son of Nancy Bankhead and probably Hark (Lay) Wales. After his family was freed, he lived in Salt Lake City. He worked as a cook in Ogden, where the newspaper called him "an expert in gastrosophical science." Valentine spent two years in the state penitentiary for larceny. After a pardon from the governor, he moved to Rock Springs, Wyoming, shortly after the large-scale murder of Chinese miners in the 1885 Rock Springs Massacre. Valentine died in Rock Springs in 1888.

Documented Family: Mother Nancy Bankhead Valentine; probably father Hark (Lay) Wales; siblings and half-siblings

Enslaver: George W. Bankhead

Burial: E-6-29-5W, Ogden City Cemetery, Ogden, Utah; shown in cemetery records as "John Valentine," son of James Valentine and Nancy Beckstead [sic]

Sources: "Random References," *Ogden Herald* (Ogden, UT), September 7, 1882. "Valentine Henry, cook, 5th Street." J. C. Graham & Co., *The Utah Directory for 1883–84* (Salt Lake City, UT: J. C. Graham & Co., 1883). "Taken to the Pen," *Ogden Herald*, May 23, 1883. "Chips," *Salt Lake Herald* (Salt Lake City, UT), May 24, 1883. "Chips," *Salt Lake Herald*, May 26, 1883. "Convicts Pardoned," *Deseret News*, September 16, 1885. "The Sheffield Mob," *Southern Utonian* (Beaver, UT), September 18, 1885. "Random References," *Ogden Standard*, February 14, 1888. Ogden City Cemetery, telephone conversation with the author, August 12, 2016.

Frank (Bankhead) Valentine (1857–)

Frank was the son of Nancy Bankhead. He lived with his mother and her husband James Valentine in Salt Lake City for many years. He disappeared from the public record after 1880, except for a possible mention in a 1901 criminal complaint in Ogden.

Documented Family: Mother Nancy Bankhead Valentine; stepfather James Valentine; siblings and half-siblings

Enslaver: George W. Bankhead

Sources: "Charged with Robbery," *Salt Lake Herald*, September 9, 1901.

Nancy (Bankhead) Valentine (1860–)

Nancy was probably the daughter of Nancy Bankhead and James Valentine. She was born in Draper, Utah. After she and her family were freed, they lived in Salt Lake City before she disappeared from the public record. She may have married and moved to Alabama, although there is no obvious tie between Nancy Valentine and Nancy, the widow of Hannibal Dunlap, who claimed she was born in Utah in 1858. However, this is a tantalizing clue that some of the children born to the enslaved residents of Utah Territory may have led full lives elsewhere after they disappeared from the records of Utah Territory.

Documented Family: Mother Nancy Bankhead Valentine; father James Valentine; siblings and half-siblings

Enslaver: George W. Bankhead

Sources: Nancy Dunlap, Jefferson County, Alabama, *1930 Census.*

Female (Bankhead)

Listed by number as a member of an 1848 Latter-day Saint wagon company, this may be an adult or child, and could be Esther Harmon. (See her entry.)

Enslaver: George W. Bankhead

Wagon Company: Heber C. Kimball (1848)

Sources: Bullock, 1847–1848 Emigration List, 33.

Barnes

Female (Barnes) (1840–) and Female Infant (Barnes) (1859–)

This unnamed woman and infant lived in Salt Lake City in 1860. Merchant and slave trader Clifton R. Barnes and his wife Martha probably took the woman from Missouri to Utah Territory and then back to Missouri. Alternatively, she could be Louisa (Moody), hired to work in the Barnes household. The woman was not living with the Barnes family in Kansas a few years later, so nothing more is known of her life.

Documented Family: Infant daughter (1859–)

Enslavers: Clifton R. Barnes (1824–1887) and Martha A. Dawson Barnes (1831–1900)

Sources: Clifton Barnes, Great Salt Lake County, Utah Territory Slave Schedule, *1860 Census*. *The History of Jackson County, Missouri* (Kansas City, MO: Union Historical Company, 1881), 957. C R Barnes, Leavenworth County, Kansas State Historical Society, 1865 Kansas Territory Census, *Kansas State Census Collection, 1855–1925*. Ancestry.com. https://www.ancestry.com/search/collections/ksstatecen.

Barnett

Camplin Barnett (1805–)

Bird and Martha Barnett enslaved as many as eight people as they left Tennessee and moved to Missouri, the Great Salt Lake Valley, and California. In 1830, they enslaved one woman or girl in Perry County, Tennessee. The couple evidently did well in land speculation and tobacco, and, by 1840, they enslaved seven individuals in Benton County, Tennessee. In 1842, five of the enslaved were taxed at a total value of $1,750. The Barnett family were baptized into the Church of Jesus Christ of Latter-day Saints. They lived near Latter-day Saint converts A. O. Smoot and Seth Utley. Barnett and Utley donated some of the labor-intensive crop of tobacco their enslaved people grew to help fund the Latter-day Saint Nauvoo Temple. Barnett took his household to St. Joseph, Missouri, and arrived in the Great Salt Lake Valley in 1848 or 1849. In 1850, Barnett went to El Dorado County, California, and since he appears to have arrived in California before statehood, he kept his enslaved people in bondage.

In 1850, Camplin Barnett worked in the mining community of Kelsey, California. The census reported that he was born in Kentucky. He appears in no known additional records.

Enslavers: Bird Braxton Barnett (1809–1891) and Martha Walker Barnett (1811–1889)

Wagon Company: Unknown (1848)

Sources: Bird Barnett, Perry County, Tennessee, *1830 Census*. Bird B. Barnet [sic], 1836, Haywood County, 1842, Benton County, Early Tax Lists of Tennessee, Tennessee State Library and Archives, *Tennessee, Early Tax List Records, 1783–1895*. Ancestry.com. https://www.ancestry.com/search/collections/2883. Bird B. Barnett, Benton County, Tennessee, *1840 Census*. April 14, 1845, Daybook C, Nauvoo Tithing Record, 1844–1845, Trustee-in-Trust Tithing Daybooks, 1842–1847, CR 5 71, CHL. A. O. Smoot Diary, Vol. 1, 1836–1846, MSS 896, Special Collections, HBLL. Willard Richards to Randolph Alexander, May 25, 1848, Willard Richards Journals and Papers, 1821–1854, MS 1490, CHL. B. B. Barnett, Nauvoo Legion Mounted Rangers, 1850, Utah Territorial Militia Records, Series 2210. *USHS and FSFT*. https://www.familysearch.org/search/collection/1462415. Camplin Barnett, El Dorado County, California, *1850 Census*. LaMar C. Berrett, "History of the Southern States Mission: 1831–1861" (master's thesis, Brigham Young University, Provo, UT, 1960). P. T. Barnett and Anonymous, Excerpts from Letter and Notes, Camden, Tennessee, 1937, typescript, copy in possession of author.

Amy or Emily (Barnett) Rogers (1817–1887)

Amy (Emma or Emily) was born in Virginia around 1817. She is in the 1852 California state census with "Slave" written in the field for "Profession, trade, or occupation." She was the mother of Lucinda and Jordan Duncan and an unnamed daughter. Her mother appears to be Lucy Auther, who died in Stockton, California, at the age of 108. Sometime before 1870, Emily married Cornelius "Colonel" Rogers and lived for many years in Concord, Contra Costa, California. Lucinda's family Bible has a record of the deaths of Emily and Cornelius Rogers and copies of their obituaries. Emily's obituary reported: "She leaves, besides an aged husband... a son and daughter [Lucinda and Jordan], living in Snelling, California, and a daughter in one of the Southern States."

Documented Family: Possible Mother Lucy Auther (1787–1896); children Lucinda Duncan, Jordan Duncan, and an unnamed daughter; husband Cornelius Rogers (1811–1889)

Enslavers: Bird Braxton Barnett (1809–1891) and Martha Walker Barnett (1811–1889)

Burial: Pacheco Cemetery, Contra Costa, California

Sources: Amy, San Joaquin County, *1852 California Census*. Emily Rodgers, Contra Costa County, California, *1870 Census*. Emma Rodgers, Concord, Contra Costa, CA, *1880 Census*. "Mrs. Emily Rogers," unlabeled newspaper clipping, November 26, 1887. "Concord, Contra Costa Co.," *Elevator* (San Francisco, CA), c. June 10, 1889. Loucina Fell Lee Bible, CA, 1890, private collection. "Mrs. Auther," *Evening Mail* (Stockton, CA), March 27, 1896.

John (Barnett) (1828–)

John was reportedly born in North Carolina or Tennessee around 1828. The 1850 census for El Dorado County, California, showed him helping Bird B. Barnett run his hotel. He appeared in the 1852 California census in San Joaquin County as a "Slave." By 1860, he was no longer in the Barnett household. A granddaughter remembered that he slept outside Martha's door when Bird was away on business. The memory also remembered him as an "old Negro," but the 1840 census claimed that all the enslaved males in the household were under twenty-three years old, so "old" appears to be a racial marker rather than statement of age. The granddaughter remembered her grandfather Barnett as an astute businessman, but "a terror": parsimonious and abusive. She also remembered John sheltering a baby from rain with his body and fetching children home from school. If John survived slavery and remained in California, he did not use the name Barnett and is currently unidentifiable.

Enslavers: Bird Braxton Barnett (1809–1891) and Martha Walker Barnett (1811–1889)

Sources: John, El Dorado County, California, *1850 Census*. John, San Joaquin County, *1852 California Census*. Martha V. Reynolds, "Bird Braxton Barnett's Father's [sic]," ed., Anonymous, n.d., partial typescript, copy in possession of author.

Sandy Barnett (1828–1864)

Sandy was reportedly born around 1828 in Tennessee. His documentable history is almost identical to John's, except the Barnett family did not preserve any separate memories of him. He died in the Stockton

State Hospital in 1864 and is buried in the cemetery associated with the hospital.

Enslavers: Bird Braxton Barnett (1809-1891) and Martha Walker Barnett (1811-1889)

Burial: Stockton State Hospital Cemetery, Stockton, California

Sources: Sandy, El Dorado County, CA, *1850 Census*. Sandy, San Joaquin County, *1852 California Census*.

James (Barnett) (1832-)

James or Jim was reportedly born around 1832 in Tennessee. The Barnett family did not preserve any separate memories of him, and his fate is unknown.

Enslavers: Bird Braxton Barnett (1809-1891) and Martha Walker Barnett (1811-1889)

Sources: James, El Dorado County, California, *1850 Census*. Jim, San Joaquin County, *1852 California Census*.

Jane (Barnett) Scott Venable Grundy (1840-1922)

Jane was reportedly born around 1840 in Tennessee. In 1850, she lived in the Barnett household in El Dorado County, and two years later, she lived with the Barnett's fifteen-year-old daughter Ann Barnett Lane in Stockton. She had ten children and was an AME preacher.

Enslavers: Bird Braxton Barnett (1809-1891) and Martha Walker Barnett (1811-1889)

Sources: Jane, El Dorado County, California, *1850 Census*. Jane, San Joaquin County, *1852 California Census*.

Lucinda or Loucina (Barnett) Duncan Davis White Fell Lee Dixon (1843-)

Lucinda "Sindy" or Loucina was born around 1843 in Tennessee. She remained in the Barnett household through at least 1860. In 1865, she married miner William Anderson Davis. They had four children. After the death of her first husband, she remarried James White, who was taken to California during the gold rush by Thomas and Mary Thorn, and they had three children. Lucinda's next marriage was to W. R. Lee. They may have had four children. She appears in her brother's obituary as Lucinda Duncan. Her death date and burial place is unknown, but she is probably buried in Stockton Rural Cemetery.

Documented Family: Mother Amy or Emily Rodgers; brother Jourdan Duncan; husband William Anderson Davis (1823–1873) and children Louisa (1862–1895, married Jesse Greenly), Eliza (1866–1957, married William Martin), Edward Augustus (1868–, married Lizzie Robertson) and William Anderson (1872–); husband James E. White (1815–1887) and children Anne Bella (1877–), James Henry (1879–1966, married Miltie Tappan), and Clara Rinda (1884–1899); husband W. R. Lee and possible children Tora, Joseph, Amanda, and Anita; husband (unknown) Dixon

Enslavers: Bird Braxton Barnett (1809–1891) and Martha Walker Barnett (1811–1889)

Burial: Probably Stockton Rural Cemetery, San Joaquin, California

Sources: Lucinda, El Dorado County, California, *1850 Census*. Sindy, San Joaquin County, *1852 California Census*. Lucinda, Mariposa County, California, *1860 Census*. Lucina Davis, Mariposa County, California, *1870 Census*. Lucinda Lee, Stockton, San Joaquin, California, *1900 Census*. Loucina Fell Lee Bible. "Duncan," *Daily Evening Record* (Stockton, CA), May 12, 1922.

Jourdan (Barnett) Duncan (1845–1922)

Jourdan was born around 1845 in Tennessee and remained in the Barnett household through at least 1860. He worked as a sheepherder and laborer in Northern California and remained unmarried until his death in 1922 at the San Joaquin General Hospital. His death notice called him, "Jordan Duncan, loving brother of Lucinda Dixon, a native of Tennessee, aged 72 years."

Documented Family: Mother Amy or Emily Rogers; sister Lucinda or Loucina Duncan

Enslavers: Bird Braxton Barnett (1809–1891) and Martha Walker Barnett (1811–1889)

Burial: 27-E-218, Stockton Rural Cemetery, Stockton, California

Sources: Jourdan, El Dorado County, California, *1850 Census*. Jordon, San Joaquin County, *1852 California Census*. Jordan, Mariposa County, California, *1860 Census*. Jordan Duncan, Mariposa County, California, *1880 Census*. Jordan Duncan, San Joaquin County, California, *1910 Census*. Jordan Duncan, San Joaquin County, California, *1920 Census*. *California, County Birth, Marriage, and Death Records*. Jordan Duncan, Stockton Rural Cemetery, *FindAGrave*. https://www.findagrave.com. Loucina Fell Lee Bible. "Duncan," *Daily Evening Record*.

Box

Female (Box) (1830–)

The Box family may have taken this unnamed woman from Texas to Utah Territory, or they may have hired her there. Unless this was Betsy Brown Flewellen, nothing more is known of her.

Enslavers: Thomas Box (1804–1881) and Clarkey Carpenter Box (1812–1881)

Wagon Company: possibly a merchant company or the Homer Duncan Company (1857)

Sources: Thomas Box, Tippah County, Mississippi, *1840 Census*. Thomas and Clarkey Box, Henderson County, Texas, *1850 Census*. Thº Box, Henderson County, Texas Slave Schedule, *1850 Census*. Thomas Box, Henderson County, Texas Productions of Agriculture, *1850 Census*. Thomas Box, Henderson County, 1851–52, 1854, Texas State Library and Archives, *Texas, County Tax Rolls, 1837–1910*. FSFT. https://www.familysearch.org/search/catalog/986276. *A Memorial and Biographical History of Navarro, Henderson, Anderson, Limestone, Freestone and Leon Counties, Texas* (Chicago, IL: Lewis Publishing, 1893). Norman B. Ferris and Morris J. Snedaker, "The Diary of Morris J. Snedaker, 1855–1856,"

Southwestern Historical Quarterly 66 (July 1962–April 1963): 534. https://www.jstor.org/stable/30236261. "The Late Outrages on the Plains," *Sacramento Daily Union*, November 14, 1857. Tho Box, Great Salt Lake County, Utah Territory Slave Schedule, *1860 Census*.

Brown

Betsy Brown Flewellen (1836/1845–1900)

Betsy may have been born in Virginia. Latter-day Saint missionary John Brown purchased her in St. Louis in 1848 and took her to Utah. In 1857, Brown listed Betsy at the high price of $1,000 in a deed of consecration, a symbolic representation that he would be willing to transfer his property to the Church of Jesus Christ of Latter-day Saints.

After Betsy was freed, she worked in Salt Lake City and Corinne, Utah Territory. She married barber John Flewellen, who may have served in the Civil War. The records of the Presbyterian Church in Corinne list three children for the couple, but two died as infants. Betsy's whereabouts after 1880 are unknown. She may have moved to Idaho and Colorado with her daughter Kate Oglesby, who also disappeared from the public record along with Betsy's grandchildren Dan and Mary Oglesby.

Documented Family: Husband John Flewellen and children Julia Ann or Kate (1872–1928?, married Posey Oglesby), infant son (1875–1876), and John C. Flewellen (1878–1878)

Enslavers: Elizabeth Crosby Brown (1822–1906) and John Brown (1820–1896)

Wagon Company: Willard Richards (1848)

Sources: John Brown's Company of 10, Report, June 1848, MS 14290, Camp of Israel Schedules and Reports, 1845–1849, CHL. John Brown, Consecration Deed, February 3, 1857, Records of Utah County (1851–1864), F:81–82, MSS 3905, Special Collections, HBLL. "Corinne," *Salt Lake Herald*, March 29, 1877. Golden Spike Chapter Utah Genealogical Association, "Historical and Genealogical Register of Indexes to Corinne, Utah Newspapers 1869–1875," typed manuscript, Brigham City, Utah, 1975, 31, 37–38. Betsy Brown, Box Elder County, Utah Territory, *1870 Census. Church Register of the Presbyterian Church, Corinne, Utah* (Philadelphia, PA: Presbyterian Board of Publication, n.d.), 79, 127, 128, microfilm 0906168, FHL. Betsy Flewelen, Box Elder County, Utah Territory, *1880 Census*. Carter, *Negro Pioneer*, 32. Jack Beller, "Negro Slaves in Utah," Utah Historical Quarterly 2, no. 4 (October 1929): 124, https://www.jstor.org/stable/45057482.

Burton-Robinson

John Burton (1797–1865)

John Burton told a Latter-day Saint patriarch late in his life that he was born in Virginia to Zachariah and Jenny. The Burton family later thought he had been enslaved by the McCord family, but his birthplace and the history of the Burton and McCord families suggest that he was enslaved by Virginia native John N. Burton, then Burton's widow, Latter-day Saint convert Susan McCord Burton.

Susan remarried Joseph Lee Robinson as a plural wife. Plural marriage complicated the question of ownership, but Robinson called John, "a colrd man a member of the [Mormon] Church which was the property of my second wife a good and faithful servant."

The first time John Burton appeared by name in any known record was when he spent January 26, 1847, digging a grave for Charity Fuller Campbell. Campbell's husband was serving in the Mormon Battalion, so neighbors, including John, helped care for the family. The same account book that showed the care of the Campbell family reported that John spent two days working in the millrace.

John Burton went to the Great Salt Lake Valley in 1847, traveling with Daniel M. and Ann Crosby Thomas and their enslaved man Philemon and girl Tennessee. The leaders of the Latter-day Saint wagon train recorded the names of John Burton and Philemon in a list of those "capable of bearing arms and of performing other camp duties."

The Burton-Robinson family arrived in 1848 and settled in Davis County before moving south to help settle Iron County. Burton appeared in the population schedule in 1850 and 1860 rather than in a slave schedule, but he did not live in his own household, and, in 1860, James Henry Martineau, a man raised in a slave household, called him "a slave." Martineau wrote in the Deseret Alphabet, a phonemic script intended to help integrate Latter-day Saint immigrants, that "Black John" was present at the deathbed of Parowan Stake President John C. L. Smith.

Although Joseph L. Robinson remembered him as "a good Saint," Burton could not participate in the Latter-day Saint lay priesthood due to his African ancestry. He participated in the religious community in other ways: he helped build the local chapel and interpreted when Job Pitcher Hall spoke in tongues. A neighbor recalled Burton speaking in a Latter-day Saint testimony meeting: "Brudders and Sisters, wen the good Lawd calls old Black John, I'se a gwine, I'se a gwine over Jordan to meet my Lawd."

Robinson took Burton to Great Salt Lake City in 1856, but Burton returned to Parowan before 1860 and lived with Susan Burton Robinson's son and daughter-in-law. He died and is buried in Parowan.

Documented Family: Parents Zachariah and Jenny

Enslavers: Susan McCord Burton Robinson (1808–1876) and Joseph Lee Robinson (1811–1893); Sidney Rigdon Burton (1838–1897) and Anna Maria Fish Burton (1842–1905)

Wagon Company: Edward Hunter-Jacob Foutz (1847)

Burial: Section 7, lot 18, site 4, Parowan City Cemetery, Parowan, Utah

Notes: Although Joseph L. Robinson called him "John Burton" in his account book, the wagon company roster listed Burton as "John Robinson," misread in later sources as "Roberson" or "Robertson." A fictionalized family history, *Five Branches of Love*, is unreliable. By all accounts, Burton was an intelligent, hard-working man, but the book portrayed him as a bumbling although well-meaning "boy" and had him speak in heavy dialect when no one else did. For his probable origin in the Burton family: John N. Burton married, first, Sally Allred of Tennessee. Her family had no enslaved laborers. John N. Burton married, second, Susan McCord of Kentucky. Her family also had no enslaved laborers.

Sources: History of Monroe and Shelby Counties, Missouri (St Louis: National Historical Company, 1884), 175–76. James McCord [Susan's father], six free White persons, no slaves or free colored, Pike County, Missouri, *1830 Census*. James McCord and four other persons matching the description of widowed Susan, her children, and an enslaved man, age 36–54, Monroe County, Missouri, *1840 Census*. Donald E.

Burton, "History of John Burton: 1797–1865," October, 2013 (digital copy of unpublished manuscript, copy in possession of author). Verbal communication of content of patriarchal blessing from Church History Department to Rance Hutchings, John Burton, Number 252, Patriarchal Blessings, 11:113, CHL, as cited in Burton, "History of John Burton," 25–26. Edward Hunter and Jacob Foutz, Letter, August 17, 1847, in *Historical Department Journal History of the Church*, Vol. 23, CR 100 137, CHL. John Robinson, Iron County, Utah Territory, *1850 Census*. Iron County, folder 3, MS 2672, Utah Territory Productions of Agriculture, *1850 Census*, CHL. John Burton, Iron County, Utah Territory, *1860 Census*. Joseph Lee Robinson, Autobiography, 1883, folder 1, 47, 67, 76–77, 113; Account book, Records, 1846–1847, folder 4, 1–2, Joseph Lee Robinson Papers 1883–1892, MS 7042, CHL. Fourth Ten, June 21, 1847, *Historical Department Journal History*. James G. Bleak, *Annals of the Southern Utah Mission, 1850–1900*, MS 318, box 1, folder 1, 3, CHL. Joseph Lee Robinson, *The Journal of Joseph Lee Robinson: Mormon Pioneer*, eds. Oliver Preston Robinson, Mary Robinson Egan, David Nielsen, Joni Nielsen, and Kevin Merrell, E-book, August 2003. https://archive.org/details/JlrBasicJournal. Parowan Minute Book III, quoted in Luella Adams Dalton, *History of Iron County Mission, Parowan, Utah* (privately printed, 1973), 320. James Henry Martineau, Parowan Stake Minutes, 1855, translated and transcribed from the Deseret Alphabet by Joseph R. Bingham, 1981, Parowan Stake Historical Record, 1855–1860, LR 6778 28, folder 2, CHL. "Br. J. P. Hall spoke in tongues, and John Burton (a slave) interpreted." January 5, 1860, Parowan Stake Historical Record. Carter, *Negro Pioneer*, 14–15. Mary West Riggs, Don L. Riggs, *Five Branches of Love*, with contributions by Christie Roberts and Kevin Merrell (Salt Lake City, UT: privately printed, 1967, reprinted as a digital book, 2006), 87, 223–24.

Camp-Greer

Charlotte (Camp) (1830–1853)

Charlotte and her younger brother Daniel were born into the household of Diannah and Williams Camp, Charlotte in Alabama, and Daniel three years later in Tennessee. The Camp family joined the Church of Jesus Christ of Latter-day Saints in the early 1840s and moved to Utah Territory in 1850. On the way across the country, young Richard and Ellen Camp almost drowned while in Charlotte's care, but she managed to rescue the children. Ellen Camp Greer recalled, "she said if we had not come to, she was going to throw us back in the river, and then jump in herself. Then no one would know any thing about it." Charlotte had reason to fear since court records document that Williams Camp was a violent man.

Charlotte helped care for several of the Camp children while Williams and Diannah Camp returned to the South to settle the estate of Diannah's father. Ellen Camp Greer later recalled, "this negro woman that was left to take care of us took sick and died, and that left us girls alone." The cemetery recorded Charlotte's death from tuberculosis when she was buried, but when a child in the Camp family died almost a decade later, someone in the Camp family must have looked for Charlotte's death record and not found it, because her death was recorded a second time with a slightly different burial location and death date.

Enslavers: Williams Camp (1800–1875) and Diannah Greer Camp (1806–1876)

Wagon Company: Shadrach Roundy (1850)

Burial: B-2-13 or 8, Salt Lake City Cemetery, Salt Lake City, Utah

Notes: Williams Camp married Diannah Greer, and their daughter Ellen married Thomas Lacy Greer. Despite the shared name, the Greer families are not related. *Negro Pioneer* confused the Camp, Greer, and Sprouse families. Anonymous editing, notable omissions, and various inaccuracies in the oldest known version of Ellen Camp Greer's autobiography compromise its reliability, but historical documentation rarely contradicts her general account.

Sources: Williams Camp, eight slaves, Tuscaloosa County, Alabama, *1830 Census*. Williams Camp, eight slaves, Weakley County, Tennessee, *1840 Census*. Williams Camp, District Seven, 1842, three slaves, value $1500; 1843, four slaves, value $1700; 1844, four slaves, value $1600; 1845, four slaves, value $1600; 1846, four slaves, value $1700; 1847 and 1848, land but no slaves, Weakley County (TN) Trustee, *Tax Books, 1842–1851*. FSFT. https://www.familysearch.org/search/catalog/57169. Captain S. Roundy's Company Report, September 1850, Brigham Young Office Emigrating Companies Reports, 1850–1862, CR 1234 5, CHL. Williams

Camp, Davis County, Utah Territory Slave Schedule [draft], 1850 [1851]. Charlotte Camp, 22 July [1853], entries 334 (grave B-2-13) and 1322 or 1324 (grave B-2-8), Utah Archives and Records Service, *Salt Lake County (UT) Death Records, 1849–1949*. FSFT. https://www.familysearch.org/search/collection/1459704. Ellen C. Greer and Anonymous, Anecdotes and Reminiscences of Her Life as Related by Grandma Ellen C. Greer, May 19, 1921, MS 7776, 8, CHL. Carter, *Negro Pioneer*, 39–44. Elizabeth Camp v. Williams Camp, Petition for Divorce, April 1856, Salt Lake County Probate Court Case Files, Series 373, box 3, folder 139, USHS. Elizabeth Camp v. Williams Camp, Petition for Divorce and Alimony, November 1861, Salt Lake County Probate Court Case Files, Series 373, box 3, folder 139, USHS. W. Paul Reeve, email message to author, September 13, 2014. Amelia Camp v. Williams Camp, Petition for Divorce and Alimony, June 1862, Salt Lake County Probate Court Case Files, Series 373, box 8, folder 48, USHS. Amelia Camp v. Williams Camp, Petition for Divorce and Alimony, September 1864, Salt Lake County Probate Court Case Files, Series 373, box 9, folder 71, USHS. Ruth Camp v. Williams Camp, Bill for Divorce, May 11, 1865, Salt Lake County Probate Court Case Files, Series 373, box 9, folder 152, USHS. "Third Judicial District Court," *Deseret News*, March 19, 1863. "Justices' Court," *Deseret News*, October 5, 1864.

Daniel (Camp) (Williams) (Hooper) (1833–)

Daniel was born in Tennessee on October 14, 1833. Williams and Diannah Camp took him to the Great Salt Lake Valley in 1850. Camp hired out Daniel to William H. Hooper around 1853. Daniel tried to escape when the Camp and Greer families planned to take him to Texas in 1856, but Latter-day Saint bishop Edwin D. Woolley intervened, beginning one of the only court cases to examine the legal implications of An Act in Relation to Service. Although the judge dismissed the case for lack of evidence, Daniel remained in Utah Territory.

Camp registered Daniel in probate court in 1856, claiming "the said Negroe, Daniel, since his birth up to the presant time," which suggests he had enslaved Daniel's mother. Camp sold Daniel to Thomas S. Williams in 1858. Williams sold him to William H. Hooper in 1859. The Salt Lake County Recorder's Office recorded the deed. Daniel disappeared from the public record after 1860, but he may be memorialized in the rural Rich County, Utah, landforms "Negro Dan Hollow" and "Negro Dan Spring."

Enslavers: Williams and Diannah Greer Camp; Thomas S. Williams (1827–1860) and Albina Merrill Williams (Lawson?) (1826–1914); William H. Hooper (1813–1882) and Mary Ann Knowlton Hooper (1829–1887)

Wagon Company: Shadrach Roundy (1850)

Burial: Unknown; possibly Rich County, Utah

Sources: Although it was a long shot and unsuccessful, the Rich County Public Library and County Clerk's offices tried to help identify the origin of the name of Negro Dan Hollow and Spring. June 9, 1856, June 16, 1856, Brigham Young Office Journal, box 72, folder 2, Office Files. Territory of Utah v. Williams Camp et al. (1856), Salt Lake County Probate Court Case Files, Series 373, box 4, folder 2, USHS. Stout, *Mormon Frontier*, 2:597. June 16, 1856, Elias Smith Journals, 1836–1888, MS 1319, box 1, folder 4, CHL. Affidavit of Williams Camp in regard to his Servant Daniel, July 10, 1856, Probate Register of Servants, Salt Lake County Probate Court Case Files, Series 373, box 4, folder 26, USHS. Bill of Sale for Dan, August 17, 1859, Great Salt Lake County Recorder's Office, as reproduced in Carter, *Negro Pioneer*, 42. Wm H Hooper, Great Salt Lake County, Utah Territory Slave Schedule, *1860 Census*. "1858 . . . Augst 9 Pd Miller, Russell & Co. in Negro 'Dan' 200.00." Hooper Account, Thomas S. Williams Probate, Third District Court, Salt Lake County (UT), Probate Case Files, 1852–1896, Series 1621, case 67, USHS. John W. Van Cott, *Utah Place Names: A Comprehensive Guide to the Origins of Geographic Names* (Salt Lake City, UT: University of Utah Press, 1990), 272.

Shepherd (Greer) (Camp) (Hooper) (1837–1859)

Shepherd was one of 132 enslaved people on the James Greer plantation in 1851. After Greer's death, his daughter Diannah and her husband Williams Camp traveled from Utah Territory to Mississippi for their share of the estate. Greer died intestate, and his executors divided his enslaved people into fourteen roughly equivalent lots. "Williams and Diannah inherited "Lot No 5" of Sam, Dary, Easter, Shepperd, Davy, Isaac, Isham, and Peter, together worth $4650, and they owed about $20 to the estate to make their share even.

Based on the 1856 Utah census, they only took Shepherd and Isaac to Utah Territory. The census also shows Daniel (Camp) and an enslaved woman named Caroline, who does not match the description of anyone in the Greer probate.

Diannah and Williams Camp registered Shepherd in the probate court in 1856. They told the court that he was born in 1837 in Henry County, Tennessee, that they took possession of him in January 1853 in Marshall County, Mississippi, and took him to Utah Territory in 1854. Fellow enslaver William Taylor Dennis appeared in probate court to confirm their claim of ownership.

Camp later sold Shepherd to William H. Hooper. In 1859, Shepherd and Thomas Bankhead Coleman were arguing over the attentions of Caroline and Tampian Hoye, then in the Williams household, and Thomas shot Shepherd. He died a few days later. The county death records do not list Shepherd's burial location, but he was probably buried in a pauper's grave in the Salt Lake City Cemetery.

Enslavers: Williams and Diannah Greer Camp; William H. and Mary Ann Knowlton Hooper

Wagon Company: Private or merchant company (1854)

Burial: Probably Salt Lake City, Utah

Sources: James Greer Sr., twenty-eight slaves, Marshall County, Mississippi, *1840 Census*. James M. Greer, eighty-eight slaves, Marshall County, Mississippi Slave Schedule, *1850 Census*. James Greer Probate, Division of Slaves, December 1851, Marshall County Chancery Court, Vol. 8, 137–143, Mississippi County Courthouses and Public Libraries, *Mississippi Probate Records, 1781–1930*. FSFT. https://www.familysearch.org/search/collection/2036959. Affidavit of Diannah Camp in regard to Negro boy Shepherd, July 10, 1856; Affidavit of Williams Camp in regard to Negro boy Shepard, July 10, 1856; Affidavit of Wm T. Dennis in regard to Negro boy Shepherd, July 10, 1856, Salt Lake County Probate Court Case Files, Series 373, box 4, folder 26, USHS. Camp and East households, Wards 13 and 14, Great Salt Lake County, *1856 Utah Territorial Census*.

Isaac (Greer) (Camp) (Greer) (1842–)

Isaac was enslaved by James Greer. After Greer died, his daughter Diannah Greer Camp and her husband traveled from Utah Territory to Mississippi to take possession of their inheritance, including Isaac, age nine. After a few years in Utah Territory, Isaac went with Camp daughter Ellen and her husband, Thomas Lacy Greer, to Bosque County, Texas, in 1856. When Diannah Greer Camp died in 1876 at her daughter's home in Texas, the probate showed that her estate included properties in Utah Territory and Arkansas, but neither her estate documents nor any family histories provide clues to Isaac's fate.

Enslavers: Williams and Diannah Greer Camp; Catherine Ellen Camp Greer (1837–1929) and Thomas Lacy Greer (1826–1881)

Wagon Company: Private or merchant company (1854)

Notes: Do not confuse Isaac with Ike (Camp), who supposedly was enslaved by Williams Camp in Tennessee. Besides Daniel, Shepherd, Isaac, and Carolina, the 1856 census lists an otherwise unknown Isaac in the home of Ellen Camp Greer's sister-in-law Wilmirth Greer East, although without the annotation "(colored)" like the others, so perhaps Isaac provided labor for multiple households or there were two Isaacs.

Sources: T. L. Greer, Bosque County, Texas Slave Schedule, *1860 Census*. Diannah Camp Probate, 1876, Utah County, District, and Probate Courts, Utah, Wills and Probate Records.

Carolina (Greer) (Camp) (Greer) (1837–)

Williams and Diannah Greer Camp took Carolina to Utah Territory in 1854. She was baptized a member of the Church of Jesus Christ of Latter-day Saints in 1855. Her baptismal record said she was born in Tennessee in 1837. She may have been enslaved by Diannah's father, James Greer, but she was not listed in his estate documents.

Thomas and Ellen Camp Greer took Carolina to Texas in 1856. The Greers were the only Latter-day Saints in Bosque County who enslaved laborers: two women, two men, and two boys born in Texas. Besides a later memory of Carolina cooking Christmas dinner in Texas and her probable appearance in the 1860 census slave schedule and tax records, nothing more is known of her. When the Greer family moved to Arizona Territory in the 1870s, they took a young Black man with them, Jeff Tribbett (1857–1917), who may have been Carolina's son. He and several members of the Greer family took part in a fatal 1882 shootout, and then he spent most of the rest of his life working at the Los Angeles County Hospital.

Enslavers: Williams and Diannah Greer Camp; Thomas Lacy and Catherine Ellen Camp Greer

Wagon Company: Private or merchant company (1854)

Sources: Carolina, Coloured, [born] Tennessee, December 25, 1837, 1st [Baptism Apl 5, 1855 by H. G. Eldredge, Confirmed Apl 5, 1855 by Daniel Shearer], Thirteenth Ward Record of Members, LR 6133 7, CHL. W. Paul Reeve, email message to author, September 10, 2018. T. L. Greer, Bosque County, Texas Slave Schedule, *1860 Census.* T. L. Greer, Bosque County, 1860, 1862, *Texas, County Tax Rolls.* Ned H. Greenwood, "The Greers of Apache County," TN-1316590, FHL. Dean Smith, "Sheepmen vs. Cattlemen: The Bloodiest Range War in Apache County," *Arizona Highways* 71, no. 2 (February 1995): 32–35. Carter, *Negro Pioneer,* 41. Jeff Tribbett, Los Angeles County, CA, *1900 Census.* Jeff Tribbett, Los Angeles County, California, *1910 Census.*

Church

Tom (Church) (Smoot) (1820–1862)

Tom was enslaved by Abraham Church, and then Church's son Haden Wells Church, who traveled from his missionary work in England to rural Hickman County, Tennessee, to help settle his father's estate. English immigrant James T. Wilson traveled to the United States with Haden W. Church and remembered that Church inherited Tom. As they crossed the country, Church left Tom with the migrating Saints. Officials arrested and beat Tom in Jackson County, Missouri, when he could not produce a slave pass. Wilson intervened on Tom's behalf, and Tom was freed to go west in the A. O. Smoot wagon company.

In 1854, Henry A. Cheever baptized "Tom Brother Churches Black man" a member of the Sugar House Ward of the Church of Jesus Christ of Latter-day Saints. The Church and Smoot families were neighbors in Great Salt Lake City, and A. O. Smoot either hired or purchased Tom. In 1855, Margaret McMeans Smoot accompanied her husband to Big Cottonwood Canyon where he was supervising the building of a road, and wrote in her diary, "the men have to work in the water and Mr Smoot too[.] A Bro. Hunt is sick and <Tom> to day from being in the water it is hard work." Margaret's diary occasionally mentioned Tom helping develop and use irrigation systems in agriculture, perhaps working both for the Smoot families and the Latter-day Saint effort to create a sugar factory. He also appears to have driven Smoot family members between Sugar House and downtown Salt Lake City. The diary situates Tom in a busy household with the Smoot family, hired laborers, and his close associate for several years, orphaned Joseph Abbott, who was killed by lightning in 1859.

The 1860 census slave schedule showed Tom in the Smoot household along with Jerry (Lewis), formerly the property of Duritha Lewis. The census listed both men as Black and forty years old. The descendants of Emanuel Murphy remembered "Old Tom" along with Phoebe, an enslaved woman in the Murphy household, and perhaps the two became friends or married. Tom and Phoebe both died just months before they would have become free when Congress ended slavery in the territories. Tom died of "Inflam of Chest," perhaps pneumonia or tuberculosis.

Enslavers: Haden Wells Church (1824–1875) and Sarah Ann Arterbury Church (1824–1889); Abraham O. Smoot and Margaret Thompson McMeans Smoot (1810–1884)

Wagon Company: Abraham O. Smoot (1852)

Burial: B-4 (Pauper), Salt Lake City Cemetery, Salt Lake City, Utah

Notes: James T. Wilson wrote his account mentioning Tom almost forty years after the events and confused a few details, but his memories agree with most contemporaneous documentation. Wilson thought Tom drowned (it was Jerry), thus placing Tom in the Smoot household: "A. O. Smoot, of Salt Lake, at last owned this nigger and finally he was drowned while bathing." An unnamed elderly resident of St. George, Utah, remembered a Black man with Haden Wells Church in St. George, but all records suggest that this was a late memory of Tom, who never would have been in St. George. (Carter, *Negro Pioneer*, 65.)

Sources: Abram Church, Hickman County, Tennessee Slave Schedule, *1850 Census.* James T. Wilson, "The Life of James Thomas Wilson," c. 1889, typescript edited by Cordelia D. W. Hortin, William W. Hortin, and Frances G. Hortin, 1992, Family Search Digital Library. *History of Jackson County*, 113, 193–94, 776, 833, 845. Isaac M. Ridge, M.D., *A Memorial and Biographical Record of Kansas City and Jackson County, Mo.* (Chicago, IL: Lewis Publishing, 1896), 19–24. William C. Jones, ed., *The Revised Statutes of the State of Missouri* (St. Louis, MO: J. W. Dougherty, 1845), 777, 1016–17. Record of Members, [1848]–1938, Sugar House Ward, microfilm 26792, FHL. Margaret T. Smoot, Journal, excerpted by Mindy Smoot Robbins, Margaret T. Smoot Papers, 1838–1884, A. O. Smoot Papers, MSS 896, Special Collections, HBLL. Margaret T. Smoot Sketch Book, Abraham Owen Smoot Family Papers, 1836–1947, MSS 3843, Special Collections, HBLL. Thomas Church, Sugar House Ward, Great Salt Lake County, *1856 Utah Territorial Census.* A. O. Smoot, Great Salt Lake County, Utah Territory Slave Schedule, *1860 Census.* "Tom a negro Belonging to Bishop Smoot 29 [Apr 1862] Inflam of Chest," Utah Archives and Records Service, Utah Death Registers. Hyrum B. Ipson, "Haden Wells Church," FSFT. Digital Copy of Typescript. Accessed March 9, 2016. https://familysearch.org/photos/stories/936637. W. Paul Reeve, email message to author, August 4, 2019.

Crosby

Toby (Crosby) Embers (1797–1866?)

Toby Embers was born in the Northwest Territory. He may have been enslaved by French settlers in the region and sold to South Carolina native John Crosby in Knox County, Indiana Territory. John Crosby's son William later purchased a man named Grief Embers from his grandfather's estate. Grief was about twenty years younger than Toby but said to be his brother. The two may have belonged to the estate of William Embry, who died in 1815. Descendants of the former Embers slaves or servants lived in Knox County until after the Civil War. Due to the laws of the territory, Toby and Grief Embers probably entered the Crosby households as indentured rather than enslaved servants, but every existing legal record treated them as chattel slaves.

William Crosby and his family moved to Mississippi. In 1848, he took many of his enslaved workers to Utah Territory. During the journey to the Great Salt Lake Valley, Homer Duncan "came across t[w]o negroes, who belonged to the Company. and they had their guns well loaded." He borrowed a weapon and shot a bear. Duncan did not name the two men in his story, a common practice if the enslaved were even mentioned at all, but they fit the description of Toby and Grief Embers.

Embers accompanied Crosby to San Bernardino in 1851, where he became a free man around 1856. Toby had two children, Charles and Martha, with Hannah Smiley, who was enslaved by Robert and Rebecca Dorn Smith. (See Hannah's entry for more about their family.) The Crosby families must have relied on their enslaved peoples' ignorance of the law and actively sought to create a fear of freedom in them since Toby's daughter remembered hearing her "people laugh in later years over the terror they felt on reaching California and learning they were no longer slaves." She said, "They did not know how they could live, and begged their former owners to take them back to a slave state."

In 1858, Toby and his family held a dance in their new home in San Bernardino. Joseph McFeely and others demanded entrance to the party. Embers objected, and McFeely beat him and drove everyone out of the home. Embers swore out a complaint with the justice of the peace. When McFeely received the complaint, he found Toby at the office of James W. Wilson. He drew a pistol and threatened "a certain couloured <man> by the name of Toby Ember that he would shoot him the said Toby Ember if he did not eat a certain a paper charging him the said McFeely with doing a certain unlawful act." Wilson swore in a subsequent complaint that he was sure that McFeely would have shot Embers if he did not eat the paper. A jury found McFeely not guilty.

Embers died around 1866, with the year suggested by a delinquent property tax notice in Hannah's name. An 1868 record named Hannah as Toby's widow when she transferred her property to her two children with Toby. San Bernardino does not have burial records from the time, but Toby and Hannah Embers would have been buried in the San Bernardino Pioneer Cemetery.

Documented Family: Possible brother Grief Embers; wife Hannah Smiley (1821/1825–1868?) and children Charles Embers (1849–1935, married Jane Thompson and Dolores Salcido) and Martha Embers (1854–1932, married Israel Beal)

Enslavers: Elizabeth Coleman Crosby (1785–1849); William Crosby (1808–1880) and Sarah Harmon Crosby (1808–1888)

Wagon Company: Willard Richards (1848)

Burial: San Bernardino Pioneer Cemetery, San Bernardino, California

Notes: Charmaine Lay Kohler's interpretation of the family history, *Southern Grace,* is historical fiction and cannot be used as a reliable source. The connection is not clear between Elizabeth Coleman Crosby and her purported parents, Joseph and Sytha Coleman, of Union District, South Carolina, since Elizabeth is not named in Coleman's will or probate, but she may be one of the otherwise unidentified daughters: Mary, Anne, or Sytha. The family used the unusual female name Sytha over multiple generations.

Sources: Joseph Coleman, Union District, South Carolina *1800 Census.* Joseph Coleman Will, 1806, Union County; Joseph Coleman Probate, box 4, Package 45, South Carolina County, District, and Probate Courts, *South Carolina, Wills and Probate Records, 1670–1980.* Ancestry.com. https://www.ancestry.com/search/collections/9080. William Embry Will, Knox County, 1815, Indiana County, District, and Probate Courts, *Indiana, Wills and Probate Records, 1798–1999.* Ancestry.com. https://www.ancestry.com/search/collections/9045. Tyre Embers, Knox County, Indiana, *1880 Census.* John Crosby, 1839, Monroe County Tax Rolls 1822–1841, box 3723, Mississippi Department of Archives and History, Various Records, 1820–1951. FSFT. https://www.familysearch.org/search/collection/1919687. John Crosby Probate, Monroe County, 1842, Mississippi County, District, and Probate Courts, Mississippi, Wills and Probate Records, 1780–1982. Ancestry.com. https://www.ancestry.com/search/collections/8995. John Brown's Company of 10, June 1848, Camp of Israel Schedules and Reports. Homer Duncan, Autobiographical Sketch, c. 1900, typescript of holograph, MS 21280, CHL. Toby, Utah County, Utah Territory Slave Schedule [draft], 1850 [1851]. William Crosby, Utah County, Utah Territory Slave Schedule [draft], 1850

[1851]. Toby, Los Angeles County, *1852 California Census*. State of California v. Joseph McFeely (1858), Justice Court of San Bernardino, case 42, SBCHA. Hannah Smiley, San Bernardino County, California, National Archives, *IRS Tax Assessment Lists, 1862–1918*. Ancestry.com. https://www.ancestry.com/search/collections/1264. Hannah Embers to Charles Embers and Martha Embers, Conveyance, June 26, 1868, San Bernardino Property Records, 288, SBCHA. Emma Lou Thornbrough, *The Negro in Indiana: A Study of a Minority* (Indianapolis, IN: Indiana Historical Bureau, 1957). Earl E. McDonald, "Disposal of Negro Slaves by Will in Knox County, Indiana," *Indiana Magazine of History* 26, no. 2 (June 1930): 145. https://www.jstor.org/stable/27786437. Robertalee Lent and June B. Barekman, *Knox Co. Indiana Early Land Records Court Indexes*, Vol. 2 (Post Falls, ID: Genealogical Reference Builders, 1966). *History of Knox and Daviess Counties, Indiana* (Chicago, IL: Goodspeed Publishing Co., 1886), 208. George W. Beattie and Helen P. Beattie, *Heritage of the Valley: San Bernardino's First Century* (Oakland, CA: Biobooks, 1951), 186, quoted in Byron R. Skinner, *Black Origins in the Inland Empire, Heritage Tales, Sixth Annual Publication of the City of San Bernardino Historical and Pioneer Society* (San Bernardino, CA: City of San Bernardino Historical and Pioneer Society, 1983), 28. "Mormon Colony in Sharp Contrast to Mother Lode," *San Bernardino County Sun* (San Bernardino, CA), September 30, 1951. Edward Leo Lyman, *San Bernardino: The Rise and Fall of a California Community* (Salt Lake City, UT: Signature Books, 1996). DeEtta Demaratus, *The Force of a Feather: The Search for a Lost Story of Slavery and Freedom* (Salt Lake City, UT: University of Utah Press, 2002), 181–82. L. A. Ingersoll, *Ingersoll's Century Annals of San Bernardino County, 1769 to 1904* (Los Angeles, CA: L. A. Ingersoll, 1904), 350–51. Charmaine Lay Kohler, *Southern Grace: A Story of the Mississippi Saints* (Boise, ID: Beagle Creek Press, 1995).

Edy (Crosby) (1827–)

Elizabeth Crosby took Edy to the Great Salt Lake Valley in 1848. She may be Esther Harmon (see later entry), but no documents connect the two women, and both disappear from known records: Edy around 1848 and Esther around 1855. Another possibility is a woman named Iddy shown with a young man named James in the draft population schedule of the

1850 census for Utah County as "Free Black" in company with the San Bernardino settlers.

Enslavers: Elizabeth Coleman Crosby

Wagon Company: Willard Richards (1848)

Notes: See the entry for Esther Harmon. Due to dates and listed cash value, Edy in the John Crosby Jr. probate is not Edy in the William Jeter will. (William Jeter Will, 1797, South Carolina County, District, and Probate Courts, *South Carolina, Wills and Probate Records.*)

Sources: James and Iddy, Utah County, Utah Territory population schedule [draft], 1850 [1851], MS 2672, box 1, folder 9, CHL.

Mary (Crosby) Bankhead Sampson Chism (1827–1884)

Mary (Crosby) Bankhead Sampson Chism was a member of a Latter-day Saint wagon company, an early settler of San Bernardino, and eventually a successful property owner. She may be Mariah, inherited by Ann Crosby Thomas upon the death of her father, and then taken by Ann's mother, Elizabeth Coleman Crosby, to Utah Territory.

Mary shows up next as the property of Ann's brother William, who took her to San Bernardino with her two children. Crosby also took her unnamed enslaved husband from the Bankhead household. She had one additional child with the unnamed man.

When Mary was freed, Daniel M. Thomas wrote, "And Sallys [Sarah Harmon Crosby's] maid Servant Mary did find favor in the Eyes of Samuel [Sampson] a man of light color who came down with the Bishop from the land of Ophor [sic]." Thomas continued, "and he did look upon Mary and behold She did look fair and he did take her for a wife, and there is a Saying that they will only Sojourn with her mistress a few days."

Mary and Samuel Sampson did not remain together after the birth of their two sons, and Mary remarried barber Andrew Chism of Kentucky. Her sons Robert and Thomas were active in Black Los Angeles politics. When Mary Chism died in 1884, her children were spread throughout the region working mostly in service or transient occupations, and the government sold her property at auction after her children failed to pay property taxes. Mary (Crosby) Bankhead Sampson Chism has no known living descendants.

Documented Family: Husband (Unknown) Bankhead and children Nancy Bankhead (1848–1875, married James A. Jefferson), George Bankhead Chism (1851–), and John C. Bankhead Chism (1854–); husband Samuel Sampson (1823–) and children Thomas W. Sampson (1857–1917) and Samuel Henry Sampson (1859–); husband Andrew Chism or Chisholm (1828–) and children Maggie Chism (1868–1941, married Charles Hudgins), James Chism (1870–), and Robert Chism (1871–).

Enslavers: Elizabeth Coleman Crosby; William and Sarah Harmon Crosby

Wagon Company: Willard Richards (1848)

Burial: Probably California

Notes: Sources occasionally spell Chism as "Chisolm." "Ophir" may mean Ophir, Placer County, California, mostly destroyed by fire in 1853, or it may be a general reference to the gold mining regions of California. Mary Chism is not in the burial records of the cemetery in Santa Monica, where she lived when she died.

Sources: Mary, Utah County, Utah Territory Slave Schedule [draft], 1850 [1851]. Daniel M. Thomas to Amasa Lyman, Incoming Letters P–Y 1856, box 4, folder 1, Amasa M. Lyman Collection, MS 829, CHL (hereafter, Lyman Collection). "The Ophir Fire—Additional Particulars," *Sacramento Daily Union*, July 15, 1853. Mary Chism, San Bernardino County, California, *1860 Census*. Mary Bankhead and Andrew Chism, Marriage, May 1, 1864, California Department of Public Health, *California, County Birth, Marriage, and Death Records, 1830–1980*, Ancestry.com. Samuel Samson, paralyzed, Los Angeles County, California Schedules of Defective, Dependent, and Delinquent Classes, *1880 Census* (Berkeley, CA: Bancroft Library, University of California, and Provo, UT: Ancestry.com, 2010). Mary Sumption, Los Angeles County, California, *1870 Census*. "Local Brevities," *Los Angeles Herald*, October 24, 1874. Mary Chism, Los Angeles County, California, *1880 Census*. "City Property ... Delinquent Taxes," *Los Angeles Herald*, February 3, 1882. "The Courts [Mary Chism estate]," *Los Angeles Times* (Los Angeles, CA), November 4, 1884. "The Emancipation Hall," *Los Angeles Herald*, January 3, 1886. "Santa Monica," *Los Angeles Herald*, May 8, 1892. "In Santa Monica City," *Los Angeles Herald*, June 23, 1894. "To Quiet Title," *Los Angeles Herald*, April 1,

1896. "Official Public Records," *Los Angeles Herald*, May 11, 1901. "Attachments," *Los Angeles Herald*, July 10, 1902. "Charles Morrell and Robert Chism, colored, are looking for H. L. Leggett of the California Carnival Company. They want to collect $200 alleged to be due them in salaries." "Alameda County News," *San Francisco Call* (San Francisco, CA), June 17, 1905. Woodlawn Cemetery, Santa Monica, California, telephone conversation with the author, January 9, 2018.

Oscar (Crosby) Smith (1815–1872)

When John Crosby died, executors set Oscar's value at $550, and he became the property of Crosby's son William. The census stated twice that Smith was born in Virginia, so he could have been inherited from Crosby grandparents in Virginia or purchased from slave traders, but a granddaughter of Martha Flake remembered that he was born in Mississippi and was the brother of Hark Wales and Martha Flake. There is no known contemporaneous documentation of the relationships among the enslaved people from the John Crosby plantation. Martha's granddaughter also remembered that Smith tried to escape in the South. "His head was through the rails and he could not get his body through as he was a large man. He was caught & beat. He went through life with his head twisted to one side."

The Crosby family sent Smith in the first Latter-day Saint wagon company to the Great Salt Lake Valley in 1847 so he could prepare a home for the family's arrival the next year. Two weeks after Smith reached the Great Salt Lake Valley, he participated in the Latter-day Saint practice of baptism or rebaptism and confirmation. Nelson Higgins baptized him, and Apostle George A. Smith confirmed him.

William Crosby took Smith to San Bernardino in 1851. When he was freed in 1856, he moved to Los Angeles with Grief and Harriet Embers, where he was active in political and religious life. Along with Biddy Mason, he was one of the founders of the AME Church in Los Angeles.

Smith appeared twice in the 1860 census, both times listed with a Native American man, Juan Jose, and associated with the African American families of John and Mandy Ballard and Daniel and Sarah Jefferson. Multiple census entries are no surprise: Mary Chism's son George appeared three times in the same census.

When Smith helped celebrate the Fifteenth Amendment to the Constitution and his new right to vote, local Democratic politicians were courting the Black vote. Mississippi native Col. Edward K. C. Kewen addressed "'his colored brethren, ladies and gentlemen,' saying that he and his friend Oscar Smith, colored, were born in the same State, and had always been friends. . . . He had loved the negroes as slaves and hoped that they would love him now that they were free." The newspaper editorialized, "The scene was quite touching, and might have brought tears to the eyes of some of the Colonel's partisans, but we regret to say that some of the profane have since swore about it."

Although later reports said Smith died in 1870, he and a widowed housekeeper, Doña Antonia Slater (1815–), lived that year by Elizabeth Flake Rowan and her family. Despite his participation in the Fifteenth Amendment celebrations, Oscar Smith never had the chance to vote. His heart gave out in 1872, and he was buried in the old Los Angeles City Cemetery. The cemetery was paved over, or burials were moved over the years without records kept of the removals, so Oscar Smith's final resting place is unknown.

Enslavers: William and Sarah Harmon Crosby

Wagon Company: Brigham Young (1847)

Burial: Old Los Angeles City Cemetery, Los Angeles, California

Notes: None of those enslaved by the Crosby family is known to have used the surname Crosby, so a researcher would not expect to find Oscar under that name. Daniel Thomas wrote in early 1856 that Oscar moved with Grief and Harriet Embers to Los Angeles, and Daughters of Utah Pioneers said he died in Los Angeles in 1870. The only Black man in Los Angeles named Oscar was Oscar Smith, and he was closely associated with Elizabeth Flake Rowan and Biddy Mason. Oscar is an infrequently used name, and there were no discernable alternate identities for Oscar Smith. His age and both birthplaces appear within acceptable margins of error, and his 1872 death was close to the reported death date. An 1873 city directory, printed after his death, showed Smith twice, once on Fort Street and once at the U.S. Hotel.

Sources: For 1847 sources, see Green Flake. Daniel M. Thomas to Lyman, Lyman Collection. Carter, *Negro Pioneer*, 8. Oscar Crosby, Rebaptism record, 1850–1863, Historian's Office Rebaptism Records, 1848–1876, CR 100 591, folder 1, 3, CHL. Oscar, Utah County, Utah Territory Slave Schedule [draft], 1850 [1851]. Oscar Smith and Juan Jose; Juan Jose and Oscar Smith, Los Angeles County, California, *1860 Census*. "Letter from Bishop Ward," *Elevator*, September 3, 1869. "Housebreaking [Doña Antonia Slater victim]," *Los Angeles Star* (Los Angeles, CA), January 28, 1860. Antonia A. Slater, Los Angeles County, California, *1860 Census*. Oscar Smith and Antonia Slater, Los Angeles County, California, *1870 Census*. "Los Angeles," *Elevator*, March 11, 1870. "Celebration of the Fifteenth Amendment by the Colored People," *Elevator*, April 22, 1870. Oscar Smith, March 13, 1872, 72 [sic] years old, "Negro—heart disease," Southern California Genealogical Society, "Los Angeles City Cemetery," *SCGS Genealogy*. http://www.scgsgenealogy.com/free/LACC-Title.html. *Los Angeles City and County Directory* (Los Angeles, CA: King & Stratton, 1873), 11. "Oscar Crosby (colored), born in Virginia about 1815." "Genealogy: Genesis of the Hundred and Forty-Three Utah Pioneers," *Salt Lake Herald*, May 30, 1915. Notes from Udell Home.

Violet (Crosby) (Bankhead) Vallentyne Litchford (1798–)

Violet was one of the oldest of all the enslaved African American people in Utah Territory. The loss of Violet's memories is particularly keen, as she would have had extensive information about the workings of a slave society and life in the Crosby and Bankhead households.

From the time Violet appeared in John Crosby's probate in the 1840s until the unknown end of her life, she lived with a younger woman named Rose. They seem to be mother and daughter, but no documents confirm the relationship. On some plantations, all the children were given into the care of one woman while their mothers worked, so Violet may have been the mother of Rose, Martha, Oscar, and Hark as some later remembered, or she may have been their caretaker. Oscar and Hark have no known descendants, so DNA tests cannot confirm relationships. Violet may have had a husband with a given or family name of Morris, since Martha's grandchildren claimed Morris as her maiden name.

The census listed Violet's birthplace as South Carolina, Virginia, and Georgia, which suggests that those who provided the information did not know where she was born. However, some of her children or foster children consistently claimed to be from Virginia, so she may have been enslaved since birth by the Coleman or Jeter families of Virginia.

When John Crosby died, Violet became the property of William and Sarah Harmon Crosby. They took Violet to the Great Salt Lake Valley in 1848. Crosby planned to take Violet and Rose to California in 1851 but left them to work for his brother-in-law John H. Bankhead. The two women lived in a home with Green Flake. Violet, Rose, Rose's children, and a succession of partners or husbands lived together until Violet's death.

Documented Family: None, although based on later memories, she may have been the wife of Morris and the mother of Oscar Smith, Hark Wales, Martha Flake, and Rose Crosby; possible relative Miles Litchford (1805–c.1899)

Enslavers: William and Sarah Harmon Crosby; probably John and Nancy Crosby Bankhead

Wagon Company: Willard Richards (1848)

Burial: I-11, Union Fort Pioneer Cemetery, Cottonwood Heights, Utah

Notes: Violet's name was alternately spelled Vilet (Crosby probate and 1848 wagon roster), Vilate (1850 census and Daughters of Utah Pioneers sources), Violate (1860 and 1870 census and Fretwell Collection), Violett (1855 newspaper notice), Violet (1856 newspaper notice and cemetery record), and Villott (1872 petition). In consultation with her family, she appears as Violet throughout this book. (Juanita Reynolds, email message to author, July 11, 2020.) For documentation that Crosby left Violet and Rose with the Bankhead family, see a list of letters at the post office. "Bankhead Violett ... Bankhead Thomas ... Bankhead Nathan ... Esther (a colored woman." ("List of Letters," *Deseret News*, April 4, 1855; see also Violet Bankhead in "List of Letters," *Deseret News*, July 2, 1856.)

Sources: Vilate, Utah County, Utah Territory Slave Schedule [draft], 1850 [1851]. Vilate Crosby, Great Salt Lake County, Utah Territory, *1850 Census*. Violate Vollantyne, Salt Lake County, Utah Territory, *1860 Census*. Violate Litchford, Salt Lake County, Utah Territory, *1870 Census*. "Against the

Admission of Utah as a State. Memorial of the Citizens of Utah against the Admission of the Territory as a State, May 6, 1872," *The Miscellaneous Documents Printed by Order of the House of Representatives* (Washington, DC: Government Printing Office, 1872), 24. Notes from Udell Home. Daughters of Utah Pioneers, "Fort Union Pioneer Cemetery Memorial."

Rose Harmon Crosby (Flake?) (Bankhead) (Priesly) Vallentyne/ Banks Litchford Catlin (1835–)

William Crosby left Rose and her mother Violet in the Great Salt Lake Valley when he went to California in 1851. The two women moved into a home with Green Flake, so Rose, not Martha, may have been Green's wife mentioned in a letter to Brigham Young. Rose gained her freedom through the intervention of Brigham Young in the early 1850s and named her first son Daniel Freeman to celebrate their liberation. Daughter of Utah Pioneers remembered the historic occasion in a garbled form: "Rose, the daughter of Vilate Crosby, was the mother of . . . Dan Bankhead, who was called 'Dan Freeman' as he was the first Negro child born after they arrived in Utah." Daniel would have been the twelfth to fourteenth Black child born in the valley since 1847, but the first among the small group of newly freed, and the claim would have changed as people forgot its original context.

Violet and Rose made a life for themselves in Union, south of downtown Salt Lake City. Rose had eight known children with at least four fathers: an unnamed Bankhead man, Scottish immigrant John Priestly, Ohio native Miles Litchford, and James Vallentyne or Valentine, later Banks, a different man than the older James Valentine, who married Nancy Bankhead. There is no known documentation for any marriage, and sometimes her relationships overlapped. Carrie Bankhead Leggroan and Celia Bankhead Leggroan remembered her as "the old lady that lived back of us" and confirmed that Rose "wasn't married . . . she was going with . . . two or three fellas at that time," although they recalled that she married someone named Valentine.

Rose's longest relationship or marriage may have been with freeborn Ohio native Miles Litchford, who mined with Green Flake and others in the mountains above the Salt Lake Valley. Rose and Miles may have had five children: Catherine, Rose, Susannah, Caroline, and Cordelia or Martha.

After Violet died, Rose lived with her son Daniel Freeman Bankhead and his wife Celia Douglass (later Grice). Her two youngest daughters lived with Green and Martha Flake. Based on many such clues, Rose may have had a disability and been unable to care for her family. There is no record of her death date or burial place, but her family may have buried her by Violet in the Union Pioneer Cemetery. Her descendants still live in the Salt Lake Valley.

Documented Family: Possible mother Violet and father Morris; possible husband Green Flake; son with (unknown) Bankhead: Daniel Freeman Bankhead (1854–, married Celia Douglass Bankhead Grice); son with John Priestly: John Priesly or Priestly (1858–1921, married Sarah); children with Miles Litchford (1805–c.1899): Catherine Litchford (1860–1917, married John Patterson and J. R. Walker, and had a child with William Bergen), Rose Litchford (1863–), Susannah Litchford (1867–), Caroline Litchford (1869–), and Cordelia or Martha Litchford (1871–1891); child with James Vallentyne/Banks (1830–): Isaac Frederic Valentine/Banks (1866–1939, married Sina Bankhead)

Enslavers: William and Sarah Harmon Crosby; probably John and Nancy Crosby Bankhead

Wagon Company: Willard Richards (1848)

Burial: Possibly Union Fort Pioneer Cemetery, Cottonwood Heights, Utah

Notes: Rose appeared in records with the last names Catlin and Miles, but Miles may be a reference to Miles Litchford, since her sister was listed once as Martha Green, possibly in reference to her husband Green Flake. In 1860, James Vallentyne/Banks was arrested for theft. In 1862, he led a group of about twenty-five youth in a rowdy celebration of a marriage called a "charivari," and he was arrested along with Nephi Owen and William Woolsey. Banks may have moved back and forth between Utah and Nevada. He appeared last in any known record in 1870.

Sources: Rose, Utah County, Utah Territory Slave Schedule [draft], 1850 [1851]. Rose, Great Salt Lake County, Utah Territory, *1850 Census.* Rosannah Vollantyne, Salt Lake County, Utah Territory, *1860 Census.* Rose Litchford, Salt Lake County, Utah Territory, *1870 Census.* Rosanna Miles [perhaps meaning Miles Litchford], Salt Lake County, Utah Territory, *1880 Census.* "Local News," *Mountaineer* (Salt Lake City, UT), September 8, 1860. "Doings of the Probate Court," *Deseret News,* September 12, 1860. "A Colored Gentleman in Trouble," *Deseret News,* April 13, 1870. "Agents for the Elevator," *Elevator,* June 24, 1870. Carter, *Negro Pioneer,* 22–23. Leggroan and Leggroan Interview, 19. "Against the Admission of Utah as a State," 24 [487]. John Priesly, son of Rose Harmon, August 16, 1921, Salt Lake City, death certificate 2102581, Utah Department of Health, USHS.

Grief (Crosby) Embers (1816–1873)

Grief was born in Indiana and may have belonged by life interest to Sarah Jeter Crosby the first twenty-five years of his life. When Sarah died, her grandson William Crosby purchased Grief from his grandfather's estate. On the day that William purchased Grief, neither of them could have imagined that ten years later, they would be living not in Mississippi, but in San Bernardino, California, after having moved to Utah Territory in 1848, then California in 1851.

A San Bernardino historian remembered, "Uncle Grief, a colored man, had a large tin horn, about six feet long . . . He acted as bugler and blew his horn to assemble the men, or for other purposes."

Daniel M. Thomas wrote in a letter that when they discovered they were free, Grief and his wife Harriet (Lay) and Oscar Smith immediately left San Bernardino for Los Angeles. Grief and Harriet Embers provided homes to their niece Martha and Tennessee "Harriet" Jackson's daughters Louisa and Harriet.

Despite the initial lure of Los Angeles, Grief and Toby Embers returned to San Bernardino and purchased property vacated by the Latter-day Saints. Grief and Harriet eventually owned three of the four lots on the south side of the block fronting West 4th Street between F and G Streets.

Not long before Embers died, an inebriated Michael Murphy accosted him on the street. In his attempt to defend himself, Grief broke Murphy's leg, but since he acted in self-defense, he suffered no legal consequences.

The *San Bernardino Guardian* described Grief upon his death as "respected by all who knew him." Harriet died about four years later. Two decades after Grief died, the man who purchased their land discovered that the estate never went through probate, so he filed documents in court, including one that stated, "That the true name of said decedent was and is Grief Embers, but he was often called and known by the name of Grief Crosby."

In a puzzling addendum to Grief's story, John Brown wrote during a trip to Mississippi in 1867: "Here I met a colored man named Grief. He once belonged to Mother Crosby. He was glad to see me." Brown explained that all the freed enslaved people had left the area and moved into towns and cities. Perhaps Grief sought his family or friends in Mississippi, and hopefully he found them.

Documented Family: Possible brother Toby Embers; wife Harriet Lay and foster children Louisa Jackson (1857–1913, married George Pollard) and Harriet Jackson (1860–, married George Washington)

Enslavers: William and Sarah Harmon Crosby

Wagon Company: Willard Richards (1848)

Burial: Probably San Bernardino Pioneer Cemetery, San Bernardino, California

Notes: Do not confuse Harriet Embers or Harriet Jackson Washington with Harriet Mason Washington, the daughter of Biddy Mason. The account of Grief returning to Mississippi is in John Brown's autobiography, but not in his holograph diary, so the editor presumably added the story from the letters Brown mentions writing home.

Sources: William Jeter Will, 1793, Edgefield County, South Carolina County, District, and Probate Courts, *South Carolina, Wills and Probate Records*. John Crosby Sr., Probate, 1841, case 158, Monroe County, Mixed Estate and Probate Court Files, Mississippi County Courthouses, *Mississippi Probate Records*. Grief, Utah County, Utah Territory Slave Schedule [draft], 1850 [1851]. Grief, Los Angeles County, *1852 California Census*. Daniel M. Thomas to Lyman, Lyman Collection. Grief Embers, San Bernardino County, California, *1860 Census*. Grief Ambrose, San Bernardino County, California, *1870 Census*. Transfer, William Baxter to Grief Embers, July 30, 1861, 213–215; Transfer, Q. S. Sparks to Grief Embers, January 23, 1867, 456, SBCHA. Grief Embers Death, October 8, 1873, San Bernardino Death Records, SBCHA. Petition for Letters of Administration for Harriet Embers Estate, June 8, 1878, Probate Book D, 78–80,

SBCHA. "Grief Embers, a well-known colored man, died suddenly about noon yesterday, from the bursting of a blood vessel. He died respected by all who knew him." *San Bernardino Guardian*, as quoted in Nicholas R. Cataldo, "Man Called Grief Brought Much Joy," *San Bernardino Sun* (San Bernardino, CA), April 20, 2009. https://www.sbsun.com/general-news/20090420/man-called-grief-brought-much-joy. Ingersoll, *Annals of San Bernardino*, 135. "Town of San Bernardino–1853–1854," Map, *City of San Bernardino* (website). Accessed March 1, 2017. http://www.ci.san-bernardino.ca.us/about/history/fort_san_bernardino.asp. Joan Hedges McCall, *Redlands Remembered: Stories from the Jewel of the Inland Empire* (Charleston, SC: History Press, 2012), 12–15. Skinner, *Black Origins*, 47, based on an account in *San Bernardino Guardian*, April 5, 1873. "Real Estate Troubles," *Herald* (Los Angeles, CA), March 2, 1898. *In the matter of the Estate of Grief Embers, Deceased*, Decree of Distribution, Superior Court, San Bernardino County, February 25, 1898, Probate Book 17, 288–289, SBCHA. John Brown and John Z. Brown, *Autobiography of Pioneer John Brown 1820–1896* (Salt Lake City, UT: Press of Stevens and Wallis, 1941).

Nelson or Knelt (Crosby) Price (1833–1882)

William Crosby took Nelson from Mississippi to the Great Salt Lake Valley in 1848 and to San Bernardino in 1851. He worked for rancher Francisco Vejar in Pomona, halfway between San Bernardino and Los Angeles, in 1860. After a series of natural disasters forced Vejar from his ranch, Nelson worked in the Plummer boarding house in Los Angeles, and then as a bootblack. He died in Los Angeles.

Enslavers: William and Sarah Harmon Crosby

Wagon Company: Willard Richards (1848)

Sources: Nelson, Utah County, Utah Territory Slave Schedule [draft], 1850 [1851]. Nelson, Los Angeles County, CA, *1860 Census*. Nelson Price, Los Angeles County, California, *1870 Census*. "Council Proceedings," *Los Angeles Herald*, August 1, 1878. Nelson Price, December 9, 1882, dropsy, *California, County Birth, Marriage, and Death Records*. Paul R. Spitzzeri, "No Place Like Home: The Francisco Vejar Adobe, Pomona, ca. 1872," *The*

Homestead Blog. https://homesteadmuseum.wordpress.com/2017/01/31/no-place-like-home-the-francisco-vejar-adobe-pomona-ca-1872.

Henderson (Crosby) Houstin (1836–)

Henderson was not in the John Crosby probate, but William Crosby took him to Utah Territory in 1848 and then to San Bernardino in 1851. In 1860, he lived with Biddy Mason in Los Angeles. Nothing more is known of him.

Enslavers: William and Sarah Harmon Crosby
Wagon Company: Willard Richards (1848)
Sources: Henderson, Utah County, Utah Territory Slave Schedule [draft], 1850 [1851]. Henderson, Los Angeles County, *1852 California Census*. Henderson Houstin, Los Angeles County, California, *1860 Census*.

Nancy (Crosby) Bankhead Jefferson (1848–1875)

Nancy was one of the first Black children born in the Salt Lake Valley. Her mother was Mary Crosby Bankhead and her father an unnamed Bankhead. William Crosby took the enslaved family to San Bernardino in 1851. When Nancy's family learned they were free, they moved to Los Angeles. After Nancy's husband James Jefferson died in 1870 and her son Joseph in 1871, she worked as a household servant. When Nancy died by suicide in 1875, the newspaper reported that she had been living with an unnamed man, had been drinking, "and probably took the dose [of poison] in a fit of despondency." The newspaper did not mention that she had been freed from slavery as a child but wrote as a memorial: "Nancy was 26 years of age, and American by birth."

Documented Family: Mother Mary (Crosby) Bankhead Sampson Chism; father Unknown (Bankhead); stepfathers and siblings and half-siblings; husband James A. Jefferson (1840–1870), son Joseph Jefferson (1864–1871)
Enslavers: William and Sarah Harmon Crosby
Burial: Probably Los Angeles, California

Sources: Nancy, Utah County, Utah Territory Slave Schedule [draft], 1850 [1851]. Nancy Bankhead, San Bernardino County, California, *1860 Census*. Marriages, Marriage Licenses A, 45, James A. Jefferson, Nancy Bankhead, February 3, 1864, San Bernardino County Recorder, SBCHA. Nancy Jefferson, Los Angeles, California, *1870 Census*. James A. Jefferson, April 22, 1870; Joseph Jeferson, May 18, 1871, Southern California Genealogical Society, "Los Angeles City Cemetery." Nancy Jefferson Inquest, *Los Angeles Herald*, September 28, 1875. Nancy Jefferson Death, *Daily Alta California* (San Francisco, CA), October 1, 1875.

George (Crosby) Bankhead Chism (1850–)

George was born in the Great Salt Lake Valley to an enslaved woman named Mary and an unnamed enslaved man from the Bankhead household. When his mother discovered she was free by early 1856, she moved to Los Angeles with her children and second husband, Samuel Sampson. George Bankhead appeared three times in the 1860 census. He then took the name of his second stepfather, Andrew Chism, and learned his trade as a barber. He last appeared in a public record living with his parents in Santa Monica in 1880.

Documented Family: Mother Mary (Crosby) Bankhead Sampson Chism; father Unknown (Bankhead); stepfathers and full- and half-siblings

Enslavers: William and Sarah Harmon Crosby

Sources: George, Utah County, Utah Territory Slave Schedule [draft], 1850 [1851]. George Bankhead, San Bernardino County; George Bulkhead [*sic*], Los Angeles County; George Bankhead, Los Angeles County, CA, *1860 Census*. George Chism, Santa Monica, California, *1880 Census*.

Dennis

Nancy Lines (Bankhead) (Dennis) Smith (1816–1877)

Along with Betsy Brown Flewellen, Nancy Smith was one of two enslaved women symbolically dedicated to the work of the Church of Jesus Christ of Latter-day Saints. In 1857, Dr. William Taylor Dennis created a deed listing "1 African Servant Girl [$]500.00." The Dennis family remembered

Nancy only as a "Black Mammy" and did not preserve any personal information, including whether she left her own family in the South.

Nancy was probably enslaved from birth by George and Jane Greer Bankhead, and then given to their daughter, Talitha Bankhead, upon her marriage to Dr. Dennis, or else Talitha inherited Nancy upon her father's death. Nancy lived on the edges of American settlement her entire life, including in the Chickasaw Cession. Nancy was the only enslaved person to remain with the Dennis family after the townspeople of Tabor, Iowa, helped the others escape.

Nancy became a member of the Church of Jesus Christ of Latter-day Saints in 1857. The record of her baptism by English immigrant Thomas Karren showed her as "Nancy Lines [Dennis] Co[lored]," born on July 4, 1816 in White County, Tennessee, with parents Jerrimiah and Mary Jane White. Church records show that she paid a modest amount of tithing.

Life in the Dennis household was plagued by violence and scandal. When one of Dr. Dennis's plural wives filed for divorce, the divorce proceedings documented claims of death threats, violent beatings, and lack of financial support. The Dennis family later concluded that Nancy was buried in Piute County, Utah, but the census shows that she stayed in Utah County with Talitha Dennis when Talitha left her husband after the scandal of his illegitimate child with Marinda Redd. Nancy was buried in the Spanish Fork Cemetery along with Samuel (Bankhead) Smith, who moved from Cache Valley to join her after he was freed. He may have been a relative or husband.

Documented Family: Parents Jerrimiah [Lines?] and Mary Jane White; possible husband or relative Samuel (Bankhead) Smith

Enslavers: William Taylor Dennis (1810–1894) and Talitha Cumi Bankhead Dennis (1809–1882)

Wagon Company: Private or merchant company (1855)

Burial: Spanish Fork City Cemetery, Spanish Fork, Utah

Notes: The 1870 census shows Nancy Smith next to Talitha Dennis in Salem. They lived in two of a group of three houses, with the third house vacant. The information matches, except her color was listed as White. Since there is no alternate identity for Nancy Smith, the census taker may have mistaken "M" (Mulatto) in the draft census for "W" (White), or perhaps he did not ask about race.

Sources: George Bankhead, Marion County, Alabama, *1830 Census.* William T. Dennis, Pontotoc County, Mississippi, *1840 Census.* William T. Dennis, 1839, 1840, 1841, 1843, 1845, Pontotoc County, County Tax Rolls, box 3932, Mississippi Department of Archives and History, *Various Records.* William T. Dennis, Pontotoc County, Mississippi Slave Schedule, *1850 Census.* "Nancy (A negro)," Stone City, Cedar [later Utah] County, *1856 Utah Territorial Census.* Nancy [Dennis], Utah County, Utah Territory, *1860 Census.* Nancy Lines Dennis, Lehi Ward Book A 1856–1876, microfilm 889413, FHL. Palmyra Ward Tithing Office Ledger, 1851–1857, LR 6700 21, CHL. William Taylor Dennis, Consecration Deed, February 7, 1857, Records of Utah County (1851–1864), F:111–12. Nancy Smith, Utah County, Utah Territory, *1870 Census.* Sarah Z. Dennis v. William T. Dennis (1873), Utah County Probate Court, USHS. Nancy Bankhead, October 24, 1877, Spanish Fork (UT) Cemetery Records. "Slavery in Utah," *Broad Ax.* Anonymous, "The Life History of William Taylor Dennis and His Wife Talitha Cumi Bankhead," n.d., digital manuscript, copy in possession of author. Dennis Jones, FamilySearch message to author, September 14, 2017. Anonymous, "1. In 1856." Carl Carter, email message to author, February 28, 2020.

Dotson

Frank? (Dotson) (–1858)

Although his origins are unknown, Frank was probably enslaved by US Marshal Peter K. Dotson. Dotson was not raised in a slave household, so he may have purchased Frank during a trip to Washington, DC, in 1857, or purchased or hired him from someone in Utah Territory, perhaps business associates Thomas S. Williams or John M. Hockaday.

Robert Taylor killed Frank in 1858. A newspaper noted the rapid increase in crime following the arrival of the US Army and reported, "A short time past two colored gentlemen quarreled in the streets; one was stabbed and the other shot dead by his antagonist." When Dotson left the territory after he falsely accused Brigham Young of counterfeiting, he left unpaid bills, including a $10 charge shown in Thomas S. Williams's probate as the "Use of Carriage to Grave Y[ar]d to Convey P. K. Dodson's Negro."

Enslavers: Peter Kessler Dotson (1823–1898) and Emily Wingfield Kebbell Dotson (1827–1891)

Burial: B_4_Pauper_167, Salt Lake City Cemetery, Salt Lake City, Utah

Sources: Thomas Dotson, Greenbrier County, Virginia, *1830 Census*. Thomas Dottson, Greenbrier County, Virginia, *1840 Census*. Frank Black man, Shot by Robt Taylor, September 1, 1858, Utah Archives and Records Service, *Utah Death Registers*. August 1859, Accounts, Thomas S. Williams Probate, Third District Court Probate Case Files, Series 1621, USHS. Burton v. Dotson, Whitmore, and Burr (1861), Great Salt Lake County Probate Court. Hubert H. Bancroft, *History of Utah, 1540–1886* (San Francisco, CA: History Company, 1889), 573. "US Mail Line," *Valley Tan*, March 1, 1859. "Progress of Civilization (!)," *Deseret News*, September 15, 1858. "Progress of Civilization," *Sacramento Daily Union*, October 11, 1858.

Drummond

Cato (Harkreader) (Drummond) Smith? (1830?–)

Cato arrived in the Great Salt Lake Valley in the possession of James A. Harkreader of Tennessee, then on his way to California. Cato was attempting to liberate himself when Harkreader sold him to federal appointee Judge William W. Drummond. Cato was later arrested for beating one of Drummond's enemies. Cato may have ended up in Carson Valley, Nevada, shown as Cato Smith in the 1860 census with a man reportedly from Missouri, John Coagner, who may be one of two Civil War soldiers with similar names, Pennsylvania native John Coughenour or French immigrant John Coignier. Alternately, Drummond may have taken Cato back to the states since a New Orleans newspaper reported the arrival of "Judge Drummond, lady and servant." However, the newspaper did not provide a name for the servant, so this may or may not be a last reference to Cato.

Enslavers: James A. Harkreader (1813–); William W. Drummond (1819–1888)

Note: In describing the criminal actions, later historians used the nickname "Cuffy" for Cato, probably not realizing it was a pejorative. (*Oxford English Dictionary*, s.v. "Cuffee, Cuffy, *n.*," accessed February 9, 2021, https://www.oed.com.)

Sources: William W. Drummond, Stark County, Illinois, *1850 Census*. Hosea Stout, "A Short Sketch of the History of Judge W. W. Drummond," n.d., Governor's Office Files, 1850–1867, box 53, folder 23, Office Files. "Popular Sovereignty in Utah," *New York Tribune* (New York, NY), April 23, 1856. "A Fugitive Slave Advertised There," *National Era* (Washington, DC), May 1, 1856. "Slavery in Utah," *Portland Advertiser* (Portland, ME), April 29, 1856. "Impositions Upon Utah," *Deseret News*, May 20, 1857. Ronald W. Walker, "'Proud as a Peacock and Ignorant as a Jackass': William W. Drummond's Unusual Career with the Mormons," *Journal of Mormon History* 42, no. 3 (July 2016): 1–34. https://doi.org/10.5406/jmormhist.42.3.0001. Juanita Brooks, *History of the Jews in Utah and Idaho* (Salt Lake City, UT: Western Epics, 1973), 32. William Chandless, *A Visit to Salt Lake; Being a Journey Across the Plains, and a Residence in the Mormon Settlements at Utah* (London: Smith, Elder, and Co., 1857), 278. Peter J. Smith, Nevada Judicial Historical Society, email message to author, December 22, 2015. James A. Harkreader v. James C. Hamilton (1836), Wilson County (TN) Circuit Court, Tennessee State Library and Archives, *Minute Books, Civil and Criminal, 1810–1965*. FSFT. https://www.familysearch.org/search/catalog/256096. Jas A. Harkrider, Sacramento County, California, *1850 Census*. Cato Smith, Carson County, Utah Territory, *1860 Census*. Illinois State Archives, *Databases of Illinois Veterans Index, 1775–1995*. Ancestry.com. https://www.ancestry.com/search/collections/9759. National Archives in Washington, DC, *Civil War Draft Registrations Records, 1863–1865*. Ancestry.com. https://www.ancestry.com/search/collections/1666. "Later from Nicaragua," *New Orleans Daily Crescent* (New Orleans, LA), March 28, 1857. *Slave Manifests of Coastwise Vessels Filed at New Orleans, Louisiana, 1807–1860* (National Archives Microfilm Publication M1895). Jules Remy and Julius Brenchley, *A Journey to Great-Salt-Lake City* (London: W. Jeffs, 1861), 2, 341, 343. Russell W. McDonald, "William Wormer Drummond," in *Biographical Summaries: Nevada's Territorial, District, Supreme Court and Federal Judges, 1856–1993* (digital copy of unpublished manuscript), partial copy in possession of author (Reno, NV: Nevada Judicial Historical Society, n.d.), 155–58. W. W. Drummond, Cook County, Illinois, *1860 Census*. "Judge W. W. Drummond Dying in a Grog Shop," *New York Tribune*, November 22, 1888. "Once He Was Supreme Judge of Utah," *Knoxville Journal* (Knoxville, TN), November 25, 1888.

Fango

Gobo Fango (1855–1886)

Gobo Fango entered the South African household of Henry and Ruth Sweetnam Talbot after being abandoned during the Frontier Wars of the 1850s. The British government outlawed slavery in South Africa but settlers used Indigenous unpaid labor. Gobo provided child labor on the ship *Race Horse* after the Talbot family joined the Church of Jesus Christ of Latter-day Saints and left for America. Although Talbot descendants later claimed their ancestors adopted Fango, there was no legal way to do so in South Africa or America.

Gobo was not on the list of arrivals in Boston, so there may be truth to a later memory that the Talbot family smuggled him into the United States rolled in a carpet. South African writer Patric Tariq Mellet concluded that Fango was enslaved and kidnapped. It was a serious crime: the shipowner could have been fined $20,000 and lost his ship, and Talbot could have been arrested, fined $5,000, and sentenced to five to ten years in prison. In addition, anyone involved in any transactions involving Fango's labor could have been fined $800. Some free Black men in Chicago noticed Fango and attempted to rescue him, but the Talbot family concealed him and continued to Utah Territory.

Although no primary documentation remains, family histories indicate that Fango was sold or hired out in Utah Territory, first to Lewis and Susannah Perkins Whitesides. Fango was not provided sufficient clothing or shelter and lost part of his foot to frostbite. Edward and Mary Ann Whitesides Hunter of Grantsville offered to hire him. They freed him and put him on their payroll.

Fango was a mild-mannered and kindly sheepherder and accumulated significant property through a business partnership with Walter Mathews. In 1886, cattleman Frank Bedke shot Fango without provocation during an Idaho range war. Members of the Bedke family later shared theories with historian Dean Garrett, although the newspaper accounts of the murder disprove their claims. Garrett wrote, "[T]he Bedkes are proud of their grandfather for killing Gobo rather than possibly allowing his own life to be taken." Gobo died a week after the shooting, and in the meantime, Swedish immigrant and justice of the peace Claus Karlson helped him write a will that left modest bequests to the Hunter and Mathews families. He left the rest of his estate to the poor of Grantsville and the building of the Latter-day Saint temple in Salt Lake City.

Enslavers or Employers: Henry Talbot (1812–1895) and Ruth Sweetnam Talbot (1817–1903); Lewis Whitesides (1828–1899) and Susannah Perkins Whitesides (1830–1913); Edward Hunter (1821–1892), Mary Ann Whitesides Hunter (1825–1914), and Martha Ann Hyde Hunter (1841–1924)

Wagon Company: Homer Duncan (1861)

Burial: Lot 233, Oakley Cemetery, Oakley, Idaho

Notes: Susannah Perkins Whiteside was the niece of Utah enslaver Reuben Perkins. Edward Hunter was the nephew of Edward Hunter, the Presiding Bishop of the Church of Jesus Christ of Latter-day Saints. The children's magazine *Friend* included the claim of adoption in an inaccurate fictionalized account of Fango's life. (Tess Hilmo, "Gobo Fango," *Friend*, March 2003, The Church of Jesus Christ of Latter-Day Saints, https://www.churchofjesuschrist.org/study/friend/2003/03/gobo-fango.) The Hunter family later remembered, without any confirming documentation: "When slavery was abolished, Edward Hunter stopped paying the thirty dollars [a month] to Gobo's 'owner' and began paying it to Gobo. The owner sued Mr. Hunter on this matter but was not able to change this." (John P. Millward, "An Account of the Life of Gobo Fango," photocopy of typescript, MS 13543, folder 1, CHL.)

Sources: Patric Tariq Mellet, "A South African amaGaleca Slave in the USA," *Camissa People: Cape Slavery & Indigene Heritage*, March 29, 2014. https://camissapeople.wordpress.com/2014/03/29/a-south-african-amagaleca-slave-in-the-usa. Tim Keegan, *Colonial South Africa and the Origins of the Racial Order* (London: Leicester University Press, 1997), 145–47. "An Act to Prohibit the Importation of Slaves into any Port or

Place Within the Jurisdiction of the United States," 9 U.S.C., 2 Stat. 426 (1807). *Race Horse*, Port Elizabeth, South Africa, to Boston, April 19, 1861, Passenger Lists of Vessels Arriving at Boston, 1820–1891, National Archives Microfilm Publication M277:58. F. W. Blake, Diary, April–December 1861, CHL, quoted at *Saints by Sea*. https://saintsbysea.lib.byu.edu/mii/account/1233. Gobo Fango, Tooele County, Utah Territory, *1880 Census*. "A Negro Shepherd Shot in Idaho," *Idaho Statesman* (Boise, ID), February 16, 1886. "Oakley Homicide: Particulars of the Shooting and Death of the Negro Gobo," *Deseret News*, March 3, 1886. "Late News," *Owyhee Avalanche* (Silver City, ID), April 9, 1887. "Bedke Not Guilty," *Owyhee Avalanche*, April 16, 1887. Gobo Fango, Will and Probate, 1886, Third District Court, Tooele County (UT), Probate Case Files, Series 83314, box 1, folder 32, USHS. Eli Wiggill, "History," at Paul Tanner-Tremaine, *1820 Settlers to South Africa*. Accessed December 5, 2016. https://www.1820settlers.com/genealogy/Media/documents/Eli%20Wiggill%20History.pdf. Eli Wiggill Autobiography, 1883, microfilm of manuscript, MS 8344, CHL. H. Dean Garrett, "The Controversial Death of Gobo Fango," *Utah Historical Quarterly* 57, no. 3 (Summer 1989), 264–72. https://www.jstor.org/stable/45061873.

Flake

Green Flake (1828–1903)

Flake was born near Wadesboro, Anson County, North Carolina. Clues, including his son's death certificate, suggest that Flake's father may have been the Abram or Abraham shown in two generations of Flake wills. His mother may have been Haly, and his siblings Arter, Jude, and Liz or Elizabeth. When Jurden Flake died, Green and Elizabeth became the property of James Madison Flake, who was married to Agnes Love.

In 1843, Latter-day Saint missionary Benjamin Clapp baptized James and Agnes Flake in Kemper County, Mississippi. The next April, missionary John Brown recorded, "I also baptised two black men Allen & Green belonging to brother Flake." Much later, a newspaper said that Green knew Joseph Smith, so perhaps Green accompanied Flake to Nauvoo before Smith's death in 1844, but more likely, someone confused Green with Isaac James or Isaac Manning. The Flakes lived briefly in Nauvoo starting in late 1845 before they moved in 1846 to Winter Quarters, a Latter-day Saint refugee settlement on the Missouri River. Sarah DeArmon Pea Rich wrote about her family's struggle to survive with her husband away. Someone introduced her to James Flake, and he told her, "'Sister Rich send that man here and get a quarter of this calf.' I did so, and reached home with plenty to eat, and I found the family ready to thank the Lord." Flake's phrase "that man" likely meant Green.

The Flakes sent nineteen-year-old Green with the first 1847 wagon company to prepare a home. He and other enslaved men were to travel under the direction of John Brown, the missionary who baptized Green. Many years later, Green told of traveling along the Platte River, meeting Pawnee, and seeing bison. In July, the leaders of the wagon company sent an advance company ahead, including Flake, Oscar Smith, and Hark Wales. As the advance company began its final approach into the Great Salt Lake Valley, Flake hitched the mules to his enslaver's carriage and became the first to drive into Emigration Canyon. Flake arrived in the Great Salt Lake Valley on July 21 or 22, 1847. When Brigham Young entered the valley on July 24, apostle Wilford Woodruff drove him in Woodruff's carriage.

On August 8, Flake participated in Latter-day Saint religious ordinances of rebaptism and confirmation. Tarleton Lewis baptized Flake, and Wilford Woodruff confirmed him.

Later accounts suggested that Flake returned to Winter Quarters, but it would have defeated the purpose of sending the enslaved men ahead to prepare homes and crops if they had almost immediately headed back, and Flake, Hark Wales, and Oscar Smith are not on the list of those who returned to Winter Quarters.

The Flakes arrived in 1848. Scotsman Robert L. Campbell traveled in their company and wrote as they neared the Great Salt Lake Valley, "a negro from the valley yesterday came into Camp pretty loquacious & intelligent." Perhaps he meant Green.

Green's granddaughter later remembered, "When they reached the Salt Lake Valley, B. Young said, 'Brothers you are now free as I am.'" However, James Flake and others, notably William Crosby and John H. Bankhead, prevailed on questions of enslavement, even though Green continued to speak of freedom.

After the death of James Madison Flake in 1850, Agnes Love Flake left Green to work for Brigham Young in exchange for the means to resettle in California. Correspondence between Brigham Young and William Crosby mentioned Green's wife. Several clues, including his first child's birth date, suggest that Flake may have divorced a first wife, possibly Rose, and married Martha (Crosby) (Bankhead) around 1853. In 1854, Martha gave birth to Lucinda not long after Rose gave birth to Daniel Freeman, the son of an unnamed man. Daniel's surname commemorated the liberation of the small group of former Mississippi slaves. Brigham Young settled them on land in Union, and the Flake family remembered him with respect and affection. Many years after both men died, a descendant recalled, "Green shed tears at the death of Brigham Young, helped dig his grave, and was at the funeral of the beloved President."

When a mining boom began around 1870, Flake mined with Miles Litchford, Hark Wales, and others. Many in the small Black community signed the petition, "Against the Admission of Utah as a State."

Although Flake was a Latter-day Saint, he could not hold the lay priesthood due to his color and status as a slave. He did not receive a patriarchal blessing as others in the faith did. As he aged, Flake spoke at Pioneer Day celebrations. When organizers planned the 1897 commemorations, the *Salt Lake Herald* included a suggestion that Green Flake should drive Latter-day Saint President Wilford Woodruff's carriage, and it should look like Woodruff's carriage as Woodruff drove Brigham Young into the Salt Lake Valley in 1847. The *Salt Lake Tribune* coverage reported, "One of the most interesting of these old-timers was Green Flake, the only colored survivor of the band of '47. Green is a vigorous, broad-shouldered, good-natured, bright old gentleman." The reporter continued, "He wears glasses, but that is the only sign of old age about him. His voice might do for a trumpet, and he steps off like a West Pointer when he walks." The reporter mentioned Flake's conversation with Aaron Farr, "about the days when sagebrush was their staple scenery and Indians their nearest neighbors."

After Martha's death, Green moved to the African American settlement of Grays Lake, Idaho. When he died, his death was news throughout Utah. His family buried him in Union Cemetery next to Martha.

Documented Family: Possible wife Rose Crosby (1835–); wife Martha Morris (Crosby) (1828–1885) and children Lucinda Flake (1854–1937, married George Stevens) and Abraham Flake (1857–1936, married Mary Ann Steele and Levora Litcherl)

Enslavers: James Madison Flake (1815–1850) and Agnes Love Flake (1819–1855)

Wagon Company: Brigham Young (1847)

Burial: I-7, Union Fort Pioneer Cemetery, Cottonwood Heights, Utah

Sources—Vital and Government Records: William Love, Richmond County, North Carolina, *1790 Census*. William Love Probate, 1792, Richmond County; Samuel Flake Will, 1802, Anson County; Jurden Flake Will, 1843, Anson County; Thomas G. Flake Will, 1850, Anson County, North Carolina County, District, and Probate Courts, *North Carolina, Wills and Probate Records, 1665–1998*. Ancestry.com. https://www.ancestry.com/search/collections/9061. Jourden Flake, twenty slaves, Anson County, North Carolina, *1830 Census*. Jordan Flake, seventeen slaves, Anson County, North Carolina, *1840 Census*. Jas M Flake, eight slaves, Anson County, North Carolina, *1840 Census*. R[ichmond] J Love, 1841, Thos J Love, 1842, Richmond Love, 1842, James M Flake, 1843, Jas M Flake, 1844, Richd Love, 1844, Jas M Flake, 1845, R J Love, 1845, R Loves Est., 1846, Agustus Love, 1846, Kemper County Tax Rolls 1841–1852, Mississippi Department of Archives and History, *Various Records*. Erasmus Love v. Richmond Love, 38 N.C. 104, 85 (N.C. 1843). Agness Flake, Utah County, Utah Territory, *1850 Census*. Agnes Flake, Utah County, Utah Territory Slave Schedule [draft], 1850 [1851]. Brigham Young, Great Salt Lake County, Utah Territory Slave Schedule [draft], 1850 [1851]. Green Flake, Vilate Crosby, Rose Crosby, Great Salt Lake County, Utah Territory, *1850 Census*. Green Flake, Salt Lake County, Utah Territory, *1860 Census*. Green Flake v. Nils Mason (1864), Salt Lake County Probate Court Case Files, Series 373, box 8, folder 144. Green Flake, Salt Lake County, Utah Territory, *1870 Census*. Greene Flack, Salt Lake County, Utah Territory, *1880 Census*. Green Flake, Bingham County, Idaho, *1900 Census*. Abraham Flake, January 28, 1936, Bonneville County, death certificate 96944, Idaho Bureau of Vital Records, *Idaho, Death Records, 1890–1967*. Ancestry.com. https://www.ancestry.com/search/collections/60566.

Sources—Primary Documents and Interviews: Joseph L. Robinson Account book, Records, 1846–1847, Joseph Lee Robinson Papers 1883–1892, MS 7042, folder 4, CHL. Sarah DeArmon Pea Rich, 1814–1893, Autobiography (1814–1893), digital transcript, W. V. Smith, *BOAP*. Accessed April 21, 2021. http://www.boap.org/LDS/Early-Saints/SRich.html. John Brown, Journal, box 1, folder 1, images 30–117, MS 1636, Reminiscences and Journals, CHL. "Pres^t Young rode in W. Woodruff's Carriage." July 24, 1847; Military Organization, Return Pioneer Journal, Thomas Bullock, Journals, MS 1385, folder 2, vol. 3–5, CHL. William Clayton, Diary, 1847, William Clayton Diaries, 1846–1853, MS 1406, CHL. Albert Perry Rockwood, Journal, April–July 1847, MS 1449, folder 1, 34, 35, CHL. Green Flake, August 8, 1847, Historian's Office Rebaptism Records. "Against the Admission of Utah as a State." Robert L. Campbell, Journal, October 11, 1848, Historical Department Office Journal, 1844–2012, July 15, 1848–October 19, 1848, CR 100 1, vol. 12, CHL. William Crosby to Brigham Young, c. March 12, 1851; Brigham Young to William Crosby, March 12, 1851; Amasa Lyman to Brigham Young, July 27, 1854, box 40, folder 21; Brigham Young to Amasa Lyman and C. C. Rich, August 19, 1854, box 17, folder 14, Office Files. Green Flake, Utah Semi-Centennial Commission, *The Book of the Pioneers* (Salt Lake City, UT: Utah Semi-Centennial Commission, 1897), 1, 242, USHS. William Jordan Flake, box 37, folder 13, CR 100 18, Biographical Sketches, 1891–2013, CHL. Green and Martha Flake gravestone, Union Fort Pioneer Cemetery, Cottonwood Heights, Utah. Beller, "Negro Slaves in Utah," 125. Notes from Udell Home. Fretwell, "Green Flake."

Sources—Newspaper: "100 Dollars Reward [fugitive slave notice, E[rasmus?] Love]," *Carolina Observer* (Fayetteville, NC), January 15, 1840. "Mining in Utah," *Elevator*, December 14, 1872. Francis H. Grice, "From Our Salt Lake Correspondent," *Elevator*, June 28, 1873. "Notice [Flake property used as landmark]," *Deseret News*, March 24, 1875. "Delinquent Sale," *Salt Lake Tribune*, November 23, 1875. "Mining Notices: Delinquent Sale," *Salt Lake Tribune*, April 5, 1876. "Pioneers," *Salt Lake Herald*, July 3, 1880. "The Pioneers," *Deseret News*, April 12, 1890. "The Twenty-Fourth at Union," *Deseret Evening News*, July 26, 1888. "The Pioneers," *Deseret News*, April 12, 1890. "Green Flake to P. J. Stone, part of section 21, township 2 south, range 1 east. 50 [dollars]." "Real Estate Transfers," *Salt Lake*

Herald, April 1, 1893. "Echoes of the 24th," *Salt Lake Herald*, July 26, 1893. "Green Flake to James Honeysett et al., part section 21, township 2 south, range 1 east . . . 600 [dollars]." "Real Estate Transfers," *Salt Lake Herald*, December 2, 1893. "Fifty Years Ago Today," *Salt Lake Tribune*, April 15, 1894. "Pioneer Day," *Salt Lake Herald*, August 16, 1894. "Salt Lake News," *Ogden Standard*, August 21, 1894. "The Veterans' Reunion," *Salt Lake Herald*, August 21, 1894. "The Pioneers of 1847," *Deseret News*, August 25, 1894. "Green Flake to John A. Durall, part section 20, township 2 south, range 1 east . . . 800 [dollars]." "Real Estate Transfers," *Salt Lake Herald*, August 28, 1895. "Dr. Faust's Ideas for the Carnival," *Salt Lake Herald*, May 28, 1896. "Fifty Years Ago Today," *Salt Lake Tribune*, May 31, 1897. "Some Living Pioneers," *Salt Lake Herald*, June 29, 1897. "The Utah Pioneer Jubilee," *Lehi Banner* (Lehi, UT), July 6, 1897. "Fifty Years Ago Today," Salt Lake Tribune, July 13, 1897. "More Pioneers," *Deseret News*, July 19, 1897. "The Opening Day of the Jubilee," *Salt Lake Tribune*, July 20, 1897. "Some Jubilee Visitors," *Salt Lake Tribune*, July 26, 1897. "Green Flake to John A. Durrell, part of section 21, township 2 south range 1 east . . . 50 [dollars]." "Real Estate Transfers," *Salt Lake Herald*, July 29, 1897. "Idaho Seems to be Well Represented," *St. George Union* (St. George, UT), August 7, 1897. "Slavery in Utah," *Broad Ax*. "Green Flake Passes Away," *Deseret News*, October 22, 1903. "Death of Green Flake," *Idaho Register* (Idaho Falls, ID), October 23, 1903. "Green Flake is No More," *Salt Lake Tribune*, October 23, 1903. "Utah Pioneer Laid to Rest," *Deseret Evening News*, October 23, 1903. "Pioneer Colored Man Dies at Home of Son," *Ogden Standard*, October 23, 1903. "Died." *Salt Lake Herald*, October 23, 1903. "Funeral of Green Flake," *Deseret Evening News*, October 31, 1903. Ellen Carney, "Blacks Were First to Settle Idaho's Grays Lake Valley," *Idaho State Journal*, March 3, 2013. https://www.idahostatejournal.com/news/local/blacks-were-first-to-settle-idaho-s-grays-lake-valley/article_b82435f6-83d0-11e2-b4da-001a4bcf887a.html.

Sources—Additional: Andrew Jenson, *Latter-day Saint Biographical Encyclopedia* (Salt Lake City, UT: Andrew Jenson History Company and Andrew Jenson Memorial Association, 1914, 1920, 1936), 2:218, 3:372, 4:703. Osmer D. Flake, *William J. Flake: Pioneer-Colonizer* (printed by author, 1948). Verbal communication of content of Patriarchal Blessing Index from Church History Department to author, 2016. LaMar C.

Berrett, "History of the Southern States Mission: 1831–1861" (master's thesis, Brigham Young University, Provo, UT, 1960). Dennis L. Lythgoe, "Negro Slavery in Utah" (master's thesis, University of Utah, 1966), 27–28. Dennis L. Lythgoe, "Negro Slavery in Utah," *Utah Historical Quarterly* 39, no. 1 (Winter 1971): 42. https://doi.org/10.2307/272985. Carter, *Negro Pioneer*, 4–8. Augusta Flake to Elizabeth DeBrouwer, February 22, 1979, San Bernardino Public Library, San Bernardino, CA. Udell, Interview. Charles L. Keller, *The Lady in the Ore Bucket: A History of Settlement and Industry in the Tri-Canyon Area of the Wasatch Mountains* (Salt Lake City, UT: University of Utah Press, 2010). Ron Freeman, "James Madison Flake (1815–1850)" (unpublished manuscript), 2011, 35–36, 42, FSFT. https://familysearch.org/photos/artifacts/3394048.

Elizabeth Flake Rowan (1833–1908)

Elizabeth Flake Rowan is one of the few women and African American settlers listed on a monument in downtown San Bernardino commemorating the city's first residents. In 1848, she crossed the plains to the Great Salt Lake Valley as an enslaved teenager with James and Agnes Love Flake. After she was freed, she always used the name Elizabeth. Although her name was Elizabeth on the wagon roster, and she always used that name for herself, the White Flake family later remembered her as "Liz," so she was probably "Lyse" in Jurden Flake's will. Flake descendants remembered that Agnes Love's parents gave her to the family, but all the enslaved people from the Love side of the family appear to have stayed in Mississippi pending the resolution of a court battle among Love relatives.

After James Flake died in 1850, Agnes took her three surviving children and Elizabeth and moved to San Bernardino. Agnes died in 1855, and Maria Tanner Lyman took in the Flake children and Elizabeth. When the enslaved people in San Bernardino learned they were free by early 1856, Daniel M. Thomas wrote to Amasa Lyman that Elizabeth had been to Los Angeles and met someone she planned to marry, but that those plans were delayed. The 1860 census showed Elizabeth Flake as a single mother and laundress in San Bernardino.

Elizabeth married Charles Rowan. He had served on the *USS Jacob Bell* in the Potomac Flotilla during the Civil War. His obituary said that he was freed as a young man and was a valet and barber to Abraham

Lincoln, Secretary of War Edwin Stanton, and others. A reporter from the *San Bernardino Sun* later saw a letter of recommendation from Abraham Lincoln in the possession of the family, but the whereabouts of the letter is unknown. Charles Rowan helped found the Los Angeles African Methodist Episcopal (AME) Church in Los Angeles before he and Elizabeth moved to San Bernardino. Elizabeth did not contribute to the church with her husband and sons; she appears to have been a Latter-day Saint, and since there was no congregation in San Bernardino after 1857, she eventually joined the Reorganized Church of Jesus Christ of Latter Day Saints (now Community of Christ).

Elizabeth and Charles raised four children: Walter, Byron Thomas, Alice, and Charles. Walter died shortly after he married Emma Richards. Byron married Mary Young and lived in Daggett and San Bernardino, but his only daughter died young, and he did not leave known descendants. Alice became the first African American teacher in an integrated school in California. She married Frank H. Johnson and had five children. Charles suffered from alcoholism. He and his wife Agnes Henderson Rowan divorced after he attempted to murder her.

Elizabeth Flake Rowan and her daughter Alice visited Salt Lake City in 1877 and stayed with Susan Steele Blanchard, a sister of Green Flake's daughter-in-law. Diarist Mary Lois Walker Morris described Alice as "very Ladylike and refined."

When her former enslavers' son William married, Elizabeth sent him a set of silver. William's son and daughter-in-law visited Elizabeth in 1904. Their daughter wrote, "She took them in her carriage around the city, recounting the history of the place to them. How I wish we had written it all down."

In early 1901 when Rowan was taken ill, she received several visitors, including Biddy Mason's daughter, Ellen Huddleston.

Rowan died three years after her husband and is buried in the San Bernardino Pioneer Memorial Cemetery. Her estate was initially valued at $5,000, including real estate and mining stock. She left extensive personal property to friends and family. The newspaper wrote a glowing obituary, and her family thanked the community for "the loving sympathy shown us in our great bereavement; for the appreciative remembrance of our dear mother . . . [for] the beautiful floral tributes, and the many acts of untiring service during her last illness."

Documented Family: Son Walter James Rowan (1858–1886, married Emma Jane Richards) with an unknown father; husband Charles Rowan (1837–1905) and children Byron Thomas Rowan (1862–1934, married Mary Young), Alice Ann Rowan (1868–1912, married Frank H. Johnson), and Charles Henry Rowan (1874–1910, married Agnes Ann Henderson)

Enslavers: James M. and Agnes Love Flake

Wagon Company: Willard Richards (1848)

Burial: San Bernardino Pioneer Cemetery, San Bernardino, California

Sources: First 50, Reports, circa June 1848, box 2, folder 32, Camp of Israel Schedules and Reports. Agnes Flake slave 2, female, Utah County, Utah Territory Slave Schedule [draft], 1850 [1851]. Daniel M. Thomas to Lyman, Lyman Collection. Elizabeth Flake, San Bernardino County, CA, *1860 Census.* "Letter from Bishop Ward," *Elevator.* Elizabeth Rowan, Los Angeles County, California, *1870 Census.* Elizabeth Rowan, San Bernardino County, California, *1880 Census.* Walter James Rowan and Emma Jane Richards, November 29, 1882, Recorder, Marriage Licenses D, 20, SBCHA. Walter J. Rowan Death, June 7, 1886, San Bernardino County Recorder, Deaths Book 2, 38, SBCHA. Charles Rowan Jr., November 4, 1895, San Bernardino Courts, Insanity and Intemperance Cases, Book 1, Inebriate Commitments 1895–1897, CC box, 12, SBCHA. "Notes of the Day," *Los Angeles Herald*, November 5, 1895. Byron Thomas Rowan, Gary [sic] Young, March 15, 1898, San Bernardino County Recorder, Marriage Licenses K, 350, SBCHA. "From Friday's Daily," *San Bernardino Weekly Sun* (San Bernardino, CA), February 3, 1899. "His Big Bail," *San Bernardino Evening Transcript* (San Bernardino, CA), March 17, 1900. Elizabeth Rowan, San Bernardino County, California, *1900 Census.* "City in Brief," *San Bernardino Evening Transcript*, January 18, 1901. "City in Brief," *San Bernardino Evening Transcript*, January 19, 1901. "Prof. Lorenz Treated Daggett Child," *San Bernardino Evening Transcript*, November 15, 1902. Charles Rowan, alias Charles Rone or Rohan, National Archives and Records Administration, *U.S. Civil War Pension Index: General Index to Pension Files, 1861–1934.* Ancestry.com. https://www.ancestry.com/search/collections/4654. "Charles Rowan Joins His Fathers," *San Bernardino Sun*, September 20, 1905. "Mrs. Elizabeth Rowan," *San Bernardino Daily Sun* (San Bernardino, CA), March 31, 1908. "Card of Thanks," *San*

Bernardino Daily Sun, April 2, 1908. "Will Filed in Estate of the Late Mrs. Rowan," *San Bernardino Sun*, April 15, 1908. "Has Priceless Lincoln Relic," *San Bernardino Sun*, February 17, 1909. "Official Record," *San Bernardino Sun*, October 20, 1911. "Mrs. Liz Flake Rowan," Settlement of San Bernardino Monument, northeast corner of N. Arrowhead Avenue and West 3rd Street in front of the Historic San Bernardino County Courthouse, Daughters of Utah Pioneers, Monument 302, Settlement of San Bernardino, 1964, San Bernardino, CA. Melissa Lambert Milewski, *Before the Manifesto: The Life Writings of Mary Lois Walker Morris* (Logan, UT: Utah State University Press, 2007), 516–18. Skinner, *Black Origins*, 74–75. Charles Henry Rowan Jr. and Agnes Ann Sophia Henderson, January 10, 1903, San Bernardino County Recorder, Marriage Licenses N, 238, SBCHA. Rowan v. Rowan (1909), San Bernardino Courts, case 11034, cases 11021–58, SBCHA. "Tries to Murder Wife for Refusing to Give Him Money," *Los Angeles Herald*, May 29, 1908. Susan Easton Black and Harvey B. Black, *Early Members of the Reorganized Church of Jesus Christ of Latter Day Saints* (Provo, UT: Religious Studies Center Brigham Young University, 1993). Carter, *Negro Pioneer*, 18–20.

Harper

Male (Harper) (1830–)

Irish immigrant John Harper was a skilled stonecutter and therefore in great demand in Utah Territory, but he suffered from "liver complaint," which could mean anything from malaria to leukemia. He wrote, "In the spring of 1860, I wrote to President Brigham Young, and made him acquainted with my situation. Then he instructed Bishop Edward Hunter to give me a yoke of oxen and a wagon." Harper did not have any funds to buy an enslaved laborer, but due to the demand for his trade, someone may have donated the labor of an enslaved worker. The man shown in the Harper household in the 1860 census slave schedule was probably Thomas Bankhead Coleman on early work release from prison. The Harpers were called to the Cotton Mission in Southern Utah in 1861, which would be when Coleman began to work at the hotel next door to the Harper residence, and where he worked until his murder in 1866.

Enslavers: Probably renters or borrowers John Harper (1812–1863) and Isabella Mitchell Harper (1819–1889)

Notes: The 1852 wagon roster does not list an extra member of the Harper household, nor does the 1856 Utah territorial census, so the identity of John and Isabella Harper as "J. & I. Harper" in the 1860 slave schedule was an open question. However, Elizabeth Whitmore in the Fifteenth Ward was listed third on the slave schedule, the Harpers lived in the Thirteenth Ward and were fourth, and William H. Hooper was also in the Thirteenth Ward and was listed fifth. There are no other likely options. Harper lived by Justice of the Peace Jeter Clinton who presided over Coleman's first trial in 1859, and neighbors included enslaver William Hooper and slave renter Horace S. Eldredge. Researcher Connell O'Donovan also concluded John and Isabella Harper were the correct couple. (Connell O'Donovan, comment on "Utah Slaves 1850 and 1860," April 4, 2007, AfriGeneas Slave Research Forum, http://www.afrigeneas.com/forumd/ index.cgi/md/read/id/6904/sbj/utah-slaves-1850-and-1860.)

Sources: If the man in the slave schedule was Thomas Bankhead Coleman, see Coleman's entry for additional sources. "9th Company," *Deseret News*, September 18, 1852. John Harper, Great Salt Lake County, *1856 Utah Territorial Census*. J. & I. Harper, Great Salt Lake County, Utah Territory Slave Schedule, *1860 Census*. John Harper, Jewel B. Furniss, Alice M. Rich, and Brenda Anderson, "Autobiography of John Nelson Harper," MS 7766, CHL. John and Isabella Harper, Great Salt Lake County, Utah Territory, *1860 Census*. Debra Holm, email message to author, November 5, 2015.

Hockaday

George (Hockaday) (1830–1860)

George may have been enslaved by William Hockaday in Kentucky. Hockaday enslaved two people in 1820, three in 1830, and seven in 1840. No one matched George's description in the 1830 census, but one child matched his description in 1840, suggesting that George was born after 1830. George went with merchant, adventurer, and West Point dropout John M. Hockaday to Utah Territory where Hockaday ran stagecoach, mail, and merchant routes between Great Salt Lake City and Missouri.

John Hockaday may have enslaved other men in the territory. George died shortly after the 1860 census and was buried in a pauper's grave.

Enslaver: John M. Hockaday (1823–1865)

Burial: E-5-14-1W or N-1/2, Salt Lake City Cemetery, Salt Lake City, Utah

Sources: William Hockaday, Winchester, Clark County, Kentucky, *1820 Census*. William F. Hockaday, Winchester, Clark County, Kentucky, *1830 Census*. Wm F. Hockaday, Winchester, Clark County, Kentucky, *1840 Census*. John M. Hockaday, Union County, Kentucky Slave Schedule, *1850 Census*. John M. Hockaday, Great Salt Lake County, Utah Territory Slave Schedule, *1860 Census*. George Hockaday, negro, [August 1860], *Salt Lake County (UT) Death Records*. George (Negro) Hockaday, August 1860, grave E_5_14_1W, Salt Lake City Cemetery, Salt Lake City, Utah Division of State History, *Cemeteries and Burials*. William P. MacKinnon, email messages to author, October 11, 2016, November 28, 2017. William P. MacKinnon, "Predicting the Past: The Utah War's Twenty-First Century Future," *Arrington Annual Lecture*, 2008, Paper 13. https://digitalcommons.usu.edu/arrington_lecture/13. W. W. Phelps, *Almanac for the Year 1860* (Great Salt Lake City, UT: J. McKnight, 1860), 6. "Affairs in Utah: Interesting Letter from Judge Drummond," *New York Tribune*, May 27, 1857. William P. MacKinnon, "The Buchanan Spoils System and the Utah Expedition: Careers of W. M. F. Magraw and John M. Hockaday," *Utah Historical Quarterly* 31, no. 2 (April 1963): 127–50. https://www.jstor.org/stable/45059094. "West Point Cadets," *New York Commercial Advertiser* (New York, NY), May 5, 1842. United States Military Academy, *Official Register of the Officers and Cadets of the U.S. Military Academy, West Point, N.Y.* (West Point, NY: United States Military Academy Printing Office, 1843), 249, 271, 296, 303.

Johnston

Randolph (Johnston) Hughes (1832–)

Albert Sidney Johnston enslaved Randolph "Ran" Hughes, born to parents who had been enslaved by Johnston's first wife, Henrietta Preston. Hughes accompanied Johnston to Utah Territory as a cook, personal servant, and bodyguard. After they left Utah Territory, Johnston converted Hughes's chattel slavery to a paid indenture of five years at $12 a month plus room and board. The two went to California, and then back to the South where Johnston fought for the Confederacy. Johnston died at the Battle of Shiloh, and Hughes continued to serve other army officers. Parts of Hughes's life are documented by the extensive Johnston correspondence, but his whereabouts after the war are unknown.

Documented Family: Brother John (Unknown)

Enslaver: Albert Sidney Johnston (1803–1862)

Military Expedition: Utah War (1857–1858)

Sources: Charles Pierce Roland, *Albert Sidney Johnston, Soldier of Three Republics*, 2nd ed. (Lexington: University Press of Kentucky, 2001), 141, 181–82. William Preston Johnston, *The Life of Gen. Albert Sidney Johnston* (New York, NY: D. Appleton, 1878), 15, 178–79, 279–81. Bexar County, Texas Slave Schedule, *1850 Census*. Randolph Hughes, Contract, December 10, 1860, Johnston Papers, Barret Collection, Tulane University, New Orleans, LA, in Roland, *Johnston*, 241–42.

Jolley

Lambson or Lamb (Jolley) (1838–1849)

Lambson was born January 4, 1838, probably in Weakley County, Tennessee, to an unnamed woman who was the only enslaved servant in the household of Henry and Frances Manning Jolley. The woman probably came from the Manning family, but both Jolley and Manning families participated in slave patrols and occasionally placed fugitive slave notices in the North Carolina newspapers. Most of those in the notices (Frank, Peter, Isaac, Frank, Steward, Judy, Isham, Alfred, Gabriel, Richard, and Noah) were said to be seeking freedom or their families. One notice placed in 1811 had an extralegal threat of capital punishment: "All Masters of vessels and others strictly forbid harboring [or] employing . . . said fellow off under the severe penalty of the law—which is Death."

Lambson's mother may have died or been sold not long after his birth since he is the only enslaved person listed in the 1840 census. There is no record of the identity of Lambson's father, and whether

Henry Jolley separated father and son when he moved to Nauvoo, Illinois. Frances Manning Jolley died when Lambson was six years old. Henry Jolley remarried New Hampshire native Susannah Law Taggart, so Lambson lived in her household until she died a year and a half later and then in a household with Jolley's third wife, widow Barbara Spangler Creager.

After two years in Iowa, the family headed to the Great Salt Lake Valley. The wagon roster showed Henry (age fifty-nine), Barbara (age fifty), and "Lamb (a black boy)" (age ten), traveling with one wagon, six oxen, one cow, six other cattle, seven chickens, and a dog. Nine months after he arrived in the Salt Lake Valley, Lambson died by drowning. The burial record shows "Lambson Servant of Henry Jolly." Lambson's death record suggests that Jolley's understanding of the responsibilities and relationships of Southern slavery were typical for the time and that he and his community considered Lambson a chattel slave.

Enslavers: Henry Jolley (1789–1850) and Barbara Spangler Creager Jolley Sherwood (1799–)

Wagon Company: Willard Richards (1848)

Burial: C-10-14, Salt Lake City Cemetery, Salt Lake City, Utah

Notes: Errors within a document believed to be Henry Jolley's autobiography suggest that it was written about a century after Jolley's death. Its anachronistic ideas about slavery and race should be attributed to its unnamed author and not to Henry Jolley. (Carter, *Negro Pioneer*, 44–46.) Its story about a boy's death in Pleasant Grove, Utah, was a late memory of Benjamin Price (1842–1850) who died after falling from a log (Utah Archives and Records Service, *Utah Death Registers*). A Jolley family source of unknown origin and no documentation suggests Lambson's parents were Nellie and Abraham.

Sources: Howard R. Driggs and J. Rulon Hales, *Timpanogos Town: Story of Old Battle Creek and Pleasant Grove, Utah* (Manchester, NH: Clarke Press, 1948), 33. "Nellie," FSFT. Accessed February 1, 2019. https://www.familysearch.org/tree/person/details/LKFW-GY6. Weakley County Court, Minutes, 1827-1838, Tennessee County Courthouses, *Tennessee, Probate Court Books, 1795–1927*. FSFT. https://www.familysearch.org/search/collection/1909088. Henry Jolly, Weakley County, Tennessee, *1830*

Census. Henry Jolly, Weakley County, Tennessee, *1840 Census.* Henry Jolley, 1842, no taxable slaves, Weakley County (TN) Trustee, *Tax Books.* "Lamb (a black boy)," Willard Richards Company, 1848, Camp of Israel Schedules and Reports. Lambson, Servant of Henry Jolly, July 17, 1849, *Salt Lake County (UT) Death Records.* Bryant Manning Jolley and Jolley Family Organization, *The Jolley Family Book: The Story of Henry Jolley and His Wife, Frances Manning Jolley* (Provo, UT: Brigham Young University Press, 1966), I, 6–7. University of North Carolina at Greensboro, *N.C. Runaway Slave Advertisements*, Digital Library on American Slavery. https://library.uncg.edu/slavery. "15 Dollars Reward" [Benjamin Manning advertising for the return of Frank], *State Gazette of North Carolina* (Edenton, NC), August 24, 1797. "Run-Away" [Joseph Manning advertising for the return of Frank], *Edenton Gazette and North Carolina General Advertiser* (Edenton, NC), October 15, 1811. "$20 Reward" [John Manning advertising for return of Peter], *Free Press* (Halifax, NC), July 12, 1831. "$25 Reward" [Reuben S. Manning advertising for the return of Isaac], *Tarboro Press* (Tarboro, NC), September 14, 1839. "$100 Reward" [Reuben S. Manning advertising for return of Steward], *Tarboro Free Press* (Tarboro, NC), April 30, 1842. "$20 Reward" [W. H. Manning advertising for return of Judy], *Albemarle Bulletin* (Edenton, NC), July 12, 1851. "$50 Reward" [Benjamin Manning advertising for the return of Isham], *Wilmington Journal* (Wilmington, NC), August 28, 1857. "Look Out for the Runaways!! Abolitionism!!! $150 Reward" [John Jolly of Cass County, Georgia, advertising for the return of Alfred, Gabriel, Richard, and Noah], *Ashville News* (Ashville, NC).

Lay

Hark (Crosby) (Lay) Wales (1825–1887)

Hark Wales was one of the three enslaved men who entered the Great Salt Lake Valley ahead of the first Latter-day Saint wagon company. His name is incorrectly shown as "Hark Lay" on the Brigham Young Memorial in downtown Salt Lake City. Wales was born in Mississippi and enslaved by John Crosby. The Lay family later created a fanciful story to explain what they considered an unusual given name, but the name Hark appeared in both Black and White populations of the South. Upon Crosby's death,

Wales became the property of Crosby's daughter Sytha and her husband, William H. Lay. The couple sent Wales ahead to the valley in 1847 to prepare a home. Charmaine Lay Kohler later claimed that Hark was baptized in Mormon Springs in Mississippi but did not provide a source for the claim, and Hark does not appear in 1847 Latter-day Saint rebaptism records with Green Flake and Oscar (Crosby) Smith.

In 1848, enslaved single mother Nancy (Bankhead) arrived in the valley with her two sons. She and Wales married and had sons Howard and probably Henry. The couple named Howard after Major Howard Egan, who was in the 1847 wagon company with Wales and an 1848 company with Nancy.

William and Sytha Lay took Wales to California in 1851 and separated him from his young family. Wales learned he was free by early 1856. He farmed in San Timoteo Canyon above San Bernardino and eventually moved back to Utah Territory in the early 1870s. His former wife Nancy had been married to James Valentine for many years. He boarded in the home of Green and Martha Flake's daughter Lucinda Stevens in the small African American community in Union Fort and farmed and worked in the Evergreen Mine with Green Flake and Miles Litchford and in the Decomposed Mine with Daniel Freeman Bankhead. He died in the 1880s and is buried in Union Cemetery.

Documented Family: Wife Nancy Bankhead Valentine (1823–1894); sons Howard Egan Wales (1849–) and probably Henry Bankhead Valentine (1852–1888)

Enslavers: Sytha Crosby Lay (1817–1881) and William Harvey Lay (1817–1886)

Wagon Company: Brigham Young (1847)

Burial: I-12, Union Fort Pioneer Cemetery, Cottonwood Heights, Utah

Notes: The records of the Union Cemetery were reconstructed in the mid-twentieth century, and provide death dates of 1881, 1887, or 1890. The most likely is 1887. No known records document William Lay and his family enslaving people before he married Sytha Crosby.

Sources: For 1847 sources, see the entry for Green Flake. Hark, Utah County, Utah Territory Slave Schedule [draft], 1850 [1851]. Hark Lay,

Utah County, Utah Territory, *1850 Census*. Hark, Los Angeles County, *1852 California Census*. Hark Wales, San Bernardino County, California State Library, *California Voter Registers*. "Notice [Hark Wales mining]," *Salt Lake Tribune*, May 6, 1876. "Notice [Hark Wales mining]," *Salt Lake Tribune*, August 10, 1878. Harks Wales, Salt Lake County, Utah Territory, *1880 Census*. H. L. A. Culmer, *Utah Directory and Gazetteer for 1879-80* (Salt Lake City, UT: J. C. Graham & Co., 1879), 203. Hark Wales, 1881, row I grave 12, Union Fort Cemetery, Sandy, Utah Division of State History, *Cemeteries and Burials*. "Hark or Hark Whales Lay (col.), born in Mississippi, 1825." "Genealogy: Genesis of the Hundred and Forty-Three Utah Pioneers," *Salt Lake Herald*, May 30, 1915. Daughters of Utah Pioneers, "Fort Union Pioneer Cemetery Memorial." Kohler, *Southern Grace*, 58, 60. Vincent Lay, Will, Lawrence County, Tennessee, 1836, 96–97. Ancestry.com. *Tennessee, Wills and Probate Records, 1779–2008*, https://www.ancestry.com/search/collections/9176. Rhoda Lay, Lawrence County, Tennessee, *1840 Census*.

Harriet (Lay) Embers (1820–1877)

Harriet was born in North Carolina. Daniel M. Thomas described her as "that beautifull piece of Ebony." She entered the William and Sytha Lay household in Mississippi sometime after the John Crosby probate showed Sytha inheriting an enslaved woman named Milly. Perhaps Milly died before the Lay family went west, and they purchased Harriet, or perhaps Milly had a husband in Monroe County, and Sytha and William Lay exchanged her for Harriet. Several women in 1870 Mississippi match Milly's description, including Milly Troup of Monroe County, who was treated for illness in Georgia during the war.

William and Sytha Lay took Harriet to the Great Salt Lake Valley in 1848 and to San Bernardino in 1851. She gained her freedom by 1856 and moved to Los Angeles with her husband, Grief Embers. The 1870 census shows Grief's niece Martha and the two daughters of Tennessee "Harriet" (Thomas) Jackson living with them. The couple returned to farm in San Bernardino, where they both died in the 1870s.

Documented Family: Husband Grief Embers (1816–1873); foster daughters Louisa Jackson (1857–1913, married George Pollard), Harriet Jackson

(1860–, married George Washington), and Martha Embers (1854–1932, married Israel Beal)

Enslavers: Sytha and William Harvey Lay

Wagon Company: Willard Richards (1848)

Burial: San Bernardino Pioneer Cemetery, San Bernardino, California

Sources: Harriett, Utah County, Utah Territory Slave Schedule [draft], 1850 [1851]. Harriet, Los Angeles County, *1852 California Census*. Daniel M. Thomas to Lyman, Lyman Collection. Millie Troup, *Georgia Freedmen's Bureau Field Office Records, 1865–1872* (National Archives Microfilm Publication M1903). Millie Troup, Monroe County, Mississippi, *1870 Census*.

Lucy (Crosby) (Lay) (Smoot/Williams?) (1836–)

Lucy was probably born into the John Crosby household and may be Violet's daughter. She was about six years old when Crosby daughter Sytha Lay inherited her. Lucy disappeared from the Lay household at the same time a girl of the same age named Lucy appeared in the Smoot household in Utah Territory, so Sytha or William Lay probably sold her to A. O. or Margaret Smoot. The next year, Margaret Smoot sold Lucy to Thomas S. Williams for $400. After Williams registered the sale in probate court four years later, Lucy disappeared from the public record. Williams probably took her to Missouri when he moved there temporarily, and perhaps she died, or he sold her to help finance the purchase of a hotel. She matches the general description of Lucy Green, who worked as a servant in St. Louis in 1870.

Enslavers: Sytha and William Harvey Lay; probably A. O. and Margaret McMeans Smoot; probably Thomas S. and Albina Merrill Williams

Wagon Company: Willard Richards (1848)

Note: Other than A. O. Smoot's grandmother who hired out enslaved people in exchange for a home and food and clothing, none of the Smoot or McMeans families seemed to enslave people before the 1850s in Utah Territory.

Sources: Abraham Smoot, Great Salt Lake County, Utah Territory Slave Schedule [draft], 1850 [1851]. Salt Lake City Probate Court, A. O. Smoot's Bill of Sale of Negro to Thos. S. Williams, 1856, Salt Lake County Probate Court Case Files, Series 373, box 4, folder 26, USHS. Lucinda Williams, Utah Territory Census Returns, February 1856, Great Salt Lake County, Ward 13, MS 2929, box 1, folder 11, CHL. Lucy Green, St. Louis, Missouri, *1870 Census.* Ron Freeman, "Smoot, George (Washington)," digital file, FSFT. Accessed February 18, 2017. https://familysearch.org/photos/artifacts/6137791. Freeman, "Rowlett, Nancy Ann," digital file, FSFT. Accessed February 18, 2017. https://familysearch.org/photos/artifacts/7470319. George Smoot, Franklin County, Kentucky, *1810 Census.* Anthony McMeans Probate, 1816, case 633, South Carolina County, District, and Probate Courts, *South Carolina, Wills and Probate Records.* Esther [Hunter] McMein, Cherokee County, Alabama, *1850 Census.*

Lewis

Jerry (Lewis) (Smoot) (1820–1861)

Solomon Trail enslaved Jerry in Kentucky. Trail's daughter Duritha and her husband David Lewis were Latter-day Saint converts and survivors of the 1838 Haun's Mill Massacre in Missouri. After the massacre, they returned to Kentucky to recuperate in the Trail home, where they probably interacted again with Jerry. When Solomon Trail died, Duritha Lewis, then living in the Midwest, inherited Jerry and two young sisters, Caroline and Tampian. With the proceeds of the Trail estate, David and Duritha Lewis moved to the Great Salt Lake Valley.

Jerry helped support the family after David Lewis's death. The David Lewis probate showed him as "1 coloured man (35 yrs old)" with a value of $700. Duritha Lewis named him in a Utah Territory slave registration in 1858. She claimed to be "the true and Lawful owner of three persons of African blood, whose names and ages are <as> follows, to wit Jerry, Caroline, & Tampian, aged 38, 18, and 14. That she the said Duritha Lewis inherited them from her father Solomon Trail according to the Laws of the state of Kentucky." Brigham Young heard Lewis was trying to sell Jerry in 1860 and inquired about the "industrious <and> faithful" man and offered to purchase him himself and "set him at liberty." However, Lewis either sold or hired Jerry to A. O. Smoot.

In 1861, the *Deseret News* reported, "[A] colored man in the service of Mayor Smoot, was drowned while bathing in one of the sloughs between the city and the Jordan, which are now filled with water, as the river is at full banks. The body was found and recovered that evening." Based on multiple accounts, Jerry drowned near where I-15 now joins I-80, about where West Millcreek Road meets South 900 West in South Salt Lake. The death record shows, "Blackman Jeremiah of A. O. Smoot[,] 16 [June] 1861 Drowned in Millcreek." He was buried in a pauper's grave.

Enslavers: David Lewis (1814–1855) and Duritha Trail Lewis (Hendricks Andrew) (1813–); A. O. and Margaret McMeans Smoot

Wagon Company: David Lewis (1851)

Burial: B-4-168, Salt Lake City Cemetery, Salt Lake City, Utah

Notes: James T. Wilson heard about Jerry's death and concluded that Tom (Church) (Smoot) had drowned; he may not have known that Smoot hired or enslaved both Jerry and Tom.

Sources: Solomon Trail, Simpson County, Kentucky, *1820 Census*. Solomon Trail, Simpson County, Kentucky, *1830 Census*. David Lewis and Juanita Brooks, "Excerpt from the Journal of David Lewis," typescript, no date, Ancestry.com, 3. Solomon Trail, Simpson County, Kentucky, *1840 Census*. Solomon Trail, Simpson County, Kentucky Slave Schedule, *1850 Census*. Captain David Lewis's Company Report, August 22, 1851, box 1, Brigham Young Office Emigrating Companies Reports. David Lewis, Autobiography, 1854, microform, anonymous holograph copy of original, MSS MFilm 00157, Huntington Library, San Marino, CA. "Died" [David Lewis], *Deseret News*, September 26, 1855. David Lewis Probate, 1855, Third District Court Probate Case Files, Series 1621, box 1, folder 41, case 39, USHS. Duritha Lewis, Slave Registration, August 4, 1858, Salt Lake County Probate Court Case Files, Series 373, box 5, folder 11, USHS. Brigham Young to Mrs. David Lewis, January 3, 1860, box 19, folder 1, Office Files. Brigham Young to Mrs. David Lewis, March 31, 1860, box 19, folder 5, Office Files. A. O. Smoot, Great Salt Lake County, Utah Territory Slave Schedule, *1860 Census*. "Smoots Negro drowned named Jerry," Patty Bartlett Sessions, *Mormon Midwife: The 1846–1888 Diaries of Patty*

Bartlett Sessions, ed. Donna Toland Smart (Logan: Utah State University Press, 1997), 286. "Drowned," *Deseret News*, June 19, 1861. Wilson, "Life of James Thomas Wilson." "Blackman Jeremiah," Utah Archives and Records Service, *Utah Death Registers.* Jeremiah Blackman, June 16, 1861, grave B_4_Pauper_168, Salt Lake City Cemetery, Salt Lake City, Utah Division of State History, *Cemeteries and Burials.* William G. Hartley, *Kentucky Converts and Utah Pioneers: The Story of Five Brothers* (Salt Lake City, UT: Lewis Brothers Family Organization, 2014), 86.

Caroline Hoye (Lewis) (Williams) Bankhead Jackson (1841–1904)

Caroline was the daughter of Nathan and Hagar Hoye. After Solomon Trail died, his daughter Duritha Trail Lewis inherited Caroline and her sister Tampian and took them to Utah Territory in 1851. The 1858 David Lewis probate shows her as "1 [coloured] woman (16 [yrs old])" with a value of $500. Duritha Lewis registered the sisters in the probate court to comply with An Act in Relation to Service and then sold them to merchant Thomas S. Williams. In 1859, A. B. Miller and Williams fought in court over the ownership of Caroline and Tampian. The federal judge disagreed with the jury verdict, and the case was never reheard before Indigenous raiders murdered Williams in California. During the Williams probate, Seth M. Blair wrote to probate court judge Elias Smith about the ownership of Caroline and Tampian, including an unpaid mortgage on one of the girls. He asked that the administrator of the Williams estate "take possession of two Negresses belonging to the Estate of Said T. S. Williams[,] One in the hands of Horace S. Eldridge the other in the possession of the Widow of Said Williams." The probate case file includes no reply.

Newspapers mentioned the sisters, "the reigning ebony belles of Great Salt Lake City," as the reason for an 1859 fight between Thomas Bankhead Coleman and Shepherd Camp that ended in Shepherd's death.

Either Caroline or Tampian may have been in the Williams home when federally appointed territorial governor John W. Dawson propositioned widowed Albina Williams. Williams drove him off, and, after word spread, he fled the state.

After she was freed, Caroline married Samuel Bankhead, a pioneer of 1848. Samuel and their daughter Luela died, and Caroline remarried

Andrew Jackson, a Civil War veteran and later member of the Grand Army of the Republic. They had three children. Caroline and Andrew divorced, and later remarried each other. When Caroline died of typhoid fever in Ogden, Utah, her neighbor, Ella Smith, provided the information for her death certificate and named her parents as Nathan and Hagar Hoye. A year later, Andrew Jackson died by suicide, "despondent over the loss of his wife."

Documented Family: Father Nathan Hoye, mother Hagar Hoye; sister Tampian; husband Samuel Bankhead (1844–1871) and daughter Luela Bankhead (1866–1872); husband Andrew Jackson (1840–1905) and children William Sinclair Jackson (1872–1943, married Ada A. Wallace), Georgia Jackson (1876–1892), and Vincent Jackson (1877–1931, married May E. Chambers)

Enslavers: David and Duritha Trail Lewis; Thomas S. Williams, Albina Merrill Williams, and Priscilla Mogridge Smith Williams Staines (1818–1881)

Wagon Company: David Lewis (1851)

Burial: Annex-16-23-4E, Ogden City Cemetery, Ogden, Utah, with husband Andrew Jackson and daughter Georgia

Notes: The wagon roster numbers but does not name Caroline and Tampian. The 1870 census showed Caroline's family twice, living in the Ninth and Thirteenth Wards.

Sources: Captain David Lewis's Company Report, August 22, 1851, Brigham Young Office Emigrating Companies Reports. Duritha Lewis, Slave Registration, August 4, 1858, Salt Lake County Probate Court Case Files, Series 373, box 5, folder 11, USHS. Seth M. Blair to Elias Smith, c. 1860, Thomas S. Williams Probate, Third District Court Probate Case Files, Series 1621, USHS. "Shooting Affair," *Valley Tan*, April 19, 1859. "Third Judicial District Court," *Deseret News*, August 10, 1859. "Third Judicial District Court," *Deseret News*, August 24, 1859. "More Murders on the Mohave," *Los Angeles Star*, March 31, 1860. "Mormon Policy," *Los Angeles Star*, March 31, 1860. "Murders on The Mohave by Indians," *Sacramento Daily Union*, April 2, 1860. "The Murder of Williams," *Deseret News*, April 25, 1860. Stout, *Mormon Frontier*, 2:701. Percilla Williams and Albina Williams, Great Salt Lake County, Utah Territory Slave Schedule,

1860 Census. Carline Bankhead, Ward 9, Caroline Bankhead, Ward 13, Salt Lake County, Utah Territory, *1870 Census.* Samuel Bankhead, November 19, 1871, grave B_4_Pauper_151; Luella Bankhead, October 29, 1872, grave B_4_Pauper_150, Salt Lake City Cemetery, Salt Lake City, Utah Division of State History, *Cemeteries and Burials. Ogden City Directory for 1892–1893* (Ogden, UT: R. L. Polk & Co., 1892), 180. Caroline Jackson, October 18, 1904, grave Annex-16-23-4E, Ogden City Cemetery, Ogden, Utah Division of State History, *Cemeteries and Burials.* Caroline Jackson, October 18, 1904, Ogden, death certificate 0403216, Utah Department of Health, USHS. "Suicides at the 'White Elephant': Andrew Jackson, Colored," *Deseret Evening News,* August 7, 1905. "Utah State News," *Spanish Fork Press* (Spanish Fork, UT), August 10, 1905.

Tampian Simpson Hoye (Lewis) (Williams) Campbell (1844–1916)

David and Duritha Trail Lewis took Tampian and her older sister Caroline to Utah Territory in 1851. The David Lewis probate shows her as "1 [coloured] girl (11 [yrs old])" with a value of $300. In a time of great need, Duritha sold the sisters to merchant Thomas S. Williams. After she was freed, Tampian married Andrew Campbell, who arrived in the territory with the army and became a leading Utah civil rights activist. The couple had five children named after abolitionists or emancipators. Emma and Roscoe died young, but the others survived and did well in the integrated Utah schools. Daughter Nellie married and moved to West Virginia where she died. Her family transported her body back to Utah for burial.

Tampian died in 1916. Her husband survived her by six years. They have no known descendants.

Documented Family: Father Nathan Hoye, mother Hagar Hoye; sister Caroline; husband Andrew Campbell (1842–1922); children Emma B. Campbell (1874–1885), Sumner Lincoln Trowbridge Campbell (1877–1924), Ulysses Webster Campbell (1878–1940, married Myrtle Scaggs Grimes), Nellie Campbell (1880–1907, married William B. Walker), and Roscoe Campbell (1889–1889).

Enslavers: David and Duritha Trail Lewis; Thomas S. Williams, Albina Merrill Williams, and Priscilla Mogridge Smith Williams Staines

Wagon Company: David Lewis (1851)

Burial: B-24-11, Mount Olivet Cemetery, Salt Lake City, Utah, near husband Andrew and son Sumner Campbell

Notes: The name Tampian's son remembered as her maiden name, "Simpson," was the county where she was born. There was not a Simpson family there when Tampian was born, and those named Simpson in the area in previous generations did not enslave workers. She and her sister Caroline should share the family name Hoye, but Simpson appears here since her son used the name. William Jackson's draft registration shows Ulysses Campbell as his cousin. Daughters of Utah Pioneers documented Andrew Campbell and his four children, but missed Tampian, Caroline, and Jerry (Carter, *Negro Pioneer*, 70).

Sources: William Sinclair Jackson, Alameda, CA, United States, Selective Service System, *World War I Selective Service System Draft Registration Cards, 1917–1918*, National Archives Microfilm Publication M1509. Ancestry.com. https://www.ancestry.com/search/collections/6482. Tampica Ann Campbell, July 13, 1916, grave B_24_11, Mount Olivet Cemetery, Salt Lake City, Utah Division of State History, *Cemeteries and Burials*. Gampia Ann Campbell, July 11, 1916, Salt Lake City, death certificate 1602253, Utah Department of Health, USHS. "To the Colored Citizens of Utah," *Salt Lake Tribune*, November 7, 1873. "Amusements and Social," *Salt Lake Daily Tribune* (Salt Lake City, UT), January 2, 1892. "Names of Graduates," *Salt Lake Daily Tribune*, June 4, 1897. Nellie Campbell Walker, August 20, 1907, West Virginia County Courthouses, *West Virginia, Deaths Index, 1853–1973*. FamilySearch.org and Ancestry.com. https://www.ancestry.com/search/collections/2568. Nellie Walker, Wheeling, West Virginia, *Salt Lake County (UT) Death Records*. "Death Claims Old Negro Resident," *Salt Lake Telegram* (Salt Lake City, UT), March 30, 1922. "Deaths and Funerals," *Salt Lake Tribune*, March 31, 1922.

McKown

Female (McKown) (1825?–)

Francis McKown told Brigham Young that this unnamed woman was born into his household. By 1830, she was left motherless. McKown took her and her brother to Utah Territory where she served as the housekeeper since Francis's wife Margaret Lockhart died while traveling to Utah Territory.

When McKown decided to return to Mississippi, the enslaved woman sought refuge in Brigham Young's home. McKown wrote to Brigham Young: "my Negro Girl is at your house and is desirous to not leave the Valley." McKown said that he knew she expected him to "Correct hur if I get hur but this is the first offence She Ever was guilty of and I am persuaded to think my self that She is not to Blame." He thought an unnamed neighbor had encouraged her to run away. McKown asked Young to send her back and promised that he would not whip her. "She was Borne mine and I raised hur till and it seems as though there was one out of the family ever since she has bin away." The woman probably accompanied McKown back to Mississippi around 1850, since she matches the description of a woman in McKown's household in 1860 and no one of her description appears in the records of the American West.

Enslaver: Francis McKown (1791–1869?)

Wagon Company: Heber C. Kimball (1848)

Notes: After McKown returned to Mississippi, two of the enslaved people in his household in the 1860 census were male, thirty-one, and female, thirty-five. Although no documentation confirms their identities, the dates match the 1830 and 1840 censuses and suggest the two were siblings, male and female, and between nineteen and twenty-seven years old when they crossed the country and back.

Sources: Francis McKown, Union County, South Carolina, *1830 Census*. Francis McKown, Monroe County, Mississippi, *1840 Census*. Brown, box 1, folder 1, images 27–28, Reminiscences. Report of Mississippi Co^y, May 23, 1848, Camp of Israel Schedules and Reports. Francis McKown to Brigham Young, March 31, 1849, box 21, folder 16, Office Files. Sampson McKown and Tabitha E. Box, June 28, 1854, Itawamba, Hunting for Bears Genealogy Society, *Mississippi, Compiled Marriage Index, 1776–1935*, Ancestry.com. https://www.ancestry.com/search/collections/7842. Frank McKown, Itawamba County, Mississippi Slave Schedule, *1860 Census*.

Male (McKown) (1829?–)

This man was born to a woman enslaved by Francis and Margaret Lockhart McKown. He went to Utah Territory and probably accompanied McKown back to Mississippi around 1850. Nothing more is known of him.

Enslaver: Francis McKown
Wagon Company: Heber C. Kimball (1848)

Moody

Louisa (Moody) (1838–)

Preston Thomas baptized Louisa into the Church of Jesus Christ of Latter-day Saints in Texas in 1853 along with members of the William C. Moody family who enslaved her. Tax records suggest that she had not been in the household long. The family took Louisa to Utah Territory in 1853 where she appeared on a list of rebaptisms two or three years later, with her birthplace shown as Alabama. She does not appear in any additional known records.

Enslavers: William C. Moody (1819–1906) and Harriet Henson Moody (1820–1884)
Wagon Company: Moses Daley Freight Train (1853)
Notes: The 1850 slave schedule for Grimes County, Texas, is badly damaged, and the legible part does not show William C. Moody. The Preston Thomas diary transcription is closed to researchers at the Church History Library, but derivative versions are available.
Sources: William C. Moody, *Texas, County Tax Rolls.* Wm C. Moody, Grimes County, Texas, *1850 Census.* Preston Thomas, Daniel H. Thomas, and Annette Taylor, "Preston Thomas [Diaries and Biography]," digital copy of typescript, 1940; n.d. https://docs.wixstatic.com/ugd/78a476_22 d3bdc50ebe4f0398ed3e288858d84e.pdf. Loisa, Alabama, 1838, baptized April 22 [year unknown], "Black," Record of Members, 1849–1941, Salt Lake City Fifteenth Ward, microfilm 26675, FHL. Jeffery O. Johnson,

email message to author, May 27, 2014. W. Paul Reeve, email message to author, August 4, 2019. E. Grant Moody, Michael F. Moody, Penelope Moody Allen, and Elaine McAllister Harry Moody, *The John Wyatt Moody Family: Past and Present* (Tempe, AZ: Dr. Thomas Moody Family Organization, 1985).

Murphy

Phoebe (Murphy) (1810–1862?)

Explorer Richard Burton noted the presence in an 1860 Latter-day Saint wagon company of "an exceedingly plain middle-aged and full-blooded negro woman, who was fairly warned—the children of Ham are not admitted to the communion of the Saints, and consequently to the forgiveness of sins and a free seat in Paradise—that she was 'carrying coals to Newcastle.'" Burton's comment is the only known contemporaneous description of Phoebe, a fifty-year-old woman enslaved by Emanuel M. and Nancy Easters Murphy, but Burton did not report what, if anything, Phoebe said in response.

Nancy Murphy probably inherited Phoebe from her father around 1851. Murphy descendants later remembered an additional enslaved man they called "Old Tom," but no documents support him being a part of the household, and they probably remembered Tom (Church) (Smoot), since Tom's enslaver A. O. Smoot helped the Murphy family settle in Utah. The family also remembered that Tom and Phoebe died of the cold. Tom died in early 1862, and a few lines later, the burial record shows an unnamed person who died in January 1862 in the general neighborhood. Combined with the family memory and in the absence of other documentation, the blank entry may be the last record of Phoebe's life.

Enslavers: Emanuel Masters Murphy (1809–1871) and Nancy Easters Murphy (1813–1898)

Wagon Company: Jesse Murphy (1860)

Burial: Possibly E-12-8, Salt Lake City Cemetery, Salt Lake City, Utah

Note: Murphy descendants wondered if a man in the household named Jacob Dalson was "Old Tom," but Dalson was White and born about 1840.

Sources: Richard F. Burton, *The City of the Saints, and Across the Rocky Mountains to California* (New York, NY: Harper & Brothers, 1862), 181. E. M. Murphy, 1851, 1859, Weakley County (TN) Trustee, *Tax Books.* Robert Easter Will, 1845, Union District, South Carolina County, District, and Probate Courts, *South Carolina, Wills and Probate Records.* Emanuel M. Murphy, Fayette County, Georgia, *1850 Census.* "Phoebe (colored) [age] 50," Jesse Murphy Company, 1860, Brigham Young Office Emigrating Companies Reports. Don E. Norton Jr., *Emanuel Masters Murphy: 1809-71, Ancestry, Life, Children* (Provo, UT: Stevenson's Genealogical Center, 1980), 98. Entry 1461, Twelfth Ward, grave E-12-8, Utah Archives and Records Service, *Utah Death Registers.* Salt Lake City Cemetery, telephone conversation, December 8, 2017.

Pearson

Laura Pearson (1831–1878)

Richard Pearson bought Laura in South Carolina in 1847 and immediately took her to Missouri. After Pearson divorced his young wife Martha Powers (Pearson Luzzadder), he took Laura and her daughter, Susan Price, to Utah Territory, and he and Laura married there before they moved to Colusa County, California. Richard died in 1865 and left his estate to Laura and her children. Pearson's daughter from his first marriage, Adelaide Pearson De Loge, sued for his estate over the question of whether an enslaved person could marry. The California Supreme Court eventually ruled in favor of Laura Pearson, finding, "The marriage of a master with his female slave amounts to a relinquishment of his right to hold her as a slave." Laura died not long after, much of the estate spent in legal fees. Several of her children passed as White, and one of her grandsons served as an army officer during the First World War.

Documented Family: Daughter Susan Price Halley (see below); husband Richard Pearson (1818–1865) and children Theodore Pearson (1856–1921, married Belle Scott, Hannah Farmer, and Bessie Gebbett), Henry Pearson (1857–1876), Mary Pearson (1858–1875), William Pearson (1859–1883?), Richard Pearson (1862–1883), and Jefferson Pearson (1865–1941?); daughter Josephine Pearson (1868–1877) with an unknown father

Enslaver: Richard Pearson (1818–1865)

Wagon Company: Probably merchant company

Burial: College City Cemetery, College City, California

Sources: Adelaide Pearson v. Laura Pearson et al., *Reports of Cases Determined in the Supreme Court of the State of California, Vol. 51, 1875–1877,* ed. Charles A. Tuttle (San Francisco, CA: Bancroft-Whitney, 1906), 120–24. "Rocky Point, Humboldt River," *Sacramento Daily Union,* June 4, 1852. Richard Pearson, Colusa County, California Census of Agriculture, *1860 Census.* Richard Pearson Will, 1865, California County, District, and Probate Courts, *California, Wills and Probate Records,* Ancestry.com, https://www.ancestry.com/search/collections/8639. "A Fortune Saved—A California Romance," *Daily Alta California,* January 8, 1872. "Supreme Court Decisions, October Term, 1873, Pearson vs. Pearson," *Sacramento Daily Union,* October 25, 1873. "Supreme Court Decisions, October Term, 1875," *Sacramento Daily Union,* January 26, 1876. Richard Pearson Probate, 1865, Colusa County, *California, Wills.* Guardianship of Theodore Pearson, Richard Pearson, William Pearson, and Jefferson Pearson, Minors, 1876, case 111, Colusa County, *California, Wills.* James T. Halley, New Philadelphia, OH, 1949, National Archives in Washington, DC, *Headstone Applications for Military Veterans, 1925–1963.* Ancestry.com. https://www.ancestry.com/search/collections/2375.

Susan Price Halley (1852–1930)

Born in Missouri to Laura and an unknown father, Susan went west as a small child with her mother and the man soon to be her stepfather, Richard Pearson. The family settled in Colusa County, California. Susan Price eventually married Frederick F. Halley, and she and her children passed as White. She moved to Oregon with her children but is buried in California; her gravestone is inscribed, "Darling Mother."

Documented Family: Mother Laura Pearson; husband Frederick Francis Halley (1826–1905) and children William P. Halley (1867–1889), Mary Ellen Halley (1871–1940, married Warren H. Leach), Frederick Francis Halley Jr. (1872–1948, married Mabel Richardson), Laura Halley (1877–1946, married Charles Farmer and Josephus Damsell), Nellie Maude

Halley (1882–1932, married Ellis Evans), and James Theodore Halley (1894–1949)

Enslaver: Richard Pearson

Burial: 14-J, College City Cemetery, College City, California

Sources: Susan Halley, June 24, 1930, College City, California, *FindAGrave*.

Perkins

Frank Perkins (1810–1888)

Frank was probably born to an enslaved woman, Dawney or Rondowney, not long after she was deeded to Reuben and Elizabeth Petillo Perkins by Elizabeth's father. Frank Perkins lived with his enslavers in Jackson County, Tennessee, and then in the late 1830s, Livingston (later Grundy) County, Missouri. Census records support the memory that Frank had a wife in Tennessee, perhaps the mother of his older children, and a second wife, Esther, in Missouri, probably the mother of his younger children.

Many of Reuben and Elizabeth's children joined the Church of Jesus Christ of Latter-day Saints in Illinois, and the extended family went west in 1849. During the journey, Frank was injured in a stampede.

Reuben Perkins established residence in Session Settlement (now Bountiful), Davis County. He was far from wealthy, but due to Frank and Esther's increasing family, he was the largest enslaver in Utah Territory after Bird B. Barnett and Robert M. Smith left for California. Frank's family appears in the 1860 census slave schedule but not in the 1850 census or Reuben Perkins's consecration deed. Reuben appears in labor tithing records, but Frank does not.

Although there is no independent documentation, a neighbor later remembered that Reuben Perkins sent the enslaved Perkins children to school. Another neighbor recalled that a company of Latter-day Saint immigrants had just arrived in the valley. "Uncle Ike Atkinson said that he had heard [Frank Perkins] say [to his son], 'Wesley, get your hat on or you'll be as brown as the emigrants.'"

No records document when Frank and his family knew they were free, but it might have been at the end of the Civil War when the family moved to Great Salt Lake City. Within a short time, Esther and many of the surviving children died, leaving only Frank, Ben, Mary Ann, Charlotte, and Sylvester. The grieving family sent Sylvester to live with Elizabeth Edwards Jones.

Frank was briefly married to Connecticut native Jane Manning James. He was a member of the Church of Jesus Christ of Latter-day Saints, and he, Jane, and his daughter Mary Ann Perkins James participated in 1875 Latter-day Saint proxy baptisms for the dead in the Endowment House. Frank and Mary were baptized on behalf of Mary's grandmother Dawney and aunts Darkous, Lousindy, Maria, and Seely; some of Jane's relatives; and Frank's nephew George Green and cousin Jack Vose.

His complete work history is unknown, but the census records show that Perkins worked for Mary Ann Gurnsey Young and Ann Oliver Young, sisters-in-law of Brigham Young, and Dr. Washington F. Anderson.

Documented Family: Mother Dawney or Rondowney; sisters Darkous, Lousindy, Maria, and Seely; relative Benjamin Perkins (1819–1909); wife Esther Perkins and children Mary Ann Perkins (1840–1917, married Sylvester James), Sarah Perkins (1842–1866), Downey Perkins (1848–1869, married Silas Woolridge), Ephraim Perkins (dates unknown), Wesley Perkins (1852–1866), Alma/Albert Perkins (1858–1866), Manissa Perkins (dates unknown), Thomas Perkins (dates unknown), Sylvester Perkins (1856/1866–1934, married Martha Stevens), Charlotte Perkins (1862–1898, married Charles Campbell); wife Jane Elizabeth Manning James (1813/1822–1908; divorced)

Enslavers: Reuben Perkins (1783–1871) and Elizabeth Petillo Perkins (1782–1863)

Wagon Company: Allen Taylor (1849)

Burial: UK 6429, Salt Lake City Cemetery, Salt Lake City, Utah

Notes: Do not confuse Frank Perkins with Franklin Monroe Perkins (1829–1865), son of Reuben Perkins. Frank Perkins's entry in *Pioneers and Prominent Men of Utah* is partially correct. The correct page of the 1840 census shows the Perkins household with four males under the age of ten, one male under the age of twenty-three (Ben), one male under the age of thirty-five (Frank), and one female under ten (Mary Ann).

Based on the 1840 census, Frank was born between 1805 and 1816, so the birth date used for this book is from the next time his age is given in the 1860 census.

Sources: "A Bill of sale from Littleton Petillo to Reuben Perkins & wife dated Aug. 10th 1808, proved by Wm Ghent ... to my beloved son-in-law [Reuben Perkins] & his wife Elizabeth ... a Negro girl named Rondowney." Lincoln County (NC) Court of Pleas and Quarter Sessions, January Term, 1809, *Minutes, 1806–1813*; Anne McAllister and Kathy Sullivan, *Lincoln County Court of Pleas and Quarter Sessions* (Lenoir, NC: privately published, 1989), 6, quoted in Eugene H. Perkins, *The First Mormon Perkins Families: Progenitors and Utah Pioneers of 1847–1852; A Contemporary History of the Ute Perkins Line* (privately printed, 2008), 86. Reuben Perkins, Jackson County, Tennessee, *1830 Census*. Reuben Perkins, Early Tax Lists of Tennessee, 1836, 67–69, Tennessee State Library and Archives, *Tennessee, Early Tax List*. Reuben Perkins, Marion Township, Livingston County, Missouri, *1840 Census*. Allen Taylor's 100, Report, c. October 1849, Camp of Israel Schedules and Reports. Margaret Gay Judd Clawson, Reminiscences, c. 1904–1911, 57 [image 131], MS 3712, CHL. Reuben Perkins, Time Book of Tithing Hands for the Year 1850, 18, CR 104 28, General Tithing Office Tithing Labor Time Books, 1850–1854, CHL. Reuben Perkins, Davis County Transfer Book, 1857–1858, box 4, folder 2, 3, CR 5 53, Consecration Deeds, 1854–1867, CHL. Frank Perkins, North Kanyon Ward, Davis County, *1856 Utah Territorial Census*. Reuben Perkins, ten slaves, Davis County, Utah Territory Slave Schedule, *1860 Census*. Frank Perkins, Salt Lake City Ward 13, Utah Territory, *1870 Census*. Frank Perkins, Salt Lake City Ward 13, Utah Territory, *1880 Census*. Frank Perkins, January 22, 1888, grave UK6429, Salt Lake City Cemetery, Salt Lake City, Utah Division of State History, *Cemeteries and Burials*. "Perkins, Franklin [sic]," in Frank E. Esshom, *Pioneers and Prominent Men of Utah* (Salt Lake City, UT: Utah Pioneers Book Publishing Company, 1913), 1096. Daughters of Utah Pioneers, Davis County Company, *East of Antelope Island: History of the First Fifty Years of Davis County* (Bountiful, UT: Carr Printing Company, 1948), 154, 158. "Record of Baptisms for the Dead for the Seed of Cain," September 3, 1875, Endowment House, Salt Lake City, Utah Territory, microfilm 255498, FHL. Tonya Reiter, "Black Saviors on Mount Zion: Proxy Baptisms and Latter-day

Saints of African Descent," *Journal of Mormon History* 43, no. 4 (October 2017): 100–23. https://doi.org/10.5406/jmormhist.43.4.0100. Bankhead, interview by Lawrence. Mary Lucile Bankhead, interview by Alan Cherry, April 11, 1985, interview CRC-P2, transcript, LDS Afro-American Oral History Project, Charles Redd Center for Western Studies, Brigham Young University, Provo, UT.

Esther Perkins (1820–1865)

Esther was from Missouri. Her great-granddaughter remembered that she was Native American, so she may have been part or all Indigenous or perhaps enslaved by a Native American. She married Frank Perkins and may have had eleven children, although no documentation confirms the names and birth dates of the children in the family. Reuben Perkins took Esther and her family to the Salt Lake Valley in 1849. The settlers' cattle were spooked by the bison on the plains, and Esther started a stampede when she waved a dishtowel out the end of a wagon.

The White Perkins family later remembered Esther as "Old Ess," but she was around forty-five years old when she died of tuberculosis right before Christmas in 1865. She was buried in a pauper's grave.

Documented Family: Husband Frank Perkins; children (possible stepdaughter) Mary Ann, Sarah, Downey, Ephraim, Wesley, Albert/Alma, Manissa, Thomas, Sylvester, and Charlotte

Enslavers: Reuben and Elizabeth Petillo Perkins

Wagon Company: Allen Taylor (1849)

Burial: B-4-446, Salt Lake City Cemetery, Salt Lake City, Utah

Sources: Esther Perkins, North Kanyon Ward, Davis County, *1856 Utah Territorial Census*. Esther Perkins, "coloured woman, wife of Frank, supposed to be 45 years old," December 20, 1865, Utah Archives and Records Service, *Utah Death Registers*. Perkins, *First Mormon Perkins Families*, 309. Emily L. Snyder Thompson, "History of Emily Lydia Snyder Thompson," typescript, n.d. FSFT. https://www.familysearch.org/photos/artifacts/22922719.

Benjamin Perkins (1819–1909)

Records give a range of ages for Benjamin Perkins. When he died, Sylvester Perkins reported that Ben's father was Frank Perkins and his mother was unknown. However, in 1860, Reuben Perkins reported that Benjamin was forty-seven years old, and Frank was fifty, so the biological relationship is unknown. A neighbor later remembered that his enslavers sold or hired out Perkins to merchants Livingston & Kinkead. The neighbor reported that the children in the family "were heart broken and the white children's fun was all killed for that day."

Perkins testified as a witness in court during an 1859 murder trial, a rare event in the United States since most jurisdictions did not allow the enslaved to testify in court.

After he was freed, Ben worked at William H. Kimball's hotel and stage station in Summit County, and then he made his way north to Butte, Montana. He was a member of the Butte AME Church. A newspaper reporter thought it was rare sport when Ben Perkins claimed he was descended from the "kings of San Domingo," but the memory situates his family in the Caribbean prior to their arrival in the United States. As he aged, he was injured several times and began to act erratically, so Butte officials sent him on the train to Salt Lake City. He eventually lost his sight and died at Sylvester Perkins's home in Millcreek.

Documented Family: Possible father Frank Perkins; possible stepmother Esther and half-siblings

Enslavers: Reuben and Elizabeth Petillo Perkins

Wagon Company: Allen Taylor (1849)

Burial: A-131-7, Elysian Burial Gardens, Millcreek, Utah

Notes: The age on his death certificate of "abt 90" is within two years of his age given in the 1860 census when he lived with Reuben Perkins, suggesting an approximate birth year of 1819.

Sources: Benjamin Perkins, North Kanyon Ward, Davis County, *1856 Utah Territorial Census*. "Third Judicial District Court," *Deseret News*, September 21, 1859. Reuben Perkins, ten slaves, Davis County, Utah Territory Slave Schedule, *1860 Census*. Benjamin Perkins, Summit County,

Utah Territory, *1870 Census*. "Butte in Brief," *Montana Standard* (Butte, MT), February 13, 1896. "A Church Debate," *Montana Standard*, August 20, 1896. "City News in Brief," *Butte Daily Post* (Butte, MT), May 10, 1897. "City News in Brief," *Butte Daily Post*, January 18, 1898. "Ben [Perkins] is Unlucky," *Anaconda Standard* (Anaconda, MT), January 18, 1898. "May Have Wheels: A Colored Man Detained in Jail on the Charge of Insanity," *Butte Daily Post*, February 21, 1898. "Shipped to Salt Lake," *Anaconda Standard*, February 27, 1898. "Town Talk," *Salt Lake Herald*, March 1, 1898. "In Police Circles," *Salt Lake Tribune*, October 16, 1898. Benj. Perkins, Salt Lake County, Utah, *1900 Census*. Leggroan and Leggroan Interview, 33. Benjimin [sic] Perkins, June 14, 1909, grave A-131-7, Elysian Burial Gardens, Salt Lake City, Utah Division of State History, *Cemeteries and Burials*. Benjiman [sic] Perkins, June 14, 1909, Wilford Ward, Salt Lake County, death certificate 0901978, Utah Department of Health, USHS. Daughters of Utah Pioneers, *East of Antelope Island*, 158.

Mary Ann Perkins James (1840–1917)

Mary was born in Missouri and accompanied her enslaved family to the Great Salt Lake Valley in 1849. She and her family lived in Davis County. They moved to Great Salt Lake City after they were freed. There she married Sylvester James, the son of Jane Manning James. Mary had eight children, but only two of them outlived her.

Mary and Sylvester owned a farm in Millcreek, Salt Lake County. They grew vegetables, fruit, and wheat; raised chickens, turkeys, and geese; and hunted game. The women in the family preserved food from their garden and took in laundry. Although the community did not segregate schools, and both White and Black children played together, it did segregate work and church. Black families could attend church services, picnics, and programs, as well as quilting bees, but not dances or most temple ceremonies, although Mary and her father and stepmother did Latter-day Saint baptisms for the dead in the Endowment House in 1875.

Lucile Perkins Bankhead remembered Mary and Sylvester: "They did the best they could. Whoever was over them they abided by that. As for them complaining about themselves, I never heard it." She explained that the only criticism she heard was when Sylvester talked about Brigham Young. "He did not like him. As for the others, it just seemed like they were moving in a smooth line . . . They thought that was their life, and that was it." Descendants of the family have maintained residence in Utah since their ancestors arrived in 1847 and 1849.

Documented Family: Parents Frank and (possibly) Esther Perkins; siblings; husband Sylvester L. (Sherman) James (1838–1920); children William Henry James (1866–1921), Esther Jane James (1869–1945, married Henry A. Leggroan), Nella James (1871–1887), Sylvester James (1874–1874), Albert Sherman James (1876–1879), Nettie James (1878–1911, married Louis B. Leggroan), Manissa or Massa James (1881–1881), and Mary Ann James (1885–1888)

Wagon Company: Allen Taylor (1849)

Enslavers: Reuben and Elizabeth Petillo Perkins

Burial: A-50-7, Elysian Burial Gardens, Millcreek, Utah

Note: Sylvester James used his stepfather's surname although he was listed as Sherman in the 1847 wagon roster. Sylvester's family recalled that his father was French Canadian, but the Sherman family of Connecticut was closely related to General William Tecumseh Sherman and not French Canadian.

Sources: Mary Perkins, North Kanyon Ward, Davis County, *1856 Utah Territorial Census.* "Record of Baptisms for the Dead." Reiter, "Black Saviors." Tonya Reiter, "Life on the Hill: The Black Farming Families of Millcreek," *Journal of Mormon History* 44, no. 4 (October 2018): 68–89. https://doi.org/10.5406/jmormhist.44.4.0068. Brigham Young's 1847 Emigration Division (First Division) Daniel Spencer's 100, Schedules, c. February 1847, box 1, folder 16, Camp of Israel Schedules and Reports. Mary James, Salt Lake City Ward 1, Utah Territory, *1870 Census.* Mary Ann James, Salt Lake City Ward 1, Utah Territory, *1880 Census.* Mary James, Millcreek, Utah, *1900 Census.* Mary James, Wilford, Utah, *1910 Census.* Bankhead, interview by Lawrence. Bankhead, interview by Cherry, 10. Mary Ann Perkins James, October 18, 1917, grave A-50-7, Elysian Burial Gardens, Salt Lake City, Utah Division of State History, *Cemeteries and Burials.* Mary Ann James, November 16, 1917, Salt Lake City, death certificate 1703061; Sylvester James, March 5, 1920, Millcreek, death certificate 2002152, Utah Department of Health, USHS.

Sarah Perkins (1842–1866)

Sarah was a daughter of Frank and Esther Perkins, born the property of Reuben and Elizabeth Petillo Perkins. Sarah spent more than a decade in Session Settlement (Bountiful), before the family was freed and moved to Great Salt Lake City. Three months after her mother's death, Sarah died from "milk fever" (puerperal or childbed fever) after giving birth in 1866. Both the identity of the father and the fate of the infant are unknown. Sarah's family recalled that she married a man named Peter Livingston. The death record does not list a husband, and there is no documentation of a Peter Livingston in Utah. There was, however, her half-brother Benjamin's employer, Howard Livingston (1823–1898), who was still in the area when Sarah's child was conceived. He or an unknown Black man in his employ may have fathered the child. Sarah is buried in a pauper's grave in the Salt Lake City Cemetery.

Documented Family: Parents Frank and Esther Perkins; siblings; child, unknown (Perkins or Livingston) (1865–)

Wagon Company: Allen Taylor (1849)

Enslavers: Reuben and Elizabeth Petillo Perkins

Burial: B-4-447, Salt Lake City Cemetery, Salt Lake City, Utah

Sources: Sarah Perkins, North Kanyon Ward, Davis County, *1856 Utah Territorial Census*. Sarah Perkins (colored), March 24, 1866, Utah Archives and Records Service, *Utah Death Registers*. Esshom, *Pioneers and Prominent Men*, 1096. Joseph P. Smallwood v. Howard Livingston (1865), Salt Lake County Probate Court Case Files, Series 373, box 10, folder 37, USHS. Walker Bros. v. Howard Livingston (1865), Salt Lake County Probate Court Case Files, Series 373, box 10, folder 78, USHS.

Downey Perkins Woolridge (1848–1869)

Downey was named after her grandmother Dawney or Rondowney. In the mid-1860s, she married Silas Woolridge, formerly enslaved by the Sprouse-Wooldridge family. Downey died after the birth of her first child, Silas. Downey's sister Mary may have taken the baby since she had a baby herself, but two weeks after Downey died, newborn Silas died of "innutrition," meaning he starved to death. The diagnosis did not mean Silas did not have food; most cases of innutrition were caused by an illness or birth defect. Mother and son were buried next to each other in the Salt Lake City Cemetery.

Documented Family: Parents Frank and Esther Perkins; siblings; husband Silas Woolridge (1814/1836–1917); son Silas Woolridge (1869–1869)

Enslavers: Reuben and Elizabeth Petillo Perkins

Wagon Company: Allen Taylor (1849)

Burial: Buried next to infant son Silas, REM 27 and 28, Salt Lake City Cemetery, Salt Lake City, Utah

Sources: Dorney Woolrich, October 30, 1869; Silas Woolrich, November 9, 1869, Utah Archives and Records Service, *Utah Death Registers.* E. H. Gibbs, "Bowel Complaints of Children," *Hall's Journal of Health* 24, no. 11 (November 1877): 320–21.

Ephraim Perkins (dates unknown)

The family reported Ephraim's name and that he died at age twenty-one. He appeared in the 1856 Utah territorial census without an age, but nothing more is known about him. He may have been born in Missouri and traveled across the plains with his family, or he may have been born in Utah Territory.

Documented Family: Parents Frank and Esther Perkins

Enslavers: Reuben and Elizabeth Petillo Perkins

Sources: Ephraim Perkins, North Kanyon Ward, Davis County, *1856 Utah Territorial Census.* Esshom, *Pioneers and Prominent Men*, 1096.

Wesley Perkins (1852–1866)

Wesley was a son of Frank and Esther Perkins, born around 1852 in Davis County, Utah Territory. He died of a lung disease in April 1866, perhaps the tuberculosis that killed his mother and brother Alma. He is buried in a pauper's grave in the Salt Lake City Cemetery.

Documented Family: Parents Frank and Esther Perkins; siblings

Enslavers: Reuben and Elizabeth Petillo Perkins

Burial: B-4-448, Salt Lake City Cemetery, Salt Lake City, Utah

Sources: Wesley Perkins, North Kanyon Ward, Davis County, *1856 Utah Territorial Census*. Daughters of Utah Pioneers, *East of Antelope Island*, 158. Wesley Perkins, April 30, 1866, *Salt Lake County (UT) Death Records*. Wesley Perkins, Salt Lake City Cemetery, Salt Lake City, Utah Division of State History, *Cemeteries and Burials*.

Manissa Perkins (dates unknown)

Manissa died as an infant. None of the Perkins children are listed in Davis County burials, but perhaps Manissa was among unidentified remains moved from the original cemetery to the Bountiful City Cemetery.

Documented Family: Parents Frank and Esther Perkins; siblings
Enslavers: Reuben and Elizabeth Petillo Perkins
Burial: Possibly the Bountiful City Cemetery, Bountiful, Utah
Sources: Esshom, *Pioneers and Prominent Men*, 1096. "History of Bountiful City Cemetery," *Bountiful, Est. 1847*, website. Accessed March 27, 2019. https://www.bountifulutah.gov/Cemetery-History.

Thomas Perkins (dates unknown)

Thomas died as an infant. He does not appear in vital records.

Documented Family: Parents Frank and Esther Perkins; siblings
Enslavers: Reuben and Elizabeth Petillo Perkins
Burial: Possibly the Bountiful City Cemetery, Bountiful, Utah
Sources: Esshom, *Pioneers and Prominent Men*, 1096.

Alma (Albert) Perkins (1858–1866)

Alma was a son of Frank and Esther Perkins, born around 1858, and given a name from the Book of Mormon. The family later remembered his name as "Albert." He died of a lung disease. He was buried in a pauper's grave, but in the White Perkins family section of the Salt Lake City Cemetery. Perhaps news of the multiple deaths reached the Perkins family in Bountiful, and they were able to assist with his burial.

Documented Family: Parents Frank and Esther Perkins; siblings

Enslavers: Reuben and Elizabeth Petillo Perkins

Burial: C-2-1-5W, Salt Lake City Cemetery, Salt Lake City, Utah

Sources: Alma Perkins, May 25, 1866, *Salt Lake County (UT) Death Records*. Alma Perkins, Salt Lake City Cemetery, Salt Lake City, Utah Division of State History, *Cemeteries and Burials*, Esshom, *Pioneers and Prominent Men*, 1096.

Sylvester Perkins (1856/1865–1934)

Birth dates given for Sylvester range from 1856 to 1865. The 1856 territorial census lists Sylvester, which means he would have been enslaved at his birth and would have been the next-to-the-last living of those enslaved in Utah. *Pioneers and Prominent Men of Utah* supports this birth date and birth order in the family. Sylvester's family recalled that his parents could not care for him and "gave him to Mrs. [Elizabeth Edwards] Jones," and that he worked on her ranch for many years "on the Promotory [sic] out there herding horses and breaking horses for them." He worked as a cowboy in Colorado for many years before he married Martha Stevens, a granddaughter of Green and Martha Flake. He purchased Elizabeth Jones's farm, and he and his family lived in Millcreek. His daughter Lucile Perkins Bankhead was a member of Daughters of Utah Pioneers and the first Relief Society president of the Genesis Group, an organization of the Church of Jesus Christ of Latter-day Saints in Salt Lake City.

Documented Family: Probable parents Frank and Esther Perkins and siblings; wife Martha Stevens (1875–1954); children Mary Lucile Perkins (1902–1994, married Thomas LeRoy Bankhead), Frank S. Perkins (1904–1977, married Carrie Washington), Huron Perkins (1908–1976, married Sammie Davidson Haynes), George S. Perkins (1913–2005, married Lillie Ellis and Sammia Morgan or Heath)

Enslavers: Possibly Reuben and Elizabeth Petillo Perkins

Burial: A-131-8, Elysian Burial Gardens, Millcreek, Utah

Sources: Sylvester Perkins, North Kanyon Ward, Davis County, *1856 Utah Territorial Census*. Sylvester Perkins, Millcreek, Utah, *1900 Census*.

Figure 10.1. William James and Sylvester Perkins. Used by permission, Utah State Historical Society.

Sylvester Perkins, Wilford, Utah, *1910 Census*. Sylvester Perkins, Salt Lake County, Utah, *1920 Census*. Sylvester Perkins, Salt Lake County, Utah, *1930 Census*. Sylvester Perkins, March 9, 1934, grave A-131-8, Millcreek Cemetery (Elysian Burial Gardens), Salt Lake City, Utah Division of State History, *Cemeteries and Burials*. Elizabeth Jones, Homestead Patent, Certificate 2233, Application 3191, Salt Lake City, Utah Territory, June 20, 1883, US Department of the Interior and Bureau of Land Management,

General Land Office Records. Bankhead, interview by Cherry. Ronald G. Coleman, "African-American Community," in *Missing Stories: An Oral History of Ethnic and Minority Groups in Utah*, eds. Leslie G. Kelen and Eileen Hallet Stone (Salt Lake City, UT: University of Utah Press, 1996), 73–77.

Charlotte Perkins Campbell (1862–1898)

Depending on her exact birth date, Charlotte "Lottie" was probably born to still-enslaved Esther in Davis County. She lived with her sister Mary Ann Perkins James in Great Salt Lake City after they were freed. She found work as a servant in the house of notorious madam Kate Flint, and she eventually became a prostitute herself. She married prizefight organizer Charles Campbell in the 1890s and died of tuberculosis not long afterward.

Documented Family: Parents Frank and Esther Perkins; siblings; husband Charles Campbell (1855–)

Enslavers: Reuben and Elizabeth Petillo Perkins?

Burial: L-90-11, Mount Olivet Cemetery, Salt Lake City, Utah

Notes: Charlotte is not in the 1860 census slave schedule, so she was probably born after mid-June 1860. The birth date of 1862 comes from the 1870 census.

Sources: Charlotte Perkins [James], Salt Lake City Ward 1, Utah Territory, 1870 *Census*. Lotta Perkins, Summit County, Utah Territory, 1880 *Census*. "In the Police Court," *Salt Lake Herald*, June 13, 1886. "Before Judge Pyper," *Salt Lake Herald*, June 16, 1886. "Before Judge Pyper," *Salt Lake Herald*, January 9, 1887. "A Round-Up," *Salt Lake Herald*, March 8, 1888. "Police Court," *Salt Lake Herald*, March 9, 1888. "In the Law's Clutches," *Salt Lake Herald*, April 5, 1889. "Police Court," *Deseret Evening News*, December 17, 1890. "For Vagrancy," *Salt Lake Times* (Salt Lake City, UT), December 17, 1890. "The Frail Again Raided," *Salt Lake Herald*, February 11, 1891. "In Handcuff Circles," *Salt Lake Herald*, May 2, 1891. "Griffith an Angel," *Salt Lake Herald*, June 5, 1892. "In Police Circles," *Salt Lake Times*, November 1, 1892. "The Police Round-up," *Salt Lake Herald*, March 14, 1893. "Brief and Breezy," *Salt Lake Herald*, April 13, 1893. "Late Arrests,"

Salt Lake Herald, July 8, 1893. "Police Pointers," *Salt Lake Tribune*, May 6, 1894. "Coontown Raided," *Salt Lake Tribune*, August 30, 1894. "G. W. Bell, charged with an assault and battery upon Lottie Perkins, a colored prostitute . . . was held in bonds of $50." "Police Court Record," *Salt Lake Herald*, October 5, 1894. "Charles Campbell, who was held on the charge of residing in a house of ill-fame, was discharged." "Police Court," *Salt Lake Herald*, August 3, 1894. "Colored Men Fight a Duel," *Salt Lake Tribune*, November 7, 1895. "Thompson's Hearing," *Salt Lake Herald*, August 4, 1896. "Jim Williams Won," *Salt Lake Herald*, February 16, 1898. "Died," *Salt Lake Tribune*, September 2, 1898. Charlotte Perkins Campbell, grave L-90-11, Mount Olivet Cemetery, Salt Lake City. Mount Olivet Cemetery, telephone conversation, August 1, 2016.

Redd

Venus (Hancock) Redd (1810–1875)

Descendants of the family who enslaved Venus Redd remembered that her name was pronounced "ven-is" like the city in Italy, not "veen-us." John Hardison Redd kept a partial record of the members of his household, free and enslaved. (All later strikeouts removed here.)

> Moriah Daughter of Cupit and Amy was born October the 9th AD 1809
>
> Venius Daughter of Cupit and Amy was born August the 25th AD 1810
>
> Abram son of Cupit and Amy was born October the 9th AD 1812
>
> Chaney Daughter of Cupit and Amy was born March the 26th AD 1817
>
> Fanetty Daughter of Cupit and Amy was born June the 26th AD 1819
>
> Luke son of Venius was born Janry the 9th AD 1828
>
> Thomas son of Moriah was born Janry 23rd AD 1828

Cupit or Cupid was probably sold in 1796 between two members of the Williams family of Onslow County, North Carolina. Amy and her

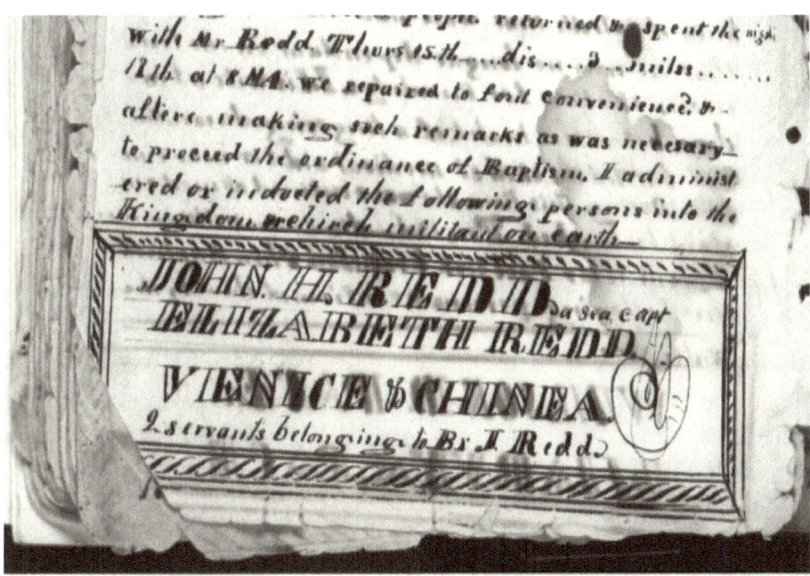

Figure 10.2. The baptisms of Venus Redd and Chaney Redd as recorded by John D. Lee. Church History Library, Salt Lake City, Utah.

children were probably enslaved by Zebedee Hancock. Zebedee Hancock left Chaney to his wife Nancy Rial Hancock and Venus to his daughter Elizabeth. When Nancy died, Chaney went to Elizabeth, then married to John Hardison Redd. Redd fathered a child, Luke, with eighteen-year-old Venus, and may have fathered additional children with Venus or her sisters Chaney and Moriah. The family later recalled that Redd was possessive of his enslaved women. A grandchild of John's son Lemuel recalled that Redd "was away from home and a neighbor's slave came over and slept in their slave quarters." When the neighbor located the slave, "How he begged and pleaded and cried for mercy, but they whipped him. They whipped him with a shovel. If pap had been home no one would have dared to come prowling around our slave quarters like that."

Latter-day Saint missionary John D. Lee recorded his baptisms of John and Elizabeth Redd, and "VENICE & CHINEA 2 servants belonging to Br J. Redd." In April 1845, John and Elizabeth Redd visited the headquarters of the Church of Jesus Christ of Latter-day Saints in

Nauvoo, Illinois. Tithing records show that John paid tithing donations for himself, Elizabeth, and their daughters of two pair of socks, $1.25 in silver, a shot gun, and a pistol. He paid $1.00 in silver in Venus's name.

It took several years for Redd to decide to go west. Historian Merina Smith wrote that John D. Lee courted already-married Caroline Gilliam, and she left for the West. Redd and Gilliam's husband went to retrieve her from Nebraska Territory in 1847. Redd and the reunited couple returned to Tennessee, and it was not until 1850 that the Redd family started west.

Redd and his household settled in Utah Valley and built homes and a sawmill. Redd descendants thought that Redd freed his enslaved people in the South, but they appeared in both 1850 population and slave schedules. Venus was rebaptized in 1852. She received a Biblical-style patriarchal blessing in 1855 that decreed solemn warnings and blessings for her life. Venus's blessing did not declare her lineage in the House of Israel, as most blessings did, but it promised her that "there is no difference whether . . . bond or free . . . Thou shalt be blest . . . [and] rejoice in a day to come."

Elizabeth Hancock Redd died in 1853, and John Hardison Redd died in 1858. After his death, his legal heirs divided his property between themselves and Venus, Luke, and Marinda. Since the enslaved could not own property, this suggests that the family considered them free.

Venus, Luke, and Marinda remained in Spanish Fork. Venus worked as a midwife. One family remembered that Venus delivered Serine Torjusdatter Evensen Gardner's twins. She also may have delivered Marinda's sons and Luke's children.

Spanish Fork bishop Albert King Thurber wrote that he ate dinner with "Canaanites" Luke and Venus Redd. He said he "enjoyed a good time. Cabbage and pork with other good articles of food were on the table." A traveler wrote that in Spanish Fork, "There were no Irish, but there was one family of Africans, who seemed to be held in esteem." Most memories of Venus were recorded seventy or eighty years after her death, so their accuracy is unknown. *Negro Pioneer* included a story about her wish to participate in temple rites. As mentioned in the introduction, the story is not possible to confirm, and there are many reasons to disbelieve it.

Luke moved between Spanish Fork and Southern Utah, and eventually to California. Venus continued to live with Marinda and Alexander

Bankhead. The 1870 census listed Venus's surname as "Cupid." Perhaps when the census taker asked for her family name, he prompted her for her father's name. Her descendants use the name Venus Redd for her, including on her gravestone.

Documented Family: Parents Cupid and Amy; sisters Moriah (1809-), Chaney (1817-1872), and Fanetty (1819-); brother Abram (1812-); son Luke Ward Redd (1828-1883)

Enslavers: Elizabeth Hancock Redd (1798-1853) and John Hardison Redd (1799-1858); possibly John H. Redd heirs Mary Lewis Redd Hawkes (1839-1920), Ann Moriah Redd Pace (1830-1908), Ann Elizabeth Redd Pace (1831-1897), Lemuel Hardison Redd (1836-1910), Benjamin Jones Redd (1842-1887), and Mary Ann (Redd) Hawkes (1857-1911)

Wagon Company: James Pace (1850)

Burial: Spanish Fork City Cemetery, Spanish Fork, Utah

Notes: In his anecdote about "one family of Africans," Thaddeus Kenderdine thought he was in Battle Creek (Pleasant Grove), but his description is of Spanish Fork. (Thaddeus S. Kenderdine, *A California Tramp and Later Footprints* [Newton, PA: Globe Printing House, 1888], 98.) Manumission records for Rutherford County, Tennessee, are held by the county. A graduate research assistant found a few manumission records in the County Archives for a family named Reed, but the Reeds are a different family, as shown in the census agricultural schedule. (Beth Cavanaugh, Rutherford County [TN] Archives, email message to author, December 8, 2014.)

Sources: John Hardison Redd, Family Record, n.d., private collection. Zae Hargett Gwynn, *Abstracts of the Records of Onslow County, North Carolina, 1734-1850* (Onslow County, NC: Z. H. Gwynn, 1961), 1:446, 480, 540; 2:1217, 1220, 1225. Zebedee Hancock Probate, 1824, Onslow County, *North Carolina, Wills and Probate Records*. John H. Redd, Onslow County, North Carolina, *1830 Census*. John D. Lee, Journal, March 1842-August 1843, MS 2092, 149, CHL. Venus Redd, April 3, 1845, Daybook C, Trustee-in-Trust Tithing Daybooks. John H. Redd letter, December 27, 1848, Rutherford County, Tennessee, to Druzilla Holt Pearson (Thompson), MS 3663, CHL. John H. Redd, Utah County, Utah Territory Slave Schedule [draft], 1850 [1851]. Spanish Fork (UT) Ward Record, 1852-1864, LR

8611 29, 2, 3–5, CHL. Division of John H. Redd's Property, c. 1858, folder 8, Farozine R. Bryner Collection, 1847–1956, MS 8865, CHL. Venes Redd, Utah County, Utah Territory, *1860 Census*. Venus Cupid, Utah County, Utah Territory, *1870 Census*. Venus Redd, 1875 [alternately 1876], Spanish Fork (UT) Cemetery Records. Merina Smith, *Revelation, Resistance, and Mormon Polygamy: The Introduction and Implementation of the Principle, 1830–1853* (Logan: Utah State University Press, 2013), 223–24. John C. Hurd, *The Law of Freedom and Bondage in the United States* (Boston, MA: Little, Brown & Company, 1862), 2, 212. John H. Redd, Consecration Deed, January 5, 1858, Records of Utah County (1851–1864), H:132–33. Leonard J. Arrington, *Great Basin Kingdom: An Economic History of the Latter-day Saints, 1830–1900, New Edition* (Boston, MA: Harvard University Press, 1958; Urbana and Chicago, IL: University of Illinois Press, 2005), 146–48. Reiter, "Redd Slave Histories." William G. Hartley, *Another Kind of Gold: The Life of Albert King Thurber* (Troy, ID: John Lowe Butler Family Association, 2011), 176. Lura Redd, Amasa Jay Red, and Amasa Mason Redd, *The Utah Redds and Their Progenitors* (Salt Lake City, UT: Privately Printed, 1973). Tonya Reiter, conversation with the author, June 27, 2017. *Redd Family History Y-DNA Project, Family Tree DNA*. Accessed November 30, 2018. https://www.familytreedna.com/groups/reddfamilyhistoryydnaproject. Elisha Warner, *The History of Spanish Fork* (Spanish Fork, UT: The Press Publishing Company, 1930), 31. Lura Redd and William Howard Prince, "John Hardison and Elizabeth Hancock Redd," typescript, FSFT. Accessed October 11, 2014. https://familysearch.org/photos/artifacts/8170300. Annie Gardner Francis, "Serena Evensen," FSFT. Accessed October 4, 2016. https://familysearch.org/photos/artifacts/2162690. Carter, *Negro Pioneer*, 25–27.

Chaney (Hancock) (Redd) (Cunningham) (1812–1872)

Chaney was one of Venus Redd's sisters. She was the mother of Amy and may be the mother of Marinda. When Zebedee Hancock died, Chaney became the property of his second wife, Nancy, and upon Nancy's death, she became the property of Elizabeth Hancock and John Hardison Redd. Chaney became a member of the Church of Jesus Christ of Latter-day Saints in 1843 and went west with the Redds in 1850.

Daughters of Utah Pioneers later concluded that Chaney died in the 1850s in Spanish Fork, but although she is missing from the 1860 census, she appears in the 1870 federal census with Samuel and Mary Cunningham in St. George. Perhaps she was taken to Texas in the late 1850s by a Latter-day Saint convert, where she matches the description of an enslaved woman in the Cunningham household, and perhaps she returned with them to Utah Territory in the early 1860s. Alternatively, if Chaney remained in Utah Territory, she may have been missed in the census, although she should have been listed in the settlement of the John H. Redd estate. If she did remain in the territory, perhaps Cunningham hired her on his journey to St. George in 1862, or perhaps she went south to New Harmony with the Redd family and eventually worked for Cunningham in St. George.

After the Civil War, Chaney arranged to move an unnamed woman and a girl named Julia from the South to Utah Territory. The woman died, and Chaney could no longer care for Julia, so the William B. Maxwell family took her in. They also took in a Pahvant (Ute) boy named Jack. The Maxwell family remembered that Julia married George Waters and had a daughter named Lizzie Ann.

Documented Family: Parents Cupid and Amy; sisters Moriah (1809–), Venus (1810–1875), and Fanetty (1819–), and brother Abram (1812–); daughter Amy (1836–1854) and possible daughter Marinda Caroline Redd Bankhead (1831–1907)

Enslavers: John H. and Elizabeth Hancock Redd; possibly Samuel Cunningham (1824–1889) and Mary Ellis Cunningham (1824–1903); possibly Redd heirs as shown in Venus's entry

Wagon Company: James Pace (1850)

Burial: A-J-197-3, St. George City Cemetery, St. George, Utah

Note: Chaney's name appears with a variety of spellings, but the evidence favors "Chaney," a female name used throughout the United States during the nineteenth century, perhaps a variation of the French *chêne*, meaning oak tree.

Sources: Cheney Redd, Spanish Fork, Utah County, *1856 Utah Territorial Census*. Saml Cunningham, Ellis County, Texas Slave Schedule, *1860*

Census. Wesley W. Craig and Roberta Blake Barnum, "Pioneer Indexes, Washington County, Utah, 1852–1870: St. George, Male Pioneer Index, A–E Surnames," *Washington County Utah History and Genealogy,* 1998–1999. https://www.rootsweb.ancestry.com/~utwashin/settlers/sg-ae.html (site discontinued). Chaney Cunningham, Washington County, Utah Territory, *1870 Census.* Carter, *Negro Pioneer,* 25. Julia (Maxwell), Lincoln County, Nevada, *1870 Census.* Alvin C. Warner, "William B. Maxwell and Some of His Descendants, 1821–1959," 1960, quoted in Dale Maxwell Holyoak, "Life History of William Bailey Maxwell 1821–1895," 1997, TN-980012, 49, FHL. Daniel Bay Gibbons, "Jack Maxwell, Adopted Son of William and Lucretia Maxwell," *Bay & Gibbons Family History* (blog), February 6, 2019. https://baygibbons.blogspot.com/2019/02/jack-maxwell-adopted-son-of-james-and.html. Chauncy Cunningham, August 31, 1872, grave A-J-197-3, St. George City Cemetery, St. George, Utah Division of State History, Cemeteries and Burials.

Luke Ward Redd (1828–1883)

Luke Ward Redd was the son of John Hardison Redd and enslaved eighteen-year-old Venus. John and Elizabeth Redd took Venus, Luke, and four other enslaved or indentured people west with them in 1850. After he was freed, Luke continued to live in Spanish Fork, where he fathered two children with English immigrant Emma Love Ainge. Perhaps their grandmother Venus served as midwife at their births and gave his daughter her Southern name. Luke's daughter and son, Flady and John, passed as White as adults.

No official record remains of Luke and Emma's appearance in court in Provo not long after Flady's birth. Albert K. Thurber wrote to George Albert Smith that he was in Provo by request of the court "as a witness against Luke Redd and Emma Ainge of Spanish Fork for Lewdness resulting in her having a child which today she declared in open court to belong to Redd." He continued, "he denies its being his [redacted] . . . I trust this arrest and trial will put a stop to such conduct in Spanish Fork."

Luke moved south to New Harmony with the Redds and fathered a child there with a married neighbor. The community kept the story a secret for more than a century, but the relationship is now confirmed by DNA. Luke's son from New Harmony, like his half-brother and sister, also passed as White. One of Luke's grandsons served as a flight engineer during the Second World War and was killed in a 1944 plane crash in India.

In the wake of the New Harmony scandal, Redd moved to California and worked as a carpenter. He died in the Placer County Hospital and was buried in the adjoining cemetery.

Documented Family: Father John Hardison Redd, mother Venus Redd; partner Emma Love Ainge Harris (1840–1905) and children Flady Ainge (1864–1953, married Christian Morrison) and John Ainge or Haynes (1866–1918, married Sarah Elizabeth Hemenway Carter Vaughn Ainge/Haynes Wagner); son George Clarence Goddard (1872–1939, married Sarah Ann Lambeth) with Mary Ann Pace Goddard (1835–1915)

Enslavers: John H. and Elizabeth Hancock Redd; possibly Redd heirs

Wagon Company: James Pace (1850)

Burial: 317, Placer County Hospital Cemetery, Auburn, California, under the name L. M. Reed

Sources: Luke Redd, Utah County, Utah Territory, *1860 Census*. Luke Redd, Utah County, MS 9234, Utah Territory Productions of Agriculture, *1860 Census*, CHL. A. K. Thurber to G. A. Smith, June 17, 1864, box 6, folder 14, 54–55, MS 1322, George A. Smith Papers, 1834–1877, CHL. Reiter, "Redd Slave Histories," 109–26. Tonya Reiter, email message to author, July 22, 2015. Vivian Harris Evans, Fern Thorne Bigelow, and Mildred C. Cook, "Life Sketch of Emma (Love) Ainge," Daughters of Utah Pioneers History Files, Daughters of Utah Pioneers, Salt Lake City, UT, cited in Reiter, "Redd Slave Histories," 120, n85. Redd, *Utah Redds*, 25. Luke W. Redd, Kane County, Utah Territory, *1870 Census*. Luke Ward Redd, Nevada County, 1873, 1875; Placer County, 1879, California State Library, *California Voter Registers*. L. W. Redd, Placer County, California, *1880 Census*. "L. M. Reed," Placer County Hospital Cemetery, California, August 25, 1883, *FindAGrave*. "Sgt. G. C. Goddard Killed in Plane Crash in India," *Iron County Record* (Cedar City, UT), April 6, 1944.

Marinda Caroline Redd Bankhead (1831–1907)

Marinda's death certificate gives a birth date of October 1831. Age estimates from the census put her year of birth between 1829 and 1835. If she was one of the children listed in the Redd household in the 1840 census, as the Redd family history suggests, she was born between 1830 and 1835. The Redd family recalled that Marinda was the daughter of Chaney, but when she died, the doctor wrote in the space for parents' names on her death certificate, "Could not get more information. Did not know much about herself."

Marinda was baptized a Latter-day Saint in Spanish Fork, Utah Territory, in 1852, and was freed after the deaths of John and Elizabeth Redd. After she was freed, she had two illegitimate sons. The first, David William Pace, was the son of John Alma Lawrence Pace, and passed as White as an adult. After his birth, Marinda was "transferred" to Dr. Pinney of nearby Salem, as she told journalist Julius Taylor in an 1899 interview, one of the few accounts of the slave experience in Utah Territory. (See Appendix 6.) There was only one doctor in the area, hot-tempered, polygamous, former enslaver William Taylor Dennis, and no one with a similar name, so "Pinney" would be Julius Taylor's error. Perhaps the townspeople hoped to provide Marinda with some stability with most of the Redd family deceased or elsewhere in the territory, but in the long tradition of the sexual abuse of Black women, Marinda gave birth to a second son, Edward, and named Dr. Dennis as the father.

Edward died as an infant, and Marinda married Alexander Bankhead. They raised David William and spent the rest of their lives in Spanish Fork. They lived on 100 East between 200 and 300 South in a home surrounded by asparagus plants, which grew to the roof of the house in the summer. Julius Taylor reported, "They are both devout and strict Mormons. She belongs to the Ladies' Relief Society of her Ward, and takes an active part with her white sisters in all work of that character."

Alexander died in 1902. Five years later, Marinda died of breast cancer in the county infirmary, known locally as the "poorhouse." The couple's property went to Marinda's son. Alex and Marinda never learned to read or write, but her son did, and he settled the estate with the assistance of Latter-day Saint bishop Marinus Larsen. David William Pace died in Salt Lake City in 1951. Census and death records suggest that he may have been married, but little is known about his life.

Documented Family: **Possible mother Chaney (Redd) (Cunningham) and father John Hardison Redd; son David William Pace (1862–1951,** widowed or divorced, wife unknown) with John A. L. Pace (1841–1929); son Edward T. Dennis or Redd (1867–1867) with William Taylor Dennis (1810–1894); husband Alexander Bankhead (1836–1902)

Enslavers: John H. and Elizabeth Hancock Redd; possibly Redd heirs as shown in Venus's entry

Wagon Company: James Pace (1850)

Burial: 09.09.23, Spanish Fork City Cemetery, Spanish Fork, Utah

Notes: Tonya Reiter discovered the identity of Marinda's son, David William Pace. The Bankhead probates included actions against Emily Monroe to quiet title on the Bankhead home. Monroe probably moved into the home after Alexander and Marinda died.

Sources: "[M]irendy and Amy servants of John H. Redd Snr.," Rebaptisms, Spanish Fork (UT) Ward Record. Marinda Redd, Utah County, Utah Territory, *1860 Census*. "Edward T Dennis <Redd> [father] William T Dennis [mother] Miranda C Redd [birth] April 12th 1867 Sph Fork Utah Spy [death] Oct$\underline{r}$ 29th 1867 [cause] Flux [medical attendant] Venis Redd." Spanish Fork (UT) Cemetery Records. Marinda Bankhead, Utah County, Utah Territory, *1870 Census*. Marinda Bankhead, Utah County, Utah Territory, *1880 Census*. Julius Taylor, "Slavery in Utah," *Broad Ax*. Carter, *Negro Pioneer*, 24–25. Rindy Bankhead, Utah County, Utah, *1900 Census*. Alexander Bankhead Probate, 1905, 1912, No. 1361, Fourth District Court, Utah County, Utah. Marinda Redd Bankhead, January 20, 1907, Provo, death certificate 0703608, Utah Department of Health, USHS. "Jots," *Spanish Fork Press*, January 24, 1907. "Provo News Notes," *Salt Lake Tribune*, July 22, 1909. Alexander Bankhead Probate, 1905, 1912, Marinda Bankhead Probate, 1912, Fourth District Court, Utah County, District, and Probate Courts, *Utah, Wills and Probate Records*. David William Pace, September 10, 1951, Salt Lake City, death certificate 0005102556, Utah Department of Health, USHS. "David William Pace," *Salt Lake Telegram*, September 12, 1951. Reiter, "Redd Slave Histories," 116–17. Louisa Price Trotter, "History of Mary Ann Gardner Price, Native Pioneer," May 19, 2013. FSFT. https://www.familysearch.org/photos/artifacts/1061903. Pat Sagers, email message to author, June 7, 2013.

Amy (Redd) (1836–1854)

Amy was the daughter of Chaney and was named after her grandmother. She went west with the Redd family in 1850 and was baptized a Latter-day Saint in 1852. During all the strife with native tribes and difficulties of securing food and establishing new homes, the Spanish Fork ward records recorded, "Amy daughter of Chany died on Saturday morn[ing] Nov . . . the 4th 1854."

Documented Family: Mother Chaney Redd (1812–1872)

Enslavers: John H. and Elizabeth Hancock Redd

Wagon Company: James Pace (1850)

Burial: Spanish Fork Pioneer Heritage Cemetery, Spanish Fork, Utah

Note: Amy's name is sometimes shown as Anna or Ama.

Sources: "[M]irendy and Amy servants of John H. Redd Snr." Rebaptisms, Spanish Fork (UT) Ward Record.

Sam Franklin (Redd) (1833–)

Sam Franklin appears in the 1850 census slave schedule as an indentured servant. Nothing more is known about him than his age (seventeen), his color (yellow, meaning biracial), and that he was to be freed when he turned twenty-one. He was not in the household in 1840, so his indenture might indicate that he was the son of a White woman in the extended family, that his mother negotiated his freedom at age twenty-one, or that Redd needed temporary labor and purchased his indenture. He was too young to be the illegitimate child born to John Hardison Redd and Peggy Breece in 1821. Franklin may have been living under the name Samuel Redd in nearby Payson in 1856, but nothing more is known of him.

Enslavers: John H. and Elizabeth Hancock Redd

Wagon Company: James Pace (1850)

Sources: Samuel Redd, Payson, Utah County, *1856 Utah Territorial Census*. John H. Redd's Bastard Bond, May 7, 1821, Onslow County, North Carolina, North Carolina State Archives, *Bastardy Bonds and Records*

(North Carolina), 1736–1957, FSFT. https://www.familysearch.org/search/catalog/766391.

Rich

Richard "Dick" (Minter) (Rich?) Jackson (1827–)

Richard Jackson went to California with John S. Minter (1825–1895) during the gold rush. Minter was from Kentucky and Missouri, and his obituary claimed he was in one of the Frémont expeditions. He was said to have traveled to California in 1846, back to Missouri, and then returned to California around 1849. The facts are unclear since Minter does not appear in works about the Frémont expeditions. If Minter took Richard to California before it became a state in 1850, he could have enslaved him there; if he arrived afterwards, his claim was tenuous.

Jackson fled his enslaver. He took refuge with the Latter-day Saints in San Bernardino and began a family with Tennessee "Harriet" (Thomas). David Seely wrote to Amasa Lyman and Latter-day Saint apostle Charles C. Rich, "Negro Dick was arrested and about to be taken unless we would pay 750 Dollars for him poor fellow it seemed as though his heart would brake the Girls thought that they could not get along with out him." Seeley wrote that he and Hyrum H. Blackwell arranged to pay Minter either $500 cash or one hundred bushels of wheat. They gave Minter wheat belonging to Rich. Seely reported to Rich that Jackson "says he will stay with you as long as he lives." The bond that secured Jackson's freedom showed a payment of $750. No document shows whether Jackson placed himself into indentured service to pay back the wheat. Due to the unsettled laws of slavery, Jackson may have been free or indentured rather than enslaved. When Jack Beller wrote about Utah slavery in the 1920s, Benjamin L. Rich mistakenly told him that his grandfather, Charles C. Rich, owned "three pairs of slaves that were later liberated in California when Rich went there in 1851." The families of Rich and his wife Sarah DeArmon Pea Rich had not enslaved people since before they moved from the South to the Midwest starting in the 1810s, so Benjamin Rich was probably remembering the other enslaved people in San Bernardino. Whatever the legal arrangement, Dick traveled with Charles C. Rich between California and Utah Territory. Rich wrote in 1855, "I in company with Bro Geo. Cannon... [and nine others] and my negro Dick started for San Bernardino." Jackson accompanied Rich and most of the San Bernardino settlers to Utah Territory in 1857. By 1860, the Jackson family lived in Los Angeles. Ten years later, their surviving daughters lived in San Bernardino with Grief and Harriet (Lay) Embers, so Richard Jackson may have been dead by 1870.

Documented Family: Tennessee or Harriet (Thomas) Jackson and children (see his wife's entry)

Enslaver: Charles C. Rich? (1809–1883)

Wagon Company: Amasa M. Lyman/Charles C. Rich Company (1857) (California to Utah Territory)

Notes: President of the San Bernardino Latter-day Saint Stake David Seely wrote to Lyman and Rich about Jackson in 1853, but his letter is filed with 1855 correspondence. Charles C. Rich's consecration deeds list property of almost $10,000 in both Great Salt Lake and Davis counties but does not include Richard Jackson as enslaved property. The Church History Library in Salt Lake City contains a picture of a Black woman with a penciled description on the back: "Julia Brown, wife of the only slave owned by C. C. Rich. Husband and wife given their freedom in California about 1855." The handwriting is typical of the mid- to late-twentieth century and suggests that the picture was labeled years after Benjamin Rich's claim. No woman matching her description appears in public records, so perhaps the name and identity are faulty memories. Hopefully more information will surface.

Sources: Dick, Los Angeles County, *1852 California Census*. David Seely to Amasa M. Lyman and C. C. Rich, February 8, 1853, Correspondence, 1841–1877, box 3, folder 11, Lyman Collection. Lyman, *San Bernardino*, 290. Bond for The Delevy [sic] of Richard "Nigger Dick," Business Papers, box 3, folder 8, Charles C. Rich Collection, MS 889, CHL. Stacey L. Smith, *Freedom's Frontier: California and the Struggle Over Unfree Labor* (Chapel Hill, CA: University of North Carolina Press, 2015). Salt Lake County Transfer Book, C, 1855–1857, box 4, folder 3; Davis County Transfer Book, 1855–1856, box 4, folder 1, 5, Consecration Deeds. "Memorandom of Company that travied to Utah with Elders Lyman & Rich starting from the, 16th to the 18th of April 1857 . . . Dick a Black Man." Amasa

Lyman, Diary, 16:5–6, Lyman Collection. Beller, "Negro Slaves in Utah," 124. Sarah DeArmon Pea Rich, 1814–1893, Autobiography (1814–1893), digital transcript, W. V. Smith, *BOAP*. Accessed April 21, 2021. http://www.boap.org/LDS/Early-Saints/SRich.html. "Julia Brown," Standley Rich Family Photograph Collection, PH 1960, CHL.

Smith-Mason-Smiley

Biddy (Smith) Mason (1818/1825–1891)

Biddy Mason's family reported that she was born in Hancock County, Georgia. If so, she may be the enslaved woman named Barbara in the probate of Thomas Mason Sr., who died in Hancock County, Georgia, in 1837, one year before Biddy was first known to be in Mississippi, or she may be one of Barbara's unnamed children. Six years of Mason's life are lost to history, but she gave birth to two daughters before she, her children, and Rande became the property of Robert and Rebecca Dorn Smith in Franklin County, Mississippi. Although the Smiths joined the Church of Jesus Christ of Latter-day Saints, Mason's biographer DeEtta Demaratus suggested that the Smiths planned to move to California, and only went to Utah Territory with John Brown's company of Mississippi converts when circumstances delayed their travel.

Biddy Mason was the mother of three young daughters with unknown fathers when she helped drive the Smith livestock across the plains. The household went to San Bernardino, California, in 1851. In 1856, not long before the Supreme Court case *Dred Scott* may have altered the outcome of the case, Judge Benjamin Hayes freed Mason and Hannah Smiley and their families in *In re Hannah* (1856).

Mason lived in Los Angeles, where she used her income as a nurse to invest in real estate. Few details of her work remain, but Georgia Herrick Bell testified during an 1887 court case, "Had several women to work before I went [into care for a postpartum illness] . . . [including] Aunt Biddy Mason and her daughter Harriet." Mason eventually became a well-to-do philanthropist. She was a member of the Fort Street Methodist Episcopal Church, cementing her ties to the White community, and she helped found and support the First African Methodist Episcopal Church in Los Angeles, cementing her ties to the Black community.

Mason lived to see her grandson Henry Owens become active in local politics, and her other grandson, Robert Owens, manage the family property, but as she aged, her family began a battle over her estate that would last for years after her death. When she died in 1891, the *Los Angeles Herald* wrote, "These forty years have been filled with good works, and we are sure she has been welcomed into the 'Better Land' with the plaudit 'Well done!'" Mason is remembered with a public memorial in downtown Los Angeles.

Documented Family: Daughters Ellen Mason (1838–1921), Ann Mason (1844–1857), and Harriet Mason (1847–1914)

Enslavers: Robert Mays Smith (1804–1891) and Rebecca Dorn Smith (1810–1899)

Wagon Company: Willard Richards (1848)

Burial: Section G, lot 320, Evergreen Cemetery, Los Angeles, California

Notes: Mason lived with Robert and Winnie Owens in 1860 when the census showed her as "Bridget Owens." The census does not specify who provided the name, and Mason and her family never used the name Bridget otherwise, so she should be named only as "Biddy Mason." Mason's daughter gave a birth date for her mother, but the range of dates provided in earlier documents suggest Mason did not know her birth date. Some community histories later claimed she took her surname in homage to Amasa Mason Lyman, but primary sources provide neither documentation for the claim nor reason to believe it.

Sources: Thomas Mason Probate, 1837, Hancock County, Wills and Administration of Estates, 1794–1958, Georgia County Courthouses, *Georgia Probate Records, 1742–1990,* FSFT. https://www.familysearch.org/search/collection/1999178. Report of Mississippi Coy, May 23, 1848, John Brown's Company of 10, Report, June 1848, Camp of Israel Schedules and Reports. Robert M. Smith, Utah County, Utah Territory Slave Schedule [draft], 1850 [1851]. Biddy, Utah County, Utah Territory Slave Schedule, *1850 Census.* Biddy, Los Angeles County, *1852 California Census.* Daniel M. Thomas to Lyman, Lyman Collection. "Suit for Freedom," *Los Angeles Star,* February 2, 1856. "Suit for Freedom," *Daily Democratic State Journal* (Sacramento, CA), February 19, 1856. Delilah Beasley and Monroe N.

Work, "Documents: California Freedom Papers," *Journal of Negro History* 3, no. 1 (January 1918): 51–53. Biddy Mason, Physician, 1862, CA, National Archives, *IRS Tax Assessment Lists*. "Letter from Bishop Ward," *Elevator*. "An Appeal for the Colored People of Los Angeles," *Los Angeles Herald*, July 19, 1884. "Criminal Libel," *Los Angeles Herald*, March 17, 1887. "The Short Hairs: Will Manage the Republican Convention," *Los Angeles Herald*, September 28, 1890. "Mrs. Biddy Mason," *Los Angeles Herald*, January 16, 1891. "The Negro Woman in Los Angeles and Vicinity—Some Notable Characters," *Los Angeles Daily Times* (Los Angeles, CA), February 12, 1909, Special Section. Delilah L. Beasley, *The Negro Trail Blazers of California* (Los Angeles, CA: Times Mirror Printing and Binding House, 1919), 88–90, 109–11. Dolores Hayden, "Biddy Mason's Los Angeles 1856–1891," *California History* 68, no. 3 (Fall 1989): 86–99. https://doi.org/10.2307/25462395. Demaratus, *Force of a Feather*. Smith, *Freedom's Frontier*, 127–131. John Mack Faragher, *Eternity Street: Violence and Justice in Frontier Los Angeles* (New York, NY: W. W. Norton and Company, 2016). "A Relic of Pueblo Days," *Los Angeles Herald*, May 12, 1901. "With a Vengeance," *Daily Evening Herald* (Stockton, CA), October 11, 1867. "Biddy Mason Memorial Park," *Atlas Obscura*. Accessed October 17, 2018. https://www.atlasobscura.com/places/biddy-mason-memorial-park.

Ellen (Smith) Mason Owens Huddleston Taft (1838–1921)

The father of Biddy Mason's daughter Ellen is unknown. She lived in Utah Territory for a few years before Robert and Rebecca Smith took her and her family to California in 1851. After her liberation, she married Charles Owens. They had two sons, Robert and Henry. When the boys were old enough, Charles sent them and Ellen to be educated in Northern California. Ellen later provided journalist and author Delilah Beasley with family information and memories for her book, *The Negro Trail Blazers of California*. Beasley described Ellen as "one of the most charming ladies the writer has been privileged to interview, a perfect inspiration."

Owens and her family helped found the First AME Church in Los Angeles. After her first husband's death, she remarried and divorced twice. Ellen and her son Robert managed the family's extensive real estate holdings. Robert and his wife Anna were active in Los Angeles society. Their daughters Manilla and Gladys ran a music shop, and Gladys married jazz musician and composer Benjamin F. "Reb" Spikes and, later, real estate developer Garrie Harrison. Robert and Anna Owens separated or divorced, and Anna moved in with her daughter. In 1932 Robert Owens went to his daughter's house, shot and killed Anna and his son-in-law, and then turned the gun on himself. Since he spared his daughter and grandson, Biddy Mason has living descendants.

Documented Family: Mother Biddy Mason; husband Charles P. Owens (1832–1882) and children Robert C. Owens (1859–1932, married Anna Frances Dugged) and Henry Louis Owens (1861–1893, married Louise Kruger); husband Granville Huddleston (1844–1900); husband Samuel S. Taft (1852–1933)

Enslavers: Robert M. and Rebecca Dorn Smith

Wagon Company: Willard Richards (1848)

Burial: Section G, lot 320, Evergreen Cemetery, Los Angeles, California

Sources: See legal sources under sister Harriet Washington. Ellen, Utah County, Utah Territory Slave Schedule [draft], 1850 [1851]. Ellen Owens, Los Angeles, California, *1860 Census*. Ellen Owens, Los Angeles, California, *1870 Census*. Hellen Owens, Los Angeles, California, *1880 Census*. Ellen Huddleston, Los Angeles, California, *1900 Census*. Ellen Taft, Los Angeles, California, *1910 Census*. Ellen Huddleston, Los Angeles, California, *1920 Census*. "Ellen Huddleston against Granvile Huddleston," *Los Angeles Herald*, August 14, 1897. "Marriage Licenses," *Los Angeles Herald*, October 1, 1909. "Three Lives Toll of Family Quarrel," *Riverside Daily Press* (Riverside, CA), February 15, 1932. "Kills 2, Self in Jealousy Over Wealth," *Evening Tribune* (San Diego, CA), February 15, 1932.

Ann (Smith) Mason (1844–1857)

Ann was Biddy Mason's second daughter, born in Mississippi. She was missed in the Latter-day Saint wagon company roster, probably because Hannah Smiley also had a daughter named Ann. She lived in Utah Territory before going to California in 1851. She died a year after she and her family were freed.

Documented Family: Mother Biddy Mason

Enslavers: Robert M. and Rebecca Dorn Smith

Wagon Company: Willard Richards (1848)
Burial: Probably Los Angeles, California
Sources: Ann, Utah County, Utah Territory Slave Schedule [draft], 1850 [1851]. Ann, Los Angeles County, *1852 California Census*. Beasley, *Negro Trail Blazers*, 109–10.

Harriet (Smith) Mason Ward Sargent Brown Washington (1847–1914)

Harriet was Biddy Mason's third daughter, born right before the Smith household left for Utah Territory. Judge Benjamin Hayes freed her family in California. Newspapers across the country mentioned her rescue of passengers after the explosion of the steamer *Ada Hancock*. At the time, she worked for Phineas and Rebecca Banning, and she saved their sons from drowning. The *New York Times* wrote that she "displayed undaunted courage and rendered great assistance to numbers of others. During the whole excitement she remained perfectly calm, and was the means of keeping several of the ladies' heads above water." When Michael Sanborn of the Banning Museum in Los Angeles gave a lecture about Harriet in 2013, the audience included descendants of Biddy Mason, the Banning family, and Judge Benjamin Hayes.

Harriet helped found the First AME Church in Los Angeles. She married Edward Ward or Brown, then William Sargent, then resumed her first married name, then married William H. Washington, a charismatic preacher who had served six years for second-degree murder. She had no children.

Her mother's real estate investments, improved by her heirs, kept them in comfort for many years. A newspaper account described Harriet Washington as the richest Black woman in Los Angeles. She and her family battled over their property for most of a decade before Harriet found good legal representation from Los Angeles attorney Elizabeth Kinney and won a case in the California Supreme Court. After she was lured to San Bernardino in what she described as an attempted murder, she filed a lawsuit against her nephew for intimidation. The battles eventually calmed, and the families managed to go about their business peacefully. Harriet is buried beside her mother and half-sister Ellen in the Evergreen Cemetery in Los Angeles.

Documented Family: Mother Biddy Mason; husband Edward Brown Ward (1843–); husband William Sargent (1837–); husband William H. Washington (1857–1934)

Enslavers: Robert M. and Rebecca Dorn Smith

Wagon Company: Willard Richards (1848)

Burial: Section G, lot 320, Evergreen Cemetery, Los Angeles, California

Sources: Harriet, Utah County, Utah Territory Slave Schedule [draft], 1850 [1851]. Harriett, Los Angeles County, *1852 California Census.* DeEtta Demaratus, email message to author, September 21, 2016, citing communication from Hal Eaton. "A Terrific Explosion: Destruction of the Ada Hancock at San Pedro, Cal.," *New York Times*, May 31, 1863. "From Darkness to Light: Discovering Harriet Mason," notice of lecture, *The Banning Museum*, April 3, 2013. https://www.thebanningmuseum.org/from-darkness-to-light-discovering-harriet-mason. Harriett Masen and Edward Ward, February 18, 1865, *California, Select Marriages, 1850–1945.* Ancestry.com. https://www.ancestry.com/search/collections/60241. "Letter from Bishop Ward," *Elevator*. "A Clergyman Convicted of Murder," *Sacramento Daily Record-Union* (Sacramento, CA), March 22, 1888. William H. Washington, California State Archives, and Department of Corrections, *California, Prison and Correctional Records, 1851–1950.* Ancestry.com. https://www.ancestry.com/search/collections/8833. Harriett Ward, Los Angeles, California, *1870 Census.* Harriett Ward, Los Angeles, California, *1880 Census.* Harriett Washington, Los Angeles, California, *1900 Census.* Harriet Washington, Los Angeles, California, *1910 Census.* "New Suits Filed," *Los Angeles Herald*, November 5, 1897. "Among Relatives: An Aunt Sues Her Nephew and Niece for an Accounting," *Los Angeles Herald*, March 9, 1898. "Swore in Church," *Los Angeles Herald*, May 25, 1898. "A Tax Controversy," *Los Angeles Herald*, May 5, 1899. "Mason Children: In Court Over the Same Spring St. Property," *Los Angeles Herald*, April 1, 1900. "Colored Family's Dispute," *Los Angeles Herald*, June 22, 1900. Huddleston v. Washington, 69 P. 146 (Cal. 1902). "Fright Worth $10,000," *Los Angeles Herald*, December 28, 1904. Harriett Washington, 1914, California Department of Health and Welfare, *California, Death Index, 1905–1939.* Ancestry.com. https://www.ancestry.com/search/collections/5187. Evergreen Cemetery, Los Angeles, telephone conversation with the author, December 19, 2017.

Rande (Smith) (1822–)

Rande is listed on the Latter-day Saint wagon company roster as one of the workers enslaved by Robert M. Smith, but the roster does not specify sex, and he or she does not appear in any later document. Rande may be the "Negro boy Belonging to Mr Smith" who attempted to free himself and sought refuge in the Root and McMurtrey homes in 1849. (See Appendix 4.)

Enslavers: Robert M. and Rebecca Dorn Smith
Wagon Company: Willard Richards (1848)
Sources: Robert M. Smith, Franklin County Tax Rolls, 1844, box 3633, Mississippi Department of Archives and History, *Various Records*. John Brown's Company of 10, Report, June 1848, Report of Mississippi Coy, May 23, 1848, Camp of Israel Schedules and Reports. Benjamin Mathews to Brigham Young, March 31, 1849, box 21, folder 16, Office Files.

Hannah (Dorn) (Smith) Smiley Embers (1821/1825–1868?)

Hannah was born in South Carolina and was enslaved by John Dorn. Little Steven's Creek Baptist Church later recorded the baptism of "John Dorn Senr' Hannah." In 1856, Benjamin Hayes described Hannah as "a woman nearly white, whose children are all nearly so." When Dorn died, his executors listed the contents of the estate in the newspaper, including more than sixteen hundred acres, "ALSO Thirty-two Negroes, about 2500 bushels of Corn, and Fodder. 10 Horses, 2 good Road Wagons." John's daughter Rebecca and her husband Robert Mays Smith purchased Hannah and her three children Ann, Lawrence, and Nelson, sometimes called Nat or Nathaniel. Hannah eventually had nine known children, the first born when she was about fifteen years old and the last about twenty years later. After they were freed, Hannah and many of her children used the surname Smiley, suggesting a connection to the Smyley family of Edgefield County, South Carolina. They enslaved a man named Nelson, perhaps Hannah's male relative. Biographer DeEtta Demaratus concluded that Hannah's first husband was a man named Frank shown with Hannah in the Dorn estate.

Robert and Rebecca Smith took Hannah and her children to Mississippi, where they joined four other enslaved people in the household. Hannah gave birth to Jane, father unknown, while traveling to the Salt Lake Valley. She gave birth to Charles Embers, son of Toby Embers, in Utah Territory. After Smith took her to San Bernardino, California, she gave birth to four additional children: Marion, probably fathered by Latter-day Saint convert John Heath; Martha Embers, daughter of Toby Embers; and Henry and Catherine, with an unknown father.

Hannah had a new baby and could not appear in court in 1856, but Judge Benjamin Hayes secured witnesses and questioned her privately. She eventually admitted that Rebecca Smith made her take an oath that she would stay with the family, and that she preferred to stay in California, but "she felt compelled to observe [the oath], and would have to do so if brought up in Court again, but IT WAS NOT HER WISH TO RETURN TO TEXAS." Hayes concluded that she "has either been under actual duress . . . or she has been imposed upon, in her ignorance, by 'false promises,' and 'misrepresentations' of law and fact." Hayes declared Hannah and her children free and granted Hannah custody of her children.

She lived in San Bernardino with Toby Embers, who died about 1866. Hannah inherited his property and almost immediately transferred it to their children Charles and Martha. She signed the document with an X, suggesting that she never learned to write. She died not long afterwards and is probably buried in the San Bernardino Pioneer Cemetery.

Hannah's children mostly remained in California. Her son Marion was convicted of arson but freed ten years into his twelve-year sentence when law enforcement discovered that the main witness to the case had perjured himself. According to news reports, in 1905, Marion took what he thought was a bottle of beer from a stable, drank it quickly, and died a painful and lingering death since it was formaldehyde.

Their father was part of their life, and Martha and Charles had stability that their half-brothers and sisters lacked. In 1870, Martha married Civil War veteran Israel Beal (1848–1929). The community-minded couple raised their family in Redlands, California. Their grandson Charlie Beal worked with Louis Armstrong, and he and his brother Eddie worked internationally as pianists. In 2010, the city of Redlands named a park after Israel Beal.

Documented Family: (children not listed in order of birth) Possible husband Frank and children Ann Smith (1840–1904, married Emanuel Peppers and Henry Daniels), Lawrence Embers (1841–), Nelson or Nathaniel Smiley (1843–1880, married Juana Biggs); daughter Jane Smiley Embers (1847–, married George Goins); husband Toby Embers and children Charles Embers (1850–1935, married Jane Thompson and Dolores Salcido) and Martha Embers (1854–1932, married Israel Beal); possibly John Heath (1823–) and son Marion Heath Smith (1852–1905); unknown partner and children Henry Smiley (1856–, married Jennie Guzman), and Catherine Smiley (1859–1860)

Enslavers: Robert M. and Rebecca Dorn Smith

Wagon Company: Willard Richards (1848)

Burial: Probably San Bernardino Pioneer Cemetery, San Bernardino, California

Notes: A Henry Smiley worked for Biddy Mason's grandson in 1890, but San Quentin State Prison records gave his age as nineteen in 1891, so he may have been a grandchild, and nothing more is known of Hannah's son Henry. Son Marion's inquest documents noted that he had a dark complexion but blue eyes. (See "Eye Color," *Stanford at The Tech: Understanding Genetics*, The Tech Museum of Innovation, San Jose, California, October 8, 2004, https://genetics.thetech.org/ask/ask57.) Louis Armstrong introduced pianist Charlie Beal twenty-four minutes into the movie *New Orleans*. (*New Orleans*, YouTube video, from United Artists, 1947, featuring Charlie Beal, posted by Gonzalo WebMusic, January 7, 2015, https://youtu.be/Mgp6Etsy_WI?t=24m.)

Sources: John Dorn, seventeen slaves, Edgefield County, South Carolina, *1830 Census*. John Dorn, thirty-one slaves, Edgefield County, South Carolina, *1840 Census*. Estate of John Dorn, 1834, box 9, Package 313; Estate of James Smyley, 1839–1844, box 27, Package 965; John Dorn, Letters of Administration, 1846, South Carolina County, District, and Probate Courts, *South Carolina, Wills and Probate Records*. Gloria Ramsey Lucas, *Slave Records of Edgefield County, South Carolina* (Edgefield, SC: Edgefield County Historical Society, 2010; digitized book and electronic index, Ancestry.com, 2014), 117. Membership Book of Little Steven's Baptist Church, September 9, 1843, Tompkins Library, Edgefield, South Carolina, quoted in Demaratus, *Force of a Feather*, 22. "Notice [John Dorn estate]," *Edgefield Advertiser* (Edgefield, SC), October 7, 1846. The Smith homestead in Mississippi is at Lilly Lane SW, Bogue Chitto, Lincoln, Mississippi, 39629. Franklin County Land Commissioner Records, 1842, Bbox 3445, 34, 37, Mississippi Department of Archives and History, *Various Records*. Hannah, Utah County, Utah Territory Slave Schedule [draft], 1850 [1851]. John Heath, Utah County, Utah Territory, *1850 Census*. Hannah, Los Angeles County, *1852 California Census*. "Suit for Freedom," *Los Angeles Star*. "Suit for Freedom," *Daily Democratic State Journal*. Hannah Smiley, San Bernardino County, California, *1860 Census*. Catherine Smiley, croup, Los Angeles County, California Mortality Schedule, *1860 Census*. "Smiley Hannah, San Bernardino, Penalties for [tax] default . . . 1.00." Hannah Smiley, 1866, San Bernardino County, California, National Archives, *IRS Tax Assessment Lists*. Hannah Embers to Charles Embers and Martha Embers, Conveyance, June 26, 1868, Property Records, 288, SBCHA. Heather Hardy, "Remembered and Known: Latter-day Saints in the Antebellum South," unpublished manuscript, 2001, CHL. Demaratus, *Force of a Feather*, 22–26. Henry Smiley, 1890, 254 South Spring Street, Los Angeles, California State Library, *California Voter Registers*. Henry Smiley, 1891, San Quentin, California State Archives, and Department of Corrections, *California, Prison and Correctional Records*. Marion Heath, Los Angeles County, California, *1870 Census*. "Weather in San Bernardino—Sentenced for Arson," *San Francisco Bulletin* (San Francisco, CA), March 18, 1879. "Sentence Commuted," *San Francisco Chronicle* (San Francisco, CA), April 24, 1886. "Stolen Drink May Cause San Bernardino Man's Death," *San Francisco Call*, June 30, 1905. Marion Smith, Inquest, July 2, 1905, San Bernardino, California, Coroner's Record, 86, SBCHA. Marriage License, Marriage Certificate, December 25–26, 1870, Marriages A, San Bernardino Court Records, SBCHA. "China Wedding," *San Bernardino Weekly Courier* (San Bernardino, CA), January 3, 1891. "Died [Martha Beal]," *San Bernardino Sun*, May 8, 1932. Eugene Chadbourne, "Eddie Beal," *AllMusic*. Accessed November 25, 2016. https:// www.allmusic.com/artist/eddie-beal-mn0000166097. Eugene Chadbourne, "Charlie Beal," *AllMusic*. Accessed November 25, 2016. https:// www.allmusic.com/artist/charlie-beal-mn0000804648/biography. "Pianist, Charley Beal: In the Right Place, Again," *Desert Sun* (Palm Springs, CA), April 14, 1978. Jesse B. Gill, "Park Named After Beal," *Redlands Daily*

Facts, March 3, 2010. https://www.redlandsdailyfacts.com/2010/03/03/park-named-after-beal.

Ann (Dorn) (Smith) Smiley Peppers Daniels (1837/1840–1904)

Ann accompanied her mother Hannah Smiley from South Carolina to Mississippi and then to Utah Territory and California, where she gave birth to a daughter, Mary, perhaps the child of William "Seco" Smith. Hannah had just given birth at the time of the writ of *habeas corpus* that freed the family, so Ann spoke on behalf of her family. She told the judge that she "knows her mother would rather die than go and leave her children." She asked Hayes, "If I go back to Texas, will I be as free as here?" He told her that she would not be, and she replied, "I cannot say now whether to stay or go; I want to stay where my mother Hannah stays. If she stays, I want to stay—it is hard to be scattered so."

After she was freed, Ann married Manuel Peppers and had six more children. Her family helped found the First AME Church in Los Angeles. Manuel became a violent alcoholic, and they divorced, or he died. She remarried and had a daughter with husband Henry Daniels. Her daughter Alice Baldridge was a renowned Los Angeles spiritualist, and her son Henry "Harry" Peppers was a professional boxer. Ann died of cancer in 1904. Her funeral was at First AME.

Documented Family: Mother Hannah Smiley; siblings and half-siblings; daughter Mary Peppers (1853–); husband Emanuel Peppers (1833–) and children Caroline Peppers (1856–1890, married Thomas Grice), Alice Peppers (1859–1930, married John H. Baldridge), Manuel Peppers (1863–1906), Louis Peppers (1863–1922, married Mollie Patterson), Maria Peppers (1867–), Nelson Peppers (1868–1870), Henry Peppers (1872–1911), and Jane Peppers (1873–); husband Henry Daniels and child Eliza Daniels (1877–1953, married Edward Zimmons)

Enslavers: Robert M. and Rebecca Dorn Smith

Wagon Company: Willard Richards (1848)

Burial: Rosedale Cemetery, Los Angeles, California

Sources: Ann, Utah County, Utah Territory Slave Schedule [draft], 1850 [1851]. Ann, Los Angeles County, *1852 California Census*. Ann Pepper, Los

Angeles, California, *1860 Census*. Ann Peppers, Los Angeles, California, *1870 Census*. Ann Danniels, Los Angeles, California, *1880 Census*. Ann Pepper, Los Angeles, California, *1900 Census*. "Suit for Freedom," *Daily Democratic State Journal*. Demaratus, *Force of a Feather*, 152–53. "Local Brevities," *Los Angeles Herald*, July 24, 1874. "Items in Brief," *Los Angeles Daily Star* (Los Angeles, CA), September 13, 1873. "Local News in Brief," *Los Angeles Daily Star*, July 21, 1874. "Died [Caroline Peppers]," *Daily Alta California*, February 11, 1890. "Deaths [Ann Peppers Daniels]," *Los Angeles Herald*, March 10, 1904. "Among Colored Citizens," *Los Angeles Herald*, March 13, 1904. "Big Birthday Party for Spirits Given by Woman [Alice Peppers Baldridge] in L. A.," *Los Angeles Herald*, March 12, 1921.

Lawrence (Dorn) (Smith) Smiley Embers (1842–)

Lawrence accompanied his mother to Mississippi, Utah Territory, and California. He missed most of the court proceedings of *In re Hannah* (1856) so he could attend to his mother and newborn brother. After he was freed, he killed German immigrant Henry Ferling in an election day brawl. The same judge who freed his family sentenced him to five years in San Quentin. Lawrence was injured in a mass escape in 1862. His whereabouts are unknown after his release from prison.

Documented Family: Mother Hannah Smiley; siblings and half-siblings

Enslavers: Robert M. and Rebecca Dorn Smith

Wagon Company: Willard Richards (1848)

Sources: Lawrence, Utah County, Utah Territory Slave Schedule [draft], 1850 [1851]. Lawrence, Los Angeles County, *1852 California Census*. Lawrence Smiley, San Bernardino County, California, *1860 Census*. "Caught," *Sacramento Daily Union*, November 21, 1860. "Murder by a Negro," *Los Angeles Star*, November 3, 1860. "District Court," *Los Angeles Star*, December 15, 1860. "Bound for San Quentin," *Los Angeles Star*, December 29, 1860. Lawrence Embers, 1860, San Quentin, California State Archives, and Department of Corrections, California, Prison and Correctional Records. Hubert H. Bancroft, *History of California, 1860–1890* (San Francisco, CA: History Company, 1890), 7:217.

Nelson or Nathaniel (Dorn) (Smith) Smiley (1845–1880)

Nelson or Nathaniel "Nat" was Hannah Smiley's third child born in South Carolina. His enslavers usually gave his name as Nat or Nathaniel, while Hannah used the name Nelson. The name variation may show disagreement between his mother and enslavers. Nelson went with the Smith family to Mississippi, Utah Territory, and California. He married Juana Biggs. Her mother was Refugio Redondo and father was Peter Biggs, formerly enslaved by an army officer who led the Mormon Battalion to California. Juana died before 1880. Nelson found work in a hotel in California's Central Valley and died by suicide in 1880.

Documented Family: Mother Hannah Smiley; siblings and half-siblings; wife Juana Biggs (1848–)

Enslavers: Robert M. and Rebecca Dorn Smith

Wagon Company: Willard Richards (1848)

Burial: A/PG2/5/5, Visalia Public Cemetery, Visalia, California

Sources: Nelson, Utah County, Utah Territory Slave Schedule [draft], 1850 [1851]. Nelson Smiley, San Bernardino County, California, *1860 Census.* Nelson Smiley and Juana Biggs, September 1, 1867, Los Angeles, California Department of Public Health, *California, County Birth, Marriage, and Death Records.* Nelson Smiley, widower, Tulare County, California, *1880 Census.* Nelson Smiley, *Tulare County, California Mortality Schedule, Tenth Census of the United States, 1880* (Berkeley, CA: Bancroft Library, University of California, 1880), 7, 97. Kendra Field and Daniel Lynch, "'Master of Ceremonies': The World of Peter Biggs in Civil War–Era Los Angeles," *Western Historical Quarterly* 47, no. 3 (August 2016): 1–27. https://doi.org/10.1093/whq/whw160. Faragher, *Eternity Street,* 201–02, 446.

Jane (Smith) Smiley Goins (1847–)

Jane was an infant when she crossed the plains. During *In re Hannah,* Judge Benjamin Hayes described Jane and her family as "nearly white" and wrote that Jane "can not easily be distinguished from the white race." After she married George Goins, they seem to have lived in Sacramento

288 | Chapter Ten

and been active in the AME Church, but nothing more is known of their lives.

Documented Family: Mother Hannah Smiley; half-siblings; husband George Goins

Enslavers: Robert M. and Rebecca Dorn Smith

Wagon Company: Willard Richards (1848)

Note: Do not confuse Jane Smiley Goins with Jane Thompson Embers, the wife of Charles Embers.

Sources: Jane, Utah County, Utah Territory Slave Schedule [draft], 1850 [1851]. "Suit for Freedom," *Los Angeles Star*. Jane Smiley, San Bernardino County, California, *1860 Census*. "District Court—Divorce [George and Pocahontas Goins]," *Sacramento Daily Union*, March 12, 1860. Jane Smiley and George Goins, April 10, 1862, Marriage, Los Angeles, California Department of Public Health, *California, County Birth, Marriage, and Death Records*. "Sabbath School Exhibition at Sacramento," *Pacific Appeal* (San Francisco, CA), March 28, 1863.

Charles (Smith) Embers (1849–1935)

Charles or Charley Embers was one of the early Black settlers of Tucson, Arizona, and the last to die of all the known enslaved African American residents of Utah Territory. He was the son of Toby Embers and Hannah Smiley, born in Utah Territory and taken as a small child to San Bernardino, where his family was freed. He married Jane Thompson and had a daughter Eliza. He moved to Arizona, where he lived for six decades. He remarried Dolores Salcido, and they had one daughter who did not survive childhood. Embers spent his last years in the county hospital, where he was photographed and interviewed by graduate student James W. Yancy about his experiences in Arizona. The hospital attendants estimated his age at death as sixty, rather than his actual age of eighty-six.

Documented Family: Father Toby Embers; mother Hannah Smiley; sister Martha Embers Beal (1854–1932); half-siblings; wife Jane Thompson (1846–) and daughter Eliza (1870–); wife Dolores Salcido (1860–1925), stepdaughter Trefulio Salcido, and daughter (unknown name) (1895–before 1900)

Enslavers: Robert M. and Rebecca Dorn Smith

Burial: Pima County Cemetery, Tucson, Arizona

Notes: Charles Embers is occasionally called Cato in early records. James Y. Yancy included a picture of Charles in his thesis, and it can be seen in the original source. The obituary of Dolores Embers reported that upon her death she had many living descendants from a previous marriage.

Sources: James W. Yancy, "The Negro of Tucson, Past and Present" (master's thesis, University of Arizona, 1933), 15–17, https://repository.arizona.edu/handle/10150/306668. Charley, Utah County, Utah Territory Slave Schedule [draft], 1850 [1851]. Cato [Charles], Los Angeles County, *1852 California Census*. Charles Embers, Los Angeles County and San Bernardino County, California, *1860 Census*. Charles Embers and Jane Thompson, Marriages, Book A, 1855–1870, SBCHA, cited in Demaratus, *Force of a Feather*, 227n75. Charles Embers and Jane Thompson, married July 20, 1858, California Department of Public Health, *California, County Birth, Marriage, and Death Records*. Charles Embers, Pima County, Arizona Territory, *1870 Census*. Janie and Eliza Embers, Los Angeles County, California, *1870 Census*. "City in Brief," *Arizona Daily Star* (Tucson, AZ), July 27, 1895. Charles and Dolores Embers, Pima County, Arizona Territory, *1900 Census*. "Tucson Woman, 103 [sic] Years Old Dies Saturday," *Arizona Daily Star*, November 8, 1925. Dolores Salcido de Embers, November 6, 1925, Tucson; Charles Embers, November 27, 1935, Tucson, Arizona Department of Health Services, *Arizona, Death Records, 1887–1960*. Ancestry.com. https://www.ancestr.com/search/collections/8704.

Sprouse-Wooldridge

Silas (Sprouse) Woolridge (1814/1836–1917)

Silas Woolridge was born in Alabama. He was enslaved by a succession of related families, probably beginning with Thomas and Keziah Wooldridge, then their daughter Emily Wooldridge Hundley Rooker and her first husband Jordan Hundley, and then Emily and Jordan's daughter Catherine Hundley Sprouse and her husband John Sprouse. Woolridge probably went from Texas to Utah with John Sprouse in the mid-1850s. Sprouse remarried Nancy R. Greer Johnson Sprouse, the sister of Nathaniel Hunt Greer, whose family was also involved in slavery in Utah Territory. Since John Sprouse died in 1858, Nancy is listed as the enslaver in the 1860 census slave schedule.

In the late 1860s, Silas Woolridge married Downey Perkins. Downey and her son Silas died shortly after his birth. After his wife and son died, Woolridge moved to the Pioche mining area of southern Nevada and worked with African American brothers Lorenzo Dow Barton (1832–1919) and Isaac Barton (1844–1926). The three men later moved to California. Woolridge's burial record said he was 103 years old. Despite the wide variation shown in his age in legal documents, his actual age was probably around ninety. Whatever his actual age, Silas would have experienced decades of life in slavery, followed by more than fifty years as a free man.

Documented Family: Wife Downey Perkins (1848–1869); son Silas Woolridge (1869–1869)

Enslavers: John Sprouse (1802–1858) and Nancy Reddick Greer Johnson Sprouse (1805–1878)

Burial: Haven of Rest 874–13, Historic Union Cemetery, Bakersfield, California

Notes: Negro Pioneer badly garbled the story of Silas and Downey Woolridge. Silas spelled his surname without the first "d" used in the name of his first enslavers. Silas's probable former enslaver Emily Wooldridge Hundley Rooker was in Utah by 1851. She is not known to have taken enslaved people to Utah, and she and her husband Samuel Rooker lived in Colorado by 1860.

Sources: Thomas Wooldridge, October 24, 1798, Petition 20679804, Elbert County Georgia, Race & Slavery Petitions Project, Digital Library on American Slavery, University of North Carolina at Greensboro. John Sprous, Neshoba County, Mississippi, *1840 Census.* John Sprouse, Grimes County, Texas Slave Schedule, *1850 Census.* Catharine Sprouce, 1849, John Sprouce, 1849–1852, Grimes County, *Texas, County Tax Rolls.* N. R. Sprows [Nancy Reddick Greer Johnson Sprouse], Great Salt Lake County, Utah Territory Slave Schedule, *1860 Census.* S. M. and Emily Rooker, Denver, Kansas Territory, *1860 Census.* Dorney Woolrich, October 30,

1869, *Salt Lake County (UT) Death Records*. Silas Woolrich, November 9, 1869, *Salt Lake County (UT) Death Records*. Sloan, *Salt Lake City Directory*, 151. Silas Woolridge, Lincoln County, Nevada, *1880 Census*. Silas Woolridge, Lincoln County, Nevada, *1900 Census*. Silas Woolridge, Lincoln County, Nevada, *1910 Census*. Silas Woolridge, January 25, 1917, Historic Union Cemetery, Bakersfield, CA, *FindAGrave*.

Thomas

Philemon (Crosby) (Thomas) (1810–)

Philemon was enslaved by or indentured to John Crosby. Upon Crosby's death, Philemon became the property of Crosby's daughter Ann. Crosby's estate documents show a small wage paid by his son-in-law Kemp Watts to Philemon "Phill" and Toby Embers. Ann Crosby and her husband Daniel M. Thomas took Philemon to Utah Territory in 1847. The leaders of the wagon train included Philemon in a list of men who could bear arms and perform camp duties.

Philemon appears in the 1850 census as the Mississippi settlers headed to California. Perhaps the census-taker, Thomas Bullock, paused a moment to ponder the irony of an enslaved man named Philemon, since in the Bible Philemon was the enslaver and Onesimus the slave.

Philemon discovered he was free by 1856. Later that year, Caroline Barnes Crosby (not related to the Southern family) wrote, "Negro Phill called in the evening. Told us many anecdotes of the southern states, and the slaves." Philemon worked for Louis Glaser in San Bernardino and Los Angeles, and then he disappeared from the public record.

Enslavers: Ann Crosby Thomas (1811–1878) and Daniel Monroe Thomas (1809–1894)

Wagon Company: Edward Hunter-Jacob Foutz (1847)

Notes: Louis Glaser had shops in San Bernardino and Los Angeles. He may be the same man as Charles Glaser, who is traceable in census and vital records, but Philemon did not appear in any records with Charles or Louis Glaser or any Glaser business partner. One compiled database claimed without documentation that Philemon was born in Knox County, Indiana.

Sources: John Crosby Probate, Monroe County, 1842, Mississippi County, District, and Probate Courts, Mississippi, Wills and Probate Records. Edward Hunter and Jacob Foutz, Letter, August 17, 1847, in *Historical Department Journal History*. Philemon, Utah County, Utah Territory Slave Schedule [draft], 1850 [1851]. Philip, Los Angeles County, *1852 California Census*. Daniel M. Thomas to Lyman, Lyman Collection. "Caroline Barnes Crosby," *No Place to Call Home: The 1807–1857 Life Writings of Caroline Barnes Crosby, Chronicler of Outlying Mormon Communities*, ed. Edward Leo Lyman, Susan Ward Payne, and S. George Ellsworth (Logan, UT: Utah State University Press, 2005), 399, 423. "San Bernardino Store," *Los Angeles Star*, October 20, 1855. "Dissolution of Partnership," *Los Angeles Star*, April 26, 1856. "A New Grocery Store," *Los Angeles Star*, June 14, 1856. "To the Public! L. Glaser," *Los Angeles Star*, April 25, 1857. "Highway Robbery," *Los Angeles Star*, July 11, 1857. LDS Pioneer and Handcart Companies, 1847–1856. Ancestry.com. https://www.ancestry.com/search/collections/5146.

Tennessee or Harriet (Crosby) (Thomas) Jackson (1836–)

Upon the death of John Crosby, Tennessee became the property of Ann Crosby and her husband Daniel M. Thomas, who took her to Utah Territory in 1847 and to California in 1851. Tennessee appears to be Harriet Jackson and may have been the daughter of Grief Embers. She married Richard Jackson of Kentucky, who appears to be Dick (Rich), who fled his enslaver to live in the San Bernardino settlement. The couple had four or five children. Two of her daughters died young. Harriet was active in the AME Zion Church.

Jackson daughters Harriet (or Mary) and Louisa lived with Grief and Harriet Embers in 1870. Louisa was married to George Pollard in San Bernardino in 1877 by Latter-day Saint John Ellis Garner, which links Harriet Jackson to the San Bernardino African American community and confirms that she may have returned to San Bernardino and died there.

Documented Family: Possible father Grief Embers; Richard Jackson (1832–) and children William Jackson (1852–), Elizabeth E. Jackson (1856–1859), Louisa Jackson (1858–1859) (possibly misnamed in record),

Louisa Jackson (1858–1913, married George Pollard), and Mary or Harriet Jackson (1860–, married George Washington)

Enslavers: Daniel M. and Ann Crosby Thomas

Wagon Company: Edward Hunter-Jacob Foutz (1847)

Burial: Probably California

Sources: Tennessee, Utah County, Utah Territory Slave Schedule [draft], 1850 [1851]. Tennessee, Los Angeles County, *1852 California Census*. Richard and Harriet Jackson, Los Angeles County, California, *1860 Census*. Elizabeth and Louisa Jackson, Los Angeles County, California Mortality Schedule, *1860 Census*. "Proceedings of the Annual Conference of the A. M. E. Zion Church," *Pacific Appeal*, July 26, 1873. Louisa Jackson to George Pollard, San Bernardino, January 12, 1877, California Department of Public Health, *California, County Birth, Marriage, and Death Records*. Lyman, *San Bernardino*, 290–91n49.

Unidentified Individuals

Betty (unknown) (1825–) and Harriet (1844–)

The 1850 census for Utah County shows Betty, twenty-five, and Harriet, six, among the Latter-day Saints from Mississippi headed to San Bernardino. They were listed after John and Catherine Higgins Holladay and before Allen Freeman Smithson and his second wife, Jennette Burton Taylor Smithson. The scarce details suggest that this was Biddy Mason and her daughter Harriet, since no documentation indicates that the Smithson, Holladay, or Harmon families enslaved any people in Utah Territory. The census entry may document Biddy working as a hired or loaned nurse.

Sources: Betty and Harriet, Utah County, Utah Territory, *1850 Census*.

Esther Harmon (1824–)?

Esther Harmon was from North Carolina and in her twenties when she appeared in the draft copy of the 1850 census living with free Black Jane Manning James in Great Salt Lake City. She did not appear in the copy of the census sent to the federal government. Esther next appeared in an 1855 list of letters at the post office: "Esther (a colored woman)," along with Violet (Crosby), Thomas Bankhead, and Nathan Bankhead. She is probably "Hammon" in a list of unmarried African American enslaved people in the Great Salt Lake Valley found in the Brigham Young Office Collection.

The use of the surname Harmon in the 1850 census suggests that she may be associated with the Smithson–Holladay–Harmon–Crosby extended family. She was the right age to be Ede, a woman enslaved by Elizabeth Crosby, but several details do not match. In another possibility, Elizabeth Crosby's daughter-in-law Sarah Harman, or Harmon, from Monroe County, Mississippi, was the daughter of Stephen Harman, who died after Sarah and her brother James left for Utah Territory. Stephen left his children several enslaved people, and his estate file includes correspondence between a lawyer in Mississippi and William and Sarah Crosby in San Bernardino, California. However, his will does not name Esther.

Sources: Esther Harmon, Great Salt Lake County, Utah Territory [draft copy], *1850 Census*. Unknown to Brigham Young, c. 1851–1854, Ecclesiastical Files, Office Files. "List of Letters," *Deseret News*, April 4, 1855. Thomas Bullock, Names of Pueblo Soldiers and Mississippi Brethren, 1847, MS 15561, CHL. John Brown Company of Ten, 1848, box 2, folder 31, Camp of Israel Schedules and Reports. Stephen Harman, Monroe County, Mississippi, *1840 Census*. Stephen Harmon Probate, 1850, case 431, Monroe County, Mixed Estate and Probate Court Files, Mississippi County Courthouses, *Mississippi Probate Records*.

Thompson (1825–)?

Thompson, a twenty-five-year-old Black man from Mississippi, is in the 1850 census population schedule next to Hark (Lay) Wales and between the Lay and Robert M. Smith households. There is no further record of Thompson or whether he was enslaved. He may be the unnamed man in the Bankhead household and the father of Mary Crosby's older children.

Sources: Thompson, Utah County, Utah Territory, *1850 Census*.

Whitmore

Female (Whitmore) (1846–)

Elizabeth Whitmore enslaved or hired an unnamed teenage girl in Great Salt Lake City in 1860. Whitmore may have taken her from Texas to California in 1857 or hired or purchased her in Utah. She may be Downey Perkins (Woolridge) or Betsy Brown (Flewellen). She is too young to be the woman enslaved by Elizabeth Whitmore in Ellis County, Texas, who joined the Church of Jesus Christ of Latter-day Saints and was remembered by Whitmore descendants as "a negro servant whom [Elizabeth] would leave to care for the house and tend the baby while she went into the fields to pick cotton." Whitmore may have sold the baptized woman along with any other people she enslaved before she left Texas.

Elizabeth Whitmore is listed as the enslaver in the 1860 slave schedule since much of her property was an inheritance from her first husband, Michael T. Flaherty. After the murder of her second husband, Elizabeth turned the remains of the Flaherty estate into a fortune in territorial Utah. Nothing in any family record explains the identity or fate of the teenager listed in the slave schedule, and there is no evidence that she went with Whitmore to Southern Utah in the early 1860s.

Enslavers: Elizabeth Carter Flaherty Whitmore Casey (1827–1892) and James Montgomery Whitmore (1826–1866)

Notes: The Flaherty estate is not in the tax rolls in 1853 but appeared under James Whitmore's name in 1854 through 1857. In 1855, the family had $500 in the bank; the next year they had no money in the bank and four enslaved people, valued at $2,575. Shortly before they left Texas, tax records showed the same land, $2,000 cash, and two enslaved people valued at $1,250. A slave sale accounts for the large infusion of cash. James Whitmore created a consecration deed in 1858 showing a small amount of property, but Elizabeth did not create a consecration deed showing the bulk of their property. Elizabeth Whitmore's father wrote her out of his will and a large inheritance of land and enslaved people if she did not leave her new faith, while her husband James M. Whitmore's parents may have died as Union sympathizers in a Confederate prison.

Sources: Elizabeth Whitmore, Great Salt Lake County, Utah Territory Slave Schedule, *1860 Census*. Ferris, "Diary of Morris J. Snedaker," 535–37. M T Flaherty, Ellis County, Texas Productions of Agriculture, *1850 Census*. M T Flaherty, Ellis County, 1850–1852; J M Whitmore, Ellis County, 1854–1857, *Texas, County Tax Rolls*. M. T. Flaherty Probate, 1852–53, Ellis County; Richard Carter Probate, 1860, Brazos County, Texas County, District, and Probate Courts, *Texas, Wills and Probate Records, 1833–1974*. Ancestry.com. https://www.ancestry.com/search/collections/2115. James M. Whitmore, no. 595, Salt Lake County Transfer Book, 1857–1867, Consecration Deeds, 1854–1867, CR 5 53, box 4, folder 4, 212, CHL. B. P. Pendleton, J. E. J. [pseud., Joseph Ellis Johnson], "More from Dixie," *Salt Lake Daily Telegraph*, February 3, 1866. Le Landgren, *A Whitmore Family History, 1793–1990* (West Linn, OR: Family Gathering, 1990), 3, 10–11.

Eleven

ASSOCIATED ENSLAVED INDIVIDUALS

Richard Camper (1795-1884)

When wealthy Utah politician and businessman William H. Hooper (1813–1882) died, his executors valued his estate at more than $500,000. Hooper's family had enslaved people in Dorchester County, Maryland, the birthplace of Harriet Tubman and Frederick Douglass, but Hooper did not take enslaved people to Utah Territory, although he hired and purchased Daniel and Shepherd Camp there. The estate files of Hooper and his widow, Mary Ann Knowlton Hooper (1829–1887), confirm a family story that Hooper paid a pension to a man formerly enslaved by his family. Journalist Edward Tullidge reported that "Old Charley" was a playmate of Hooper's father. The Hooper family said he died after being bedridden for ten years. "He was not forgotten, however, nor forsaken, by him to whose rearing he had contributed in earlier times. He was cared for to the last, receiving a liberal stipend regularly from Mr. Hooper."

Estate papers show a small pension paid to Richard Camper (1795–1884) of Dorchester County, Maryland, then to Camper's widow Harriet (1805–). The Hooper family ended the pension when Mary Ann Hooper died.

Sources: Bill of Sale for Dan, August 17, 1859, Great Salt Lake County Recorder's Office, as reproduced in Carter, *Negro Pioneer*, 42. William H. Hooper, Great Salt Lake County, Utah Territory Slave Schedule, *1860 Census*. William H. Hooper Probate, 1883, box 27, folder 3; Mary Ann Knowlton Hooper Probate, box 38, folder 20, Third District Court Probate Case

Files, Series 1621, USHS. Richard Camper, Dorchester County, MD, *1860 Census*. Richard and Harriet Camper, Dorchester County, MD, *1870 Census*. Richard and Harriet Camper, Dorchester County, MD, *1880 Census*. "Hon. W. H. Hooper," *Tullidge's Quarterly Magazine* 2, no. 4 (July 1883): 663. Kate B. Carter, *The Negro Pioneer* (Salt Lake City: Daughters of Utah Pioneers, 1965), 35.

Jacob (Crosby) (Bankhead) (1829–1847)

Jacob was a young teenager when he became the property of John Henderson and Nancy Crosby Bankhead. Jacob was on his way to help settle the Great Salt Lake Valley when he died at Winter Quarters near today's Omaha, Nebraska.

Enslavers: John H. and Nancy Crosby Bankhead

Burial: Grave 126, Winter Quarters (Mormon Pioneer) Cemetery, Omaha, Nebraska

Sources: John Crosby Probate, Monroe County, 1842, Mississippi County, District, and Probate Courts, Mississippi, Wills and Probate Records. "Jacob; age 17 years, 6 months; Servant of John Bankhead; Deceased, April 7, 1847; Disease, Winter fevur; Birthplace, Monroe C<u>o</u> Missipi; Time, Oct 1829; Grave 126." Sexton's Records, Cutler's Park and Winter Quarters, LR 6359 24, CHL.

Henry (Crosby) (Brown) (–1847)

Henry was enslaved by John Crosby and then by John and Elizabeth Crosby Brown. He was going to be in the first Latter-day Saint wagon company with John Brown, but he died at Round Prairie, Missouri. Based on locations given in accounts of the travel and local histories, Henry is probably buried near North Andrew High School in Rosendale, Missouri.

Enslavers: John and Elizabeth Crosby Brown

Burial: Round Prairie, Rosendale, Andrew County, Missouri

Sources: John Crosby Probate, Monroe County, 1842, Mississippi County, District, and Probate Courts, Mississippi, Wills and Probate Records. Brown, box 1, folder 1, images 41–71, Reminiscences. Connie Johnson,

Rolling Hills Consolidated Library, Savannah, Missouri, telephone conversation with the author, May 19, 2016. *History of Andrew and DeKalb Counties Missouri, From the Earliest Time to the Present* (St. Louis and Chicago: Goodspeed Publishing Co., 1888), 268. Marceline Simerly and Martie Schuman, "The Round Prairie Trail," Fillmore History Archives, Schuman Auction Service, http://www.schumanauction.com/RoundPrarie.htm (site discontinued).

Harman or Harmon

Stephen Harman or Harmon (1779–1850) of Monroe County, Mississippi, died after his daughter Sarah Harmon Crosby and her husband William Crosby, and son James Harman and his wife Mary Ann Blanks Smithson Harman left for Utah Territory. Harman left Toby or Felix, Polly, and Coleman to Sarah, and he left Nathan and Sam to James. The probate file shows incomplete correspondence between a lawyer in Mississippi and William and Sarah Crosby in California but does not document that any of the enslaved people went to Utah Territory or California.

Sources: Stephen Harman, Monroe County, Mississippi, *1840 Census*. Stephen Harmon Probate, 1850, case 431, Monroe County, Mixed Estate and Probate Court Files, Mississippi County Courthouses, Mississippi Probate Records.

Five Unknown (Dennis)

Five people enslaved by William and Talitha Bankhead Dennis liberated themselves in Tabor, Iowa, in 1854. The 1850 census slave schedule listed a thirty-year-old man, a twenty-six-year-old woman (possibly Nancy Lines Smith, who continued to Utah), an eighteen-year-old woman, and an eighteen-year-old man. Accounts from residents of Tabor mention two children. (See Chapter 3, "Exodus and Escape.")

Sources: William T. Dennis, Pontotoc County, Mississippi Slave Schedule, *1850 Census*. John Todd, *Early Settlement and Growth of Western Iowa or Reminiscences* (Des Moines, IA: Historical Department of Iowa, 1906), 134–37. Dennis L. Lythgoe, "Negro Slavery in Utah," (master's thesis, University of Utah, 1966), 32–33, https://collections.lib.utah.edu/details?id=1602212. Catherine Grace Barbour Farquhar, "Tabor and Tabor College," *Iowa Journal of History and Politics* 41, no. 4 (October 1943): 358–59. https://archive.org/details/iowajournalofhisoostat. Mary Ellen Snodgrass, *The Underground Railroad: An Encyclopedia of People, Places, and Operations* (Armonk, NY: M.E. Sharpe, 2008), 244. Louis T. Jones, *The Quakers of Iowa* (Iowa City, IA: State Historical Society of Iowa, 1914).

Ike (Camp)

Ike (Camp), as remembered in the autobiography of Ellen Camp Greer, is not Isaac (Greer) (Camp) (Greer), taken by Diannah and Williams Camp to Utah Territory and then by Thomas and Ellen Camp Greer to Texas. Ellen Greer recalled that in her childhood, fifteen men came to her father's blacksmith shop to tar and feather him due to his conversion to the Latter-day Saints. Ike supposedly hid while Camp drove off the attackers, and when chastised by Camp, Ike reportedly said, "Well, Massa William, I thought you was enough for them men."

Ellen claimed that Camp took Ike to Illinois with a promise that he would be freed, but that he ran away. On a return trip to the South, Camp came across him working in an inn and took him back to Tennessee where Camp supposedly freed Ike and his wife Darcy and gave them land. Census and tax records and manumission laws make this memory improbable. The family later remembered an additional enslaved man "Ben," but there is no trace of a man by that name in Greer probate or other documents. The memory may be of Benjamin Perkins.

Sources: See the entry for Charlotte (Camp).

Harriet Burchard Church (1843–1922)

After Haden W. Church died in Tennessee in 1875, his brother Thomas Church moved his family from Tennessee to Utah Territory. Thomas's first wife, Nancy Bryan Church, was still alive when Thomas began living with Harriet, an enslaved girl Nancy brought into their household. When he returned to Tennessee after fighting in the Civil War, Thomas housed Harriet and their children in one home and, Nancy having died, lived in another home with Nancy's only surviving child. Latter-day Saint missionary Joseph Argyle wrote, "went and saw Bro Thomas Churches wife we had prayed to the Lord and hast him to rase her up from the aflection that was troubling her and we found her better and she told us that she would be Baptized." Although the 1870 census showed Harriet and her children as Black, missionaries did not mention Harriet's color, and she and her children passed as White in Utah Territory.

Author Connell O'Donovan wrote that the family came to the attention of Latter-day Saint leaders. Church President Lorenzo Snow and the Quorum of the Twelve said a son, John Taylor Church, should not hold the lay priesthood or serve a mission because of his Black ancestry. Despite that decision, Harriet and Thomas Church participated in Latter-day Saint temple sealing rites three years later. Although other formerly enslaved men and women participated in the temple ordinance of baptism for the dead, Harriet Church and Rebecca Foscue are currently the only formerly enslaved African American people known to have participated in other temple ordinances.

Sources: Joseph Argyle, image 77, MS 340, Reminiscences and Journal 1870–1894, CHL. Bruce Crow, email message to author, October 11, 2017. H. Church, Maury County, Tennessee, *1870 Census*. Harriet Church, Millard County, Utah Territory, *1880 Census*. First Presidency Minutes, March 1, 1900; Quorum of the Twelve Minutes, March 1, 1900; George F. Gibbs to John M. Whitaker, January 18, 1909; Abraham Owen Woodruff diary, March 1, 1900; cited in Connell O'Donovan, "'I would confine them to their own species': LDS Historical Rhetoric and Praxis Regarding Marriage Between Whites and Blacks," Website of Connell O'Donovan, paper presented at Sunstone West, March 28, 2009, Cupertino, CA. http://www.connellodonovan.com/black_white_marriage.html.

Rebecca Foscue Meads (1833–1881)

Rebecca Foscue was the daughter of Lewis Foscue and Easter, a woman he enslaved. Lewis Foscue wrote an unenforceable provision into his Mississippi will desiring to free Rebecca upon his death, but his family did not honor his wishes, and Rebecca remained in slavery. In 1860, she was living as a free woman in Ohio, where she married English immigrant Nathan Meads and joined the Church of Jesus Christ of Latter-day

Saints. The two moved to Utah Territory. Both Rebecca Foscue Meads and Harriet Burchard Church, also formerly enslaved, passed as White, were married to White men, were known to be of African descent, and are the only formerly enslaved people known to have participated in their own Latter-day Saint temple rites before 1978.

Source: Tonya S. Reiter, "Rebecca Henrietta Foscue Bentley Meads," *Century of Black Mormons.* Accessed April 21, 2021, https://exhibits.lib.utah.edu/s/century-of-black-mormons/page/meads-rebecca-henrietta-foscue-bentley.

Twelve

BLACK RESIDENTS OF UTAH TERRITORY

This section contains brief explanations about several individuals or families who had connections to those in the main chapters or were misrepresented in family or community histories. Many, but not all, had been enslaved elsewhere.

Blanchard and Steele

Mary Ann Steele (1856–1916) was the first of five siblings to move to Utah or Idaho. In 1881, she married Abraham Flake, son of Green and Martha Flake. Their daughter Blanche (1883–1948) married into the Leggroan family and is the only member of the Steele family known to have living descendants. *Susan Steele Blanchard* (1867–1926) and her husband Lloyd Blanchard (1849–1900) moved to Utah in 1883 when Susan took a job with Governor Eli Houston Murray. The couple was active in politics, Freemasonry, and the Calvary Baptist Church. Susan hosted Elizabeth Flake Rowan and her daughter during their trip to Utah in 1887. After Lloyd died, Susan remarried Joseph Grant Smith (1867–1932). *Lovell R. Steel* (1864–1903), married Jane Manning James's granddaughter, Melvina Robinson. Steel surprised Salt Lake City when he left substantial legacies to his family. *Lucretia Steel Green Perkins* (1860–) married Daniel H. Stevens (1878–1955), a grandson of Green and Martha Flake. *Charles Steele* (1865–1907) lived in Idaho but is buried in the Mount Olivet Cemetery in Salt Lake City like most of the family.

Sources: "Big Oquirrh Victory," *Salt Lake Herald*, August 21, 1895. "Town Talk," *Salt Lake Herald*, April 29, 1898. "Was Real 'Possum Dinner,'" *Salt Lake Herald*, February 8, 1902. Milewski, *Before the Manifesto*, 30n75. "Colored Man's Will. Lovell R. Steel Left Good Estate for An Afro-American," *Deseret Evening News*, January 21, 1903. "Died [Charles Steele]," Salt Lake Herald, September 1, 1907.

Burtch

Negro Pioneer mentions "Burtch," who crossed the plains in 1850 and went to California. There is no trace of a man of this name in Latter-day Saint or government records, so this is probably a memory of the Bird B. Barnett household.

Sources: Kate B. Carter, *The Negro Pioneer* (Salt Lake City: Daughters of Utah Pioneers, 1965), 39.

Carson

Robert Carson died in 1865 of tuberculosis and was buried in the pauper's section of the Salt Lake City Cemetery. He may be "Negro Bob" who was called as a witness in *Utah v. Colburn* (1859).

Sources: Robert Carson, "Colored Man," Consumption, May 3, 1865, *Salt Lake County (UT) Death Records*. United States v. Colburn (1859), Salt Lake County Probate Court Case Files, Series 373, box 6, folder 12, USHS.

Chambers and Leggroan

Samuel and Amanda Leggroan Chambers were important Black residents of early Utah, as were Amanda's brother, Edward "Ned" Leggroan and his family. Many family members moved from the South to Utah Territory and Idaho and married into the families mentioned in this book.

Sources: William G. Hartley, "Samuel D. Chambers," *New Era*, June 1974, https://www.churchofjesuschrist.org/study/new-era/1974/06/samuel-d-chambers.

Grice

In 1872, Haitian-born Francis H. Grice (1836–1893) filed for citizenship in Salt Lake City. His father, Hezekiah Grice, was a Black Maryland activist. Daughters of Utah Pioneers thought Frank Grice arrived in the Salt Lake Valley in 1848, but he moved to Utah Territory in the 1870s from Nevada, which is probably where he married Martha (1836–1918). Grice ran the Elevator Prospecting Company on behalf of Philip Alexander Bell, a civil rights activist, capitalist, and owner of the San Francisco African American newspaper, *Elevator*. Grice wrote about mining and civil rights for the *Elevator* and Utah newspapers. Grice's son Albert married Celia Freeman, the widow of Daniel Freeman Bankhead, and raised her daughters Celia (Elkins) and Mary Adelle. An acquaintance reported three other children in *Negro Pioneer*: Wallace, who married Emma Stewart; Ella; and Ida. "Ella and Ida" were step-granddaughters Celia and Mary Adelle, and Emma and Wallace may be a confused memory of the Stewart-Thurman family.

After selling shares in a mine, Frank and Martha Grice farmed and ran a restaurant at 135 S. Main Street in Salt Lake City. In 1883, Grice offered Joe or Sam Harvey a job on his farm. Martha ran Harvey out of the restaurant when he became agitated, but he seemed dangerous, so she and Frank notified Salt Lake City Police Chief Andrew Burt. Burt and Grice were standing outside the restaurant when Harvey returned and shot Burt. After Harvey was jailed, a mob stormed the jail and lynched him.

Frank Grice died in 1893. Martha moved to Idaho and remarried Perry Horton and later Harry T. Taylor. She left her property to an adopted grandson, Thomas M. Brown, who was briefly married to Beulah Jackson Thurman, the mother of Harlem Renaissance author Wallace Thurman.

Sources: Carter, *Negro Pioneer*, 32–33. "Mining in Utah," *Elevator* (San Francisco, CA), December 14, 1872. "From Our Salt Lake Correspondent," *Elevator*, June 28, 1873. Harvey, Colored, August 25, 1883, "Lynched Homicide," *Salt Lake County (UT) Death Records*. "Bloody and Brutal. Chief of Police Burt Shot and Killed on Main Street by a Vagabond Negro," *Salt Lake Daily Herald* (Salt Lake City, UT), August 26, 1883. Christopher Jones, "From the Archives: Black Internationalism in 19th Century Salt Lake City; or a Haitian-born African American in Utah Reports on the

Fourth of July, 1873," *Juvenile Instructor*, July 4, 2018, https://juvenileinstructor.org/from-the-archives-a-black-mormon-view-of-the-fourth-of-july-1873. Hezekiah Grice and Others, *Men of Maryland*, ed. George F. Bragg (Baltimore, MD: Church Advocate Press, 1914), 59–60.

Hannah Maria

When Venna Smart reconstructed the Union Cemetery records, she added a woman named "Hannah Maria" with a note that she could have been a Graham slave. The name is unlikely to have come from a written record, and the list is unreliable.

Sources: Venna Smart, Union Cemetery, in John D. Fretwell, Compiled Material on Black Mormons, c. 1982, Chapter 4, 89, MS 6968, CHL.

Hook

Richard and Daisy Hook are listed as Black in the Union Cemetery records, but they do not appear in other records and are not buried in the Black section of the cemetery.

Sources: Graves A-20 and A-19, Venna Smart, History of Union Fort Cemetery, John D. Fretwell Collection.

James and Manning

Jane Elizabeth Manning James is the best-known African American woman in early Latter-day Saint history. She joined the Church of Jesus Christ of Latter-day Saints in Connecticut and took her extended family to Nauvoo, where she lived in the household of Latter-day Saint founder Joseph Smith. She married Isaac James from New Jersey. They went to the Great Salt Lake Valley in 1847. Their daughter Mary Ann James Robinson was probably the first Black child born in Utah.

The James family lived in Brigham Young's household for several years. After Jane and Isaac divorced, Jane remarried Frank Perkins, but the marriage did not last. While they were married, they participated in Latter-day Saint baptisms for the dead in the Endowment House. Jane's brother Isaac Manning eventually joined her in Salt Lake City, and the two were well known in the city and at Latter-day Saint worship services.

Sources: Quincy D. Newell, *Your Sister in the Gospel: The Life of Jane Manning James, a Nineteenth-Century Black Mormon* (New York, NY: Oxford University Press, 2019). Henry Wolfinger, "A Test of Faith: Jane Elizabeth James and the Origins of the Utah Black Community," in *Social Accommodations in Utah*, American West Occasional Papers, ed. Clark S. Knowlton (Salt Lake City, UT: University of Utah, 1975), 126–72. Brigham Young's 1847 Emigration Division (First Division), Camp of Israel Schedules and Reports. Family Record, c. 1855, Miscellaneous Files, 1832–1878, box 170, folder 25, Office Files. Family Record, 1853–1858, box 170, folder 26, Office Files. Record of Baptisms for the Dead.

Kane Servants

In 1858, Philadelphia native and abolitionist Thomas L. Kane helped negotiate the end of the Utah War. He traveled incognito to Utah Territory, using the surname of his Black servant, Anthony Osborne, who remained in California.

Alfred Cumming of Georgia became territorial governor in 1858. He wrote to Albert Sidney Johnston, "I left camp on the 5th inst . . . accompanied by Col. Kane, as my guide, and two servants." The servants he mentioned may have worked for Kane or Cumming, but Cumming is not in the 1860 slave schedule.

Thomas Kane and his wife Elizabeth traveled with an unnamed Black servant when they visited Utah Territory in the 1870s.

Sources: Matthew J. Grow and Ronald W. Walker, *The Prophet and the Reformer: The Letters of Brigham Young and Thomas L. Kane* (New York, NY: Oxford University Press, 2015), 237, 240, 456. LeRoy R. Hafen and Ann W. Hafen, *The Utah Expedition: 1857–1858* (Glendale, CA: Arthur H. Clark Company, 1958), 286. Carter, *Negro Pioneer*, 65–66. Anthony Osborn, Alameda County, CA, *1860 Census*.

Lewis

Black Massachusetts abolitionist Q. Walker Lewis (1798–1856) joined the Church of Jesus Christ of Latter-day Saints and traveled to Utah Territory in 1851 but returned to Massachusetts the next year. He left no record of his reaction to An Act in Relation to Service, passed while he was in

Utah, and whether changing Latter-day Saint racial views contributed to his departure from the territory.

Source: Connell O'Donovan, "The Mormon Priesthood Ban and Elder Q. Walker Lewis: 'An Example for His More Whiter Brethren to Follow,'" *John Whitmer Historical Association Journal* 26 (2006): 48–100. https://www.jstor.org/stable/43200236.

Pope

Virginia native and blacksmith Frank or Francis Pope (1800–) worked in downtown Great Salt Lake City. He testified in court in 1859 about the killing of Shepherd Camp and in 1860 in a case against James Valentine/Banks. His name last appeared in the Thomas S. Williams probate.

Sources: Frank Pope, Fourteenth Ward, Great Salt Lake County, *1856 Utah Territorial Census*. Francis Pope, Great Salt Lake County, Utah Territory, *1860 Census*. "Third Judicial District Court," *Deseret News*, September 21, 1859. "Local News," *Mountaineer*, September 15, 1860. June 13, 1860, Williams Probate.

Sion

English Latter-day Saint converts Frederick Sion (1814–1905) and Ellen Hill Sion (1819–1903) moved to Utah Territory in 1862. Frederick had some African ancestry. They left no indication of whether it was due to racial tensions that they left Cache Valley for Oregon in the 1870s, but Sion and his family, along with other Black residents of Utah Territory, signed the 1872 petition to Congress, "Against the Admission of Utah as a State," with their names recorded as "Tion."

Sources: "Captain Miller's Company," *Deseret News*, September 17, 1862. "Against the Admission of Utah as a State," 31. Fredrick Sion, Cache County, Utah Territory, *1870 Census*. Fredrick Sion, Union County, Oregon, *1880 Census*.

Xhosa Immigrants

Umlemle or Wmlemle (1845–) and Enyanke or Enganke (1846–) were probably Xhosa from the Eastern Cape, South Africa. They traveled with

Latter-day Saint converts to Utah Territory on the brig *Mexicana* in 1865. Due to the British laws of South Africa, they could not be enslaved, but the ship register listed them as servants. When the converts arrived at Castle Garden, Minor G. Atwood went ashore with the captain and told officials that he had a company of immigrants from South Africa. "They said I could not land them there supposing they were negroes but when I informed them that they were Mormons they showed us every attention." The only suggestion that the two men made it past Castle Gardens is a note from English immigrant Thomas Alston about his childhood experience crossing the plains: "Among the members of the company . . . was also two colored men from Africa" who asked not to be called American racial epithets. The only Latter-day Saint converts likely to have had two Black men with them and to have traveled both on the *Mexicana* and with the Alston family were Henry and Martha Knight Smith, but none of the South African families left information about the two men. The section "Lynchings" mentions the death of three unnamed men at a railroad camp in the winter of 1868–1869. Perhaps the two men died in these or similar circumstances.

Sources: Umlemle and Enyanke, British brig "Mexicana," Port Elizabeth, South Africa, to New York, June 20, 1865, *Passenger Lists of Vessels Arriving at New York, New York, 1820–1897* (National Archives Microfilm Publication T715;253, list 532, line 46–47), Records of the US Customs Service, Record Group 36. Miner G. Atwood, Diary, April 12, 1865, South African Mission, Manuscript History, CHL, quoted at *Saints by Sea*, https://saintsbysea.lib.byu.edu/mii/account/869. Thomas Alston, Autobiography, in Ray Lester Alston, comp., "Thomas Alston and Mary Ellen Holt Alston," 1975, 16–19, as cited at *Pioneer Database*. Accessed October 3, 2016, https://history.churchofjesuschrist.org/overlandtravel/sources/13790599138166828810-eng/thomas-alston-and-mary-ellen-holt-alston-compiled-by-ray-l-alston-1975-16-19. LaDonna Petersen, "Life History of Henry Smith Sr. (1815–1872), digital copy of typescript, FSFT. Accessed October 3, 2016, https://familysearch.org/photos/artifacts/21201462.

Taylor (Julius and Anna)

Julius F. Taylor (1854–1934) was the charismatic editor of the African American newspaper, *The Broad Ax*. His wife, Anna Emogene Taylor

(1872–1932), taught art. Taylor published his newspaper for four years in Salt Lake City before he moved to a larger market in Chicago.

Sources: Michael S. Sweeney, "Julius F. Taylor and the Broad Ax of Salt Lake City," *Utah Historical Quarterly* 77, no. 3 (Summer 2009): 204–21, https://www.jstor.org/stable/45063211.

Taylor (W. W. and Elizabeth)

William Wesley Taylor (1865–1907), no relation to Julius, edited one of the Black newspapers in Salt Lake City, *Utah Plain Dealer* (1895–1909). Taylor was a devoted Republican and was mentioned in the national press due to the furor over prospective US Senator Reed Smoot inviting him and his wife and other Black Republicans to a political dinner. His wife, Elizabeth Austin Taylor Morris (1874–1932), edited the paper after Taylor's death. She was one of the founders of the African Methodist Episcopal (AME) churches in Salt Lake City and Grand Junction, Colorado.

Sources: *Plain Dealer* (Salt Lake City, UT), January 9, 1897, CHL. Jeffrey D. Nichols, "The Broad Ax and the Plain Dealer Kept Utah's African Americans Informed," *Utah History to Go*, State of UT. https://historytogo.utah.gov/broad-ax. Amy Tanner Thiriot, "Elizabeth Taylor, Newspaper Woman and Activist," *Better Days 2020*. Accessed April 21, 2021, https://www.utahwomenshistory.org/bios/elizabeth-taylor.

Taylor

Robert Taylor shot Frank (Dotson?) in 1858. Perhaps he was "Negro Bob" who was called as a witness in *United States v. Colburn* (1859), and Robert Carson, who died in 1865 of tuberculosis.

Sources: "Progress of Civilization (!)," *Deseret News*, September 15, 1858. United States v. Colburn (1859), Salt Lake County Probate Court Case Files, Series 373, box 6, folder 12, Utah State Archive.

Wood

Negro Pioneer mentioned a couple named Edwin and Ann Wood, but got details wrong, including a claim that they arrived in the Great Salt

Lake Valley in 1847. Edwin Wood ran the farm of Virginia widow Martha Fortune Howerton in Missouri. He and his family lived in the Howerton home through at least 1878 and moved to Utah Territory before 1880. Martha Howerton's husband Joseph traveled to California around 1849 and could have taken young Edwin with him. They could have spent time in the Salt Lake Valley, but the most likely explanation for the information in *Negro Pioneer* is that someone confused Edwin Wood with another man.

Sources: Edward [sic] Wood, Chariton County, Missouri, *1870 Census*. Edwin Wood, Salt Lake County, Utah Territory, *1880 Census*. *The History of Cass and Bates Counties, Missouri* (St. Joseph, MO: National Historical Company, 1883), 1197. Carter, *Negro Pioneer*, 31.

Valentine and Banks

Two unrelated men named James Valentine lived in the Salt Lake Valley: James Valentine or Vallentyne/Banks and Canadian James Valentine, who married Nancy Bankhead. The first James may be a man who traveled to Utah with the Amasa Lyman wagon company in 1848. The draft copy of the 1850 census for Utah Territory showed James and an otherwise unknown twenty-year-old Iddy as free Blacks from Missouri. The official copy of the census showed them as James and Lizzy, ages twenty-five and eighteen, with no indication of race. James may be James Valentine/Banks, who remained in Great Salt Lake City and had at least one child with Rose (Crosby).

Canadian James Valentine had a family with Nancy Bankhead and a son named Morena or Marine Valentine (1861–1883) with an unknown woman. Morena worked in a livery stable in downtown Salt Lake City and was known as "Cooney" or "Snowflake." When Morena contracted tuberculosis and could no longer care for himself city officials temporarily housed him in the jail. He died before they could move him to the county hospital. The burial record showed that he was born in 1861 in Union Fort, the son of James Valentine, but did not specify which James Valentine; however, another newspaper article reported that he was a half-brother to James and Nancy Bankhead Valentine's children.

Sources: James and Iddy, Utah County, Utah Territory population schedule [draft], 1850 [1851], MS 2672, box 1, folder 9, CHL. James and Lizzy, Utah County, Utah Territory, *1850 Census.* "A State Road Accident," *Salt Lake Tribune,* January 9, 1880. "Chips," *Salt Lake Herald,* April 13, 1883. "Died in Jail," *Deseret News,* April 18, 1883. Morena Valentine, April 12, 1883, Salt Lake City, Utah Archives and Records Service, *Utah Death Registers.* "A Valentine," *Salt Lake Herald,* April 27, 1883.

Thirteen

FORMER OR UNPROVEN ENSLAVERS

This chapter provides explanatory notes about a few of the families connected to Utah who may or may not have had enslaved laborers in the South. Most family memories of slavery are inaccurate and must be checked against government and legal records. For example, a grandson remembered that Charles C. Rich owned "three pair of slaves" although he enslaved either one or no people, and despite detailed memories, an enslaved woman named "Mammy Chloe" may not have existed, or if she did exist, cannot be traced into Utah Territory. Surveys of Southern Latter-day Saint converts found no additional documentation of enslaved people taken to Utah Territory besides the ones listed in this book.

Blair

Utah lawyer Seth M. Blair was involved in several legal actions involving enslaved residents of Utah Territory. His widowed mother held a life interest in the family property and died after the Civil War, so Blair never inherited enslaved people from his parents. He is not known to have enslaved people in Texas or Utah Territory, but he does appear to have had a financial interest in a mortgage with either Caroline or Tampian Hoye as collateral. (See Appendix 5.)

Sources: James Blair Will and Probate, 1846, Dewitt County, Transcribed Probate Minutes, Vol. A1–B1, 1846–1851, 26, Texas County, District, and Probate Courts, Texas, Wills and Probate Records.

Butler

John Lowe and Caroline Skeen Butler joined the Church of Jesus Christ of Latter-day Saints and moved to Utah Territory. Descendants later claimed that when Butler and Skeen married in Tennessee in 1831, Caroline's father gave them an enslaved couple, but Butler did not care for slavery and freed the couple. The marriage happened months before Tennessee strengthened its slave codes to prevent most manumissions, but while the claim is legally possible, it is unlikely. Caroline's father enslaved twelve people in 1830, most of them children under the age of ten, and it would have been unusual for him to give the equivalent of much of his farm's labor capacity to one of his ten or more children, especially since he had three disabled daughters who would need long-term care. William G. Hartley also questioned details of the family history in his biography of John Lowe Butler.

Many years afterward, John D. Lee told a story about election day violence in the South in which Butler, "professed to be half white and free born," but Lee's story makes better sense without the word "half." There is no known picture of Butler, but his children and grandchildren appear to be of Scots-Irish or German descent, so Lee's claim serves best as an example of the use of race as a rhetorical weapon in nineteenth-century America.

Sources: William G. Hartley, *My Best for the Kingdom: History and Autobiography of John Lowe Butler, a Mormon Frontiersman* (Salt Lake City, UT: Aspen Books, 1993). Jesse Skeen, Sumner County, Tennessee, *1830 Census.* John L. Butler to Caroline Skeen, January 29, 1831, Sumner County, Tennessee State Library and Archive, *Tennessee State Marriages, 1780–2002,* Ancestry.com, https://www.ancestry.com/search/collections/1169. Hurd, *Law of Freedom and Bondage* (Clark, NJ: The Lawbook Exchange, Ltd., 2006), 2–92. John D. Lee and W. W. Bishop, *Mormonism Unveiled; or, The Life and Confessions of the Late Mormon Bishop, John D. Lee* (St. Louis, MO: Bryan, Brand, 1877), 60.

Covington and Collins

George Armstrong Hicks (1835–1926), who married into the Jolley family with its history of slavery, helped settle "Utah's Dixie" in the early 1860s.

He wrote a memoir that included anecdotes about neighbors Robert D. Covington (1815–1902) and Covington's brother-in-law Albert W. Collins (1814–1873). Hicks called Covington a barely literate "Rebel sympathizer" and Mississippi slave driver, and Collins another slave driver who "used to often entertain his hearers at places where people were gathered for public work . . . by narrating acts of cruelty which he had committed in whipping slaves while on plantations in the South." Hicks wrote that Collins claimed to have beaten an enslaved man to death and to have raped multiple enslaved women.

Covington and Collins are not listed as landowners in tax records for Noxubee County, Mississippi, which supports the claim about their employment overseeing forced labor. Tax records show that in 1840, Covington enslaved one person. This disagrees with the census record that showed more enslaved people in his household, but the 1840 census and Noxubee County tax records disagree for multiple enslavers. In 1842, Covington enslaved two people and Collins one. The next year Covington joined the Church of Jesus Christ of Latter-day Saints. By 1845, the tax records show that he owned no taxable property. Even if he desired to do so, Covington could not have manumitted the enslaved except with an act of the state legislature, so he likely sold them for funds to move across the country. Covington and Collins traveled from Winter Quarters to Utah Territory in the same company as enslaved John Burton, but no record shows that Covington or Collins took enslaved people to Utah.

Sources: Polly Aird, Jeff Nichols, and Will Bagley, eds., *Playing with Shadows: Voices of Dissent in the Mormon West*, Kingdom in the West: The Mormons and the American Frontier Series (Norman, OK: Arthur H. Clark, 2011), 172–73. R D Covington and Albert W Collins, 1837–1845, Noxubee County Tax Rolls 1834–1847, box 3732, Mississippi Department of Archives and History, Various Records.

Cropper and Croft

George W. and Sebrina Land Matheny Cropper enslaved two people in Texas: a man listed as George's property, and a girl listed as Sebrina's property. In an 1850 letter to his wife, George Cropper mentioned enslaved people as currency: "I would give a little negro if I had one to be with you." After George died, Sebrina remarried Jacob Croft, and they left for Utah

Territory. Just before they entered Kansas Territory, then gripped with the violent conflicts over slavery that gave it the name "Bleeding Kansas," the couple sold "A woman about thirty seven years of age named Patricia and a boy four years old named Andrew, a boy two years old named Landy" to Cherokee leader and later Confederate General Stand Watie for $1,300. In 1860, Watie enslaved seventeen people, including three who fit the description of Patricia and her boys. Jacob Croft's consecration deed confirms that he was among the wealthier settlers in Utah Territory.

Deed, Jacob and Sabrina Croft sale of slaves Patricia, Andrew, and Landy to Stand Watie, June 7, 1856, Cherokee Nation Collection in Western History Collections of the University of Oklahoma, box 41, folder 125, published in R. Halliburton Jr., *Red Over Black: Black Slavery among the Cherokee Indians* (Westport, CT: Greenwood Press, 1977), 114, in Jeffery O. Johnson, "Cattle, Slaves, Missionaries and Mormon Converts from Texas, 1850s" (lecture, Mormon History Association, San Antonio, TX, June 2014). Jeffery O. Johnson, email message to author, February 8, 2013. Stand Watie, Cherokee Nation Slave Schedule, *1860 Census*. Jacob Croft, Consecration Book Index, 1857–1858, box 1, 34, Consecration Deeds.

Sources: Geo W and Sebrina Cropper, Harris County, Texas Slave Schedule, *1850 Census*. George W. Cropper to Mrs. Geo. W. Cropper, July 21, 1850, ed. Kimberly Spendlove, FSFT. Accessed February 28, 2020. https://www.familysearch.org/tree/person/memories/KWJC-9YS.

Cunningham

Samuel and Mary Ellis Cunningham enslaved one woman (1820–) in Ellis County, Texas. There is no record that they took her to Utah Territory. They settled in St. George, Utah Territory, in the fall of 1862 after any enslaved person would have been freed by act of Congress. In 1870, the census shows that they employed a servant named Chaney, likely Chaney (Redd). There is no detailed record of the family's movements, but Chaney's presence in the household raises the question of whether Cunningham could have accompanied other Texas converts to Utah Territory in the mid-1850s, purchased or hired Chaney there, taken her back to Texas, and then returned to Utah Territory.

Sources: Ferris, "Diary of Morris J. Snedaker," 534. Edith Smith and Vivian Lehman, "*No Land . . . Only Slaves!*" Vol. 11. *Abstracts from the Deed*

Books of Upshur & Ellis Counties in Texas (Balch Springs, TX: privately printed, 2005), 91–141.

Ewell

The "autobiography" of Mary or Polly Blann Ewell Jones (1817–1898) tells of "Mammy Chloe," who helped her young "mistress" through many dramatic trials in the American South and then through the vicissitudes of Latter-day Saint pioneer life. The short document reads like fiction, but, for many years, its place in Kate B. Carter's *Negro Pioneer* meant that it was treated as fact. The document does not hold up to verification. Its excessive errors, use of language, and thematic elements about slavery date it to the mid-twentieth century. The author was probably one of seven granddaughters who may have known Jones at least briefly during her lifetime. A version of the family history by Manila Campbell suggests that the family originally enslaved two people but does not claim the presence of Chloe in Utah Territory. A dialect-laden version by Eddavene Houtz Bean takes Chloe into Utah Territory and adds intricate details about her supposed life there.

Census records show no enslaved people in the Blann or Ewell households for decades before the family arrived in Utah Territory. The 1850 census does not show Black members of the Ewell household. The 1852 Latter-day Saint wagon company roster shows only the widowed Mary and her six children. No one matching Chloe's description appears in Utah census, death, or burial records, even under alternate names, and if she had been in Utah until well past 1865, as later stories claimed, she should be in multiple records. In the absence of any documentary corroboration, the family stories should be classed as historical fiction, including a dramatic anecdote about Chloe's reaction to segregated Latter-day Saint temple worship.

Sources: Carter, *Negro Pioneer*, 36–39. Manila Bybee Campbell, "Mary Lee Bland (Blann) History," Digital File, March 9, 2017, FSFT. https://www.familysearch.org/photos/artifacts/34378667. Eddavene Houtz Bean, "History of Mary Lee Bland," digital file, FSFT. Accessed November 14, 2016, https://familysearch.org/photos/artifacts/17797928. John Blann, Ray County, Missouri, *1830 Census*. John Blan, Livingston County, Missouri, *1840 Census*. Pleasant Ewell, Bedford County, Tennessee, *1830 Census*.

Pleasant Ewel, Hancock County, Illinois, *1840 Census*. Polly Ewell, Pottawattamie County, Iowa, *1850 Census*. Emigration of 1852, Sixteenth Company, Second Ten, *Historical Department Journal History*.

Foscue

In 1924, Eliza Foscue Lee Wells's family had proxy baptisms done in the Salt Lake Temple for seventy-six Black individuals. Around 1920, she sent a daughter to the South to collect genealogy, a trip likely the source for the names of the deceased enslaved people, among them Big George, Big Bill, Mammy Jane, and Cudjo. Wells was not known to take any enslaved people with her to Utah.

Sources: "All Negro Blood: Baptisms and Confirmations for the Dead," Salt Lake Temple, F 183511, 1924–1942, John D. Fretwell Collection. Eliza Foscue Lee Wells, "Autobiography of Eliza's Youth," digital file, partial transcript of autobiography, May 26, 2008, copy in possession of the author. Bonnie Black Wilkerson, Ancestry.com message to author, June 1, 2016.

Graham

In 1840, Thomas B. Graham (1807–1864) and his wife Sarah McCrory Graham (1811–1847) enslaved a young girl. She was not in the household long, since Mississippi tax records showed that Graham employed no free Blacks and enslaved no one between the ages of five and sixty from 1841 through 1843 and had no Black household members of any age in 1844. An 1847 letter from Graham's daughter and son-in-law pled with the family to return to Arkansas and mentioned that Thomas's father inherited "a very likely negro fellow <and fifty dollars in money> when Old Grandfather Bradford divided out his property." *Negro Pioneer* shared Graham memories of "possibly Aunt Hannah, Robert and Isaac." However, the 1850 census, 1851 Iowa census, and Latter-day Saint wagon company roster do not show enslaved people in the household, and Thomas Graham's deed of consecration showed a net worth around $300.

One of the daughters in the family, Caroline Graham Hill, told a story about Brigham Young's coachman Isaac James, but her family later mistakenly assumed James was a family slave. Her family also told of Caroline crying for her deceased mother "and being comforted by one of their slaves." The memory could have been about any of the enslaved people traveling with the Latter-day Saint wagon companies. The family story continued, "They arrived in the Salt Lake Valley on 19 October 1948 [1852]. Thomas B. Graham hurried and built a house, he also let all the slaves go free." Again, the anecdote is meaningless without supporting documentation.

After a bear killed Graham in Cache Valley in 1864, some of his children continued to live in Union, Salt Lake County. When Venna Smart compiled the Union Cemetery records, she added a woman named "Hannah Maria" to the list and wondered if she could have been a Graham slave. It is unlikely.

In recent years, family members puzzled over a picture of a Black couple and child found in Graham family collections. Someone wrote on the back, "Mr. and Mrs. Taylor—slaves worked on Thomas Bradfords [sic] Graham's Farm. They came to Utah with the Bradfords to help with the children." Based on the handwriting, the note was written after *Negro Pioneer* and is likely incorrect. However, the name "Taylor" provides a clue. The unreliable 1856 Utah territorial census showed an otherwise unidentified man named Robert in the Graham household. A Black man named Robert Taylor shot Frank (Dotson?) in 1858 and could have been the same man, but the connection is speculative.

Sources: Thomas Graham, Kemper County, Mississippi, *1840 Census*. Thomas Grayham or Graham, 1841, 1842, 1843, 1844, Kemper County, County Tax Rolls, 1841–1852, box 3677, Mississippi Department of Archives and History, Various Records. Carter, *Negro Pioneer*, 34. Edwin R. Shipman and Mary Jane Graham Shipman to Thomas and Sarah Graham, November 25, 1847, Pickens County, Alabama, digital copy of holograph, courtesy of Gloria Ann Smith, February 11, 2017, FSFT. https://www.familysearch.org/photos/artifacts/33360519. Thomas Grayham, Pottawattamie County, Iowa, *1850 Census*. Thomas B. Graham, 1851, Iowa State Historical Society, *Iowa, State Census Collection, 1836–1925*, Ancestry.com, https://www.ancestry.com/search/collections/1084. "T[homas]. B. Graham and 9 persons [identifiable as family members Sarah, Martha, Frances, John, William, Caroline, Amanda, George, and another Thomas]" "7th Company," *Deseret News Weekly (Great Salt Lake City, UT)*, September 18, 1852. Thomas B. Graham, Robert Graham, Mill

Creek, Great Salt Lake County, *1856 Utah Territorial Census.* Thomas B. Graham, Consecration Book Index, 110. Anonymous, "Caroline Graham Hill," FSFT, accessed April 11, 2016, https://familysearch.org/photos/stories/3402434. Venna Smart, History of Union Fort Cemetery, typescript, John D. Fretwell Collection. "Mr. and Mrs. Taylor," digital copy of photo, private collection, digital copy in possession of author.

Heath and Marler

John Heath may be the father of Marion Heath Smith, born to enslaved woman Hannah Smiley when the Mississippi Saints and their enslaved people went to settle San Bernardino. (See the entry for Hannah Smiley Embers.) Heath may be related to Harriet Heath Marler (1813–1869). Her family recalled that an enslaved woman in the household died while traveling from Mississippi to Utah Territory. There is no record that the family enslaved people in Utah Territory.

Sources: Allen Marlow [*sic*], Claiborne, Mississippi, *1840 Census.* Adolph Heath (father), fifteen slaves, Claiborne County, Mississippi Slave Schedule, *1850 Census.* John Heath, Utah County, Utah Territory, *1850 Census.* Lola Taylor Wells and Arline Martindale Scott Brinton, "Harriett Heath Marler," FSFT. Accessed February 22, 2019, https://www.familysearch.org/photos/artifacts/75280830.

Holladay and Smithson

When Bartlett Smithson died in the 1830s, his son Allen Smithson (1816–1877) bought a boy named Lid from his estate. However, there were no enslaved people in the households of either of Allen Smithson's wives or documentation that Smithson took enslaved people when he went to Utah Territory.

The 1850 census shows Smithson traveling with John Holladay (1798–1862) and Catherine Higgins Holladay (1797–1877), the parents of his deceased first wife, Lutisha Holladay (1824–1849). Holladay descendants later recalled that two formerly enslaved people followed their ancestors to Utah Territory. However, no known documentation confirms that John Holladay enslaved anyone. Catherine's parents enslaved people, but the executors to their estates sold them at auction, and Catherine did not appear in records as an enslaver. An autobiography by Holladay son-in-law Absalom Dowdle (1819–1897) mentions many enslaved people in the family but is an unreliable source due to multiple suspect claims. There is often a kernel of truth behind family legends, though. The Holladay family lived by John H. and George Bankhead in Alabama, and the Bankhead brothers took enslaved people to Utah Territory. After they were freed, some of them lived near Holladay descendants in Union, and this may be the source of the legends.

Sources: Benjamin Higgins Probate, Estate Papers, box 14, Package 340, Richland County, South Carolina County, District, and Probate Courts, South Carolina, Wills and Probate Records. John Holliday, no slaves, Marion County, Alabama, *1830 Census*. Daniel Holiday Sr., Marion County, Alabama, *1830 Census*. Bartlet Smithson Probate, 1839, Inventory Records of Estates, 1839–1921, Mississippi County Courthouses, Mississippi Probate Records. John Holliday, no slaves, Marion County, Alabama, *1840 Census*. (This census shows four children at home, no adults.) Sarah Smithson, Monroe County, Mississippi, *1840 Census*. Absalom P. Dowdle, "Absalom Porter Dowdle (Taken from His Diary)," MS 9266, CHL. Carter, Negro Pioneer, 50.

Holt and Pearson

John H. Redd's niece Drusilla Holt Pearson left her husband Amos Pearson and headed west with the Latter-day Saints. After Pearson died, Elza Taylor petitioned the Onslow County, North Carolina, court for Drusilla and her daughter to receive the proceeds of the sale of Sophy, age thirteen, and Charles, two. When Taylor filed the petition, Drusilla's daughter had already died of measles at Winter Quarters, and Drusilla was on her way to the Great Salt Lake Valley. The estate documents do not specify whether she received any proceeds from the sale of the two children. Drusilla's parents, John and Mary Redd Holt, enslaved three people in 1830, but none in 1840, and no reliable documentation suggests they enslaved people in Utah Territory.

Sources: Amos Pearson, 1847, *North Carolina, Wills and Probate Records*. Jno Holt, Rutherford County, Tennessee, *1830 Census; 1840 Census*. Sexton's Records, Cutler's Park and Winter Quarters, LR 6359 24, CHL.

Kinney

A newspaper article reported that Judge John F. Kinney "is also in the slave trade, as well as the principal men of the Territory." Kinney was born in New York to parents from New England. He served on the Supreme Court of Iowa and was appointed twice as chief justice of the Utah Territory Supreme Court, after which he served as delegate from Utah Territory to the US Congress. He then returned home to Nebraska. He supported popular sovereignty, but there is no known documentation to support the newspaper's claim.

Sources: "Popular Sovereignty in Utah," *New York Tribune*, April 23, 1856. J. Sterling Morton, *Illustrated History of Nebraska* (Lincoln, NE: Jacob North & Company, 1907), 2, 65–68.

Lane and Phelps

James Addison Lane and M. Harrison Phelps were traveling to Utah Territory in 1856, each with an enslaved man, when they received a letter from Lane's son-in-law Gilbert Greer in Great Salt Lake City. "It breathed the spirit of apostacy and produced a bad effect," wrote Philip Hosking. Weeks later, the wagon train met the Greer family returning to Texas, and Lane and Phelps went with them.

Sources: Philip W. Hosking, Journal, September 17, 1856, 2, 3, 5, CR 100 137, Vol. 41, Historian's Office Journal History of the Church, CHL.

Lee

John D. Lee (1812–1877) is best known for his role in the 1857 Mountain Meadows Massacre. He was raised by an unnamed Black wet nurse. Even after he was weaned, his mother was unable to care for him, so he lived in the nurse's home. Later during a time of poverty, Barton, a man formerly enslaved by his mother, found him work. After Lee joined the Church of Jesus Christ of Latter-day Saints, he served a mission in the South and baptized enslaved sisters Venus and Chaney Redd. No known reliable documentation connects him to Black slavery in Utah Territory.

Sources: Lee, *Mormonism Unveiled* (Albuquerque, NM: University of New Mexico Press, 2008), 37–38, 44. John D. Lee, Journal, March 1842–August 1843, MS 2092, CHL.

Martineau

Diarist James Henry Martineau (1828–1921) left records of Black pioneer John Burton in his accounts of Parowan, Utah Territory. Martineau's autobiographical claim that his father manumitted an enslaved mother and son may be reliable due to his family's origin in the Northeast and residence in Washington, DC, and New York. Martineau recalled that a boat captain threw the family's enslaved man overboard while the family traveled from Alabama to Washington, DC, "without trying to save him or to let any one else do so, notwithstanding all my father could say. All the redress the law allowed, was his price as a chattel." Martineau's cousin later went to Washington, DC, and located their old nurse, Margaret Jackson. Martineau wrote, "She hugged and kissed him, and also inquired of me—her other son."

Sources: James H. Martineau, *An Uncommon Common Pioneer: The Journals of James Henry Martineau, 1828–1918*, ed. Donald G. Godfrey and Rebecca S. Martineau-McCarty (Provo, UT: Religious Studies Center, Brigham Young University, 2008), 5, 162–63. Margaret Jackson, Queen Anne's County, MD, *1870 Census*. Parowan Stake Historical Record.

Moody and Slade

William C. Moody (1819–1906) enslaved Louisa in Texas and took her to Utah Territory. (See her entry.) The family later said that Moody's sister, Dorinda Moody Salmon Goheen Slade (1808–1895) "owned male and female slaves and a large herd of cattle . . . Dorinda freed her slaves and bought wagons and ox-teams." No tax records clearly show enslaved people in the Goheen or Slade households in Harris or Grimes counties. Even if Dorinda did enslave anyone, Texas made manumission almost impossible, and those freed illegally would be seized by the government.

Dorinda's third husband was New York native Washington Slocum, aka William Rufus Slade (1811–1872). Slade's granddaughter Clara Slade Rollins Hutchinson was born several years after his death. At age eighty-eight, she recalled, "Father [William Slade (1834–1902)] had a Negro nanny and also a Negro boy for his servant. This servant refused to leave the family and accompanied them when they journeyed to Southern Utah." She recalled that Mose was the only Black man in the region. "Mose, the Negro of Father's, was still with them in Pine Valley [in 1872] and died there." Texas tax and census records show that Slade enslaved no people. Wagon company, census, and Pine Valley burial records do not show Mose or anyone matching his description. The definitive history of Pine Valley does not mention him, and there is no indication of a slave dwelling on the hand-drawn map of the valley in the history. There are a few unidentified burials in Pine Valley, and Slade took three wagons to Utah Territory with only two obvious drivers, so it is possible that he took an enslaved man to Utah without his name being recorded on the wagon roster. However, the Croft family traveled west in the same company and sold a woman and two children before they entered Kansas, then in a violent battle over slavery. It is likely that if there was a man named Mose in Pine Valley, he may have arrived in Utah later than the Slade family.

Sources: Jeffery O. Johnson, email message to author, May 27, 2014. E. Grant Moody, Michael F. Moody, Penelope Moody Allen, and Elaine McAllister Harry Moody, *The John Wyatt Moody Family: Past and Present* (Tempe, AZ: Dr. Thomas Moody Family Organization Inc., 1985), 41. D M Goheen, Harris County, Grimes County, Texas, *1850 Census.* Hurd, *Law of Freedom and Bondage* (Clark, NJ: The Lawbook Exchange, Ltd, 1958), 2:195-200. Clara Slade Rollins Hutchinson, "Life Story of William Slade," FSFT. https://www.familysearch.org/patron/v2/TH-300-39743-299-39/dist.txt. Wm Slade, Harris County, 1846–1852; Michael and Dorinda Goheen, Harris County, 1843, 1845, 1848, 1850; D. M. Goheen, Grimes County, 1851–1852, Agt. for D. M. Slade, Grimes County, 1853, Texas State Archives, *Texas, County Tax Rolls.* Harris County, Texas Slave Schedule, *1850 Census.* Jacob Croft Company Reports, 1856, Brigham Young Office Emigrating Companies Reports. "Pine Valley Cemetery, Washington County, UT," *Utah Gravestones.* https://www.utahgravestones.org/cemetery.php?cemID=518. Elizabeth Beckstrom and Bessie Snow, *"Oh Ye Mountains High": History of Pine Valley, Utah* (St. George, UT: Heritage Press, 1980), 24.

Morehead and Thomas

Elizabeth Thomas Morehead may have taken an older enslaved woman west with her; her grandson later reported that when they lived by Kanesville (Council Bluffs, Iowa), "The old negro woman that came With ma named Sue died ... of brain fever." Morehead's brother, Latter-day Saint missionary Preston Thomas, baptized enslaved Samuel Davidson Chambers, who moved to Utah Territory with his family after the Civil War.

Sources: James M. Moorhead, Noxubee County Tax Rolls, 1844–1845, Mississippi Department of Archives and History, Various Records. Joseph Harrison Thomas, "Biographical Sketch of the Life of Ann Morehead Thomas, 1841–1917," FSFT. https://www.familysearch.org/photos/artifacts/4057518. Hardy, "Remembered and Known."

Nowlin

When Bryan Ward Nowlin (1815–1877) headed west with the Latter-day Saints, his wife Jane Hardin Nowlin (Dillard) (1817–1911) took their "children and two young negro slaves and quite an amount of property in team carriage and dry goods" and went to live with her parents in Mississippi. Two Nowlin sons fought for the Confederacy. One died at Antietam and the other was wounded at Gettysburg.

Bryan W. Nowlin, his brother Jabus Nowlin, and their father Peyton Nowlin donated several hundred dollars to help the poor move to the West. Bryan accompanied his sister-in-law Amanda Thomas Nowlin (Starr Durfee) to the Great Salt Lake Valley. Jabus joined the Mormon Battalion and went to the Great Salt Lake Valley by way of California. Parents Peyton and Margaret Nowlin may have died while moving west. No known documentation shows the family with enslaved people in Utah Territory.

Sources: March 30, 1846, Daybook D, Nauvoo Tithing Record, 1835–1847, Trustee-in-Trust Tithing Daybooks. Benjamin Franklin Cummings, MS 1684, Reminiscences and Diaries, 1842–1879, CHL, as cited at *Pioneer Database,* https://history.churchofjesuschrist.org/overlandtravel/sources/25258339192005642630-eng/cummings-benjamin-franklin-reminiscences-and-diaries-1842-1879-fd-1-8-p. Peyton Nowlin, Bedford County, Tennessee, *1830 Census.* Jane Hardin, Pontotoc County, Mississippi, *1850 Census.* Mark Hardin, Pontotoc County, Mississippi Slave Schedule, *1850 Census.* Mark H. and William C. Nowlin, "Biographies Company G, 2nd Mississippi Infantry, Pontotoc County," *Pontotoc County, Mississippi Genealogy and History,* 1999–2002, *MSGenWeb.* http://msgw.org/pontotoc/cw/CoGMNOPZ.htm.

Powell

When the Mississippi Saints headed west, several families planned to send enslaved men ahead to prepare homes in the West. John Powell had to decide whether to send an enslaved man, but instead he sent his brother, David Powell, with John Brown, Oscar Smith, and Hark Wales. David Powell was in California by 1852. John Powell did not take any enslaved people to Utah Territory, and he and his family went almost immediately to California.

Sources: Brown, box 1, folder 1, Images 56–58, Reminiscences. Report of Mississippi Co^y, May 23, 1848, Camp of Israel Schedules and Reports. Powell, David, *Latter-day Saint Biographical Encyclopedia*, ed. Jenson (Salt Lake City, UT: Western Epics, 1971) 4:715. David Powell, Sacramento, *1852 California Census*. John Powell, Sonoma County, California, *1860 Census*.

Rencher

Umpstead Rencher and his family went west in 1854 in the Washington Lafayette Jolley wagon company. Rencher enslaved four people in 1850: a young woman and an infant probably hers, and two boys. Rencher may have sold them in Anderson or Corsicana, Texas, when he and Washington Lafayette Jolley outfitted the wagon company to go to Utah Territory. Rencher's father had died before he was born, and his uncles Abraham and Daniel helped raise him. As governor of New Mexico Territory, Abraham Rencher helped create one of the harshest slave codes in the country and provided the best-known estimate of about two dozen enslaved Black people in New Mexico Territory.

Sources: Umpstead Rencher, Sumter, Alabama Slave Schedule, *1850 Census*. Washington Lafayette Jolley, Biographical Information, as Cited at Pioneer Database, https://history.churchofjesuschrist.org/overland-travel/sources/15812810796384699175-eng/washington-lafayette-jolley-biographical-information-relating-to-mormon-pioneer-overland-travel-database-2003-2017. Mark J. Stegmaier, "A Law That Would Make Caligula Blush: New Mexico Territory's Unique Slave Code, 1859–1861," *New Mexico Historical Review* 87, no. 2 (Spring 2012): 209–42, https://digitalrepository.unm.edu/nmhr/vol87/iss2/3.

Richards

John Alexander Richards (1826–1889) became a Latter-day Saint missionary in 1855 and spent the rest of his life in the Cherokee Nation. A biography recalled that he married a widowed Cherokee enslaver, but she died not long afterward. Richards did not appear in the 1860 census slave schedule.

Sources: Richards, John A., *Latter-Day Saint Biographical Encyclopedia*, ed., Andrew Jenson (Salt Lake City, UT: Western Epics, 1971), 3, 702–703. Cherokee Nation, Indian Nations Indian Territory Archives, 1860 Federal Census of Indian Territory, *USGenWeb Archives*. http://www.usgwarchives.net/ok/nations/1860_federal_census_of_indian_te.htm.

Ricks

Joel Ricks was the ancestor of a large Latter-day Saint family, including a son, Thomas E. Ricks, the founder of the educational institution now called Brigham Young University–Idaho. Joel and his brother Lewis were executors of their father's estate in the mid-1840s and sold the enslaved people from their father's estate. Joel Ricks did not take enslaved workers to Utah Territory.

Sources: Guy S. Rix, *History and Genealogy of the Ricks Family of America* (Salt Lake City, UT: Skelton Publishing Co., 1908), 73. Jonathan Ricks, Trigg County, Kentucky, *1840 Census*.

Stewart

Brothers James, William, and George W. Stewart sent donations of $195.70 from Alabama to help build the Nauvoo Temple in 1845. In his 1831 will, their father, George Stuart of Cumberland, North Carolina, left James an enslaved man named Harry, William an enslaved five-year-old named Ephram, and George W. a twelve-year-old girl named Annaca. James Stewart remained in Alabama. William Stewart went to Utah in 1847. The 1840 census showed that he had enslaved five people in Alabama. The 1847 wagon roster showed ten unnamed people in his household, with nine of them known members of the family, so it is likely that he sold most of his enslaved workers in Alabama and possible that he took one to Utah, but there is no known documentary confirmation, including the 1850 census. George W. Stewart started west but died in Missouri. His family continued to Utah. Descendants remembered that his death left his family destitute, and his widow, Georgia native Ruthinda Baker Stewart, sold "a large ******* [sic], named Anne [sic], who had been a personal servant for many years," for two yoke of oxen, two cows, and $50. Anne or Annaca may be Anica Young, whose descendants lived in Clinton County, Missouri, for many years.

Sources: George Stewart, Cumberland County, NC, *1830 Census*. George Stewart [Jr.], Tuscaloosa County, Alabama, *1830 Census*. George Stuart Estate, 1831, Cumberland County, North Carolina County, District, and Probate Courts, North Carolina, *Wills and Probate Records*, 1665–1998, Ancestry.com, https://www.ancestry.com/search/collections/9061. William Stewart, James Stewart, George Stewart, Tuscaloosa County, Alabama, *1840 Census*. William Stewart, James Stewart, George Stewart, April 12, 1845, Daybook C, Trustee-in-Trust Tithing Daybooks. William Stewart, Great Salt Lake County; Ruth Stewart, Weber County, Utah Territory, *1850 Census*. Anica Young, Clinton County, Missouri, *1870 Census*. Laura Moench Jenkins, "The Life Story of Ruthinda Baker Stewart" (digital copy of unpublished manuscript, 2013), FSFT. https://familysearch.org/photos/artifacts/2894992.

Stout

The diaries of attorney Hosea Stout (1810–1889) detail the early legal history of Utah Territory. Stout was from Kentucky, but his parents belonged to the Society of Friends (Quaker) and United Society of Believers in Christ's Second Appearing (Shaker) and did not enslave people.

Sources: Stout, *On the Mormon Frontier* (Salt Lake City, UT: University of Utah Press, 2009).

Utley (Littlejohn)

A grandson of Latter-day Saint converts Littlejohn and Elizabeth Rutledge Utley incorrectly recalled, "[Utley] owned and was the overseer of hundreds of slaves. His father owned the plantation." Littlejohn's father, also named Littlejohn Utley, inherited one enslaved woman, Nancy, from his father, but does not appear in other records as an enslaver. Elizabeth Rutledge Utley's father Richard left her an enslaved woman named Patsey in his 1832 will, but Patsey was not in the household in 1840, and there is no record that the family took enslaved people to Utah.

Sources: Jacob Utley Probate, 1796, Wake County, *NC, Wills and Probate Records.* Littlejohn Utley (Sr.), one female slave over fifty-five years old, Wake County, NC, *1830 Census.* Richd Rutledge, seven slaves, Perry County, Alabama, *1830 Census.* Richard Rutledge Will, 1832, Will Records, Vol. A, 1821–1855, Alabama County Courthouses, *Alabama Probate Records, 1809–1985,* FamilySearch. https://www.familysearch.org/search/collection/1925446. Littlejohn Utley (Jr.), Perry County, Alabama, *1840 Census.* Maggie Bell Tolman Porter, "Margaret Eliza Utley (1835–1902)," FSFT. Accessed February 21, 2019, https://www.familysearch.org/photos/artifacts/37109706.

Utley (Seth)

In late 1844, enslavers Seth Utley and Bathsheba Woods Utley of Benton County, Tennessee, donated 157 pounds of tobacco grown and harvested with enslaved labor to help build the Nauvoo Temple. They do not appear to have moved to Nauvoo or Utah Territory.

Sources: Seth Utly, Humphreys, Tennessee, *1830 Census.* Seth Utley, Benton, Tennessee, *1840 Census.* Seth Utley, November 11, 1844, Daybook C, Trustee-in-Trust Tithing Daybooks. Seth Utley, Prairie, Arkansas Slave Schedule, *1850 Census.*

Williams

Traveler Richard Ackley mentioned, "Negro Bill, the largest Negro I ever saw. He was a native of Missouri and belonged to Tom [Thomas S.] Williams and had lived in the valley for years." Perhaps Ackley remembered Daniel or Shepherd Camp, or perhaps Williams took an enslaved man from Missouri to Utah Territory after his brief stay there in the mid-1850s. There is no additional documentation of "Bill," so the note was either a mistake of name or the mention of an additional unknown enslaved man in the Salt Lake Valley.

Sources: Richard Thomas Ackley, "Across the Plains in 1858," *Utah Historical Quarterly* 9 (July–October 1941): 215, https://www.jstor.org/stable/45063456.

Fourteen

RELATED TOPICS

Carson Valley

Latter-day Saints settled Carson Valley, about six hundred miles west of Salt Lake City, in the early 1850s. It was part of Utah Territory until 1861, when it became part of Nevada Territory.

In 1855, Latter-day Saint apostle Orson Hyde traveled to Carson Valley as its probate court judge. His first criminal case was that of a Black man named only as Thacker, who had threatened to cut out and roast the heart of Sophronia Allen Rose. Fearing that the community would lynch Thacker, Hyde arrested him, fined him court costs, and suggested that for his own protection, he should join his unnamed enslaver in California. "Thacker" may be Robert Thacker (1832–) of Tennessee, who worked five years later as a waiter in Marysville, California.

Although Latter-day Saints were the first to build towns in the area, the 1860 census shows a predominantly non–Latter-day Saint mining population. Carson Valley's forty-nine Black residents worked as barbers, cooks, bakers, laborers, miners, and washerwomen, and mostly lived in their own households, sometimes with children. The census does not specify legal status, and none of the Black or interracial families appear to be connected to the Latter-day Saint settlers. Only two residents meet the criteria for likely enslavement, which was living in a household headed by a Southerner. William Davis of Maryland lived in a household with Southerners in the army outpost of Fort Churchill. Cato Smith lived with Missourian John Coagner in Jacks Valley and may be the enslaved man who traveled to Carson Valley with Judge William W. Drummond several years earlier.

Sources: Sam P. Davis, ed., *The History of Nevada* (Reno, NV: Elms Publishing Company, 1913), 1:275. Myrtle Stevens Hyde, *Orson Hyde: Olive Branch of Israel* (Salt Lake City, UT: Agreka Books, 2000), 345. Albert R. Page, "Orson Hyde and the Carson Valley Mission, 1855–1857" (master's thesis, Brigham Young University, 1970). Susan Southwick, email message to author, December 23, 2015. Wm Davis, Fort Churchill; Cato Smith, Jacks Valley, Carson Valley, Carson County, Utah Territory, *1860 Census*. Robert Thacker, Marysville, California, *1860 Census*.

Federal Census Classification Errors

The racial categories provided in the census during the nineteenth century depended on the perceptions of the census taker and local communities, so it was not always a cohesive system. The 1850 federal census mortality schedule showed Jane Clark, age six, Black, who died in Weber County. The census said she was born in Deseret (Utah), so she would have been Indigenous. Other Indigenous people classified as Black in the census in Utah include Bessie Johnson, Zenos Hill, and Barbara Allred.

Sources: Jane Clark, Weber County, Utah Territory Mortality Schedule, 1850 [1851], MS 2672, box 1, folder 12, CHL. Bessie Johnson, *Indian Census Rolls, 1885–1940*, M595;143, Records of the Bureau of Indian Affairs, Record Group 75. Zenos Hill, Sanpete County; Barbara Allred, Salt Lake County, UT, Bessie Johnson, Cache County, Utah, *1900 Census*.

Lynching

Lynching is an extrajudicial killing by a mob, often used to intimidate a minority population. There are two reliable accounts of Black lynching in Utah. Joe or Sam Harvey found his way to Utah Territory after the Civil War and, in 1883, killed Salt Lake police chief Andrew Burt. A mob lynched him in downtown Salt Lake City. Robert Marshall killed Deputy Sheriff J. Milton Burns and was lynched by a mob in Price, Utah, in 1925. Based on the existing documentation, the killing of Thomas Coleman in 1866 was murder rather than lynching. Two additional accounts are not well documented enough to categorize as lynching rather than murder.

First is a reported killing at a railroad camp in northern Utah Territory: "There was a man shot and hung at Wasatch tonight . . . Reason given: He is a Dammed Nigger." Additionally, three men of unknown names and ethnicities were said to have been killed at a railroad camp during the winter of 1868–1869.

Sources: O. C. Smith, Diary, cited in Robert G. Athearn, *Union Pacific Country* (Lincoln, NE: University of Nebraska Press, 1976), 86–87, 409. Ronald G. Coleman, "Blacks in Utah History: An Unknown Legacy," in *The Peoples of Utah*, ed. Helen Z. Papanikolas (Salt Lake City, UT: Utah State Historical Society, 1976), 115–40. Kimberley Mangun and Larry R. Gerlach, "Making Utah History: Press Coverage of the Robert Marshall Lynching, June 1925," in *Lynching Beyond Dixie: American Mob Violence Outside the South*, ed. Michael J. Pfeifer (Urbana, Chicago, and Springfield: University of Illinois Press, 2013), 133–64, 303–04.

Latter-day Saint Converts among the Enslaved in the South

Latter-day Saint missionaries occasionally baptized enslaved Black people in the South. The records do not document or suggest compulsory baptism; for example, Biddy Mason remained Methodist, and Hannah Smiley remained Baptist. Those who were baptized in the South and went to Utah Territory with their enslavers included Green Flake and Venus and Chaney Redd. Not all went to Utah. John Brown baptized Hager, enslaved by Elias Arterbury, and Jack, enslaved by James Turnbow, but the two remained in the South. For a comprehensive treatment, see W. Paul Reeve's *Century of Black Mormons*.

Sources: W. Paul Reeve, *Century of Black Mormons*, J. Willard Marriott Library, University of Utah, https://exhibits.lib.utah.edu/s/century-of-black-mormons/page/welcome. Brown, box 1, folder 1, image 26, Reminiscences. Hardy, "Remembered and Known."

Utah's Dixie

After the Latter-day Saints arrived in the Great Salt Lake Valley, they began to establish settlements along the trade route to California, from the Great Salt Lake Valley through the southwestern corner of the current state of Utah to San Bernardino, California.

In 1852, settlers began to move into Washington County near the junction of the Santa Clara and Virgin Rivers. John D. Lee wrote to Brigham Young about the possibilities of growing "cotton Flax Hemp grapes Figs sweet potatoes Fruits of almost every kind & be independent of our kind christian Friends who drove us from their Midst." The settlers first grew cotton in 1854. Many of the earliest residents of Washington County, including a group of 1857 settlers, were from the South, and many participated in the Mountain Meadows Massacre, but records show that most of them were small farmers, few had enslaved people in the South, and none appear to have enslaved African Americans in Utah. The territory did not create an 1860 slave schedule for the county.

Due to the moderate climate, the attempt to grow cotton, the early presence of Southern families, and the region's location south of the main settlements, settlers soon called the region "Dixie" or "Utah's Dixie." The first known recorded use of "Dixie" was in January 1860. Brigham Young said: "Why, instead of ... going to St. Louis to buy goods, we can go down to our Dixie land, the southern part of our Territory, and raise cotton and manufacture goods for ourselves." The *Deseret News* joked that the large number of settlers moving to settle St. George in 1861 were "Going South, But Not Seceding."

When Brigham Young discussed cotton, it was always in the context of home industry and territorial self-sufficiency. When the price of cotton soared during the Civil War and Washington County farmers had more cotton than they could make into cloth, they sold several tons in California and the East. Out-of-territory sales ended when the territory created manufacturing facilities.

Some may draw the borders of Utah's Dixie as far as Parowan with John Burton, its one enslaved Black resident, but as part of the Iron Mission, Parowan was not historically part of the Cotton Mission. John Burton died in 1865, but others nearby eventually included Luke Ward Redd in New Harmony; Dow Barton, Isaac Barton, and Silas Woolridge outside Panaca, Nevada; and in Utah's Dixie: Chaney (Redd) (Cunningham), Julia (Maxwell) Waters, Benjamin Polk, Edward Taylor, and possibly others in the mining community of Silver Reef. *Negro Pioneer* reported that Haden Wells Church took an enslaved man to Washington County, but the anecdote appears to be a late memory of Tom (Church) (Smoot), who was not in Washington County. The family of William Rufus Slade much later thought he had an enslaved man named Mose with him in Pine Valley, but no known evidence supports the claim.

Beginning in the twentieth century, residents erroneously began to connect the term "Dixie" to the Confederacy. Institutions in the region continue to address this historical error.

Sources: John D. Lee to Brigham Young, March 17, 1852, box 22, folder 17, Office Files. Brigham Young, "Sufferings of the Saints—Overcoming Evil with Good, &c.," January 5, 1860, G. D. Watt and J. V. Long, *Journal of Discourses* (Liverpool, England: George Q. Cannon, 1862), 9:105. "Going South, But Not Seceding," *Deseret News*, October 23, 1861. Brigham Young, "Call for Teams to Go to the Frontiers—Encouragement of Home Manufactures," April 7, 1861, *Journal of Discourses* (Liverpool, England: George Q. Cannon) 9:190. Brigham Young, "How and By Whom Zion is To Be Built.—Sanctification.—General Duties of the Saints," G. D. Watt and J. V. Long, *Journal of Discourses* (Liverpool, England: Daniel H. Wells, 1865), 10:170. Brigham Young. "Love for the Things of God.—The Temporal Nature of the Kingdom.—The Proper Use of Grain.—The Love of God Should Rule in Every Heart, Etc.," June 22–29, 1864, *Journal of Discourses* (Liverpool, England: Daniel H. Wells), 10:334. Ivan J. Barrett, "History of the Cotton Mission and Cotton Culture in Utah" (master's thesis, Brigham Young University, 1947). Leonard J. Arrington, "The Mormon Cotton Mission in Southern Utah," *Pacific Historical Review* 25, no. 3 (August 1956): 221–38, https://doi.org/10.2307/3637013. Carter, *Negro Pioneer*, 85–86. Andrew Karl Larson, *I Was Called to Dixie: The Virgin River Basin: Unique Experiences in Mormon Pioneering* (Salt Lake City, UT: Deseret News Press, 1961; repr., 1979). W. Paul Reeve, "From Cotton to Cosmopolitan: Local, National, and Global Transformations in Utah's Dixie" (Opening Plenary Session Lecture, Mormon History Association, St. George, UT, May 2011). Gregory A. Prince, "Keep it Dixie," *Salt Lake Tribune*, January 1, 2013, https://archive.sltrib.com/article.php?id=55507090&itype=CMSID. Amy Tanner Thiriot, "Guest Post: A Response to the Salt Lake Tribune on Utah's Dixie and Slave Culture," *Keepapitchinin: The Mormon History* (blog), February 7, 2013, http://www.keepapitchinin.org/2013/02/07/guest-post-a-response-to-the-salt-lake-tribune-on-utahs-dixie-and-slave-culture. "Utah's Dixie State University Back in Focus as Confederate Flags Come Down." *The Guardian* (US edition), July 11, 2015, https://www.theguardian.com/us-news/2015/jul/11/utah-dixie-state-university-name-change-confederate-flags.

AFTERWORD

The enslaved African American children, women, and men of Utah Territory were part of a historic westward migration. They lived in the Latter-day Saints settlements in the West, some for months, some for years. More than half of them were enslaved by an interrelated group of Latter-day Saint converts from the Mississippi-Alabama border. Some were enslaved by merchants and army officers, but most were enslaved by farmers, so they had the experiences and skills gained from work on rural farms. Most had lived their lives in bondage on the far reaches of the American settlements. They knew the sound of wolves and bears. They knew how to create settlements and build roads, homes, and churches. They knew the pull of the westward movement.

The journey to the Great Salt Lake Valley was a new adventure, although it came at great cost as enslavers separated the enslaved from their families and communities in the South. As they went west, they walked through prairie grass and wildflowers and saw herds of bison. They cared for livestock and participated in all the work of a wagon train. They met Indigenous peoples, who reminded some of them of the memories of their own Indigenous heritage. Many were of mixed African and Indigenous or European descent. Their ancestors had probably been in the Americas for generations, perhaps hundreds of years, before they set foot in Utah Territory. Benjamin Perkins told a reporter that his ancestors had been the "kings of San Domingo."

Their lives were representative of the experiences of the oppression of enslaved peoples in the mid-nineteenth century: the yearning for freedom, the children born without the consent of their mothers, parents unable to protect their sons and daughters, the marks of the whip on their backs, and the scars on their hands. They crossed the Plains carrying the heart-rending memories of separations from their mothers and fathers, brothers and sisters, and even their own children. They went west not knowing where their parents, brothers, and sisters would be buried when they died.

Some of them must have carried generational memories of the Middle Passage—that searing separation from Africa with the memories so deep that they carried them in their bones—but arriving in Utah Territory, they passed those stories no further, since the most common factor of their lives in the West was isolation. When they set their feet to cross the Great Plains, they became part of a group so secluded and small within a larger White population that often the societal requirements against intermarriage meant they had little or no opportunity for marriage and families of their own and had no ability to pass their memories further.

They were enslaved by hard people who were teaching their children to be hard, people who did all they could to preserve the ownership of their labor even in the legal uncertainties of the western settlements. When the first wave of families took their enslaved people to the West, about half of the enslaved entered land just barely claimed from Mexico. The isolation of the Latter-day Saint settlements meant that the authority of international, Mexican, and American law and the formation of slave law in Utah Territory had little practical effect on the lives of the enslaved. Brigham Young initially thought that their arrival in the Great Salt Lake Valley freed the enslaved. The enslavers convinced him otherwise and largely prevailed on questions of ownership of labor. During the process, the enslavers likely communicated Protestant theories of African American slavery that entered Latter-day Saint theology and helped shape the church's racial practices for generations. The creation of slave law in Utah Territory happened within the context of conflicts with Indigenous and Mexican slave traders and was shaped both by an ongoing battle with the federal government over control of the territory and the inexperience of those writing the law. All this had little effect on the day-to-day lives of the enslaved, except for a small group who lived at the foot of Big Cottonwood Canyon. For them, An Act in Relation to Service (1852) meant that Brigham Young was able to provide them freedom. But for the rest, their lives remained much like they were in the South.

Some of the enslaved had the experience of crossing the Plains and crossing them again not long afterward to return to the South, since the uncertainties of the law in the West together with the experience of life in the Latter-day Saint settlements drove some of the enslavers back to the South. Due to legal battles, notably *In re Hannah* (1856) and *Territory of Utah v. Williams Camp* (1856), some saw their enslavers return to the South without them.

Their total number was around one hundred. Despite their isolation, they found friends, both Black and White, and created communities that made it possible to live among strangers. They found ways to get word to each other. Word from home would have come from Southern merchant wagon trains and soldiers. Although unlikely that they would have heard news of their own families, they did occasionally hear "news of 'de wah,'" as a young man remembered Samuel Smith saying.

Those who bore the scars of enslavement were the backbone of the early Mormon settlements in the Great Salt Lake Valley. They planted crops, churned butter, made cheese, and helped keep the settlers alive those first few years. In 1850 and 1851, many left for California, most never to return to Utah Territory, and as tens of thousands of new Latter-day Saint converts poured into the Great Salt Lake Valley from the northeast United States and Europe, those who remained became even more isolated.

When descendants of their enslavers started to tell their stories two or three generations later, they got the details badly wrong. The long-standing inaccuracies preserved in family and community histories make it doubly important to leave the myths behind and discover the faint actual traces that remain of the lives of the enslaved settlers so the community and nation can again tell their stories.

Above all, the most important part of their story is that they were a part of all this. They ran the farms, drove the wagons, raised the livestock, delivered the babies, wiped away the blood, boiled the water for laundry, built the fences, and made the food. Their experience was connected to the earth they set their feet upon. Their footsteps and their labor became a part of the creek beds, the gravel, the canyons and rivers, and the very rocks of the Great Salt Lake Valley and Utah Territory.

Appendix 1

AN ACT IN RELATION TO SERVICE, UTAH TERRITORIAL LEGISLATURE (1852)

AN ACT IN RELATION TO SERVICE.

Sec. 1. *Be it enacted by the Governor and Legislative Assembly of the Territory of Utah,* That any person or persons coming to this Territory and bringing with them servants justly bound to them, arising from special contract or otherwise, said person or persons shall be entitled to such service or labor by the laws of this Territory: *Provided,* That he shall file in the office of the Probate Court, written and satisfactory evidence that such service or labor is due.

Sec. 2. That the Probate Court shall receive as evidence any contract properly attested in writing or any well proved agreement wherein the party or parties serving have received or are to receive a reasonable compensation for his, her, or their services: *Provided,* That no contract shall bind the heirs of the servant or servants to service for a longer period than will satisfy the debt due his, her, or their master or masters.

Sec. 3. That any person bringing a servant or servants, and his, her, or their children from any part of the United States, or other country, and shall place in the office of the Probate Court the certificate of any Court of record under seal, properly attested that he, she, or they are entitled lawfully to the service of such servant or servants, and his, her, or their children, the Probate Justice shall record the same, and the master or mistress, or his, her, or their heirs shall be entitled to the services of the said servant or servants unless forfeited as hereinafter provided, if it shall appear that such servant or servants came into the Territory of their own free will and choice.

SEC. 4. That if any master or mistress shall have sexual or carnal intercourse with his or her servant or servants of the African race, he or she shall forfeit all claim to said servant or servants to the commonwealth; and if any white person shall be guilty of sexual intercourse with any of the African race, they shall be subject, on conviction thereof to a fine of not exceeding one thousand dollars, nor less than five hundred, to the use of the Territory, and imprisonment, not exceeding three years.

SEC. 5. It shall be the duty of masters or mistresses, to provide for his, her, or their servants comfortable habitations, clothing, bedding, sufficient food, and recreation. And it shall be the duty of the servant in return therefor, to labor faithfully all reasonable hours, and do such service with fidelity as may be required by his, or her master or mistress.

SEC. 6. It shall be the duty of the master to correct and punish his servant in a reasonable manner when it may be necessary, being guided by prudence and humanity; and if he shall be guilty of cruelty or abuse, or neglect to feed, clothe, or shelter his servants in a proper manner, the Probate Court may declare the contract between master and servant or servants void, according to the provisions of the fourth section of this act.

SEC. 7. That servants may be transferred from one master or mistress to another by the consent and approbation of the Probate Court, who shall keep a record of the same in his office; but no transfer shall be made without the consent of the servant given to the Probate Judge in the absence of his master or mistress.

SEC. 8. Any person transferring a servant or servants contrary to the provisions of this act, or taking one out of the Territory contrary to his, or her will, except by decree of Court in case of a fugitive from labor, shall be on conviction thereof, subject to a fine, not exceeding five thousand dollars, and imprisonment, not exceeding five years, or both, at the discretion of the Court, and shall forfeit all claims to the services of such servant or servants, as provided in the fourth section of this act.

SEC. 9. It shall further be the duty of all masters or mistresses, to send their servant or servants to school, not less than eighteen months between the ages of six years and twenty years.

Approved Feb. 4th, 1852.

Appendix 2

SLAVE REGISTRATIONS AND BILL OF SALE

Four 1856 affidavits begin this collection of legal documents. The Probate Court recorded most of the following documents after Utah Terr. v. Camp (1856). They were supposed to be recorded in a Probate Register of Servants, but the register is not known to be in existence. The affidavits name enslaved Daniel (Camp) and Shepherd (Greer) (Camp); court clerk William Ivins Appleby and deputy Curtis E. Bolton; and enslavers Williams Camp, Diannah Greer Camp, Diannah's deceased father James Greer, and Dr. William Taylor Dennis. Next is an 1856 copy of an 1852 bill of sale that names enslaved Lucy (Crosby or Lay); enslavers Margaret T. Smoot, Abraham Owen Smoot, and Thomas S. Williams; witness to the sale, Hugh Sutherland, who worked for Williams; and probate court judge Elias Smith. The next document is an 1858 registration that names enslaved Jerry (Lewis or Smoot), Caroline Hoye Bankhead Jackson, and Tampian Hoye Campbell; enslavers Duritha Trail Lewis and her deceased father Solomon Trail; and court officials James W. Cummings and John G. Lynch. The final document is a copy of an 1859 bill of sale that names enslaved Daniel (Camp); Salt Lake County recorder Franklin B. Woolley; lawyer Seth M. Blair; enslavers Thomas S. Williams, William H. Hooper, and Williams Camp; and two witnesses, accountant Charles Evans and probably Albert Brady Jackman.

Williams Camp, Registration for Daniel, July 10, 1856, Probate Register of Servants, Slave Registrations, Salt Lake County (UT) Probate Court, Civil and Criminal Case Files, 1852–1887, Series 373, box 4, folder 26, Utah State Archives.

Affidavit of Williams Camp in regard to his Servant "Daniel"
Filed July 10° 1856
Recorded Page 3 of Probate Register of Servants

Utah Territory   }
Salt Lake County   } ss

Personally appeared before me, W. I. Appleby, Clerk of the Supreme Court of the united States of Amarica, for the Territory of Utah, Williams Camp, who being duly sworn, <According to law> deposeth and sayeth, that a certain Negroe boy named Daniel, was born a slave for life, in his house, the 14th day of October 1833, in the state of Tennessee, Weakly County; and the said deponent has owned the said Negroe, Daniel, since his birth up to the presant time. Said deponent brought the said Negroe boy, Daniel, in to the Territory of Utah, a slave for life, in the year 1850. <u>Now</u> this deponent makes this Affidavit in order that the said Negroe boy, Daniel, may be registered a slave for life in the Probate Court <of Great Salt Lake County in said Territory> according to the statutes of the said Territory of Utah

W^{ms} Camp

Subscribed and Sworn to before me at Great Salt Lake City Utah Territory this 10th day of July AD 1856

W I Appleby Clerk
p[er] Curtis E Bolton
Deputy

Diannah Camp, Registration for Shepherd, July 3, 1856, Probate Register of Servants, Slave Registrations, Salt Lake County (UT) Probate Court Civil and Criminal Case Files, 1852–1887, Series 373, box 4, folder 26, Utah State Archives.

Affidavit of Dianah Camp in regard to Negro boy Shepherd.
Filed July 10º 1856.
Rec^d on page 4 of Probate Register of Servants

Terrytory of Utah   }
County of Great Salt lake   } ss

Personally appeard before me—W. I. Appleby clerk of the first Juditial district court of the United States for the Terytory of Utah Dianah Camp who being first duly sworn according to law deposeth and saith that a certain negro boy named Shepherd was bornd in the year 1837 in the State of Tennessee—Henry County that the said negro boy Shepherd was bornd a slave then belonging to my Father one James Greer Resident of the afore said county of Henry in the State of Tennessee that the said James Greer died in the year 1851 in the State of arkansas Previous to his death the said Greer made a will that after his debts were canciled all of his property Remaining should be Equally divided among his children fourteen in number, that according to the said will of the deceased the property Remaining was divided and the wife of the afore said Dianah wife and consort of Williams Camp was one of the heirs of the afore said deceased Greer did Receive the said negro boy named Shepherd as afore said in the month of January 1853 in the State of Mississippi county of Marshal of the administrator of the estate of the afore said deceased Greer and deponent further says that since the month of January 1853 the said negro boy named Shepherd as afore said has belonged to Williams Camp Husband of the afore said Dianah Camp and that the afore said Williams Camp is Justly Entitled to the labor of the afore said negro boy named Shepherd through life and further that the said Camp is a Resident of the County and Terrytory afore said and that the afore said negro boy was brought by him to the Terrytory afore said a slave for life in the year 1854 the said deponent makes this declaration in order that the said negro boy may be Registered as a slave in the court of Probates as is made and provided for by the statutes of the Territory afore said

              Diannah Camp

Subscribed and sworn to before me this third day of July AD 1856

W I Appleby Clerk
p[er] Curtis E Bolton
Deputy

Williams Camp, Registration for Shepherd, July 3, 1856, Probate Register of Servants, Slave Registrations, Salt Lake County (UT) Probate Court Civil and Criminal Case Files, 1852–1887, Series 373, box 4, folder 26, Utah State Archives.

Affidavit of Williams Camp in regard to Negro boy Shepard.
Filed July 10º 1856
Recorded on pages 5 & 6 of Probate Register of Servants
*

Territory of Utah }
County of Great Salt Lake } ss

Personally appeared before me W. I. Appleby, Clerk of the First Judicial District Court of the United States for the Territory of Utah, Williams Camp, who being first duly sworn according to law deposeth and says, that a certain Negro boy named Shepard was born in the year 1837 in the State of Tennessee, Henry County, that the said Negro boy Shepard was born a Slave, then belonging to one James Greer, resident of the aforesaid County of Henry in the State of Tennessee; that the said James Greer died in the year 1851 in the State of Arkansas. Previous to his death the said Greer made a will, that after his debts were cancelled, all of his property, remaining, should be equally divided among his children, fourteen in number, that according to the said will of the deceased the property remaining was divided, and the wife of the aforesaid Williams Camp, was one of the heirs of the said deceased Greer. And deponent further says that in January 1853 he, the said Camp and his wife, the heir of the aforesaid deceased Greer, did receive the said Negro boy named Shepard as aforesaid, in the month of January 1853 in the State of Mississippi, County of Marshal, of the Administrator of the estate of the aforesaid deceased Greer. And deponent further says that since the month of January 1853, the said Negro boy named Shepard as aforesaid has belonged to this deponent W^ms Camp aforesaid; that I the aforesaid Camp am justly and lawfully entitled to the labor of the aforesaid Negro boy named Shepard through life; And further that he the said Camp is a resident of the County and Territory aforesaid, and that the aforesaid Negro boy was brought by him to the Territory aforesaid a slave for life in the year 1854. The said deponent makes this declaration in order that the said Negro boy may be registered as a slave in the Court of Probate, as is made and provided for by the statute of the Territory aforesaid

                Williams Camp

                Subscribed and sworn to before me this third day of July AD 1856

                W I Appleby Clerk
                p[er] Curtis E Bolton
                Deputy

William T. Dennis, Affidavit regarding the registration for Shepherd, July 3, 1856, Probate Register of Servants, Slave Registrations, Salt Lake County (UT) Probate Court Civil and Criminal Case Files, 1852–1887, Series 373, box 4, folder 26, Utah State Archives.

Affidavit of Wm T. Dennis in regard to Negro boy Shepherd.
Filed July 10th 1856
Recorded on page 7 of Probate Register of Servants

Terytory of Utah   }
County of Great Salt lake   } ss

Personally appeard before me W. I. Appleby Clerk of the first Juditial district Court of the United States for the Terytory of Utah W^m T Dennis after being duly qualified & deposeth and saith that his personal acquaintance commenced with Williams Camp at St Louis, Misarie some time in the Spring of 1854 and that he had with him at that time a certain negro boy named shepherd claimed him as the said negro boy shepherd as his property as a slave for life the boy shepherd Recognising the said Camp as his master deponent further states he was in company with Camp and said boy Shep some two or three weeks at St Louis at the time above Refered to. then traviled the great portion of the way (an over Land Rout) from St Louis to St Joseph M$^{\underline{o}}$ since my arival in the vally of the Great Salt Lake on the 22nd day of August 1855 our acquaintance with the said Camp and boy Shep has bin Renewed and I never heard Camps title to the boy Shepherd Questioned at any time

        W^{m} T Dennis

        Subscribed and sworn to before me this third day of July AD 1856

        W I Appleby Clerk
        p[er] Curtis E Bolton
         Deputy

Thomas S. Williams, Registration for Lucinda, July 10, 1856, Probate Register of Servants, Slave Registrations, Salt Lake County (UT) Probate Court Civil and Criminal Case Files, 1852–1887, Series 373, box 4, folder 26, Utah State Archives.

A. O. Smoots Bill of Sale of Negro To Thos. S. Williams
Filed July 10th 1856
Recorded on page 8 of Probate Register of Servants

G. S. L. City March 1 1852
   Thomas S. Williams
     To A. O. Smoot Dr.
To 1 Negro Girl named Lucinda $400.00
Witness   } Recd. Payment

H. Sutherland   }   Margaret T. Smoot
I approve of the above sale or transfer

                                        E Smith Probate Judge
                                        GSL County UT

Mr. A O. Smoot

Dear Sir,

I have this day Received the above amount of Mr. Thomas S. Williams in full Payment for One Negro Girl Lucinda as above described

Witness   }   Margaret T. Smoot
H. Sutherland   }

Duritha Lewis, Registration for Jerry, Caroline, and Tampian, August 4, 1858, Slave Registrations, Salt Lake County (UT) Probate Court Civil and Criminal Case Files, 1852–1887, Series 373, box 5, folder 11, Utah State Archives.

Affidavit of Duritha Lewis in regard to certain Negro slaves the property of the said Lewis
Filed in the Office of the Probate Court G.S.L. County, Augt 4, 1858
Recorded on Page 9. Probate Register of Servants

Territory of Utah
Great Salt Lake county   ss

Personally appeared before <me> James W Cummings clerk of the third Judicial District Court for said Territory, Duritha Lewis who being duly sworn states on oath that she is the true and Lawful owner of three persons of Affrican blood, whose names and ages are <as> follows to wit Jerry, Caroline, & Tampian, aged 38, 18, and 14. That she the said Duritha Lewis inherited them from her father Soloman Trail according to the Laws of the state of Kentucky. That by virtue of such inheritance she is entitled to the services of the said Jerry, Caroline, and Tampian during their lives according <to> the Laws of the said Territory and further saith not. that she makes for this affidavit that they may be registered as Slaves according to the requirements of the Laws of said Territory for life

Duritha Lewis

Sworn and subscribed to before }
me this 4th day of Aug. AD 1858 }
J. W. Cummings Clerk U.S. 3rd }
Dist Court Utah Territory }
p[er] John G. Lynch Depy }

Bill of Sale for Dan, August 17, 1859, Great Salt Lake County Recorder's Office, as reproduced in Kate B. Carter, The Negro Pioneer *(Salt Lake City: Daughters of Utah Pioneers, 1965), 42. Tonya Reiter attempted to find the original bill of sale in 2015 and 2016, but neither the Recorder's Office nor any other local government office or archives could locate it. This transcription is from the image in* Negro Pioneer.

Territory of Utah }
County of Great Salt Lake } I Franklin B. Woolley recorder in and for the county of Great Salt Lake and Territory of Utah, duly qualified by law to take acknowledgements, certify that Seth M Blair, Personally known to me appeared this Seventeenth day of August A. D. 1859 and acknowledged that he of his own choice executed the foregoing transfer and mortgage for the uses and purposes therein Set forth.

Recorded Aug 22nd 1859.   Franklin B. Woolley

Know all men by these presents. That I Thomas S. Williams of Great Salt Lake City in the Territory of Utah, for and in consideration of the sum of eight hundred dollars, to me in hand paid at and before the ensealing and delivery of these presents by W^m H Hooper of the city and territory aforesaid, the receipt whereof is hereby acknowledged, have bargained and sold and by these presents, do grant bargain and sell and convey unto the said W^m H Hooper, his heirs, executors, administrators and assigns, one Negro boy "Dan"; the said negro boy is twenty-six years of age was born the property and Slave of Williams Camp on the 15th day of October A. D. 1833 in the town of Dresden Weekley County State of Tennessee; and by the said Williams Camp was sold to me in the year 1858 a bill of sale having been executed to me by the said Williams Camp for the said negro boy "Dan," To have and to hold the said Negro boy "Dan" unto the said W^m H Hooper, his executors administrators and assigns forever And I do for myself my heirs executors and administrators covenant and agree to and with the said Wm H. Hooper to warrant and defend the sale of the said negro boy, hereby sold unto the said W^m H Hooper, his Executors administrators and assigns, against all and every person and persons whomsoever

Attest

A. R. Jackman
Charles Evans
Great Salt Lake City
Sept 7th 1859

T.S. Williams

Recorded September 8th 1859
F B Woolley Recorder

Appendix 3

DEEDS OF CONSECRATION

The only enslavers known to include enslaved people in their deeds of consecration were John Brown and William T. Dennis of Utah County. Their 1857 deeds named Betsy Brown Flewellen and Nancy Lines Smith. Utah County Recorder Lucius N. Scovil and Probate Judge Dominicus Carter recorded the deeds.

John Brown, Deed of Consecration, February 3, 1857, Records of Utah County (1851–1864), Book F, 81–83, MSS 3905, L. Tom Perry Special Collections, Harold B. Lee Library, Brigham Young University, Provo, Utah.

John Brown's Cons^r Deed.
Recorded February 3rd 1857
<u>Be it known by these Presents</u>
That I John Brown of Lehi City, in the County of Utah and Territory of Utah for and in consideration of the good will which I have to the <u>Church of Jesus Christ of Latter Day Saints</u> give and convey unto <u>Brigham Young</u> Trustee in Trustee for said Church, his successors in office, and assigns, all my claim to an ownership of the following described property to wit:—Lot 7 in Bl. 9. Containing 50/160 of an Acre in the Lehi City Survey
of Building Lots with improvements thereon   150.00
Also Lot 7 in Bl. 10. Containing One Ac.
in the Lehi Survey of Garden Lots   75.00
[List of other real estate   550.00]
3 Yoke of Oxen and one Wagon   300.00
6 Cows @ $30 & two Calves 8$each   196.00
1 Yearling 15$& two pigs @ 5$each   25.00
Farming tools 75$& one Rifle 30$ 105.00
Household Furniture Beds Bedding &   150.00
12 Sheep at 5$per head & Two Horse Pistoles 10$ 72.00
1 Silver Watch $25 & 1 Cooking Stove $30   55.00

60 Bushels of Wheat @ 2$per Bu.	120.00
5 " " Corn @ 1.50 " "	7.50
60 " " Potatoes @ 1 " "	60.00
Garden Vegetables 30$& 6 Tons of Hay $48	78.00
Cloth in Progress $25 & outstanding Ac/ts 50$	75.00
1 African Servant Girl	<u>1000.00</u>
Total Value of John Browns Property	<u>$3038.50</u>

Three thousand and Thirty Eight Dollars & 50¢. Together with all the rights privileges and appurtenances thereunto belonging or appertaining. I also covenant and agree that I am the lawful claimant and owner of said property, and will warrant and forever defend the same, unto the said Trustee in Trust, his successors in office, and assigns, against the claim of my heirs, assigns or any person whomsoever.

<u>John Brown</u> {Seal}

Witnesses
Thomas Taylor
Canute Peterson
Joseph Dobson

William Taylor Dennis, Deed of Consecration, February 7, 1857, Records of Utah County (1851–1864), Book F, 111–112, MSS 3905, L. Tom Perry Special Collections, Harold B. Lee Library, Brigham Young University, Provo, Utah. See also, Consecration Deeds, 1855–1858, Deeds, D, no. 61, box 2, folder 16, CR 5 53, Consecration Deeds, 1854–1867, Church History Library, Salt Lake City, Utah.

William Taylor Dennis Cons^r Deed
Recorded February 7th 1857.
Be it known by these Presents. That I Wm Taylor Dennis of Lehi City, in the County of Utah, and Territory of Utah, for and in Consideration of the good will which I have to the Church of Jesus Christ of Latter Day Saints give and covey unto Brigham Young Trustee in Trust for said Church his successors in office and assigns, all my claim to and ownership of the following described property to wit:—Household Furniture Beds Bedding & c $300.00

1 Cook Stove Building Material &c	200.00
1 Carriage & Harness	150.00
3 Wagons & 2 Yoke of Oxen	475.00
Machinery Saw & Grist Mill Draws Fixtures with 2 4 8 in Circular Saws	1800.00
1 Cow $20 1 Hog $30	50.00
4 Horses	400.00
1 Gold Watch $60. 1 Silver Watch 5$.	65.00
2 Rifles $30. 1 Gun Barrel 2 1/2$	32.50
1 Double barrell Shot Gun	20.00
1 Single " " "	10.00
1 Colts revolver	25.00
2 Tons of Hay @ 8$pr Ton	16.00
Garden Vegetables	25.00
Wheat Flour & Corn $25. Tools 20$	45.00
1 African Servant Girl	500.00
Total Value of Wm Dennis Property	4113.50

Four thousand one hundred & thirteen dollars & 50¢.

Together with all the Rights, privileges and appurtenances thereunto belonging or appertaining. I also covenant and agree that I am the lawful claimant and owner of said property, and will warrant and forever defend the same unto the said Trustee in Trust, his successors in office, and assigns, against the claims of my heirs, assigns, or any person whomsoever.

Witnesses
Thomas Taylor   Wm T. Dennis {seal}
Orrin D Farlin
John Folker

Appendix 4

BRIGHAM YOUNG CORRESPONDENCE

Benjamin Mathews to Brigham Young, March 31, 1849, box 21, folder 16, Brigham Young Office Files, CR 1234 1, CHL. The letters from Mathews and Francis McKown (below) are in the same handwriting.

March the 31 1849
I take the opportunity of writing you a few lines concerning the buisness I Came here on I am Satisfyed my Self and Severel others that the Negro boy Belonging to Mr Smith is here but not Comatable yet he has bin See by Severel Persons on last Saturday the 24 and Sunday he Stayed during the knight in this Settle ment one knight at [Jeremiah and Emeline Davis] Roots & the other at [Samuel and Julia Ann Morris] McMurtrys

    I am verry well Convinced in my own mind there is people in the Company going to Calafornia that is knowing to this Boys Runing a way and is interested in getting him of and provided the martial does not come I want you to Send me further orders By Mr Hopper

    I think that the Negro Boy Called Jim that Come through in A. Lymans Company is knowing to the whole matter ~~the~~ there is a good many people [indecipherable] gong to Calafornia that has objections to Jim going being that he has a owner in Missourea and in fact they think that the Martial will be after him before he crosses Bear River and I Could mention names but for fear of being mistaken I will not do it that I thing is Concerned in this matter

    B. Mathews
    To Presadent Young

Francis McKown to Brigham Young, March 31, 1849, box 21, folder 16, Brigham Young Office Files, CR 1234 1, CHL.

March the 31 1849
Brother Young I Received your letter dated the 30. of this inst whiceh informs me that my Negro Girl is at your house and is desirous to not leave the Valley

Brother young my Opinion about this matter is this S[h]e Expects perhaps that I will Correct hur if I get hur but this is the first offence She Ever was guilty of and I am persuaded to think my self that She is not to Blame there must be Some person that lived knot Exceedeing and is Living forty Rods from the place that I Left from what I can Larn that is more guilty than [s]he is an as for me Coorrecting hur for such an offence I Shal not do it She has bin my Cook & did all of my washing Since my wife died my Oldest Daughter is not fourteen years of age yet and if yow please Send hur By Mr Hopper the Barrer of this Letter

She was Borne mine and I raised hur till and it Seems as though there was One out of the family ever since She has bin away

I want [indecipherable] that when Benjamine Mathews returns that you Should ask him Concerning Some person that hunted his Horse too days to go and get permission of yow So as to pre vent B. Mathews provided he gat hur from [indecipherable] from bringing hur to me

Remains yow Brothr   F,, McKown
                                        To B. Young

William Crosby to Brigham Young, c. March 12, 1851, box 22, folder 6, Brigham Young Office Files, CR 1234 1, CHL.

Brother Brigham Young by request of William Lay I write you these Lines to inform you that nothing but the Cash Can git harks wife and [William] Lay has not got it and his Black man wants to go with him and he wants you to Send him word by the Boy what he shall do if his boy is to go and if not the result of the matter Hark is a good boy and will do right I Believe I will speek of Green the Boy that Came with hark to see you he is a mean dirty I sarvace [savage] Lying disafected Saucy to Brother Flakes wife Disobediant I think that if you had him as you have Isaac that you would see the 2 Extreams he supposes that if he was free that he would never hav to do any thing on earth a gain and he would leave his Black wife and git him a white woman and insult Every person he met that did not please him and I think from what I no of him he have a man take him that would treat him right and make him work and behave him self one word from you will settle the whole matter this only my Judgement my health is improving fast

> I am your Dear Brother and never Deviating Friend
> William Crosby

Brigham Young to William Crosby, March 12, 1851, box 22, folder 6, Brigham Young Office Files, CR 1234 1, CHL.

G.S.L. City March 12 1851
Bro Crosby
I have just received your letter and say to you that it would not be wisdom to part Man and Wife and inasmuch as Greene abuses Sister Fleak how would it do for Bro Lay to take Greene and leave Hark perhaps Bro Bankhead woud do somthing for Sister Fleak in consideration thereof altho we do not wish to encourage the Sale of Blacks in these vallies yet it seems as tho Sister fleak might need some assistance perhaps that an Exchange might be made Either for the woman or man there is little doubt but they will all go free as soon as they shall arrive in California. I therfor would not advise you to be very Strenous to take many of them to that country

> Your affectionate brother
> Brigham Young

Brigham Young to Mrs. David [Duritha Trail] Lewis, January 3, 1860, box 19, folder 1, Brigham Young Office Files, CR 1234 1, CHL.

G.S.L. City, Jan. 3, 1860.
Mr's David Lewis
   3d Ward, City,

Dear Sister:—

I understand that you are frequently importuned to sell your negro man Jerry, but that he is industrious <and> faithful, and desires to remain in this Territory. Under these circumstances I should certainly deem it most advisable for you to keep him, but should you at any time conclude otherwise ~~I [indecipherable]~~ and determine to sell him, ordinary kindness would require that you should sell him to some kind, faithful member of the Church, that he may have a fair opportunity for doing all the good he desires to do or is capable of doing. I have been told that he is about forty years old, if so, it <is> not presumeable that you will, in case of ~~his~~ sale, ask so high a price as ~~you would a younger~~ you might expect for a younger person. If the price is sufficiently made, I may conclude to purchase him and set him at liberty.

Your Bro. in the Gospl
B Y

Brigham Young to Mrs. David [Duritha Trail] Lewis, March 31, 1860, box 19, folder 5, Brigham Young Office Files, CR 1234 1, CHL.

G.S.L. City, March 31, 1860.
Mr's Lewis, wife of the late David Lewis,
3ᵈ Ward, City,

Dear Sister:—Since I last saw you I have been informed that Jerry claims that he is free, and that you have no papers or <other> evidence to prove that he is your slave. Still he told me that <he> is willing <and much prefers> to live with and serve you, but it is very uncertain whether he will stay long with any one else ~~since he claims that he is free, and~~ I know of no one, under ~~the this~~ <these> ~~[indecipherable] such~~ circumstances, that would deem it a safe investment to buy him. For these reasons I think it much the best for you to retain him in your service.

Your Brother in the Gospel,
BY

Appendix 5

MISCELLANEOUS DOCUMENTS

Seth M. Blair to Judge Elias Smith, c. 1860, Thomas S. Williams Probate, Third District Court, Salt Lake County (UT), Probate Case Files, Series 1621, case 63, USHS.

Territory of Utah
Co. of Gr Salt Lake
Hon. E. Smith
Judge of Probate
For Said Co.

Your petitioner would respectfully represent that the anexed a/c for mony furnished Tho. S. Williams was obtained & loaned to the Said Williams on a pledge of <u>Honor</u> that your petitioner should be secured by Mortgage on one <of> the Negre<u>ss</u>es bot by him of Mrs. Lewis which pledge he failed to fullfill. Your petitioner further represents that He is able to prove that Said Negre<u>ss</u> on the belongs to the Estate of T. S. Williams your petitioner further represents that great injustice is done him by thom who hold the said Negress & other property belonging to the s[ai]d Estate of T. S. Williams. Your petitioner further represents that the Note Executed to B[radford] Leonard is yet drawing 10 pr c per month <interest> And prays the Court to allow the a/c anexed of principal & interest up to date with 10 pr C pr month untill paid to meet the said interest. Your petitioner further prays that the Court will decree & sett apart so mutch of the property of Said Estate of Williams as to ~~meet~~ pay said a/c & interest of your petitioner

Your petitioner further prays that the Administrator of the Said Estate of Williams be instructed by the Court to take possession of two <u>Negresses</u> belonging to the Estate of Said T. S. Williams One in the hands of Horace S. Eldridge the other in the possession of the Widow of Said Williams

Your petitioner further represents that their is Certain assets in Esse belonging to the Said Estate in Suits pending in the U. S. Destrict Court which has not been reported to the Judge of Probate. to the great damage of the creditors of said Estate

And in duty bound would be

Yours
S. M. Blair

Daniel M. Thomas to Amasa Lyman, February 4, 1856, Incoming Letters P–Y 1856, box 4, folder 1, Amasa M. Lyman Collection, MS 829, CHL.

San Bernardino Feb 4 1856

Dear Bro Lyman

According to promise I will trespass upon your time a Short time by a perusal of a few lines from your humble Se[r]vant, and <as> I kept the chronicles of San Bernardino for one year, and got my hand in a little, I thought I would give you Some Short extracts from my book of chronicles, even the town talk and doings in a Small way as the more important matters I presume are given by Bro Rich and others

Myself and numerous family are enjoiying good health at present, but one of my men Servants even Philemon did on or about the 1st day of the 1st month leave the premises of Daniel the Judge of his own Free will and accord, to the City near ~~the~~ by the Sea Shore called the Angeles Speaking after the manner of the Amerecans And he has entired into partnership with L Glazier in his Store (ie) Blacking Boots and carrying water and also in the latter part of the reign of [California governor] John whose Sirname is bigler two of the chief Bishops [William Crosby's] men Servants did also conceive in their hearts not to abide in the house of their master ~~And~~ <evene> Grief and Oscar, they went and behold they pitched their tents in the city of the angels likewise together with that beautifull piece of Ebony called Harriet his wife also dwelt with them in the Same Land

And there was one of our Brethren even Robert Smith who did abide in San Bernardino under the reign of ~~Lym~~ Lyman at Said city many years, and the Lord did prosper Robert in the Land untill he did possess much flocks & herds and came to pass that there was not enough Substance in the land of San Bernardino for his flocks and herds and he Said I will depart to the land of the Gentiles where I will not have to pay tithing neither pay pieces of gold & Silver for an inheritance and after he did dwell there a few days he Said I will arise and Sell my flocks & and herd that the Lord gave me in San Bernardino and I will go and Sojourn in the land of Texas and he did according to his Saying. but It came to pass that when he was about to arise and depart those Sons of Belial the Abolishest [abolitionists] was Stired up against him because he was going to take his men and maid Se<r>vants and behold they went unto the chief men of the city and consulted togather what they Should do, and they Said we will Send the chief officer even the Sheriff and take those Servants from him which they did accordingly and Charles the Son of Toby was at San Bernardino and the chief Judge Hays Sent up a writing to our chief officer to take charly in his care that Robert might not carry him to the Land of bondage

And Sallys [Sarah Harmon Crosby] maid Servant Mary did find favor in the Eyes of Samuel a man of light color who came down with the Bishop from the land of Ophor and he did look upon Mary and behold She did look fair and he did take her for a wife, and there is a Saying that they will only Sojourn with her mistress a few day

And Mariah [Tanner Lyman] had also a ~~handmaid~~ <maid Servants> from the land of ham And at the end of the year when the people all were giving feasts behold the ~~handmaid~~ <maid Servant> of Mariah went down among the gentiles and behold one of the Sons of Ham Saw her even Elizabeth and promised to marry her and She has made the wedding garments ~~are made~~, and all things are ready but the Son of ham has not come up yet

thus ends the cronicles of Daniel

You will excuse my foolishness I thought Bro R. & H. would advise you of all important matters and I would mention a few unimportant ones Yours with High Esteem

D M Thomas

Excerpts from Anonymous, "Slavery in Draper," c. 1935, handwritten manuscript, MS 6017, CHL. Explanatory notes and corrections in brackets.

Nancy with her five boys had been given to George Bankhead of Kentucky [Tennessee or Alabama] who had heard the call of Joseph, the Mormon Prophet, and had decided to cast his destiny with him and his people. . . . George and John [Bankhead], the two older [younger] sons . . . were off for the West, away in the Rocky Mountains. There was nothing could stop them. The father was loathe to see his sons go, but they departed with his benedictions. [Their father died before they left Alabama.] A wagon, horses, bedding, clothing, cooking utensils and ample provisions were provided. Five of his best slaves and the mother were given into their charge.

George Bankhead settled in Draper and his brother John, in Cache Valley. . . . George engaged in farming and cattle raising. He had no children of his own. The negro boys helped him in his labors and Mammy Nancy did the housekeeping. There were Sambo [Samuel], and Howard, and [Walter] Roll, and Henry and Alex. They were as black as coal and had lips as red as rubies. [Based on the 1850 census, none of them fit this description.] Here was the runt-skin and agile. The other boys were large and vigorous for their age. Socially they were on a par with the rest of the children of the community. [The rest of the document contradicts this claim.] They commanded the attention of their associates by reason of their teasing disposition. Roll became an efficient dancer and later went to California where his art and skill continued. [He died of tuberculosis in Salt Lake City in 1866.]

Mr. William Brown [(1856–1941)], now in his 79th year . . . related the following incident: "It was at a children's dance [c. 1862]. Boys and girls were seated upon benches around the room. Hen was there in his best attire. He was about 12 years old. In his effort to secure a partner, he asked the girls one after another down the line and finally Hannah Heward [(1856–1871)] responded to his invitation and they went whirling on the floor."

Mr. Brown and Joseph M. Smith [(1856–1948); son of Danish immigrants] . . . are responsible for this story: "George Bankhead was want to gather wood from Butterfield Canyon. Upon one of these trips they were cutting a big tree when Roll exclaimed, 'Which way shall I run, Massa George?' 'Run the way the tree falls, you fool!' replied Mr. Bankhead. In his attempt to get away some of the branches hit Roll, whereupon Mr. Bankhead remarked, 'Did you get hurt, Roll?' 'No,' said the boy, 'not much.' 'Wish the hell it had killed you,' thundered Mr. Bankhead."

Upon another occasion the boys were gathered at Henry Day's on the west. Nora (Mrs. Nora Stringfellow [(1860–1944); thus too young to have had any independent memories] tells this episode) . . . They were playing around the house and in the yard and having a general good time. Differences arose between the blacks and the whites. Among the latter were Jim [(1853–1903)] and Elestra Day [probably Joseph Elisha Day (1856–1932)], Frank Smith, Jos. L. Rawlins [(1850–1926); later US Senator], and others. Words passed back and forth and their it was proposed to hang one of the slaves to the crosspiece over the front gate. A rope was secured and in the scuffle which ensued, Henry Day [(1824–1898)], the father of the house, who had been watching from the window, suddenly made his appearance with a big stick in his hand and the proceedings came to a hasty termination.

Joseph [M. Smith]'s father had made him an iron wagon. It had four big wheels and a box painted red. It was the pride of its owner and the envy of every boy. "Wha ah yo' goin' wid dat wagon, boy?" shouted Sambo as he saw Joseph coming down the road. And soon the quintette was upon him. "Dat haint yo' wagon, chile!" chirped Howard. "Dat am my wagon," said Alex. [Alexander was too old for this story to be plausible as told.] "Dat am my wagon," said Hen and the tug of war was on. The wagon was wrenched from the hands of little Joe and hurled into a slough on the side of the road. Joe immediately set up a howl that could be heard for blocks around and in a few minutes his father was upon the scene. The negro boys were not slow in grasping the situation and when the wagon was again in the possession of its rightful owner his assailants were nowheres to be seen.

Thirteen years had passed since they came to Draper. The war was over. Freedom had been established. And like the fledgelings ready to leave their mother's nest, their hearts began to swell, new thoughts and new aspiration began to dawn upon their minds and ere long they were away upon their own resources.

John D. Fretwell (1917–2011) spent many years collecting materials related to early Black pioneers. Part of the collection is at the Church History Library in Salt Lake City, but his family holds most of his research, and they provided generous access. The following documents from the collection are, first, a note from Bertha Stevens Udell (1896–1994), the youngest granddaughter of Green and Martha Flake. The second is a compiled mix of personal interviews and memories probably taken from later print sources and written into the first person. As with other late sources, it should be used with caution. The document includes the story of Flake speaking at a Pioneer Day celebration led by Fretwell's grandfather, Alphonzo Bert Simmons (1861–1938). Due to the lapse of years and the anomalous claim that Flake was shy, the account is probably best understood as a fictionalized representation of a strong but distant community memory. The third selection is from Fretwell's interviews with Bertha Udell as excerpted from Fretwell's biography of Green Flake. Spelling and punctuation are as found in the original documents.

Notes from Bertha Stevens Udell Home, n.d., 2 pp., John D. Fretwell Collection, private collection. Page numbers refer to Carter's Negro Pioneer.

Page 5

Brigham Young gave a yoke of oxen for Green Flake. When they reeched <reached> Salt Lake Valley B. Young said "Brothers you are now free as I am"

Martha Crosby's back was marked with whelps from beating she received from the white master.

Martha Crosby's mother—Violate ~~Morris~~ <Crosby> the fingers were burned off her hand as a child.

page 6
George Stevens was 33 years of age and Lucinda Violate was 18 when they married.

page 8
Hark Lay & Oscar Crosby were Lucinda Violate Stevens great Uncles. Crosby was born in Miss. He was running from the slave masters trying to escape through a rail fence. His head was through the rails and he

could not get his body through as he was a large man. He was caught & beat. He went through life with his head twisted to one side.

Page 29
Lucinda Violate was not a mid wife. When women had babies she helped take care of the babies after they were born. She took a 4 day old infant who belonged to a white couple home with her for 3 w weeks and slept with and took care of the baby tt until the mother was able to care for it as the mother had complications after child birth.

Excerpts from John D. Fretwell, "Green Flake," n.d., Typescript, 4 pp., John D. Fretwell Collection.

Green Flake was invited as a special guest to speak and tell about himself at the Willow Creek Ward, Bannock Stake, Idaho

[Sources]George Washington Stevens; Ned [Leggroan];—David Oglesby—Udell—Bankhead—All these families have made a contribution to my research project

Green Flake thought the members of the Willow Creek Ward would make fun of him and it was his good friend Ned Leggroan who showed him that he was an honored guest and no one wouldn't make light of any message or thing he talked about. [At] first he was shy and hesitated but he over come his fears and began to speak freely. He never told all his story and it was said he came back again and entered into the discussion when others told their story.... Green Flake claims that he had a Mother and he was sure that he had some brothers and sisters. It was the Masters and Slave Owners who said his Mother had died A friendly and caring Negro woman told him she and another woman nursed him as well as his own Mother As a child he grew up with other Colored children, about his own age, and the was cared for by different women in the Negro Quarters. They were given plenty to eat, did their assigned chores and learned to fear and respect all White folks. He remembers getting his first whipping for [not] acting quickly enough when the White Man spoke:

"I drove a team and wagon to the Salt Lake Valley for my Master James Flake and helped build him a home and a fit place to live. They moved into the home and I was moved out most of the time to live in a dugout and a shed. I would gather and cut fire wood for another person's fire and [then] I would have to scrounge wood for myself."

Green liked to work on the Temples and church buildings. "I never could give anything to the church except my hands."

THE PRIESTHOOD
Green claimed he was given the Aaronic Priesthood and ordained as a Deacon but all the papers and proof he held the priesthood were lost or not written down. [This is probably a misunderstanding between generations. Samuel Chambers was a contemporary of Green Flake who also fulfilled the duties of a deacon without being ordained to the priesthood.] In some wards and gatherings he told that he passed and prepared the sacrament but that only happened a few times. He was often called to provide clean pure water and at time he walked a distance to find clear water, He helped build and set up the sacrament table and shined the cups and glasses until they would glisten. He was called on to visit special families and do their chores. Such as chopping wood, help with farm animals and tend to the widows, the sick and in firmed.

CONSECRATED OLIVE OIL
Green Flake families always kept a bottle of Consecrated Oil in their home and used it freely when there was any injury, hurt or illness around. He would rub the oil over the where the hurt or affliction was and pray for the those who were in need. The olive oil was the first thing he or his wife would reach for in case of injure or disease. They would use the oil even before they called on the Elders to administer to them. He claimed Brigham Young gave him a bottle of Concentrated Olive Oil and he used it sparingly for many years.

When I first met Bertha Stevens Udell in Fresno several years ago she wanted me to get her a bottle of consecrated oil. I told her I would have to check with the Bishop and he sent me to the Stake President and they claimed the Church didn't do that anymore. When I told her, of course she was disappointed and was some what hurt. "What happened to the Church when they don't follow what Brigham Young taught the Saints?" inquired Sister Udell. I was called on to administer her, her husband and members of her family. When I spoked to one of the General Authorities he told me to get them a bottle of olive oil and say a prayer over it and explain to the family it was blessed but not consecrated by one who held the priesthood.

Many times President found a seat for Green and other Colored folks at General Conference and other meetings up front and sometimes on the front row. It was said that Green shed tears at the death of Brigham Young and helped dig his grave and was at the funeral of the beloved President. He remembered that his children Abraham and Lucinda, Green's two children, was allowed to play with the children of Brigham Young.

Excerpts from John D. Fretwell, History of Green Flake, 1999, typescript, 4 pp., John D. Fretwell Collection.

Mrs Oscar [John or William] Crosby brought with her and old Negro maid named Violate. Violate had two of her daughters with her Rose and Martha. A romance blossomed between Green and Martha and it took time in making all the arrangements between the Crosby [Bankhead] and Flake families. It was said that both Green and Martha had to work for the Crosby [Bankhead] family until her Master decided they had fulfilled their obligation in paying a fair price for a colored girl. Also, they gave the Crosbys [Bankheads] produce form their garden and farm. Brigham Young was upset with the Crosbys and said the debt was paid in full. Sic ... Berth Marie Stevens Udell—-grand daughter

(19) A fire destroyed everything [Green and Martha Flake] owned. The only thing that survived the fire was a large porcelain cup. This treasure stayed with the family for years. The cup was handed down to the oldest child then the oldest grandchild. The oldest [surviving] granddaughter was Bertha Marie Stevens Udell. A few years before her death she felt the cup should be given to the Church in memory of her Grandfather Green Flake. She asked if John D. Fretwell would take the cup to the Church Historians Officer and present to [them] in her name. [As of February 2018, the cup was on display at the Church History Museum in Salt Lake City.]

(20) Martha Ann Morris Flake hand was burned, withered and scarred. After Martha married Green Flake she wanted to be known as Martha Ann Morris rather than having the name of Crosby. Family tradition and stories handed down through Green Flakes families tell this story. When Martha Ann was a young slave in the Oscar [John] Crosby's home one of her main duties was to care for the Crosby's children. One day her mistresses young girl was playing in the kitchen and

during the children's play the Crosby child put her hand on a very hot kettle. The child received a large burn on her hand. The girls cries brought Mrs. [Elizabeth Coleman] Crosby who came to comfort and care for her daughters burns. Mrs Crosby was very upset with her slave girl Martha who was tended the children and said she was to be punished. Mrs. Crosby shouted out. "Do you know how it feels to be burned, you wicked girl?" The angry Mistress then took Martha's hand and held it on the hot iron kettle until the hand sizzled and fried. Because the girl was shouting and crying out in pain the woman forced her hand again to the hot kettle She fainted and lay very still. Another slave picked up the girl and took her to the slaves quarters and tended her burns. Some of the tendons in the girls arm were damaged and after that she wasn't a good worker in the fields. The slave on the Crosby plantation remembered the incident and avoided Mrs Crosby whenever possible. She was known for punishing her slaves in a cruel way. Sic Bertha Marie Steven Udell—Interview with John D. Fretwell . . . 1990 . . . Fresno, CA

Appendix 6

SELECTED NEWSPAPER ARTICLES

Orson Hyde, "Slavery Among the Mormons," Frontier Guardian *(Kanesville, IA), December 11, 1850.*

We feel it to be our duty to define our position in relation to the subject of Slavery. There are several men in the Valley of the Salt Lake from the Southern States, who have their slaves with them. There is no law in Utah to authorize Slavery, neither any to prohibit it. If the slave is disposed to leave his master, no power exists there, either legal or moral that will prevent him. But if the slave choose to remain with his master; none are allowed to interfere between the master and the slave. All the slaves that are there appear to be perfectly contented and satisfied.

When a man in the Southern States embraces our faith and is the owner of slaves, the church says to him, if your slaves wish to remain with you, and to go with you, put them not away; but if they choose to leave you, or are not satisfied to remain with you, it is for you to sell them, or to let them go free, as your own conscience may direct you. The church on this point, assumes not the responsibility to direct. The laws of the land recognize slavery,—we do not wish to oppose the laws of the country. If there is sin in selling a slave, let the individual who sells him, bear that sin, and not the church. Wisdom and prudence dictate to us this position, and we trust that our position will henceforth be understood!

Our counsel to all our ministers in the North and in the South is, to avoid contention upon this subject, and to oppose no institution which the laws of the country authorize; but labor to bring men into the Church and kingdom of God, and then teach them to do right, and honor their God and his creatures.

If every enthusiastic spirit would be still, and allow Southern men a little time to reflect without being thorned, goaded, and nettled by restless aspirants, there might be more accomplished by a generosity that generally characterizes the South, than all the heated and misguided zeal of fanatical men, the zenith of whose ambition is, to make a smoke and a fuss.

Julius F. Taylor, "Slavery in Utah," Broad Ax (Salt Lake City, UT), March 25, 1899. It is not clear whether certain errors in the article originated in the telling of the stories or in Julius Taylor's account. The story of the escape was an experience of Marinda's long-time associate, Nancy Lines Smith, rather than Marinda. There is no historical record of "many slaveholders [who] left this Territory," so this could be a memory of the Greer family departure for Texas or army officers and merchants leaving with their enslaved people between the Utah War and the Civil War. Due to household timelines, the claims about Marinda being transferred to William Taylor Dennis and Alexander belonging to A. O. Smoot probably do not indicate legal enslavement in either household.

SLAVERY IN UTAH.

IT is very hard for the younger generation, especially those who are unfamiliar with the early history of this Territory, and those who later became residents of it, to comprehend or realize the fact, that African slavery existed within its borders, and that quite a few slaves were brought to these valleys by the pioneers, in 1847, and many more were brought in by those who followed later.

There are some few negroes still residing in various parts of this State and in Idaho, who were brought here as slaves, and held as such until the close of the civil war. When the war broke out, many slaveholders left this Territory with their slaves, and returned to the Southern States; because they believed by so doing, the risk of losing them would not be so great.

One of these unique characters, who was brought here in 1847 [1848], by the pioneers, resides in Spanish Fork, and his name is Alex. Bankhead. He is greatly respected, and held in high esteem by all the people of that flourishing little city.

While visiting their home, the latter part of last December, Mr. and Mrs. Bankhead, at our request, related their early experience in Utah. Mr. Bankhead belonged to the famous family of Bankheads of Alabama; and several male members of that family became converts to Mormonism. And when they came to the Territory they brought their slaves with them. Two or three members of the family located at Wellsville; and some of their ex-slaves, who still reside in that place and Corinne, assumed the names of their masters.

In time, Alex. Bankhead became the property of Bishop Smoot, who located at Provo. Mr. Bankhead is now well on to 70 years of age, and he well remembers Brigham Young and the other early leaders of the Mormon Church. He informed us, that when this city was in its infancy, the slaves always congregated in a large room or hall on State street, almost opposite the city and county building. There they would discuss their condition, and gaze in wonderment at the lofty mountains, which reared their snowy peaks heavenward, and completely forbade them from ascertaining how they could make their escape back to the South, or to more congenial climes. For we were assured that their lives in the then new wilderness, was far from being happy, and many of them were subjected to the same treatment that was accorded the plantation negroes of the South.

Mrs. Bankhead was born in North Carolina, not very far from Newburn. She was the property of a gentleman by the name of Redd. She, in company with a number of other slaves, were on their way to Utah; and while passing through the State of Kansas, during the dark hours of the night, the majority of them made good their escape, which was a great loss to their owner. But Mrs. Bankhead was not so successful in that direction, and she was brought on to Utah. After residing in this city for some years, she finally was transferred to Dr. Pinney [Dennis], of Salem. In the course of time she married Mr. Bankhead.

They both have a very distinct recollection of the joyful expressions which were upon the faces of all the slaves, when they ascertained that they had acquired their freedom through the fortunes of war. At that time many negroes, according to Mr. Bankhead's statement, "Left Salt Lake City and other sections of the Territory, for California and other States."

Mr. and Mrs. Bankhead now own a little home, including twenty acres of land. They are both devout and strict Mormons. She belongs to the Ladies' Relief Society of her Ward, and takes an active part with her white sisters in all work of that character. Mrs. Bankhead visited Salt Lake during the Pioneer Jubilee, and observed in the parade, Flake Green, who now lives in Idaho, and Mrs. Jane James, of this city, who formerly lived with Prophet Joseph Smith, and her brother, Isaac Manning, who assisted to erect the Nauvoo Temple.

The last named persons and other members of our race, came here with the Pioneers.

NOTES

SANKOFA

1. "Adinkra Symbols," *twi.bb: Online Dictionary for the Twi Language of the Akan People of Ghana in West Africa*, accessed August 24, 2017, http://www.twi.bb/akan-adinkra.php (site discontinued).
2. Robert S. Rattray, *Religion and Art in Ashanti* (Oxford: Clarendon Press, 1927), 265–67.
3. Erik R. Seeman, "Reassessing the 'Sankofa Symbol' in New York's African Burial Ground," *William and Mary Quarterly* 67, no. 1 (January 2010): 122, https://doi.org/10.5309/willmaryquar.67.1.101.
4. John Hardison Redd, Family Record (Digital copy of holograph, n.d.), private collection; Tonya Reiter, "Redd Slave Histories: Family, Race, and Sex in Pioneer Utah," *Utah Historical Quarterly* 85, no. 2 (Spring 2017): 108–26, https://www.jstor.org/stable/10.5406/utahhistquar.85.2.0108.

INTRODUCTION

1. William Crosby to Brigham Young, c. March 12, 1851, box 22, folder 6, CR 1234 1, Brigham Young Office Files (hereafter Office Files), Church History Library, The Church of Jesus Christ of Latter-day Saints, Salt Lake City, Utah (hereafter CHL).
2. Brigham Young to Mrs. David Lewis, March 31, 1860, box 19, folder 5, Office Files.
3. "Slavery in Utah," *Broad Ax* (Salt Lake City, UT), March 25, 1899.
4. Kate B. Carter, *The Negro Pioneer* (Salt Lake City: Daughters of Utah Pioneers, 1965), 4, 19.
5. Joseph Smith and William W. Phelps, *General Smith's Views of the Powers and Policy of the Government of the United States* (Nauvoo, IL: John Taylor, Printer, 1844), 9. https://www.josephsmithpapers.org.
6. W. Paul Reeve, *Religion of a Different Color: Race and the Mormon Struggle for Whiteness* (Oxford: Oxford University Press, 2015), 195–97.
7. Brigham Young to William Crosby, March 12, 1851, box 22, folder 6, Office Files.

8. Wilford Woodruff to Thomas L. Kane, November 27, 1849, box 16, folder 28, MSS 792, Thomas L. Kane Collection, L. Tom Perry Special Collections, Harold B. Lee Library, Brigham Young University, Provo, Utah (hereafter Special Collections, HBLL).
9. Ira Berlin, *Many Thousands Gone: The First Two Centuries of Slavery in North America* (Cambridge, MA: Harvard University Press, 1998), 369.
10. Young's sermon addressed previous remarks about constitutional law and abolitionism by merchant and missionary Alexander Robbins Jr. (1818–1902): "Brother Robbins also spoke of what they term the 'nigger drivers and nigger worshippers,' and observed how keen their feelings are upon their favorite topic slavery." The newspaper did not print Robbins's comments. Robbins had traveled to Utah Territory with merchants Charles Kinkead and William S. Godbe and did not remain in the territory. Alexander Robbins, "Arrived," *Deseret News* (Salt Lake City, UT), September 3, 1856; Alexander Robbins, "Sermon," *Deseret News*, September 17, 1856.
11. Frederick Douglass, *The Life and Times of Frederick Douglass: From 1817–1882* (London: Christian Age Office, 1882), 195.
12. 2 Nephi 26:33, Book of Mormon.
13. Austin Steward, *Twenty-Two Years a Slave, and Forty Years a Freeman* (Rochester, NY: William Alling, 1857), 133–37; Records of the Bureau of the Census, *1820 Census: Fourth Census of the United States* (National Archives Microfilm Publication M33, 142 rolls, Record Group 29), Ontario County, New York, 1820; Records of the Bureau of the Census, *1830 Census: Fifth Census of the United States* (National Archives Microfilm Publication M19, 201 rolls, Record Group 29), Ontario County, New York, 1830. For more on Young's racial views, see John G. Turner, *Brigham Young: Pioneer Prophet* (Cambridge, MA: Harvard University Press, 2012) and for a directed analysis, see Reeve, *Religion of a Different Color*.
14. Notes from Bertha Stevens Udell Home, n.d., 2 pp., John D. Fretwell Collection, private collection; Bertha Stevens Udell with John D. Fretwell, 1990 (Interview, Fresno, California), cited in John D. Fretwell, "Green Flake," (typescript, private collection, 1999), 3.
15. Francis McKown to Brigham Young, March 31, 1849, box 21, folder 16, Office Files.
16. Benjamin Mathews to Brigham Young, March 31, 1849, box 21, folder 16, Office Files.
17. "A Stew," *Frontier Guardian* (Kanesville, IA), September 5, 1849.
18. "Slaves Among the Mormons," *Natchez Weekly Courier* (Natchez, MS), October 2, 1850.
19. "From Utah," *New York Weekly Tribune* (New York, NY), February 8, 1851.
20. The Georgia Platform appears in the historical record as other communities adopted it; for example, "Patriotic Demonstrations in Alabama," *Weekly National Intelligencer* (Washington, DC), April 26, 1851.
21. See Appendix 6. Orson Hyde, "Slavery Among the Mormons," *Frontier Guardian*, December 11, 1850.
22. John C. Hurd, "§578. Legislation of Utah Territory," in *The Law of Freedom and Bondage in the United States* (Boston: Little, Brown and Company, 1862), 2:212.
23. No manumissions or court cases appear in Illinois records for enslaved people taken into Illinois by Latter-day Saints. Iowa law allowed travelers to pass through the territory without losing their enslaved people. M. Scott Heerman, "In a State of Slavery: Black Servitude in Illinois, 1800–1830," *Early American Studies: An Interdisciplinary*

Journal 14, no. 1 (Winter 2016): 114–39, Project MUSE; Illinois State Archives, *Illinois Servitude and Emancipation Records (1722–1863)*, https://cyberdriveillinois .com/departments/archives/databases/servant.html; Hancock County, Illinois, Misc. Court Records, 1844–1858, Misc. Court Records, 1845–1853, Misc. Court Records, [?]–1839, *Illinois Probate Records, 1819–1988*, FSFT, https://www.familysearch .org/search/collection/1834344; Hurd, *Law of Freedom and Bondage*, 2:132–37, 174–77.

24. John W. Gunnison, *The Mormons, or, Latter-day Saints, in the Valley of the Great Salt Lake* (Philadelphia: Lippincott, Grambo & Co., 1852), 143.

25. Mark J. Stegmaier, "A Law That Would Make Caligula Blush?: New Mexico Territory's Unique Slave Code, 1859–1861," *New Mexico Historical Review* 87, no. 2 (Spring 2012): 209–42, https://digitalrepository.unm.edu/nmhr/vol87/iss2/3.

26. Christopher B. Rich, Jr., "The True Policy for Utah: Servitude, Slavery, and 'An Act in Relation to Service,'" *Utah Historical Quarterly* 80, no. 1 (Winter 2012): 54–74, https:// www.jstor.org/stable/45063378.

27. Brigham Young [by Daniel Wells] to Horace S. Eldredge, July 12, 1852, box 17, folder 3, Office Files.

28. Ronald G. Coleman, "A History of Blacks in Utah, 1825–1910" (PhD diss., University of Utah, 1980), 44–48. For more on how the conflict between popular sovereignty and federal power played out in Utah Territory, see Brent M. Rogers, *Unpopular Sovereignty: The Mormons and the Federal Management of Early Utah Territory* (Lincoln: University of Nebraska Press, 2017).

29. John Bernhisel to Brigham Young, July 3, 1850, box 60, folder 10, Office Files.

30. Davis County, box 1, folder 2; Great Salt Lake and Davis Counties, box 1, folder 6; Utah County, box 1, folder 10, Utah Territory Slave Schedule [draft], 1850 [1851] Utah Territorial Census, MS 2672, CHL.

31. Records of the Bureau of the Census, *1850 Census: Seventh Census of the United States* (National Archives Microfilm Publication M432, 1009 rolls, Utah Territory Slave Schedule, Record Group 29), Utah County, 1850.

32. Ardis E. Parshall, "Comment on *Keepapitchinin: The Mormon History Blog*," April 30, 2013, http://www.keepapitchinin.org/2013/04/30/a-historical-mystery-thomas -bullock-and-the-utah-county-census.

33. Bureau of the Census, *A Century of Population Growth from the First Census of the United States to the Twelfth, 1790–1900* (Washington, DC: Government Printing Office, 1909), 132.

34. Bureau of the Census, *Population Growth*, 133.

35. Brigham Young, Great Salt Lake County, Utah Territory Slave Schedule [draft], 1850 [1851], CHL; Agnes Flake, Utah County, Utah Territory Slave Schedule [draft], 1850 [1851], CHL; Records of the Bureau of the Census, *1850 Census: Seventh Census of the United States* (National Archives Microfilm Publication M432, 1009 rolls, Record Group 29), Green Flake, Great Salt Lake County, Utah Territory, 1850.

36. Crosby to Young, c. March 12, 1851, Office Files.

37. Stacey L. Smith, *Freedom's Frontier: California and the Struggle Over Unfree Labor* (Chapel Hill: University of North Carolina Press, 2015), 1–79, 109–140; Delilah L. Beasley, *The Negro Trail Blazers of California* (Los Angeles, CA: Times Mirror Printing and Binding House, 1919); Delilah L. Beasley and Monroe N. Work, "Documents: California Freedom Papers," *Journal of Negro History* 3, no. 1 (January 1918): 50–54,

https://www.journals.uchicago.edu/doi/pdf/10.2307/2713793; and Delilah L. Beasley, "Slavery in California," *The Journal of Negro History* 3, no. 1 (January 1918): 33–44, https://www.journals.uchicago.edu/doi/10.2307/2713792.

38. Reeve, *Religion of a Different Color*, 140–70; Utah Territorial Legislative Assembly, *Acts, Resolutions and Memorials Passed by the First Annual, Special Sessions, of the Legislative Assembly, of the Territory of Utah* (Salt Lake City, UT: Brigham H. Young, 1852a), 80–82; Utah Territorial Legislative Assembly, *Journals of the House of Representatives, Council and Joint Sessions of the First Annual and Special Sessions of the Legislative Assembly of the Territory of Utah* (Salt Lake City, UT: Brigham H. Young, 1852b), 88, 90, 108–10, 122; Kevin Waite, *West of Slavery: The Southern Dream of a Transcontinental Empire* (Chapel Hill: University of North Carolina Press, 2021), 125–134; Nathaniel R. Ricks, "A Peculiar Place for the Peculiar Institution: Slavery and Sovereignty in Early Territorial Utah" (master's thesis, Brigham Young University, 2007).

39. Historians previously relied on Wilford Woodruff's version of Young's remarks, but the definitive version is LaJean Purcell Carruth's transcription of a shorthand report. Brigham Young, February 5, 1852, Church History Department Pitman Shorthand transcriptions: Addresses and Sermons, 1851–1874, box 2, folder 9, CR 100 912, CHL.

40. "Adelaide Pearson v. Laura Pearson et al.," in Charles A. Tuttle, ed., *Reports of Cases Determined in the Supreme Court of the State of California, Vol. 51, 1875–1877* (San Francisco: Bancroft-Whitney, 1906), 120–25; "Supreme Court Decisions, October Term, 1873, Pearson vs. Pearson," *Sacramento Daily Union* (Sacramento, CA), October 25, 1873; "Supreme Court Decisions, October Term, 1875," *Sacramento Daily Union*, January 26, 1876.

41. Slave Registrations, Salt Lake County (UT) Probate Court Civil and Criminal Case Files, 1852–1887, Series 373, box 4, folder 26; box 5, folder 11, USHS.

42. John Brown, Consecration Deed, February 3, 1857, Records of Utah County (1851–1864), F:81–82, MSS 3905, Special Collections, HBLL.

43. Leonard J. Arrington, *Great Basin Kingdom: An Economic History of the Latter-day Saints, 1830–1900, New Edition* (Boston: Harvard University Press, 1958; Champaign, IL: University of Illinois Press, 2005), 133–45.

44. Do not confuse the Mississippi and Nova Scotia Crosby families in Nauvoo, Utah Territory, and San Bernardino. There were multiple men named John Brown in Nauvoo tithing records; journal entries help single out the enslaver. John Brown's account of his trip from Mississippi to Nauvoo mentioned seven travelers at the beginning and six when he reached Nauvoo, including "Brother Matthews" and "Brother Bankhead." The other names come from the tithing record. May 27, 30, 31, June 2, 4, 1845, Daybook D, Nauvoo Tithing Record, 1835–1847, Trustee-in-Trust Tithing Daybooks, 1842–1847, CR 5 71, CHL; John Brown and John Z. Brown, *Autobiography of Pioneer John Brown 1820–1896* (Salt Lake City, UT: Press of Stevens and Wallis, Inc., 1941), 56–62.

45. "Venius a Slave <of John H. Redd>," April 3, 1845; "Benjn Holladay (negro)," April 4, 1845; "Widow Susan Burton's (Negro John)," April 22, 1845, Daybook C, Nauvoo Tithing Record, 1844–1845, Trustee-in-Trust Tithing Daybooks, 1842–1847, CR 5 71, CHL. Venus Redd is indexed as "Venius a (Nigger)" in Index to Tithing and Donation Record, 1844–1846, Trustee-in-Trust Indexes, 1842–1852, CR 5 72, CHL; Palmyra

Ward Tithing Office Ledger, 1851–1857, LR 6700 21, CHL; Carl Carter, email message to author, February 28, 2020.

46. The names of the enslaved are known for the Jolley, Crosby, Redd, and Burton households; partially known for the Bankhead, Stewart, Nowlin, Flake, and Barnett households; and unknown for the rest. The tithing books show occasional duplicate entries, including for James M. Flake. Several other enslavers may have made donations, but the ones listed here are those with identifiable church and government records, and who were documented to be enslavers when the donation was made. Some donors remained in the South and lost contact with the church. Haden W. Church and A. O. Smoot are not known to have enslaved anyone until around 1851, so they are not in this list. Although Samuel Heath was raised in a slave household, he is not known to have been an enslaver himself. James Poe enslaved no taxable people in 1844, but six in the 1846 tax record, so his $5 donation in 1845 may or may not belong in this list. Tax records suggest that the 1845 cash donations from Robert D. Covington and Washington N. Cook may have come from the proceeds from selling people. November 4, 11, 1844, February 15, March 26, April 3–4, 12, 14, 22, May 27, 30–31, June 4, 1845, Daybook C; September 8, 22, October 1, 24, November 21, 24, December 1, 1845, January 6, 23, March 30, April 3, 6–7, August 20, 1846, Daybook D, Trustee-in-Trust Tithing Daybooks; James Poe, 1844, 1846, Choctaw County Tax Rolls, 1835–1893; R D Covington, Washington N Cook, Noxubee County Tax Rolls, 1844–1845, Mississippi Department of Archives and History, *Various Records, 1820–1951*, FSFT, https://www.familysearch.org/search/collection/1919687.

47. *Hancock Eagle*, "The Temple in the Market," (Nauvoo, IL, May 8, 1846); Richard Bennett, "'Has the Lord Turned Bankrupt?' The Attempted Sale of the Nauvoo Temple, 1846–1850," *Journal of the Illinois State Historical Society* 95, no. 3 (Autumn 2002): 254–55n13, https://scholarsarchive.byu.edu/facpub/1080; Jeffrey Mahas, Facebook message to author, August 21, 2020.

48. Existing records suggest that most of the early Utah settlers who donated labor toward communal projects donated one or two days and few donated more than four or five days in a year. *The Time Book of Tithing Hands for the Year 1850* shows that Reuben Perkins provided five and a half days of labor tithing, but the book specifies when someone other than the tithe payer provided the labor and does not indicate that anyone other than Perkins himself provided the labor. See additional discussion in the chapter "Green Flake and the Tithing Myth." Reuben Perkins, Time Book of Tithing Hands for the Year 1850, 18, CR 104 28, General Tithing Office Tithing Labor Time Books, 1850–1854, CHL.

49. Thomas S. Williams paid tithing in 1851 from merchanting profits, but neither he nor his parents appear to have enslaved anyone until he purchased Lucy from Margaret Smoot in 1852, and he doesn't appear in tithing records afterward. Trustee-in-Trust Tithing and Donation Records, 1846–1879, CR 5 79, CHL.

50. [Entry 484] 1850, June 3, 8, [July] 1852, Trustee-in-Trust Tithing and Donation Records; March 22, 1852, April 13, June 15, October 11, 1853, San Bernardino Branch Tithing Accounts, 1851–1857, LR 1594 21. Around 1855 the church decentralized tithing payments and any further donations would appear in records kept by individual congregations. Wards did not always preserve tithing records. For example, only an

1859 record appears to exist for the Sugar House Ward. Index Entry, CR 5 79, Trustee-in-Trust Tithing and Donation Records, CHL.

51. Leonard J. Arrington, Feramorz Y. Fox, and Dean L. May, *Building the City of God: Community and Cooperation among the Mormons* (Urbana: University of Illinois Press, 1992), 70, 75.

52. By 1857, it was clear that the church would not take any property, so the creators of earlier deeds risked more financially than later ones. Arrington, *Great Basin Kingdom*, 146–48; Consecration Book Index, 1857–1858, box 1, image 486, CR 5 53, Consecration Deeds, 1854–1867, CHL; Feramorz Y. Fox, "The Consecration Movement of the Middle Fifties Part II, Conclusion," *Improvement Era* 47, no. 2 (February 1944): 80–81, 120–21, 124–25, https://archive.org/details/improvementera4702unse. Those known to have sold enslaved people before they traveled to Utah Territory were Jacob Croft, $4,582, and Joel Ricks, $3,620. Consecration Index, 34, 339. Although he had enslaved a young girl in the South, Thomas B. Graham listed property worth only $325. Consecration Index, 110. Enslavers in Utah Territory included John Brown, $3,038.50; Haden W. Church, $1,576; William Taylor Dennis, $4,113.50; Reuben Perkins, $1,916; John H. Redd, $2,350; Abraham O. Smoot $7,250; James M. Whitmore, $600. Elizabeth Carter Flaherty Whitmore held most of the property in her family and did not create a deed. Consecration Book Index, 20, 34, 54, 291, 336, 365, 441; Franklin Monroe Perkins, Reuben Perkins, January 6, 1857, Davis County Transfer Book, 1857–1858, Consecration Deeds, box 4, folder 2, 1, 3; John H. Redd, Consecration Deed, Records of Utah County, H:132–33.

53. John Brown, Records of Utah County, February 3, 1857; William Taylor Dennis, January 20, 1857, Consecration Deeds, Records of Utah County, F:81–82, 111–112.

54. Ardis E. Parshall, email message to author, May 2, 2016.

55. "An Overland Journey. XXI. Two Hours with Brigham Young," *New-York Daily Tribune* (New York, NY), August 20, 1859.

56. Thomas D. Brown, *Journal of the Southern Indian Mission: Diary of Thomas D. Brown*, ed. Juanita Brooks (Logan: Utah State University Press, 1972), 111.

57. Bill of Sale for Dan, August 17, 1859, Great Salt Lake County Recorder's Office, as reproduced in Carter, *Negro Pioneer*, 42; Seth M. Blair to Elias Smith, n.d., Thomas S. Williams Probate, Third District Court, Salt Lake County (UT), Probate Case Files, Series 1621, case 63, USHS.

58. Records of the Bureau of the Census, *1860 Census: Eighth Census of the United States* (National Archives Microfilm Publication M653, Utah Territory Slave Schedule, Record Group 29), William H. Hooper, Great Salt Lake County, 1860; William H. Hooper & Thos. S. Williams lately trading under the firm of Hooper & Williams, to the use of William H. Hooper v. George W. Belt, Henry Coleman and Thos. A Stoddard, trading under the firm of Belt, Coleman & Co. (1859), Salt Lake County Probate Court Case Files, Series 373, box 5, folder 90, USHS.

59. "Third Judicial District Court," *Deseret News*, August 10, 1859.

60. "Third Judicial District Court," *Deseret News*, August 10, 1859.

61. Thomas D. Morris, *Southern Slavery and the Law, 1619–1860* (Chapel Hill: University of North Carolina Press, 1999), 132.

62. Richard F. Burton, *The City of the Saints, and Across the Rocky Mountains to California* (New York, NY: Harper & Brothers, 1862), 181.

63. George P. Sanger, ed., *The Statutes at Large, Treaties, and Proclamations, of the United States of America* (Boston: Little, Brown and Company, 1863), 432.
64. "From Washington," *Deseret News*, July 2, 1862.
65. John M. Bernhisel to Brigham Young, June 13, 1862, box 61, folder 6; Journal of President B. Young's Office, box 72, folder 5, Office Files.
66. "Another Pioneer Laid at Rest—Funeral Services of Mrs. Nancy Bankhead," *Logan Journal* (Logan, UT), March 6, 1915.
67. The enslaved members of the Bankhead household appeared in the population schedule. They also appeared in the draft slave schedule, all shown as enslaved by John Bankhead, although some were enslaved by his brother George. John H. Bankhead, Great Salt Lake County, Utah Territory Slave Schedule [draft], 1850 [1851]; Sam, Nancy, Alexander, Thomas, Nathan, Miram, Sam, Rolly, Howard, Great Salt Lake County, Utah Territory, *1850 Census*.
68. Carter, *Negro Pioneer*, 25.
69. Beth Cavanaugh, Rutherford County (TN) Archives, email message to author, December 8, 2014; Tonya Reiter, "Redd Slave Histories: Family, Race, and Sex in Pioneer Utah," *Utah Historical Quarterly* 85, no. 2 (Spring 2017): 108–26; John H. Redd, *Utah Territory Slave Schedule* [draft], Utah County, 1850 [1851].
70. Lewis Ricks, Autobiography, in *History and Genealogy of the Ricks Family of America*, ed. Guy S. Rix (Salt Lake City, UT: Skelton Publishing Co., 1908), 73.
71. Hurd, *Law of Freedom and Bondage*, 2:93, 152, 172.
72. George Stuart Will, 1831, Cumberland County, North Carolina County, District, and Probate Courts, *North Carolina, Wills and Probate Records, 1665–1998*, Ancestry.com, https://www.ancestry.com/search/collections/9061; Laura Moench Jenkins, "The Life Story of Ruthinda Baker Stewart" (digital copy of unpublished manuscript, 2013), FSFT, https://familysearch.org/photos/artifacts/2894992.
73. Jeffery O. Johnson, "Cattle, Slaves, Missionaries and Mormon Converts from Texas, 1850s" (lecture, Mormon History Association, San Antonio, TX, June 2014).
74. Samuel H. Williamson and Lawrence Officer created a calculator to convert historical prices to current equivalents. Some of their conversions will be used with permission throughout this book. Their *MeasuringWorth* calculator takes a dollar amount and estimates a range of modern equivalents. Using one value, *real price*, based on the goods and services an average household would buy, Crosby's estate valuation of $16,929 would be worth around half a million dollars today. However, since his estate was mostly income-generating land and an enslaved labor force, a better calculation may be the *relative income value*, based on the "relative 'prestige value' [of] the owners of this income or wealth because of their rank in the income distribution," using GDP (gross domestic product), or total of the goods and services produced at a given time. Using the relative income value, Crosby's estate, including the enslaved people that his widow and children took to Utah Territory, would be worth more than $12 million today. The family's status in the community suggests that the income value may be the most accurate. The prices for enslaved humans in estate inventories were based on age, sex, training, physical condition, reproductive potential, reputation, and local, national, and international markets. Samuel H. Williamson and Louis P. Cain, "Measuring Slavery in 2016 Dollars," *MeasuringWorth*, accessed April 27, 2021,

https://www.measuringworth.com/calculators/uscompare; Williamson and Cain, "Measuring Slavery in 2016 Dollars*," *MeasuringWorth*, 2016, https://www.measuringworth.com/slavery.php. Used by permission.
75. William W. Hening, *The Statutes at Large; Being a Collection of All the Laws of Virginia* (New York, NY: Bartow, 1823), 2:170.
76. Sam Franklin, Utah County, Utah Territory Slave Schedule [draft], 1850 [1851].
77. Heather Hardy, "Remembered and Known: Latter-day Saints in the Antebellum South" (unpublished manuscript, 2001), CHL.
78. Williamson and Cain, "Measuring Slavery."
79. Lura Redd, Amasa Jay Red, and Amasa Mason Redd, *The Utah Redds and Their Progenitors* (Salt Lake City, UT: privately printed, 1973), 292.
80. Carter, *Negro Pioneer*, 20.
81. Carter, *Negro Pioneer*, 33–34.
82. Italics in original. Carter, *Negro Pioneer*, 48.
83. In 1870, Americus Greer estimated his personal estate at $400 with no servants in the household. Eliza M. Wakefield, *Texas and the Greers* (privately printed, 1953), 24; Records of the Bureau of the Census, *1870 Census: Ninth Census of the United States* (National Archives Microfilm Publication M593, 1,761 rolls), Americus Greer, Bosque County, Texas, 1870.
84. Wakefield, *Texas and the Greers*, 6.
85. See Kimberly Wallace-Sanders, *Mammy: A Century of Race, Gender, and Southern Memory* (Ann Arbor, MI: University of Michigan Press, 2009).
86. Carter, *Negro Pioneer*, 27.
87. Carter, *Negro Pioneer*, 36–39.
88. "Gobo Fango," FSFT, accessed June 20, 2020, https://www.familysearch.org/tree/person/collaborate/LZFT-3ZF.
89. For the spread of the legend, see, for example, Joseph Walker, "Flake Descendant Ironically Embodies LDS, Pioneer History," *Deseret News*, July 23, 2012, https://www.deseretnews.com/article/765591796/Flake-descendant-ironically-embodies-LDS-pioneer-history.html.
90. Jane Manning James and Elizabeth J. D. Roundy, Autobiography, c. 1902, MS 4425, CHL; Carter, *Negro Pioneer*, 20.
91. Carter, *Negro Pioneer*, 28.
92. Carter, *Negro Pioneer*, 44–46. A list of fugitive slave notices from the Jolley and Manning families is in Section 2 under "Lambson or Lamb (Jolley)."
93. Jennifer L. Hochschild and Brenna M. Powell, "Racial Reorganization and the United States Census 1850–1930: Mulattoes, Half-Breeds, Mixed Parentage, Hindoos, and the Mexican Race," Harvard University Department of Government, *Studies in American Political Development* 22, no. 1 (Spring 2008): 59–96, https://doi.org/10.1017/s0898588x08000047.
94. Thomas A. Foster, *Rethinking Rufus: Sexual Violations of Enslaved Men* (Athens: University of Georgia Press, 2019), 62–63. Kohler's claim about sex trafficking is not possible to verify and appears among many other errors in her fictionalized history, including incorrect prices for the men enslaved in the Crosby household. Charmaine Lay Kohler, *Southern Grace: A Story of the Mississippi Saints* (Boise, ID: Beagle Creek Press, 1995), 42.

95. Notes from Udell Home; Daniel M. Thomas to Amasa Lyman, February 4, 1856, Incoming Letters P–Y 1856, box 4, folder 1, Amasa M. Lyman Collection, MS 829, CHL (hereafter Lyman Collection).
96. "Criminal action concerning the 1831 insurrection of slaves," *Miscellaneous Records of Slaves and Freemen* (Onslow County, North Carolina, 1763–1912), 937–44, https://www.familysearch.org/search/catalog/1594521; Charles E. Morris, "Panic and Reprisal: Reaction in North Carolina to the Nat Turner Insurrection, 1831," *North Carolina Historical Review* 62, no. 1 (1985): 29–52, https://www.jstor.org/stable/23518997; Donnie D. Bellamy, "Slavery in Microcosm: Onslow County, North Carolina," *Journal of Negro History* 62, no. 4 (1977): 339–50, https://doi.org/10.2307/2717110.
97. Journal of President B. Young's Office, December 28, 1860, box 72, folder 5, 194, Office Files; Doctrine and Covenants 87:4, ed. Church of Jesus Christ of Latter-day Saints (Salt Lake City: Church of Jesus Christ of Latter-day Saints, 1981).
98. Reeve, *Religion of a Different Color*, 143.
99. Junius P. Rodriguez, "Running Away," in *Encyclopedia of Slave Resistance and Rebellion, Volume 2: O–Z and Primary Documents*, ed. Junius P. Rodriguez (Westport, CT: Greenwood Press, 2007), 428–31.
100. A journalist concluded in 1855 that women in Utah Territory were in "slavery worse than can be realized in the South." "Interesting from the Mormons," *New York Herald* (New York, NY), May 4, 1855. Although abuses occurred during plural marriage, the institution was not in any way equivalent to hereditary enslavement in the South. Although plural marriage in the Lewis, Williams, and Burton-Robinson households raised questions about slave ownership, the questions were never legislated or addressed by a judge. For more on plural marriage, see Laurel Thatcher Ulrich, *A House Full of Females: Plural Marriage and Women's Rights in Early Mormonism, 1835–1870* (New York, NY: Knopf, 2017); and Kathryn M. Daynes, *More Wives Than One: Transformation of the Mormon Marriage System, 1840–1910* (Champaign, IL: University of Illinois Press, 2008).
101. "Slavery in Utah," *Broad Ax*.
102. "Slavery in Utah," *Broad Ax*.
103. Donald E. Burton, "History of John Burton: 1797–1865" (unpublished manuscript), copy in possession of author, 24.
104. National Humanities Center, "'Slaves for Life, and Servants for a Time': Servitude in British America: Five European Perspectives, 1705–1750," *Becoming American: The British Atlantic Colonies, 1690–1763*, https://nationalhumanitiescenter.org/pds/becomingamer/economies/text6/servitude.pdf.
105. Charles Ball and Mr. Fisher, *Fifty Years in Chains, or, the Life of an American Slave* (New York, NY: H. Dayton, 1859), 54.
106. Elizabeth Fox-Genovese, *Within the Plantation Household: Black and White Women of the Old South* (Chapel Hill: University of North Carolina Press, 1988), 31.
107. Fox-Genovese, *Within the Plantation Household*, 101.
108. John H. Redd to Druzilla Holt Pearson (Thompson), December 27, 1848, MS 3663, folder 1, CHL (digital copy of photocopy of holograph; Rutherford County, TN).
109. "Knocked Down," *Valley Tan* (Salt Lake City, UT), November 19, 1858.

110. George Q. Cannon, *Journal of George Q. Cannon* (The Church of Jesus Christ of Latter-day Saints, Salt Lake City, Utah: Church Historian's Press, May 5, 1855), https://www.churchhistorianspress.org/george-q-cannon.
111. Even the terms "Black" and "African American" raise issues of class and opportunity. Erika V. Hall, Katherine W. Phillips, and Sarah S. M. Townsend, "A Rose by Any Other Name?: The Consequences of Subtyping 'African-Americans' from 'Blacks,'" Journal of Experimental Social Psychology 56 (2015): 183–90, https://dx.doi.org/10.1016/j.jesp.2014.10.004.
112. Anonymous, "Slavery in Draper," c. 1935, handwritten manuscript, MS 6017, 5–6, 7, CHL.
113. Kohler, *Southern Grace*, 40, 46; Mary West Riggs, Don L. Riggs, Christie Roberts, and Kevin Merrell, *Five Branches of Love* (Salt Lake City, UT: Don L. Riggs, 1967, reprinted as a digital book, 2006), 65; Margaret Blair Young and Darius Aidan Gray, *Standing on the Promises*, 3 vols. (Provo, UT: Zarahemla Books, 2012, 2013).
114. This may be an unsolvable puzzle since the Hancock family enslaved Amy when her children were born. Zae Hargett Gwynn, *Abstracts of the Records of Onslow County, North Carolina, 1734–1850* (Onslow County, NC: Z. H. Gwynn, 1961), 1:581.
115. For an example of the use of surnames, Celia Bankhead of Corinne, Utah, placed an ad seeking her mother, Mary Halingworth. "Mrs. Celia Bankhead," *Richmond Planet* (Richmond, VA), February 27, 1897, in "Last Seen: Finding Family After Slavery," Department of History, Villanova University and Mother Bethel AME Church, http://informationwanted.org; David E. Paterson, "A Perspective on Indexing Slaves' Names," *The American Archivist* 64 (Spring/Summer 2001): 132–42, https://www.americanarchivist.org/doi/pdf/10.17723/aarc.64.1.th18g8t6282h4283; Robyn N. Smith, "The Complexity of Slave Surnames," *Reclaiming Kin: Taking Back What Was Once Lost*, March 14, 2017, https://www.reclaimingkin.com/the-complexity-of-slave-surnames.
116. Original photo from Emmeline B. Wells, ed., *Charities and Philanthropies: Woman's Work in Utah* (Salt Lake City, UT: George Q. Cannon & Sons Co., 1893), 10. Tonya Reiter found the second picture. It is in the collections of the Utah State Historical Society and cropped from a commemorative book. General Board of Relief Society, *A Centenary of Relief Society, 1842–1942* (Salt Lake City, UT: General Board of Relief Society, 1942); Fifteenth Ward Relief Society Building, Nicholas G. Morgan Collection, USHS, https://collections.lib.utah.edu/details?id=435724.

CHAPTER 1: SOUTHERN ORIGINS: MISSISSIPPI AND ALABAMA

1. "A Sudden Death. Cordelia Litchford Dies of Hemorrhage of the Lungs," *Salt Lake Herald* (Salt Lake City, UT), February 24, 1891.
2. John Crosby Probate, Monroe County, 1842, images 226–27, 236–39, Mississippi County, District, and Probate Courts, "Mississippi, Wills and Probate Records, 1780–1982," Ancestry.com, https://www.ancestry.com/search/collections/8995.
3. Williamson and Cain, *MeasuringWorth*, accessed April 27, 2021.
4. Knox County records make few references to the Crosby family, with none about slavery or indenture. Joseph Coleman Will, Union County, 1806, South Carolina County, District, and Probate Courts, South Carolina, Wills and Probate Records,

1670–1980, Ancestry.com, https://www.ancestry.com/search/collections/9080; Emma Lou Thornbrough, *The Negro in Indiana: A Study of a Minority* (Indianapolis: Indiana Historical Bureau, 1957), 1–54; Earl E. McDonald, "Disposal of Negro Slaves by Will in Knox County, Indiana," *Indiana Magazine of History* 26, no. 2 (June 1, 1930): 145, https://www.jstor.org/stable/27786437; Robertalee Lent and June B. Barekman, *Knox Co. Indiana Early Land Records Court Indexes*, 2 vols. (Post Falls, ID: Genealogical Reference Builders, 1966), 74.

5. *History of Knox and Daviess Counties, Indiana* (Chicago: Goodspeed Publishing Co., 1886), 208.
6. John Crosby, 1839, Monroe County Tax Rolls, 1822–1841, box 3723, Mississippi Department of Archives and History, *Various Records*.
7. John Crosby Probate, Mississippi County, District, and Probate Courts, "Mississippi, Wills and Probate Records," 196, 206, 229, 242, 252.
8. John Crosby's final estate settlement was in 1844, when the youngest child came of age and her mother revalued the property and gave an accounting to the court. John Crosby Probate, Mississippi County, District, and Probate Courts, "Mississippi, Wills and Probate Records," 267–68; John Crosby, Final Settlement, Monroe County, Inventories 1839–1844, 2:173–77; Guardianship of Elizabeth and Nancy Crosby, 1840, case 140.1, Monroe County, Mixed Estate and Probate Court Files, Mississippi County Courthouses and Public Libraries, Mississippi Probate Records, 1781–1930, FSFT, https://www.familysearch.org/search/collection/2036959.
9. A different account may suggest that Violet was the victim, but the accounts favor Martha. The other account says, "the fingers were burned off her hand as a child." Udell, Interview, 3; Notes from Udell Home.
10. Brown, *Autobiography*, 46; John Brown, Journal, box 1, folder 1, images 31–33, MS 1636, Reminiscences and Journals, CHL.
11. "A Big Fire. Marion County's Temple of Justice," *Marion County Herald* (Hamilton, AL), April 5, 1887. Newspaper notices about the estate do not provide additional details. See, for example, "Administrator's Notice," *Huntsville Democrat* (Huntsville, AL), July 23, 1842.
12. "Petition to the President and Congress by Intruders on Chickasaw Lands, September 5, 1810," in *The Territorial Papers of the United States, Vol. VI: The Territory of Mississippi, 1809–1817 Continued*, ed. Clarence E. Carter (Washington, DC: United States Government Printing Office, 1938), 111; Records of the Bureau of the Census, *1850 Census: Seventh Census of the United States* (National Archives Microfilm Publication M432, 1009 rolls, Record Group 29), John Bankhead, Marion County, Alabama, 1850.
13. "Jacob; age 17 years, 6 months; Servant of John Bankhead; Deceased, April 7, 1847; Disease, Winter fevur; Birthplace, Monroe Cº Missipi; Time, Oct 1829; Grave 126." Sexton's Records, Cutler's Park and Winter Quarters, LR 6359 24, CHL; Wellsville History Committee, *Windows of Wellsville, 1856–1984* (Providence, UT: Wellsville History Committee, 1985), 51; "The Recent Murder," *Daily Union Vedette* (Camp Douglas, UT), December 13, 1866.
14. Thomas Bullock, 1847–1848 Emigration List, Nauvoo City Court Docket Book, February 1844–May 1845, MS 3441, 33, CHL.
15. "Another Pioneer Laid at Rest," *Logan Journal*; see also, "Nancy Bankhead," *Logan Journal*, May 1, 1909.

16. John H. Bankhead, Utah Territory Slave Schedule [draft], Great Salt Lake County, 1851 [1851].
17. Records of the Bureau of the Census, *1860 Census: Eighth Census of the United States* (National Archives Microfilm Publication M653, Utah Territory Slave Schedule, Record Group 29), Geo Bankhead, Great Salt Lake County, 1860.
18. Records of the Bureau of the Census, *1860 Census: Eighth Census of the United States* (National Archives Microfilm Publication M653, Record Group 29), Jno H. Bankhead, Cache County, Utah Territory, 1860; Charles W. Nibley and Preston Nibley, "Reminiscences of Charles W. Nibley," *Improvement Era* 37, no. 10 (October 1934): 598, https://archive.org/details/improvementera3710unse.
19. DeEtta Demaratus, *The Force of a Feather: The Search for a Lost Story of Slavery and Freedom* (Salt Lake City, UT: University of Utah Press, 2002), 30–36.
20. Carter, *Negro Pioneer*, 4.
21. Alvaretta K. Register, *State Census of North Carolina, 1784–1787* (Baltimore, MD: Genealogical Publishing Co., 2001), 139; Records of the Bureau of the Census, *1790 Census: First Census of the United States* (National Archives Microfilm Publication M637, 12 rolls, Record Group 29), William Love, Richmond County, North Carolina, 1790.
22. Samuel Flake Will, 1802, Anson County, *North Carolina, Wills and Probate Records*.
23. Jurden Flake Will, 1843, Anson County, *North Carolina, Wills and Probate Records*; Thomas G. Flake Will, 1850, Anson County, *North Carolina, Wills and Probate Records*.
24. James Boone, Remarks, "Tribute to the Life of James M. Flake, 1859–1946," CR 712 2, box 73, folder 15, 14, CHL. As of December 2018, the genealogical database FSFT showed Green Flake as the son of Jordan Flake and "Mrs. Jordan Flake." "Green Flake," FSFT, accessed February 15, 2019, https://www.familysearch.org/tree/person/details/KWVP-Q8J.
25. William Love Probate, 1792–1845, Richmond County, *North Carolina, Wills and Probate Records*.
26. R[ichmond] J Love, 1841, Thos J Love, 1842, Richmond Love, 1842, James M Flake, 1843, Jas M Flake, 1844, Richd Love, 1844, Jas M Flake, 1845, R J Love, 1845, R Loves Est., 1846, Agustus Love, 1846, Kemper County Tax Rolls 1841–1852, Mississippi Department of Archives and History, *Various Records*.
27. Carter, *Negro Pioneer*, 4.
28. The North Carolina Supreme Court requested more information before rendering a decision, and the case does not include a record of the final disposition of the enslaved people. Erasmus Love v. Richmond Love, 38 N.C. 104, 85 (N.C. 1843); Osmer D. Flake, *William J. Flake: Pioneer-Colonizer* (Printed by author, 1948), 21–22.
29. No law appears to have superseded An Act Respecting Slaves (1805), which left manumission to the state legislature with payment of a security. Hurd, *Law of Freedom and Bondage*, 2:143. Legislative books do not show manumissions. See, for example, *Laws of the State of Mississippi, Passed at a Regular Biennial Session of the Legislature, Held in the City of Jackson in January, February and March, A. D. 1846* (Jackson, MS: C. M. Price and G. R. Fall, 1846); Carter, *Negro Pioneer*, 4.

CHAPTER 2: SOUTHERN ORIGINS: TENNESSEE, MISSOURI, AND KENTUCKY

1. John H. Redd to Druzilla Holt Pearson (Thompson), December 27, 1848. MS 3663, CHL, Rutherford County, TN.
2. "Redd Family History Y-DNA Project," *Family Tree DNA*, https://www.familytreedna .com/groups/reddfamilyhistoryydnaproject/about; Reiter, "Redd Slave Histories," 122. For explanation of "my family both white and black," see Fox-Genovese, *Within the Plantation Household*, 101.
3. "Samuel Majors exhibited ten wolf scalps in open court and proved to the satisfaction of the court (Four justices being present) that he killed them within the limits of Weakley County." David "Davy" Crockett is occasionally mentioned in court records alongside the Jolley family. July 13, 1830, Weakley Minutes, 1827–1835, 1:185, A:23–31, Tennessee County Courthouses, *Tennessee, Probate Court Books, 1795–1927*, FSFT, https://www.familysearch.org/search/collection/1909088; *Index to the Compiled Military Service Records for the Volunteer Soldiers Who Served During the War of 1812* (National Archives Microfilm Publication M602); North Carolina Adjutant-General, *Muster Rolls of the Soldiers of the War of 1812* (Raleigh, NC: Times Office, 1851), 88.
4. Gwynn, *Records of Onslow County*, 1:446.
5. Gwynn, *Records of Onslow County*, 1:540.
6. "John H. Redd, attorney for Anson Hancock of Gadsden County, Florida, sold for 400 dollars paid by Richard Collins, a negro named Elias, formerly the property of Benjm. Farnell, deceased, first sold by his excrs. To William Hancock and then transferred to Anson Hancock. May, 1832. Tests: B. J. Pollard." Gwynn, *Records of Onslow County*, 2:1217, 1220.
7. "James Williams to Benjamin Williams, Sr., for 250 pounds sold three negroes, Lucy, Lancy, and boy Cupid, horses and furniture. Tests: John Hatch, Edward Young." September 21, 1796, Gwynn, *Records of Onslow County*, 1:480.
8. Zebedee Hancock Probate, 1824, Onslow County, *North Carolina, Wills and Probate Records*.
9. Anson Hancock Will, 1860, Franklin County, Florida County, District, and Probate Courts, *Florida, Wills and Probate Records, 1810–1974*, Ancestry.com, https://www .ancestry.com/search/collections/8993; Records of the Bureau of the Census, *1860 Census: Eighth Census of the United States* (National Archives Microfilm Publication M653, Record Group 29), Hellen Hancock, Colorado County, Texas, 1860; William Hancock Probate, 1854, Onslow County, North Carolina State Archives, North Carolina Estate Files, 1663–1979, FSFT, https://www.familysearch.org/search/collection/1911121.
10. Roy W. Copeland, "The Nomenclature of Enslaved Africans as Real Property or Chattels Personal: Legal Fiction, Judicial Interpretation, Legislative Designation, or Was a Slave a Slave by Any Other Name," *Journal of Black Studies* 40, no. 5 (2010): 950, https://www.jstor.org/stable/40648615.
11. William Blackstone, et al., *Commentaries on the Laws of England* (New York: E. Duyckinck, G. Long, Collins & Hannay, 1827), 1:343.
12. James M. Lyon v. John Knott Et Ux., "Mississippi Court of Appeals, October Term, 1853," *American Law Register (1852–1891)* 2, no. 10 (August 1854): 604–18, https://www .jstor.org/stable/3302032; George L. Haskins, "Curtesy in the United States," *University

of Pennsylvania Law Review 196 (1951): 196–223, https://scholarship.law.upenn.edu/penn_law_review/vol100/iss2/3.

13. For a detailed treatment, see Stephanie E. Jones-Rogers, *They Were Her Property: White Women as Slave Owners in the American South* (New Haven, CT: Yale University Press, 2019).
14. Oliver L. Barbour and Ebenezer B. Harrington, *An Analytical Digest of the Equity Cases Decided in the Courts of the Several States, and of the United States, from the Earliest Period* (Springfield, MA: Merriam, 1837), 1:219–20, 242, https://catalog.hathitrust.org/Record/008595509.
15. Gwynn, *Records of Onslow County*, 2:1225.
16. Division of John H. Redd's Property, c. 1858, folder 8, Farozine R. Bryner Collection, 1847–1956, MS 8865, CHL.
17. Carter, *Negro Pioneer*, 25.
18. Hurd, *Law of Freedom and Bondage*, 2:90–94.
19. A graduate research assistant, Beth Cavanaugh, found no manumission records for the Redds. Beth Cavanaugh, Rutherford County (TN) Archives, email message to author, December 8, 2014.
20. Hurd, *Law of Freedom and Bondage*, 2:212.
21. Daughters of Utah Pioneers and Davis County Company, *East of Antelope Island: History of the First Fifty Years of Davis County* (Bountiful, UT: Carr Printing Company, 1948), 154.
22. Hurd, *Law of Freedom and Bondage*, 1:42; Morris, *Southern Slavery*, 193–96.
23. See Jim Downs, *Sick from Freedom: African-American Illness and Suffering during the Civil War and Reconstruction* (Oxford: Oxford University Press, 2012).
24. Littleton Petillo to Reuben Perkins and wife, August 10, 1808, Lincoln County (NC) Court of Pleas and Quarter Sessions, January Term, 1809, *Minutes, 1806–1813*, North Carolina Department of Archives and History, "North Carolina, Civil Action Court Papers, 1712–1970," FSFT, https://www.familysearch.org/search/collection/1930242; Eugene H. Perkins, *The First Mormon Perkins Families: Progenitors and Utah Pioneers of 1847–1852; a Contemporary History of the Ute Perkins Line* (privately printed, 2008), 86.
25. Mary Ann James, November 16, 1917, Salt Lake City, death certificate 1703061, Utah Department of Health, Office of Vital Records and Statistics, Utah State Archives, Death Certificates, Series 81448, USHS; "Record of Baptisms for the Dead for the Seed of Cain," (Salt Lake City, Utah: Endowment House, September 3, 1875), microfilm 255498, FHL.
26. Records of the Bureau of the Census, *1830 Census: Fifth Census of the United States* (National Archives Microfilm Publication M19, 201 rolls, Record Group 29), Reuben Perkins, Jackson County, Tennessee, 1830; Reuben Perkins, Early Tax Lists of Tennessee, 1836, 67–69, Tennessee State Library and Archives, Tennessee, Early Tax List Records, 1783–1895, Ancestry.com, https://www.ancestry.com/search/collections/2883.
27. Records of the Bureau of the Census, *1840 Census: Sixth Census of the United States* (National Archives Microfilm Publication M704, 580 rolls, Record Group 29), Reuben Perkins, Wilson G. Perkins, and John H, Perkins, Marion Township, Livingston County, Missouri, 1840; Henrietta Bankhead, "Interview with Florence

Lawrence"(Helen Z. Papanikolas papers, 1954–2001, MS 471), Marriott Library Special Collections, University of Utah, November 22, 1977, 24; see also Mary Lucile Bankhead, interview with Alan Cherry (CRC-P2, transcript, LDS Afro-American Oral History Project), Charles Redd Center for Western Studies, Brigham Young University, Provo, Utah, April 11, 1985.

28. Henrietta Bankhead, interview with Florence Lawrence (Helen Z. Papanikolas Papers, 1954–2001, MS 471), Marriott Library Special Collections, University of Utah, November 22, 1977, 24.
29. "Ben [Perkins] is Unlucky," *Anaconda Standard* (Anaconda, MT), January 18, 1898.
30. Caroline Jackson, October 18, 1904, Ogden, death certificate 0403216, Utah Department of Health, USHS.
31. David Lewis and Juanita Brooks, "Excerpt from the Journal of David Lewis," typescript (copy in possession of author, n.d.), 3; David Lewis, Autobiography, 1854, microform, anonymous holograph copy of original, MSS MFilm 00157, Huntington Library, San Marino, California.
32. "Died [David Lewis]," *Deseret News*, September 26, 1855; William G. Hartley, *Kentucky Converts and Utah Pioneers: The Story of Five Brothers* (Salt Lake City, UT: Lewis Brothers Family Organization, 2014), 86, PDF e-book; Records of the Bureau of the Census, *1850 Census: Seventh Census of the United States* (National Archives Microfilm Publication M432, 1009 rolls, Record Group 29), Solomon Trail, Simpson County, Kentucky Slave Schedule, 1850; Duritha Lewis, Slave Registration, August 4, 1858, Salt Lake County Probate Court Case Files, Series 373, box 5, folder 11, USHS.
33. Captain David Lewis's Company Report, August 22, 1851, Brigham Young Office Emigrating Companies Reports, 1850–1862, box 1, CR 1234 5, CHL.

CHAPTER 3: EXODUS AND ESCAPE

1. The 1850 census slave schedule listed a thirty-year-old man, a twenty-six-year-old woman, and another woman and man both aged eighteen. The older woman does not match the age later given for Nancy Lines Bankhead Smith. If the description of the escape is accurate, the two children would have been younger than four years old. Records of the Bureau of the Census, *1850 Census: Seventh Census of the United States* (National Archives Microfilm Publication M432, 1009 rolls, Record Group 29), William T. Dennis, Pontotoc County, Mississippi Slave Schedule, 1850.
2. As recorded in the Mississippi chapter, the local courthouse burned, so there are no Bankhead estate records. Records of the Bureau of the Census, *1830 Census: Fifth Census of the United States* (National Archives Microfilm Publication M19, 201 rolls, Record Group 29), George Bankhead, Marion County, Alabama, 1830; Anonymous, "The Life History of William Taylor Dennis and His Wife Talitha Cumi Bankhead" (digital manuscript, copy in possession of author, n.d.); Nancy Bankhead, October 24, 1877, Spanish Fork (UT) Cemetery Records, microfilm 1654570, FHL; Records of the Bureau of the Census, *1840 Census: Sixth Census of the United States* (National Archives Microfilm Publication M704, 580 rolls, Record Group 29), William T. Dennis, Pontotoc County, Mississippi, 1840.
3. Talitha's brother William wrote in his Confederate Application for Presidential Pardon that he was in poor health and unable to perform manual labor. He said, "The

freeing of the negros and the general depression of private property and uncertainty of the future condition of this section of country has left no criterion upon which to make a correct estimate of the value of your petitioners estate." Records of the Bureau of the Census, *1860 Census: Eighth Census of the United States* (National Archives Microfilm Publication M653, Record Group 29), William G. Bankhead, Noxubee County, Mississippi Slave Schedule, 1860; William Bankhead, *Case Files of Applications from Former Confederates for Presidential Pardons, 1865–1867*, M1003, Records of the Adjutant General's Office, 1780s–1917, Record Group 94.

4. Several people in the Upper Midwest or Canada generally match the description of the five members of the Dennis household, but none so closely as to confirm a connection. The Tabor townspeople named in the accounts of the escape are Massachusetts native Samuel Holten Adams (1823–1910), English immigrant John Hallam (1832–1896), Massachusetts native James Kasson Gaston (1832–1891), New York native and educator George Belcher Gaston (1814–1873), New York native Charles Wesley "Hundred Weight" Tolles (1823–1923), Connecticut native Cephas Case (1783–), a man remembered as "Irish Henry," and William L. Clark, probably a Virginia native from nearby Fremont City. John Todd, *Early Settlement and Growth of Western Iowa or Reminiscences* (Des Moines: Historical Department of Iowa, 1906), 134–37; Dennis L. Lythgoe, "Negro Slavery in Utah" (master's thesis, University of Utah, 1966), 32–33, https://collections.lib.utah.edu/details?id=1602212; Catherine Grace Barbour Farquhar, "Tabor and Tabor College," *Iowa Journal of History and Politics* 41, no. 4 (October 1943): 358–59, https://archive.org/details/iowajournalofhisoostat; Mary Ellen Snodgrass, *The Underground Railroad: An Encyclopedia of People, Places, and Operations* (Armonk, NY: M.E. Sharpe, 2008), 244; Louis T. Jones, *The Quakers of Iowa* (Iowa City: State Historical Society of Iowa, 1914), 187–202.

5. Anonymous, "Life History of William Taylor Dennis and His Wife Talitha Cumi Bankhead."

6. "Slavery in Utah," *Broad Ax* (Salt Lake City, UT), March 25, 1899.

7. John Brown, Journal, box 1, folder 1, image 60, MS 1636, Reminiscences and Journals, 1843–1896, CHL.

8. Green and Martha's granddaughter later remembered, "Hark Lay & Oscar Crosby were Lucinda Violate Stevens great Uncles." The granddaughter did not differentiate between the use of "uncle" as an honorific or a description of a biological relationship. Notes from Udell Home.

9. Green Flake and Utah Semi-Centennial Commission, *The Book of the Pioneers* (Salt Lake City: Utah Semi-Centennial Commission, 1897), 1:242, USHS.

10. Thomas Bullock, May 7, 1847, April–June 1847, Journals, MS 1385, CHL.

11. The advanced company consisted of "O.P. Rockwell, Jack Redding<en>, Nathaniel Fairbanks, Joseph Egbert, John S. Freeman, Marcus B. Thorpe, Robert Crow, Ben B. Crow, John Crow, W<alter>. H. Crow, Walter Crow, G<eorge>. W. Therlkill, James Chesney, Lewis B. Meyers, John Brown, Shadrach Roundy, Hans C. Hanson, Levi Jackman, Lyman Curtis, David Powell, Oscar Crosby, Hark Lay, Joseph Mathews, Gilbard Summe, Green Flake, John S. Gleason, Charles Burke, Norman Taylor, A<lexander>. P. Chessley, Seth Taft, Horace Thornton, Stephen Kelsey, James Stewart, Robert Thomas, C<harles> D. Burnham, John S. Eldredge, Elijah Newman,

Francis Boggs, Levi N. Kendall, [and] David Grant." Thomas Bullock, July 13, 1849, June–September 1847, Journals.

12. "This afternoon two Pioneers called at the News in the persons of Green Flake, a colored man who was one of the original Pioneers and who lived in Salt Lake for forty-nine years, and who last year moved to Idaho, and James T. S. Allred of Spring City, Utah. The former is 70 years of age and claims to have driven the first wagon that entered Emigration canyon." "More Pioneers," *Deseret News*, July 19, 1897; Thomas Bullock's journal has a date of July 22 for the arrival of the advance company, but some traveled ahead, and Green Flake later mentioned the date of July 21. "Some Jubilee Visitors," *Salt Lake Tribune* (Salt Lake City, UT), July 26, 1897; Thomas Bullock, July 22, 1849, June–September 1847, Journals.

13. Thomas Bullock, "Military Organization," September–October 1847, Journals, MS 1385, CHL.

14. For the earliest migration, an 1846–1847 Mississippi company may have taken several enslaved people to the Great Salt Lake Valley, but there is no documentation of them in the company or the valley. The Pioneer Database has identified ninety-one members of the company, but Howard Egan's account suggests additional members. Howard Egan, *Pioneering the West 1846 to 1878: Major Howard Egan's Diary*, ed., William M. Egan (Richmond, UT: Howard R. Egan Estate, 1917), 64. The Barnett household went to the Great Salt Lake Valley in either 1848 or 1849, but most family memories suggest 1849. (See the Camplin (Barnett) biography in Part 2.) Among the 1849 migration, there is not adequate information about the birth dates of some of the Perkins family, including Ephraim. "Perkins, Franklin [sic]," in Frank E. Esshom, *Pioneers and Prominent Men of Utah* (Salt Lake City, UT: Utah Pioneers Book Publishing Company, 1913), 1096. In the 1857 migration, Texans Thomas and Clarkey Carpenter Box and Elizabeth Carter Flaherty Whitmore may have taken enslaved people to Utah Territory, but they may have hired the enslaved women shown in the 1860 census in Utah Territory. In 1861, Gobo Fango's place in this list is based on later reminiscences that the Talbot family smuggled him to Utah Territory and illegally sold or hired him out there, rather than independent documentation.

15. Homer Duncan, Autobiographical Sketch, c. 1900, typescript of holograph, MS 21280, CHL.

16. Margaret Gay Judd Clawson, Reminiscences, c. 1904–1911, 57 [image 131], MS 3712, CHL.

17. The wagon roster is vague, but the "colored woman" is probably Esther, since it is unlikely that there were other Black women in the wagon train. Emily L. Snyder Thompson, "History of Emily Lydia Snyder Thompson," typescript (n.d.), FSFT, https://www.familysearch.org/photos/artifacts/22922719.

18. Wilson remembered the men he worked for as "Bridget" and "Mr. Smart." They were Dr. Isaac M. Ridge (1825–1907) and Ridge's father-in-law Thomas A. Smart (1806–1879). *The History of Jackson County, Missouri* (Kansas City, MO: Union Historical Company, 1881), 113, 193–94, 776, 833, 845; "Isaac M. Ridge, M.D.," in *A Memorial and Biographical Record of Kansas City and Jackson County, Mo.* (Chicago: Lewis Publishing, 1896), 19–24. James T. Wilson, "The Life of James Thomas Wilson,"

c. 1889, typescript edited by Cordelia D. W. Hortin, William W. Hortin, and Frances G. Hortin, 1992, 30–32, Family Search Digital Library.
19. Wilson, "Life of James Thomas Wilson."
20. William C. Jones, ed., *The Revised Statutes of the State of Missouri* (St. Louis, MO: J. W. Dougherty, 1845), 777, 1016–17.
21. Wilson, "Life of James Thomas Wilson."
22. Hosea B. Horn, "History of Davis County, Iowa, Chapter II," *The Annals of Iowa* 10, no. 2 (1865): 445–47.

CHAPTER 4: THE SETTLEMENT OF UTAH

1. Hubert H. Bancroft, *History of Utah, 1540–1886* (San Francisco: History Company, 1889), 258–59, 266.
2. "White Girls Served Negroes," *Butler Weekly Times* (Butler, MO), February 19, 1903. See, also, "Reed Smoot Dined Negroes and There is a Row in Utah Similar to That Following Roosevelt's Entertainment of a Distinguished Colored Guest," *Tucson Citizen* (Tucson, AZ), February 17, 1903; "Teddy's and Hanna's Rival. Smoot Bids Fair to Eclipse Them—Dines Negroes at Banquet," *New York Daily People* (New York, NY), February 14, 1903.
3. "The Veterans' Reunion," *Salt Lake Herald*, August 21, 1894; C. Elliott Berlin, "Abraham Owen Smoot, Pioneer Mormon Leader" (master's thesis, Brigham Young University, 1955), https://scholarsarchive.byu.edu/etd/4523.
4. Carter, *Negro Pioneer*, 25.
5. Augustus Koch, *Bird's Eye View of Salt Lake City, Utah Territory 1870* (Chicago: Chicago Lithographing Co., 1870, Library of Congress Geography and Map Division), https://www.loc.gov/resource/g4344s.pm009280/?r=0.056,0,1.389,0.925,0.
6. "Later from Salt Lake," *Sacramento Daily Union*, May 6, 1859; Hosea Stout, *On the Mormon Frontier: The Diary of Hosea Stout, 1844–1861*, ed. Juanita Brooks (Salt Lake City: University of Utah Press and Utah State Historical Society 1964), 2:699.
7. "Thomas Bankhed, Nathan B, Harks wife, Hammon, Alexander." Unknown to Brigham Young, c. 1851–1854, Ecclesiastical Files, 1841–1877, Files Relating to Marriage and Other Ordinances, Letters, 1845–1854, box 64, folder 1, Office Files.
8. Bankhead, interview with Lawrence.
9. Chad M. Orton, "The Martin Handcart Company at the Sweetwater: Another Look," *BYU Studies* 45, no. 3 (2006): 4–37, https://scholarsarchive.byu.edu/byusq/vol45/iss3/1; LeRoy R. Hafen and Ann W. Hafen, *Handcarts to Zion: The Story of a Unique Western Migration, 1856–1860* (Glendale, CA: A.H. Clark Co, 1960); and David Roberts, *Devil's Gate: Brigham Young and the Great Mormon Handcart Tragedy* (New York: Simon & Schuster, 2008).
10. Daniel W. Jones, *Forty Years Among the Indians* (Salt Lake City, UT: Juvenile Instructor Office, 1890), 63.
11. For more on Thomas Bankhead Coleman, see his biographical entry.
12. "Shooting Affair," *Valley Tan*, April 19, 1859; "Interesting from Utah," *New York Times* (New York, NY), June 17, 1859; David H. Schenk, "Freedmen with Firearms: White Terrorism and Black Disarmament During Reconstruction," *The Gettysburg College*

Journal of the Civil War Era 4, Article 4 (2014): 9–44, https://cupola.gettysburg.edu/gcjcwe/vol4/iss1/4.
13. Editorial, *Deseret News*, April 20, 1859.
14. Stout, *Mormon Frontier*, 2:695; United States v. Colburn (1859), Salt Lake County Probate Court Case Files, Series 373, box 6, folder 12, USHS; "Third Judicial District Court," *Deseret News*, September 21, 1859.
15. The county jail contained one inmate and the state penitentiary contained eight inmates during the census, none of them Coleman or two other men sentenced to a year of hard labor. "Third Judicial District Court," *Deseret News*, September 21, 1859; Records of the Bureau of the Census, *1860 Census: Eighth Census of the United States* (National Archives Microfilm Publication M653, Record Group 29), County Jail, Great Salt Lake County, Utah Territory, 1860; Records of the Bureau of the Census, *1860 Census: Eighth Census of the United States* (National Archives Microfilm Publication M653, Record Group 29), Penitentiary, Warden Alexander McRae, Great Salt Lake County, Utah Territory, 1860; Records of the Bureau of the Census, *1860 Census: Eighth Census of the United States* (National Archives Microfilm Publication M653, Utah Territory Slave Schedule, Record Group 29), J. & I. Harper, Great Salt Lake County, 1860.
16. "The Killing of Thos. Coleman Monday Night," *Daily Union Vedette*, December 15, 1866.
17. "Murder," *Daily Union Vedette*, December 12, 1866.
18. "The Recent Murder," *Daily Union Vedette*, December 13, 1866.
19. "The Killing of Thos. Coleman Monday Night."
20. Kenneth L. Cannon II, "'Mountain Common Law': The Extralegal Punishment of Seducers in Early Utah," *Utah Historical Quarterly* 51, no. 4 (Fall 1983): 308–27, https://www.jstor.org/stable/45061124; Connell O'Donovan, "'Let This Be a Warning to All Niggers': The Life and Murder of Thomas Coleman in Theocratic Utah," *Website of Connell O'Donovan*, June 2008, www.connellodonovan.com/coleman_bio.pdf.
21. Thomas Coleman, December 11, 1866, grave B_4_Pauper_216, Salt Lake City Cemetery, Salt Lake City, Utah Division of State History, *Cemeteries and Burials* (Salt Lake City: Utah Department of Heritage & Arts, 2014), https://utahdcc.secure.force.com/burials.
22. Interview with John Z. Brown, cited in Jack Beller, "Negro Slaves in Utah," *Utah Historical Quarterly* 2, no. 4 (October 1929): 124, https://www.jstor.org/stable/45057482.
23. J. M. Flake to Amasa Lyman, September 30, 1849, box 3, folder 8, Lyman Collection.
24. George Q. Cannon, *Journal of George Q. Cannon* (The Church of Jesus Christ of Latter-day Saints, Salt Lake City, UT: Church Historian's Press, October 15, 1849), https://churchhistorianspress.org/george-q-cannon; C. C. Rich Journal, November 15, 1849, cited in November 1849, n28, *Journal of George Q. Cannon*; Amasa Lyman's statement, Agnes Flake account, October 1, 1850, Gold Dust Accounts (Church Mint), 1848–1851, box 83, Office Files; Carter, *Negro Pioneer*, 21; Ron Freeman, "James Madison Flake (1815–1850)" (unpublished manuscript, 2011), 35–36, 42, 55–56, FSFT, https://familysearch.org/photos/artifacts/3394048.
25. "2nd Oldest Inhabitant Interview," *Logan Republican* (Logan, UT), July 22, 1908.

26. The Smith, Flake, Crosby, Thomas, and Lay households made 17 percent of the butter and 48 percent of the cheese reported by forty-nine households later relocating to California. George Bankhead was not in the agricultural schedule, so his brother may have cared for his property while he was in California. Robert M. Smith, Agnes Flake, William Crosby, Daniel M. Thomas, William Lay, Utah County; John Brown, Abraham Smoot, John H. Bankhead, Great Salt Lake County; Joseph Robinson, Iron County; Records of the Bureau of the Census, *1850 Census: Seventh Census of the United States* (National Archives Microfilm Publication M432, 1009 rolls, Utah Territory Productions of Agriculture, MS 2672, CHL, Record Group 29), Reuben Perkins, Davis County, 1850 [1851].
27. Thomas G. Alexander, "Brigham Young and the Transformation of Utah Wilderness, 1847–58," *Journal of Mormon History* 41, no. 1 (January 2015): 103–24, https://www.jstor.org/stable/10.5406/jmormhist.41.1.103.
28. William Crosby to Amasa Lyman, April 15, 1850, Incoming Letters, 1850–1852, box 3, folder 9, Lyman Collection.
29. The list of free Black residents in Table 2 is from Utah County, Great Salt Lake County, 1850 [1851] Utah Territorial Census, MS 2672, CHL.
30. Report of Mississippi Co^y, May 23, 1848, box 2, MS 14290, Camp of Israel Schedules and Reports, CHL.
31. Benjamin Mathews to Brigham Young, March 31, 1849, box 21, folder 16, Office Files.
32. Kentucky native William S. Hopper, subsequently of California. Francis McKown to Brigham Young, March 31, 1849, box 21, folder 16, Office Files.
33. Records of the Bureau of the Census, *1860 Census: Eighth Census of the United States* (National Archives Microfilm Publication M653, Mississippi Slave Schedule, Record Group 29), Frank McKown, Itawamba County, 1860.
34. Wilford Woodruff to Thomas L. Kane, November 27, 1849, box 16, folder 28, MSS 792, Thomas L. Kane Collection, HBLL.
35. William Taylor Dennis, Deed of Consecration, February 7, 1857, Records of Utah County (1851–1864), F:111–112, MSS 3905, HBLL; John Brown, Deed of Consecration, February 3, 1857, Records of Utah County (1851–1864), F:81–82, 111, MSS 3905, HBLL.
36. Abraham Smoot, *Utah Territory Slave Schedule* [draft], Great Salt Lake County, 1850 [1851] Census.
37. Salt Lake City Probate Court, A. O. Smoot's Bill of Sale of Negro To Thos. S. Williams, 1856, Slave Registrations, Salt Lake County Probate Court Case Files, Series 373, box 4, folder 26, USHS.
38. For more on these conflicts, see Polly Aird, "'You Nasty Apostates, Clear Out': Reasons for Disaffection in the Late 1850s," *Journal of Mormon History* 30, no. 2 (Fall 2004): 129–207, https://www.jstor.org/stable/23289370.
39. Mary Emma Rolf to R. A. Moore, December 24, 1891, Thomas S. Williams Probate, Third District Court Probate Case Files, Series 1621, case 67, USHS.
40. Sections 5, 6, 9, An Act in Relation to Service, Utah Territorial Legislature (1852).
41. "Died [David Lewis]," *Deseret News*, September 26, 1855; Brown, *Journal of the Southern Indian Mission*, 111.
42. David Lewis Probate, Third District Court Probate Case Files, Series 1621, box 1, folder 41, case 39, 14–15, USHS.
43. Duritha Lewis, Slave Registration, August 4, 1858, Salt Lake County Probate Court Case Files, Series 373, box 5, folder 11, USHS.

44. Deed of Sale, as reproduced in Kate B. Carter, *The Negro Pioneer* (Salt Lake City: Daughters of Utah Pioneers, 1965), 42–43; Williams Probate, Series 1621, case 67, USHS.
45. "Shooting Affair," *Valley Tan*, April 19, 1859. "Cuffy" was originally a personal name, but by the nineteenth century, it became a derogatory term for a Black man. Later writers repeated the use of the term for Judge William W. Drummond's enslaved servant Cato, probably not realizing it was a pejorative. *Oxford English Dictionary*, s.v. "Cuffee, Cuffy, n.," accessed February 9, 2021, https://oed.com; Catherine V. Waite, *The Mormon Prophet and His Harem* (Cambridge, MA: Riverside Press, 1866), 38.
46. Hooper & Williams v. Belt, Coleman and Stoddard (1859), Salt Lake County Probate Court Case Files, Series 373, box 5, folder 90, USHS.
47. "Third Judicial District Court," *Deseret News*, August 10, 1859.
48. The current or former enslavers on the jury were John M. Moody, Williams Camp, Edward W. East, and Thomas Box. "Third Judicial District Court," *Deseret News*, August 10, 1859; "Third Judicial District Court," *Deseret News*, August 24, 1859; Stout, *Mormon Frontier*, 2:701.
49. Williams Probate, Series 1621, case 63, USHS; "More Murders on the Mohave," *Los Angeles Star*, March 31, 1860; "Mormon Policy," *Los Angeles Star*, March 31, 1860; "Murders on The Mohave by Indians," *Sacramento Daily Union*, April 2, 1860; "The Murder of Williams," *Deseret News*, April 25, 1860. Latter-day Saint freighters feared the Indigenous people in the area and normally never separated into smaller groups, but Williams and Jackman ignored this precaution. Thaddeus S. Kenderdine, *A California Tramp: Among the Mormon Settlements, Along the Desert Border, On the Great Sandy Deseret, and From the Kingston Springs to San Bernardino* (Newtown, PA: Globe Printing House, 1888), 120–83.
50. Lawyer Seth M. Blair (1819–1875) was a business partner of Thomas S. Williams. He does not appear to have enslaved people, but his parents did. Seth M. Blair to Elias Smith, c. 1860, Williams Probate, Series 1621, case 63, USHS; Records of the Bureau of the Census, *1860 Census: Eighth Census of the United States* (National Archives Microfilm Publication M653, Utah Territory Slave Schedule, Record Group 29), Percilla Williams and Albina Williams, Great Salt Lake County, 1860.
51. Albina Williams, Affidavit, December 31, 1861, box 49, folder 5, Office Files; "Exciting and Terrifying Occurrences," *Deseret News*, January 22, 1862; "Our Fourteen Governors," *Salt Lake Herald-Republican* (Salt Lake City, UT), January 29, 1893.
52. John W. Van Cott, *Utah Place Names: A Comprehensive Guide to the Origins of Geographic Names* (Salt Lake City: University of Utah Press, 1990), 272.
53. The list of the free Black population in Table 3 is from Carson County, Great Salt Lake County, Utah County, Utah Territory, *1860 Census*.
54. John L. Edwards, "The Move South Related by John L. Edwards," *Box Elder News* (Brigham City, UT), May 25, 1917.
55. Darren Parry (former chairman of the Northwestern Band of the Shoshone Nation), in discussion with the author, May 21, 2020.
56. Charles W. Nibley and Preston Nibley, "Reminiscences of Charles W. Nibley," *Improvement Era* 37, no. 10 (October 1934): 598, https://archive.org/details/improvementera3710unse.
57. Brigham Young to Mrs. David Lewis, January 3, 1860, box 19, folder 1, Office Files.
58. Brigham Young to Mrs. David Lewis, March 31, 1860.

59. A. O. Smoot, Great Salt Lake County, Utah Territory Slave Schedule, *1860 Census*.
60. "Drowned," *Deseret News*, June 19, 1861.
61. August 9, 1855, Margaret T. Smoot, Sketch Book, Abraham Owen Smoot Family Papers, 1836–1947, MSS 3843, Special Collections, HBLL.
62. Margaret T. Smoot, Journal, excerpted by Mindy Smoot Robbins, Margaret T. Smoot Papers, 1838–1884, A. O. Smoot Papers, MSS 896, Special Collections, HBLL.
63. "Tom a negro Belonging to Bishop Smoot 29 [Apr 1862] Inflam of chest," Utah Archives and Records Service, *Utah Death Registers, 1847–1966*, Series 21866, Ancestry.com, https://www.ancestry.com/search/collections/6967.
64. Although there appears to be no remaining documentation of Smoot hiring or purchasing Jerry or Tom, the connection comes from the movements of the two men, the elimination of other possibilities, and a positive identification by James T. Wilson. For citations, see the biographical entries for Jerry and Tom. If documentation ever existed about Alexander Bankhead's legal status after he appeared in George W. Bankhead's household in 1860, it did not make it into known government records or the Smoot papers at the Church History Library and Special Collections at Brigham Young University. Claims in Carter, *Negro Pioneer*, 24, and "Slavery in Utah," *Broad Ax*, are not definitive. Content regarding slavery is limited in the following collections: Smoot Family Papers, 1836–1947, MSS 3843, Special Collections, HBLL; A. O. Smoot Papers, 1837–1894, MSS 896, Special Collections, HBLL; Margaret Thompson McMeans Smoot, Diary, MS 5204, CHL; A. O. or Margaret Smoot letters, Office Files.

CHAPTER 5: GOING TO CALIFORNIA

1. The account is not in Brown's holograph diary, so John Z. Brown presumably added it from one of Brown's many letters home. Brown, *Autobiography*, 274; John Brown, Journal, box 1, folder 4, December 1, 1867, images 128–29, MS 1636, Reminiscences and Journals, CHL.
2. Brigham Young, Heber C. Kimball, and Willard Richards to Amasa Lyman and Charles C. Rich, March 17, 1851, Incoming Letters, 1850–1852, box 3, folder 9, Lyman Collection.
3. William Crosby, *Utah Territory Slave Schedule* [draft], Utah County, Great Salt Lake County, 1850[1851].
4. William Crosby to Brigham Young, c. March 12, 1851.
5. January 1851, Great Salt Lake County, Court Papers, MS 2490, CHL.
6. Brigham Young to William Crosby, March 12, 1851.
7. William Crosby, Agnes Flake, Utah County, Great Salt Lake County; Brigham Young, Utah Territory Slave Schedule [draft], Great Salt Lake County, 1850 [1851]; Records of the Bureau of the Census, *1850 Census: Seventh Census of the United States* (National Archives Microfilm Publication M432, 1009 rolls, Utah Territory Schedule of Population, Record Group 29), Green Flake, Vilate Crosby, and Rose Crosby, Great Salt Lake County, 1850.
8. March 26, 1851, vol. 14, CR 100 1, Historical Department Office Journal, 1844–2012, CHL.
9. "Fort San Bernardino," map, *City of San Bernardino* (website), accessed March 1, 2017, http://www.ci.san-bernardino.ca.us/about/history/fort_san_bernardino.asp.

10. List of Loyalists in San Bernardino, box 3, folder 18, Charles C. Rich Collection, MS 889, CHL (hereafter Rich Collection).
11. San Bernardino Branch Tithing Record, 1853–1857, LR 1594 23, 46, CHL; June 8, 1852, Trustee-in-Trust Tithing and Donation Records; Edward Leo Lyman, *San Bernardino: The Rise and Fall of a California Community* (Salt Lake City, UT: Signature Books, 1996), 67; Amasa Lyman, Diary, July 13, 1854, Lyman Collection.
12. George W. Beattie and Helen P. Beattie, *Heritage of the Valley: San Bernardino's First Century* (Oakland, CA: Biobooks, 1951), 186, quoted in Byron R. Skinner, *Black Origins in the Inland Empire*, Heritage Tales, Sixth Annual Publication of the City of San Bernardino Historical and Pioneer Society (San Bernardino, CA: City of San Bernardino Historical and Pioneer Society, 1983), 28; "Mormon Colony in Sharp Contrast to Mother Lode," *San Bernardino County Sun* (San Bernardino, CA), September 30, 1951; Harriet A. Jacobs, *Incidents in the Life of a Slave Girl*, ed. L. Maria Child (Boston: Published for the Author, 1861), 67.
13. Dick, Los Angeles County, *1852 California Census*. John S. Minter was from Kentucky by way of Missouri. His obituary reported that he went west in one of John C. Frémont's expeditions, but he does not appear in literature about the expeditions. "Death of John Minter: A Member of Fremont's First Expedition to California," *San Diego Union* (San Diego, CA), January 31, 1895.
14. Lyman, *San Bernardino*, 290–91n49; Records of the Bureau of the Census, *1860 Census: Eighth Census of the United States* (National Archives Microfilm Publication M653, Record Group 29), Richard and Harriet Jackson, Los Angeles County, California, 1860.
15. For why the San Bernardino settlers would have paid Dick's enslaver, see Smith, *Freedom's Frontier*. David Seely to Amasa M. Lyman and C. C. Rich, February 8, 1853, Correspondence, 1841–1877, box 3, folder 11, Lyman Collection; Bond for The Delevy [sic] of Richard "Nigger Dick," Business Papers, box 3, folder 8, Rich Collection; Lyman, *San Bernardino*, 290.
16. Salt Lake County Transfer Book, C, 1855–1857, box 4, folder 3; Davis County Transfer Book, 1855–1856, box 4, folder 1, 5, Consecration Deeds; Charles C. Rich Journal, May 10, 1855, box 1, folder 9, Rich Collection; Amasa Lyman, Diary, box 2, 16:5–6, Lyman Collection.
17. "Suit for Freedom," *Los Angeles Star*, February 2, 1856; "Suit for Freedom," *Daily Democratic State Journal* (Sacramento, CA), February 19, 1856; Beasley, *Negro Trail Blazers*, 88–90, 109–11. Judge Hayes had held district court in San Bernardino multiple times and knew people there. See, for example, Amasa Lyman, Diary, February 19, 1855, Lyman Collection.
18. "Coroner's Inquest—Sudden Death," *Sacramento Daily Union*, June 2, 1856.
19. Daniel M. Thomas to Lyman, Lyman Collection.
20. Smith, *Freedom's Frontier*, 127–31.
21. Delilah Beasley and Monroe Work located, transcribed, and published the court record of *In re Hannah* in 1918. Starting that year, the Los Angeles County Archives destroyed its records or transferred them to the Huntington Library and Museum of Natural History in Los Angeles. Librarians and archivists at the Huntington Library, Museum of Natural History, San Bernardino County Historical Archives, and California State Archives could not find the original case in their collections. California

State Archives, telephone conversation with the author, May 17, 2016; Morex Arai, Huntington Library, email message to author, September 20, 2016; John Cahoon, Seaver Center, Natural History Museum of Los Angeles County, telephone conversation with the author, September 9, 2016; Beasley and Work, "California Freedom Papers," 51–53. UCLA Special Collections has photographs of a copy of the case made by a court clerk in 1860. "Freedom Papers of Biddy Mason," Collection of Miriam Matthews, UCLA Library Digital Collections.

22. "Suit for Freedom," *Los Angeles Star*; "Suit for Freedom," *Daily Democratic State Journal*.
23. Benjamin Hayes to Jack Hinton, September 20, 1863, Benjamin Hayes, Scrapbook Collection, Bancroft Library, San Francisco, California, reproduction of holograph in Demaratus, *Force of a Feather*, 185–90.
24. Daniel M. Thomas to Lyman, Lyman Collection.
25. William Chandless, *A Visit to Salt Lake; Being a Journey Across the Plains, and a Residence in the Mormon Settlements at Utah* (London: Smith, Elder, and Co., 1857), 306.
26. Lyman, *San Bernardino*, 132; "Correspondence of the Star," *Los Angeles Star*, October 22, 1853.
27. William Warren to Amasa Lyman, April 3, 1856, Incoming letters, P–Y, 1856, box 4, folder 1, Lyman Collection; December 11, 1855, San Bernardino Branch Journal, 1851–1853, 1855–1877, LR 1594 22, CHL.
28. "Suit for Freedom," *Los Angeles Star*.
29. Amasa Lyman, Diary, April 26, 1854, Lyman Collection.

CHAPTER 6: GREEN FLAKE AND THE TITHING MYTH

1. George Q. Cannon, *Journal of George Q. Cannon*, October 15, 1849; Freeman, "James Madison Flake," 55–56.
2. Colleen Barry and Paul Foy, "Story of Nobelist's Past is Inconsistent with Data," *Washington Post* (Washington, DC), November 7, 2007, https://www.washingtonpost.com/wp-dyn/content/article/2007/11/06/AR2007110602209.html.
3. William Flake's biographer wrote that no one kept a record of the family. Osmer D. Flake, *William J. Flake: Pioneer-Colonizer* (Printed by author, 1948), 15–16.
4. Freeman, "James Madison Flake," 35–36, 42.
5. First 50, Reports, c. June 1848, box 2, folder 32, Camp of Israel Schedules and Reports; Records of the Bureau of the Census, *1840 Census: Sixth Census of the United States* (National Archives Microfilm Publication M704, 580 rolls, Record Group 29), Jas M Flake, Anson County, North Carolina, 1840; Records of the Bureau of the Census, *1850 Census: Seventh Census of the United States* (National Archives Microfilm Publication M432, 1009 rolls, Record Group 29), Agnes Flake, Utah County, Utah Territory, 1850; "Elizabeth Colard," *Pioneer Database*, accessed February 16, 2021, https://history.churchofjesuschrist.org/overlandtravel/pioneers/3404/elizabeth-colard.
6. Dennis L. Lythgoe included the William J. Flake biography in his master's thesis and in Dennis L. Lythgoe, "Negro Slavery in Utah," *Utah Historical Quarterly* 39, no. 1 (Winter 1971): 40–54, https://doi.org/10.2307/272985. *Negro Pioneer* included a similar but unsourced story as if it were part of a newspaper article: "One record says,

'During [the years he supposedly lived in Joseph Smith's home in Nauvoo, which he did not] Green's work was accepted as tithing.'" Carter, *Negro Pioneer*, 6. For examples of the spread of the claim see, for example, Pat Bagley, "Living History: Slaves Arrived in Utah with Brigham Young," *Salt Lake Tribune*, February 19, 2010, https://archive.sltrib.com/story.php?ref=/ci_14437472.

7. William Jordan Flake, box 37, folder 13, CR 100 18, Biographical Sketches, 1891–2013, CHL. Although he submitted an entry, Flake was not in Jenson's *Biographical Encyclopedia*. His son James is in the second volume, his son Osmer is in the third, and Green Flake is in the fourth. "James M. Flake," "Osmer D. Flake," and "Green Flake" in Andrew Jenson, *Latter-day Saint Biographical Encyclopedia* (Salt Lake City, UT: Andrew Jenson History Company and Andrew Jenson Memorial Association, 1914, 1920, 1936), 2:218, 3:372, 4:703. The tithing story had one notable detractor in the Flake family. In 1979, family historian Augusta Flake wrote, "In various journals there are reports . . . of James M. Flake having given Green to Brigham Young and one record said that he was given as a 'payment of tithing!' I can't believe that." Augusta Flake to Elizabeth DeBrouwer, February 22, 1979, San Bernardino Public Library, San Bernardino, California.

8. Notes from Udell Home.

9. The first known estate recorded in Utah Territory was Oliver Porter Davis Estate, 1850, Great Salt Lake County, Court Papers. "Adelaide Pearson v. Laura Pearson et al." in *Reports of Cases Determined*, 1875, 51:120–24.

10. For more about the inheritance and hiring out of the enslaved, see Morris, *Southern Slavery*, and Robert W. Fogel and Stanley L. Engerman, *Time on the Cross: The Economics of American Negro Slavery*, rev. ed. (New York: W. W. Norton & Company, 1995).

11. Notes from Udell Home. For prices of oxen, see, for example, "1 yoke of Oxen 100," Joseph Dunlap Consecration Deed; "Also one yoke of oxen worth one hundred dollars 100," Thurston Simpson Consecration Deed, Great Salt Lake County Transfer Book, 1855–1857, box 4, folder 3, 8, 9, Consecration Deeds.

12. Horace E. and Eliza J. Barnes Guardianship, Jackson County, May 1856, Series 1, box 2, Missouri, County, District, and Probate Courts, *Missouri, Wills and Probate Records, 1766–1988*, Ancestry.com, https://www.ancestry.com/search/collections/9071; Harrison A. Trexler, "Slavery in Missouri, 1804–1865" (PhD diss., Johns Hopkins University, 1914), 28–29, 31–33.

13. When Flake donated a span of mules, he subtracted part of the total from his cash donations, giving a different total from the amount kept in family records. October 24, November 24, 1845, April 3, April 7, 1846, Daybook D, Trustee-in-Trust Tithing Daybooks; April 6, 1846 (duplicate), September 4, 1851, Entry 484, June 8, 1852 (duplicate), Trustee-in-Trust Tithing and Donation Records; March 22, 1852, April 13, June 15, October 11, 1853, San Bernardino Branch Tithing Accounts; James M. Flake, Tithing and Donation Receipt, April 7, 1846, reproduced in Freeman, "James Madison Flake," 33.

14. Three women gave property to the church and received it immediately in return: single mother Emily S. Frink (silver watch, 1842), missionary wife Nancy Marinda Hyde (tablecloth, 1842), and widow Agness M. Smith (curtain knobs and a fur, 1842). Alex D. Smith, Church History Library, email message to author, February 18, 2016, citing *The Joseph Smith Papers*, https://josephsmithpapers.org.

15. The general labor tithing books at the Church History Library in Salt Lake City (CR 104 27 and 104 28) show that few women paid labor tithing, except for Mary Bronson Ensign (folder 1, Time Book of Tithing Hands for the Year 1850, 8), missionary wife Sarah Bradshaw Hawkins Dunn (folder 2, Labor Time Book for 1851 & 1852; folder 3, Time Book of Tithing Labor and Team Work, 1851), widow Laurany Huffaker Molen (folder 2), Nancy Martin Perkins (folder 2), and Elmira Pinkham Tufts (folder 2, April 5, 1851; folder 3). Most of the women had older sons. Some books show a tally of days and do not record which member of a household provided the labor, so even if an enslaver donated slave labor, the record would not indicate that. Other books note the identity of the laborer. However, the tithing books list few enslavers. Haden W. Church donated one day in 1853. Reuben Perkins donated a few days. One of the labor tithing books showed that Brigham Young used the labor of "7 Hands 1 day" a few weeks after the exchange of letters with William Crosby in 1851, but the "Hands" are unnamed and may or may not have included Flake. March 22, 1851, Time Book of Tithing Labor and Team Work, 1851, General Tithing Office Tithing Labor Time Books. Agnes Flake is not in Names of Persons Who Have Paid Their Tithing, 1852, box 79, folder 10, Office Files.
16. Agnes Flake Account, October 1, 1850; Amasa Lyman's Statement, box 83, folder 3, Gold Dust Accounts. The 1850 census agricultural schedule entry showed that the Flake family owned two mules, ten oxen, ten milk cows, and five other cattle, and made more than a thousand pounds of cheese and butter. Based on the amounts shown for Williams Camp and John H. Redd, who arrived in the fall of 1850, the numbers given in the schedule pertain to the actual census dates, meaning the year ending June 1, 1850, and do not include Flake's subsequent widowhood. The poverty of many of the early immigrants may have depressed the cash price for oxen, but if she sold any livestock, she may have had several hundred dollars of cash receipts. The schedule raises the question of why she would take oxen in exchange for Green's labor, but the amount of tithing she cared to pay between her husband's death and her own death would have been a small fraction of the price for an enslaved man. Agnes Flake, Utah Territory Productions of Agriculture, box 1, folder 10, Utah County, *1850 [1851] Census*.
17. San Bernardino Branch Tithing Accounts, 111–12; San Bernardino Branch Tithing Record, 46.
18. For an explanation of Brigham Young's finances, see "Appendix D: The Settlement of the Brigham Young Estate, 1877–1879," in Leonard J. Arrington, *Brigham Young: American Moses* (New York: Alfred A. Knopf, 1985), 422–30.
19. Arrington, *Brigham Young: American Moses*, 427.
20. Brigham Young, *Utah Territory Slave Schedule* [draft], Great Salt Lake County, 1850 [1851].
21. Wilford Woodruff, June 1, 1851, Journal, box 2, folder 3, MS 1352, Wilford Woodruff Journals and Papers 1828–1898, CHL.
22. Brigham Young to Amasa Lyman and C. C. Rich, August 19, 1854, box 17, folder 14, Office Files.
23. Family Record, 1853–1858, Family Record, c. 1855, Miscellaneous Files, 1832–1878, box 170, folders 25–26, Office Files.
24. Amasa Lyman, Diary, December 24, 1854, Lyman Collection.

25. Amasa Lyman to Brigham Young, July 27, 1854, box 40, folder 21, Office Files.
26. Brigham Young to Amasa Lyman and C. C. Rich, August 19, 1854, box 17, folder 14, Office Files.
27. Fretwell, "Green Flake," 4.

CHAPTER 7: THE TEXANS

1. Ellen Greer Rees, "Greer Men and Ellen C. Greer" (unpublished typescript, n.d.), TN-117134, FHL; "My Pretty Quadroon," in *Beadle's Dime Song Book No. 10* (New York: Beadle and Company, 1863), 40–41.
2. Stout, *Mormon Frontier*, June 1, 1857, 2:627–28.
3. For more about women's control of the enslaved, see Jones-Rogers, *They Were Her Property*.
4. William N. Greer, "Greer, Nathaniel Hunt," *Handbook of Texas Online*, Texas State Historical Association, June 15, 2010, https://www.tshaonline.org/handbook/online/articles/fgr45.
5. Texas tax rolls show that the extended Greer family enslaved nine or ten people in Milam County before they left for Utah. Greer, Milam County, 1853, 1854 Texas State Library and Archives, *Texas, County Tax Rolls, 1846–1910*, FSFT, https://www.familysearch.org/search/catalog/986276; Wakefield, *Texas and the Greers*, 6, 24; Records of the Bureau of the Census, *1860 Census: Eighth Census of the United States* (National Archives Microfilm Publication M653, Texas Slave Schedule, Record Group 29), T. L. Greer, Bosque County, 1860; Records of the Bureau of the Census, *1860 Census: Eighth Census of the United States* (National Archives Microfilm Publication M653, Texas, Record Group 29), James Lane, Bosque County, 1860; Records of the Bureau of the Census, *1870 Census: Ninth Census of the United States* (National Archives Microfilm Publication M593, 1,761 rolls, Texas, Record Group 29), Thomas Greer, Americus Greer, and James Lane, Bosque County, 1870; Ellen C. Greer and Anonymous, Anecdotes and Reminiscences of Her Life as Related by Grandma Ellen C. Greer (May 19, 1921), MS 7776, 8, CHL; Emigrating Journal, 1855, box 13, MS 4806, Edward Stevenson Collection, 1849–1922, CHL.
6. "Blair & Co's. Column," *Deseret News*, December 4, 1855; "Notice! [Blair, Greer, & Basett]," *Deseret News*, March 26, 1856; "John B. Maiben, Licensed Auctioneer House," *Deseret News*, May 7, 1856; "Land Claims," *Deseret News*, February 11, 1857; "My Last," *Deseret News*, January 20, 1858.
7. Elizabeth Camp v. Williams Camp, Petition for Divorce, April 1856, Salt Lake County Probate Court Case Files, Series 373, box 3, folder 139, USHS.
8. Amelia Camp filed for divorce in 1862 and again in 1864. During the contentious proceedings, the court repeatedly ruled against Williams Camp, assessing alimony and child support after he fraudulently told the court that he had few assets. The court ruled against him for not allowing Amelia her property, for breaking into her residence and taking her property, and for violating court orders. The court appointed Edwin D. Woolley to divide property and protect Amelia's interests. Amelia Camp v. Williams Camp, Petition for Divorce and Alimony, June 1862, box 8, folder 48; Amelia Camp v. Williams Camp, Petition for Divorce and Alimony, September 1864, box 9, folder 71, Salt Lake County Probate Court Case Files, Series 373, USHS.

9. "Third Judicial District Court," *Deseret News*, March 19, 1863; "Justices' Court," *Deseret News*, October 5, 1864; Elizabeth Camp v. Williams Camp, Petition for Divorce and Alimony, November 1861, Salt Lake County Probate Court Case Files, Series 373, box 3, folder 139, USHS; W. Paul Reeve, email message to author, September 13, 2014.
10. Ellen C. Greer and Anonymous, Anecdotes and Reminiscences of Her Life as Related by Grandma Ellen C. Greer (May 19, 1921), 6, MS 7776, CHL.
11. The 1856 census lists an otherwise unknown Isaac in the home of Ellen Camp Greer's sister-in-law Wilmirth Greer East, so perhaps there were two Isaacs, perhaps Isaac provided labor for both households, or perhaps the name was one of the padded entries from the unreliable census. Camp and East households, Wards 13 and 14, Great Salt Lake County, *1856 Utah Territorial Census*, MS 2929, CHL.
12. Williams Camp to Brigham Young, March 3, 1856, box 64, folder 3, Office Files.
13. Williams Camp, Salt Lake County Transfer Book D, 1857–1867, box 4, folder 4, 10, Consecration Deeds.
14. "Notice [Camp excommunication]," *Deseret News*, March 26, 1856.
15. "Take Notice," *Deseret News*, April 9, 1856.
16. Elizabeth Camp v. Williams Camp (1861).
17. Brigham Young Office Journal, June 9, 1856, box 72, folder 2, Office Files.
18. Stout, *Mormon Frontier*, 2:597.
19. "Woolley family members . . . enjoy the story that once Brigham Young said that if Bishop Woolley should fall off his horse while crossing to the other side of the Jordan, they should not look for him floating downstream. Instead, they would find him swimming upstream, obstinately contending against the current." Leonard J. Arrington and Davis Bitton, *Saints Without Halos: The Human Side of Mormon History* (Salt Lake City, UT: Signature Books, 1982), 61.
20. Brigham Young Office Journal, June 16, 1856, box 72, folder 2, Office Files.
21. Stout, *Mormon Frontier*, 2:597.
22. Territory of Utah v. Williams Camp et. al. (1856), Salt Lake County Probate Court Case Files, Series 373, box 4, folder 2, USHS.
23. Elias Smith Journals, June 16, 1856, 1836–1888, MS 1319, box 1, folder 4, CHL.
24. Affidavit of Williams Camp in regard to Negro boy Shepard, July 10, 1856, Salt Lake County Probate Court Case Files, Series 373, box 4, folder 26, USHS.
25. Affidavit of Williams Camp in regard to Negro boy Shepard, 5–6.
26. Affidavit of Williams Camp in regard to his Servant "Daniel," July 10, 1856, Salt Lake County Probate Court Case Files, Series 373, box 4, folder 26, USHS.
27. Records of the Bureau of the Census, *1860 Census: Eighth Census of the United States* (National Archives Microfilm Publication M653, Utah Territory Slave Schedule, Record Group 29), N. R. Sprows [Nancy Reddick Greer Johnson Sprouse], Great Salt Lake County, Utah Territory Slave Schedule, 1860.
28. Annie Duckett Hundley, "Permelia Emily Wooldridge" (digital copy of typescript), FSFT, https://familysearch.org/photos/artifacts/12804863.
29. Records of the Bureau of the Census, *1880 Census: Tenth Census of the United States* (National Archives Microfilm Publication T9, 1,454 rolls, Record Group 29), Silas Woolridge, Lincoln County, Nevada, 1880; Records of the Bureau of the Census, *1900 Census: Twelfth Census of the United States* (National Archives Microfilm Publication T623, 1,854 rolls, Record Group 29), Silas Woolridge, Lincoln County, Nevada, 1900;

Records of the Bureau of the Census, *1910 Census: Thirteenth Census of the United States* (National Archives Microfilm Publication T624, 1,178 rolls, Record Group 29), Silas Woolridge, Lincoln County, Nevada, 1910; Silas Woolridge, January 25, 1917, Bakersfield, California, *FindAGrave*, https://www.findagrave.com.

30. George Armstrong Custer, *My Life on the Plains, or, Personal Experiences with Indians* (New York: Sheldon and Company, 1874), 43–45; see also, Cathy [pseud.], *clmroots: History of an American Family* (blog), 2008–2017, https://clmroots.blogspot.com.

31. The 1850 census recorded that Clarkey Box could not read or write. Records of the Bureau of the Census, *1840 Census: Sixth Census of the United States* (National Archives Microfilm Publication M704, 580 rolls, Record Group 29), Thomas Box, Tippah County, Mississippi, 1840; Records of the Bureau of the Census, *1850 Census: Seventh Census of the United States* (National Archives Microfilm Publication M432, 1009 rolls, Record Group 29), Thomas Box and Clarkey Box, Henderson County, Texas, 1850; Records of the Bureau of the Census, *1850 Census: Seventh Census of the United States* (National Archives Microfilm Publication M432, 1009 rolls, Texas Slave Schedule, Record Group 29), Thomas Box, Henderson County, 1850; *A Memorial and Biographical History of Navarro, Henderson, Anderson, Limestone, Freestone and Leon Counties, Texas* (Chicago: Lewis Publishing, 1893).

32. Norman B. Ferris and Morris J. Snedaker, "The Diary of Morris J. Snedaker, 1855–1856," *Southwestern Historical Quarterly* 66 (July 1962–April 1963): 534, https://www.jstor.org/stable/30236261.

33. "The Late Outrages on the Plains," *Sacramento Daily Union*, November 14, 1857.

34. Isabella Marden Pratt Robison, Biography (digital copy, n.d.), FSFT, https://family-search.org/photos/stories/5115493.

35. Records of the Bureau of the Census, *1860 Census: Eighth Census of the United States* (National Archives Microfilm Publication M653, Record Group 29), Thomas Box, Great Salt Lake County, Utah Territory, 1860; Records of the Bureau of the Census, *1860 Census: Eighth Census of the United States* (National Archives Microfilm Publication M653, Record Group 29), Thomas Box, Great Salt Lake County, Utah Territory Slave Schedule, 1860.

36. Preston Thomas, Daniel H. Thomas, and Annette Taylor, "Preston Thomas [Diaries and Biography]" (digital copy of typescript), accessed April 21, 2021, https://docs.wix-static.com/ugd/78a476_22d3bdc50ebe4f0398ed3e288858d84e.pdf. Loisa, Alabama, 1838, baptized April 22 [year unknown], "Black," Record of Members, 1849–1941, Salt Lake City Fifteenth Ward, microfilm 26675, FHL. W. Paul Reeve, email message to author, August 4, 2019.

37. *A Memorial and Biographical History of Ellis County, Texas* (Chicago: Lewis Publishing Co., 1892), 174. A letter from Whitmore to Brigham Young shows that Whitmore had limited education like many other Texas converts. M. T. Flaherty Probate, Ellis County, Texas County, District, and Probate Courts, *Texas, Wills and Probate Records, 1833–1974*, Ancestry.com, https://www.ancestry.com/search/collections/2115; James M. Whitmore to Brigham Young, December 25, 1865, box 30, folder 18, Office Files; Le Landgren, *A Whitmore Family History, 1793–1990* (West Linn, OR: Family Gathering, 1990), 3.

38. Ferris and Snedaker, "Diary of Morris J. Snedaker," 535.

39. Ferris and Snedaker, "Diary of Morris J. Snedaker," 536.

40. Elizabeth Carter Flaherty Whitmore's fortunes through 1857 can be traced through the census agricultural and tax records. In 1850, Michael Flaherty owned extensive property. He did not appear to enslave people. Records of the Bureau of the Census, *1850 Census: Seventh Census of the United States* (National Archives Microfilm Publication M432, 1009 rolls, Texas Productions of Agriculture, Record Group 29), M. T. Flaherty, Ellis County, 1850; M T Flaherty, Ellis County, 1850–1852; J M Whitmore, Ellis County, 1854–1857, *Texas, County Tax Rolls*. The estate is not in the tax rolls in 1853 but appeared under James Whitmore's name between 1854 and 1857. In 1855, the family had $500 in the bank; the next year, they had no money in the bank and four enslaved people, valued at $2,575. In 1857, shortly before they left for Utah Territory, the records showed four hundred acres, two enslaved people valued at $1,250, $2,000 in the bank, and miscellaneous property valued at more than $300, with the large infusion of cash probably from selling the enslaved people.
41. Hurd, *Law of Freedom and Bondage*, 2:195–200; Douglas Hales, "Free Blacks," in *Handbook of Texas Online*, June 12, 2010, https://www.tshaonline.org/handbook/online/articles/pkfbs.

CHAPTER 8: MERCHANTS, ARMY OFFICERS, AND GOVERNMENT APPOINTEES

1. One of the Livingston brothers may have fathered a child with Benjamin Perkins's relative Sarah Perkins. (See her biography.) "Past Celebrations of Pioneer Day," *Salt Lake Herald*, April 15, 1897; Daughters of Utah Pioneers, *East of Antelope Island*, 158.
2. Merchants John Probosco and Samuel Demoss subsequently moved to Mariposa County, California. Barnes and Barnes v. Probosco and Demoss (1854), Weber County (UT) Probate Court, Civil and Criminal Case Files, Series 1593, box 1, folders 13–14, USHS; Probosco v. Barnes and Barnes (1854), box 2, folder 95; Barnes and Barnes v. Demoss (1854), box 2, folder 96, Salt Lake County Probate Court Case Files, Series 373, USHS.
3. Horace E. and Eliza J. Barnes Guardianship, Jackson County, 1856, Series 1, box 2, files 1–23, Missouri, County, District, and Probate Courts, *Missouri, Wills and Probate Records*.
4. Harrison A. Trexler, "Slavery in Missouri, 1804–1865" (PhD diss., Johns Hopkins University, 1914), 28–29, 31–33.
5. Caldwell v. Porter (1855), Jackson County Records Center, Jackson County (MO) Circuit Court, 1855–1857, 7, Kansas City Public Library, Civil War on the Western Border, accessed April 21, 2021, https://civilwaronthewesternborder.org/islandora/object/civilwar%3A7874.
6. Caldwell v. Porter, Jackson County (MO) Records Center, Jackson County Circuit Court, 1855–1857 (Kansas City Public Library, Civil War on the Western Border, 1855), 15, https://civilwaronthewesternborder.org/islandora/object/civilwar%3A7874.
7. Caldwell v. Porter (1855), 60–61.
8. William W. Brown, *Narrative of William W. Brown, a Fugitive Slave* (Boston: Anti-Slavery Office, 1847), 45–46.
9. Brown, *Narrative of William W. Brown*, 49–51.
10. Records of the Bureau of the Census, *1860 Census: Eighth Census of the United States* (National Archives Microfilm Publication M653, Utah Territory Slave Schedule,

Record Group 29), Clifton Barnes, Great Salt Lake County, 1860. Union Historical Company, *History of Jackson County, Missouri* (Kansas City, MO: Union Historical Company, 1881), 957; C R Barnes, Leavenworth County, Kansas State Historical Society, 1865 Kansas Territory Census, *Kansas State Census Collection, 1855–1925*, Ancestry.com, https://www.ancestry.com/search/collections/ksstatecen.

11. "Affairs in Utah: Interesting Letter from Judge Drummond," New York Tribune (New York, NY), May 27, 1857; William P. MacKinnon, "The Buchanan Spoils System and the Utah Expedition: Careers of W. M. F. Magraw and John M. Hockaday," *Utah Historical Quarterly* 31, no. 2 (April 1963): 147, https://www.jstor.org/stable/45059094.

12. "West Point Cadets," *New York Commercial Advertiser* (New York, NY), May 5, 1842; United States Military Academy, *Official Register of the Officers and Cadets of the U. S. Military Academy, West Point, N.Y.* (West Point, NY: United States Military Academy Printing Office, 1843), 249, 271, 296, 303; "Arrivals at the Hotels," *Louisville Daily Democrat* (Louisville, KY), April 21, 1848.

13. Records of the Bureau of the Census, *1830 Census: Fifth Census of the United States* (National Archives Microfilm Publication M19, 201 rolls, Record Group 29), William F. Hockaday, Clark County, Kentucky, 1830; Records of the Bureau of the Census, *1840 Census: Sixth Census of the United States* (National Archives Microfilm Publication M704, 580 rolls, Record Group 29), William F. Hockaday, Clark County, Kentucky, 1840; Records of the Bureau of the Census, *1850 Census: Seventh Census of the United States* (National Archives Microfilm Publication M432, 1009 rolls, Kentucky Slave Schedule, Record Group 29), John M. Hockaday, Union County, 1850.

14. William P. MacKinnon, "Predicting the Past: The Utah War's Twenty-First Century Future," *Arrington Annual Lecture*, 2008, Paper 13, https://digitalcommons.usu.edu/arrington_lecture/13; MacKinnon, "The Buchanan Spoils System and the Utah Expedition," 127–50, https://www.jstor.org/stable/45059094; Dan Rottenberg, *Death of a Gunfighter: The Quest for Jack Slade, the West's Most Elusive Legend* (Yardley, PA: Westholme, 2010); W. W. Phelps, *Almanac for the Year 1860* (Great Salt Lake City, UT: J. McKnight, 1860), 6; Senate of the United States, *Journal of the Executive Proceedings of the Senate of the United States of America From December 3, 1855, to June 16, 1858, Inclusive*, Vol. 10 (Washington, DC: Government Printing Office, 1887), 148–49, 577, 725; "Utah," *Philadelphia Inquirer* (Philadelphia, PA), August 5, 1857.

15. Records of the Bureau of the Census, *1860 Census: Eighth Census of the United States* (National Archives Microfilm Publication M653, Utah Territory Slave Schedule, Record Group 29), John M. Hockaday, Great Salt Lake County, 1860; George Hockaday, negro [August 1860], Utah Archives and Records Service, *Salt Lake County (UT) Death Records, 1849–1949*, FSFT, https://www.familysearch.org/search/collection/1459704; George (Negro) Hockaday, August 1860, grave E_5_14_1W, Salt Lake City Cemetery, Salt Lake City, Utah Division of State History, *Cemeteries and Burials*.

16. Charles A. Tuttle, *Reports of Cases Determined*, 51:120.

17. "Rocky Point, Humboldt River," *Sacramento Daily Union*, June 4, 1852.

18. Records of the Bureau of the Census, *1860 Census: Eighth Census of the United States* (National Archives Microfilm Publication M653, California Census of Agriculture, Record Group 29), Richard Pearson, Colusa County, 1860.

19. Richard Pearson Will, 1865, California County, District, and Probate Courts, *California, Wills and Probate Records, 1850–1953*, Ancestry.com, https://www.ancestry.com/search/collections/8639.

20. "A Fortune Saved—A California Romance," *Daily Alta California* (San Francisco, CA), January 8, 1872.
21. "Supreme Court Decisions, October Term, 1873, Pearson vs. Pearson," *Sacramento Daily Union*, October 25, 1873.
22. *Reports of Cases Determined*, 51:120, 124.
23. "Supreme Court Decisions, October Term, 1875," *Sacramento Daily Union*, January 26, 1876.
24. Richard Pearson Probate, 1865, Colusa County; Guardianship of Theodore Pearson, Richard Pearson, William Pearson, and Jefferson Pearson, Minors, 1876, case 111, Colusa County, *California, Wills*.
25. Benjamin Allston to Adele Allston, May 19, June 6, August 24, 1854, March 15, 1855, Letters, 1854–1857, Military and Personal Correspondence (1848–1960) 12/17, Allston Family Papers, 1830–1901, South Carolina Historical Society, courtesy of William Gorenfeld.
26. Allston to Allston, "Allston Family Papers, 1830–1901," Partial typescript courtesy of William Gorenfeld (South Carolina Historical Society, Charleston, SC, March 28, 1855).
27. Records of the Bureau of the Census, *1860 Census: Eighth Census of the United States* (National Archives Microfilm Publication M653, South Carolina Slave Schedule, Record Group 29), Benjamin Allston and R. F. W. Allston, Prince George Parish, 1860.
28. John W. Phelps, Diary (manuscript, New York Public Library), April 23, 1859, as cited in Don R. Mathis, "Camp Floyd in Retrospect" (master's thesis, University of Utah, 1959), 30; see also, Thomas G. Alexander and Leonard J. Arrington, "Camp in the Sagebrush: Camp Floyd, Utah, 1858–61," *Utah Historical Quarterly* 34 (1966): 3–21, https://www.jstor.org/stable/45058591.
29. Roger Nielson counted about eight hundred civilian employees plus dependents with the army but said that names were difficult or impossible to discover. Roger B. Nielson, *Roll Call at Old Camp Floyd, Utah Territory* (Fort Crittenden, UT: R. B. Nielson, 2006), 269–75.
30. Charles Pierce Roland, *Albert Sidney Johnston, Soldier of Three Republics*, 2nd ed. (Lexington: University Press of Kentucky, 2001), 141; Records of the Bureau of the Census, *1850 Census: Seventh Census of the United States* (National Archives Microfilm Publication M432, 1009 rolls, Texas Slave Schedule, Record Group 29), Bexar County, 1850.
31. William Preston Johnston, *The Life of Gen. Albert Sidney Johnston* (New York: D. Appleton, 1878), 178–79.
32. Roland, *Johnston*, 181; Albert Sidney Johnston to William Preston Johnston, November 23, 1856, in Roland, *Johnston*, 182.
33. Randolph Hughes, Contract, December 10, 1860, Johnston Papers, Barret Collection, Tulane University, New Orleans, LA, in Roland, *Johnston*, 241–42.
34. William Preston Johnston, *The Life of Gen. Albert Sidney Johnston* (New York: D. Appleton, 1878), 279.
35. Johnston, *Life of Johnston*, 280–81.
36. "Popular Sovereignty in Utah," *New York Tribune*, April 23, 1856.
37. August 1859, Accounts, Williams Probate, Series 1621, case 67, USHS.

38. For details of the counterfeiting court actions, see Burton v. Dotson, Whitmore, and Burr (1861), Salt Lake County Probate Court Case Files, Series 373, USHS, or Bancroft, *History of Utah*, 573.
39. Frank Black man, September 1, 1858, Utah Archives and Records Service, *Utah Death Registers*.
40. "Progress of Civilization (!)," *Deseret News*, September 15, 1858; "Progress of Civilization," *Sacramento Daily Union*, October 11, 1858.
41. "In the Matter of the Petition of William W. Drummond, a Bankrupt," *Illinois Weekly State Journal* (Springfield, IL), February 9, 1843; "Drunk, Disgrace, Death: William W. Drummond, a Once Noted Lawyer, Dies in a Barrel-House," *Chicago Daily Inter-Ocean* (Chicago, IL), November 21, 1888.
42. Jemimah McClenahan Drummond's brother James K. McClenahan moved to the Great Salt Lake Valley in 1847 and her sister Elizabeth McClenahan Richards moved there in 1849. Jules Remy and Julius Brenchley, *A Journey to Great-Salt-Lake City* (London: W. Jeffs, 1861), 2:343; Russell W. McDonald, "William Wormer Drummond," in *Biographical Summaries: Nevada's Territorial, District, Supreme Court and Federal Judges, 1856–1993*, digital copy of unpublished manuscript, partial copy in possession of author (Reno: Nevada Judicial Historical Society, n.d.), 155; "Impositions Upon Utah," *Deseret News*, May 20, 1857; Records of the Bureau of the Census, *1860 Census: Eighth Census of the United States* (National Archives Microfilm Publication M653, Record Group 29), W. W. Drummond, Cook County, Illinois, 1860; "Judge W. W. Drummond Dying in a Grog Shop," *New York Tribune*, November 22, 1888; "Once He Was Supreme Judge of Utah," *Knoxville Journal* (Knoxville, TN), November 25, 1888.
43. "A Democratic Drummond Light in the East," *Albany Evening Journal* (Albany, NY), September 1, 1859. For more about the Utah War, see William P. MacKinnon, *At Sword's Point: A Documentary History of the Utah War to 1858, Part 1 and 2* (Norman, OK: Arthur H. Clark, 2008, 2016).
44. For more on the battle over the control of Utah Territory, see Rogers, *Unpopular Sovereignty*.
45. Russell W. McDonald, "William Wormer Drummond," in *Biographical Summaries: Nevada's Territorial, District, Supreme Court and Federal Judges, 1856–1993* (digital copy of unpublished manuscript, partial copy in possession of author. Reno: Nevada Judicial Historical Society, n.d.), 155.
46. Jules Remy and Julius Brenchley, *A Journey to Great-Salt-Lake City* (London: W. Jeffs, 1861), 2:341; James A. Harkreader v. James C. Hamilton (1836), Wilson County (TN) Circuit Court, Tennessee State Library and Archives, *Minute Books, Civil and Criminal, 1810–1965*, FSFT, https://www.familysearch.org/search/catalog/256096; Jas A. Harkrider, Sacramento County, California, *1850 Census*.
47. Drummond and Kinney do not appear in Latter-day Saint membership records. "Popular Sovereignty in Utah," *New York Tribune*, April 23, 1856; "A Fugitive Slave Advertised There," *National Era* (Washington, DC), May 1, 1856; and "Slavery in Utah," *Portland Advertiser* (Portland, ME), April 29, 1856.
48. William W. Drummond to Brigham Young, September 13, 1855 (box 53, folder 23), Office Files.
49. Hosea Stout, "A Short Sketch of the History of Judge W. W. Drummond," n.d., Governor's Office Files, 1850–1867, box 53, folder 23, Office Files.

50. The grand jurors would have known the name Ada used in Utah Territory, but the reference to "a certain woman" likely meant that they believed her name to be a professional or courtesan name. United States v. William W. Drummond and Woman (1856), Salt Lake County Probate Court Case Files, Series 373, box 3, folder 110, USHS; Ronald W. Walker, "'Proud as a Peacock and Ignorant as a Jackass': William W. Drummond's Unusual Career with the Mormons," *Journal of Mormon History* 42, no. 3 (July 2016): 18, https://doi.org/10.5406/jmormhist.42.3.0001.
51. Juanita Brooks, *History of the Jews in Utah and Idaho* (Salt Lake City, UT: Western Epics, 1973), 32. See also McDonald, "Drummond," in *Biographical Summaries*, 158; Chandless, *A Visit to Salt Lake*, 278; Stout, *Mormon Frontier*, 2:583–84.
52. "Later from Nicaragua," *New Orleans Daily Crescent* (New Orleans, LA), March 28, 1857; *Slave Manifests of Coastwise Vessels Filed at New Orleans, Louisiana, 1807–1860* (Washington, DC: National Archives Microfilm Publication M1895).
53. Records of the Bureau of the Census, *1860 Census: Eighth Census of the United States* (National Archives Microfilm Publication M653, Record Group 29), Cato Smith, Carson County, Utah Territory, 1860; Peter J. Smith, email message to author, December 22, 2015.

CHAPTER 9: FREE AT LAST

1. "The Veterans' Reunion," *Salt Lake Herald*, August 21, 1894; "The Pioneers of 1847," *Deseret News*, August 25, 1894.
2. Bible, King James Version, John 14:2.
3. See, for example, Carter, *Negro Pioneer*, 21–22.
4. Records of the Bureau of the Census, *1860 Census: Eighth Census of the United States* (National Archives Microfilm Publication M653, Record Group 29), Richard Camper, Dorchester County, Maryland, 1860; Records of the Bureau of the Census, *1870 Census: Ninth Census of the United States* (National Archives Microfilm Publication M593, 1,761 rolls, Record Group 29), Richard and Harriet Camper, Dorchester County, Maryland, 1870; Records of the Bureau of the Census, *1880 Census: Tenth Census of the United States* (National Archives Microfilm Publication T9, 1,454 rolls, Record Group 29), Richard and Harriet Camper, Dorchester County, Maryland, 1880; William H. Hooper Probate, box 27, folder 3; Mary Ann Knowlton Hooper Probate, box 38, folder 20, Third District Court Probate Case Files, Series 1621, USHS; "Hon. W. H. Hooper," *Tullidge's Quarterly Magazine* 2, no. 4 (July 1883): 663; Carter, *Negro Pioneer*, 35.
5. Eugene H. Perkins, telephone conversation with the author, August 12, 2016.
6. Williamson and Cain, *MeasuringWorth*, accessed April 27, 2021.
7. The census only showed personal property above $100. Samuel and Caroline Bankhead, Nancy and James Valentine, Alexander and Marinda Bankhead, Betsy Brown, Miles Litchford, Green and Martha Flake, Sylvester and Mary James, Benjamin Perkins, Chaney Cunningham, Luke Redd, Utah Territory, *1870 Census*; Census Office, Department of the Interior, *Ninth Census, United States, 1870, Instructions to Assistant Marshals* (Washington, DC: Government Printing Office, 1870), 10.
8. Despite a prohibition on interracial sex in An Act in Relation to Service (1852), Utah Territory first prohibited interracial marriage in 1888. Patrick Q. Mason, "The

Prohibition of Interracial Marriage in Utah, 1888–1963," *Utah Historical Quarterly* 76, no. 2 (Spring 2008): 108–31, https://www.jstor.org/stable/45063125.

9. See, for example, Robert John Wilkinson, "Human Genetic Susceptibility to Tuberculosis," *Journal of Infectious Diseases* 205, no. 4 (February 2012): 525–27, https://doi.org/10.1093/infdis/jir792.
10. Demaratus, *Force of a Feather*, 181–82; L. A. Ingersoll, *Ingersoll's Century Annals of San Bernardino County, 1769 to 1904* (Los Angeles: L. A. Ingersoll, 1904), 350–51; Dolores Hayden, "Biddy Mason's Los Angeles 1856–1891," *California History* 68, no. 3 (Fall 1989): 86–99, https://doi.org/10.2307/25462395.
11. State of California v. Joseph McFeely (1858), Justice Court of San Bernardino, case 42, SBCHA.
12. Skinner, *Black Origins*, 47, based on an account in *San Bernardino Guardian*, April 5, 1873.
13. U. S. Const. amend. XV.
14. "Celebration of the Fifteenth Amendment by the Colored People," *Elevator* (San Francisco, CA), April 22, 1870.
15. Southern California Genealogical Society, "Los Angeles City Cemetery," *SCGS Genealogy*, http://www.scgsgenealogy.com/free/LACC-Title.html. For the cadaver trade, see Daina Ramey Berry, *The Price for Their Pound of Flesh: The Value of the Enslaved, from Womb to Grave, in the Building of a Nation* (Boston: Beacon Press, 2017).
16. Louisa Maria Tanner Lyman went by Maria or Mariah. See, for example, Mariah Lyman to Amasa Lyman, September 30, 1849, in J. M. Flake, to Amasa Lyman, Incoming letters, 1849, box 3, folder 8, Lyman Collection; Daniel M. Thomas to Lyman, Lyman Collection.
17. Charles Rowan, alias Charles Rone or Rohan, National Archives and Records Administration, *U. S. Civil War Pension Index: General Index to Pension Files, 1861–1934*, Ancestry.com, https://www.ancestry.com/search/collections/4654.
18. "Has Priceless Lincoln Relic," *San Bernardino Sun* (San Bernardino, CA), February 17, 1909; "Charles Rowan Joins His Fathers," *San Bernardino Sun*, September 20, 1905.
19. "Letter from Bishop Ward," *Elevator*, September 3, 1869; Skinner, *Black Origins*, 74–75.
20. The conclusion that Green Flake and Elizabeth Flake were siblings is based on their listing in the Jurden Flake will and resemblance to each other. Melissa Lambert Milewski, *Before the Manifesto: The Life Writings of Mary Lois Walker Morris* (Logan: Utah State University Press, 2007), 516–18.
21. "City in Brief," *San Bernardino Evening Transcript* (San Bernardino, CA), January 18, 1901; "City in Brief," *San Bernardino Evening Transcript*, January 19, 1901.
22. "Will Filed in Estate of the Late Mrs. Rowan," *San Bernardino Sun*, April 15, 1908; "Official Record," *San Bernardino Sun*, October 20, 1911; "Mrs. Elizabeth Rowan," *San Bernardino Daily Sun* (San Bernardino, CA), March 31, 1908.
23. John Mack Faragher, *Eternity Street: Violence and Justice in Frontier Los Angeles* (New York: W. W. Norton and Company, 2016), 246–47.
24. Faragher, *Eternity Street*, 201.
25. "Death of 'Aunt Winnie,'" *Los Angeles Herald* (Los Angeles, CA), April 19, 1883; "A Relic of Pueblo Days," *Los Angeles Herald*, May 12, 1901.
26. "Letter from Bishop Ward," *Elevator*.

27. Biddy Mason, Physician, 1862, California, National Archives, *IRS Tax Assessment Lists, 1862–1918*, Ancestry.com, https://www.ancestry.com/search/collections/1264.
28. DeEtta Demaratus, email message to author, September 21, 2016, citing communication from Hal Eaton; "A Terrific Explosion: Destruction of the Ada Hancock at San Pedro, Cal.," *New York Times*, May 31, 1863.
29. "An Appeal for the Colored People of Los Angeles," *Los Angeles Herald*, July 19, 1884; "The Negro Woman in Los Angeles and Vicinity—Some Notable Characters," *Los Angeles Daily Times* (Los Angeles, CA), February 12, 1909, Special Section.
30. "The Short Hairs: Will Manage the Republican Convention," *Los Angeles Herald*, September 28, 1890. See the biographical entries for Mason and her daughters for more on the legal battles.
31. Messages from Joyce Niswander, August 13, 2018, Donna Marks, May 9, 2015, Anonymous, April 24, 2013, at "Bridget 'Biddy' Mason," *FindAGrave*.
32. Thomas M. D. Ward (1823–1894) was the tenth bishop of the African Methodist Episcopal (AME) Church. "Letter from Bishop Ward," *Elevator*; "Bishop Ward Dead," *St. Louis Republic* (St. Louis, MO), June 12, 1894.
33. Howard Wales was in California by 1869. "List of Letters Remaining," *Sacramento Daily Union*, June 25, 1869.
34. "A Cruel Practical Joke," *Sacramento Daily Union*, March 20, 1886.
35. "Just Outside," *Fresno Republican Weekly* (Fresno, CA), February 18, 1887; Howard Wales, 1888, Merced, California State Library, *California Voter Registers, 1866–1898*, Ancestry.com, https://www.ancestry.com/search/collections/2221.
36. Green Flake v. Nils Mason (1864), Salt Lake County Probate Court Case Files, Series 373, box 8, folder 144, USHS.
37. Charles L. Keller, *The Lady in the Ore Bucket: A History of Settlement and Industry in the Tri-Canyon Area of the Wasatch Mountains* (Salt Lake City: University of Utah Press, 2010).
38. "Delinquent Sale," *Salt Lake Tribune*, November 17, 1875.
39. "Fatal Avalanche," *Salt Lake Herald*, February 25, 1882; LaReah H. Toronto, Naomi G. Jimenoz, and Merle H. Yarrington, "To These, Our Grandparents" (digital copy of typescript, n.d.), FSFT, https://www.familysearch.org/photos/artifacts/25331474.
40. George A. Smith, "Patriarchal Marriage—The Settlement of Utah," May 19, 1872, D. W. Evans, J. Q. Cannon, and Julia Young, *Journal of Discourses* (Liverpool: Albert Carrington, 1873), 15:29.
41. For more on early mining in Utah, see Keller, *Lady in the Ore Bucket*. "Against the Admission of Utah as a State. Memorial of the Citizens of Utah against the Admission of the Territory as a State, May 6, 1872," *The Miscellaneous Documents Printed by Order of the House of Representatives* (Washington, DC: Government Printing Office, 1872), 18, 24, 25.
42. See, for example, "The Twenty-Fourth at Union," *Deseret News*, August 1, 1888; "Real Estate Transfers," *Salt Lake Herald*, August 28, 1895. The scholarly treatment of the early Black settlers of Idaho is currently very limited. For the history of Grays Lake, see Ellen Carney, "Blacks Were First to Settle Idaho's Grays Lake Valley," *Idaho State Journal*, March 3, 2013, https://www.idahostatejournal.com/news/local/blacks-were-first-to-settle-idaho-s-grays-lake-valley/article_b82435f6-83d0-11e2-b4da-001a4bcf887a.html.
43. "More Pioneers," *Deseret News*, July 19, 1897.

44. Accounts disagree on the date of July 21 or 22, 1847. There was no Ira in the wagon company; perhaps he confused company member John Eldredge with his brother Ira, who led a wagon company that left Nebraska two months later. Flake, *Book of the Pioneers*, 1:242.
45. "Funeral of Green Flake," *Deseret Evening News* (Salt Lake City, UT), October 31, 1903.
46. Reeve, *Religion of a Different Color*, 195–97.
47. David William Pace, September 10, 1951, Salt Lake City, death certificate 0005102556, Utah Department of Health, USHS.
48. A. K. Thurber to G. A. Smith, June 17, 1864, box 6, folder 14, 54–55, MS 1322, George A. Smith Papers, 1834–1877, CHL.
49. Redd Y-DNA Project; Reiter, "Redd Slave Histories," 122; "Luke Ward Redd," FSFT, accessed 21 April 2021, https://www.familysearch.org/tree/person/details/LWS9-Y8C.
50. "Slavery in Utah," *Broad Ax*.
51. "Edward T Dennis <Redd> [father] William T Dennis [mother] Miranda C Redd [birth] April 12th 1867 Sp^h Fork Utah Utah [death] Octr 29th 1867 [cause] Flux [medical attendant] Venis Redd." Spanish Fork (UT) Cemetery Records; Pat Sagers, email message to author, June 7, 2013.
52. Spanish Fork Ward General Minutes, 1851–1883, LR 8611 11, CHL, in Reiter, "Redd Slave Histories," 116–17.
53. Amy Tanner Thiriot, "Eminent Women: Mary Parker Chidester and Catharine Maria Sedgwick, Part 1" (*Keepapitchinin*, October 18, 2012), http://www.keepapitchinin.org/2012/10/18/eminent-women-mary-parker-chidester-and-catharine-maria-sedgwick-part-1.
54. Records of the Bureau of the Census, *1870 Census: Ninth Census of the United States* (National Archives Microfilm Publication M593, 1,761 rolls, Record Group 29), Alexander and Marinda Bankhead, Utah County, Utah Territory, 1870; Records of the Bureau of the Census, *1900 Census: Twelfth Census of the United States* (National Archives Microfilm Publication T623, 1,854 rolls), Alex and Rindy Bankhead, Utah County, Utah, 1900; "Slavery in Utah," *Broad Ax*.
55. Tonya Reiter, "Black Saviors on Mount Zion: Proxy Baptisms and Latter-day Saints of African Descent," *Journal of Mormon History* 43, no. 4 (October 2017): 100–23, https://doi.org/10.5406/jmormhist.43.4.0100; Lisle G. Brown, "'Temple Pro Tempore': The Salt Lake City Endowment House," *Journal of Mormon History* 34, no. 4 (Fall 2008): 1–68, https://mds.marshall.edu/lib_faculty/15/; "Record of Baptisms for the Dead."
56. "Butte in Brief," *Montana Standard* (Butte, MT), February 13, 1896; "A Church Debate," *Montana Standard*, August 20, 1896; "City News in Brief," *Butte Daily Post* (Butte, MT), May 10, 1897; "Ben [Perkins] is Unlucky," *Anaconda Standard*, January 18, 1898; "May Have Wheels: A Colored Man Detained in Jail on the Charge of Insanity," *Butte Daily Post*, February 21, 1898; "Shipped to Salt Lake," *Anaconda Standard*, February 27, 1898; "Town Talk," *Salt Lake Herald*, March 1, 1898.
57. Jeffrey D. Nichols, *Prostitution, Polygamy, and Power: Salt Lake City, 1847–1918* (Urbana: University of Illinois Press, 2002).
58. "In the Police Court," *Salt Lake Herald*, June 13, 1886.
59. "In the Police Court."
60. "Before Judge Pyper," *Salt Lake Herald*, June 16, 1886.

61. Records of the Bureau of the Census, *1880 Census: Tenth Census of the United States* (National Archives Microfilm Publication T9, 1,454 rolls, Record Group 29), Mrs. Nellie Kidd, Eureka County, Nevada, 1880; Records of the Bureau of the Census, *1920 Census: Fourteenth Census of the United States* (National Archives Microfilm Publication T625, 2,076 rolls), Ellen M. Mclean, Alameda County, California, 1920.
62. Records of the Bureau of the Census, *1880 Census: Tenth Census of the United States* (National Archives Microfilm Publication T9, 1,454 rolls, Record Group 29), Lotta Perkins, Summit County, Utah Territory, 1880.
63. To situate James and Perkins within the history of prostitution in Utah Territory, see Nichols, *Prostitution, Polygamy, and Power*. For more on prostitution in the American West and the reasons women entered the sex trade, see Michael Rutter, *Upstairs Girls: Prostitution in the American West* (Helena, MT: Farcountry Press, 2005) and Anne M. Butler, *Daughters of Joy, Sisters of Misery: Prostitutes in the American West, 1865–90* (1985; repr., Urbana: University of Illinois Press, 1987).
64. "Before Judge Pyper," *Salt Lake Herald*, January 9, 1887. For additional newspaper citations, see Charlotte Perkins's biographical entry.
65. "Brief and Breezy," *Salt Lake Herald*, April 13, 1893.
66. "Coontown Raided," *Salt Lake Tribune*, August 30, 1894. In the late nineteenth century, Salt Lake City had two main Black newspapers, *Utah Plain Dealer* and *Broad Ax*, plus three larger newspapers divided along religious lines. The *Salt Lake Tribune* was generally antagonistic toward the Church of Jesus Christ of Latter-day Saints; the *Salt Lake Herald* was sympathetic, and the church owned the *Deseret News*. None of the three papers provided much coverage of the local Black community. When the *Deseret News* did, it was usually straightforward, but the *Tribune* and *Herald* tended to treat the Black community as comic relief. Only fragments remain of the *Plain Dealer*. *Broad Ax* was devoted to politics, so neither paper is a source for significant amounts of biographical content except a short 1899 *Broad Ax* article, "Slavery in Utah." (See Part 2: Miscellaneous Topics for brief articles about William Wesley and Elizabeth Austen Taylor of *Plain Dealer* and Julius Taylor of *Broad Ax*, and Appendix 6 for "Slavery in Utah.")
67. "Police Court Record," *Salt Lake Herald*, October 5, 1894.
68. "Police Court," *Salt Lake Herald*, August 3, 1894; "Colored Men Fight a Duel," *Salt Lake Tribune*, November 7, 1895; "Thompson's Hearing," *Salt Lake Herald*, August 4, 1896; "Jim Williams Won," *Salt Lake Herald*, February 16, 1898; "Died," *Salt Lake Tribune*, September 2, 1898.
69. Records of the Bureau of the Census, *1860 Census: Eighth Census of the United States* (National Archives Microfilm Publication M653, Record Group 29), James Vollantyne, Great Salt Lake County, Utah Territory, 1860; "Local News," *Mountaineer* (Salt Lake City, UT), September 8, 1860; "Doings of the Probate Court," *Deseret News*, September 12, 1860; "A Colored Gentleman in Trouble," *Deseret News*, April 13, 1870; "Agents for the Elevator," *Elevator*, June 24, 1870.
70. For more on the Litchford family, see Diane Kelly Runyon and Kim Shoemaker Starr, *Secrets Under the Parking Lot: The True Story of Upper Arlington, Ohio, and the History of Perry Township in the Nineteenth Century* (Scotts Valley, CA: CreateSpace Independent Publishing, 2017).

71. "Lost, Stayed or Stolen," *Ogden Standard Examiner* (Ogden, UT), November 7, 1899; "Police Cameos," *Salt Lake Tribune*, November 12, 1899; "Yesterday's Real Estate Transfers," *Salt Lake Herald*, August 14, 1894.
72. "Inherits an Estate: Joy Comes to a Poor and Needy Colored Woman," *Salt Lake Herald*, November 13, 1899.
73. The news coverage was often incorrect about relationships. "Negro Woman to Get Fortune," *Salt Lake Herald*, January 16, 1902; "Washerwoman Wins a Fortune," *Salt Lake Telegram* (Salt Lake City, UT), April 11, 1902; Catherine Patterson, October 19, 1917, Salt Lake City, death certificate 1702930, Utah Department of Health, USHS.
74. "To the Colored Citizens of Utah," *Salt Lake Tribune*, November 7, 1873; "To the Colored Citizens of Utah," *Salt Lake Herald-Republican,* November 12, 1873.
75. "Colored Republicans Again Deceived," *Broad Ax*, January 18, 1896.
76. See, for example, "Names of Graduates," *Salt Lake Daily Tribune*, June 4, 1897.
77. William Sinclair Jackson, Alameda, California, United States, Selective Service System, *World War I Selective Service System Draft Registration Cards, 1917–1918*, National Archives Microfilm Publication M1509, Ancestry.com, https://www.ancestry.com/search/collections/6482.

BIBLIOGRAPHY

1790 Census: First Census of the United States. National Archives Microfilm Publication M637 (12 rolls), Records of the Bureau of the Census, Record Group 29, U.S. National Archives and Records Administration, Washington, DC, 1790.

1800 Census: Second Census of the United States. National Archives Microfilm Publication M32 (52 rolls), Records of the Bureau of the Census, Record Group 29, U.S. National Archives and Records Administration, Washington, DC, 1800.

1810 Census: Third Census of the United States. National Archives Microfilm Publication M252 (71 rolls), Records of the Bureau of the Census, Record Group 29, U.S. National Archives and Records Administration, Washington, DC, 1810.

1820 Census: Fourth Census of the United States. National Archives Microfilm Publication M33 (142 rolls), Records of the Bureau of the Census, Record Group 29, U.S. National Archives and Records Administration, Washington, DC, 1820.

1830 Census: Fifth Census of the United States. National Archives Microfilm Publication M19 (201 rolls), Records of the Bureau of the Census, Record Group 29, U.S. National Archives and Records Administration, Washington, DC, 1830.

1840 Census: Sixth Census of the United States. National Archives Microfilm Publication M704 (580 rolls), Records of the Bureau of the Census, Record Group 29, U.S. National Archives and Records Administration, Washington, DC, 1840.

1850 Census: Seventh Census of the United States. National Archives Microfilm Publication M432 (1,009 rolls), Records of the Bureau of the Census, Record Group 29, U.S. National Archives and Records Administration, Washington, DC, 1850.

1850 Utah Territory Agricultural Schedules: Utah Territory Productions of Agriculture [draft], 1850 [1851]. MS 2672, box 1, folders 2, 3, 6, 10, Church History Library (hereafter CHL).

1850 Utah Territory Population Schedules: Schedule of Population [draft], 1850 [1851] Utah Territorial Census. MS 2672, box 1, folders 1, 3, 4, 5, 9, CHL.

1850 Utah Territory Slave Schedules: Slave Schedule [draft], 1850 [1851] Utah Territorial Census. MS 2672, box 1, folders 2, 6, 10, CHL.

1852 California Census: California State Library. "California State Census of 1852." Ancestry.com.

1856 Utah Territorial Census. MS 2929, CHL.

1860 Census: Eighth Census of the United States. National Archives Microfilm Publication M653, Records of the Bureau of the Census, Record Group 29, U.S. National Archives and Records Administration, Washington, DC, 1860.

1860 Utah Territory Productions of Agriculture. Utah Territory Census Schedules, 1850–1860, 1870. MS 9234, CHL.

1865 Kansas Territorial Census: Kansas State Historical Society. "1865 Kansas Territory Census." *Kansas State Census Collection, 1855–1925.* Ancestry.com. https://www.ancestry.com/search/collections/ksstatecen.

1870 Census: Ninth Census of the United States. National Archives Microfilm Publication M593 (1,761 rolls), Records of the Bureau of the Census, Record Group 29, U.S. National Archives and Records Administration, Washington, DC, 1870.

1880 Census: Tenth Census of the United States. National Archives Microfilm Publication T9 (1,454 rolls), Records of the Bureau of the Census, Record Group 29, U.S. National Archives and Records Administration, Washington, DC, 1880.

1900 Census: Twelfth Census of the United States. National Archives Microfilm Publication T623 (1,854 rolls), Records of the Bureau of the Census, Record Group 29, U.S. National Archives and Records Administration, Washington, DC, 1900.

1910 Census: Thirteenth Census of the United States. National Archives Microfilm Publication T624 (1,178 rolls), Records of the Bureau of the Census, Record Group 29, U.S. National Archives and Records Administration, Washington, DC, 1910.

1920 Census: Fourteenth Census of the United States. National Archives Microfilm Publication T625 (2,076 rolls), Records of the Bureau of the Census, Record Group 29, U.S. National Archives and Records Administration, Washington, DC, 1920.

1930 Census: Fifteenth Census of the United States. National Archives Microfilm Publication T626 (2,667 rolls), Records of the Bureau of the Census, Record Group 29, U.S. National Archives and Records Administration, Washington, DC, 1930.

1940 Census: Sixteenth Census of the United States. National Archives Microfilm Publication T627 (4,643 rolls), Records of the Bureau of the Census, Record Group 29, U.S. National Archives and Records Administration, Washington, DC, 1940.

Ackley, Richard Thomas. "Across the Plains in 1858." *Utah Historical Quarterly* 9, nos. 1–4 (July–October 1941): 190–228. https://www.jstor.org/stable/45063456.

An Act in Relation to Service, Utah Territorial Legislature (1852).

"An Act to Prohibit the Importation of Slaves into any Port or Place Within the Jurisdiction of the United States." 9 U.S.C., 2 Stat. 426 (1807).

"Adinkra Symbols." *twi.bb: Online Dictionary for the Twi Language of the Akan People of Ghana in West Africa.* http://www.twi.bb/akan-adinkra.php (site discontinued).

Against the Admission of Utah as a State. "Memorial of the Citizens of Utah against the Admission of the Territory as a State, May 6, 1872." *The Miscellaneous Documents Printed by Order of the House of Representatives.* Washington, DC: Government Printing Office, 1872.

Aird, Polly. "'You Nasty Apostates, Clear Out': Reasons for Disaffection in the Late 1850s." *Journal of Mormon History* 30, no. 2 (Fall 2004): 129–207. https://www.jstor.org/stable/23289370.

Aird, Polly, Jeff Nichols, and Will Bagley, eds. *Playing with Shadows: Voices of Dissent in the Mormon West.* Kingdom in the West: The Mormons and the American Frontier Series. Norman, OK: Arthur H. Clark, 2011.

Alabama County Courthouses. "Alabama Probate Records." 1809-1985. FSFT. https:// www.familysearch.org/search/collection/1925446.

Alexander, Thomas G. "Brigham Young and the Transformation of Utah Wilderness, 1847-58." *Journal of Mormon History* 41, no. 1 (January 2015): 103-24. https://www .jstor.org/stable/10.5406/jmormhist.41.1.103.

Alexander, Thomas G., and Leonard J. Arrington. "Camp in the Sagebrush: Camp Floyd, Utah, 1858-61." *Utah Historical Quarterly*, 34, no. 1 (Winter 1966): 3-21. https://www .jstor.org/stable/45058591.

"All Negro Blood: Baptisms and Confirmations for the Dead." 1924-1942. Salt Lake Temple, F 183511. John D. Fretwell Collection. Private Collection.

Allston Family Papers, 1830-1901, South Carolina Historical Society, Charleston, SC. Partial Typescript Courtesy of William Gorenfeld, 2018.

Alston, Thomas. 1975. Autobiography. In Ray Lester Alston, comp. "Thomas Alston and Mary Ellen Holt Alston." As Cited at Pioneer Database. 16-19. Accessed October 3, 2016. https://history.churchofjesuschrist.org/overlandtravel.

Anonymous. "Caroline Graham Hill." Digital Copy of Typescript, n.p., n.d. FSFT. Accessed April 11, 2016. https://familysearch.org/photos/stories/3402434.

Anonymous. "History of John Henderson Bankhead, 1814-1884, and Nancy Coleman Crosby, 1825-1915." Unpublished manuscript, n.p., n.d., TN-2155810, FHL.

Anonymous, "1. In 1856 [excerpt from Anonymous, 'Salem Pioneers,']" Jones442 [pseud.], FSFT, August 26, 2013. https://www.familysearch.org/tree/person/collaborate/ KWNJ-L71.

Anonymous. "Slavery in Draper." Handwritten manuscript, n.p., c. 1935. MS 6017, CHL.

Anonymous. "The Life History of William Taylor Dennis and His Wife Talitha Cumi Bankhead." Digital manuscript, n.p., n.d. Copy in possession of author.

Argyle, Joseph. Reminiscences and Journal 1870-1894. MS 340, CHL.

Arizona Department of Health Services. "Arizona, Death Records, 1887-1960." Ancestry .com. https://www.ancestry.com/search/collections/8704.

Arrington, Leonard J. *Brigham Young: American Moses*. New York: Alfred A. Knopf, 1985.

Arrington, Leonard J. *Great Basin Kingdom: An Economic History of the Latter-day Saints, 1830-1900, New Edition*. Boston, MA: Harvard University Press; 1958. Champaign, IL: University of Illinois Press, 2005.

Arrington, Leonard J. "The Mormon Cotton Mission in Southern Utah." *Pacific Historical Review* 25, no. 3 (August 1956): 221-38. https://doi.org/10.2307/3637013.

Arrington, Leonard J., and Davis Bitton. *Saints Without Halos: The Human Side of Mormon History*. Salt Lake City, UT: Signature Books, 1982.

Arrington, Leonard J., Feramorz Y. Fox, and Dean L. May. *Building the City of God: Community and Cooperation among the Mormons*. Champaign, IL: University of Illinois Press, 1992.

Athearn, Robert G. *Union Pacific Country*. Lincoln, NE: University of Nebraska Press, 1976.

Ball, Charles, and Mr. Fisher. *Fifty Years in Chains, or, the Life of an American Slave.* New York, NY: H. Dayton, 1859.

Bancroft, Hubert H. *History of California, 1860–1890.* Vol. 7. San Francisco, CA: History Company, 1890.

Bancroft, Hubert H. *History of Utah, 1540–1886.* San Francisco, CA: History Company, 1889.

Bankhead, Henrietta. Interview by Florence Lawrence, November 22, 1977. Helen Z. Papanikolas Papers, 1954–2001. MS 471, Marriott Library Special Collections, University of Utah.

Bankhead, Mary Lucile. Interview by Alan Cherry, CRC-P2, transcript, LDS Afro-American Oral History Project. Provo, UT: Charles Redd Center for Western Studies, Brigham Young University, April 11, 1985.

Banks, Ray H., and Patricia Banks. *Jex Family History.* Provo, UT: BYU Press, 2004.

Barbour, Oliver L., and Ebenezer B. Harrington. *An Analytical Digest of the Equity Cases Decided in the Courts of the Several States, and of the United States, from the Earliest Period.* Vol. 1. Springfield, MA: Merriam, 1837.

Barnes and Barnes v. DeMoss (1854). USHS.

Barnes and Barnes v. Probosco and Demoss (1854). USHS.

Barnett, P. T., and Anonymous. Excerpts from Letter and Notes, Camden, Tennessee, 1937. Typescript.

Barrett, Ivan J. "History of the Cotton Mission and Cotton Culture in Utah." Master's thesis, Brigham Young University, 1947.

Beadle's Dime Song Book No. 10. New York, NY: Beadle and Company, 1863.

Bean, Eddavene Houtz. "History of Mary Lee Bland." Digital Copy of Typescript, July 24, 2015. FSFT. https://familysearch.org/photos/artifacts/17797928.

Beasley, Delilah L. *The Negro Trail Blazers of California.* Los Angeles, CA: Times Mirror Printing and Binding House, 1919.

Beasley, Delilah L. "Slavery in California." *The Journal of Negro History* 3, no. 1 (January 1918): 33–44. https://www.journals.uchicago.edu/doi/10.2307/2713792.

Beasley, Delilah L., and Monroe N. Work. "Documents: California Freedom Papers." *Journal of Negro History* 3, no. 1 (January 1918): 50–54. https://www.journals.uchicago.edu/doi/pdf/10.2307/2713793.

Beckstrom, Elizabeth, and Bessie Snow. *"Oh Ye Mountains High": History of Pine Valley, Utah.* St. George, UT: Heritage Press, 1980.

Bellamy, Donnie D. "Slavery in Microcosm: Onslow County, North Carolina." *Journal of Negro History* 62, no. 4 (October 1977): 339–50. https://doi.org/10.2307/2717110.

Beller, Jack. "Negro Slaves in Utah." *Utah Historical Quarterly* 2, no. 4 (October 1929): 122–26. https://www.jstor.org/stable/45057482.

Bennett, Richard. "'Has the Lord Turned Bankrupt?' The Attempted Sale of the Nauvoo Temple, 1846–1850." *Journal of the Illinois State Historical Society* 95, no. 3 (Autumn 2002): 235–63. https://scholarsarchive.byu.edu/facpub/1080.

Bennion, Michael K. "Captivity, Adoption, Marriage and Identity: Native American Children in Mormon Homes, 1847–1900." Master's thesis, University of Nevada, Las Vegas, 2012.

Berlin, C. Elliott. "Abraham Owen Smoot, Pioneer Mormon Leader." Master's thesis, Brigham Young University, 1955. https://scholarsarchive.byu.edu/etd/4523.

Berlin, Ira. *Many Thousands Gone: The First Two Centuries of Slavery in North America.* Cambridge, MA: Harvard University Press, 1998.

Berrett, LaMar C. "History of the Southern States Mission: 1831–1861." Master's thesis, Brigham Young University, 1960.

Berry, Daina Ramey. *The Price for Their Pound of Flesh: The Value of the Enslaved, from Womb to Grave, in the Building of a Nation.* Boston, MA: Beacon Press, 2017.

"Biddy Mason Memorial Park." *Atlas Obscura.* Accessed October 17, 2018. https://www.atlasobscura.com/places/biddy-mason-memorial-park.

Biographical Sketches, 1891–2013. CR 100 18, CHL.

"Biographies Company G, 2nd Mississippi Infantry, Pontotoc County." *Pontotoc County, Mississippi Genealogy and History*, 1999–2002. *MSGenWeb.* http://msgw.org/pontotoc/cw/CoGMNOPZ.htm.

Black, James, Parley Jacobsen, and Ellen Taggart. *Ogden, Weber County, Utah, City Cemetery Records.* Vol. 4. Salt Lake City, UT: Privately printed, 1940–1942.

Black, Susan Easton, and Harvey B. Black. *Early Members of the Reorganized Church of Jesus Christ of Latter Day Saints.* Provo, UT: Religious Studies Center, Brigham Young University, 1993.

Blackstone, William, Barron Field, John F. Archbold, Joseph Chitty, and Edward Christian. *Commentaries on the Laws of England.* New York, NY: E. Duyckinck, G. Long, Collins & Hannay, 1827.

Bleak, James G. Annals of the Southern Utah Mission, 1850–1900. MS 318, CHL.

Bragg, George F. *Men of Maryland.* Baltimore, MD: Church Advocate Press, 1914. https://archive.org/details/menofmarylandbrag.

Brigham Young Office Emigrating Companies Reports, 1850–1862. CR 1234 5, CHL.

Brigham Young Office Files. CR 1234 1, CHL.

Brooks, Juanita. *History of the Jews in Utah and Idaho.* Salt Lake City, UT: Western Epics, 1973.

Brown, John. Reminiscences and Journals. MS 1636, CHL, 1843–1896.

Brown, John, and John Z. Brown. *Autobiography of Pioneer John Brown 1820–1896.* Salt Lake City, UT: Press of Stevens and Wallis, Inc., 1941.

Brown, Lisle G. "'Temple Pro Tempore': The Salt Lake City Endowment House." *Journal of Mormon History* 34, no. 4 (Fall 2008): 1–68. https://mds.marshall.edu/lib_faculty/15/.

Brown, Thomas D. *Journal of the Southern Indian Mission: Diary of Thomas D. Brown.* Edited by Juanita Brooks. Logan, UT: Utah State University Press, 1972.

Brown, William W. *Narrative of William W. Brown, a Fugitive Slave.* Boston, MA: Anti-Slavery Office, 1847.

Bryner, Farozine R. Collection, 1847–1956. MS 8865, CHL.

Bullock, Thomas. 1847–1848 Emigration List. Nauvoo City Court Docket Book, February 1844–May 1845. MS 3441, CHL.

Bullock, Thomas. Journals, 1843–1849. MS 1385, CHL.

Bullock, Thomas. Names of Pueblo Soldiers and Mississippi Brethren, 1847. MS 15561, CHL.

Bureau of Land Management and US Department of the Interior. *General Land Office Records*. https://glorecords.blm.gov.

Bureau of the Census. *A Century of Population Growth from the First Census of the United States to the Twelfth, 1790–1900*. Washington, DC: Government Printing Office, 1909.

Burton v. Dotson, Whitmore, and Burr (1861). Great Salt Lake County Probate Court. USHS.

Burton, Donald E. "History of John Burton: 1797–1865" (Digital copy of unpublished manuscript). October 2013.

Burton, Richard F. *The City of the Saints, and Across the Rocky Mountains to California*. New York, NY: Harper & Brothers, 1862.

Butler, Anne M. *Daughters of Joy, Sisters of Misery: Prostitutes in the American West, 1865–90*. 1985. Reprint. Champaign, IL: University of Illinois Press, 1987.

Cache County, Utah, Deed Records, Vol. B, 1869–1872. Logan, UT: Cache County Courthouse, 2012.

Caldwell v. Porter (1855). "Jackson County (MO) Records Center, Jackson County Circuit Court, 1855–1857." Kansas City Public Library, Civil War on the Western Border. https://civilwaronthewesternborder.org/islandora/object/civilwar%3A7874.

California County, District, and Probate Courts. "California, Wills and Probate Records, 1850–1953." Ancestry.com. https://www.ancestry.com/search/collections/8639.

California Department of Health and Welfare. "California, Death Index, 1905–1939." Ancestry.com. https://www.ancestry.com/search/collections/5187.

California Department of Public Health. "California, County Birth, Marriage, and Death Records, 1830–1980." Ancestry.com. https://www.ancestry.com/search/collections/61460/.

California Mortality Schedule. *Tenth Census of the United States*. Berkeley, CA: Bancroft Library, University of California, 1880.

California Schedules of Defective, Dependent, and Delinquent Classes. "1880 United States Census." Bancroft Library, University of California. Ancestry.com. https://www.ancestry.com/search/collections/1634/.

California State Archives, and California Department of Corrections. "California, Prison and Correctional Records, 1851–1950." Ancestry.com. https://www.ancestry.com/search/collections/8833.

California State Library. "California Voter Registers, 1866–1898." Ancestry.com. https://www.ancestry.com/search/collections/2221.

"California, Select Marriages, 1850–1945." Ancestry.com. https://www.ancestry.com/search/collections/60241.

Camp of Israel Schedules and Reports, 1845–1849. MS 14290, CHL.

Campbell, Manila Bybee. "Mary Lee Bland (Blann) History." Digital Copy of Typescript, March 9, 2017. FSFT. https://www.familysearch.org/photos/artifacts/34378667.

Cannon, George Q. *Journal of George Q. Cannon*. Salt Lake City, UT: Church Historian's Press, The Church of Jesus Christ of Latter-day Saints, 2021. https://churchhistorianspress.org/george-q-cannon.

Cannon, Kenneth L., II. "'Mountain Common Law': The Extralegal Punishment of Seducers in Early Utah." *Utah Historical Quarterly* 51, no. 4 (Fall 1983): 308–27. https://www.jstor.org/stable/45061124.

Carruth, LaJean Purcell. Church History Department Pitman Shorthand transcriptions: Addresses and Sermons, 1851–1874. CR 100 912, CHL.

Carter, Clarence E. *The Territorial Papers of the United States, Vol. VI: The Territory of Mississippi, 1809–1817 Continued*. Washington, DC: United States Government Printing Office, 1938.

Carter, Kate B. *The Negro Pioneer*. Salt Lake City, UT: Daughters of Utah Pioneers, 1965.

Case Files of Applications from Former Confederates for Presidential Pardons, 1865–1867. M1003, Records of the Adjutant General's Office, 1780s–1917, Record Group 94. FSFT. https://www.familysearch.org/search/collection/1936545.

Cathy [pseud.]. *Clmroots: History of an American Family* (blog). https://clmroots.blogspot.com.

Census Office, Department of the Interior. *Ninth Census, United States, 1870, Instructions to Assistant Marshals*. Washington, DC: Government Printing Office, 1870.

Chadbourne, Eugene. "Charlie Beal." AllMusic. Accessed November 25, 2016. https://www.allmusic.com/artist/charlie-beal-mn0000804648/biography.

Chadbourne, Eugene. "Eddie Beal." AllMusic. Accessed November 25, 2016. https://www.allmusic.com/artist/eddie-beal-mn0000166097.

Chandless, William. *A Visit to Salt Lake; Being a Journey Across the Plains, and a Residence in the Mormon Settlements at Utah*. London: Smith, Elder, and Co., 1857.

Church Register of the Presbyterian Church, Corinne, Utah. Philadelphia, PA: Presbyterian Board of Publication, n.d.

Clawson, Margaret Gay Judd. Reminiscences, c. 1904–1911. MS 3712, CHL.

Clayton, William. Diaries, 1846–1853. MS 1406, CHL.

Coleman, Ronald G. "Blacks in Utah History: An Unknown Legacy." In *The Peoples of Utah*, edited by Helen Z. Papanikolas, 115–40. Salt Lake City, UT: Utah State Historical Society, 1976.

Coleman, Ronald G. "A History of Blacks in Utah, 1825–1910." PhD diss., University of Utah, 1980.

Consecration Deeds, 1854–1867. CR 5 53, CHL.

Copeland, Roy W. "The Nomenclature of Enslaved Africans as Real Property or Chattels Personal: Legal Fiction, Judicial Interpretation, Legislative Designation, or Was a Slave a Slave by Any Other Name." *Journal of Black Studies* 40, no. 5 (May 2010): 946–59. https://www.jstor.org/stable/40648615.

Craig, Wesley W., and Roberta Blake Barnum. "Pioneer Indexes, Washington County, Utah, 1852–1870: St. George, Male Pioneer Index, A–E Surnames." *Washington County Utah History and Genealogy*, 1998–1999. http://www.rootsweb.ancestry.com/~utwashin/settlers/sg-ae.html (site discontinued).

Crosby, Caroline Barnes. *No Place to Call Home: The 1807–1857 Life Writings of Caroline Barnes Crosby, Chronicler of Outlying Mormon Communities.* Edited by Edward Leo Lyman, Susan Ward Payne, and S. George Ellsworth. Logan, UT: Utah State University Press, 2005.

Crosby, John. *Various Records*, Monroe County Tax Rolls, 1822–1841, box 3723, Jackson, MS: Mississippi Department of Archives and History, 1839.

Culmer, H. L. A. *Utah Directory and Gazetteer for 1879–80.* Salt Lake City, UT: J. C. Graham & Co., 1879.

Cummings, Benjamin Franklin. Reminiscences and Diaries, 1842–1879. MS 1684, CHL. As cited at *Pioneer Database.*

Custer, George Armstrong. *My Life on the Plains, or, Personal Experiences with Indians.* New York, NY: Sheldon and Company, 1874.

Dalton, Luella Adams. *History of Iron County Mission, Parowan, Utah.* Privately printed, 1973.

Daughters of Utah Pioneers, Davis County Company. *East of Antelope Island: History of the First Fifty Years of Davis County.* Bountiful, UT: Carr Printing Company, 1948.

Daughters of Utah Pioneers, Far South East, Salt Lake County. "A Bicentennial Salute & Dedication, Fort Union Pioneer Cemetery Memorial." 1976. John D. Fretwell Collection. Private Collection.

Davis, Sam P., ed. *The History of Nevada.* Vol. 1. Reno, NV: Elms Publishing Company, 1913.

Daynes, Kathryn M. *More Wives Than One: Transformation of the Mormon Marriage System, 1840–1910.* Champaign, IL: University of Illinois Press, 2008.

Demaratus, DeEtta. *The Force of a Feather: The Search for a Lost Story of Slavery and Freedom.* Salt Lake City, UT: University of Utah Press, 2002.

Doctrine and Covenants, ed. *Church of Jesus Christ of Latter-day Saints.* Salt Lake City, UT: Church of Jesus Christ of Latter-day Saints, 1981.

Douglass, Frederick. *The Life and Times of Frederick Douglass: From 1817–1882.* London: Christian Age Office, 1882.

Dowdle, Absalom P. "Absolam Porter Dowdle (Taken From His Diary)." MS 9266, CHL.

Downs, Jim. *Sick from Freedom: African-American Illness and Suffering During the Civil War and Reconstruction.* Oxford: Oxford University Press, 2012.

Driggs, Howard R., and J. Rulon Hales. *Timpanogos Town: Story of Old Battle Creek and Pleasant Grove, Utah.* Manchester, NH: Clarke Press, 1948.

Duncan, Homer. Autobiographical Sketch, c. 1900. Typescript of holograph. MS 21280, CHL.

Egan, Howard. *Pioneering the West 1846 to 1878: Major Howard Egan's Diary.* Edited by William M. Egan. Richmond, UT: Howard R. Egan Estate, 1917.

Erasmus Love v. Richmond Love, 38 N.C. 104, 85 (N.C. 1843). https://casetext.com/case/love-v-love-43.

Esshom, Frank E. *Pioneers and Prominent Men of Utah*. Salt Lake City, UT: Utah Pioneers Book Publishing Company, 1913.

Evans, D. W., J. Q. Cannon, and Julia Young. *Journal of Discourses*. Vol. 15. Liverpool, England: Albert Carrington, 1873.

Evergreen Memorial Park Cemetery. "Los Angeles, Records 1877–1988 and Indexes 1877–1989." FSFT. https://www.familysearch.org/search/catalog/1143073.

"Eye Color." *Stanford at The Tech: Understanding Genetics*. San Jose, CA: The Tech Museum of Innovation, October 8, 2004. https://genetics.thetech.org/ask/ask57.

"FamilySearch Family Tree (FSFT)." *The Church of Jesus Christ of Latter-day Saints*. https://www.familysearch.org.

Faragher, John Mack. *Eternity Street: Violence and Justice in Frontier Los Angeles*. New York, NY: W. W. Norton and Company, 2016.

Farquhar, Catherine Grace Barbour. "Tabor and Tabor College." *Iowa Journal of History and Politics* 41, no. 4 (October 1943): 337–93. https://archive.org/details/iowajournalofhisoostat.

Ferris, Norman B., and Morris J. Snedaker. "The Diary of Morris J. Snedaker, 1855–1856." *Southwestern Historical Quarterly* 66, no. 4 (April 1963): 516–46. https://www.jstor.org/stable/30236261.

Field, Kendra, and Daniel Lynch. "'Master of Ceremonies': The World of Peter Biggs in Civil War–Era Los Angeles." *Western Historical Quarterly* 47, no. 3 (August 2016): 1–27. https://doi.org/10.1093/whq/whw160.

Fifteenth Ward Relief Society Building. "Nicholas G. Morgan Collection." *USHS*. https://collections.lib.utah.edu/details?id=435674.

FindAGrave. https://www.findagrave.com.

Flake, Augusta, to Elizabeth DeBrouwer. San Bernardino, CA: San Bernardino Public Library, February 22, 1979.

Flake, Osmer D. *William J. Flake: Pioneer-Colonizer*. Printed by author, 1948.

Fleming, Robert E. "The Real Utah War: The Mountaineer's Efforts to Combat the Valley Tan." Master's thesis, Brigham Young University, 1996.

Florida County, District, and Probate Courts. "Florida, Wills and Probate Records, 1810–1974." Ancestry.com. https://www.ancestry.com/search/collections/8993.

Fogel, Robert W., and Stanley L. Engerman. *Time on the Cross: The Economics of American Negro Slavery*. New York, NY: W. W. Norton and Company, 1995.

Foster, Thomas A. *Rethinking Rufus: Sexual Violations of Enslaved Men*. Athens: University of Georgia Press, 2019.

Fox, Feramorz Y. "The Consecration Movement of the Middle Fifties Part II, Conclusion." *Improvement Era* 47, no. 2 (February 1944): 80–81, 120–21, 124–25. https://archive.org/details/improvementera4702unse.

Fox-Genovese, Elizabeth. *Within the Plantation Household: Black and White Women of the Old South*. Chapel Hill: University of North Carolina Press, 1988.

Francis, Annie Gardner. "Serena Evensen." Digital Copy of Typescript, n.p., n.d. FSFT. Accessed October 4, 2016. https://familysearch.org/photos/artifacts/2162690.

"Freedom Papers of Biddy Mason." 1860. Collection of Miriam Matthews. UCLA Library Digital Collections.

Freeman, Ron. "James Madison Flake (1815–1850)." Unpublished manuscript, 2011. FSFT. https://familysearch.org/photos/artifacts/3394048.

Freeman, Ron. "Rowlett, Nancy Ann." Unpublished manuscript, 2014. FSFT. https://familysearch.org/photos/artifacts/7470319.

Freeman, Ron. "Smoot, George (Washington)." Unpublished manuscript, 2014. FSFT. https://familysearch.org/photos/artifacts/6137791.

Fretwell, John D. "Green Flake." 1999. Typescript. John D. Fretwell Collection. Private Collection.

Fretwell, John D. Compiled Material on Black Mormons, c. 1982. MS 6968, CHL.

"From Darkness to Light: Discovering Harriet Mason." Lecture. *The Banning Museum*, April 3, 2013. https://www.thebanningmuseum.org/2013/04/03/from-darkness-to-light-discovering-harriet-mason.

Garrett, H. Dean. "The Controversial Death of Gobo Fango." *Utah Historical Quarterly* 57, no. 3 (Summer 1989): 264–72. https://www.jstor.org/stable/45061873.

General Board of Relief Society. *A Centenary of Relief Society, 1842–1942*. Salt Lake City, UT: General Board of Relief Society, 1942.

General Tithing Office Tithing Labor Time Books, 1850–1854. CR 104 27 and 104 28, CHL.

Georgia County Courthouses. "Georgia Probate Records, 1742–1990." FSFT. https://www.familysearch.org/search/collection/1999178.

Georgia Freedmen's Bureau Field Office Records, 1865–1872. Washington, DC: National Archives Microfilm Publication M1903, n.d.

Gibbons, Daniel Bay. *Bay & Gibbons Family History* (blog). https://baygibbons.blogspot.com.

Gibbs, E. H. "Bowel Complaints of Children." *Hall's Journal of Health* 24, no. 11 (November 1877): 320–21.

Gold Dust Accounts (Church Mint), 1848–1851. Brigham Young Office Files. CR 1234 1, CHL.

Golden Spike Chapter Utah Genealogical Association. "Historical and Genealogical Register of Indexes to Corinne, Utah Newspapers 1869–1875." Typed manuscript, Brigham City, Utah, 1975.

Great Salt Lake County. Court Papers. 1850–1851. MS 2490, CHL.

Greenwood, Ned H. "The Greers of Apache County." Digital Copy of Typescript, n.p., n.d. TN-1316590, FHL.

Greer, Ellen C., and Anonymous. Anecdotes and Reminiscences of Her Life as Related by Grandma Ellen C. Greer, May 19, 1921. MS 7776, CHL.

Grow, Matthew J., and Ronald W. Walker. *The Prophet and the Reformer: The Letters of Brigham Young and Thomas L. Kane*. New York, NY: Oxford University Press, 2015.

Gunnison, John W. *The Mormons, or, Latter-day Saints, in the Valley of the Great Salt Lake*. Philadelphia, PA: Lippincott, Grambo & Co., 1852.

Gwynn, Zae Hargett. *Abstracts of the Records of Onslow County, North Carolina, 1734–1850*. 2 vols. Onslow County, NC: Z. H. Gwynn, 1961.

Hafen, LeRoy R., and Ann W. Hafen. *Handcarts to Zion: The Story of a Unique Western Migration, 1856–1860*. Glendale, CA: A.H. Clark Co, 1960.

Hall, Erika V., Katherine W. Phillips, and Sarah S. M. Townsend. "A Rose by Any Other Name: The Consequences of Subtyping 'African-Americans' from 'Blacks.'" *Journal of Experimental Social Psychology* 56 (January 2015): 183–90. https://dx.doi.org/10.1016/j.jesp.2014.10.004.

Hancock County, Illinois. Misc. "Court Records, 1844–1858, Misc. Court Records, 1845–1853, Misc. Court Records, 1839, Illinois Probate Records, 1819–1988." FSFT. https://www.familysearch.org/search/collection/1834344.

Handbook of Texas Online. Austin, TX: Texas State Historical Association. https://www.tshaonline.org/home.

Hardy, Heather. "Remembered and Known: Latter-day Saints in the Antebellum South." Unpublished manuscript, 2001, CHL.

Harper, John. "Autobiography of John Nelson Harper." 1861, 1931, 1935. Edited by Jewel B. Furniss and Alice M. Rich. MS 7766, CHL.

Hartley, William G. "Samuel D. Chambers." *New Era*, "June 1974." The Church of Jesus Christ of Latter-day Saints. https://www.churchofjesuschrist.org/study/new-era/1974/06/samuel-d-chambers.

Hartley, William G. *Another Kind of Gold: The Life of Albert King Thurber*. Troy, ID: John Lowe Butler Family Association, 2011.

Hartley, William G. *Kentucky Converts and Utah Pioneers: The Story of Five Brothers*. Salt Lake City, UT: Lewis Brothers Family Organization, 2014.

Hartley, William G. *My Best for the Kingdom: History and Autobiography of John Lowe Butler, a Mormon Frontiersman*. Salt Lake City, UT: Aspen Books, 1993.

Haskins, George L. "Curtesy in the United States." *University of Pennsylvania Law Review* 196 (1951): 196–223. https://scholarship.law.upenn.edu/penn_law_review/vol100/iss2/3.

Hayden, Dolores. "Biddy Mason's Los Angeles 1856–1891." *California History* 68, no. 3 (Fall 1989): 86–99. https://doi.org/10.2307/25462395.

Heerman, M. Scott. "In a State of Slavery: Black Servitude in Illinois, 1800–1830." *Early American Studies: An Interdisciplinary Journal* 14, no. 1 (Winter 2016): 114–39.

Hening, William W. *The Statutes at Large; Being a Collection of All the Laws of Virginia*. Vol. 2. New York, NY: Bartow, 1823.

Hilmo, Tess. "Gobo Fango." *Friend*, "March 2003," The Church of Jesus Christ of Latter-Day Saints. https://www.churchofjesuschrist.org/study/friend/2003/03/gobo-fango.

Historian's Office Rebaptism Records, 1848–1876. CR 100 591, CHL.

Historical Department Journal History of the Church. CR 100 137, CHL.

Historical Department Office Journal, 1844–2012. CR 100 1, CHL.

History of Andrew and DeKalb Counties, Missouri, From the Earliest Time to the Present. St. Louis and Chicago, IL: Goodspeed Publishing Co., 1888.

"History of Bountiful City Cemetery." Bountiful, Est. 1847. https://www.bountifulutah.gov/Cemetery-History.

History of Cass and Bates Counties, Missouri. St. Joseph, MO: National Historical Company, 1883.

History of Jackson County, Missouri. Kansas City, MO: Union Historical Company, 1881.

History of Knox and Daviess Counties, Indiana. Chicago, IL: Goodspeed Publishing Co., 1886.

History of Monroe and Shelby Counties, Missouri. St. Louis, MO: National Historical Company, 1884.

Hochschild, Jennifer L., and Brenna M. Powell. "Racial Reorganization and the United States Census 1850–1930: Mulattoes, Half-Breeds, Mixed Parentage, Hindoos, and the Mexican Race." Harvard University Department of Government, *Studies in American Political Development* 22, no. 1 (Spring 2008): 59–96. https://doi.org/10.1017/s0898588x08000047.

Holyoak, Dale Maxwell. "Life History of William Bailey Maxwell 1821–1895." 1997. Digital Copy of Typescript. TN-980012, FHL.

"Hon. W. H. Hooper." *Tullidge's Quarterly Magazine* 2, no. 4 (July 1883): 662–64.

Horn, Hosea B. "History of Davis County, Iowa, Chapter II." *The Annals of Iowa* 10, no. 2 (January 1865): 445–47. https://doi.org/10.17077/0003-4827.1883.

Huddleston v. Washington, 69 P. 146 (Cal. 1902).

Hundley, Annie Duckett. "Permelia Emily Wooldridge." Digital Copy of Typescript. FSFT. https://familysearch.org/photos/artifacts/12804863.

Hunting for Bears Genealogy Society. *Mississippi, Compiled Marriage Index, 1776–1935.* Ancestry.com. https://www.ancestry.com/search/collections/7842.

Hurd, John C. *The Law of Freedom and Bondage in the United States.* Vol. 2. Boston, MA: Little, Brown and Company, 1862.

Hutchinson, Clara Slade Rollins. "Life Story of William Slade." Digital Copy of Typescript. FSFT. https://www.familysearch.org/patron/v2/TH-300-39743-299-39/dist.txt.

Hyde, Myrtle Stevens. *Orson Hyde: Olive Branch of Israel.* Salt Lake City, UT: Agreka Books, 2000.

Idaho Bureau of Vital Records. "Idaho, Death Records, 1890–1967." Ancestry.com. https://www.ancestry.com/search/collections/60566.

Illinois State Archives. "Databases of Illinois Veterans Index, 1775–1995." Ancestry.com. https://www.ancestry.com/search/collections/9759.

Illinois State Archives. *Illinois Servitude and Emancipation Records (1722–1863).* https://cyberdriveillinois.com/departments/archives/databases/servant.html.

Index to the Compiled Military Service Records for the Volunteer Soldiers Who Served During the War of 1812. Washington, DC: National Archives Microfilm Publication M602, n.d.

Indiana County, District, and Probate Courts. "Indiana, Wills and Probate Records, 1798–1999." Ancestry.com. https://www.ancestry.com/search/collections/9045.

Ingersoll, L. A. *Ingersoll's Century Annals of San Bernardino County, 1769 to 1904*. Los Angeles, CA: L.A. Ingersoll, 1904.

Iowa State Historical Society. "Iowa, State Census Collection, 1836–1925." Ancestry.com. https://www.ancestry.com/search/collections/1084.

Ipson, Hyrum B. "Haden Wells Church." Digital Copy of Typescript, n.p., n.d. FSFT. Accessed March 9, 2016. https://familysearch.org/photos/stories/936637.

J. C. Graham & Co. *The Utah Directory for 1883–84*. Salt Lake City, UT: J. C. Graham & Co., 1883.

Jacobs, Harriet A. *Incidents in the Life of a Slave Girl*. Edited by L. Maria Child. Boston, MA: Published for the Author, 1861.

James M. Lyon v. John Knott Et Ux. Mississippi Court of Appeals, October Term, 1853. *American Law Register (1852–1891)* 2, no. 10 (August 1854): 604–18. https://www.jstor.org/stable/3302032.

James, Jane Manning, and Elizabeth J. D. Roundy. Autobiography, c. 1902. MS 4425, CHL.

Jenkins, Laura Moench. "The Life Story of Ruthinda Baker Stewart." Digital copy of unpublished manuscript. 2013. FSFT. https://familysearch.org/photos/artifacts/2894992.

Jenson, Andrew. *Latter-day Saint Biographical Encyclopedia, 4 vols*. Salt Lake City, UT: Andrew Jenson History Company and Andrew Jenson Memorial Association, 1901, 1914, 1920, 1936.

Johnson, Jeffery O. "Cattle, Slaves, Missionaries and Mormon Converts from Texas, 1850s." Lecture, Mormon History Association, San Antonio, TX, 2014.

Johnson, Joel Hills. "A Journal or Sketch of the Life of Joel Hills Johnson." Digital Copy of Typescript. TN-518553, FHL.

Johnston, William Preston. *The Life of Gen. Albert Sidney Johnston*. New York, NY: D. Appleton, 1878.

Jolley, Bryant Manning, and Jolley Family Organization. *The Jolley Family Book: The Story of Henry Jolley and His Wife, Frances Manning Jolley*. Provo, UT: Brigham Young University Press, 1966.

Jones, Christopher. "From the Archives: Black Internationalism in 19th Century Salt Lake City; or a Haitian-Born African American in Utah Reports on the Fourth of July, 1873." *Juvenile Instructor*, July 4, 2018. https://juvenileinstructor.org/from-the-archives-a-black-mormon-view-of-the-fourth-of-july-1873.

Jones, Daniel W. *Forty Years among the Indians*. Salt Lake City, UT: Juvenile Instructor Office, 1890.

Jones, Louis T. *The Quakers of Iowa*. Iowa City, IA: State Historical Society of Iowa, 1914.

Jones, William C., ed. *The Revised Statutes of the State of Missouri*. St. Louis, MO: J. W. Dougherty, 1845.

Jones-Rogers, Stephanie E. *They Were Her Property: White Women as Slave Owners in the American South*. New Haven, CT: Yale University Press, 2019.

Joseph Smith Papers. https://josephsmithpapers.org.

Kane, Thomas L. Collection, 1690–1982. MSS 792, Special Collections, HBLL.

Keegan, Tim. *Colonial South Africa and the Origins of the Racial Order.* London: Leicester University Press, 1997.

Kelen, Leslie G. and Eileen Hallet Stone. *Missing Stories: An Oral History of Ethnic and Minority Groups in Utah.* Salt Lake City, UT: University of Utah Press, 1996.

Keller, Charles L. *The Lady in the Ore Bucket: A History of Settlement and Industry in the Tri-Canyon Area of the Wasatch Mountains.* Salt Lake City, UT: University of Utah Press, 2010.

Kenderdine, Thaddeus S. *A California Tramp: Among the Mormon Settlements, Along the Desert Border, On the Great Sandy Deseret, and From the Kingston Springs to San Bernardino.* Newtown, PA: Globe Printing House, 1888.

Kimball, Stanley B. *Heber C. Kimball: Mormon Patriarch and Pioneer.* Champaign, IL: University of Illinois Press, 1981.

Koch, Augustus. *Bird's Eye View of Salt Lake City, Utah Territory 1870.* Chicago, IL: Chicago Lithographing Co., 1870. Library of Congress Geography and Map Division. https://www.loc.gov/resource/g4344s.pm009280/?r=0.056,0,1.389,0.925,0.

Kohler, Charmaine Lay. *Southern Grace: A Story of the Mississippi Saints.* Boise, ID: Beagle Creek Press, 1995.

Landgren, Le. *A Whitmore Family History, 1793–1990.* West Linn, OR: Family Gathering, 1990.

Larson, Andrew Karl. *I Was Called to Dixie: The Virgin River Basin: Unique Experiences in Mormon Pioneering.* Salt Lake City, UT: Deseret News Press, 1961; repr., 1979.

Last Seen: Finding Family after Slavery. Villanova, PA: Department of History, Villanova University and Mother Bethel AME Church, 2022. http://informationwanted.org.

Laws of the State of Mississippi, Passed at a Regular Biennial Session of the Legislature, Held in the City of Jackson in January, February and March, A. D. 1846. Jackson, MS: C. M. Price and G. R. Fall, 1846.

"LDS Pioneer and Handcart Companies, 1847–1856." Ancestry.com. https://www.ancestry.com/search/collections/5146.

Lee, John D. Journal, March 1842–August 1843. MS 2092, CHL.

Lee, John D., and W. W. Bishop. *Mormonism Unveiled; or, the Life and Confessions of the Late Mormon Bishop, John D. Lee.* St. Louis, MO: Bryan, Brand, 1877.

Lee, Loucina [Duncan Davis White Dixon] Fell. Family Bible. California, 1890. Private Collection (digital images of holograph record in possession of author).

Leggroan, Celia Bankhead, and Carrie Bankhead Leggroan. Interview, December 3, 1977. Helen Z. Papanikolas Papers, 1954–2001. MS 471, Marriott Library Special Collections, University of Utah, Salt Lake City.

Lent, Robertalee, and June B. Barekman. *Knox Co. Indiana Early Land Records Court Indexes.* Vol. 2. Post Falls, ID: Genealogical Reference Builders, 1966.

Lewis, David, and Juanita Brooks. "Excerpt from the Journal of David Lewis." Typescript, n.d., Copy in Possession of Author.

Lewis, David, Autobiography. Microform, anonymous holograph copy of original. MSS MFilm 00157, San Marino, CA: Huntington Library, 1854.

Los Angeles City and County Directory. Los Angeles, CA: King & Stratton, 1873.

Lucas, Gloria Ramsey. *Slave Records of Edgefield County, South Carolina*. Edgefield, SC: Edgefield County Historical Society, 2010; Digitized Book and Electronic Index, Ancestry.com, 2014.

Lyman, Amasa M. Collection, 1832–1877. MS 829, CHL.

Lyman, Edward Leo. *San Bernardino: The Rise and Fall of a California Community*. Salt Lake City, UT: Signature Books, 1996.

Lythgoe, Dennis L. "Negro Slavery in Utah." Master's thesis, University of Utah, 1966. https://collections.lib.utah.edu/details?id=1602212.

Lythgoe, Dennis L. "Negro Slavery in Utah." *Utah Historical Quarterly* 39, no. 1 (Winter 1971): 40–54. https://doi.org/10.2307/272985.

MacKinnon, William P. "Predicting the Past: The Utah War's Twenty-First Century Future." *Arrington Annual Lecture*, 2008. https://digitalcommons.usu.edu/arrington_lecture/13.

MacKinnon, William P. "Sex, Subalterns, and Steptoe: Army Behavior, Mormon Rage, and Utah War Anxieties." *Utah Historical Quarterly* 76, no. 3 (Summer 2008): 227–46. https://www.jstor.org/stable/45063621.

MacKinnon, William P. *At Sword's Point: A Documentary History of the Utah War to 1858*. 2 vols. Norman, OK: Arthur H. Clark, 2008, 2016.

MacKinnon, William P. "The Buchanan Spoils System and the Utah Expedition: Careers of W. M. F. Magraw and John M. Hockaday." *Utah Historical Quarterly* 31, no. 2 (April 1963): 127–50. https://www.jstor.org/stable/45059094.

Mangun, Kimberley, and Larry R. Gerlach. "Making Utah History: Press Coverage of the Robert Marshall Lynching, June 1925." In *Lynching Beyond Dixie: American Mob Violence Outside the South*, edited by Michael J. Pfeifer. Champaign, IL: University of Illinois Press, 2013.

Martineau, James H. *An Uncommon Common Pioneer: The Journals of James Henry Martineau, 1828–1918*. Edited by Donald G. Godfrey and Rebecca S. Martineau-McCarty. Provo, UT: Religious Studies Center, Brigham Young University, 2008.

Mason, Patrick Q. "The Prohibition of Interracial Marriage in Utah, 1888–1963." *Utah Historical Quarterly* 76, no. 2 (Spring 2008): 108–31. https://www.jstor.org/stable/45063125.

Mathews, Benjamin to Brigham Young, March 31, 1849, box 21, folder 16, Office Files.

Mathis, Don R. "Camp Floyd in Retrospect." Master's thesis, University of Utah, 1959.

McCall, Joan Hedges. *Redlands Remembered: Stories from the Jewel of the Inland Empire*. Charleston, SC: History Press, 2012.

McDonald, Earl E. "Disposal of Negro Slaves by Will in Knox County, Indiana." *Indiana Magazine of History* 26, no. 2 (June 1930): 143–46. https://www.jstor.org/stable/27786437.

McDonald, Russell W. "William Wormer Drummond." In *Biographical Summaries: Nevada's Territorial, District, Supreme Court and Federal Judges, 1856–1993*. Digital copy of unpublished manuscript, partial copy in possession of author. Reno: Nevada Judicial Historical Society, n.d.

Mellet, Patric Tariq. "A South African amaGaleca Slave in the USA." *Camissa People: Cape Slavery & Indigene Heritage* (blog), March 29, 2014. https://camissapeople.wordpress.com/2014/03/29/a-south-african-amagaleca-slave-in-the-usa.

Memorial and Biographical History of Ellis County, Texas. Chicago, IL: Lewis Publishing Co., 1892.

Memorial and Biographical History of Navarro, Henderson, Anderson, Limestone, Freestone and Leon Counties, Texas. Chicago, IL: Lewis Publishing Co., 1893.

Memorial and Biographical Record of Kansas City and Jackson County, Mo. Chicago, IL: Lewis Publishing, 1896.

Miller, Reuben. Journals, 1848–1849. MS 1392, CHL.

Millward, John P. "An Account of the Life of Gobo Fango." Digital Copy of Typescript. MS 13543, CHL.

Mississippi County Courthouses and Public Libraries. "Mississippi Probate Records, 1781–1930." FSFT. https://www.familysearch.org/search/collection/2036959.

Mississippi County, District, and Probate Courts. "Mississippi, Wills and Probate Records, 1780–1982." Ancestry.com. https://www.ancestry.com/search/collections/8995.

Mississippi Department of Archives and History. "Various Records, 1820–1951." FSFT. https://www.familysearch.org/search/collection/1919687.

Missouri, County, District, and Probate Courts. "Missouri, Wills and Probate Records, 1766–1988." Ancestry.com. https://www.ancestry.com/search/collections/9071.

Moody, E. Grant, Michael F. Moody, Penelope Moody Allen, and Elaine McAllister Harry Moody. *The John Wyatt Moody Family: Past and Present*. Tempe, AZ: Dr. Thomas Moody Family Organization Inc., 1985.

Morris, Charles E. "Panic and Reprisal: Reaction in North Carolina to the Nat Turner Insurrection, 1831." *North Carolina Historical Review* 62, no. 1 (January 1985): 29–52. https://www.jstor.org/stable/23518997.

Morris, Mary Lois Walker. *Before the Manifesto: The Life Writings of Mary Lois Walker Morris*. Edited by Melissa Lambert Milewski. Logan, UT: Utah State University Press, 2007.

Morris, Thomas D. *Southern Slavery and the Law, 1619–1860*. Chapel Hill: University of North Carolina Press, 1999.

Morton, J. Sterling. *Illustrated History of Nebraska*. Lincoln, NE: Jacob North & Company, 1907.

"Mr. and Mrs. Taylor." Photograph. Private Collection, Digital Copy in Possession of Author.

National Archives. "IRS Tax Assessment Lists, 1862–1918, Records of the Internal Revenue Service, Record Group 58." Ancestry.com. https://www.ancestry.com/search/collections/1264.

National Archives and Records Administration. "U. S. Civil War Pension Index: General Index to Pension Files, 1861–1934." Ancestry.com. https://www.ancestry.com/search/collections/4654.

National Archives in Washington, DC. "Civil War Draft Registrations Records, 1863–1865." Ancestry.com. https://www.ancestry.com/search/collections/1666.

National Archives in Washington, DC. "Headstone Applications for Military Veterans, 1925–1963." Ancestry.com. https://www.ancestry.com/search/collections/2375.

National Humanities Center. "'Slaves for Life, and Servants for a Time': Servitude in British America: Five European Perspectives, 1705–1750." *Becoming American: The British Atlantic Colonies, 1690–1763*. https://nationalhumanitiescenter.org/pds/becomingamer/economies/text6/servitude.pdf.

New Orleans [movie]. YouTube Video, from United Artists, 1947, Featuring Charlie Beal. Posted by Gonzalo WebMusic, January 7, 2015. https://youtu.be/Mgp6Etsy_WI?t=24m.

Newell, Quincy D. *Your Sister in the Gospel: The Life of Jane Manning James, a Nineteenth-Century Black Mormon*. New York, NY: Oxford University Press, 2019.

Nibley, Charles W., and Preston Nibley. "Reminiscences of Charles W. Nibley." *Improvement Era* 37, no. 10 (October 1934): 597–98, 601–03. https://archive.org/details/improvementera3710unse.

Nichols, Jeffrey D. "The Broad Ax and the Plain Dealer Kept Utah's African Americans Informed." *Utah History to Go*, State of Utah. https://historytogo.utah.gov/broad-ax.

Nichols, Jeffrey D. *Prostitution, Polygamy, and Power: Salt Lake City, 1847–1918*. Champaign, IL: University of Illinois Press, 2002.

Nielson, Roger B. *Roll Call at Old Camp Floyd, Utah Territory*. Fort Crittenden, UT: R. B. Nielson, 2006.

North Carolina Adjutant-General. *Muster Rolls of the Soldiers of the War of 1812*. Raleigh, NC: Times Office, 1851.

North Carolina County, District, and Probate Courts. "North Carolina, Wills and Probate Records, 1665–1998." Ancestry.com. https://www.ancestry.com/search/collections/9061.

North Carolina Department of Archives and History. "North Carolina, Civil Action Court Papers, 1712–1970." FSFT. https://www.familysearch.org/search/collection/1930242.

North Carolina State Archives. "Bastardy Bonds and Records (North Carolina), 1736–1957." FSFT. https://www.familysearch.org/search/catalog/766391.

North Carolina State Archives. "North Carolina Estate Files, 1663–1979." FSFT. https://www.familysearch.org/search/collection/1911121.

Norton, Don E., Jr. *Emanuel Masters Murphy: 1809–71, Ancestry, Life, Children*. Provo, UT: Stevenson's Genealogical Center, 1980.

Notes from Bertha Stevens Udell Home, n.d., Fresno, CA. Private collection (digital copy in possession of author).

O'Donovan, Connell. "'I Would Confine Them to Their Own Species': LDS Historical Rhetoric and Praxis Regarding Marriage between Whites and Blacks." *Website of

Connell O'Donovan. Paper presented at Sunstone West, Cupertino, CA, March 28, 2009. http://www.connellodonovan.com/black_white_marriage.html.

O'Donovan, Connell. "'Let This Be a Warning to All Niggers': The Life and Murder of Thomas Coleman in Theocratic Utah." *Website of Connell O'Donovan*, June 2008. www.connellodonovan.com/coleman_bio.pdf.

O'Donovan, Connell. "The Mormon Priesthood Ban and Elder Q. Walker Lewis: 'An Example for His More Whiter Brethren to Follow.'" *John Whitmer Historical Association Journal* 26 (2006): 48–100. https://www.jstor.org/stable/43200236.

Ogden City Directory for 1892–1893. Ogden, UT: R. L. Polk & Co., 1892.

Onslow County (NC). "Miscellaneous Records of Slaves and Freemen, Onslow County, North Carolina, 1763–1912." FSFT. https://www.familysearch.org/search/catalog/1594521.

Orton, Chad M. "The Martin Handcart Company at the Sweetwater: Another Look." *BYU Studies* 45, no. 3 (September 2006): 4–37. https://scholarsarchive.byu.edu/byusq/vol45/iss3/1.

Oxford English Dictionary. https://www.oed.com.

Page, Albert R. "Orson Hyde and the Carson Valley Mission, 1855–1857." Master's thesis, Brigham Young University, 1970.

Palmyra Ward Tithing Office Ledger, 1851–1857. LR 6700 21, CHL.

Parowan Stake Historical Record, 1855–1860. LR 6778 28, CHL.

Parshall, Ardis E. *Keepapitchinin: The Mormon History Blog.* http://www.keepapitchinin.org.

Passenger Lists of Vessels Arriving at Boston, 1820–1891. Washington, DC: National Archives Microfilm Publication M277: 58, n.d.

Passenger Lists of Vessels Arriving at New York, New York, 1820–1897. Washington, DC: National Archives Microfilm Publication T715. Records of the US Customs Service, Record Group 36, n.d.

Paterson, David E. "A Perspective on Indexing Slaves' Names." *The American Archivist* 64 (Spring/Summer 2001): 132–42. https://www.americanarchivist.org/doi/pdf/10.17723/aarc.64.1.th18g8t6282h4283.

Perkins, Eugene H. *The First Mormon Perkins Families: Progenitors and Utah Pioneers of 1847–1852; a Contemporary History of the Ute Perkins Line.* Privately printed: 2008.

Petersen, LaDonna. "Life History of Henry Smith Sr. (1815–1872)." Digital Copy of Typescript, n.p., n.d. FSFT. Accessed October 3, 2016. https://familysearch.org/photos/artifacts/21201462.

Phelps, W. W. *Almanac for the Year 1860.* Great Salt Lake City, UT: J. McKnight, 1860.

"Pine Valley Cemetery, Washington County, Utah." *Utah Gravestones.* 2022. https://www.utahgravestones.org/cemetery.php?cemID=518.

Pioneer Database, 1847–1868 (Pioneer Database). "Church History." *The Church of Jesus Christ of Latter-day Saints.* https://history.churchofjesuschrist.org/overlandtravel.

Porter, Maggie Bell Tolman. "Margaret Eliza Utley (1835–1902)." Digital Copy of Typescript, n.p., n.d. FSFT. Accessed February 21, 2019. https://www.familysearch.org/photos/artifacts/37109706.

Probosco v. Barnes and Barnes (1854). USHS.

Rattray, Robert S. *Religion and Art in Ashanti*. Oxford: Clarendon Press, 1927.

"Record of Baptisms for the Dead for the Seed of Cain." September 3, 1875, Endowment House, Salt Lake City, Utah Territory. Microfilm 255498, FHL.

Record of Members, [1848]–1938, Sugar House Ward, Sugar House, UT. Microfilm 26792, FHL.

Record of Members, 1849–1941, Salt Lake City Fifteenth Ward. Microfilm 26675, FHL.

Records of Utah County (1851–1864). MSS 3905, Special Collections, HBLL.

Redd Family History Y-DNA Project. *Family Tree DNA*. https://www.familytreedna.com/groups/reddfamilyhistoryydnaproject.

Redd, John H. Family Record. Digital copy of holograph. Private Collection.

Redd, John H. to Druzilla Holt Pearson (Thompson), December 27, 1848. MS 3663, CHL.

Redd, Lura, Amasa Jay Red, and Amasa Mason Redd. *The Utah Redds and Their Progenitors*. Salt Lake City, UT: Privately printed, 1973.

Redd, Lura, and William Howard Prince. "John Hardison and Elizabeth Hancock Redd." Digital Copy of Typescript. FSFT. https://familysearch.org/photos/artifacts/8170300.

Rees, Ellen Greer. "Greer Men and Ellen C. Greer." n.d. Unpublished typescript. TN-117134, FHL.

Reeve, W. Paul. "From Cotton to Cosmopolitan: Local, National, and Global Transformations in Utah's Dixie." Opening Plenary Session Lecture, Mormon History Association, St. George, Utah, May 2011.

Reeve, W. Paul. *Century of Black Mormons*. J. Willard Marriott Library, University of Utah. https://exhibits.lib.utah.edu/s/century-of-black-mormons/page/welcome.

Reeve, W. Paul. *Religion of a Different Color: Race and the Mormon Struggle for Whiteness*. Oxford: Oxford University Press, 2015.

Register, Alvaretta K. *State Census of North Carolina, 1784–1787*. Baltimore, MD: Genealogical Publishing Co., 2001.

Reiter, Tonya. "Black Saviors on Mount Zion: Proxy Baptisms and Latter-day Saints of African Descent." *Journal of Mormon History* 43, no. 4 (October 2017): 100–23. https://doi.org/10.5406/jmormhist.43.4.0100.

Reiter, Tonya. "Life on the Hill: The Black Farming Families of Millcreek." *Journal of Mormon History* 44, no. 4 (October 2018): 68–89. https://doi.org/10.5406/jmormhist.44.4.0068.

Reiter, Tonya. "Redd Slave Histories: Family, Race, and Sex in Pioneer Utah." *Utah Historical Quarterly* 85, no. 2 (Spring 2017): 108–26. https://www.jstor.org/stable/10.5406/utahhistquar.85.2.0108.

Remy, Jules, and Julius Brenchley. *A Journey to Great-Salt-Lake City*. Vol. 2. London: W. Jeffs, 1861.

Reséndez, Andrés. *The Other Slavery: The Uncovered Story of Indian Enslavement in America*. Boston, MA: Houghton Mifflin Harcourt, 2016.

Rich, Charles C. Collection, 1832–1908. MS 889, CHL.

Rich, Christopher B., Jr. "The True Policy for Utah: Servitude, Slavery, and 'An Act in Relation to Service.'" *Utah Historical Quarterly* 80, no. 1 (Winter 2012): 54–74. https://www.jstor.org/stable/45063378.

Rich, Standley. Family Photograph Collection, c. 1853–1950. PH 1960, CHL.

Richards, Willard. Journals and Papers, 1821–1854. MS 1490, CHL.

Ricks, Nathaniel R. "A Peculiar Place for the Peculiar Institution: Slavery and Sovereignty in Early Territorial Utah." Master's thesis, Brigham Young University, 2007.

Riggs, Mary West, Don L. Riggs, Christie Roberts, and Kevin Merrell. *Five Branches of Love*. Salt Lake City, UT: Don L. Riggs, 1967, reprinted as a digital book, 2006.

Rix, Guy S. *History and Genealogy of the Ricks Family of America*. Salt Lake City, UT: Skelton Publishing Co., 1908.

Robbins, Alexander, "Arrived." *Deseret News*. September 3, 1856a.

Robbins, Alexander, "Sermon." *Deseret News*, September 17, 1856b.

Roberts, David. *Devil's Gate: Brigham Young and the Great Mormon Handcart Tragedy*. New York, NY: Simon & Schuster, 2008.

Robinson, Joseph Lee. *The Journal of Joseph Lee Robinson: Mormon Pioneer*. Edited by Oliver Preston Robinson, Mary Robinson Egan, David Nielsen, Joni Nielsen, and Kevin Merrell. E-book, August 2003. https://archive.org/details/JlrBasicJournal.

Robinson, Joseph Lee. Papers, 1883–1892. MS 7042, CHL.

Robison, Isabella Marden Pratt. "Biography." Digital Copy of Typescript, n.d. FSFT. https://familysearch.org/photos/stories/5115493.

Rockwood, Albert Perry. Journals, 1847–1853. MS 1449, CHL.

Rodriguez, Junius P., ed. *Encyclopedia of Slave Resistance and Rebellion, Volume 2: O–Z and Primary Documents*. Westport, CT: Greenwood Press, 2007.

Rogers, Brent M. *Unpopular Sovereignty: The Mormons and the Federal Management of Early Utah Territory*. Lincoln, NE: University of Nebraska Press, 2017.

Roland, Charles Pierce. *Albert Sidney Johnston, Soldier of Three Republics*. 2nd ed. Lexington, KY: University Press of Kentucky, 2001.

Rottenberg, Dan. *Death of a Gunfighter: The Quest for Jack Slade, the West's Most Elusive Legend*. Yardley, PA: Westholme, 2010.

Runyon, Diane Kelly, and Kim Shoemaker Starr. *Secrets Under the Parking Lot: The True Story of Upper Arlington, Ohio, and the History of Perry Township in the Nineteenth Century*. Scotts Valley, CA: CreateSpace Independent Publishing, 2017.

Rutter, Michael. *Upstairs Girls: Prostitution in the American West*. Helena, MT: Farcountry Press, 2005.

Saints by Sea: Latter-day Saint Immigration to America. Church History Department and Family History Department, Brigham Young University. https://saintsbysea.lib.byu.edu.

Salt Lake County (UT) Probate Court. Civil and Criminal Case Files, 1852–1887. Series 373. USHS.

San Bernardino (CA) Coroner, Court, Probate, Marriage License, Death, Inebriate Commitment, and Property Records. SBCHA.

San Bernardino Branch Journal, 1851–1853, 1855–1877. LR 1594 22, CHL.

San Bernardino Branch Tithing Accounts, 1851–1857. LR 1594 21, CHL.

San Bernardino Branch Tithing Record, 1853–1857. LR 1594 23, CHL.

Sanger, George P., ed. *The Statutes at Large, Treaties, and Proclamations, of the United States of America*. Boston, MA: Little, Brown and Company, 1863.

Sarah Z. Dennis v. William T. Dennis (1873). Utah County Probate Court. USHS.

Schenk, David H. "Freedmen with Firearms: White Terrorism and Black Disarmament During Reconstruction." *The Gettysburg College Journal of the Civil War Era* 4 (April 2014): 4. https://cupola.gettysburg.edu/gcjcwe/vol4/iss1/4.

Seeman, Erik R. "Reassessing the 'Sankofa Symbol' in New York's African Burial Ground." *William and Mary Quarterly* 67, no. 1 (January 2010): 101–22. https://doi.org/10.5309/willmaryquar.67.1.101.

Senate of the United States. *Journal of the Executive Proceedings of the Senate of the United States of America from December 3, 1855, to June 16, 1858, Inclusive*. Vol. 10. Washington, DC: Government Printing Office, 1887.

Sessions, Patty Bartlett. *Mormon Midwife: The 1846–1888 Diaries of Patty Bartlett Sessions*. Edited by Donna Toland Smart. Logan, UT: Utah State University Press, 1997.

Settlement of San Bernardino Monument. *Northeast corner of N. Arrowhead Avenue and West 3rd Street in front of the Historic San Bernardino County Courthouse*. Daughters of Utah Pioneers, Monument 302. San Bernardino, CA: Settlement of San Bernardino, 1964.

Sexton's Records, Cutler's Park and Winter Quarters, 1846–1848. LR 6359 24, CHL.

Shipman, Edwin R., and Mary Jane Graham Shipman to Thomas and Sarah Graham, "November 25, 1847, Pickens County, Alabama." Digital Copy of Holograph, Courtesy of Gloria Ann Smith, FSFT. February 11, 2017. https://www.familysearch.org/photos/artifacts/33360519.

Simerly, Marceline, and Martie Schuman. "The Round Prairie Trail." Fillmore History Archives, Schuman Auction Service. http://www.schumanauction.com/Round Prarie.htm (site discontinued).

Skinner, Byron R. *Black Origins in the Inland Empire, Heritage Tales, Sixth Annual Publication of the City of San Bernardino Historical and Pioneer Society*. San Bernardino, CA: City of San Bernardino Historical and Pioneer Society, 1983.

Slave Manifests of Coastwise Vessels Filed at New Orleans, Louisiana, 1807–1860. Washington, DC: National Archives Microfilm Publication M, 1895.

Slave Registrations. Salt Lake County (UT) Probate Court. Civil and Criminal Case Files, 1852–1887. Series 373. USHS.

Sloan, Edward L. *The Salt Lake City Directory and Business Guide, for 1869*. Salt Lake City, UT: E.L. Sloan, 1869.

Smart, Venna. History of Union Fort Cemetery. Typescript. John D. Fretwell Collection. Private Collection.

Smith, Dean. "Sheepmen *vs.* Cattlemen: The Bloodiest Range War in Apache County." *Arizona Highways* 71, no. 2 (February 1995): 32–35.

Smith, Edith, and Vivian Lehman. *"No Land . . . Only Slaves!" Volume 11: Abstracts from the Deed Books of Upshur & Ellis Counties in Texas.* Balch Springs, TX: Privately printed, 2005.

Smith, Elias. Journals, 1836–1888. MS 1319, CHL.

Smith, George A. Papers, 1834–1877. MS 1322, CHL.

Smith, Joseph, and William W. Phelps. *General Smith's Views of the Powers and Policy of the Government of the United States.* Nauvoo, IL: John Taylor, Printer, 1844. https://www.josephsmithpapers.org.

Smith, Merina. *Revelation, Resistance, and Mormon Polygamy: The Introduction and Implementation of the Principle, 1830–1853.* Logan, UT: Utah State University Press, 2013.

Smith, Robyn N. "The Complexity of Slave Surnames." *Reclaiming Kin: Taking Back What Was Once Lost*, March 14, 2017. https://www.reclaimingkin.com/the-complexity-of-slave-surnames.

Smith, Stacey L. *Freedom's Frontier: California and the Struggle over Unfree Labor.* Chapel Hill: University of North Carolina Press, 2015.

Smith, W. V. *BOAP.* http://www.boap.org.

Smoot, A. O. Papers, 1837–1894. MSS 896, Special Collections, HBLL.

Smoot Family, Abraham Owen. Papers, 1836–1947. MSS 3843, Special Collections, HBLL.

Smoot, Margaret Thompson McMeans. Diary, 1868. MS 5204, CHL.

Snodgrass, Mary Ellen. *The Underground Railroad: An Encyclopedia of People, Places, and Operations.* Armonk, NY: M.E. Sharpe, 2008.

South Carolina County, District, and Probate Courts. "South Carolina, Wills and Probate Records, 1670–1980." Ancestry.com. https://www.ancestry.com/search/collections/9080.

Southern California Genealogical Society. "Los Angeles City Cemetery." *SCGS Genealogy.* http://www.scgsgenealogy.com/free/LACC-Title.html.

Spanish Fork (UT) Cemetery Records, 1866–1898. Microfilm 1654570, FHL.

Spanish Fork (UT) Ward Record, 1852–1864. LR 8611 29, CHL.

Spitzzeri, Paul R. "No Place Like Home: The Francisco Vejar Adobe, Pomona, ca. 1872." *The Homestead Blog*, January 31, 2017. https://homesteadmuseum.wordpress.com/2017/01/31/no-place-like-home-the-francisco-vejar-adobe-pomona-ca-1872.

State of California v. Joseph McFeely (1858). Justice Court of San Bernardino. Case 42, SBCHA.

Stegmaier, Mark J. "A Law That Would Make Caligula Blush: New Mexico Territory's Unique Slave Code, 1859–1861." *New Mexico Historical Review* 87, no. 2 (Spring 2012): 209–42. https://digitalrepository.unm.edu/nmhr/vol87/iss2/3.

Stevenson, Edward. Collection, 1849–1922. MS 4806, CHL.

Steward, Austin. *Twenty-Two Years a Slave, and Forty Years a Freeman*. Rochester, NY: William Alling, 1857.

Stout, Hosea. *On the Mormon Frontier: The Diary of Hosea Stout, 1844–1861*. Edited by Juanita Brooks. Vol. 2. Salt Lake City, UT: University of Utah Press and Utah State Historical Society, 1964.

Stout, Hosea. Papers, 1829–1860. Mss B 53, USHS.

"A Sudden Death. Cordelia Litchford Dies of Hemorrhage of the Lungs," *Salt Lake Herald*. Salt Lake City, UT, February 24, 1891.

Sweeney, Michael S. "Julius F. Taylor and the Broad Ax of Salt Lake City." *Utah Historical Quarterly* 77, no. 3 (Summer 2009): 204–21. https://www.jstor.org/stable/45063211.

Tanner-Tremaine, Paul. *1820 Settlers to South Africa*. https://www.1820settlers.com.

Tennessee County Courthouses. "Tennessee, Probate Court Books, 1795–1927." FSFT. https://www.familysearch.org/search/collection/1909088.

Tennessee State Library and Archives. "Tennessee State Marriages, 1780–2002." Ancestry.com. https://www.ancestry.com/search/collections/1169.

Tennessee State Library and Archives. "Minute Books, Civil and Criminal, 1810–1965." FSFT. https://www.familysearch.org/search/catalog/256096.

Tennessee State Library and Archives. "Tennessee, Early Tax List Records, 1783–1895." Ancestry.com. https://www.ancestry.com/search/collections/2883.

Territory of Utah v. Williams Camp et. al. (1856).

Texas County, District, and Probate Courts. "Texas, Wills and Probate Records, 1833–1974." Ancestry.com. https://www.ancestry.com/search/collections/2115.

Texas State Library and Archives. "Texas, County Tax Rolls, 1846–1910." FSFT. https://www.familysearch.org/search/catalog/986276.

Third District Court, Salt Lake County (UT). Probate Case Files, 1851–1896. Series 1621, USHS.

Third District Court, Tooele County (UT). Probate Case Files, 1871–1896. Series 83314, USHS.

Thiriot, Amy Tanner. "Elizabeth Taylor, Newspaper Woman and Activist." *Better Days 2020*. https://www.utahwomenshistory.org/bios/elizabeth-taylor.

Thiriot, Amy Tanner. "Eminent Women: Mary Parker Chidester and Catharine Maria Sedgwick, Part 1." *Keepapitchinin: The Mormon History Blog*, October 18, 2012. http://www.keepapitchinin.org/2012/10/18/eminent-women-mary-parker-chidester-and-catharine-maria-sedgwick-part-1.

Thiriot, Amy Tanner. "Guest Post: A Response to the Salt Lake Tribune on Utah's Dixie and Slave Culture." *Keepapitchinin: The Mormon History Blog*, February 7, 2013. http://www.keepapitchinin.org/2013/02/07/guest-post-a-response-to-the-salt-lake-tribune-on-utahs-dixie-and-slave-culture.

Thirteenth Ward Record of Members, 1859–1870. LR 6133 7, CHL.

Thomas, Joseph Harrison. "Biographical Sketch of the Life of Ann Morehead Thomas, 1841–1917." Digital Copy of Typescript. FSFT. https://www.familysearch.org/photos/artifacts/4057518.

Thomas, Preston, Daniel H. Thomas, and Annette Taylor, "Preston Thomas [Diaries and Biography]." Digital Copy of Typescript. https://docs.wixstatic.com/ugd/78a476_2 2d3bdc50ebe4f0398ed3e288858d84e.pdf.

Thompson, Emily L. Snyder. "History of Emily Lydia Snyder Thompson." Digital Copy of Typescript. FSFT. https://www.familysearch.org/photos/artifacts/22922719.

Thornbrough, Emma Lou. *The Negro in Indiana: A Study of a Minority*. Indianapolis, IN: Indiana Historical Bureau, 1957.

Todd, John. *Early Settlement and Growth of Western Iowa or Reminiscences*. Des Moines, IA: Historical Department of Iowa, 1906.

Toronto, LaReah H., Naomi G. Jimenoz, and Merle H. Yarrington. "To These, Our Grandparents." Digital Copy of Typescript, n.d. FSFT. https://www.familysearch.org/photos/artifacts/25331474.

"Town of San Bernardino–1853–1854." Map, City of San Bernardino (Website), n.d. Accessed March 1, 2017. http://www.ci.san-bernardino.ca.us/about/history/fort_san_bernardino.asp.

Trexler, Harrison A. "Slavery in Missouri, 1804–1865." PhD diss., Johns Hopkins University, 1914.

"Tribute to the Life of James M. Flake, 1859–1946." CR 712 2, CHL.

Trotter, Louisa Price. "History of Mary Ann Gardner Price, Native Pioneer." Digital Copy of Typescript. FSFT. https://www.familysearch.org/photos/artifacts/1061903.

Trustee-in-Trust Indexes, 1842–1852. CR 5 72, CHL.

Trustee-in-Trust Tithing and Donation Records, 1846–1879. CR 5 79, CHL.

Trustee-in-Trust Tithing Daybooks, 1842–1847. CR 5 71, CHL.

Turner, John G. *Brigham Young: Pioneer Prophet*. Cambridge, MA: Harvard University Press, 2012.

Tuttle, Charles A., ed. *Reports of Cases Determined in the Supreme Court of the State of California, Vol. 51, 1875–1877*. San Francisco, CA: Bancroft-Whitney, 1906.

Udell, Bertha Stevens, Interview with John D. Fretwell, 1990, Fresno, California, in John D. Fretwell, "History of Green Flake." 1999. Typescript. Private Collection.

Ulrich, Laurel Thatcher. *A House Full of Females: Plural Marriage and Women's Rights in Early Mormonism, 1835–1870*. New York, NY: Knopf, 2017.

United States Military Academy. *Official Register of the Officers and Cadets of the U. S. Military Academy, West Point, N. Y.* West Point, NY: United States Military Academy Printing Office, 1843.

United States, Selective Service System. *World War I Selective Service System Draft Registration Cards, 1917–1918*. Washington, DC: National Archives Microfilm Publication M1509, 2005. Ancestry.com. https://www.ancestry.com/search/collections/6482.

University Libraries of The University of North Carolina at Greensboro, State Library of North Carolina, and F.D. Bluford Library at North Carolina A&T State University. *Digital Library on American Slavery.* https://library.uncg.edu/slavery.

Utah Archives and Records Service. "Salt Lake County (UT) Death Records, 1849–1949." FSFT. https://www.familysearch.org/search/collection/1459704.

Utah Archives and Records Service. "Utah Death Registers, 1847–1966." Series 21866. Ancestry.com. https://www.ancestry.com/search/collections/6967.

Utah County, District, and Probate Courts. "Utah, Wills and Probate Records, 1800–1985." Ancestry.com. https://www.ancestry.com/search/collections/9082.

Utah Department of Health, Office of Vital Records and Statistics, and Utah State Archives. Death Certificates, 1904–present. Series 81448, USHS.

Utah Division of State History. *Cemeteries and Burials.* Salt Lake City, UT: Utah Department of Heritage & Arts, 2014. https://utahdcc.secure.force.com/burials.

Utah Semi-Centennial Commission. *The Book of the Pioneers.* Salt Lake City, UT: Utah Semi-Centennial Commission, 1897.

"Utah Slaves 1850 and 1860." *AfriGeneas Slave Research Forum*, April 4, 2007. http://www.afrigeneas.com/forumd/index.cgi/md/read/id/6904/sbj/utah-slaves-1850-and-1860.

Utah Terr. v. Camp (1856).

Utah Territorial Legislative Assembly. *Acts, Resolutions and Memorials Passed by the First Annual, Special Sessions, of the Legislative Assembly, of the Territory of Utah.* Salt Lake City, UT: Brigham H. Young, 1852a.

Utah Territorial Legislative Assembly. *Journals of the House of Representatives, Council and Joint Sessions of the First Annual and Special Sessions of the Legislative Assembly of the Territory of Utah.* Salt Lake City, UT: Brigham H. Young, 1852b.

Utah Territorial Militia Records. "Series 2210." USHS and FSFT. https://www.familysearch.org/search/collection/1462415.

Van Cott, John W. *Utah Place Names: A Comprehensive Guide to the Origins of Geographic Names.* Salt Lake City, UT: University of Utah Press, 1990.

Waite, Catherine V. *The Mormon Prophet and His Harem.* Cambridge, MA: Riverside Press, 1866.

Waite, Kevin. *West of Slavery: The Southern Dream of a Transcontinental Empire.* Chapel Hill: University of North Carolina Press, 2021.

Wakefield, Eliza M. *Texas and the Greers.* Privately printed, 1953.

Walker, Ronald W. "'Proud as a Peacock and Ignorant as a Jackass': William W. Drummond's Unusual Career with the Mormons." *Journal of Mormon History* 42, no. 3 (July 2016): 1–34. https://doi.org/10.5406/jmormhist.42.3.0001.

Wallace-Sanders, Kimberly. *Mammy: A Century of Race, Gender, and Southern Memory.* Ann Arbor, MI: University of Michigan Press, 2009.

Warner, Elisha. *The History of Spanish Fork.* Spanish Fork, UT: The Press Publishing Company, 1930.

Watt, G. D., and J. V. Long. *Journal of Discourses*. Vol. 9. Liverpool, England: George Q. Cannon, 1862.

Watt, G. D., and J. V. Long, *Journal of Discourses*. Vol. 10. Liverpool, England: Daniel H. Wells, 1865.

Weakley County (TN) Trustee. "Tax Books, 1842–1851." FSFT. https://www.familysearch.org/search/catalog/57169.

Weber County (UT) Probate Court. Civil and Criminal Case Files, 1852–1887. Series 1593. USHS.

Wells, Eliza Foscue Lee. "Autobiography of Eliza's Youth." Digital Copy of Typescript. May 26, 2008, Copy in Possession of the Author.

Wells, Emmeline B., ed. *Charities and Philanthropies: Woman's Work in Utah*. Salt Lake City, UT: George Q. Cannon & Sons Co., 1893.

Wells, Lola Taylor, and Arline Martindale Scott Brinton. "Harriett Heath Marler." Digital Copy of Typescript, n.p., n.d. FSFT. Accessed February 22, 2019. https://www.familysearch.org/photos/artifacts/75280830.

Wellsville History Committee. *Windows of Wellsville, 1856–1984*. Providence, UT: Wellsville History Committee, 1985.

West Virginia County Courthouses. "West Virginia, Deaths Index, 1853–1973." FSFT and Ancestry.com. https://www.ancestry.com/search/collections/2568.

Wiggill, Eli. "Autobiography, 1883. Microfilm of Manuscript." MS 8344, CHL.

Wilkinson, Robert John. "Human Genetic Susceptibility to Tuberculosis." *Journal of Infectious Diseases* 205, no. 4 (February 2012): 525–27. https://doi.org/10.1093/infdis/jir792.

Williams, Judee. "Descendants of Nathan Bankhead." Unpublished manuscript in possession of the author, 2015.

Williamson, Samuel H., and Louis P. Cain. "Measuring Slavery in 2016 Dollars." *MeasuringWorth*, 2016. https://www.measuringworth.com/slavery.php.

Williamson, Samuel H., and Louis P. Cain. *MeasuringWorth*, 2022. https://www.measuringworth.com.

Wilson, James T. "The Life of James Thomas Wilson," c. 1889. In *Typescript*, edited by Cordelia D. W. Hortin, William W. Hortin, and Frances G. Hortin. FamilySearch Digital Library, 1992.

Wolfinger, Henry. "A Test of Faith: Jane Elizabeth James and the Origins of the Utah Black Community." In *Social Accommodations in Utah*, edited by Clark S. Knowlton, 126–72. American West Occasional Papers. Salt Lake City, UT: University of Utah, 1975.

Woodruff, Wilford. Journals and Papers, 1828–1898. MS 1352, CHL.

Yancy, James W. "The Negro of Tucson, Past and Present." Master's thesis, University of Arizona, 1933. https://repository.arizona.edu/handle/10150/306668.

Young, Margaret Blair, and Darius Aidan Gray. *Standing on the Promises*. Vol. 3. Provo, UT: Zarahemla Books, 2013.

INDEX

A. B. Miller v. Thomas S. Williams, 19, 27, 92, 240
Act in Relation to Service, An, 12, 18–22, 40, 55, 89, 112, 116, 127; components of, 341–42; violating provisions of, 19–22, 132
Ada Hancock, steamer, 141–42, 279-80
African Methodist Episcopal (AME) Church, 140–42, 148, 203, 227, 275, 277, 279, 285, 310, 434n32
Alabama: Marion County, 48, 160–61; origin narrative, 53–58
Allston, Benjamin, 124, 128–29, 159–60
Allston, Robert F. W., 160
Anderson, Kirk, 84
army officers, enslaved people and, 128–30

Bankhead John H. and George W. (brothers), 16–17, 22, 23, 31, 54–55, 58–59, 73; household of, 26, 33, 43, 89, 94–95, 99–100
Bankhead, Alexander, 1, 23, 35, 40, 81–83, 96, 136, 147, 174–75
Bankhead, George A., 170–71
Bankhead, Marinda Redd, 1, 35, 65–67, 135–36, 145–47, 174, 264, 269–71, 370–71
Bankhead, Miram, 58, 163, 164, 169–70
Bankhead, Nathan, 46, 58, 83, 94, 163–65
Bankhead, Samuel, 154, 175–76, 362–63. See also Smith, Samuel
Bankhead, Thomas. See Coleman, Thomas
Bankhead, Walter (Rolly), 43, 172–73, 176, 262–63
Barker, J. D., 100-2
Barnes, Clifton R., 111, 124–26, 179–80

Barnett, Bird B., 18, 23–23, 33, 62, 87, 180–85
Barnett, Camplin, 180–81
Barnett, James, 183
Barnett, John, 182
Barnett, Sandy, 182–83
Battle of Tippecanoe, 55
Beal, Israel, 282
Beal, Martha Embers, 100, 138, 282
Beasley, Delilah L., 3, 277, 421–21
Beller, Jack, 3, 162
Bernhisel, John M., 12–13, 30
Big Cottonwood Canyon, 96, 143–44, 196
Big Field, production from, 86
Blackwell, Hyrum H., 102, 273
Blair, Seth M., 27, 92–93, 240, 313, 350, 359–60
Book of Mormon, 7–8
Book of the Pioneers, The, 143–44
Box, Thomas and Clarkey Carpenter, 120–22, 185–86
Broad Ax, 155, 309–10, 370–71, 436n66
Brown, John and Elizabeth Crosby, 20, 22, 56, 73, 85–86, 98, 169, 186, 210, 220–21, 298, 333, 402–44; deed of consecration, 25, 89, 352–53, 404–52
Buchanan, James, 126
Bullock, Thomas, 13, 73, 100
Burton, John, 22, 40–41, 62, 85, 187–88.
Burton, Richard, 30
Burton, Robert T., 118
Butler, Caroline Skeen and John Lowe, 314

Caldwell, John C., 125
California Supreme Court, 279; on marriage, 19, 126–28, 247

California, settlement in, 98–107; creating fear of freedom, 100; purchasing San Bernardino ranch, 100; questions over property in San Bernardino, 102
Calle de los Negros, Los Angeles, 140
Camp, Amelia Evans, 117
Camp and Greer households, 115–20, 189–95; slave registration, 343–48
Camp, Carolina, 62, 194–95
Camp, Charlotte, 23, 117, 137, 189–91
Camp, Daniel, 27, 118–19, 191–92, 350-351. *See also* Hooper, William H.; Williams, Thomas S.
Camp, Elizabeth Brooks, 117–18
Camp, Isaac, 62, 194
Camp, Shepherd, 20, 27, 83, 84, 118, 119, 135, 166, 192–93; slave registration, 343-48
Camp, Williams and Diannah Greer, 23, 27, 115–20, 123, 189–95
Campbell, Charlotte Perkins, 148–51, 152, 261–62.
Campbell, Tampian Hoye, 1, 20, 21, 27, 45, 63, 69–70, 84, 90–93, 95, 120, 123, 137, 154–55, 166, 193, 238, 240–43, 313. *See also* Lewis, David and Duritha Trail
slave registration, 21, 349–50
Camper, Richard, 135–36, 297–98
Cantwell, Hannah, 102
Capecchi, Mario R., 108
Carson Valley, Utah Territory and Nevada, 216, 331–32
Carter, Kate B., 3, 35, 317
Cato, 130–33, 216-17, 331–32, 419–45
Census: agricultural schedules, 86, 161, 424n16; categories and schedules, 13, 38, 112; errors, 206, 265, 276, 332; in 1850 census taken in 1851, 12–16, 31, 38, 59, 98, 162, 200–1, 291, 293–94, 311; in 1852 in California, 181; in 1856 in Utah Territory, 25–26; in 1860, 27–29, 59, 166, 203, 331; in 1870, 136, 214–15, 241; slave schedules, 112, 196
Chandless, William, 106
charivari, 151–52, 208
Chickasaw Cession, 120, 214

Chism, George Bankhead, 17, 171, 203, 213
Chism, Mary (Crosby) Bankhead Sampson, 16–17, 107, 171, 201–3, 212-13
Church, Abraham, 62, 76, 195
Church, Haden W. and Sarah Arterbury, 76–79, 96, 195–97, 334, 403–46, 404–52, 424–15
Church, Harriet Burchard, 300–1
Church of Jesus Christ of Latter-day Saints, 6–9; and census, 13; converts among enslaved, 73, 121–22, 167, 169, 194, 196, 203, 214, 220–21, 235, 245, 250, 263, 270, 272, 295, 325, 333; converts among enslavers, 32, 58, 62, 69–70, 116, 180, 218, 220; *Deseret News*, 436–66; excommunication records, 146; General Conference, 83, 367; Genesis Group, 259; missionaries, 7, 57–58, 76, 91, 98, 115, 117, 120, 121, 141, 186, 220, 263, 322, 325, 327; plural marriage, 7, 40, 89–90, 116, 118, 187, 407n100; and racial policies, 7, 18, 35–36, 148, 254, 301–2, 317, 333; Relief Society, 47–48, 259, 270, 371, 408–116; and tithing donations, 22–25, 111–12, 180, 329. *See also* consecration deeds
Church, Tom, 76, 79, 81, 95–96, 195–97
civil rights activists, 143, 154–55, 242, 305
Civil War, 6, 12, 31, 34–35, 334, 370
Clawson, Margaret Gay Judd, 74
Coleman, Thomas (Bankhead), 92, 165–69; murder of, 82–85
Collins, Albert W., 314–15
Compromise of 1850, 6, 12
consecration deeds, 22–25, 89, 111, 118, 186, 295, 316, 318, 352–54, 404–52
coverture, 64–65
Covington, Robert D., 23, 314–15, 403–46
Creek Wars, 116
Croft, Jacob, 315–16, 404n52. *See also* Cropper, Sebrina Land Matheny
Cropper, Sebrina Land Matheny, 32, 315–16
Crosby, Edy, 56, 200–1
Crosby household, 197–213; settlement of, 54–58

Crosby, John, Jr. and Elizabeth Coleman, 9, 32–33, 55, 57, 83, 199, 367–68
Crosby, Leonard, 55–56
Crosby, Sarah Jeter, 55–56, 209
Crosby, William and Sarah Harmon, 9, 22, 55–58, 73, 87, 100, 106–7, 209, 221, 299, 360–61, 418n26; Brigham Young correspondence, 1, 7–8, 17, 99, 172, 356–57; negotiations about the enslaved, 17, 99, 110, 207
Cunningham, Samuel, 266–67
Cupit, 47, 63–64, 262. *See also* Redd, Venus
Custer, George Armstrong, 120

Daily Union Vedette, 85
Daniels, Ann (Dorn) (Smith) Smiley Peppers, 283, 285–86
Daughters of Utah Pioneers, 3, 35, 135, 243, 259, 305
Daughters of Utah Pioneers Museum, 82, 166, 175
Decker, Charles, 83, 84, 119, 165
deed of consecration. *See* consecration deeds
Dennis, William Taylor and Talitha Bankhead, 1, 2, 24, 32, 34, 71–72, 119, 146, 213–15, 270, 353–54, 404–52
Deseret News, 30, 84, 109, 116, 118, 144, 145, 400n10, 436–66
dialect, use of, 43–44
documentary editing standards, 44
domicil, 11
Dotson, Peter Kessler, 130, 215–16
Douglass, Frederick, 8, 297
Dowdle, Absalom, 321
dower interest, 65
Dred Scott case, 12, 105, 275
Drummond, Cato. *See* Cato
Drummond, William Wormer, 130–33, 216–18. *See also* Cato
Duncan, Homer, 74, 198
Duncan, Jourdan (Jordan) (Barnett), 62, 181, 184–85

Duncan, Lucinda (Loucina) (Barnett), 62, 181, 183–85

Emancipation Proclamation, 30
Embers, Charles (Smith), x, 36, 107, 136, 138, 199, 200, 282-85, 288–89
Embers, Grief (Crosby), 23, 45, 74, 100, 105–6, 107, 137–38, 209–11; return to Mississippi, 98
Embers, Hannah Smiley (Smith), 17–18, 23, 59, 102, 107, 138, 142, 198-99, 200, 281-85
Embers, Harriet (Lay), 105–6, 236–37, 360
Embers, Lawrence Smiley (Dorn) (Smith), 159, 286
Embers, Toby (Crosby), 23, 45, 56, 59, 74, 100, 104, 107, 137–38, 197–200
enslaved: army officers and, 128–30; attempts to escape slavery, 10, 26, 71–72, 87, 191, 203, 243–44, 364–65, 370–71; biographical encyclopedia of, 159–296; categorizing, 137; children born to, 95; documented individuals and locations, 75–76, 88, 93, 95, 124; government appointees and, 130–33; merchants and, 123–28; transition to freedom, 112, 135–136
enslavers: 1851 negotiations with, 16–18; and 1856 census, 25–26; and Act in Relation to Service, 18–22; from Alabama, 53–61; and Church of Jesus Christ of Latter-day Saints 6–12; documented enslaved or indentured taken to Great Salt Lake Valley, 75–76, 124; ignoring ethics in family histories, 38; former or unproven, 313–30; and freedom of enslaved, 26–31; from Kentucky, 62–70; last years before freedom, 26–31; from Mississippi, 53–61; from Missouri, 62–70; myths of freedom, 31–41; negotiations over enslaved families, 16–18; scholarly treatment of, 3–5; from Tennessee, 62–70; and tithing donations, 22–25, 111–12, 180, 329

442 | INDEX

Erasmus Love v. Richmond Love, 61, 226
estate of marital right, 65
Ewell family, 317-18. *See also* "Mammy Chloe" historical fiction

family and community histories, 31-41, 69, 188, 199, 314, 317
Fango, Gobo, 30, 36, 137, 218-20
Fifteenth Amendment, U.S. Constitution, 138, 204
Finnety, 64. *See also* Hancock, Zebedee
First African Methodist Episcopal (AME) Church, Los Angeles, 140-42, 275
First District Court of California, 102
Flake, Carlotty, 109
Flake, Elizabeth. *See* Rowan, Elizabeth Flake
Flake, Green, 1, 10, 36, 60-61, 73-74, 82, 134-37, 140, 143-45, 207-8, 220-26; labor of, 23, 25, 85-86; negotiations over, 16-18, 100; tithing myth, 108-14
Flake, James M. and Agnes Love, 23, 60-61, 73, 86, 108-14, 220-29; family, 303, 364-68; negotiations over enslaved families, 16-18, 30, 99, 100, 356-57
Flake, Martha Morris, 9, 16, 39, 46, 56-57, 143-44, 152, 162-63
Flake, William Jordan, 108-9, 423-7
Flewellen, Betsy Brown, 20-21, 77, 86, 186-87; deed of consecration, 24-25, 89, 352-53
Forbush, Rufus, 53
Franklin, Sam, 33, 41, 63, 272-73. *See also* Redd, John Hardison and Elizabeth Hancock
freedom: creating fear of, 100; last years before, 26-31; myths of, 31-32; transition to, 112, 136, 141
Fretwell, John D., 57, 364-68
Frontier Guardian, 10, 11, 369
Fugitive Slave Act, 12

Goins, Jane Smiley (Smith), 283, 287-88
Gold Mission, 86, 111

government appointees, enslaved people and, 130-33
Graham, Thomas B., 318-20
Grant, George D., 83
Grant, Ulysses S., 1
Great Salt Lake Valley, 7, 10-11, 36, 73, 85-88, 96, 221, 333, 337-39; comparisons to Bible, 81; documented enslaved/indentured taken to, 16-18, 23
Greeley, Horace, 26
Greer, Americus, 34, 118-19
Greer, Nathaniel Hunt, 116, 290
Greer, Thomas Lacy and Ellen Camp, 26, 115-19, 190, 194, 300
Grice, Francis and Martha, 143, 144, 154, 305-6
Grundy, Jane Scott Venable (Barnett), 183. *See also* Barnett, Bird B.
Gunnison, John W., 12

habeas corpus, 17, 104-5
Halley, Susan Price, 123, 126-27, 247-49. *See also* Pearson, Richard
Hancock, Zebedee, 34, 63-64, 263
Harmon, Esther, 59, 83, 90, 179, 200, 293-94
Harmon, Stephen, 299
Harper household, 84, 166, 229-30
Harrison, William Henry, 55
Hartnett, John, 84
Hayes, Benjamin, 102, 104-5, 107, 141
Heath, John, 282, 320
Hendricks, James, 92
Henry, 32, 56, 73, 298-99. *See also* Brown, John and Elizabeth Crosby
Hockaday, George, 126, 230-31
Hockaday, John M., 126, 215
Holladay, John and Catherine Higgins, 293, 320-21
Holladay, Benjamin, 22
Holt, Mary Redd, 321
Hooper, Richard. *See* Camper, Richard
Hooper, William H., 27, 92, 117, 120, 123, 135-36, 191, 193, 350-51
household, definition, 41-42

Houstin, Henderson, 107, 212. *See also* Crosby, William and Sarah Harmon
Hoye, Caroline. *See* Jackson, Caroline Hoye Bankhead
Hoye, Tampian. *See* Campbell, Tampian Hoye. *See also* Lewis, David and Duritha Trail
Huddleston, Ellen Mason Owens Taft, 3, 103, 140, 227, 277-78. *See also* Smith, Robert Mays and Rebecca Dorn
Hughes, Randolph, 2, 129-30, 231-32. *See also* Johnston, Albert Sidney
Hunter, Edward and Mary Ann Whitesides, 218-19
Hunter, Edward, Presiding Bishop, 219, 229
Hurd, John C., 11-12, 67-68
Hyde, Orson, 10, 11, 369

Ike, 300. *See also* Camp, Charlotte
In re Hannah (1856), 2, 17-18, 104-7, 142, 275, 282, 286-87, 339, 421-22-21
Indiana, 45, 55, 197, 209
insults, 42-43

Jackman, Parmenio, 27, 92
Jackson, Caroline Hoye Bankhead 27, 63, 69-70, 84, 90-93, 154-55, 240-42; slave registration, 21, 349-50. *See also* Lewis, David and Duritha Trail; Williams, Thomas S.
Jackson, Richard, 100-2, 273-74. *See also* Minter, John S; Rich, Charles C.
Jackson, Tennessee or Harriet, 23, 56, 74, 85, 102, 209, 273, 292. *See also* Thomas, Daniel M. and Ann Crosby
Jacob, 57-58, 73, 298. *See also* Bankhead, John H. and George W. (brothers)
James, Jane Manning (Perkins), 59, 90, 148, 150, 250, 293
James, Mary Ann Perkins, 68, 136, 148, 149, 254-55. *See also* Perkins, Reuben
Jefferson, Nancy Bankhead, 17, 137, 212-13. *See also* Chism, Mary (Crosby)

Bankhead Sampson; Crosby, William and Sarah Harmon
Jenson, Andrew, 109, 423-7
John C. Caldwell v. Richard H. Porter, 124-25
Johnston, Albert Sidney, 2, 129-30, 141, 231-32
Jolley, Henry, 22-23, 79-80, 232-34
Jolley, Lambson, 37-38, 62-63, 232-34
Jones, Daniel W., 83
Jones, Mary Ewell, 35, 317-18
Jordan River, 81, 96

Kane, Thomas L., 8, 9, 89, 94, 307
Kimball, Heber C., 90, 100, 109, 162
Kinkead, John H., 123, 253
Kinney, John F., 130-33, 322, 431-47

Lane, James Addison, 322
Law of Freedom and Bondage in the United States, The, 11
Lay, Lucy (Lucinda), 17, 19-20, 56, 77, 89-90, 237. *See also* Crosby, John Jr. and Elizabeth Coleman; Smoot, Abraham O. and Margaret McMeans; Williams, Thomas S.
Lay, Sytha Crosby, 17, 23, 56, 89, 169, 199, 234-37. *See also* Wales, Hark
LDS. *See* Church of Jesus Christ of Latter-day Saints
Lee, John D., 263-64, 314, 322, 334
legal status, enslaved, 11-12, 33
Lewis, David and Duritha Trail, 27, 69-70, 90-91, 95-96, 238-243; Brigham Young correspondence, 357-58; slave registrations, 20-21, 349-50. *See also* Campbell, Tampian Hoye; Jackson, Caroline Hoye Bankhead
Lewis, Jerry, 1, 69-70, 81, 91-92, 95-96, 196, 238-39. *See also* Smoot, Abraham (A. O.) and Margaret McMeans
Lincoln, Abraham, 1, 138, 227
Litchford, Cordelia, 53-54

Litchford, Miles, 54, 136, 143, 152–54, 207
Litchford, Rose and Violet, 19, 56, 77, 90, 136, 151–54, 205–9; freedom of, 99–100; negotiations, 16–18. *See also* Bankhead, John H. and George W. (brothers); Crosby William and Sarah Harmon
Livingston, James M. and Howard, 123, 253, 256
Lost Cause mythology, 34–35
Lyman, Amasa, 86–87, 98, 100, 103, 106–7, 109, 112–13, 139, 273–74, 276
Lyman, Maria Tanner, 108, 113, 139, 226
lynching, 305, 332–33, 363

"Mammy Chloe" historical fiction, 313, 317–18
manumission, 2, 19, 65–66; and myths of freedom, 1–2, 31–32, 39, 58–59, 66–67, 300, 314, 323, 400–23
Marler, Harriet Heath, 320
Martineau, James Henry, 187–88, 323
Mason v. Smith. See *In re Hannah* (1856)
Mason, Ann, 278–79. *See also* Smith, Robert Mays and Rebecca Dorn
Mason, Biddy, 17–18, 23, 59, 78, 102–7, 140–42, 275–77, 293. *See also* Smith, Robert Mays and Rebecca Dorn
Mathews, Benjamin, 10, 87, 355
McBride, Reuben, 13
McFeely, Joseph, 137
McKown, Francis and Margaret Lockhart, 10, 23, 55, 59, 87, 243–45, 356
McMurtrey, Samuel and Julia Morris, 87
Meads, Rebecca Foscue, 301–2
memory, errors of, 31–32
merchants, enslaved people and, 123–28
Minter, John S., 100–2, 273
Mississippi: enslavers from, 53–61; Franklin County, 275; Kemper County, 61, 220; Marshall County, 193; Monroe County, 55–56, 236, 294, 299; Noxubee County, 315
Missouri: Andrew County, 73, 298; narrative of enslaved from, 62–70

Moody, Louisa, 121, 245
Moody, William C. and Harriet Henson, 121, 245–46, 323
Morehead, Elizabeth Thomas, 32, 324–25
Mormon Battalion, 76, 128, 187, 287, 325
Mormonism. *See* Church of Jesus Christ of Latter-day Saints
Murphy household, 30, 246–47
Murphy, Michael, 138
Murphy, Phoebe, 30, 196, 246–47
"My Pretty Quadroon," song, 115

Nauvoo Temple, 22–23, 180, 327, 329
Nauvoo, Illinois, 22, 25, 220, 233, 306
Negro Pioneer, The, 3, 35–37, 174–75
New York State, 6, 8, 33
Nibley, Charles W., 59, 94, 160–61, 163
Northwest Ordinance, 55
Northwest Territory, 55, 197
Nowlin, Bryan W., Jabus, and Peyton, 23, 325

Ockry, Nelson, 154
Old Folks' Day, 134
Owens, Charles, 102, 141–42, 277
Owens, Robert and Winnie, 140–42, 276

Pace, David William, 145, 147, 174, 270–71
partus sequitur ventrem, 33
Pearson v. Pearson, 110
Pearson, Laura, 19, 126–28
Pearson, Richard, 19, 126–28
Perkins, Alma, 258–59
Perkins, Benjamin, 23, 68, 166, 253–54
Perkins, Charlotte. *See* Campbell, Charlotte Perkins
Perkins, Ephraim, 257
Perkins, Esther, 74, 252
Perkins, Frank, 249–52
Perkins, Jasper, 67
Perkins, Manissa, 258
Perkins, Reuben, 67–68, 249–62

Perkins, Sarah, 256
Perkins, Sylvester, 259–61
Perkins, Thomas, 258
Perkins, Wesley, 257–58
Petillo, Littleton, 60, 68, 251
Phelps, M. Harrison, 332
Philemon, 23, 56, 74, 85, 98, 105, 187, 291–92. *See also* Crosby, John Jr. and Elizabeth Coleman; Thomas, Daniel M. and Ann Crosby
Pierce, Franklin, 126
Plain Dealer, 82, 155, 310
plantation, term, 34
Pope, Francis, 308
Powell, David and John (brothers), 73, 326
Pratt, Belinda Marden Hilton, 121
Pratt, Orson, 18, 24
Price, Nelson, 107, 211–12. *See also* Crosby, William and Sarah Harmon
Price, Susan. *See* Halley, Susan Price
Probate Register of Servants, 20, 343

Rande, 10, 59, 78, 87, 275, 281. *See also* Smith, Robert Mays and Rebecca Dorn
"Record of Baptisms for the Dead for the Seed of Cain," 148
Redd, Amy, 67, 272
Redd, Chaney, 63–67, 136, 262–63, 266–68, 272, 316, 322, 333. *See also* Cunningham, Samuel
Redd, John Hardison and Elizabeth Hancock, 33, 39, 44–45, 62, 63–67, 262–73; family claims, 31, 35–36, 66, 263–64; family record, 6, 46–47, 262; manumission of the enslaved, 65–67, 135–36; tithing, 23
Redd, Lemuel, 66
Redd, Luke Ward, 2, 22, 145–46, 268–69, 334
Redd, Marinda. *See* Bankhead, Marinda Redd
Redd, Venus, 22, 35–36, 47, 63–67, 135–36, 262–66, 322

reliability, historical, 33–39, 43, 159, 199, 332–333
Relief Society. *See* Church of Jesus Christ of Latter-day Saints
Rencher, Umpstead, 326
Reorganized Church of Jesus Christ of Latter-Day Saints (RLDS), 140, 227
Rich, Charles C., 98, 100–2, 273–75, 313
Richards, John Alexander, 325
Ricks, Joel and Lewis (brothers), 32, 327
Robinson, John. *See* Burton, John
Robinson, Joseph L., 187–88
Robinson, Susan McCord Burton, 74, 187–88
Rockwell, Porter, 73
Rogers, Amy, 181–82. *See also* Barnett, Bird B.
Root, Jeremiah and Emeline Davis, 87
Rose. *See* Litchford, Rose and Violet
Rowan, Elizabeth Flake, 102, 107, 139–40, 142, 204, 226–29, 303

Salt Lake Herald, 150, 436–66
Salt Lake Tribune, 109, 151, 222, 436–66
Salt Lake Valley. *See* Great Salt Lake Valley
San Bernardino Sun, 227
San Bernardino, California; fort, 100–1; *In re Hannah* case, 104–7; purchasing ranch in, 100; questions over property/autonomy, 102; recalling settlers to Utah Territory, 107
Seely, David, 102, 273
servant, term, 41
Shoshone, 94
Slade, William R. and Dorinda Moody Salmon Goheen, 323–24, 334–35
slavery. *See* enslaved; enslavers
Smart, Thomas A., 76–77, 415–18
Smiley, Nathaniel (Nelson), 137, 287. *See also* Smith, Robert Mays and Rebecca Dorn
Smith, Cato. *See* Cato
Smith, Elias, 20, 89, 92–93, 118, 143, 240, 343, 348–49, 359–60

Smith, Joseph, 6–9, 39, 220, 306, 371, 423–6
Smith, Nancy Lines, 21, 22, 24–25, 35, 71–72, 146, 160–61, 213–15, 353–54. *See also* Dennis, William Taylor and Talitha Bankhead
Smith, Oscar, 9, 10, 23, 45, 56, 73–74, 85, 100, 105–6, 110, 138, 141, 203–5, 360. *See also* Crosby, John Jr. and Elizabeth Coleman
Smith, Robert Mays and Rebecca Dorn, 10, 23, 59, 87, 100, 102, 275–89
Smith, Samuel, 94, 160–62. *See also* Bankhead, Samuel
Smithson, Allen, 320–21
Smoot, Abraham O. (A. O.) and Margaret McMeans, 17, 19–20, 76, 81–82, 89, 95–96, 120, 134, 145, 147, 174, 195–96, 237, 239, 246, 348–49, 370–71
Smoot, William C. A., 82, 134
Snedaker, Morris J., 120–21
Southern Grace: A Story of the Mississippi Saints, 35, 43, 199, 406n94
Southern origins, enslaved: Alabama, 53–61; Kentucky, 62–70; Mississippi, 53–61; Missouri, 62–70; Tennessee, 62–70
Sprouse-Wooldridge (family), 190, 256, 289–91
Sprouse, Nancy Reddick Greer Johnson, 115, 120, 289–90
Steptoe Expedition, 128–29, 159–60
Stewart, James and Ruthinda Baker, 23, 32, 327–28
Stout, Hosea, 115, 117–19, 132–33, 167, 328

Talbot, Henry and Ruth Sweetnam, 30, 218
Tanner, Sidney, 74
Taylor, W. W. and Elizabeth Austin, 82
Territory of Utah v. Williams Camp, 19, 118–19, 191–92
Texas, 115–22, 267; Box family as enslavers, 120–21, 185–86; Greer-Camp family case, 34, 194–95; Smith family case, 102–5, 281–282
Theophilus, 1, 128–29, 159–60. *See also* Allston, Benjamin
Thomas, Daniel M. and Ann Crosby, 100, 103–4, 291–93, 360–61
Thomas, Preston, 121, 245, 324–25
Thurber, Albert K., 145–46, 264, 268
tithing donations, 22–25, 100; and Green Flake, 16–18, 108–14
tithing myth, 108–14
Tubman, Harriet, 297

Udell, Bertha Stevens, 9, 57, 110–11, 364–65
unidentified individuals, 5, 293–94
unnamed woman and infant, 124–26, 179–80. *See also* Barnes, Clifton R.
US Congress, 2, 11, 13, 30, 144
Utah Territory, 337–39; and 1850 federal census, 12–16; army officers in, 128–30; Black residents of, 303–12; Box Elder County, 94, 163; Cache Valley, 59, 94, 169, 308; children born to enslaved parents in, 22, 95; dairy production, 86, 418n26, 424n16; Davis County, 25, 27, 88, 95, 187, 249, 258; government appointees in, 130–33; Great Salt Lake County, 25–26, 27–28, 59, 99, 350–51; Iron County, 88, 187–88; location of enslaved in, 88, 93; merchants in, 123–28; scholarly treatment of slavery in, 3–4; settlement of, 81–97; Southern origins of slaves entering, 53–70; Utah County, 14, 24, 87, 88, 94, 145; Utah's Dixie, 333–35
Utley, Littlejohn and Elizabeth Rutledge, 328–29
Utley, Seth and Bathsheba Woods, 329

Valentine, Henry Wales, 43, 177–78. *See also* Bankhead, John H. and George W. (brothers)

INDEX | 447

Valentine, Nancy Wales, 23, 38–39, 42, 83, 136, 172–73; children, 175–78; negotiations, 16–17. *See also* Bankhead, John H. and George W. (brothers)

Valley Tan, 42, 84–85

Violence, 5, 10, 17, 39–40, 79, 82, 84, 94, 102, 115, 117, 137, 140, 162, 195, 203, 214, 232, 263, 315, 337–39, 365, 367–68

Violet. *See* Litchford, Rose and Violet

Wales, Hark, 10, 16–17, 46, 56, 72–75, 85, 98–100, 221–22, 234–36, 356–57. *See also* Lay, Sytha Crosby

Wales, Howard Egan, 43, 99, 142–43, 177. *See also* Bankhead, John H. and George W. (brothers)

Ward, T. M. D., 141–42, 434n32

Washington, Harriet Mason, 279–80. *See also* Smith, Robert Mays and Rebecca Dorn

Watie, Stand, 32, 316

Wells, Daniel H., 12

Wells, Eliza Foscue Lee, 318

Wheeler, Lucy, 53, 143

Wheelock, Cyrus, 83

Whitmore, Elizabeth Carter Flaherty, 115, 121–22, 230, 295–96

Williams, Albina Merrill, 31, 89, 192, 241-42

Williams, Priscilla Mogridge Smith Staines, 90

Williams, Thomas S., 19–21, 23, 84, 89–90, 92, 113, 118–20, 123, 130, 154, 191, 215, 237, 240, 242, 329, 348–51. *See also* Williams, Albina Merrill

Winter Quarters, 7, 32, 58, 62, 73, 221, 298, 321

Woodruff, Wilford, 8, 36, 87–89, 134, 221–22, 402n39

Woolley, Edwin D. 19, 26, 118–19, 191, 425n8, 426n19

Woolridge, Downey Perkins, 37, 120, 137, 256–57. *See also* Perkins, Reuben

Woolridge, Silas, 120, 122, 136, 256–57, 289–91. *See also* Sprouse-Wooldridge (family)

Work, Monroe, 421n21

Young, Brigham, 1, 7–10, 16–18, 36, 39, 73, 87, 95–96, 118, 148, 243–44, 334; and Act in Relation to Service, 18–19, 40; correspondence with, 355–58; "Files Relating to Marriage and Other Ordinances," 83, 172; and Green Flake, 110–14, 135, 222, 364, 367; monument of, 41, 47, 49, 144

Zion, 7

www.ingramcontent.com/pod-product-compliance
Lightning Source LLC
Chambersburg PA
CBHW031959300426
44117CB00008B/827